CANADIAN EDITION

PERSONAL FINANCE

JEFF MADURA

FLORIDA ATLANTIC UNIVERSITY

HARDEEP S. GILL

NAIT

CANADIAN IN-CLASS EDITION

PEARSON

Addison
Wesley

Toronto

CANADIAN EDITION

PERSONAL FINANCE

JEFF MADURA
FLORIDA ATLANTIC UNIVERSITY

HARDEEP S. GILL
NAIT

CANADIAN IN-CLASS EDITION

PEARSON

Addison
Wesley

Toronto

Library and Archives Canada Cataloguing in Publication

Madura, Jeff
   Personal finance/Jeff Madura, Hardeep Gill.—Canadian ed., in-class ed.

   Includes index.

   ISBN 978-0-321-49197-8

   1. Finance, Personal—Canada—Textbooks.   I. Gill, Hardeep, 1972–   II. Title.

HG179.M3367 2009   332.02400971   C2007-906143-5

Original edition published by Pearson Education, Inc., Upper Saddle River, New Jersey, USA. Copyright © 2007 Pearson Education, Inc. This edition is authorized for sale only in Canada.

ISBN-13: 978-0-321-49197-8
ISBN-10: 0-321-49197-1

Vice President, Editorial Director: Gary Bennett
Executive Editor: Samantha Scully
Senior Marketing Manager: Leigh-Ann Graham
Developmental Editor: Eleanor MacKay
Senior Production Editor: Jennifer Handel
Copy Editor: Susan Broadhurst
Proofreader: Laura Neves
Senior Production Coordinator: Patricia Ciardullo
Composition: Integra
Permissions Research: Beth McAuley, Dayle Furlong
Art Director: Julia Hall
Interior and Cover Design: Sharon Lucas
Cover Image: Getty Images/Windsor & Wiehahn

For permission to reproduce copyrighted material, the publisher gratefully acknowledges the copyright holders listed in the source lines throughout the text and on page 527, which are considered an extension of this copyright page.

Statistics Canada information is used with the permission of Statistics Canada. Users are forbidden to copy the data and redisseminate them, in an original or modified form, for commercial purposes, without permission from Statistics Canada. Information on the availability of the wide range of data from Statistics Canada can be obtained from Statistics Canada's Regional Offices, its World Wide Web site at http://www.statcan.ca, and its toll-free access number 1-800-263-1136.

2 3 4 5   12 11 10

Printed and bound in the United States of America.

I wish to thank my wife, Mandeep; my children,
Maeva and Jeevun; and my family
and friends for their support.
I love you guys!

—*Hardeep Gill*

Brief Contents

Contents

Preface

When will you be able to buy a home? Can you afford a new car or a vacation? How can you pay off your credit card balance? What should you invest in?

The answers to these questions are tied directly to how you as a **student** manage your finances. Managing your finances wisely will bring a sense of security and freedom that you can enjoy for years to come. Very few courses you will take throughout your post-secondary career will have the potential to profoundly shape your future like a personal finance course. Taking this course is your first step on the path towards a stable financial future.

With *Personal Finance*, Canadian Edition, In-Class Edition, as your guide, you will master key concepts that will aid you in managing and increasing your personal wealth. The aim of this textbook is to equip you with knowledge and decision-making tools to help you make sound financial decisions.

HALLMARKS OF *PERSONAL FINANCE*, CANADIAN EDITION, IN-CLASS EDITION

We recognize that students who decide to take a course in personal finance have a variety of academic backgrounds, interests, and personal goals. For some, such a course might be a prerequisite to a future in finance or business. Others may decide to take the course because they want to learn more about how to create a budget or to plan for a large purchase such as a car on their current income. Our aim with this text is to provide students with all the tools they need to fully understand and plan their personal finances in a way that is useful, engaging, and rewarding.

As part of Pearson Education Canada's commitment to providing students with value, choice, and the tools for educational success, the Canadian edition of *Personal Finance* has been designed as an in-class edition. This innovative, new presentation is designed to focus on student learning and self-study.

In-Class Edition: Learning Made Easy

As an in-class edition, the Canadian edition of *Personal Finance* is specially designed to help students succeed. This innovative presentation includes the following features:

- *In-Class Notes.* Selected in-class notes (correlated to instructor PowerPoint® slides) that cover key concepts are reproduced directly in the text with space for students to make notes while in class or while reading. This encourages active reading and participation, and students can refer back to the notes in the original context when reviewing material for tests or exams.

- *Embedded Study Guide.* As a further strategy to encourage practice and mastery, study guide questions—multiple-choice and true/false—are located at the end of each chapter, with answers at the back of the text.

- *Financial Planning Study Card.* The financial planning laminated study card, bound in at the back of the text, is a handy reference that features the key formulas presented in each chapter.

Textbook Content and Organization

We have organized this text into a logical chapter order. The first chapter establishes the text's organization by introducing students to the key components of a financial plan. The text is then organized into seven parts, beginning with Chapter 2, which are keyed to the components of a comprehensive financial plan.

Part 1. Tools for Financial Planning

Part 2. Managing Your Liquidity

Part 3. Personal Financing

Part 4. Protecting Your Wealth

Part 5. Personal Investing

Part 6. Retirement and Estate Planning

Part 7. Synthesis of Financial Planning

Key Topics in the Canadian Edition of *Personal Finance*

We have included several important topics for Canadian students in this edition. You will find some examples of these key discussions in the following chapters:

Chapter 3—In Chapter 3 we provide background on taxes and then guide students step by step through the process of completing a tax return.

Chapter 5—In Chapter 5 we discuss identity theft, different identity theft tactics, and ways to protect against this kind of theft.

Chapter 9—In Chapter 9 we discuss the various levels of health insurance coverage available to Canadians, including disability, critical illness, and long-term care.

Chapter 11—In Chapter 11 we examine different types of investments and the trade-offs that need to be considered when examining investment return and risk.

Chapter 13—In Chapter 13 we show students how to complete an analysis of a firm, an economic analysis of stocks, and an industry analysis of stocks in order to determine an investment strategy.

Chapter 15—In Chapter 15 we present a comprehensive review of public and private retirement options, including the process of converting retirement assets to income.

Decision-Making Emphasis

All of the information presented in this book is geared toward equipping students with the expertise they need to make informed financial decisions. Each chapter establishes a foundation for the decisions that form the basis of a financial plan. When students complete each chapter, they are, therefore, prepared to complete the related financial plan subsection provided on the Student CD-ROM that accompanies the text. Key to understanding personal finance is knowing how to apply concepts to real-life planning scenarios. The many examples, financial planning problems, exercises, and cases place students in the role of the decision-maker and planner.

Focus on Opportunity Costs

Personal Finance calls attention to the trade-offs involved in financial decisions. The decision to buy a new car affects the amount of funds available for recreation, rent, insurance, and investments. The text uses numerous examples and exercises to illustrate and teach students about the interdependence of personal finance decisions.

Math-Friendly Presentation

The quantitative side of financial planning intimidates many students. *Personal Finance* simplifies the mathematics of personal finance by explaining its underlying logic. Formulas and calculations are explained in the text and then illustrated in examples. Examples that can be solved using a financial calculator are depicted with a keypad illustration. Students are referred to websites with online calculators whenever pertinent. The Financial Planning Problems and Financial Planning Online Exercises provide students with ample opportunity to practise applying math-based concepts.

An Interactive Approach

Personal Finance's interactive approach incorporates online resources along with many examples, problems, and ongoing case studies, all of which focus on providing students with hands-on practice applying financial concepts.

Building Your Own Financial Plan—*Personal Finance*'s structure mirrors a comprehensive financial plan. In each chapter, students learn the skills they need to build their own financial plan. The Building Your Own Financial Plan exercises are an integrated series of problems and worksheets that present a portion of a financial plan based on the concepts presented in each chapter. The exercises and associated worksheets are available on the Student CD-ROM, which is packaged with each new book. At the end of the course, students will have completed a financial plan that they can continue to implement beyond the school term.

 ON THE STUDENT CD-ROM FOR THIS CHAPTER YOU WILL FIND:

- Building Your Own Financial Plan exercise and worksheets
- The chapter-end Continuing Case about the Sampson family
- The first part-end Continuing Case about Brad Brooks
- Read through the Building Your Own Financial Plan exercise and use the worksheets to learn how to manage your income taxes.

- After reading the Sampson case study, use the Continuing Case worksheets to help the Sampsons estimate their federal income taxes.
- After reading the Brad Brooks case study, use the Continuing Case worksheets to help Brad prepare personal financial statements.

NAME

DATE

Chapter 13: Building Your Own Financial Pla

GOALS

1. Determine how to value a stock based on information about the
2. Determine a method to use for investing in stocks.

ANALYSIS

1. Select a stock in which you are considering investing.
2. Go to www.canadianeconomy.gc.ca/english/economy. Review th

NAME

DATE

News

d. Under "Recent News," do you see any significant news events that may favourably or unfavourably affect your stock?

Earnings

e. Click on the "Estimates" tab. What is the current estimate for the mean EPS? How does this compare to the EPS from a year ago?

f. Under reported quarters, evaluate how well the company has been able to meet analyst expectations.

g. What is the trend in the estimate of the EPS?

h. Is this stock a recommended "buy" or "sell"? How many brokers have evaluated this stock?

i. What is the P/E for this stock? How does it compare to the industry?

CHAPTER 13: BUILDING YOUR OWN FINANCIAL PLAN

One of the best financial instruments to accomplish many medium- and long-term goals is investment in stocks. Investment specialists have said that at any given time there are 20 to 50 stocks that could make someone a millionaire within a short time. The secret, of course, is to find just one of those 20 to 50 stocks. In this exercise, you will analyze two or three stocks to determine if they are good investments and, therefore, a suitable means to accomplish some of the medium- and long-term goals you established in Chapter 1.

When investing in stocks, it is necessary to monitor happenings in the economy and the market. Events may very quickly have a significant impact—favourable or unfavourable—on the price trends of a stock. How frequently you monitor information depends on market conditions and the volatility of your individual stocks. Websites such as www.ca.finance.yahoo.com allow you to research financial news about any firm easily.

Selecting the right stock investment method is an important decision for any investor. The second part of this case walks you through a list of questions designed to assist you in making the important decision of whether a full-service broker or online/discount broker better suits your needs. Carefully consider the types of investments you will be making, how frequently you will make transactions, and how important one-on-one advice from a broker is to you. When comparing brokerage firms' offerings, be sure to consider at least one online or discount broker.

As you get older and your portfolio grows in size and possibly in complexity, you need to review the suitability of your broker just as you do your tax preparer, as we discussed in Chapter 3.

Use the worksheet for Chapter 13: Building Your Own Financial Plan to determine how to value stocks.

the symbol of the company
te data for your company. A
the data in the tab indicated:

Snapshot

a. On the right hand side, click on "Quote." Is the price of your high or 52-week low?

b. Does this stock pay a dividend and, if so, how much?

Charting

c. Under the stock chart, click on "5yr". What has been the lon
stock?

Building Your Own Fir

Financial Planning Weblinks—In every chapter, marginal weblinks highlight useful Internet resources. You will find a website address and a description of what type of information the website provides.

Financial Planning Online Exercises—At the end of each chapter, Financial Planning Online Exercises show students how to obtain, critically evaluate, and use Internet-based resources in making personal finance decisions.

Go to www.walterharder.ca/T1.html

This website provides an estimate of your tax liability for the year and the tax refund you will receive (if you have already paid more in taxes than your tax liability), based on your total income, deductions, and tax credits.

FINANCIAL PLANNING ONLINE EXERCISES

1. Go to www.kanetix.ca/auto-insurance.

   a. Enter your postal code and select the city in which you live. Click on Next Step and enter the requested driver information. Click on Next Step and enter the requested vehicle details. Click on Next Step and select "No" for discounts. Click on Get Quotes. The screen will display quotes for coverage from various auto insurance companies.

   b. Scroll down to Coverage details. Select a $500 deductible for both comprehensive and collision coverage. What is Loss of use? What is Legal liability for damage to non-owned automobiles? How much liability coverage can you purchase?

   c. Do any of the insurance companies offer any discounts? If so, what types of discounts do they offer? What are the credit ratings for the various insurance companies? Which company has the highest credit rating?

FINANCIAL PLANNING PROBLEMS

1. Linda neglected to complete her T1 General in time for the filing deadline of April 30, 2007. This would not be a problem if she did not owe any tax. However, after completing her tax return, she realized that the amount of tax withheld by her employer was not enough to cover the amount of taxes she owed. In fact, Linda owed an additional $2000 of income tax. Linda completed her tax return and submitted it to the CRA by November 1, 2007. Calculate Linda's income tax penalty. How much will she have to pay in total?

2. Larry is in the 32 percent marginal tax bracket. Last year, he sold stock he had held for nine months for a gain of $1900. How much tax must he pay on this capital gain?

Financial Planning Problems—At the end of each chapter, Financial Planning Problems require students to demonstrate knowledge of mathematically based concepts to perform computations in order to make well-informed personal finance decisions.

A running example of Stephanie Spratt. Stephanie Spratt is a recent college graduate and a new entrant into the workforce. She helps students apply financial planning concepts to real-life situations. Students are commonly faced with dilemmas similar to those Stephanie faces, such as how to control recreational spending or whether to buy or lease a car.

EXAMPLE

Stephanie Spratt reviews the T4 slip that her employer provided to determine what deductions she can take against her total income. Box 20 of her T4 indicates that she has $2000 in RPP contributions. In addition, Box 44 indicates that she has paid $400 in union dues. Stephanie has also received a slip from her bank indicating that she has contributed $2000 to her RRSP. Finally, Stephanie reviews her bank statement and finds that she has paid $600 for the year to maintain a safety deposit box at her bank. Her total deductions are:

Deductions

RPP Contributions	$2000
RRSP Contributions	$2000
Union Dues	$400
Safety Deposit Box Fees	$600
Total	$5000

Real-Life Scenarios

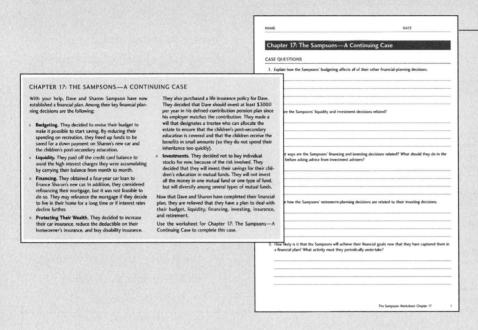

Build a financial plan for the Sampson family! The parents of two children, Dave and Sharon Sampson, have made few plans regarding their financial future. They are eager to start saving towards a new car, their children's post-secondary education, and their retirement. Students apply chapter concepts to counsel the Sampsons. The Sampsons —A Continuing Case chapter-end cases and accompanying worksheets are provided on the Student CD-ROM that accompanies the text.

PART 1: BRAD BROOKS—A CONTINUING CASE

Brad Brooks, your childhood friend, has asked you to help him gain control of his personal finances. Single and 30 years old, Brad is employed as a salesperson for a technology company. His annual salary is $48 000. After payroll deductions, EI and CPP contributions, and income taxes, his monthly disposable income is $2743. Brad has recently moved from his comfortable two-bedroom apartment with rent of $600 per month to a condo that rents for $1000 per month. The condo is in a plush property owner's association with two golf courses, a lake, and an activity center. You review his other monthly expenses and find the following:

Tenant's insurance	$20
Car payment (balance on car loan $10,000; market value of car $11,000)	500
Utilities (gas, electric, cable)	100
Cell phone (personal calls)	250
House phone	30
Food (consumed at home)	200
Clothes	100
Car expenses (gas, insurance, maintenance)	250
Entertainment (dining out, golf, weekend trips)	400

Brad is surprised at how much money he spends on clothes and entertainment. He uses his credit cards for these purchases (the balance is $8000 and climbing) and has little trouble making the required monthly payments. He would, however, like to see the balance go down and eventually pay it off completely.

Brad's other goal is to save $4000 a year so that he can retire 20 years from now. He would like to start saving in five years, as he does not think the delay will affect the final amount of retirement savings he will accumulate.

Brad currently has about $4000 in his chequing account and $200 in his savings account. He has furniture valued at $1500 and owns $1300 of tech stocks, which he believes have the potential to make him rich.

Use the worksheet for Part 1: Brad Brooks—A Continuing Case to prepare financial statements for Brad.

At the end of each part, students are prompted to **build a financial plan for Brad Brooks** using the Brad Brooks—A Continuing Case scenarios and accompanying worksheets provided on the Student CD-ROM. Brad has expensive tastes—as evidenced by his soaring credit card balance—and he needs assistance in gaining control over his finances.

Learning Tools

Chapter 3

Using Tax Concepts for Planning

The Kapoors sat down at the beginning of the year to complete their tax return for the previous year. The Kapoors realized that they would have to pay more in taxes than they had anticipated. The couple wondered if there was anything they could do to reduce the amount of tax they had to pay.

John Kapoor called his uncle Sam to see if there was anything the couple could do to reduce their taxes. Sam told them they would have been eligible for a number of deductions if they had taken the appropriate steps before December 31. If the couple had maximized their RRSPs and made additional contributions to their favourite charity, they would have saved an additional $2100 in taxes.

The moral of this story is that you, as a taxpayer, may be able to take advantage of significant tax breaks. However, while an accountant can help you complete your tax return correctly, it is your responsibility to take actions during the tax year that will allow you to take full advantage of available tax reduction strategies.

This chapter explains the basics of individual taxation. Knowledge of tax laws can help you conserve your income, enhance your investments, and protect the transfer of wealth when you die. Understanding the taxation of income and wealth is crucial to sound financial planning.

Chapter Introductions
The opening of each chapter provides an interest-grabbing scenario that previews the chapter's content.

Learning Objectives
Corresponding to the main headings in each chapter, and indicated by marginal callouts throughout the chapter, the list of learning objectives guides students through the material.

The objectives of this chapter are to:

1. Explain when you have to file a tax return
2. Demonstrate how to calculate your total income
3. Describe the major deductions available to a taxpayer
4. Show how deductions can be used to reduce total income
5. Show how tax credits can be used to lower tax payable
6. Explain how to determine your tax liability and whether you are owed a refund or owe additional tax

EXAMPLE

Helen turned 65 on October 8, 2006. Her taxable income for 2006 was $42 000. Although Helen qualifies for the age amount credit, it will be reduced because her income is above the threshold amount of $30 270. The maximum age amount for 2006 is $5066. Helen qualifies for a reduced age amount calculated as:

$$\$5066 - [(\$42\ 000 - \$30\ 270) \times 0.15]$$
$$= \$5066 - (11\ 730 \times 0.15)$$
$$= \$5066 - \$1759.50$$
$$= \$3306.50$$

As a result, Helen will record an age amount of $3306.50 on her Schedule 1 form.

excise taxes
Special taxes levied on certain consumer products such as cigarettes, alcohol, and gasoline.

Marginal Glossary
Throughout the text, key terms and their definitions appear in the text margin where they are first discussed.

Explanation by Example
Practical examples applying concepts in realistic scenarios throughout the chapters help cement student understanding of key concepts.

Ethical Dilemmas

At the end of each chapter, real-life ethical situations are presented along with critical thinking questions. These exercises are designed to help students apply ethical principles to financial situations and problems.

Summary

In paragraph form, the summaries present the key points from each chapter.

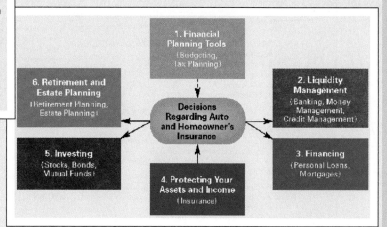

Integrating the Key Concepts

This section emphasizes the relationship between chapter topics and the six components of a financial plan.

SUMMARY

Your risk management decisions determine whether and how to protect against risk. Your alternatives are to avoid, reduce, accept, or share risk. Some types of risk are difficult to avoid and dangerous to accept. For these types of risk, insurance is needed. Once you decide whether to obtain a particular type of insurance, you must decide on the amount of coverage and on where to purchase the insurance.

Automobile insurance insures against the legal liability that may arise if your property (car) causes death or injury to others, as well as the expense associated with providing medical care to you, your passengers, and pedestrians, and the costs associated with damage to your automobile. The premium paid for auto insurance depends on how you use the vehicle, the vehicle's value and repair record, where you live, your driving record, your age and sex, as well as the features of the policy you choose, including the insurance deductible.

Review Questions

The Review Questions test students' understanding by asking them to compare and contrast concepts, interpret financial quotations, and decide how financial data can be used to make personal finance decisions.

End-of-Chapter Study Guide

Each chapter concludes with 10 multiple-choice and 10 true/false study questions for extra review.

Study Guide

Circle the correct answer and then check the answers in the back of the book to chart your progress.

Multiple Choice

1. Which of the following is not a bond feature that is desirable for bond investors?
   a. Put feature
   b. Convertible feature
   c. Call feature
   d. Extendible feature

2. An investor may be interested in investing in a Government of Canada bond because:
   a. They are a safe investment.
   b. They are available with a term to maturity of anywhere between 1 and 30 years.
   c. They can be sold easily in the secondary market.
   d. All of the above.

3. Which of the following types of bonds is subject to the most default risk?
   a. Corporate bonds
   b. Federal Crown corporation bonds
   c. Municipal bonds
   d. Provincial bonds

4. Which of the following short-term debt securities is issued by the Government of Canada?
   a. Banker's acceptances
   b. Strip bonds
   c. Commercial paper
   d. T-Bills

5. Real return bonds protect you from inflation risk by:
   a. Increasing your coupon payments every six months.
   b. Adjusting the par value of the bond for changes in the inflation rate.
   c. Offering a term to maturity that will result in a very safe, low-risk investment.
   d. All of the above.

6. All of the following are types of investment income that can be earned from owning a bond, except:
   a. Capital gains
   b. Dividends
   c. Capital losses
   d. Interest

7. With respect to bond valuation, which of the following statements is true?
   a. A bond's value is determined as the future value of the future cash flows to be received by the investor, which are the periodic coupon payments and the principal payment at maturity.
   b. A bond's value is determined as the future value of the future cash flows to be received by the investor, which are the periodic coupon payments.
   c. A bond's value is determined as the present value of the future cash flows to be received by the investor, which are the periodic coupon payments and the principal payment at maturity.
   d. A bond's value is determined as the present value of the future cash flows to be received by the investor, which are the periodic coupon payments.

8. Calculate the value of a $1000 par value bond that has five years until maturity and a coupon rate of 8 percent, paid semi-annually. New $1000 par value bonds offer a coupon rate of 6 percent.
   a. $1085
   b. $915
   c. $1045
   d. $1084

9. To minimize the effects of default risk, an investor should choose which one of the following corporate bonds?
   a. AAA-rated corporate bonds with the shortest term to maturity
   b. AA-rated short-term corporate bonds with the shortest term to maturity
   c. AAA-rated long-term corporate bonds with the longest term to maturity
   d. AA-rated long-term corporate bonds with the longest term to maturity

10. Darvin and Kim would like to purchase a portfolio of bonds that will mature when their kids are ready to attend a post-secondary institution. What would be the most appropriate bond investment strategy given their objectives?
    a. Interest rate strategy
    b. Passive strategy
    c. Bond laddering strategy
    d. Maturity matching strategy

True/False

1. True or False? The coupon payments for a bond are normally paid quarterly.

2. True or False? A bond that is trading at a price below its par value is said to be trading at a discount.

INSTRUCTOR AND STUDENT SUPPORT PACKAGE

The following array of supplementary materials is available to help busy instructors teach more effectively and to allow busy students to learn more efficiently.

For Instructors

Instructor's Resource CD-ROM   Fully compatible with the Windows and Macintosh operating systems, this CD-ROM provides a number of resources.

- *Instructor's Solutions and Resource Manual*—This comprehensive manual pulls together a wide variety of teaching tools and resources. Each chapter contains an overview of key topics, teaching tips, and detailed answers and step-by-step solutions to the Review Questions, Financial Planning Problems, and Sampsons family case questions. Each part concludes with solutions to the Brad Brooks case questions.

- *TestGen*—The TestGen test bank contains over 2000 questions in true-false, multiple-choice, and short-essay format that can be used for quick test preparation. Qualifiers with each multiple-choice question indicate the level of difficulty. The test bank has been created in easy-to-use testing software (TestGen EQ with QuizMaster-EQ for Windows and Macintosh). It is a valuable test preparation tool that allows instructors to view, edit, and add questions.

- *PowerPoint® Slides*—This useful tool provides PowerPoint slides illustrating key points from each chapter. Instructors can easily convert the slides to transparencies or view them electronically in the classroom during lectures.

For Students

Financial Planning Workbook on the Student CD-ROM   At the end of each chapter, a box titled "On the Student CD-ROM for This Chapter You Will Find" details the relevant exercises and case studies that are associated with each chapter. Students are prompted to complete the Building Your Own Financial Plan exercises and the continuing case about the Sampson family. At the end of each part, the student is prompted to complete the Brad Brooks continuing case. The Student CD-ROM contains all of these items in the Financial Planning Workbook, which is a robust and integrated Excel file.

The software templates guide students through the key steps in the financial decision-making process as they complete these exercises and case studies. The software's true power lies in the linking of all the worksheets; students are prompted to revise financial goals, cash flow statements, and personal balance sheets to demonstrate their understanding of the interrelationships among their financial decisions. Creating complete and integrated plans has never been this easy!

Additional software features include the following:

- New calculation-based templates on topics such as determining your federal income tax liability, estimating the time it will take to pay off credit card debt, and determining disability insurance needs.

- For decisions that require time value of money analysis, the software directs students for input and then performs the calculations.

The CD-ROM also contains the Building Your Own Financial Plan, The Sampsons—A Continuing Case, and Brad Brooks—A Continuing Case cases and worksheets in Adobe PDF format.

Companion Website

Available at **www.pearsoned.ca/madura**, the Companion Website provides online access to innovative teaching and learning tools, including the following:

- Online Study Guide, featuring additional true/false, multiple-choice, and essay questions

- Important key features from the textbook, including learning objectives, chapter summaries, weblinks, and a key term interactive glossary

- Up-to-date links to the Financial Planning Online features and Financial Planning Online Exercises

LIST OF REVIEWERS

We sought the advice of many excellent reviewers, all of whom strongly influenced the organization, substance, and approach of this book. We would like to extend a special thanks to Maureen Rolland who provided an additional technical review of the final manuscript.

The following individuals provided extremely useful evaluations:

Bill Bradburn
Durham College

Ken Brightling
Fanshawe College

Derek Cook
Okanagan College

Bill Giglio
Camosun College

James D. Hebert
Red River College

D. J. Nick Sunday

Donald Wheeler
College of the North Atlantic

Maureen Rolland
Georgian College

ACKNOWLEDGMENTS

I wish to acknowledge the help and support of many people associated with Pearson Education Canada who made this textbook possible. First and foremost, the contributions of Eleanor MacKay, Developmental Editor, were invaluable. Her experience and feedback helped me better understand the development process as I worked to integrate new and existing material. Also, thanks to Samantha Scully, Executive Editor, for her support and positive energy.

I would also like to thank Jennifer Handel, Senior Production Editor, for working under very tight deadlines as we tried to get this project completed. Also, I wish to thank Susan Broadhurst, who integrated the technical reviewer's suggestions and copyedited the text to ensure clarity and consistency. Another pair of eyes was very much appreciated. I would also like to thank Ross Meacher, who technically reviewed the text during production. On a similar vein, this book would not be what it is without the input from the many reviewers who had a chance to review the material. At the end of the day, your suggestions have made this an infinitely better text. I also wish to thank Cecile Wendlandt, who provided the initial spark that gave me the energy to work on this project.

—Hardeep Gill

A Great Way to Learn and Instruct Online

The Pearson Education Canada Companion Website is easy to navigate and is organized to correspond to the chapters in this textbook. Whether you are a student in the classroom or a distance learner you will discover helpful resources for in-depth study and research that empower you in your quest for greater knowledge and maximize your potential for success in the course.

Companion Website

[www.pearsoned.ca/madura] Enter

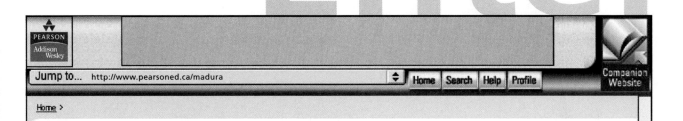

Jump to... http://www.pearsoned.ca/madura ⬆⬇ | Home | Search | Help | Profile | Companion Website

Home >

AW Companion Website

Personal Finance, Canadian Edition, In-Class Edition, by Madura and Gill

Student Resources

The modules in this section provide students with tools for learning course material. These modules include:

- Learning Objectives
- Chapter Summaries
- Self-Study Questions
- Financial Planning Online Exercises
- Glossary Flashcards
- In-Class Notes
- Weblinks and annotations
- Financial Calculator Guide

In the quiz modules students can send answers to the grader and receive instant feedback on their progress through the Results Reporter. Coaching comments and references to the textbook may be available to ensure that students take advantage of all available resources to enhance their learning experience.

Instructor Resources

A link to this book on the Pearson Education Canada online catalogue (vig.pearsoned.ca) provides instructors with additional teaching tools. Downloadable PowerPoint Presentations and an Instructor's Solutions and Resource Manual are just some of the materials that may be available. The catalogue is password protected. To get a password, simply contact your Pearson Education Canada Representative or call Faculty Sales and Services at 1-800-850-5813.

Overview of a Financial Plan

magine that you are taking a vacation next year. This is a major event for you and you wish to plan thoroughly so that nothing goes wrong. You have many choices to make. Where should you go? How big is your vacation budget and how do you want to allocate it? Vacations require detailed planning. You choose your itinerary, carefully save your money, and have the time of your life.

Now, imagine that you are planning for your financial future. You have major events ahead of you and you wish to plan thoroughly so that nothing goes wrong. You have many choices to make. Should you invest in an RRSP? What type of house should you buy? How much of your budget should be allocated to food and utilities? How much can you afford to spend on clothes? Should you spend all of your money as you earn it, or should you use some money for investment opportunities? When do you want to retire? Do you want to leave an estate for your heirs? All of these decisions require detailed planning.

In a world where there are few guarantees, thorough financial planning, prudent financial management, and careful spending can help you achieve your financial goals.

The personal financial planning process enables you to understand a financial plan and to develop a personal financial plan. The simple objective of financial planning is to make the best use of your resources to achieve your financial goals. The sooner you develop your goals and a financial plan to achieve those goals, the easier it will be to achieve them.

The objectives of this chapter are to:

1. Explain how you could benefit from personal financial planning
2. Identify the key components of a financial plan
3. Outline the steps involved in developing a financial plan

personal finance (personal financial planning)
The process of planning your spending, financing, and investing activities, while taking into account uncontrollable events such as death or disability, in order to optimize your financial situation over time.

personal financial plan
A plan that specifies your financial goals, describes the spending, financing, and investing activities that are intended to achieve those goals over time, and uses the risk management strategies that are required to protect against uncontrollable events such as death or disability.

per capita debt
The amount of debt each individual in Canada would have if total debt (consumer debt plus mortgages) was spread equally across the population.

opportunity cost
What you give up as a result of a decision.

HOW YOU BENEFIT FROM AN UNDERSTANDING OF PERSONAL FINANCE

Personal finance, also referred to as **personal financial planning**, is the process of planning your spending, financing, and investing activities, while taking into account uncontrollable events such as death or disability, in order to optimize your financial situation over time. A **personal financial plan** specifies your financial goals, describes the spending, financing, and investing activities that are intended to achieve those goals, and uses the risk management strategies that are required to protect against uncontrollable events such as death or disability. Although Canada is one of the world's wealthier countries, many Canadians do not manage their financial situations well. Consequently, they tend to rely too much on credit and have excessive debt. Excessive debt levels will affect your ability to achieve important financial goals. Consider the following statistics from Statistics Canada:

- From 1990 to 2005, consumer bankruptcies increased 97.8 percent.

- For each dollar of personal income received in 1982, Canadians saved 17 cents. As of the third quarter of 2006, the personal savings rate had decreased to 1.3 cents per dollar of personal income received.

- Total family debt increased 47.5 percent between 1999 and 2005. During this period, credit card and instalment debt rose 59.4 percent, while line-of-credit debt increased almost 77 percent.

- The per capita debt of Canadians has multiplied 5.2 times over the last 25 years, from $5470 in 1980 to $28 390 in 2006. **Per capita debt** represents the amount of debt each individual in Canada would have if total debt (consumer debt plus mortgages) was spread equally across the population.

- Thirty-four percent of Canadians do not have a retirement plan.

You have numerous options regarding the choice of bank deposits, credit cards, loans, insurance policies, investments, and retirement plans. All of these options involve decisions you will have to make for yourself. Relying on government benefits alone may not provide you with the financial future you imagine for yourself. With an understanding of personal finance, you will be able to make decisions that can enhance your financial situation. An understanding of personal finance is beneficial to you in many ways, including the following:

Make Your Own Financial Decisions

An understanding of personal finance enables you to make informed decisions about your financial situation. Each of your spending decisions has an **opportunity cost**, which represents what you give up as a result of that decision. By spending money for a specific purpose, you forgo alternative ways that you could have spent the money and also forgo saving the money for a future purpose. For example, if your decision to use your cellphone costs $100 per month, you have forgone the possibility of using that money to buy new clothes or to save for a new car. Informed financial decisions increase the amount of money that you accumulate over time and give you more flexibility to purchase the products and services you want in the future.

Opportunity cost will also affect your savings decisions. In Chapter 2, we will discuss how you can use budgeting tools to increase your savings. Savings can then be used toward short-, medium-, or long-term goals. Generally, the savings in an emergency fund, a short-term goal, will earn less interest than your investments in a retirement plan, a long-term goal. Although an emergency fund is very important to your personal financial plan, saving too much for short-term needs does limit your opportunity for long-term growth. You should strive to balance your savings goals among short-, medium-, and long-term goals.

Judge the Advice of Financial Advisers

The personal financial planning process will enable you to make informed decisions about your spending, saving, financing, and investing. Nevertheless, you may prefer to rely on advice from various types of financial advisers. An understanding of personal finance allows you to judge the guidance of financial advisers and to determine whether their advice is in your best interest rather than their best interest.

> Throughout each chapter you will find examples that put the material you have learned up to that point into context.

EXAMPLE

You want to invest $10 000 of your savings. A financial adviser guarantees that your investment will increase in value by 20 percent ($2000) this year, but he will charge you 4 percent of the investment ($400) for his advice. If you had a background in personal finance, you would know that no investment can be guaranteed to increase in value. Therefore, you would realize that you should not trust this financial adviser. You could either hire a more reputable financial adviser or review investment recommendations made by financial advisers on the Internet (often at no cost). Choosing a financial adviser is no different than hiring other professionals such as doctors, mechanics, or plumbers. It is important to ask for references, conduct an interview, and use common sense when choosing an adviser.

Financial Planners Standards Council (FPSC) A not-for-profit organization that was created to benefit the public through the development, enforcement, and promotion of the highest competency and ethical standards in financial planning.

The Financial Planners Standards Council (FPSC) is a not-for-profit organization that was created to benefit the public through the development, enforcement, and promotion of the highest competency and ethical standards in financial planning. It provides a forum in which you can email questions to individuals who have earned the Certified Financial Planner (CFP) designation. This panel of experts offers advice in the areas of investment, tax, estate, and insurance planning. You can access this forum through the FPSC website, www.cfp-ca.org/aae.asp. The expert you email will personally respond to your question.

Become a Financial Adviser

Although a single course such as this is not sufficient to become a financial adviser, an interest in and aptitude for the myriad products and ideas discussed in this course may lead you to consider a career in the financial services sector. Financial advisers are in demand because many people lack an understanding of personal finance, are not interested in making their own financial decisions, or simply do not have the time necessary to research and educate themselves on financial issues in order to make informed decisions. (It should be clearly stated, though, that most advisers cannot make decisions for their clients. An individual must give permission to the financial adviser before any action can be taken.)

The FPSC website, www.cfp-ca.org, provides a description of the steps needed to earn the Certified Financial Planner (CFP) designation. Obtaining this credential is a significant step to building a successful career as a financial adviser because it indicates that you have met the education, examination, experience, and ethical requirements set by the FPSC. Education involves the successful completion of an approved educational program and fulfillment of annual continuing education requirements to keep abreast of planning strategies and financial trends. As well, a minimum of two years' work experience in a financial planning–related position is required to earn the designation. The CFP examination covers the financial planning process, income tax planning, retirement planning, estate planning, investment planning, family law, risk management, general principles including the Code of Ethics, and small business applications in financial planning. Finally, you must adhere to a professional Code of Ethics that requires you to act in an ethically and professionally responsible manner in all services and activities. Meeting these requirements allows you to be identified by potential clients as a financial adviser who is dedicated to a high level of professionalism in providing financial planning advice.

IN-CLASS NOTES

How You Benefit from an Understanding of Personal Finance

- Make Your Own Financial Decisions
  - Know there is an opportunity cost to your decisions
- Judge the Advice of Financial Advisers
  - Be informed
  - Seek the advice of an adviser with the Financial Planners Standards Council (FPSC)
- Become a Financial Adviser
  - Take courses to gain the education and experience you would need to become a financial adviser

---

<table><tr><td>L.O. 2</td></tr></table>

COMPONENTS OF A FINANCIAL PLAN

A complete financial plan contains your personal finance decisions related to six key components:

1. Budgeting and tax planning

2. Managing your liquidity

3. Financing your large purchases

4. Protecting your assets and income (insurance)

5. Investing your money

6. Planning your retirement and estate

These six components are very different; decisions concerning each component are captured in separate plans that, taken together, form your overall financial plan. To begin your introduction to the financial planning process, let's briefly explore each component.

> When your instructor reviews each chapter using the PowerPoint slides that accompany the text, you will have an opportunity to follow along and take notes about the material you have learned.

A Plan for Your Budgeting and Tax Planning

budget planning (budgeting)
The process of forecasting future income, expenses, and savings goals.

Budget planning (also referred to as budgeting) is the process of forecasting future income, expenses, and savings goals. That is, it requires you to decide whether to spend or save money. If you receive $750 in income during one month, the amount you save is the amount of money (say, $100) that you do not spend. The relationship between income received, spending, and savings is illustrated in Exhibit 1.1. Some individuals are "big spenders": they focus their budget decisions on how to spend most or all of their income and therefore have little or no money left for saving. Others are "big savers": they set a savings goal and consider spending their income received only after allocating a portion of it toward saving. Budgeting can help you estimate how much of your income will be required to cover monthly expenses so that you can set a reasonable and practical goal for saving each month.

assets
What you own.

liabilities
What you owe; your debt.

net worth
The value of what you own minus the value of what you owe.

A first step in budgeting should be to evaluate your current financial position by assessing your income, your expenses, your assets (what you own), and your liabilities (debt, or what you owe). Your net worth (or wealth) is the value of what you own minus

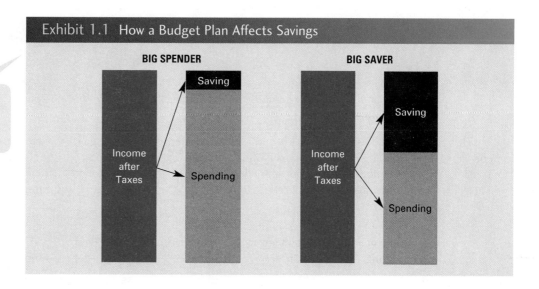

Exhibit 1.1 How a Budget Plan Affects Savings

The exhibits act as a visual reference for important concepts in each chapter.

the value of what you owe. You can measure your wealth by your net worth. As you save money, you increase your assets and therefore increase your net worth. Budgeting enables you to build your net worth by setting aside part of your income to either invest in additional assets or reduce your liabilities.

Your budget is influenced by your income, which in turn is influenced by your life stage. Exhibit 1.2 provides an overview of the six major life stages and the key financial considerations you will make at each of those stages. Individuals who are pursuing post-secondary education during their pre-career stage of life tend to have smaller incomes, usually from part-time jobs, and thus smaller budgets. At this stage, it is important to establish good money management habits, through budgeting, and to establish a credit rating. After completing their education, individuals advance to the early earning stage of life and are able to obtain jobs that pay higher salaries, which result in larger budgets. Adopting the pay-yourself-first principle, managing your debt, balancing your savings, and building your investment portfolio by starting with a mutual fund are important considerations for someone at this life stage.

As you progress through the next three life stages, you may experience various milestones. Milestones, such as getting married, having children, or starting a new job, will often result in a need or desire to update your personal financial plan. However, waiting for milestones before creating a personal financial plan can be very dangerous because you may not have any time to prepare. For example, when you reach the milestone of marriage, you may find that the expense of planning a wedding requires you to change your spending habits. At that point, you will have to ask yourself how much you can afford to spend on a wedding. If you haven't been planning ahead, you may have to scale back on your wedding plans. As a student, not planning ahead for a milestone would be the same as studying for your final exam the day before you are supposed to write it—not a good idea! Budget planning is the first step in building a successful plan so that you do not have to sacrifice what you really want when the time comes.

Although the majority of your personal financial plan will be in place by the time you reach the post-retirement life stage, it is still important to be aware of any issues that are outstanding. In particular, you may need to review your wealth management options and your estate plan. Managing your money will become more difficult as you move through this life stage. Therefore, it is important to understand what wealth management options are available and to plan accordingly. In addition, your estate plan should be reviewed to ensure that it reflects your wishes at death. As you can see, personal finance is a subject that you will encounter throughout your life. Refer back to Exhibit 1.2 as you read this textbook. The alternatives you will consider at each life stage and/or milestone will be discussed at various points in the textbook.

Exhibit 1.2 Typical Financial Planning Life Stages

	Pre-Career	Early Earning	Mid Earning	Prime Earning	Retirement	Post-Retirement
Life Stages						
Age Group	0 to 22	23 to 30	31 to 44	45 to 59	60 to 74	75 +
Consider Your Current Financial Position	■ Establish good money management habits ■ Establish a credit rating	■ Follow the pay-yourself-first principle ■ Manage your debt, don't let your debt manage you ■ Balance your savings goals ■ Consider a mutual fund, inside or outside an RRSP	■ Consider RESPs ■ Have an adequate amount of life insurance ■ Continue with your RRSPs ■ Have a will and power of attorney ■ Investigate your pension plan at work	■ How much do you need to save? ■ Are all debts paid? ■ Job security? ■ Elder care?	■ What can you expect from government programs? ■ RRSP/LIRA maturity options? ■ Review workplace pension benefits ■ Account for all assets ■ Retirement income distribution patterns ■ What happens if a spouse dies?	■ RRSP/LIRA maturity options? ■ Wealth management: how, who, where? ■ Estate planning
Milestones	Graduation	First Job New Job/Raise	Marriage First House First Baby	Empty Nest Parental Care Ten Years Till Retirement	Retirement Empty Nest Travel Parental Care	

Source. Adapted from www.bmonesbittburns.com/personalinvest/InvestorLearning/FinancialPlanning/Lifestages/default.asp (accessed June 27, 2007). Reprinted with permission of BMO Nesbitt Burns.

Another key part of budgeting is estimating the typical expenses that you will incur each month. If you underestimate expenses, you will not achieve your savings goals. Achieving future wealth requires you to sacrifice by moderating your spending today.

Many financial decisions are affected by tax laws, as some forms of income are taxed at a higher rate than others. By understanding how your alternative financial choices would be affected by taxes, you can make financial decisions that have the most favourable effect on your after-tax cash flows. Budgeting and tax planning are discussed in Part 1 because they underpin decisions about all other parts of your financial plan.

A Plan to Manage Your Liquidity

liquidity
Access to ready cash, including savings and credit, to cover short-term or unexpected expenses.

Short-term cash needs and unexpected expenses, such as emergencies, are a fact of life, and you must plan how you will cover them. Your ability to cover these expenses depends on your liquidity. Liquidity refers to your access to ready cash, including savings and credit, to cover short-term or unexpected expenses. The budget planning process described above will help you reach your savings goals. Your liquidity can be

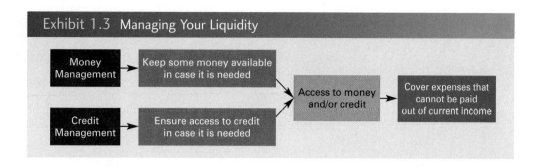

Exhibit 1.3 Managing Your Liquidity

allocated to short-term needs, such as a cup of coffee or an unexpected car repair, or to long-term needs, such as retirement. You can enhance your liquidity through money management and credit management.

money management
Decisions regarding how much money to retain in liquid form and how to allocate the funds among short-term investment instruments.

emergency fund
A portion of savings that you have allocated to short-term needs such as unexpected expenses in order to maintain adequate liquidity.

credit management
Decisions regarding how much credit to obtain to support your spending and which sources of credit to use.

Money management involves decisions regarding how much money to retain in liquid form and how to allocate the funds among short-term investment instruments. If you do not have access to money to cover short-term needs, you may have insufficient liquidity. As a result, it is important to set up an emergency fund to cover short-term needs. An emergency fund contains the portion of savings that you have allocated to short-term needs such as unexpected expenses in order to maintain adequate liquidity. Finding an effective liquidity level involves deciding how to invest your money so that you can earn a return but also have easy access to cash if needed. Money management is discussed in Chapter 4.

As an alternative to establishing an emergency fund by investing some of your savings for short-term needs, many individuals rely on credit to supplement their liquidity. As a result, credit and credit management are important aspects of liquidity. Credit management involves decisions regarding how much credit to obtain to support your spending and which sources of credit to use. Credit is commonly used to cover both large and small expenses when you are short on cash, so it enhances your liquidity. Credit should be used only when necessary since you must repay borrowed funds with interest (and the interest expenses may be very high). Unfortunately, the use of consumer credit has steadily increased since 1980. As of 2005, consumer credit represented 38 cents of each dollar of personal spending in Canada. Combined with the steady decline in the personal savings rate that was mentioned earlier in this chapter, it is clear that credit management has become a very important part of liquidity for many Canadians. Credit management is discussed in Chapter 5. The use of money management and credit management to manage your liquidity is illustrated in Exhibit 1.3.

A Plan for Your Financing

Loans are typically needed to finance large expenditures, such as university or college tuition, a car, or a home. The amount of financing needed is the difference between the amount of the purchase and the amount of money you have available, as illustrated in Exhibit 1.4. Managing loans includes determining how much you can afford to borrow, deciding on the maturity (length of time) of the loan, and selecting a loan that charges an appropriate interest rate.

A Plan for Protecting Your Assets and Income

risk
Exposure to events (or perils) that can cause a financial loss.

risk management
Decisions about whether and how to protect against risk.

insurance planning
Determining the types and amount of insurance needed to protect your assets.

In the context of insurance, the term risk can be defined as exposure to events (or perils) that can cause a financial loss. Risk management represents decisions about whether and how to protect against risk. Individuals may avoid, reduce, accept, or share (insure) their exposure to risk. Insuring against risk involves insurance planning, which is discussed in Part 4 of this text.

To protect your assets, you can conduct insurance planning, which determines the types and amount of insurance that you need. In particular, automobile insurance and homeowner's insurance protect your assets, while health insurance and life insurance protect your income.

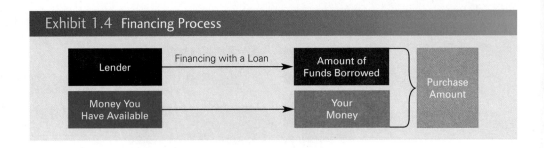

Exhibit 1.4 Financing Process

A Plan for Your Investing

Any savings that you have beyond what you need to maintain liquidity should be invested. Because these funds normally are not used to satisfy your liquidity needs, they can be invested with the primary objective of earning a return. Potential investments include stocks, bonds, mutual funds, and real estate. You must determine how much you wish to allocate toward investments and what types of investments you wish to consider. Since investments are subject to investment risk (uncertainty surrounding their potential return and future potential value), you need to understand your personal tolerance to risk in order to manage it. There are many different kinds of risk; however, at this point in our discussion, risk can most easily be defined as a potential loss of return and/or loss of capital. Your ability to accept such potential losses is your risk tolerance.

investment risk
Uncertainty surrounding not only the potential return on an investment but also its future potential value.

risk tolerance
A person's ability to accept risk, usually defined as a potential loss of return and/or loss of capital.

retirement planning
Determining how much money you should set aside each year for retirement and how you should invest those funds.

estate planning
Determining how your wealth will be distributed before and/or after your death.

A Plan for Your Retirement and Estate

Retirement planning involves determining how much money you should set aside each year for retirement and how you should invest those funds. Retirement planning must begin well before you retire so that you can accumulate sufficient money to invest and support yourself after you retire. Money contributed to various kinds of retirement plans is sheltered from taxes until it is withdrawn from the retirement account.

Estate planning is the act of determining how your wealth will be distributed before and/or after your death. Effective estate planning protects your wealth against unnecessary taxes, and ensures that your wealth is distributed in the manner that you desire.

How the Text Organization Relates to the Financial Plan's Components

Each of the first six parts of this text covers one specific component of the financial plan. The relationship among the components of the financial plan is illustrated in Exhibit 1.5. Part 1 (Tools for Financial Planning) describes budgeting, which focuses on how cash received (from income or other sources) is allocated to savings, spending, and taxes.

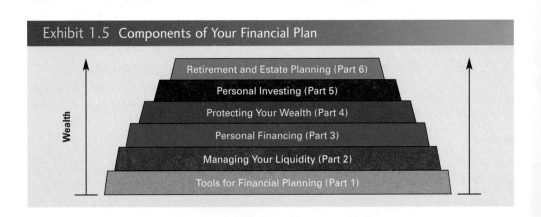

Exhibit 1.5 Components of Your Financial Plan

Exhibit 1.6 Examples of Decisions Made in Each Component of a Financial Plan

A Plan for:	Types of Decisions
1. Managing your income	What expenses should you anticipate?
	How much money should you attempt to save each month?
	How much money must you save each month toward a specific purchase?
	What debt payments must you make each month?
2. Managing your liquidity	How much money should you maintain in your chequing account?
	How much money should you maintain in your savings account?
	Should you use credit cards as a means of borrowing money?
3. Financing	How much money can you borrow to purchase a car?
	Should you borrow money to purchase a car or should you lease a car?
	How much money can you borrow to purchase a home?
	What type of mortgage loan should you obtain to finance the purchase of a house?
4. Protecting your assets and income	What type of insurance do you need?
	How much insurance do you need?
5. Investing	How much money should you allocate toward investments?
	What types of investments should you consider?
	How much risk can you tolerate when investing your money?
6. Your retirement and estate	How much money will you need for retirement?
	How much money must you save each year so that you can retire in a specific year?
	How will you allocate your estate among your heirs?

Budget planning serves as the foundation of the financial plan, as it is your base for making personal financial decisions.

The next component is managing your liquidity (Part 2) because you must have adequate liquidity before financing or investing. Once your budget plan and your liquidity are in order, you are in a position to plan your financing (Part 3) for major purchases such as a new car or a home. Part 4 explains how to use insurance to protect your wealth. Next, you can consider investment alternatives such as stocks, bonds, and mutual funds (Part 5). Finally, planning for retirement and estate planning (Part 6) focus on the wealth that you will accumulate by the time you retire.

An effective financial plan builds your wealth and therefore enhances your net worth. In each part of the text, you will have the opportunity to develop a component of your financial plan. By completing the Building Your Own Financial Plan exercises, you will build a personal financial plan by the end of the school term. Exhibit 1.6 lists examples of the decisions you will make in each component.

How the Components Relate to Your Cash Flows. Exhibit 1.7 illustrates the typical types of income (cash that you receive) and expenses (cash that you spend). This exhibit also shows how each component of the financial plan reflects decisions on how to obtain or use cash. You receive income in the form of a salary from your employer and use some of that cash to spend on products and services. Other examples of income include rental income from property, interest income from GICs, and capital gains income from stocks that you own. Budgeting (Part 1) focuses on the relationship between your income and

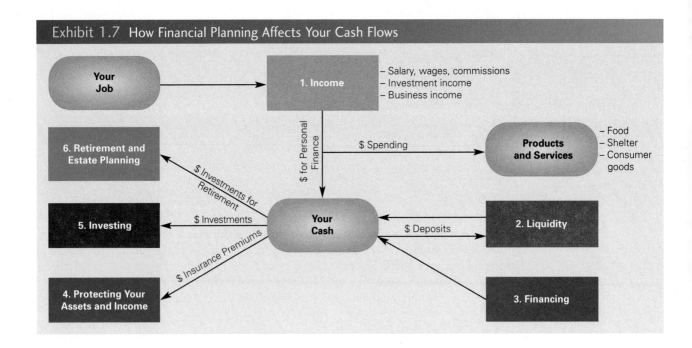

Exhibit 1.7 How Financial Planning Affects Your Cash Flows

your expenses. Your budgeting decisions determine how much of your income you spend on products and services. The residual income can be allocated for your personal finance needs. Liquidity management (Part 2) focuses on depositing a portion of your excess cash in an emergency fund or obtaining credit if you are short on cash. Financing (Part 3) focuses on obtaining cash to support your large purchases. Protecting your assets and income (Part 4) focuses on determining your insurance needs and spending money on insurance premiums. Investing (Part 5) focuses on using some of your excess cash to build your wealth. Planning for your retirement (Part 6) focuses on periodically investing cash in your retirement account.

If you need more cash inflows beyond your income, you may decide to rely on savings that you have already accumulated or obtain loans from creditors. If your income exceeds the amount that you wish to spend, you can use the excess funds to make more investments or to repay some or all of the principal on existing loans. Thus, your investment decisions can serve as a source of funds (selling your investments) or a way of using additional funds (making additional investments). Your financing decisions can serve as a source of funds (obtaining additional loans) or a use of funds (repaying existing loans).

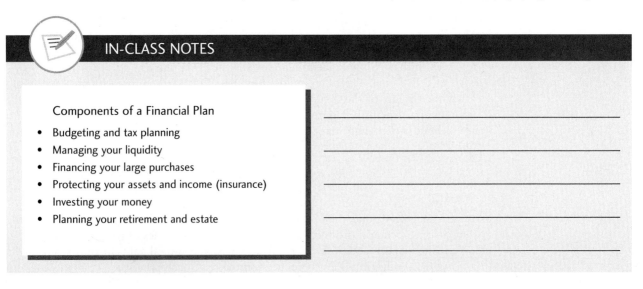

IN-CLASS NOTES

Components of a Financial Plan
- Budgeting and tax planning
- Managing your liquidity
- Financing your large purchases
- Protecting your assets and income (insurance)
- Investing your money
- Planning your retirement and estate

L.O. 3   DEVELOPING THE FINANCIAL PLAN

Six steps are involved in developing each component of your financial plan.

Step 1: Establish Your Financial Goals

You must determine your financial goals.

Specify Your Goals. Goals can be specified in a number of ways. One goal could be to save a specific amount of money so that you can make a down payment on a house. Another could simply be to pay down your debt and improve your creditworthiness. Goals may also be specified in the form of an amount of cash flow that you hope to have someday, such as $25 000 per year in income from your RRSP during your retirement.

Measure Your Goals. Whether you are saving a fixed dollar amount, paying down debt, or building a nest egg for retirement, you must determine how much cash you will need to accomplish each of these goals. Financial calculators available on the Internet can help you plan your goals. For example, Service Canada offers a Retirement Income Calculator on its website at https://srv111.services.gc.ca that can be used to measure your retirement income, including personal and government benefits.

Set Realistic Goals. You need to be realistic about your goals so that you can have a strong likelihood of achieving them. A financial plan that requires you to save almost all of your income is useless if you are unable or unwilling to follow that plan. When this overly ambitious plan fails, you may become discouraged and lose interest in planning. By reducing the level of wealth you wish to attain to a realistic level, you will be able to develop a more achievable plan.

Timing of Goals. Financial goals can be characterized as short term (within the next year), medium term (typically between one and five years), or long term (beyond five years). For instance, a short-term financial goal may be to accumulate enough money to purchase a car within six months. A medium-term goal would be to pay off a school loan in the next three years. A long-term goal would be to save enough money so that you can maintain your lifestyle and retire in 25 to 30 years. The more aggressive your goals, the more ambitious your financial plan will need to be.

Step 2: Consider Your Current Financial Position

Your decisions about how much money to spend next month, how much money to place in your savings account, how often to use your credit card, and how to invest your money depend on your financial position. A person with little debt and many assets will clearly make different decisions than a person with mounting debt and few assets. And a single individual without dependants will have different financial means than a couple with children, even if the individual and the couple have the same income. The appropriate plan also varies with your age and wealth. If you are 20 years old with zero funds in your bank account, your financial plan will be different than if you are 65 years old and have saved much of your income over the last 40 years.

Step 3: Identify and Evaluate Alternative Plans That Could Help You Achieve Your Goals

You must identify and evaluate the alternative financial plans that could achieve your financial goals (specified in Step 1), given your financial position (determined in Step 2). For example, to accumulate a substantial amount of money in 10 years, you could decide either to save a large portion of your income over that period or to invest your initial savings in an investment that may grow in value over time. The first plan is a more conservative approach, but requires you to save money consistently over time. The second plan does not require as much discipline, because it relies on the initial investment to grow substantially over time. However, the second plan has a greater chance of failure because there is risk related to whether the value of the initial investment will increase as expected.

Step 4: Select and Implement the Best Plan for Achieving Your Goals

You need to analyze and select the plan that will be most effective in achieving your goals. Individuals in the same financial position with the same financial goals may decide on different financial plans. For example, you may be willing to save a specific amount of money every month to achieve a particular level of wealth in 10 years. Another individual may prefer to make some risky investments today (rather than save money every month) in order to achieve the same level of wealth in 10 years. The type of plan you select to achieve your financial goals is influenced by your willingness to take risk and by your self-discipline.

Using the Internet. The Internet provides you with valuable information for making financial decisions. Your decision to spend money on a new music system or to save the money may depend on how much you can earn from depositing the money. Your decision of whether to purchase a new car depends on the prices of new cars and financing rates on car loans. Your decision of whether to purchase a home depends on the prices of homes and the financing rates on mortgages. Your decision of whether to invest in stocks is influenced by the prices of stocks and potential returns. Your decision of where to purchase insurance may be influenced by the insurance premiums quoted by different insurance agencies and policy options. All of these financial decisions require knowledge of prevailing prices or interest rates, which are literally at your fingertips on the Internet.

The Internet also provides updated information on all parts of the financial plan, such as:

- Current tax rates and rules that can be used for tax planning

- Recent performances of various types of investments

- New regulations for retirement plans

As mentioned earlier, many websites offer online calculators that you can use for a variety of financial planning decisions, such as:

- Estimating your taxes

- Determining how your savings will grow over time

- Determining whether buying or leasing a car is more appropriate for your circumstances

- Planning for your retirement

Financial Planning Online Exercises are provided at the end of each chapter so that you can practise using the Internet for financial planning purposes. URLs in this text are available and updated on the text's website for easy navigation.

When you use online information for personal finance decisions, keep in mind that some information may not be accurate. Use reliable sources, such as websites of government agencies or financial media companies that have proven track records of reporting financial information. Also, recognize that free personal finance advice provided online does not necessarily apply to every person's unique situation. Get a second opinion before you follow online advice, especially when the advice recommends that you spend or invest money.

A magnifying glass icon in the margin will alert you to the Focus on Ethics features, which highlight important ethical questions related to personal finance.

Focus on Ethics: Personal Financial Advice

Many individuals have a limited background in financial planning and rely on professionals in the financial services industry for advice when developing their financial plans. While most advisers take their responsibilities seriously and are very ethical, there are some unethical and incompetent advisers.

One facet of financial services products that creates a potential conflict of interest for your adviser is the many fee and commission structures available on even a single product such as a life insurance policy. Your objective is to get the best advice appropriate to your needs. The adviser's objective should be the same, but the method (or product) selected could possibly be recommended because of the commission structure that the product offers. Let's face it: there is always a conflict of interest any time a salesperson charges a fee or commission. You certainly should inquire about the commission or fees involved in any transaction. You must learn to temper any advice received.

You should be wary of two things: unethical behaviour and incompetent advice. Unethical behaviour can range from touting a stock as a "Buy" when it clearly is not, to outright theft or fraud. Incompetent advice is hard to discern. If you clearly state that you have a low risk tolerance and you are persuaded to buy a risky stock, you probably are receiving incompetent advice, or perhaps even unethical advice.

How do you avoid unethical and incompetent advisers? The solution is to do your homework. By being alert, asking questions, and carefully considering advice received, you may be able to avoid advisers who do not put your interests first. Ask questions of them and ask questions of their current clients. In many cases you will be referred to an adviser by a friend or acquaintance. Ask about his or her experience with the adviser. After you meet the adviser, you can make your own judgments. Check the adviser's credentials. Financial services professionals are licensed for the products they sell and they must meet continuing education requirements to maintain those licences. Throughout the textbook, you will find information that will lead you to the various self-regulatory organizations (SROs) that govern licensed financial services professionals in the financial services industry. For example, The Investor Education Fund website, www.investored.ca, is dedicated to helping you improve your financial know-how and make better investing decisions. Funding for the site is provided by the Ontario Securities Commission (OSC), so the information is objective and can be trusted.

While most financial services professionals are indeed professionals and knowledgeable in their field, it is still your responsibility to monitor your investments. In the final analysis, it should be your decision on which product to buy, how much insurance coverage you should have, and when you should change investments. Educating yourself on these financial products is key to making sound decisions.

Step 5: Evaluate Your Financial Plan

After you develop and implement each component of your financial plan, you must monitor your progress to ensure that the plan is working as you intended. Keep your financial plan easily accessible so that you can evaluate it over time. In general, you should review your plan annually. You should also review your plan if you experience one of the milestones listed in Exhibit 1.2 on page 6.

Step 6: Revise Your Financial Plan

If you find that you are unable or unwilling to follow the financial plan that you developed, you need to revise the plan to make it more realistic. You may need to adjust your financial goals if you are unable to maintain the plan for achieving a particular level of wealth.

We thought you could use some humour every now and again. Enjoy!

Source: www.cartoonstock.com

Go to

http://ca.finance.yahoo.com

This website provides much information and many tools that can be used for all aspects of financial planning, including tax rates, bank deposit rates, loan rates, credit card information, mortgage rates, and quotations and analysis of stocks, bonds, mutual funds, and insurance policies. It also provides information for creating retirement plans and wills.

Throughout each chapter, we have included interesting Weblinks and annotations.

Exhibit 1.8 Summary of Steps Used to Develop a Financial Plan

1. Establish your financial goals.

   - What are your short-term financial goals?
   - What are your medium-term financial goals?
   - What are your long-term financial goals?

2. Consider your current financial position.

   - How much money do you have in savings?
   - What is the value of your investments?
   - What is your net worth?

3. Identify and evaluate alternative plans that could achieve your goals.

   - Given your goals and existing financial position described in the previous steps, how can you obtain the necessary funds to achieve your financial goals?
   - Will you need to reduce your spending to save more money each month?
   - Will you need to make investments that generate a higher rate of return?

4. Select and implement the best plan for achieving your goals.

   - What are the advantages and disadvantages of each alternative plan that could be used to achieve your goals?

5. Evaluate your financial plan.

   - Is your financial plan working properly? That is, will it enable you to achieve your financial goals?

6. Revise your financial plan.

   - Have your financial goals changed?
   - Should parts of the financial plan be revised in order to increase the chance of achieving your financial goals? (If so, identify the parts that should be changed, and determine how they should be revised.)

As time passes, your financial position will change, especially upon specific events such as graduating from a post-secondary institution, marriage, a career change, or the birth of a child. As your financial position changes, your financial goals may change as well. You need to revise your financial plan to reflect such changes in your means and priorities.

The steps to developing a financial plan are summarized in Exhibit 1.8. To see how the steps can be applied, consider the example on the next page.

IN-CLASS NOTES

Developing the Financial Plan

1. Establish your financial goals
   - Ensure they are specific, measurable, realistic, and timely
2. Consider your current financial position
3. Identify and evaluate alternative plans
4. Select and implement the best plan
5. Evaluate your financial plan
6. Revise your financial plan

EXAMPLE

Stephanie Spratt graduated from college last year with a diploma in finance. After searching for a job for several months, she was hired by the Sudbury Tax Services Office at an annual salary of about $38 000. She is eager to have money from her salary to spend and to give up her interim part-time job waiting tables.

Stephanie plans to save a portion of every paycheque so that she can invest money to build her wealth over time. She realizes that by establishing a financial plan to limit her spending today, she can increase her wealth and therefore her potential spending in the future. At this point, Stephanie decides to develop an overview of her current financial position, establish her goals, and map out a plan for how she might achieve those goals, as shown in her financial plan below.

Key decisions that relate to Stephanie's financial plan will be summarized at the end of each chapter. Your financial planning decisions will differ from Stephanie's, or anyone else's. Nevertheless, the process of building a financial plan is the same. You need to establish your goals, assess different methods for achieving those goals, and decide on a financial plan that can achieve those goals.

> Stephanie Spratt is a fictional person who lives in Sudbury, Ontario, and works for the federal government at the Sudbury Tax Services Office. In each chapter, you will find examples of her progress in building her personal financial plan.

> At the end of each chapter you will have an opportunity to apply the concepts you have learned and help Stephanie Spratt further develop her financial plan.

STEPHANIE SPRATT'S FINANCIAL PLAN: Overview

STEP 1: FINANCIAL GOALS

I would like to:

- *buy a new car within a year,*
- *buy a home within two years,*
- *make investments that will allow my wealth to grow over time, and*
- *build a large amount of savings for retirement in 20 to 40 years.*

STEP 2: CURRENT FINANCIAL POSITION

I have very little savings at this time and own an old car. My current income is about $38 000 a year before taxes and payroll deductions. This should increase over time.

STEP 3: PLANS TO ACHIEVE THE GOALS

Since my current financial position does not provide me with sufficient funds to achieve these financial goals, I need to develop a financial plan to accomplish all of these goals. One possible plan would be to save enough money until I could purchase the car and home with cash. With this plan, however, I would not have sufficient savings to purchase a home for many years. An alternative is to save enough money to make a down payment on the car and home and to obtain financing to cover the rest of the cost. This alternative plan allows me to allocate some of my income toward investments. My financing decisions will determine the type of car and home that I will purchase and the amount of funds I will have left to make other investments so that I can build my wealth over time.

STEP 4: SELECTING AND IMPLEMENTING THE BEST PLAN

Financing the purchase of a car and a home is a more appropriate plan for me. I will prepare a budget so that over time I can accumulate savings for a down payment on a new car. Then, I will attempt to accumulate savings to make a down payment on a new home. I need to make sure that I can afford financing payments on any money that I borrow.

STEP 5: EVALUATING THE PLAN

Once I establish a budget, I will monitor it over time to determine whether I am achieving the desired amount of savings each month. As well, I must ensure that all credit payments are covered.

STEP 6: REVISING THE PLAN

If I cannot save as much money as I desire, I may have to delay my plans for purchasing a car and a home until I can accumulate enough funds to make the down payments. If I am able to exceed my savings goal, I may be able to purchase the car and the home sooner than I had originally expected.

You will find the chapter summaries useful tools to review the key points in each chapter; the summaries are organized by learning objective.

The Integrating the Key Concepts features summarize how to apply the concepts you have covered in the chapter to your own financial plan.

SUMMARY

Personal financial planning is the process of planning your income spending, financing, and investing activities, while taking into account uncontrollable events such as death or disability, in order to optimize your financial situation.

A financial plan has six components: (1) budgeting and tax planning, (2) managing your liquidity, (3) financing large purchases, (4) protecting your assets and income, (5) investing, and (6) planning your retirement and estate.

The financial planning process involves six steps: (1) establishing your financial goals, (2) considering your current financial position, (3) identifying and evaluating alternative plans that could achieve your goals, (4) selecting and implementing the best plan for achieving your financial goals, (5) evaluating the financial plan over time to ensure that you are meeting your goals, and (6) revising the financial plan when necessary.

INTEGRATING THE KEY CONCEPTS

All of the components of the financial plan are related. In general, the financial planning tools (such as budgeting and tax planning) are used for the financial planning decisions discussed in the following parts of this text. For example, your budget (Part 1) determines how much money you can set aside to maintain liquidity (Part 2) or to invest in long-term investments (Part 5). The other components of the financial plan are also related. The way you obtain funds to finance large purchases such as a car or a home (Part 3) depends on whether you sell any of your existing investments (Part 5) to obtain all or a portion of the funds needed. Your need for insurance (Part 4) depends on the types of assets you own (e.g., a car or a home). Your ability to save for retirement (Part 6) depends on the amount of funds you need to pay off any existing credit balance (Part 2) or loans (Part 3).

The Integrating the Key Concepts diagrams provide a visual reference of the important points in each chapter.

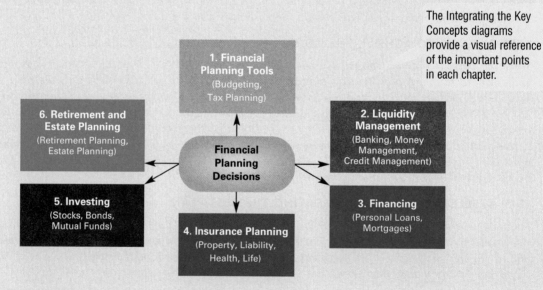

The Review Questions provide you with an opportunity to practise and review the key concepts in each chapter.

REVIEW QUESTIONS

1. Define personal financial planning. What types of decisions are involved in a personal financial plan?

2. What is an opportunity cost? What might be some of the opportunity costs of spending $10 per week on lottery tickets?

3. How can an understanding of personal finance benefit you?

4. What are the six key components of a financial plan?

5. Define budget planning. What elements must be assessed in budget planning?

6. How is your net worth calculated? Why is it important?

7. What factors influence income? Why is an accurate estimate of expenses important in budget planning? How do tax laws affect the budgeting process?

8. What is liquidity? What two factors are considered in managing liquidity? How are they used?

9. What factors are considered in managing financing?

10. What is the primary objective of investing? What else must be considered? What potential investment vehicles are available?

11. What are the three elements of planning to protect your assets? Define each element.

12. How does each element of financial planning affect your cash flows?

13. What are the six steps in developing a financial plan?

14. How do your financial goals fit into your financial plan? Why should goals be realistic? What are three time frames for goals? Give an example of a goal for each time frame.

15. Name some factors that might affect your current financial position.

16. How do your current financial position and goals relate to your creation of alternative financial plans?

17. Once your financial plan has been implemented, what is the next step? Why is it important?

18. Why might you need to revise your financial plan?

19. List some information available on the Internet that might be useful for financial planning. Describe one way you might use some of this information for financial planning purposes.

20. What are some of the different types of unethical behaviour financial advisers might engage in? How can an understanding of personal financial planning help you deal with this potential behaviour?

The Financial Planning Problems will help you review your knowledge of financial planning.

FINANCIAL PLANNING PROBLEMS

1. Julia brings home $1600 per month after taxes. Her rent is $350 per month, her utilities are $100 per month, and her car payment is $250 per month. Julia is currently paying $200 per month to her orthodontist for her braces.

   a. If Julia's groceries cost $50 per week and she estimates her other expenses to be $150 per month, how much will she have left each month to put toward savings to reach her financial goals?

   b. Julia is considering trading in her car for a new one. Her new car payment will be $325 per month, and her insurance cost will increase by $60 per month. Julia determines that her other car-related expenses (gas, oil) will stay about the same. What is the opportunity cost if Julia purchases the new car?

2. Mia has $3000 in assets, a finance company loan for $500, and an outstanding credit card balance of $135. Mia's monthly disposable income is $2000, and she has monthly expenses of $1650. What is Mia's net worth?

3. At the beginning of the year, Arianne had a net worth of $5000. During the year she set aside $100 per month from her paycheque for savings and borrowed $500 from her cousin that she must pay back in January of next year. What was her net worth at the end of the year?

4. Anna has just received a gift of $500 for her graduation, which increased her net worth by $500. If she uses the money to purchase a stereo, how will her net worth be affected? If she invests the $500 at 10 percent interest per year, what will it be worth in one year?

5. Jason's car was just stolen and the police informed him that they will probably be unable to recover it. His insurance will not cover the theft. Jason has a net worth of $3000, all of which is easily convertible to cash. Jason requires a car for his job and his daily life.

Based on Jason's net cash flow, he cannot afford more than $200 per month in car payments. What options does he have? How will these options affect his net worth and net cash flow?

Test your knowledge of how to handle specific ethical questions related to personal finance with the Ethical Dilemma problems.

ETHICAL DILEMMA

Sandy and Phil have recently married and are both in their early twenties. In establishing their financial goals, they determine that their three long-term goals are to purchase a home, to provide their children with college educations, and to plan for their retirement.

They decide to seek professional assistance in reaching their goals. After considering several financial advisers who charge an annual fee based on the size of their portfolio, they decide to go to Sandy's cousin Larry, who is a stockbroker. Larry tells them that he is happy to help them, and that his services will not cost them anything out of pocket. In their initial meeting, Larry discusses several possibilities, including a whole life insurance policy and an investment product called a segregated fund. The segregated fund guarantees that Sandy and Phil will not lose any money that they initially deposit into the fund. Because Sandy and Phil have established their long-term goals, Larry's recommendations sound appropriate and the cost is right. Both plans have a savings component that can be used for a down payment in the future when they purchase their first home.

Several years later, Sandy and Phil have diligently paid down their college debt and have also paid their life insurance premiums as well as made several large lump sum deposits into the segregated fund recommended by Larry. They are ready to purchase their first home.

Larry tells them that their life insurance has a very low surrender value at this time. In addition, segregated investment funds are at a low right now because the stock market is down. While they can cash in their fund now, they will lose about 45 percent of their original deposits. The guarantee does not apply unless the investment is kept for the contracted holding period. This information was included in their policies.

a. Did Larry act ethically in his dealings with Sandy and Phil?

b. What did Sandy and Phil fail to do?

c. How could these problems be handled in the future?

Use the Internet to learn more about planning your finances online.

FINANCIAL PLANNING ONLINE EXERCISES

1. Go to www.careers-in-finance.com/fpskill.htm.

   a. What are the most important skills needed to perform the job of a financial planner? Which skills are your strengths and which are your weaknesses?

   b. How can you obtain the skills you lack?

2. The purpose of this exercise is to familiarize you with the wide variety of personal finance resources on Yahoo! Canada. Go to http://ca.pfinance.yahoo.com.

   a. Determine how long it will take you to reach your financial goals. In the Tools section, click on "Financial Goals". How many years will it take you to reach your goal of saving $100 000 if you have already saved $5000, you are able to make a monthly contribution of $200, and you expect an average annual return of 6 percent on your investments?

   b. Using the information in Financial Planning Problem 2, determine Mia's net worth using the Net Worth Calculator located in the Tools section.

Here you will find information about what is on the Student CD-ROM for each chapter.

ON THE STUDENT CD-ROM FOR THIS CHAPTER YOU WILL FIND:

- Building Your Own Financial Plan exercise and worksheets

- The first chapter-end Continuing Case about the Sampson family.

   Read through the Building Your Own Financial Plan exercise. Then use the worksheets to review your current

financial situation and anticipate your future situation by creating short-, medium-, and long-term goals.

   After reading the case study, use the Continuing Case worksheets to help the Sampsons summarize their current financial position and plan for the future.

Study Guide

Circle the correct answer and then check the answers in the back of the book to chart your progress.

Multiple Choice

1. Personal finance is:
   a. The process of planning your spending, financing, and investing activities, while taking into account controllable events such as death or disability, in order to optimize your financial situation.
   b. The process of planning your spending and investing activities, while taking into account uncontrollable events such as death or disability, in order to optimize your financial situation.
   c. The process of planning your spending, financing, and investing activities, while taking into account uncontrollable events such as death or disability, in order to optimize your financial situation.
   d. The process of planning your spending and investing activities, while taking into account controllable events such as death or disability, in order to optimize your financial situation.

2. An understanding of personal finance is beneficial to you in many ways, including the following:
   a. Helping you make informed decisions about your financial situation.
   b. Helping you judge the guidance of financial advisers.
   c. Helping you determine whether a career as a financial adviser is right for you.
   d. All of the above.

3. Which of the following individuals would be considered a "big saver"?
   a. Jill has recently inherited $20 000 from her aunt's estate. Jill is unsure whether she should use this money to pay off her student loans or buy a new car. She decides to put this money in a savings account until she can figure out what to do with it.
   b. Ted earns $1000 per month, after deductions and taxes. Before he spends any of this money, he allocates 10 percent ($100) to his savings plan and then considers spending the rest of his money.
   c. Maria earns $1200 per month, after deductions and taxes. Maria has always been nervous about spending money, fearing that she may not have enough when she needs it. She only spends money on the bare essentials of life. As a result,

she is often able to save more than half of her monthly income.
   d. Frank earns $1100 per month, after deductions and taxes. He has a very active social life and spends most of his time out of the house with friends. Frank usually spends all of his take-home pay and sometimes is rejected by the ABM machine because he has no money in his account.

4. Olani Waters, 32, and his spouse, Vanessa, 28, are expecting their first child in a few months. David, their financial adviser, has agreed to help them determine how much life insurance they need and what their options are with respect to RESPs. What life stage would most appropriately describe the Waters' current financial position?
   a. Early earning
   b. Pre-career
   c. Mid earning
   d. Prime earning

5. Finding an effective liquidity level involves:
   a. Deciding how to invest your money in order to maximize your return.
   b. Deciding how to invest your money in order to maximize your return, before considering whether you need easy access to cash.
   c. Deciding how to invest your money in order to maximize your return, such that you will never have to rely on credit management to cover short-term needs.
   d. Deciding how to invest your money so that you can earn a return but also have easy access to cash if needed.

6. Risk management represents decisions about whether and how to protect against risk. Individuals may _____, _____, _____, or _____ their exposure to risk.
   a. Avoid, remove, accept, insure
   b. Avoid, reduce, accept, insure
   c. Avoid, reduce, acknowledge, insure
   d. Avoid, remove, acknowledge, insure

7. Place the following six steps of the financial plan in the correct order
   1. Select and implement the best plan for achieving your goals
   2. Consider your current financial position
   3. Evaluate your financial plan

4. Establish your financial goals
5. Revise your financial plan
6. Identify and evaluate alternative plans
    a. 4, 2, 6, 1, 3, 5
    b. 2, 4, 6, 1, 3, 5
    c. 4, 2, 6, 3, 1, 5
    d. 2, 4, 6, 3, 1, 5

8. Raj and Chandan have established their financial goals. Given their current financial position, they have decided to invest $100 per month in a mutual fund every year for 10 years (Plan A). Raj's co-worker suggests that, instead of saving for 10 years, the couple should immediately contribute a large lump sum, such as $1200, into a mutual fund (Plan B). Although both plans may allow the couple to achieve their goals, which of the following statements should be considered before the couple makes a decision?
    a. Plan A is a more aggressive approach that requires them to save money consistently over time, whereas Plan B does not require as much discipline, and is more likely to fail because there is risk related to whether the value of the initial investment will increase as expected.
    b. Plan A is a more conservative approach that requires them to save money consistently over time, whereas Plan B requires more discipline, and is more likely to fail because there is risk related to whether the value of the initial investment will increase as expected.
    c. Plan A is a more conservative approach that requires them to save money consistently over time, whereas Plan B does not require as much discipline, and is more likely to fail because there is risk related to whether the value of the initial investment will increase as expected.
    d. Plan A is a more conservative approach that requires them to save money consistently over time, whereas Plan B requires more discipline, and is more likely to succeed because the value of the initial investment will increase as expected.

9. When implementing the best plan to meet your financial goals, you can use information available on the Internet or the advice of a financial adviser. When deciding which products to buy, how much insurance coverage you should have, and when you should change investments, who is responsible for the plan that you implement?

a. It is your responsibility to monitor your financial plans.
b. If you have established a long-term relationship with your financial adviser, it is his or her responsibility to monitor your financial plans.
c. The company whose products you have purchased should monitor your financial plans.
d. All of the above.

10. Why might you need to revise your plan from time to time in order to make it more realistic?
    a. You are unable to follow the financial plan.
    b. You are unwilling to follow the financial plan.
    c. Your financial position has changed.
    d. All of the above.

True/False

1. True or False? The per capita debt of Canadians has risen over the last 25 years.

2. True or False? In order to become a financial adviser, you must meet the education, examination, and experience requirements set by the FPSC.

3. True or False? A single course in personal finance will allow you to start a career as a financial adviser.

4. True or False? Your net worth is the value of what you own (your assets) minus the value of what you owe (your liabilities).

5. True or False? Credit management is not a very important part of overall liquidity management for many Canadians.

6. True or False? Loans are typically needed to finance large and small expenditures.

7. True or False? The best choice for savings above and beyond what is required for liquidity purposes is low-risk, low-return investments.

8. True or False? Your personal tolerance to risk should be understood if you are considering investments such as stocks, bonds, mutual funds, and real estate.

9. True or False? Your financial goals must be specific, measurable, realistic, and timely if you wish to achieve them.

10. True or False? In general, you should review your financial plan once every two years.

Tools for Financial Planning

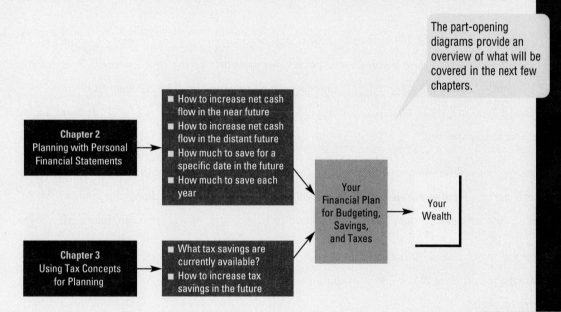

The part-opening diagrams provide an overview of what will be covered in the next few chapters.

Chapter 2
Planning with Personal Financial Statements

- How to increase net cash flow in the near future
- How to increase net cash flow in the distant future
- How much to save for a specific date in the future
- How much to save each year

Chapter 3
Using Tax Concepts for Planning

- What tax savings are currently available?
- How to increase tax savings in the future

Your Financial Plan for Budgeting, Savings, and Taxes

Your Wealth

The part-opening summary outlines how to use the chapters to create your own financial plan.

THE CHAPTERS IN THIS PART INTRODUCE THE KEY TOOLS USED to make financial planning decisions. Chapter 2 describes the personal financial statements that help you monitor your spending and guide your budgeting and savings decisions. Chapter 3 explains how to use tax concepts to assess and minimize your tax liability. Your budget, savings, and tax plans all influence your cash flows and wealth.

Chapter 2

Planning with Personal Financial Statements

W here does it all go? It seems as if the last paycheque is gone before the next one comes in. Money seems to burn a hole in your pocket, yet you don't believe that you are living extravagantly. Last month you made a pledge to yourself to spend less than the month before. Somehow, though, you are in the same position as you were last month. Your money is gone. Is there any way to plug the hole in your pocket?

What are your expenses? For many people, the first obstacle is to correctly assess their true expenses. Each expense seems harmless and worthwhile. But when combined, they can be like a school of piranhas that quickly gobble up your modest income. What can you do to gain control of your personal finances?

This chapter will show you how to take control of your finances. However, your task is not easy because it takes self-discipline and there may be no immediate reward. The result is often like a diet: easy to start, but hard to carry through.

Your tools are the personal balance sheet, the personal cash flow statement, and a budget. These three personal financial statements show you where you are, predict where you will be after three months or a year, and help you control expenses. The potential benefits are moderate spending, increased savings and investments, and peace of mind knowing that you are now in control.

The objectives of this chapter are to:

1. Explain how to create your personal cash flow statement
2. Identify the factors that affect your cash flows
3. Explain how to create a budget based on your forecasted cash flows
4. Describe how to create your personal balance sheet
5. Explain how your net cash flows are related to your personal balance sheet and how these cash flows affect your wealth

L.O. 1

PERSONAL CASH FLOW STATEMENT

personal cash flow statement
A financial statement that measures a person's income and expenses.

As mentioned in Chapter 1, budgeting is the process of forecasting future income, future expenses, and savings. When budgeting, the first step is to create a personal cash flow statement, which measures your income and expenses. Comparing your income and expenses allows you to see where your money is going. This is necessary so you can then monitor your spending and determine the amount of cash that you can allocate toward an emergency fund, investments, and other purposes.

Income

The main source of income for working people is their salary, but there can be other important sources of income. Deposits in various types of savings accounts and other forms of debt investments can generate income in the form of interest income. Some stocks also generate income in the form of dividends, and maybe capital gains.

Expenses

Expenses are both large (for example, monthly rent) and small (for example, dry cleaning costs). It is not necessary to document every expenditure, but you should track how most of your money is spent. Monitoring your expenses is much easier if you use your debit card to pay bills. If you use online banking, you will be able to clearly see any expenses that are paid using your debit card. In contrast, if you pay for most of your expenses using cash, you will have to keep a record of all receipts in order to effectively monitor your spending. Recording transactions in your chequebook register when you write cheques will also help you identify how you spend your money. Using a credit card for your purchases also provides a written record of your transactions. Many people use software programs such as Quicken (www.quicken.ca) and Microsoft Money (www.microsoft.com/money) to record and monitor their expenses.

Creating a Personal Cash Flow Statement

You can create a personal cash flow statement by recording how you received income over a given period and how you used cash for expenses.

EXAMPLE

Stephanie Spratt tried to limit her spending in college but never established a personal cash flow statement. Now that she has begun her career and is earning a salary, she wants to monitor her spending on a monthly basis. She decides to create a personal cash flow statement for the previous month.

Stephanie's Monthly Income. Stephanie's present salary is about $1460 biweekly ($37 960 annually) before taxes and payroll deductions. For budgeting purposes, she is interested in the income she receives from her employer after taxes.

About $238 of her biweekly salary goes to taxes. In addition, she contributes approximately $66 toward CPP and $26 toward EI at each pay period. Her disposable (after-tax) income is:

Biweekly Salary		$1460
Biweekly Taxes	($238)	
CPP Contribution	($66)	
EI Contribution	($26)	
Total Payroll Deductions		($330)
Biweekly Take-Home Pay		$1130
Monthly Income ($1130 × 2)		$2260

Stephanie calculates her monthly income by multiplying her take-home pay by two. Then she considers other potential sources of income. She does not receive any dividend income from stock and she does not have any money deposited in an account that pays interest. Thus, her entire monthly income comes from her paycheque. She inserts the monthly income of $2260 at the top of her personal cash flow statement.

Stephanie's Monthly Expenses. Stephanie logs into her online bank account to see how she spent her money last month. Her household payments for the month were as follows:

- $600 for rent
- $50 for cable TV
- $60 for electricity and water
- $60 for telephone expenses
- $200 for groceries
- $60 for a disability insurance plan provided by her employer (this expense is deducted directly from her pay)

Next, Stephanie reviews several credit card bills to estimate her other typical monthly expenses:

- About $100 for clothing
- About $200 for car expenses (insurance, maintenance, and gas)
- About $600 for recreation (including restaurants and a health club membership)

Stephanie uses this expense information to complete her personal cash flow statement, as shown in Exhibit 2.1. Her total expenses were $1930 last month.

net cash flows
Disposable (after-tax) income minus expenses.

Stephanie's Net Cash Flows. Monthly income and expenses can be compared by estimating net cash flows, which is equal to disposable (after-tax) income minus expenses. Stephanie estimates her net cash flows to determine how easily she covers her expenses and how much excess cash she can allocate to an emergency fund, investments, or other purposes. Her net cash flows during the last month were:

$$
\begin{aligned}
\text{Net Cash Flows} &= \text{Income} - \text{Expenses} \\
&= \$2260 - \$1930 \\
&= \$330
\end{aligned}
$$

Stephanie enters this information at the bottom of her personal cash flow statement.

IN-CLASS NOTES

Personal Cash Flow Statement
- Record Your Income
  - Salary, interest income, dividends
- Record Your Expenses
  - Rent, living expenses, credit card payments
  - Monitor expenses by recording chequing transactions and checking bank statements
- Net Cash Flows
  - Income − expenses = excess cash

Exhibit 2.1 Personal Cash Flow Statement for Stephanie Spratt

Income	Last Month
Disposable (after-tax) income	$2260
Interest on deposits	0
Dividend payments	0
Total Income	**$2260**

Expenses	Last Month
Rent	$600
Cable TV	50
Electricity and water	60
Telephone	60
Groceries	200
Disability insurance	60
Clothing	100
Car expenses (insurance, maintenance, and gas)	200
Recreation	600
Total Expenses	**1930**
Net Cash Flows	**+$330**

L.O. 2 FACTORS THAT AFFECT CASH FLOWS

To enhance your wealth, you want to maximize your (or your household's) income and minimize expenses. Your income and expenses depend on various factors, as will be described next.

Factors Affecting Income

The key factors that affect your income level are the stage of your career path, your job skills, and the number of income earners in your household.

Stage in Your Career Path. Income is low to moderate for people who are in post-secondary education or just starting a career (like Stephanie Spratt). Income tends to increase as you gain job experience and progress within your chosen career. The relationship between income and job experience is reinforced by the life stage exhibit discussed in Chapter 1 (refer back to Exhibit 1.2). Younger people in the early earning life stage tend to have lower income than older people who are in their prime earning years. This is because older people tend to have more work experience and are thus farther along in their career paths.

There are many exceptions to this tendency, however. Some older people switch careers and therefore may be set back on their career path. Other individuals who switch careers from a low-demand industry to a high-demand industry may earn higher income. Many individuals put their careers on hold for several years to raise children and then resume their professional lives.

During the retirement life stage, income from a salary may be discontinued. After retirement, individuals rely on their RRSPs and other retirement benefits, as well as interest or dividend income earned on investments for most of their income. Consequently, retired individuals' income tends to be smaller than it was when they were working. Your retirement income will come from your investments and your retirement plan. The manner in which age commonly affects income is summarized in Exhibit 2.2. Notice that there are three distinct phases.

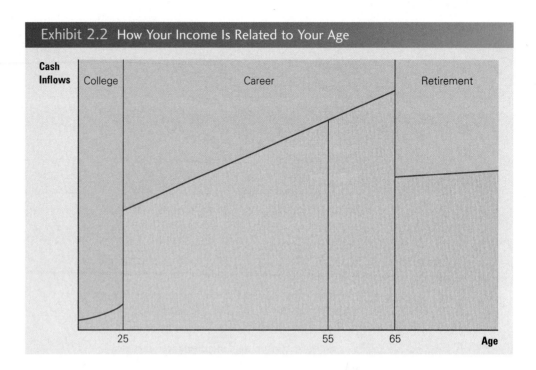

Exhibit 2.2 How Your Income Is Related to Your Age

Type of Job. Income also varies by job type. Jobs that require specialized skills tend to pay much higher salaries than those that require skills that can be obtained very quickly and easily. The income level associated with specific skills is also affected by the demand for those skills. The demand for people with a nursing licence has been very high in recent years, so hospitals have been forced to pay higher salaries to attract employees.

Number of Income Earners in Your Household. If you are the sole income earner, your household's income will typically be less than if there is a second income earner. Many households now have two income earners, a trend that has substantially increased the net cash flows to these households.

Factors Affecting Expenses
The key factors that affect expenses are a person's family status, age, and personal consumption behaviour.

Size of Family. A person who is supporting a family will normally incur more expenses than a single person without dependants. The more family members there are, the greater the expenses for food, clothing, daycare, and school tuition.

Age. As people get older, they tend to spend more money on houses, cars, and vacations. This adjustment in spending may result from the increase in their income over time as they progress along their career path. At the end of their career—that is, during their retirement and post-retirement years—people tend to spend less money as they adjust to a decrease in their income and required living expenses.

Personal Consumption Behaviour. People's consumption behaviour varies substantially. At one extreme are people who spend their entire paycheque within a few days of receiving it, regardless of its size. Although this behaviour is understandable for people who have low incomes, it is also a common practice for some people who have very large incomes, perhaps because they do not understand the importance of saving for the future. At the other extreme are "big savers" who minimize their spending and focus on saving for the future. Most people's consumption behaviour is affected by their income. For example, a two-income household tends to spend more money when both income earners are working full-time.

IN-CLASS NOTES

Factors That Affect Cash Flows

- Income
  - Stage in your career path
  - Type of job
  - Number of income earners in your household
- Expenses
  - Size of family
  - Age
  - Personal consumption behaviour

_____

_____

_____

_____

_____

L.O. 3 CREATING A BUDGET

The next step in the budgeting process is an extension of the personal cash flow statement. You can forecast net cash flows by forecasting the income and expenses for each item on the personal cash flow statement. We refer to a cash flow statement that is based on forecasted cash flows for a future time period as a **budget**. For example, you may develop a budget to determine whether your income will be sufficient to cover your expenses. If you expect your income to exceed your expenses, you can also use the budget to determine the amount of excess cash that you will have available to build an emergency fund, to invest in additional assets, or to make extra payments to reduce your personal debt.

budget
A cash flow statement that is based on forecasted cash flows (income and expenses) for a future time period.

EXAMPLE

Stephanie Spratt wants to determine whether she will have sufficient income this month. She uses the personal cash flow statement she developed last month to forecast this month's cash flows. However, she adjusts that statement for the following additional anticipated expenses:

> Car maintenance expenses will be $800 this month, primarily because Stephanie's car needs to have its brakes replaced.

Stephanie revises her personal cash flow statement from last month to reflect the expected changes this month, as shown in Exhibit 2.3. The numbers in boldface show the revised cash flows as a result of the unusual circumstances for this month.

The main effects of the unusual circumstances regarding Stephanie's expected cash flows for this month are summarized in Exhibit 2.4. Notice that the expected expenses for this month are $2530, or $600 higher than the expenses in a typical month. In this month, the expected net cash flows are:

Expected Net Cash Flows = Expected Income − Expected Expenses

= $2260 − $2530

= −$270

The budgeting process has alerted Stephanie to this $270 cash shortage.

Exhibit 2.3 Stephanie Spratt's Revised Personal Cash Flow Statement

Income	Actual Amounts Last Month	Expected Amounts This Month
Disposable (after-tax) income	$2260	$2260
Interest on deposits	0	0
Dividend payments	0	0
Total Income	**$2260**	**$2260**

Expenses	Actual Amounts Last Month	Expected Amounts This Month
Rent	$600	$600
Cable TV	50	50
Electricity and water	60	60
Telephone	60	60
Groceries	200	200
Disability insurance	60	60
Clothing	100	100
Car expenses (insurance, maintenance, and gas)	200	**800**
Recreation	600	600
Total Expenses	**$1930**	**$2530**
Net Cash Flows	**+$330**	**−$270**

Anticipating Cash Shortages

In the example above, Stephanie was able to anticipate the expense of having her car's brakes replaced. If she had been able to save her net cash flow of $330, calculated in Exhibit 2.1, in an emergency fund for a few months prior to having her brakes replaced, Stephanie could have covered her cash shortage. If she did not have sufficient money in her emergency fund, she could have temporarily used a line of credit to meet her cash needs. The money management and credit management discussions in Chapters 4 and 5, respectively, will provide you with a better understanding of how to meet short-term liquidity needs. If used consistently over time, the budgeting process can warn you of cash shortages well in advance so that you can determine how to cover the deficiency. Setting aside funds in a savings account that can serve as an emergency fund in the event of a cash shortage should be a top priority for Stephanie.

Assessing the Accuracy of the Budget

Periodically compare your actual income and expenses over a recent period (such as the previous month) to the forecasted income and expenses in your budget to determine whether your forecasts are on target. Many individuals tend to be overly optimistic in their forecasts.

Exhibit 2.4 Summary of Stephanie Spratt's Revised Cash Flows

	Last Month's Cash Flow Situation	Unusual Cash Flows Expected This Month	This Month's Cash Flow Situation
Income	$2260	$ 0	$2260
Expenses	$1930	$600	$2530
Net cash flows	$ 330	−$600	−$270

They overestimate their income and underestimate their expenses; as a result, their net cash flows are lower than expected. By detecting such forecasting errors, you can take steps to improve your budgeting. You may decide to limit your spending to stay within your budgeted expenses, or you may choose not to adjust your spending habits but to increase your forecast of expenses to reflect reality. By budgeting accurately, you are more likely to detect any future cash flow shortages and therefore can prepare in advance for any deficiencies.

EXAMPLE

Recall that Stephanie Spratt forecasted income and expenses to create a budget for the coming month. Now it is the end of the month, so she can assess whether her forecasts were accurate. Her forecasted income and expenses are shown in the second column of Exhibit 2.5. She compares the actual income and expenses (third column) to her forecast and calculates the difference between them (shown in the fourth column). The difference between columns two and three is referred to as the forecasting error; a positive difference means that the actual income or expense level was less than forecasted, while a negative difference means that the actual income or expense level exceeded the forecast.

While reviewing the fourth column of Exhibit 2.5, Stephanie notices that total expenses were $100 more than expected. Her net cash flows were –$370 (a deficiency of $370), which is worse than the expected level of –$270. Stephanie assesses the individual expenses to determine where she underestimated. Although grocery expenses were slightly lower than expected, her clothing and recreation expenses were higher than anticipated. She decides that the expenses were abnormally high in this month only, so she believes that her budgeted expenses should be reasonably accurate in most months.

Exhibit 2.5 Comparison of Stephanie Spratt's Budgeted and Actual Cash Flows for This Month

Income	Expected Amounts (forecasted at the beginning of the month)	Actual Amounts (determined at the end of the month)	Forecasting Error
Disposable (after-tax) income	$2260	$2260	$0
Interest on deposits	0	0	0
Dividend payments	0	0	0
Total Income	**$2260**	**$2260**	**$0**
Expenses	**Expected Amounts**	**Actual Amounts**	**Forecasting Error**
Rent	$600	$600	$0
Cable TV	50	50	0
Electricity and water	60	60	0
Telephone	60	60	0
Groceries	200	180	+20
Disability insurance	60	60	0
Clothing	100	170	−70
Car expenses (insurance, maintenance, and gas)	800	800	0
Recreation	600	650	−50
Total Cash Outflows	**$2530**	**$2630**	**−$100**
Net Cash Flows	**−$270**	**−$370**	**−$100**

Forecasting Net Cash Flows over Several Months

To forecast your net cash flows for several months, you can follow the same process as for forecasting one month ahead. Whenever particular types of income or expenses are expected to be normal, they can be forecasted from previous months when the levels were normal. You can make adjustments to account for any income or expense amounts that you expect to be unusual in a specific month in the future. (For example, around the winter holidays you can expect to spend more on gifts and recreation.)

Expenses such as prescription drugs, car repairs, and household repairs often occur unexpectedly. Although such expenses are not always predictable, you should budget for them periodically. You should assume that you will likely incur some unexpected expenses for repairs on a car or on household items over the course of several months. Thus, your budget may not be perfectly accurate in any specific month, but it will be reasonably accurate over time. If you do not account for such possible expenses over time, you will likely experience lower net cash flows than expected.

Budgeting with a Biweekly Pay Period

Recall that Stephanie is paid biweekly. A biweekly pay period means that she is paid every two weeks. Another way of looking at this is that Stephanie will have 26 pay periods during the year. The exhibits above only include 24 pay periods—that is, two pay periods per month for 12 months. Stephanie's budgeting method points out an interesting fact about biweekly pay periods. In order to allow for the additional two pay periods under a biweekly structure, an individual will receive an additional paycheque twice a year. During a calendar year, there will be two months during which Stephanie will be paid three times. Exhibit 2.6 provides an example of a biweekly pay period schedule for the 2008 calendar year (Friday pay dates are in red). This exhibit assumes that the first pay period continues from the end of 2007 until the first pay date of January 4. As you will notice, February and August contain three pay periods. These extra pay periods provide an ideal opportunity for Stephanie to boost her emergency fund or long-term savings plan.

Creating an Annual Budget

If you are curious about how much money you may be able to save in the next year, you can extend your budget for longer periods. You should first create an annual budget and then adjust it to reflect anticipated large changes in your cash flows. A large change in cash flow could be due to a change in income and/or expenses. The biweekly bonus discussed above is an example of a change in income. If you pay your car insurance on an annual basis, your car insurance payment is an example of a change in expense.

EXAMPLE

Stephanie Spratt believes her budget for the previous month (except for the unusual car expense) is typical for her. She wants to extend it to forecast the amount of money she might be able to save over the next year. Her disposable income is predictable because she already knows her salary for the year. Some of the monthly expenses (such as rent and the cable bill) in her monthly budget are also constant from one month to the next. To forecast these types of expenses, she simply multiplies the monthly amount by 12 to derive an estimate of the annual expenses, as shown in the third column of Exhibit 2.7.

Some other items vary from month to month, but last month's budgeted amount seems to be a reasonable estimate for the next 12 months. Over the next 12 months, Stephanie expects net cash flows of $3960. As well, Stephanie realizes that she will receive an additional $2260 from the two bonus pay periods throughout the year. Therefore, she sets a goal of saving $3960, or $330 per month, in an emergency fund, while the $2260 will be put into long-term investments.

Exhibit 2.6 Example of a Biweekly Pay Period Schedule

January 2008
S	M	T	W	T	F	S
		1	2	3	4	5
6	7	8	9	10	11	12
13	14	15	16	17	18	19
20	21	22	23	24	25	26
27	28	29	30	31		

February 2008
S	M	T	W	T	F	S
					1	2
3	4	5	6	7	8	9
10	11	12	13	14	15	16
17	18	19	20	21	22	23
24	25	26	27	28	29	

March 2008
S	M	T	W	T	F	S
						1
2	3	4	5	6	7	8
9	10	11	12	13	14	15
16	17	18	19	20	21	22
23	24	25	26	27	28	29
30	31					

April 2008
S	M	T	W	T	F	S
		1	2	3	4	5
6	7	8	9	10	11	12
13	14	15	16	17	18	19
20	21	22	23	24	25	26
27	28	29	30			

May 2008
S	M	T	W	T	F	S
				1	2	3
4	5	6	7	8	9	10
11	12	13	14	15	16	17
18	19	20	21	22	23	24
25	26	27	28	29	30	31

June 2008
S	M	T	W	T	F	S
1	2	3	4	5	6	7
8	9	10	11	12	13	14
15	16	17	18	19	20	21
22	23	24	25	26	27	28
29	30					

July 2008
S	M	T	W	T	F	S
		1	2	3	4	5
6	7	8	9	10	11	12
13	14	15	16	17	18	19
20	21	22	23	24	25	26
27	28	29	30	31		

August 2008
S	M	T	W	T	F	S
					1	2
3	4	5	6	7	8	9
10	11	12	13	14	15	16
17	18	19	20	21	22	23
24	25	26	27	28	29	30
31						

September 2008
S	M	T	W	T	F	S
	1	2	3	4	5	6
7	8	9	10	11	12	13
14	15	16	17	18	19	20
21	22	23	24	25	26	27
28	29	30				

October 2008
S	M	T	W	T	F	S
			1	2	3	4
5	6	7	8	9	10	11
12	13	14	15	16	17	18
19	20	21	22	23	24	25
26	27	28	29	30	31	

November 2008
S	M	T	W	T	F	S
						1
2	3	4	5	6	7	8
9	10	11	12	13	14	15
16	17	18	19	20	21	22
23	24	25	26	27	28	29
30						

December 2008
S	M	T	W	T	F	S
	1	2	3	4	5	6
7	8	9	10	11	12	13
14	15	16	17	18	19	20
21	22	23	24	25	26	27
28	29	30	31			

Improving the Budget

As time passes, you should review your budget to determine whether you are progressing toward the financial goals you established. To increase your savings or pay down more debt so that you can more easily achieve your financial goals, you should identify the components within the budget that you can change to improve your financial position over time.

EXAMPLE

Recall that Stephanie Spratt expects to spend about $1930 per month and invest her net cash flow in assets (such as a savings account or stocks). She would like to save a substantial amount of money so that she can purchase a new car and a home someday, so she considers how she might increase her net cash flows.

Stephanie assesses her personal income statement to determine whether she can increase her income or reduce her expenses. She would like to generate more income than $2260, but she is already paid well, given her skills and experience. She considers pursuing a part-time job on weekends, but does not want to use her limited free time to work. Therefore, she realizes that given her present situation and preferences, she will not be able to increase her monthly income. She decides to reduce her monthly expenses so that she can save more than her current level of net cash flows.

Stephanie reviews the summary of expenses on her budget to determine how she can reduce spending. Of the $1930 that she spends per month, about $1330 is spent on what she

Exhibit 2.7 Annual Budget for Stephanie Spratt

Income	Typical Month	This Year's Cash Flows (equal to the typical monthly cash flows × 12)
Disposable (after-tax) income	$2260	$27 120
Interest on deposits	0	0
Dividend payments	0	0
Total Income	**$2260**	**$27 120**

Expenses	Typical Month	This Year's Cash Flows
Rent	$600	$7200
Cable TV	50	600
Electricity and water	60	720
Telephone	60	720
Groceries	200	2400
Disability insurance	60	720
Clothing	100	1200
Car expenses (insurance, maintenance, and gas)	200	2400
Recreation	600	7200
Total Expenses	**$1930**	**$23 160**
Net Cash Flows	**+$330**	**$3960** (difference between income and expenses)

Go to
www.yourmoney.cba.ca and
click on "budget, budget!"

This website provides
tips on effective budgeting
based on your goals.

considers to be necessities (such as her rent and utilities). The remainder of the expenses (about $600) is spent on recreation. Stephanie realizes that any major reduction in spending will have to be as a result of a decrease in recreation expenses.

Most of her recreational spending is on her health club membership and eating at restaurants. She recognizes that she can scale back her spending while still enjoying these activities. Specifically, she observes that her health club is overpriced. She can save about $60 per month by joining a different health club that offers essentially the same services. She also decides to reduce her spending at restaurants by about $40 per month. By revising her spending behaviour in these ways, she can reduce her expenses by $100 per month, as summarized here:

	Previous Cash Flow Situation	Planned Cash Flow Situation
Monthly income	$2260	$2260
Monthly expenses	$1930	$1830
Monthly net cash flows	$330	$430
Yearly net cash flows	$3960 + $2260 = $6220	$5160 + $2260 = $7420

This reduction in spending will increase Stephanie's net cash flows. Over the course of a year, her net cash flows will now be $7420. Although Stephanie had hoped to find a solution that would improve her personal cash flow statement more substantially, she believes this is a good start. More importantly, her budget is realistic.

Focus on Ethics: Excessive Financial Dependence

Have you ever been faced with a large unexpected expense that forced you to ask for financial assistance from your family or friends? Perhaps your car breaks down and needs some expensive repairs. Or perhaps you see something that you would really like to buy, but you know you cannot afford it. If you have not planned for such a large expenditure, you may not have money to pay for it. Faced with a looming debt, it may seem easy to fall back on your family or friends for support. Beware of relying too much on such support, however. When you fail to control your own budget, your reliance on others over long periods of time can create tension and ultimately destroy relationships.

You must become self-reliant. Create a budget and stay within it. Build and maintain an emergency fund so that you need not rely on others in times of financial crisis. Remember, they are making a sacrifice to help you. Their opportunity cost is either forgone consumption or perhaps an investment opportunity delayed. So, before you seek help from family members or friends, ask yourself if you have done all you can on your own. Are you a careful spender or are you buying luxury items that you really cannot afford? Is your financial crisis an unforeseen emergency or did you spend the money earlier instead of saving it for this expense? Careful budgeting and controlled spending lead to self-reliance and a feeling of financial freedom. You are in control.

IN-CLASS NOTES

Creating a Budget

A budget is a forecast of your cash flows for a future time period. It does the following:

- Helps you anticipate cash surpluses and shortages
- Allows you to assess the accuracy of your cash flow
- Allows you to forecast your cash flow over several months or the coming year
- Allows you to reassess your cash flow and improve your budget

_____

_____

_____

_____

_____

L.O. 4 — PERSONAL BALANCE SHEET

The next step in the budgeting process is to create a personal balance sheet. A budget tracks your cash flows over a given period of time, whereas a personal balance sheet provides an overall snapshot of your wealth at a specific point in time. The personal balance sheet summarizes your assets (what you own), your liabilities (what you owe), and your net worth (assets minus liabilities).

personal balance sheet
A summary of your assets (what you own), your liabilities (what you owe), and your net worth (assets minus liabilities).

Assets

The assets on a balance sheet can be classified as liquid assets, household assets, and investments.

liquid assets
Financial assets that can be easily converted into cash without a loss in value.

Liquid Assets. Liquid assets are financial assets that can be easily converted into cash without a loss in value. They are especially useful for covering upcoming expenses. Some of the more common liquid assets are cash, chequing accounts, and savings accounts. Cash is handy to cover small purchases, while a chequing account is convenient for larger

Go to
http://strategis.ic.gc.ca/
epic/site/oca-bc.nsf/en/
ca01808e.html

This website provides
an estimate of the savings
you can accumulate over
time if you can reduce your
spending on daily and/or
weekly expenses, such as a
cup of coffee or lunch.
information that can help
you decide whether an
Internet bank suits your
needs

household assets
Items normally owned by a
household, such as a car
and furniture.

bonds
Certificates issued by
borrowers to raise funds.

stocks
Certificates representing
partial ownership of a firm.

mutual funds
Investment companies that
sell units to individuals and
invest the proceeds in an
overall portfolio of
investment instruments
such as bonds or stocks.

real estate
Rental property and land.

rental property
Housing or commercial
property that is rented out
to others.

purchases. Savings accounts are desirable because they pay interest on the money that is deposited. For example, if your savings account offers an interest rate of 4 percent, you earn annual interest of $4 for every $100 deposited in your account. The amount of interest you earn will be based on the lowest balance in your account during the month. For example, if you have $500 in an account for 21 days, withdraw $400 for one day and replace it the next day, interest earned for that month will be calculated based on the minimum balance of $100. The management of liquid assets to cover day-to-day transactions is discussed in Part 2.

Household Assets. Household assets include items normally owned by a household, such as a car and furniture. The financial planning involved in purchasing large household assets is discussed in Part 3. Over time, these items tend to make up a larger proportion of your total assets than do liquid assets.

When creating a personal balance sheet, you need to assess the value of your household assets. The market value of an asset is the amount you would receive if you sold the asset today. For example, if you purchased a car last year for $20 000, the car may have a market value of $14 000 today, meaning that you could sell it to someone else for $14 000. Although establishing the precise market value of some assets may be difficult, you can use recent listing prices of other similar items nearby to obtain a reasonable estimate.

Investments. Some of the more common investments are in bonds, stocks, and rental property.

Bonds are certificates issued by borrowers (typically, firms and government agencies) to raise funds. When you purchase a $1000 bond that was just issued, you provide a $1000 loan to the issuer of the bond. You earn interest while you hold the bond for a specified period. (Bonds are the subject of Chapter 14.)

Stocks are certificates representing partial ownership of a firm. Firms issue stock to obtain funding for various purposes, such as purchasing new machinery or building new facilities. Many firms have millions of stockholders who own part of the firm.

The investors who purchase stock are referred to as stockholders or shareholders. You may consider purchasing stocks if you have excess funds. You can sell some of your stock holdings when you need funds. The terms *shares* and *shareholder* mean the same as *stock* and *stockholder*, respectively. Another word you may come across is *equity*. If you own shares in a company, you have equity in that company.

The market value of stocks changes daily. You can find the current market value of a stock at many websites, including http://ca.finance.yahoo.com/investing. Stock investors can earn a return on their investment if the stock's value increases. They can also earn a return if the firm pays dividends to its shareholders.

Investments such as stocks normally are not liquid assets because you will incur a loss if you have to sell your investment at less than you paid for it. Stocks are commonly viewed as a long-term investment and therefore are not used to cover day-to-day expenses. (Stocks will be discussed in detail in Chapter 13.)

Mutual funds are investment companies that sell units to individuals and invest the proceeds in an overall portfolio of investment instruments such as bonds or stocks. They are managed by portfolio managers who decide what securities to purchase so that individual investors do not have to make these investment decisions themselves. The minimum investment varies depending on the particular fund, but it is usually between $500 and $5000. The value of the units of any mutual fund can be found in periodicals such as *The Globe and Mail* or on various websites. (We'll examine mutual funds in detail in Chapter 12.)

Real estate includes holdings in rental property and land. Rental property is housing or commercial property that is rented out to others. Some individuals purchase a second home and rent it out to generate additional income every year. Others purchase apartment complexes for the same reason. Some individuals purchase land as an investment, with an eye to future development.

Liabilities

Liabilities represent personal debts (what you owe) and can be segmented into current liabilities and long-term liabilities.

current liabilities
Personal debts that will be paid in the near future (within a year).

Current Liabilities. Current liabilities represent personal debts that will be paid in the near future (within a year). The most common example of a current liability is a credit card balance. Credit card companies send the cardholder a monthly bill that itemizes all purchases made in the previous month. If you pay your balance in full upon receipt of the bill, no interest is charged on the balance. The liability is then eliminated until you receive the next monthly bill.

long-term liabilities
Debt that will be paid over a period longer than one year.

Long-Term Liabilities. Long-term liabilities are debts that will be paid over a period longer than one year. A common long-term liability is a student loan, which reflects debt that a student must pay to a lender over time after graduation. This liability requires you to pay an interest expense periodically. Once you pay off this loan, you eliminate this liability and do not have to pay any more interest expenses. In general, you should limit your liabilities so that you can limit the amount of interest owed.

Other common examples of long-term liabilities are car loans and mortgage (housing) loans. Car loans typically have a maturity of between 3 and 5 years, while mortgages typically have a maturity of 15 to 30 years. Both types of loans can be paid off before their maturity.

Net Worth

Your net worth is the difference between what you own and what you owe.

$$\text{Net Worth} = \text{Value of Total Assets} - \text{Value of Total Liabilities}$$

In other words, if you sold enough of your assets to pay off all of your liabilities, your net worth would be the amount of assets you have remaining. Your net worth is a measure of your wealth because it represents what you own after deducting any money that you owe. If your liabilities exceed your assets, your net worth is negative. A negative net worth technically means you are bankrupt. If you sold all of your assets, you could not cover all of your liabilities. Students or those in the early earning life stage may have a negative net worth. As long as the amounts are reasonable, this may be acceptable. However, those in the latter stages of the life cycle with a negative net worth would have serious financial concerns. Insolvency means that one cannot pay the monthly bills; this usually leads to bankruptcy.

Creating a Personal Balance Sheet

You should create a personal balance sheet to determine your net worth. Update it periodically to monitor how your wealth changes over time.

EXAMPLE

Stephanie Spratt wants to determine her net worth by creating a personal balance sheet that identifies her assets and her liabilities.

Stephanie's Assets. Stephanie owns:

- $500 in cash
- $3500 in her chequing account
- Furniture in her apartment that is worth about $1000
- A car that is worth about $1000
- 100 shares of stock, which does not pay dividends, which she just purchased for $3000 ($30 per share)

Stephanie uses this information to complete the top of her personal balance sheet, shown in Exhibit 2.8. She classifies each item that she owns as a liquid asset, a household asset, or an investment asset.

Stephanie's Liabilities. Stephanie owes $2000 on her credit card. She does not have any other liabilities at this time, so she lists the one liability on her personal balance sheet under "Current Liabilities" because she will pay off the debt soon. Since she has no long-term liabilities at this time, her total liabilities are $2000.

Stephanie's Net Worth. Stephanie determines her net worth as the difference between her total assets and total liabilities. Notice from her personal balance sheet that her total assets are valued at $9000, while her total liabilities are valued at $2000. Thus, her net worth is:

Net Worth = Total Assets − Total Liabilities

= $9000   − $2000

= $7000

Exhibit 2.8 Stephanie Spratt's Personal Balance Sheet

Assets

Liquid Assets	
Cash	$500
Chequing account	3500
Savings account	0
Total liquid assets	$4000
Household Assets	
Home	$0
Car	1000
Furniture	1000
Total household assets	$2000
Investment Assets	
Stocks	$3000
Total investment assets	$3000
Total Assets	**$9000**

Liabilities and Net Worth

Current Liabilities	
Credit card balance	$2000
Total current liabilities	$2000
Long-Term Liabilities	
Mortgage	$0
Car loan	0
Total long-term liabilities	$0
Total Liabilities	**$2000**
Net Worth	**$7000**

Changes in the Personal Balance Sheet

If you earn new income this month but spend it all on products or services that are not personal assets (such as rent, food, and concert tickets), you will not increase your net worth. As you invest in assets, your personal balance sheet will change. In some cases, such as when you purchase a home, your assets increase at the same time that your liabilities increase by taking on a mortgage. In any case, your net worth will not grow unless the increase in the value of your assets exceeds the increase in the value of your liabilities.

EXAMPLE

Stephanie Spratt is considering purchasing a new car for $20 000. To make the purchase, she would:

- Trade in her existing car, which has a market value of about $1000.
- Write a cheque for $3000 as a down payment on the car.
- Obtain a five-year loan for $16 000 to cover the remaining amount owed to the car dealer.

Her personal balance sheet would be affected as shown in Exhibit 2.9 and explained next.

Change in Stephanie's Assets. Stephanie's assets would change as follows:

- Her car would now have a market value of $20 000 instead of $1000.
- Her chequing account balance would be reduced from $3500 to $500.

Thus, her total assets would increase by $16 000 (her new car would be valued at $19 000 more than her old one, but her chequing account would be reduced by $3000).

Change in Stephanie's Liabilities. Stephanie's liabilities would also change:

- She would now have a long-term liability of $16 000 as a result of the car loan.

Therefore, her total liabilities would increase by $16 000 if she purchases the car.

Change in Stephanie's Net Worth. If Stephanie purchases the car, her net worth would be:

$$\text{Net Worth} = \text{Total Assets} - \text{Total Liabilities}$$
$$= \$25\ 000 - \$18\ 000$$
$$= \$7000$$

Stephanie's net worth would remain unchanged as a result of buying the car because her total assets and total liabilities would increase by the same amount.

Stephanie's Decision. Because the purchase of a new car will not increase her net worth, she decides not to purchase the car at this time. Still, she is concerned that her old car will require a lot of maintenance in the future, so she will likely buy a car in a few months once she improves her financial position.

Analysis of the Personal Balance Sheet

The budgeting process helps you monitor your income and expenses and evaluate your net worth. In addition, by analyzing some financial characteristics within your personal balance sheet or cash flow statement, you can monitor your level of liquidity, your amount of debt, and your ability to save.

Liquidity. Recall that liquidity represents your access to funds to cover any short-term cash deficiencies. You need to monitor your liquidity over time to ensure that you have sufficient funds when they are needed. Your liquidity can be measured by the liquidity ratio, which is calculated as:

$$\text{Liquidity Ratio} = \text{Liquid Assets/Current Liabilities}$$

Exhibit 2.9 Stephanie's Personal Balance Sheet if She Purchases a New Car

Assets

	Present Situation	If She Purchases a New Car
Liquid Assets		
Cash	$500	$500
Chequing account	3500	500
Savings account	0	0
Total liquid assets	$4000	$1000
Household Assets		
Home	$0	$0
Car	1000	20 000
Furniture	1000	1000
Total household assets	$2000	$21 000
Investment Assets		
Stocks	$3000	$3000
Total investment assets	$3000	$3000
Total Assets	**$9000**	**$25 000**
Liabilities and Net Worth		
Current Liabilities		
Credit card balance	$2000	$2000
Total current liabilities	$2000	$2000
Long-Term Liabilities		
Mortgage	$0	$0
Car loan	0	16 000
Total long-term liabilities	$0	$16 000
Total Liabilities	**$2000**	**$18 000**
Net Worth	**$7000**	**$7000**

A high liquidity ratio indicates a higher degree of liquidity. For example, a liquidity ratio of 3.0 implies that for every dollar of liabilities you will need to pay off in the near future, you have $3 in liquid assets. Thus, you could easily cover your short-term liabilities.

A liquidity ratio of less than 1.0 means that you do not have sufficient liquid assets to cover your upcoming payments. In this case, you might need to borrow funds.

EXAMPLE

Based on the information in her personal balance sheet shown in Exhibit 2.8, Stephanie measures her liquidity:

Liquidity Ratio = Liquid Assets/Current Liabilities

= $4000/$2000

= 2.0

Stephanie's liquidity ratio of 2.0 means that for every dollar of current liabilities, she has $2 of liquid assets. This means that she has more than enough funds available to cover her current liabilities, so she is maintaining sufficient liquidity.

Debt Level. You also need to monitor your debt level to ensure that it does not become so high that you are unable to cover your debt payments. A debt level of $20 000 would not be a serious problem for a person with assets of $100 000, but it could be quite serious for someone with hardly any assets. Thus, your debt level should be measured relative to your assets, as shown here:

$$\text{Debt-to-Asset Ratio} = \text{Total Liabilities/Total Assets}$$

A high debt-to-asset ratio indicates an excessive amount of debt. This debt should be reduced over time to avoid any debt repayment problems. An individual's debt-to-asset ratio should be directly related to the financial planning life stages outlined in Exhibit 1.2 on page 6. The pre-career, early earning and mid earning life stages are often characterized by a relatively high debt-to-asset ratio. During those life stages, you may not have adequate resources to own a car without a car loan or purchase a home without a mortgage. As a result of these potential debts, your debt-to-asset ratio will likely be higher than that of someone in the prime earning life stage. Ideally, you should have no debt when you reach the retirement life stage. A successful financial plan should result in a debt-to-asset ratio that decreases as you pass through the various life stages outlined in Exhibit 1.2. In other words, your level of debt will decrease as you pay off any loans or mortgage debt that you have, and your level of assets should increase as your home and other appreciating assets increase in value. If you feel your debt-to-asset ratio is high, you should review your cash flows to maximize income and minimize expenses.

EXAMPLE

Based on her personal balance sheet, Stephanie calculates her debt-to-asset ratio as:

$$\text{Debt-to-Asset Ratio} = \text{Total Liabilities/Total Assets}$$
$$= \$2000/\$9000$$
$$= 22.22\%$$

This 22.22 percent debt level is not overwhelming. Even if Stephanie lost her job, she could still pay off her debt.

Savings Rate. To determine the proportion of disposable income that you save, you can measure your savings over a particular period in comparison to your disposable income (income after taxes are taken out) using the following formula:

$$\text{Savings Rate} = \text{Savings During the Period/Disposable Income During the Period}$$

EXAMPLE

Based on her cash flow statement, Stephanie earns $2260 in a particular month and expects to have net cash flows of $330 for savings or investments. She calculates her typical savings rate per month as:

$$\text{Savings Rate} = \text{Savings During the Period/Disposable Income During the Period}$$
$$= \$330/\$2260$$
$$= 14.60\%$$

Thus, Stephanie saves 14.60 percent of her monthly disposable income. In addition, Stephanie will save a total lump sum of $2260 during the months in which there is an extra pay period.

IN-CLASS NOTES

Personal Balance Sheet

- Assets (what you own):
  - Liquid assets (e.g., cash, chequing account)
  - Household assets (e.g., furniture, car)
  - Investments (e.g., bonds, stocks)
- Liabilities (what you owe):
  - Current liabilities (e.g., credit card debt)
  - Long-term liabilities (e.g., student loan)
- Net Worth
  - Value of total assets − Value of total liabilities

_____

_____

_____

_____

_____

L.O. 5

RELATIONSHIP BETWEEN CASH FLOWS AND WEALTH

The relationship between the personal cash flow statement and the personal balance sheet is shown in Exhibit 2.10. This relationship explains how you build wealth (net worth) over time. If you use net cash flows to invest in more assets, you increase the value of your assets without increasing your liabilities. Therefore, you increase your net worth. You can also increase your net worth by using net cash flows to reduce your liabilities. So, the more income that you allocate to savings and investing in assets or to reducing your debt, the more wealth you will build.

Your net worth can change even if your net cash flows are zero. For example, if the market value of your car declines over time, the value of this asset is reduced and your net worth will decline. Conversely, if the value of an investment that you own increases, the value of your assets will rise, and your net worth will increase. This can happen when you purchase stock for $3000 and its market value increases to $4000.

IN-CLASS NOTES

Relationship between Cash Flows and Wealth

- Net cash flows = Income − Expenses
  - Use your net cash flows to build your net worth over time
- Your net worth = Value of your assets − Value of liabilities
  - Increase your net worth by:
- Investing in more assets
- Reducing your liabilities

_____

_____

_____

_____

_____

Exhibit 2.10 How Net Cash Flows Can Be Used to Increase Net Worth

HOW BUDGETING FITS WITHIN YOUR FINANCIAL PLAN

The key budgeting decisions for building your financial plan are:

- How can I improve my net cash flows in the near future?
- How can I improve my net cash flows in the distant future?

These decisions require initial estimates of your income and expenses and an assessment of how you might change your spending behaviour to improve your budget over time. By limiting your spending, you may be able to increase your net cash flows and your net worth.

STEPHANIE SPRATT'S FINANCIAL PLAN: Application of Budgeting Concepts

GOALS FOR A BUDGETING PLAN

1. *Determine how I can increase my net cash flows in the near future.*
2. *Determine how I can increase my net cash flows in the distant future.*

ANALYSIS

Present Situation:

Income = $2260 per month

Expenses = $1930 per month

Net Cash Flows = $330 per month

Estimated Savings per Year = $3960 ($330 per month × 12 months) + $2260 = $6220

Increase Net Cash Flows by:

Increasing my salary? (New job?)	*No. I like my job and have no plans to search for another job right now, even if it would pay a higher salary.*
Increasing my income provided by my investments?	*No. My investments are small at this point. I cannot rely on them to provide much income.*
Other? (If yes, explain.)	*No.*

Reduce Expenses by:

Reducing my household expenses?	*No.*
Reducing my recreation expenses?	*Yes (by $100 per month).*
Reducing my other expenses?	*No.*

Overall, I identified only one adjustment to my budget, which will increase monthly net cash flows by $100.

DECISIONS

Decision to Increase Net Cash Flows in the Near Future

I initially established a budget to save $6220 per year. During the next year, I can attempt to save an additional $100 per month by reducing the amount I spend on recreation. I can increase my savings if I reduce expenses. By reducing expenses by $100 per month, my monthly savings will increase from $330 to $430 per month. The only way I can reduce expenses at this point is to reduce the amount I spend for recreation purposes.

Decision to Increase Net Cash Flows in the Distant Future

My income will rise over time if my salary increases. If I can keep my expenses stable, my net cash flows (and therefore my savings) will increase. When I buy a new car or a home, my monthly expenses will increase as a result of the monthly loan payments. If I buy a new car or a home, I need to make sure that I limit my spending (and therefore limit the loan amount) so that I have sufficient income to cover the monthly loan payments along with my other typical monthly expenses.

If I get married someday, my spouse would contribute to the income, which would increase net cash flows. We would be able to save more money and may consider buying a home. If I marry, my goal will be to save even more money per month than I save now, to prepare for the possibility of raising a family in the future.

Discussion Questions

1. How would Stephanie's budgeting decisions be different if she were a single mother of two children?

2. How would Stephanie's budgeting decisions be affected if she were 35 years old? If she were 50 years old?

SUMMARY

The personal cash flow statement measures your income, your expenses, and their difference (net cash flows) over a specific period. Income results from your salary or from income generated by your investments. Expenses result from your spending.

Your income is primarily affected by the stage in your career path and your type of job. Your expenses are influenced by your family status, age, and personal consumption behaviour. If you develop specialized skills, you may be able to obtain a job position that increases your income. If you limit your personal consumption, you can limit your spending and therefore reduce your expenses. Either of these actions will increase net cash flows and thus allow you to increase your wealth.

You can forecast net cash flows (and therefore anticipate cash deficiencies) by creating a budget, which is based on forecasted income and expenses for an upcoming period.

The budgeting process allows you to control spending. Comparing your forecasted and actual income and expenses will show whether you were able to stay within the budget. By examining the difference between your forecast and the actual income and expenses you incur, you can determine areas of your budget that may need further control or areas that required less in expenditures than you predicted. This analysis will help you modify your spending in the future or perhaps adjust your future budgets.

The personal balance sheet measures the value of your assets, your liabilities, and your net worth. The assets can be categorized into liquid assets, household assets, and investments. Liabilities can be categorized as current or long-term liabilities. The difference between total assets and total liabilities is net worth, which is a measure of your wealth.

The net cash flows on the personal cash flow statement are related to the net worth on the personal balance sheet. When you have positive net cash flows over a period, you can invest that amount in additional assets, which results in an increase in your net worth (or your wealth). Alternatively, you may use the net cash flows to pay off liabilities, which also increases your wealth.

INTEGRATING THE KEY CONCEPTS

Budgeting is a starting point for developing your financial plan. Before you can look for ways to improve your cash flows, you need to recognize how you spend or save your money. Your budget decisions dictate your level of spending and savings and therefore affect the other parts of the financial plan. The amount you save affects your liquidity (Part 2), the amount of financing necessary (Part 3), the amount of insurance you can afford and need (Part 4), the amount of funds you can invest (Part 5), and the level of wealth you will need for retirement (Part 6).

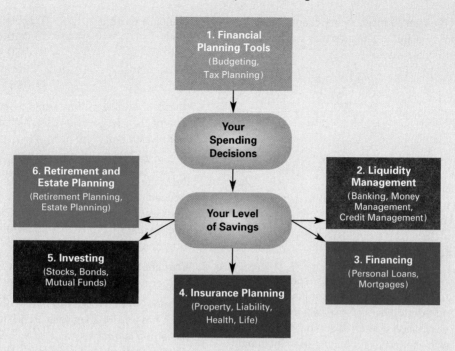

REVIEW QUESTIONS

1. What two personal financial statements are most important to personal financial planning?

2. Define income and expenses and identify some sources of each. How are net cash flows determined?

3. In general, how can you modify your cash flows to enhance your wealth?

4. Identify some factors that affect income.

5. Identify some factors that affect expenses.

6. What is a budget? What is the purpose of a budget? How can a budget help when you are anticipating cash shortages or a cash surplus?

7. How do you assess the accuracy of your budget? How can finding forecasting errors improve your budget?

8. How should unexpected expenses be handled in your budget? How might these expenses affect your budget for a specific month? Over time?

9. Describe the process of creating an annual budget.

10. Suppose you want to change your budget to increase your savings. What could you do?

11. How do you think people who do not create a budget deal with cash deficiencies? How can this affect their personal relationships?

12. What is a personal balance sheet?

13. Name three classifications of assets. Briefly define and give examples of each.

14. What are bonds? What are stocks? What are mutual funds? Describe how each of these provides a return on your investment.

15. Describe two ways that real estate might provide a return on an investment.

16. What are liabilities? Define current liabilities and long-term liabilities.

17. How is net worth a measure of wealth?

18. When does your net worth increase? Will the purchase of additional assets always increase your net worth? Why or why not?

19. What three financial characteristics can be monitored by analyzing your personal balance sheet?

20. What is the liquidity ratio? What does it indicate? How is the debt-to-asset ratio calculated? What does a high debt-to-asset ratio indicate? How is your savings rate determined? What does it indicate?

21. Describe how wealth is built over time. How do your personal cash flow statement and your personal balance sheet assist in building wealth?

FINANCIAL PLANNING PROBLEMS

1. Angela earns $2170 per month before taxes in her full-time job and $900 per month before taxes in her part-time job. About $650 per month is needed to pay taxes and other payroll deductions. What is Angela's disposable income?

2. Angela (from Problem 1) inspects her chequebook and credit card bills and determines that she has the following monthly expenses:

Rent	$500
Cable TV	30
Electricity	100
Water	25
Telephone	40
Groceries	400
Car expenses	350
Disability insurance	100
Critical illness insurance	100
Clothing and personal items	175
Recreation	300

What is Angela's net cash flow?

3. Angela makes a budget based on her personal cash flow statement. In two months, she must pay $375 for registration and taxes on her car. How will this payment affect her net cash flow for that month? Suggest ways in which Angela might handle this situation.

4. From the information provided in Problems 1 through 3, how much can Angela expect to save in the next 12 months?

5. Angela analyzes her personal budget and decides that she can reduce her recreational spending by $50 per month. How much will that increase her annual savings? What will her annual savings be now?

6. If Angela is saving $350 per month, what is her savings rate (that is, savings as a percentage of disposable income)?

7. Peter is a student. All of Peter's disposable income is used to pay for his post-secondary education expenses. While he has no liabilities (he is on a scholarship), he does have a credit card that he typically uses for emergencies. He and his friend went on a shopping spree in Toronto costing $2000, which Peter charged to his credit card. Peter has $20 in his wallet, but his bank accounts are empty. What is Peter's liquidity ratio? What does this ratio indicate about his financial position?

8. Peter (from Problem 7) has an old TV worth about $100. His other assets total about $150. What is Peter's debt-to-asset ratio? What does this indicate about his financial position?

9. Bill and Ann have the following assets:

Fair Market Value	
Home	$85 000
Cars	22 000
Furniture	14 000
Stocks	10 000
Savings account	5000
Chequing account	1200
Bonds	15 000
Cash	150
Mutual funds	7000
Land	19 000

What is the value of their liquid assets? What is the value of their household assets? What is the value of their investments?

10. Bill and Ann have the following liabilities:

Mortgage	$43 500
Car loan	2750
Credit card balance	165
Student loans	15 000
Furniture loan (6 months)	1200

What are their current liabilities? What are their long-term liabilities? What is their net worth?

11. Bill and Ann would like to trade in one of their cars, which has a fair market value of $7000, for a new one with a fair market value of $21 500. The dealer will take their car and provide a $15 000 loan for the new car. If they make this deal, what will be the effect on their net worth?

12. What is Bill and Ann's liquidity ratio? What is their debt-to-asset ratio? Comment on each ratio.

ETHICAL DILEMMA

Dennis and Nancy are in their early twenties and have been married for three years. They are eager to purchase their first house, but they do not have sufficient money for a down payment. Nancy's uncle Charley has agreed to lend them the money to purchase a small house. Uncle Charley requests a personal balance sheet and a cash flow statement as well as tax returns for the previous two years to verify their income and their ability to make monthly payments.

For the past two years, Dennis has been working substantial overtime, which has increased his income by more than 25 percent. The cash flow statements for the last two years show that Nancy and Dennis will have no difficulty making the payments Uncle Charley requires. However, Dennis's company has informed its employees that the overtime will not continue in the coming year. Nancy and Dennis are concerned that if they prepare their personal cash flow statement based on Dennis's base salary, Uncle Charley will not lend them the money because it will show the loan payments can only be made with very strict cost-cutting and financial discipline. Therefore, they elect to present just what Uncle Charley requested, which was the previous two years' personal cash flow statements and tax returns.

They decide not to provide any additional information unless he asks for it.

a. Comment on Nancy and Dennis's decision not to provide the information underlying their cash flow statement. What potential problems could result from this decision?

b. Discuss the disadvantages of borrowing money from relatives in general.

FINANCIAL PLANNING ONLINE EXERCISES

1. Go to http://strategis.ic.gc.ca/epic/site/oca-bc.nsf/en/ca01807e.html and click on "Daily Spending Habits."

   You can input various expenses that most people incur on a regular basis. Reducing these expenses increases the savings you will accrue over time. Input your age, your age at retirement, 3 percent for the expected inflation rate, and 8 percent for the rate you can earn on savings. The following example is for a 20-year-old who would like to retire at age 65.

   Under the "Quantity" heading, first make sure that all boxes read 0. Enter 5 under the quantity column for "Eating-out Lunch." Change the per-unit cost of "Eating-out Lunch" to $10. The "Total Today" column shows that the weekly savings from not eating out is $50. Scroll down to see the future value if you save your "Eating-out Lunch" money instead of spending it today. You should find that the "Future (nominal) Value if You Save Instead" is $1 153 656.70!

   Calculate the "Future (nominal) Value if You Save Instead" for the following examples based on the assumptions made above.

   a. If you drank one fewer cup of coffee per day and a cup of coffee costs $3.00.

   b. If you stop smoking, assuming that you smoke one pack per day and the cost of cigarettes is $9.50 per pack.

ON THE STUDENT CD-ROM FOR THIS CHAPTER YOU WILL FIND:

- Building Your Own Financial Plan exercise and worksheets

- The chapter-end Continuing Case about the Sampson family.

   Read through the Building Your Own Financial Plan exercise and use the worksheets to create a personal cash flow statement and personal balance sheet, and to set personal financial goals.

   After reading the case study, use the Continuing Case worksheets to prepare a personal cash flow statement and a personal balance sheet for the Sampsons.

Study Guide

Circle the correct answer and then check the answers in the back of the book to chart your progress.

Multiple Choice

1. The _____, _____, and _____ are three personal financial statements that provide an overall snapshot of your wealth at a specific point in time, allow you to compare your income and expenses, and provide a forecast of future cash flows, respectively.
   a. Personal balance sheet, the personal income statement, a budget
   b. Personal balance sheet, the personal cash flow statement, a budget
   c. Personal balance sheet, the personal income statement, a net worth report
   d. Personal balance sheet, the personal cash flow statement, a net worth report

2. Which of the following transaction methods can be used effectively to monitor your expenses?
   a. Debit card, credit card, chequebook, cash
   b. Debit card, credit card, chequebook
   c. Debit card, credit card, chequebook, receipts
   d. Debit card and credit card

3. Estimated net cash flow =
   a. Monthly income (after payroll deductions) − estimated monthly expenses
   b. Monthly income (before payroll deductions) − monthly expenses
   c. Monthly income (after payroll deductions) − monthly expenses
   d. Monthly income (after payroll deductions) − realized monthly expenses

4. Which of the following situations appears to be the most likely?
   a. A two-income household tends to spend more money when at least one income earner is working part-time.
   b. A two-income household tends to spend more money when both income earners are working part-time.
   c. A two-income household tends to spend more money, per capita, than a one-income household.
   d. A two-income household tends to spend more money when both income earners are working full-time.

5. A budget is a cash flow statement that is based on forecasted cash flows for a future time period. Which of the following may be reasons for developing a budget?
   a. To determine whether your income will be sufficient to cover your expenses
   b. To determine the amount of excess cash that you will have available to invest in additional assets
   c. To determine the amount of extra payments you can make to reduce your personal debt
   d. All of the above

6. If you run into unexpected financial difficulties, your choices may be limited. What are your best options?
   a. Use your emergency fund to cover cash shortages.
   b. Borrow from your relatives. Maybe you won't have to pay them back.
   c. Use your credit card. You can pay off this debt over time.
   d. Delay payment on your other bills to ensure you can pay this bill on time.
   e. Both a and b.
   f. Both b and c.
   g. Both a and c.

7. Bahni had expected to spend $100 on clothing and $300 on groceries during the month of May. She actually spent $150 on clothing and $275 on groceries. Her forecasting error for clothing was _____; her forecasting error for groceries was _____.
   a. +$50, −$25
   b. +$50, +$25
   c. −$50, −$25
   d. −$50, +$25

8. The assets on a personal balance sheet can be classified as _____, _____, and _____
   a. Current assets, short-term investments, long-term investments
   b. Current assets, household assets, investments
   c. Liquid assets, household assets, investments
   d. Liquid assets, short-term investments, long-term investments

9. Which of the following debts would be considered long-term liabilities?
   a. Student loans
   b. Car loans
   c. Mortgages
   d. All of the above

10. By analyzing some financial characteristics within your personal balance sheet and cash flow statement, you can monitor your financial health. All else being equal, a _____ liquidity ratio, combined with a _____ debt ratio, and a _____ savings rate indicate good financial health.
    a. High, low, high
    b. Low, low, high
    c. Low, low, low
    d. High, high, high

True/False

1. True or False? It is important to document every expenditure that you make.

2. True or False? The key factors that influence your level of income are the stage of your career path, your job skills, and the number of income earners in your household.

3. True or False? The budgeting process will make it more difficult for you to discover any cash shortage you may have in a typical month.

4. True or False? Many individuals tend to be overly pessimistic about their cash flow forecasts.

5. True or False? Your budget may not be perfectly accurate in any specific month, but it will be perfectly accurate over time.

6. True or False? Being paid biweekly means that you will receive 27 paycheques during the year instead of the 22 you would receive if you were paid semi-monthly.

7. True or False? Liquid assets are financial assets that can be easily converted to cash without a loss in value.

8. True or False? The minimum cash investment in a mutual fund varies depending on the particular fund, but is usually between $500 and $1000.

9. True or False? Credit card debt is a type of current liability.

10. True or False? Your net worth can change even if your net cash flows are zero.

Chapter 3

Using Tax Concepts for Planning

T he Kapoors sat down at the beginning of the year to complete their tax return for the previous year. The Kapoors realized that they would have to pay more in taxes than they had anticipated. The couple wondered if there was anything they could do to reduce the amount of tax they had to pay.

John Kapoor called his uncle Sam to see if there was anything the couple could do to reduce their taxes. Sam told them they would have been eligible for a number of deductions if they had taken the appropriate steps before December 31. If the couple had maximized their RRSPs and made additional contributions to their favourite charity, they would have saved an additional $2100 in taxes.

The moral of this story is that you, as a taxpayer, may be able to take advantage of significant tax breaks. However, while an accountant can help you complete your tax return correctly, it is your responsibility to take actions during the tax year that will allow you to take full advantage of available tax reduction strategies.

This chapter explains the basics of individual taxation. Knowledge of tax laws can help you conserve your income, enhance your investments, and protect the transfer of wealth when you die. Understanding the taxation of income and wealth is crucial to sound financial planning.

The objectives of this chapter are to:

1. Explain when you have to file a tax return
2. Demonstrate how to calculate your total income
3. Describe the major deductions available to a taxpayer
4. Show how deductions can be used to reduce total income
5. Show how tax credits can be used to lower tax payable
6. Explain how to determine your tax liability and whether you are owed a refund or owe additional tax

BACKGROUND ON TAXES

Taxes are an integral part of our economy. They are paid on earned income, consumer purchases, wealth transfers, and capital assets. Special taxes, called excise taxes, are levied on certain consumer products such as cigarettes, alcohol, and gasoline. Corporations pay corporate income tax on operating profits. Homeowners pay property tax on the value of their homes and land. Billions of dollars are paid in taxes each year in Canada. These taxes are a significant source of funding for governments and governmental agencies and are used to pay for a wide variety of governmental services and programs, including national defence, Canada Health and Social Transfer (CHST) benefits, support for the elderly, employment insurance, fire and police protection, government employees, road construction and maintenance, and our education systems.

Individuals pay tax at the federal, provincial, and municipal levels. The federal tax system is administered by the Canada Revenue Agency (CRA). While the federal government drafts and revises the *Income Tax Act*, the CRA administers the Act and distributes and collects the forms and publications that taxpayers use to calculate their income tax.

Many taxes, such as the goods and services tax (GST), are paid at the time of a transaction. Such taxes, which include provincial sales taxes, are consumer taxes. Some consider this form of taxation extremely fair, as one only pays tax when one consumes. The higher one's income, the higher one's consumption will be. Income taxes, however, are applied in a different manner. Income taxes are generally paid as income is earned during the year in a process called withholding. In other words, taxes are withheld (from each paycheque) as income is earned throughout the year. Employees file a form, called a TD1, with their employer, which helps the employer calculate the amount of taxes to withhold. You will complete this form when you start your first job. If you are already working, you will have completed this form. Individuals can opt to withhold more than the minimum amount from each paycheque, but are not allowed to reduce the amount of withholding below the amount specified by the CRA. Tax money that is withheld is forwarded by your employer to the federal government and held in an account that is credited to you. Self-employed individuals must estimate the amount of taxes to withhold based on projected earnings and pay estimated tax withholdings quarterly.

The tax year for federal income taxes ends on December 31. Individual income tax returns must be filed and taxes must be paid by April 30 of the following year. Self-employed individuals have until June 15 to file their income tax returns, although any taxes owing must be paid by April 30. If a taxpayer does not file his or her tax return on time, an interest penalty may be payable. The amount of the penalty will be determined by the amount of any unpaid taxes owing. If you do not file a tax return and you do not owe any additional taxes, no penalty is charged. However, if you owe taxes, you will be charged 5 percent of the amount owing plus 1 percent for each additional full month that your return is late, to a maximum of 12 months.

Personal Income Taxes

Your income is subject to personal income taxes, which are taxes imposed on income you earn. For any year that you earn income, you must file a tax return that consists of a completed T1 General, plus supporting documents. Your tax return will show whether a sufficient amount of taxes was already withheld from your paycheques, whether you still owe taxes, or whether the government owes you a refund. If you still owe taxes, you should include a cheque for the taxes owed along with your completed T1 General return. Tax forms can be downloaded from the Canada Revenue Agency website. An example of the T1 General is shown in Exhibit 3.1. It is important to note that the T1 General was created with all taxpayers in mind. The majority of taxpayers will use only a very small portion of the actual form. As a result, the discussion below only makes reference to the most commonly completed areas of the T1 General. Refer to the exhibit as you read through the chapter.

Exhibit 3.1 T1 General

Canada Revenue Agency / Agence du revenu du Canada

T1 GENERAL 2006
Income Tax and Benefit Return
Complete all the sections that apply to you in order to benefit from amounts to which you are entitled.

Identification

ON 8

Attach your personal label here. Correct any wrong information.
If you are not attaching a label, print your name and address below.

First name and initial: Stephanie

Last name: Spratt

Mailing address: Apt No – Street No Street name: 48 St. Christopher St.

PO Box: 	RR:

City: Sudbury 	Prov./Terr.: ON 	Postal code: P3E 8J1

Information about you

Enter your social insurance number (SIN) if you are not attaching a label: 1 2 3 4 5 6 7 8 9

Enter your date of birth: Year Month Day

Your language of correspondence / Votre langue de correspondance: English ☒ Français ☐

Check the box that applies to your marital status on December 31, 2006:
(see the "Marital status" section in the guide for details)
1 ☐ Married 2 ☐ Living common-law 3 ☐ Widowed
4 ☐ Divorced 5 ☐ Separated 6 ☒ Single

Information about your residence

Enter your province or territory of residence on **December 31, 2006:**

Enter the province or territory where you **currently** reside if it is not the same as that shown above for your mailing address:

If you were self-employed in 2006, enter the province or territory of self-employment:

If you **became** or **ceased** to be a **resident of Canada in 2006**, give the date of:
entry Month Day or departure Month Day

Information about your spouse or common-law partner (if you checked box 1 or 2 above)

Enter his or her SIN if it is not on the label, or if you are not attaching a label:

Enter his or her first name:

Enter his or her net income for 2006 to claim certain credits: (see the guide for details)

Enter the amount of Universal Child Care Benefit included in his or her net income above (see the guide for details):

Check this box if he or she was self-employed in 2006: 1 ☐

Person deceased in 2006

If this **return** is for a **deceased person**, enter the date of death: Year Month Day

Do not use this area

Elections Canada

THIS SECTION APPLIES **ONLY** TO CANADIAN CITIZENS.
DO **NOT** ANSWER THIS QUESTION IF YOU ARE NOT A CANADIAN CITIZEN.

As a Canadian citizen, I authorize the Canada Revenue Agency to provide my name, address, and date of birth to Elections Canada for the National Register of Electors. .... Yes ☒ 1 No ☐ 2
Your authorization is required each year. This information will be used only for purposes permitted under the *Canada Elections Act*.

Goods and services tax/harmonized sales tax (GST/HST) credit application

See the guide for details.
Are you applying for the GST/HST credit? .... Yes ☒ 1 No ☐ 2

Do not use this area 172   171

5006-R

Exhibit 3.1 continued

2

Your guide contains valuable information to help you complete your return.
When you come to a line on the return that applies to you, look up the line number in the guide for more information.

Please answer the following question:

Did you own or hold foreign property at any time in 2006 with a total cost of more than
CAN$100,000? (read the "Foreign income" section in the guide for details) .... **266** Yes ☐ 1   No ☒ 2
If *yes*, attach a completed Form T1135.

If you had dealings with a non-resident trust or corporation in 2006, see the "Foreign income" section in the guide.

As a Canadian resident, you have to report your income from all sources both inside and outside Canada.

Total income

Employment income (box 14 on all T4 slips)		101	38,000	00
Commissions included on line 101 (box 42 on all T4 slips)	102			
Other employment income		104 +		
Old Age Security pension (box 18 on the T4A(OAS) slip)		113 +		
CPP or QPP benefits (box 20 on the T4A(P) slip)		114 +		
Disability benefits included on line 114 (box 16 on the T4A(P) slip)	152			
Other pensions or superannuation		115 +		
Universal Child Care Benefit (see the guide)		117 +		
Employment Insurance and other benefits (box 14 on the T4E slip)		119 +		
Taxable amount of dividends (eligible and other than eligible) from taxable Canadian corporations (see the guide and **attach** Schedule 4)		120 +		
Taxable amount of dividends other than eligible dividends, included on line 120, from taxable Canadian corporations	180			
Interest and other investment income (**attach** Schedule 4)		121 +	0	00
Net partnership income: limited or non-active partners only (**attach** Schedule 4)		122 +		
Rental income Gross 160		Net 126 +		
Taxable capital gains (**attach** Schedule 3)		127 +	0	00
Support payments received Total 156		Taxable amount 128 +		
RRSP income (from all T4RSP slips)		129 +		
Other income Specify:		130 +		

Self-employment income (see lines 135 to 143 in the guide)

Business income	Gross 162		Net 135 +	
Professional income	Gross 164		Net 137 +	
Commission income	Gross 166		Net 139 +	
Farming income	Gross 168		Net 141 +	
Fishing income	Gross 170		Net 143 +	

Workers' compensation benefits (box 10 on the T5007 slip)	144			
Social assistance payments	145 +			
Net federal supplements (box 21 on the T4A(OAS) slip)	146 +			
Add lines 144, 145, and 146 (see line 250 in the guide).	=		▶ 147 +	
Add lines 101, 104 to 143, and 147. This is your **total income**.	150 =	38,000	00	

Exhibit 3.1 continued

 Attach your Schedule 1 (federal tax) and Form 428 (provincial or territorial tax) here. Also attach here any other schedules, information slips, forms, receipts, and documents that you need to include with your return.

3

Net income

Enter your **total income** from line 150. 150 38,000 |00

Pension adjustment
(box 52 on all T4 slips and box 34 on all T4A slips)   206

Registered pension plan deduction (box 20 on all T4 slips and box 32 on all T4A slips)	207	2,000 |00
RRSP deduction (see Schedule 7 and **attach** receipts)	208+	2,000 |00
Saskatchewan Pension Plan deduction (maximum $600)	209+	
Annual union, professional, or like dues (box 44 on all T4 slips and receipts)	212+	400 |00
Child care expenses (**attach** Form T778)	214+	
Disability supports deduction	215+	
Business investment loss Gross 228	Allowable deduction 217+	
Moving expenses	219+	
Support payments made Total 230	Allowable deduction 220+	
Carrying charges and interest expenses (**attach** Schedule 4)	221+	600 |00
Deduction for CPP or QPP contributions on self-employment and other earnings (**attach** Schedule 8)	222+	•
Exploration and development expenses (**attach** Form T1229)	224+	
Other employment expenses	229+	
Clergy residence deduction	231+	
Other deductions Specify:	232+	

Add lines 207 to 224, 229, 231, and 232. 233= 5,000 |00 ▶ − 5,000 |00
Line 150 minus line 233 (if negative, enter "0"). This is your **net income before adjustments**. 234= 33,000 |00

Social benefits repayment (if you reported income on line 113, 119, or 146, see line 235 in the guide) 235− •
Line 234 minus line 235 (if negative, enter "0"). If you have a spouse or common-law partner, see line 236 in the guide.
This is your **net income**. 236= 33,000 |00

Taxable income

Canadian Forces personnel and police deduction (box 43 on all T4 slips)	244	
Employee home relocation loan deduction (box 37 on all T4 slips)	248+	
Security options deductions	249+	
Other payments deduction (if you reported income on line 147, see line 250 in the guide)	250+	
Limited partnership losses of other years	251+	
Non-capital losses of other years	252+	
Net capital losses of other years	253+	
Capital gains deduction	254+	
Northern residents deductions (**attach** Form T2222)	255+	
Additional deductions Specify:	256+	

Add lines 244 to 256. 257= 0 |00 ▶ − 0 |00
Line 236 minus line 257 (if negative, enter "0")
This is your **taxable income**. 260= 33,000 |00

Use your taxable income to calculate your federal tax on Schedule 1 and your provincial or territorial tax on Form 428.

Exhibit 3.1   continued

Refund or Balance owing

4

Net federal tax: enter the amount from line 50 of Schedule 1 (**attach** Schedule 1, even if the result is "0")	420	3,315 75
CPP contributions payable on self-employment and other earnings (**attach** Schedule 8)	421 +	
Social benefits repayment (enter the amount from line 235)	422 +	

Provincial or territorial tax (attach Form 428, even if the result is "0")	428 +	0 00

Add lines 420 to 428.
This is your **total payable**. 435 = 3,315 75 •

Total income tax deducted (from all information slips)	437	6,000 00 •
Refundable Quebec abatement	440 +	•
CPP overpayment (enter your excess contributions)	448 +	•
Employment Insurance overpayment (enter your excess contributions)	450 +	•
Refundable medical expense supplement	452 +	•
Refund of investment tax credit (**attach** Form T2038(IND))	454 +	•
Part XII.2 trust tax credit (box 38 on all T3 slips)	456 +	•
Employee and partner GST/HST rebate (**attach** Form GST370)	457 +	•
Tax **paid** by instalments	476 +	•
Provincial or territorial credits (attach Form 479)	479 +	•

Add lines 437 to 479.
These are your **total credits**. 482 = 6,000 00 ▶ − 6,000 00

Line 435 minus line 482 = −2,684 25

If the result is negative, you have a **refund**. If the result is positive, you have a **balance owing**.
Enter the amount below on whichever line applies.

Generally, we do not charge or refund a difference of $2 or less.

Refund 484 2,684 25 •

Balance owing (see line 485 in the guide) 485 _____ •

Amount enclosed 486 _____ •

--- Direct deposit – Start or change (**see line 484 in the guide**) ---

You do not have to complete this area every year. Do not complete it this year if your direct deposit information for your refund has not changed.
Refund and GST/HST credit – To start direct deposit or to change account information only, **attach** a "void" cheque or complete lines 460, 461, and 462.
Notes: To deposit your **CCTB** payments (including certain related provincial or territorial payments) into the **same** account, also check box 463.
To deposit your **UCCB** payments into the **same** account, also check box 491.

Branch number	Institution number	Account number	CCTB	UCCB
460 _____	461 _____	462 _____	463 ☐	491 ☐
(5 digits)	(3 digits)	(maximum 12 digits)		

Attach to page 1 a **cheque** or **money order** payable to the Receiver General. Your payment is due no later than April 30, 2007.

Ontario Opportunities Fund

You can help reduce Ontario's debt by completing this area to donate some or all of your 2006 refund to the Ontario Opportunities Fund. Please see the provincial pages for details.

Amount from line 484 above		1
Your donation to the Ontario Opportunities Fund	465 −	• 2
Net refund (line 1 minus line 2)	466 =	• 3

I certify that the information given on this return and in any documents attached is correct, complete, and fully discloses all my income. **Sign here** _____ It is a serious offence to make a false return. Telephone − − Date	490 For professional tax preparers only	Name: _____ Address: _____ Telephone: − −		

Do not use this area	487 ☐	488 ☐	•

Source: www.cra-arc.gc.ca/E/pbg/tf/5006-r/5006-r-06e.pdf (accessed January 4, 2007). Reproduced with permission of the Minister of Public Works and Government Services Canada, 2008.

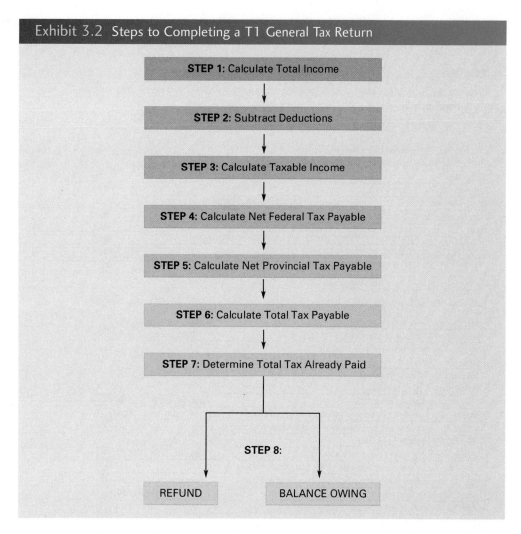

Exhibit 3.2 Steps to Completing a T1 General Tax Return

STEP 1: Calculate Total Income

STEP 2: Subtract Deductions

STEP 3: Calculate Taxable Income

STEP 4: Calculate Net Federal Tax Payable

STEP 5: Calculate Net Provincial Tax Payable

STEP 6: Calculate Total Tax Payable

STEP 7: Determine Total Tax Already Paid

STEP 8:

REFUND   BALANCE OWING

Go to
www.cra-arc.gc.ca/
formspubs/t1general/
menu-e.html

Click on
your province of residence
and then on "Provincial information and forms." Select
Form 428 for your province.

This website provides
a convenient location from
which you can download
Form 428 for your province
and any additional sched-
ules and/or forms you
might need to complete
your tax return.

T4 slip
A document provided to
you by your employer that
displays your salary and all
deductions associated with
your employment with that
specific employer for the
previous year. Your
employer is required to
provide you with a T4 slip
by February 28.

As shown in Exhibit 3.2, the calculation of income tax requires the completion of eight major steps. Step 1 requires you to calculate your total income—line 150 of the T1 General. Step 2 requires you to determine whether you have any deductions that you can subtract from your total income. Step 3 requires you to calculate your taxable income—line 260 of your T1 General—after taking into account any deductions you have. Your taxable income is then used to determine your federal and provincial tax payable. At this point, you will need to refer to the many supporting documents that the CRA has created. These documents are called schedules or forms. Schedule 1 is used to determine your net federal income tax payable. Form 428 is used to determine your net provincial income tax payable. An example of Schedule 1 is shown in Exhibit 3.3. Notice that the first line of Schedule 1 requires you to enter your taxable income from line 260 of your T1 General. This brings us to Step 4, in which you determine the amount of federal tax you owe and apply any federal non-refundable tax credits that you are eligible for. At the end of Schedule 1, page 2 of Exhibit 3.3, you are directed to enter your net federal tax on line 420 of your T1 General. You will need Form 428 to determine your provincial income tax payable (Step 5); this form is different for each province. The federal government collects taxes on behalf of all provinces and territories with the exception of Quebec.

Step 6 requires you to total your federal and provincial tax payable. Step 7 requires you to enter the total income tax deducted on line 437. Your total income tax deducted can be found on your T4 slip and any other information slips you have received. A T4 slip is a document provided to you by your employer that displays your salary and all deductions

Exhibit 3.3 Schedule 1: Federal Tax

T1-2006　　　　　　　　　　**Federal Tax**　　　　　　　　　　**Schedule 1**

Complete this schedule to claim your federal non-refundable tax credits and to calculate your net federal tax.
You must attach a copy of this schedule to your return.

Enter your **taxable income** from line 260 of your return. _____ | ___ | **1**

Use the amount on line 1 to determine which **ONE** of the following columns you have to complete.	If line 1 is $36,378 or less		If line 1 is more than $36,378 but not more than $72,756		If line 1 is more than $72,756 but not more than $118,285		If line 1 is more than $118,285	
Enter the amount from line 1.	33,000 00	**2**		**2**		**2**		**2**
Base amount	00,000 00	**3**	− 36,378 00	**3**	− 72,756 00	**3**	− 118,285 00	**3**
Line 2 minus line 3 (cannot be negative)	= 33,000 00	**4**	=	**4**	=	**4**	=	**4**
Rate	× 15.25%	**5**	× 22%	**5**	× 26%	**5**	× 29%	**5**
Multiply line 4 by line 5.	= 5,032 50	**6**	=	**6**	=	**6**	=	**6**
Tax on base amount	0,000 00	**7**	+ 5,548 00	**7**	+ 13,551 00	**7**	+ 25,388 00	**7**
Add lines 6 and 7.	= 5,032 50	**8**	=	**8**	=	**8**	=	**8**

Federal non-refundable tax credits (Read the guide for details about these credits.)

Basic personal amount		claim $8,839 **300**	8,839 00	**9**
Age amount (if you were born in 1941 or earlier)		(maximum $5,066) **301** +		**10**
Spouse or common-law partner amount:				
Base amount	8,256 00			
Minus: his or her net income (from page 1 of your return)	−			
Result: (if negative, enter "0")	=	(maximum $7,505) ▶ **303** +		**11**
Amount for an eligible dependant (**attach** Schedule 5)		(maximum $7,505) **305** +		**12**
Amount for infirm dependants age 18 or older (**attach** Schedule 5)		**306** +		**13**
CPP or QPP contributions:				
through employment from box 16 and box 17 on all T4 slips	(maximum $1,910.70) **308** +	1,707 75	•**14**
on self-employment and other earnings (**attach** Schedule 8)		**310** +		•**15**
Employment Insurance premiums from box 18 and box 55 on all T4 slips	(maximum $729.30) **312** +	710 60	•**16**
Canada employment amount (see the guide)		(maximum $250) **363** +		**17**
Public transit passes amount (see the guide)		**364** +		**18**
Adoption expenses		**313** +		**19**
Pension income amount		(maximum $2,000) **314** +		**20**
Caregiver amount (**attach** Schedule 5)		**315** +		**21**
Disability amount (for self)		**316** +		**22**
Disability amount transferred from a dependant		**318** +		**23**
Interest paid on your student loans		**319** +		**24**
Tuition, education, and textbook amounts (**attach** Schedule 11)		**323** +		**25**
Tuition, education, and textbook amounts transferred from a child		**324** +		**26**
Amounts transferred from your spouse or common-law partner (**attach** Schedule 2)		**326** +		**27**

Medical expenses for **self, spouse or common-law partner, and your dependent children born in 1989 or later** (see the guide)　**330**

Minus: $1,884 or 3% of line 236, whichever is **less**　−

Subtotal (if negative, enter "0")　=　(A)

Allowable amount of medical expenses for **other dependants**
(see the calculation at line 331 in the guide and **attach** Schedule 5)　**331** +　(B)

Add lines (A) and (B).　=　▶ **332** +　**28**

Add lines 9 to 28. **335** = 11,257 35 **29**

Multiply the amount on line 29 by 15.25%. **338** = 1,716 75 **30**

Donations and gifts (**attach** Schedule 9)　**349** +　**31**

Total federal non-refundable tax credits: add lines 30 and 31. **350** = 1,716 75 **32**

continue on the back ⇨

Exhibit 3.3 continued

Net federal tax

Enter the amount from line 8 on the other side.		5,032 50	33
Federal tax on split income (from line 5 of Form T1206)	424 +		• 34
Add lines 33 and 34. 404 =		▶ 5,032 50	35

Enter the amount from line 32 on the other side.	350	1,716 75	36
Federal dividend tax credit (see line 425 in the guide)	425 +		• 37
Overseas employment tax credit (**attach** Form T626)	426 +		38
Minimum tax carryover (**attach** Form T691)	427 +		• 39
Add lines 36 to 39. =	1,716 75	▶ − 1,716 75	40

Basic federal tax: line 35 minus line 40 (if negative, enter "0") 429 = 3,315 75 41

Federal foreign tax credit:
Where you **only** have foreign non-business income, calculate your federal foreign tax credit below. Otherwise, use Form T2209, *Federal Foreign Tax Credits*, if you have foreign business income. **Enter on this line the amount that you calculated.**   405 −   42

Federal tax: line 41 minus line 42 (if negative, enter "0") 406 = 3,315 75 43

Total federal political contributions (**attach** receipts)	409		
Federal political contribution tax credit (see the guide)	410		• 44
Investment tax credit (**attach** Form T2038(IND))	412 +		• 45
Labour-sponsored funds tax credit			
Net cost 413	Allowable credit 414 +		• 46
Add lines 44 to 46. 416 =		▶ −	47

Line 43 minus line 47 (if negative, enter "0")
(if you have an amount on line 34 above, see Form T1206) 417 = 3,315 75 48

Additional tax on RESP accumulated income payments (**attach** Form T1172)	418 +		49

Net federal tax: add lines 48 and 49.
Enter this amount on line 420 of your return. 420 = 3,315 75 50

Federal foreign tax credit: (see lines 431 and 433 in the guide)

Make a separate calculation for each foreign country. Enter on line 42 above the result from line (i) or (ii), whichever is **less**.

Non-business income tax paid to a foreign country   431   •(i)

$\dfrac{\text{Net foreign non-business income} * \boxed{433}}{\text{Net income } **}$ X Basic federal tax ***   =   (ii)

* Reduce this amount by any income from that foreign country for which you claimed a capital gains deduction, and by any income from that country that was, under a tax treaty, either exempt from tax in that country or deductible as exempt income in Canada (included on line 256). Also reduce this amount by the lesser of lines E and F on Form T626.

** Line 236 plus the amount on line 4 of Form T1206, minus the total of the amounts on lines 244, 248, 249, 250, 253, 254, and minus any amount included on line 256 for foreign income deductible as exempt income under a tax treaty, income deductible as net employment income from a prescribed international organization, or non-taxable tuition assistance from box 21 of the T4E slip. If the result is less than the amount on line 433, enter your **Basic federal tax***** on line (ii).

*** Line 41 plus the amount on lines 37 and 38, and minus any refundable Quebec abatement (line 440) and any federal refundable First Nations abatement (line 441 on the return for residents of Yukon).

5000-S1

Source: www.cra-arc.gc.ca/E/pbg/tf/5000-s1/5000-s1-06e.pdf (accessed January 4, 2007). Reproduced with the permission of the Minister of Public Works and Government Services Canada, 2008.

associated with your employment with that specific employer for the previous year. Your total tax payable (line 435) minus your tax already paid (line 482) will determine your refund or balance owing. This represents Step 8 in completing your T1 General. Each of the steps highlighted above and in Exhibit 3.2 on page 53 are covered in this chapter so that you will be ready to fill out a T1 General and any supporting documents to determine your taxes.

IN-CLASS NOTES

Background on Taxes

- Taxes are a source of revenue for our federal, provincial, and municipal governments
- We pay taxes on personal income, consumer purchases, property, wealth transfers, and capital assets

_____

_____

_____

_____

_____

L.O. 1 DO YOU HAVE TO FILE A RETURN?

Prior to submitting your income tax return, it is important to understand the circumstances under which you must file a tax return. You must file a return for a calendar year if any of the following situations apply:

- you have to pay tax for a calendar year

- the CRA sent you a request to file a return

- you disposed of property in a calendar year or you realized a taxable capital gain

- you have to repay any of your Old Age Security (OAS) or Employment Insurance (EI) benefits

- you have not repaid all of the amounts you withdrew from your registered retirement savings plan (RRSP), Home Buyers' Plan (HBP), or Lifelong Learning Plan (LLP)

- you have to contribute to the Canada Pension Plan (CPP)

Capital gains and their taxation is discussed later in this chapter. Old Age Security (OAS) is covered in Chapter 15. Employment Insurance (EI) benefits are government benefits that are payable for periods of time when you are away from work due to specific situations. Some examples of situations where EI benefits are payable include a parental leave of absence and a leave of absence as a result of injury, illness, or layoff. The Home Buyers' Plan, Lifelong Learning Plan, and Canada Pension Plan are discussed in Chapter 15.

Employment Insurance (EI) Government benefits that are payable for periods of time when you are away from work due to specific situations.

Generally, you should keep a copy of your tax return and all supporting documents indefinitely. While many recommend keeping documents for seven years, the government may request earlier documents during audits.

Why Students Should File Tax Returns

Students should file tax returns for a number of reasons. First, you may be eligible for a refundable GST/HST credit. The GST/HST credit is a quarterly tax-free payment made to low- and modest-income earners. There is no cost to apply. All you need to do is mark the "Yes" box on page 1 of the T1 General (see Exhibit 3.1) next to the question "Are you applying for the GST/HST credit?" To be eligible for this benefit you must meet one of the following criteria:

- you are 19 years of age or older

- you have, or previously had, a spouse or common-law partner

- you are, or previously were, a parent and live, or previously lived, with your child

If you do apply for this benefit, make sure that you complete the box regarding your marital status (if applicable) located on page 1 of the T1 General. Your eligibility will also be affected if you have children who have registered to receive the Canada Child Tax Benefit.

Second, if you have tuition, education, or textbook credits that you will not be using to reduce your taxes, filing a return makes the CRA aware that you have these credits. By doing this, you will be able to apply these credits to taxes payable in the future.

Third, consider that your RRSP contribution room is based on every dollar of income you earn minus pension plan adjustments. By filing a return and declaring income, you will have more room to contribute to your RRSP in the future. Your RRSP is your personal pension plan—it is in your best interest to maximize your future contributions to it.

The CRA allows taxpayers to file tax returns in two different manners. You can mail hard copies with receipts attached prior to the April 30 deadline (the postmark must be made before midnight). You can also file your return by email (NETFILE), in which case you do not have to mail the CRA receipts supporting your deductions and tax credits. The CRA has made it easier for you to find reliable tax preparation software online by listing certified software providers at www.netfile.gc.ca/software-e.html. Through this website, you can access income tax preparation software programs that are compatible with the CRA's NETFILE program. Many of these software providers will let you use their software at no charge if your income is below a certain amount.

Once the CRA has processed your return, you will receive a Notice of Assessment from the government. This notice will either confirm your calculations or provide corrections that may result in additional taxes owing or a larger tax refund. If you are expecting a refund, a cheque will be attached. The Notice also includes a box outlining your RRSP contribution limits for the following tax year. You should file the Notice of Assessment with the copy of your tax return.

L.O. 2

STEP 1: CALCULATE TOTAL INCOME (LINES 101 TO 150)

total income
All reportable income from any source, including salary, wages, commissions, business income, government benefits, pension income, interest income, dividend income, and capital gains received during the tax year. Income received from sources outside Canada is also subject to Canadian income tax.

To calculate your federal income tax, first determine your total income. Total income consists of all reportable income from any source. Some of the items included in total income are your salary, wages, commissions, government benefits, pension income, interest income, dividend income, and capital gains received during the tax year. It also includes income from your own business, as well as from tips, prizes and awards, rental property, and various taxable benefits. Examples of taxable benefits include the use of a company automobile, employer-paid education and life insurance, and employer RRSP contributions. Some types of income are not taxed, including GST credits, Canada Child Tax Benefit payments, lottery winnings, most gifts and inheritances, and most life insurance death benefits.

Wages and Salaries
If you work full-time, your main source of total income is probably your salary. Wages and salaries, along with any bonuses, are subject to federal income taxes. The calculation of the federal income tax payable on your salary is discussed later in this chapter. Some benefits are taxable. These will be included on your T4.

Interest Income

interest income
Interest earned from investments in various types of savings accounts at financial institutions; from investments in debt securities such as term deposits, GICs, and CSBs; and from loans to other individuals, companies, and governments.

Individuals can earn interest income from investments in various types of savings accounts at financial institutions. They can also earn interest income by investing in debt securities such as term deposits, guaranteed investment certificates (GICs), and Canada Savings Bonds (CSBs) and through loans to other individuals, companies, and governments. Interest income is recorded on line 121 of the T1 General. You will receive information slips (T4A) from institutions that pay you interest. Another point to remember is that tax is due on interest in the year it is earned, not in the year it is received.

Dividend Income

dividend income
Income received from corporations in the form of dividends paid on stock or on mutual funds that hold stock. Dividend income represents the profit due to part owners of the company.

Individual taxpayers can earn dividend income by investing in stocks or mutual funds. Dividend income represents income received from corporations in the form of dividends paid on stock or on mutual funds that hold stock. Some corporations pay dividends to their shareholders quarterly. Other corporations elect not to pay dividends to their shareholders and instead reinvest all of their earnings to finance their operations. This can benefit shareholders because a corporation's share price is more likely to appreciate over time if the corporation reinvests all of its earnings. Dividends are paid to shareholders from after-tax earnings. Since the firm has paid corporate income tax prior to the dividend distribution, the federal government has created a dividend adjustment calculation that will reduce the income tax payable by shareholders who receive the dividends. The dividend adjustment was created to recognize that the federal government has already collected some tax from the corporation and that it would be unfair to collect a regular amount of tax from the taxpayer, as this would constitute double taxation. The calculation of the dividend adjustment is discussed in Chapter 13.

Capital Income

capital gain
Money earned when you sell an asset at a higher price than you paid for it.

taxable capital gain
The portion of a capital gain that is subject to income tax. The portion included in income is called the inclusion amount and currently stands at 50 percent.

capital loss
Occurs when you sell an asset for a lower price than you paid for it.

allowable capital loss
The portion of a capital loss that you can deduct from taxable capital gains.

You can purchase securities (also called financial assets) such as stocks or debt instruments (such as bonds) that are issued by firms to raise capital. You can also invest in other income-producing assets such as rental properties. When you sell these types of assets at a higher price than you paid for them, you earn a capital gain. A taxable capital gain represents the portion of a capital gain that is subject to income tax. If you sell an asset for a lower price than you paid for it, you sustain a capital loss. An allowable capital loss represents the portion of a capital loss that you can deduct from taxable capital gains. A taxable capital gain is currently equal to 50 percent of the capital gain. Similarly, an allowable capital loss is currently equal to 50 percent of the capital loss. For example, in 2006, Fatima sold her shares in TD Bank for a $20 000 capital gain. Her taxable capital gain was equal to $10 000 ($20 000 × 50%). To reduce the amount of capital gain subject to personal income tax, Fatima sold her shares in Bombardier for a $10 000 capital loss. The allowable capital loss of $5000 ($10 000 × 50%) could be used to offset the $10 000 taxable capital gain. As a result, Fatima was able to record taxable capital gains of $5000 on line 127 of her T1 General. Only 50 percent of capital gains is taxed to encourage people to invest in capital assets, such as the stock of a company.

EXAMPLE

Recall from Chapter 1 that Stephanie Spratt was hired by the Sudbury Tax Services Office at an annual salary of $38 000. She earned no income from interest, dividends, or capital gains. Her total income for the year is:

Salary	$38 000
+ Interest Income	0
+ Dividend Income	0
+ Capital Gain	0
= Total Income	$38 000

L.O. 3   STEP 2: SUBTRACT DEDUCTIONS (LINES 207 TO 257)

You may be able to claim deductions and exemptions, which reduce the amount of your total income subject to taxation. The discussion below focuses on the more common deductions you will encounter, as covering all potential deductions available to you is beyond the scope of this text. You can research other potential deductions on the CRA website (www.cra-arc.gc.ca).

Deductions

deduction
An expense that can be deducted from total income to determine taxable income.

A **deduction** represents an expense that can be deducted from total income to determine taxable income. The more deductions you have, the less tax you will pay. The most common deductions include contributions to a registered pension plan (RPP), contributions to an RRSP, union/professional dues, child care expenses, support payments, carrying charges, moving expenses, and employment expenses.

Registered Pension Plan (RPP). Generally, you can deduct the total of all amounts shown in Box 20 of your T4 slips, in Box 32 of your T4A slips, and on your union or RPP receipts. As discussed earlier in this chapter, a T4 slip displays your salary and all deductions associated with your employment with a specific employer. Exhibit 3.4 provides an example of a T4 slip. Some of the boxes on the T4 slip are discussed throughout the remainder of this chapter. Refer to Exhibit 3.4 whenever necessary. A T4A slip is a document provided to you when you receive income other than salary income. The slip is created by the individual or organization that pays you these other forms of income.

T4A slip
A document provided to you when you receive income other than salary income.

Exhibit 3.4 T4 Slip

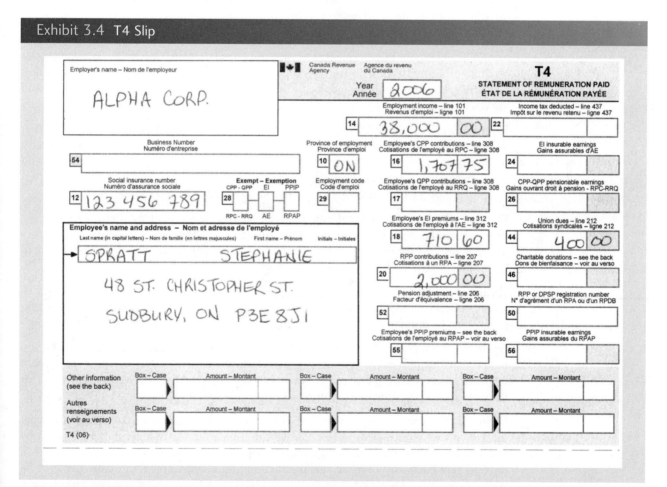

Source: www.cra-arc.gc.ca/E/pbg/tf/t4_flat/t4flat-06b.pdf (accessed January 4, 2007). Reproduced with permission of the Minister of Public Works and Government Services Canada, 2008.

Some examples of income shown on a T4A slip include pension income, a retiring allowance, and self-employed commissions. RPPs are discussed in Chapter 15.

Registered Retirement Savings Plan (RRSP). RRSP contributions made by you and/or your employer are deductible in the calculation of net income. The RRSP deduction limit is subject to change every year. Assuming that you or your employer do not contribute to an RPP, the deduction limit for 2006 is the lesser of 18 percent of your total income or $18 000.

Registered Education Savings Plan (RESP). RESP contributions made by you, your spouse, or another family member are not deductible in the calculation of net income. Starting in 2007, the annual limit on RESP contributions has been removed. The lifetime contribution limit has been increased to $50 000. In addition, the first $2500 of annual RESP contributions will be matched by a 20 percent Canada Education Savings Grant (CESG) from Human Resources and Social Development Canada. Based on their incomes, families may be eligible for an enhanced CESG rate on the first $500 of annual contributions. In addition, families entitled to the National Child Benefit Supplement (NCBS) may be eligible for the Canada Learning Bond. Children born in Alberta after December 31, 2004, are eligible for the Alberta Centennial Education Savings Plan (ACES). The tax implications of any payments received from an RESP vary depending on whether RESP beneficiaries attend a post-secondary institution. Since an RESP is a registered plan, any beneficiaries must have a social insurance number (SIN) prior to the time of application. For more information on RESPs, go to www.cra-arc.gc.ca/tax/individuals/topics/resp/menu-e.html.

Union/Professional Dues. The amount shown in Box 44 of your T4 slip is deductible in the calculation of net income.

Child Care Expenses. Child care expenses are deductible if the child was under 16 or had a mental or physical infirmity during the year of your tax return. Generally, only the spouse or common-law partner with the lower net income can claim these expenses. The amount deductible will depend on the income of the lower-income spouse, the age of the child, and the dollar amount of child care expenses being claimed.

Support Payments. Spousal support payments are deductible in the calculation of net income. Child support payments are deductible if the payments are being made with respect to a court order or written agreement established before May 1, 1997. Child support payments are not deductible if the payments are being made with respect to a court order or written agreement established on or after May 1, 1997.

Carrying Charges. The general rule is that an expenditure paid by a taxpayer to earn income from business or property is deductible from that income. The types of expenses included are fees for certain investment advice, safety deposit box fees, and interest paid on money borrowed for investment purposes.

Moving Expenses. Moving expenses incurred for the purpose of starting a new job or to attend college or other post-secondary education are deductible. The rule is that the taxpayer must be moving at least 40 kilometres closer to their job or educational institution.

Employment Expenses. You can deduct certain expenses (including any GST/HST) you paid to earn employment income. You can claim the expenses only if your employment contract requires you to pay those expenses and if you did not receive an allowance for the expenses or the allowance you received is included in your income.

Summary of Deductible Expenses. Taxpayers total their deductions to determine their net income, which is recorded on line 236 of the T1 General. Your net income is used by the federal government to calculate amounts such as the GST/HST credit, whether you have to pay back any of your social benefits, and certain non-refundable tax credits. Social benefits include Old Age Security (OAS) and Guaranteed Income Supplement (GIS). These benefits are discussed in detail in Chapter 15.

EXAMPLE

Stephanie Spratt reviews the T4 slip that her employer provided to determine what deductions she can take against her total income. Box 20 of her T4 indicates that she has $2000 in RPP contributions. In addition, Box 44 indicates that she has paid $400 in union dues. Stephanie has also received a slip from her bank indicating that she has contributed $2000 to her RRSP. Finally, Stephanie reviews her bank statement and finds that she has paid $600 for the year to maintain a safety deposit box at her bank. Her total deductions are:

Deductions

RPP Contributions	$2000
RRSP Contributions	$2000
Union Dues	$400
Safety Deposit Box Fees	$600
Total	$5000

IN-CLASS NOTES

Do You Have to File a Return?

You must file a tax return if you have earned income for one calendar year.

- Step 1: Calculate Total Income
  - Wages and salaries
  - Interest income
  - Dividend income
  - Capital income
- Step 2: Subtract Deductions
  - RPPs and RRSPs
  - Union/professional dues
  - Child care expenses, support payments, carrying charges, moving expenses, and employment expenses

(continued on page 66)

_____
_____
_____
_____
_____
_____
_____
_____

L.O. 4

STEP 3: CALCULATE TAXABLE INCOME (LINE 260)

Before calculating the taxes you owe, you need to determine your taxable income. Taxable income is equal to your net income minus some additional deductions. These deductions are more specific than the ones discussed above and often will not apply to the average taxpayer. As a result, they will not be covered in this text. For our purposes, your taxable income will be the same as your net income. You may wonder why the federal government doesn't simply allow taxpayers to total all of their deductions and determine taxable income without first having to calculate net income. As already discussed, net income serves a different purpose. Net income is used by the government to make adjustments to certain benefits, whereas the calculation of net federal and provincial income tax is based on your taxable income. This system is in place to ensure that all taxpayers are treated fairly with regards to the receipt of social benefits and the calculation of taxes payable.

EXAMPLE

Recall that Stephanie Spratt's total income is $38 000 and her deductions total $5000. Therefore, her taxable income for the year is:

Total Income	$38 000
− Deductions	$5 000
= Taxable Income	$33 000

L.O. 5

STEP 4: CALCULATE NET FEDERAL TAX PAYABLE (LINE 420)

Once you know your taxable income, you can use the table in Exhibit 3.5 to determine the federal taxes you owe. Taxes are dependent not only on your taxable income, but also on your non-refundable tax credits. Notice that the income tax system in Canada is progressive. That is, the higher an individual's income, the higher the percentage of income paid in taxes. The federal tax rates displayed in Exhibit 3.5 are known as marginal tax rates. A marginal tax rate represents the percentage of tax you pay on your next dollar of taxable income. For example, if you have taxable income of $80 000, you pay 26 percent on the next dollar of taxable income you earn.

marginal tax rate
The percentage of tax you pay on your next dollar of taxable income.

Determining Your Tax Liability

To determine your tax liability, simply refer to Schedule 1, Federal Tax (see Exhibit 3.3 on page 54), and follow the instructions at the top of the columns of the tax schedule. Converting the instructions into a formula gives the following equation for the tax liability:

Tax Liability = Tax on Base Amount + [Percentage on Excess over the Base Amount × (Taxable Income − Base Amount)]

Since Stephanie's taxable income falls within the first tax bracket, her average tax rate will be the same as her marginal tax rate. Therefore, her tax liability of 15.25 percent, calculated as ($5032.50 ÷ $33 000) x 100, may also be referred to as her average

EXAMPLE

Stephanie Spratt's taxable income is $33 000. She enters this amount on line 1 of Schedule 1.

Stephanie uses the following steps to determine her federal taxes:

- Her income falls within the first bracket in Schedule 1: $36 378 or less.
- The base amount of this bracket is $0.
- The tax rate applied to her excess income over the base amount is 15.25 percent, as shown in the first column of Schedule 1. This means that Stephanie's marginal tax bracket is 15.25 percent, so any additional income she earns is subject to a 15.25 percent tax.

In summary, her tax liability is:

Tax Liability = Tax on Base Amount + [Percentage on Excess over the Base Amount × (Taxable Income − Base Amount)]

= $0 + [15.25% × ($33 000 − $0)]	
= $0 + [15.25% × ($33 000)]	
= $0 + $5032.50	
= $5032.50.	

Exhibit 3.5 Federal Personal Income Tax Brackets and Rates

2006 Taxable Income	Tax Rate
First $36 378	15.25%
Over $36 378 up to $72 756	22.00%
Over $72 756 up to $118 285	26.00%
Over $118 285	29.00%

Source: Federal Tax Brackets and Rates / Federal Personal Income Tax Rates Table, 2006 Taxable Income and Tax Rate columns. www.taxtips.ca/fedtax.htm (accessed January 4, 2007). Reprinted with permission of Taxtips.ca.

average tax rate
The amount of tax you pay as a percentage of your total taxable income.

tax rate. Your average tax rate represents the amount of tax you pay as a percentage of your total taxable income. If Stephanie's taxable income had been in any other tax bracket, her marginal tax rate would have been greater than her average tax rate. As a general rule, an individual's marginal tax rate is greater than their average tax rate, unless their income does not exceed the income limit for the first tax bracket.

Tax Credits

tax credits
Specific amounts used directly to reduce tax liability.

refundable tax credit
The portion of the credit that is not needed to reduce your tax liability (because it is already zero) may be paid to you.

non-refundable tax credit
The portion of the credit that is not needed to reduce your tax liability will not be paid to you and cannot be carried forward to reduce your tax liability in the future.

You may be able to reduce your tax liability if you are eligible for tax credits. Tax credits are specific amounts used directly to reduce tax liability. Tax credits may be characterized as refundable or non-refundable. With respect to a refundable tax credit, the portion of the credit that is not needed to reduce your tax liability (because it is already zero) may be paid to you. The GST credit for low-income individuals and the Ontario Property Tax Credit are examples of refundable tax credits. With a non-refundable tax credit, the portion of the credit that is not needed to reduce your tax liability will not be paid to you and cannot be carried forward to reduce your tax liability in the future. Most tax credits are considered non-refundable because they can only be used to reduce your taxes. If the amount of taxes you owe is zero, your tax credits will generally be of no use to you. Exhibit 3.6 lists the 2006 federal base amounts for the most commonly used non-refundable tax credits. Generally, the base amount is multiplied by the lowest marginal federal tax bracket (15.25 percent for 2006) to determine the amount of the non-refundable tax credit. For example, the base amount for the basic personal amount tax credit is $8839 for 2006. The amount of the federal non-refundable tax credit associated with this base amount is $8839 × 15.25% = $1347.95. The effect of this tax credit is to reduce your taxes payable by $1347.95. The dollar values of the base amounts change every tax year.

It is important to realize that the lowest federal marginal tax bracket (15.25 percent for 2006) is used to calculate the dollar value of the tax credit. By contrast, a tax deduction reduces your tax owing based on your highest marginal tax bracket. Exhibit 3.5 clearly shows that tax deductions will reduce tax more effectively for taxpayers who have taxable income greater than $36 378 in 2006. For example, if you have taxable income of $37 000, a $1 deduction will result in a tax savings of 22 percent on that $1. The higher your marginal tax bracket, the greater the savings you will receive from a tax deduction relative to a tax credit. Therefore, in general, it is better to have a tax deduction than a tax credit. With respect to your income tax return, federal non-refundable tax credits are listed on page 1 of Schedule 1: Federal Tax (see Exhibit 3.3 on page 54).

clawback
Used to reduce (i.e., claw back) a particular government benefit provided to taxpayers who have an income that exceeds a certain threshold amount.

Basic Personal Amount. The basic personal amount of $8839 may be claimed by all taxpayers. Essentially, the first $8839 of taxable income earned by a taxpayer in Canada is tax-free.

Age Amount. The age amount may be claimed by a taxpayer who was 65 or older on December 31 of the tax year in question. This tax credit is subject to a clawback based on income. A clawback is used to reduce (i.e., claw back) a particular government benefit provided to taxpayers who have an income that exceeds a certain threshold amount.

Exhibit 3.6 Federal Base Amounts, 2006

Non-Refundable Tax Credit	Federal Base Amount, 2006
Basic personal amount	$8839
Age amount	5066
Spousal/equivalent-to-spouse amount	7505
Infirm dependant amount (18+ years of age)	3933
CPP/QPP contributions (employee)	1910.70
EI premiums	729.30
Public transit passes amount (maximum)	960
Pension income amount	2000
Caregiver amount	3933
Disability amount	6741
Disability amount supplement for taxpayers under 18 years of age	3933
Interest paid on your student loans	Amount paid
Tuition, education, and textbook amount (full-time)	Tuition paid + $400 education amount + $65 textbook amount
Medical expenses amount	Amount paid in excess of 3% of net income or $1884, whichever is less

Source: 2006 Non-Refundable Tax Credits - Base Amounts, excerpts to demonstrate Tax Credit Type. www.taxtips.ca/nonrefundablecredits.htm#2006baseamts (accessed January 4, 2007). Reprinted with permission of Taxtips.ca.

The idea is that as your income increases, you do not need the full financial assistance that results from tax credits and other government benefit programs. With respect to the age amount, you lose 15 percent of the age amount credit for every dollar of income greater than a certain amount ($30 270 in 2006).

EXAMPLE

Helen turned 65 on October 8, 2006. Her taxable income for 2006 was $42 000. Although Helen qualifies for the age amount credit, it will be reduced because her income is above the threshold amount of $30 270. The maximum age amount for 2006 is $5066. Helen qualifies for a reduced age amount calculated as:

$$\$5066 - [(\$42\ 000 - \$30\ 270) \times 0.15]$$
$$= \$5066 - (11\ 730 \times 0.15)$$
$$= \$5066 - \$1759.50$$
$$= \$3306.50$$

As a result, Helen will record an age amount of $3306.50 on her Schedule 1 form.

Spousal or Equivalent-to-Spouse Partner Amount. This non-refundable tax credit is available to a taxpayer who supported a spouse or equivalent-to-spouse partner who had a net income below $751 in the 2006 tax year. This tax credit is subject to a clawback based on income: $1 of income above $751 reduces the amount by $1. This is referred to as a dollar-for-dollar clawback. The benefit is eliminated once the spouse or equivalent-to-spouse partner's income exceeds $8256.

Infirm Dependant Amount (18-Plus Years of Age). You can claim an amount up to a maximum of $3933 for each of your or your spouse's or common-law partner's dependent children or grandchildren only if the children or grandchildren were mentally or physically infirm and were born in 1988 or earlier. As well, you can claim an amount only if the dependant's net income is less than $9513 in the 2006 tax year.

CPP/QPP Contributions. Claim the amount shown in boxes 16 and 17 of your T4 slips. Do not enter more than the maximum amount you can claim for the tax year, which is currently $1910.70. This amount is subject to change from time to time.

EI Premiums. Claim the amount shown in Box 18 of your T4 slips. Do not enter more than the maximum amount you can claim for the tax year, which is currently $729.30. This amount is subject to change from time to time.

Public Transit Passes Amount. After June 20, 2006, you can claim the cost of monthly public transit passes or passes of a longer duration, such as an annual pass. Do not enter more than the maximum amount you can claim for the tax year, which is currently $960.

Pension Income Amount. You can claim a credit on the first $2000 of eligible pension or annuity income reported on line 115 or line 129 of your T1 General (see page 2 of Exhibit 3.1 on page 50).

Caregiver Amount. You may be eligible to claim a caregiver amount if you provided in-home care to a parent or grandparent 65-plus years of age, or to infirm adult relatives. If you qualify, you may be able to claim this credit for more than one dependant. The current maximum amount you can claim is $3933.

Disability Amount. To claim this amount, you must have had a severe and prolonged impairment in physical or mental functions during the tax year. The current maximum amount you can claim is $6741.

Disability Amount Supplement. If you qualify for the disability amount and you were under 18 at the end of the tax year, you may be able to claim up to an additional $3933 (2006 rate).

Interest Paid on Your Student Loans. You can claim the amount of interest you paid on a student loan if the loan was made to you under the *Canada Student Loans Act*, the *Canada Student Financial Assistance Act*, or similar provincial or territorial government laws for post-secondary education.

Tuition, Education, and Textbook Amount. You can claim the amount you paid for eligible tuition fees. You can also claim an education amount of $400 for each month of full-time enrolment in a qualifying education program, and $120 for each month of part-time enrolment in a qualifying education program. In addition, you can claim a textbook amount of $65 for each month that you qualify for the full-time education amount, and $20 for each month that you qualify for the part-time education amount.

Medical Expenses Amount. To qualify for the medical expenses amount, your total medical expenses must be greater than either 3 percent of your net income or $1884, whichever is less.

Go to
www.cra-arc.gc.ca/E/pub/
tg/p105/README.html

This website provides detailed tax information for students, such as taxation of the common types of income they earn and the deductions and credits they can use to reduce their taxes payable.

The non-refundable tax credits discussed above are totalled and entered on line 335 of Schedule 1. This amount is then multiplied by the lowest federal marginal tax bracket (15.25 percent in 2006). In general, this amount represents your total non-refundable tax credits. On page 2 of Schedule 1, you are asked to enter your tax payable (from line 8 of page 1) on line 33. You are also asked to enter the amount of non-refundable tax credits (from line 32 of page 1) on line 36. In general, your net federal tax will be the difference between your tax payable and your non-refundable tax credits. Your net federal tax is recorded on line 50 of Schedule 1. This amount is then entered on line 420 on page 4 of your T1 General.

Transferable Tax Credits

As discussed earlier, most tax credits are non-refundable. That is, if you have reduced your taxes to zero and have not used all of your tax credits, you will not be able to carry forward most tax credits to the following year. However, the tuition, education, and textbook amount; the pension income amount; the age amount; and the disability amount can be transferred to other individuals. The age and pension amounts can only be transferred to the taxpayer's spouse. The list of eligible transferees with respect to the other two credits is extensive and generally includes your blood relatives (parents, grandparents, brothers, sisters, etc.).

Tax Credits Eligible for Carry Forward

Certain tax credits may be carried forward by the taxpayer. These include the medical expenses amount; the tuition, education, and textbook amount; and the charitable contribution amount. Tax credits that are carried forward may be used to reduce tax payable in future tax years. It is interesting to note that the tuition, education, and textbook amount may be used to reduce tax payable immediately by the taxpayer or a relative of the taxpayer, or may be used by the taxpayer in future tax years.

EXAMPLE

John Morris has $3200 in taxes payable for the most recent year. As a student, he is eligible for a number of tax credits, including the basic personal amount, CPP/QPP contributions, EI premiums, the public transit passes amount, and the tuition, education, and textbook amount. By using his non-refundable tax credits, John is able to reduce his taxes payable to zero. However, he is not able to use $1500 of the tuition, education, and textbook amount that he has available to him. John has two options: he can carry forward the $1500 to the next tax year and apply it against his taxes payable for that year, or he can transfer this credit to an eligible transferee, who can then use it to reduce their taxable income. Note that because the tax credit was non-refundable, John cannot simply collect the $1500 directly from the CRA.

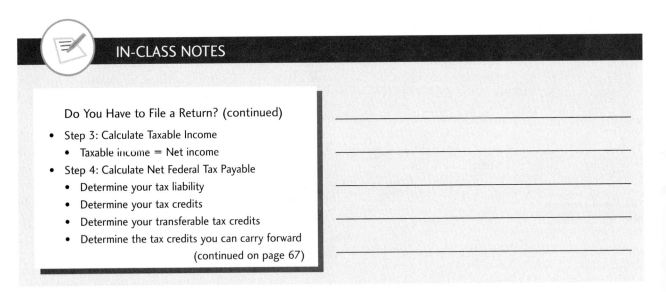

IN-CLASS NOTES

Do You Have to File a Return? (continued)
- Step 3: Calculate Taxable Income
  - Taxable income = Net income
- Step 4: Calculate Net Federal Tax Payable
  - Determine your tax liability
  - Determine your tax credits
  - Determine your transferable tax credits
  - Determine the tax credits you can carry forward

(continued on page 67)

STEP 5: CALCULATE NET PROVINCIAL TAX PAYABLE (LINE 428)

Exhibit 3.7 shows that the calculation of provincial personal income tax varies widely from province to province. Provinces calculate their marginal tax rates as a percentage of net income. This calculation is often referred to as the TONI (tax on net income) system. As discussed earlier, you need Form 428 to determine your net provincial tax payable.

The process of completing Form 428 is similar to that used to complete Schedule 1. In fact, the tax credits discussed earlier and listed in Exhibit 3.6 are available in most provinces. For the purposes of this course, a discussion of the tax differences among provinces is not required.

IN-CLASS NOTES

Do You Have To File a Return? (continued)

- Step 5: Calculate Net Provincial Tax Payable
  - You pay tax on your income to the province or territory in which you live
- Step 6: Calculate Total Tax Payable
  - The taxes you pay to the federal government plus those you pay to your provincial or territorial government equal your total tax payable
  (continued on page 69)

STEP 6: CALCULATE TOTAL TAX PAYABLE (LINE 435)

Calculating total tax payable involves adding together the amount recorded for net federal tax, line 420, and the amount for provincial or territorial tax, line 428.

Exhibit 3.7 Provincial Personal Income Tax Brackets and Rates for 2007		
Province	**Personal Income Tax Bracket**	**Marginal Tax Rate**
Newfoundland	$0–29,886	9.64%
	29,887–59,772	14.98
	59,773 and over	17.26
Prince Edward Island	$0–31,369	9.80%
	31,370–62,739	13.80
	62,740 and over	16.70
Nova Scotia	$0–29,590	8.79%
	29,591–59,180	14.95
	59,181–93,000	16.67
	93,001 and over	17.50
New Brunswick	$0–34,186	10.12%
	34,187–68,374	15.48
	68,375–111,161	16.80
	111,162 and over	17.95
Quebec	$0–29,290	16.00%
	29,291–58,595	20.00
	58,596 and over	24.00

(continued)

Exhibit 3.7 continued

Province	Personal Income Tax Bracket	Marginal Tax Rate
Ontario	$0–35,488	6.05%
	35,489–70,976	9.15
	70,977 and over	11.16
Manitoba	$0–30,544	10.90%
	30,545–65,000	13.50
	65,001 and over	17.40
Saskatchewan	$0–38,405	11.00%
	38,406–109,729	13.00
	109,730 and over	15.00
Alberta	all income	10.00%
British Columbia	$0–34,397	5.70%
	34,398–68,794	8.65
	68,795–78,984	11.10
	78,985–95,909	13.00
	95,910 and over	14.70
Yukon	$0–37,178	6.54%
	37,179–74,357	9.68
	74,358–77,959	11.44
	77,960–120,887	12.01
	120,888 and over	13.40
Northwest Territories	$0–35,315	5.40%
	35,316–37,178	8.10
	37,179–70,631	8.60
	70,632–114,830	12.20
	114,831 and over	14.05
Nunavut	$0–37,178	3.50%
	37,179–74,357	7.00
	74,358–120,887	9.00
	120,888 and over	11.50

Source: Provincial tax rates reproduced from KPMG's website at www.kpmg.ca. © 2008 KPMG LLP, a Canadian limited liability partnership and a member firm of the KPMG network of independent member firms affiliated with KPMG International, a Swiss cooperative. All rights reserved. Reproduced by permission. The tax rates for the Yukon, Northwest Territories, and Nunavut adapted from www.taxtips.ca/marginaltaxrates.htm.

Go to
www.walterharder.ca/
T1.html

This website provides an estimate of your tax liability for the year and the tax refund you will receive (if you have already paid more in taxes than your tax liability), based on your total income, deductions, and tax credits.

STEP 7: DETERMINE TOTAL TAX ALREADY PAID (LINE 482)

If you are employed by the same company throughout the year, and you do not own any other investment assets, the tax you paid in the course of the year can be determined by looking at the amount recorded in Box 22 of your T4 slip. This amount is entered on line 437 of your T1 General and then subtracted from your total tax payable, line 435.

L.O. 6 STEP 8: REFUND OR BALANCE OWING (LINE 484 OR 485)

You will receive a tax refund if the amount on line 435 is less than the amount on line 482. You will have tax owing if the amount on line 435 is greater than the amount on line 482.

Focus on Ethics: Reducing Your Taxes

tax planning
Involves activities and transactions that reduce or eliminate tax.

tax avoidance
A term used to describe the process of legally applying tax law to reduce or eliminate taxes payable in ways that the CRA considers potentially abusive of the spirit of the *Income Tax Act.*

tax evasion
Occurs when taxpayers attempt to deceive the CRA by knowingly reporting less tax payable than what the law obligates them to pay.

Do you know anyone who likes to pay taxes? Odds are you do not. Most people dislike paying taxes and put a lot of effort into reducing their tax liability. It is important to distinguish tax planning from tax avoidance and tax evasion. Tax planning involves activities and transactions that reduce or eliminate tax. Using deductions and credits for their intended purpose is a legal approach to tax planning. Tax avoidance occurs when taxpayers legally apply tax law to reduce or eliminate taxes payable in ways that the CRA considers potentially abusive of the spirit of the *Income Tax Act*. The CRA may challenge any attempt to "bend the rules" in a way that was not intended. Tax evasion occurs when taxpayers attempt to deceive the CRA by knowingly reporting less tax payable than what the law obligates them to pay. It can be tempting to report a lower salary than you earned when filing your tax return. Self-employed individuals, for example, may consider doing this. The CRA monitors tax returns to detect underestimated returns, so there is a strong likelihood that it will uncover any illegal behaviour. Attempts to reduce your taxes illegally can subject you to both criminal and civil prosecution.

Fortunately, there are many legal ways to reduce your taxes. Organize your records for things like charitable donations, medical expenses, and rent in a tax planning folder so you will not overlook a potential deduction. Prepare your return early in the year, so that you will not make a careless mistake in the rush to meet the April 30 deadline. Make sure that you have included all tax exemptions and deductions you qualify for on your return and that you have not made any miscalculations. You may even seek the advice of an accountant to ensure that you did not overlook any deductible expenses. It is important to save your receipts during the year, as you will need these when you complete your return.

IN-CLASS NOTES

Do You Have to File a Return?(continued)

- Step 7: Determine Total Tax Already Paid
  - Record the total income tax deducted (Box 22 of your T4)
- Step 8: Refund or Balance Owing
  - You will receive a refund if your total tax payable (line 435) is less than your total tax credits (line 482)
  - You will have a balance owing if your total tax payable (line 435) is more than your total tax credits (line 482)

_____

_____

_____

_____

_____

_____

HOW TAX PLANNING FITS WITHIN YOUR FINANCIAL PLAN

Tax planning involves taking actions throughout the year in order to be able to pay the lowest amount of taxes allowed by law. The key tax planning decisions in building your financial plan are:

- What tax deductions are currently available to you?

- How can you increase your tax deductions in the future?

- Should you increase or decrease the amount of your withholding tax (Form TD1 filed with your employer)?

- What records should you keep?

If you are about to file your taxes, it is generally too late to take steps to lower your tax payable other than to ensure that you include all deductions and credits for which you are eligible.

Tax planning is more effective when done in advance of the tax year-end, throughout the tax year. When considering whether to purchase a vehicle to travel to and from school, you should recognize that public transit passes are eligible for a non-refundable tax credit. Other tax credits that are non-refundable, such as those from tuition, can be carried forward or transferred to someone who has paid tax and will receive a refund for the current taxation year.

Because individuals who earn a high level of income can be exposed to very high tax rates, they should consider ways to reduce their tax liability. Some of the most useful strategies to reduce tax payable are maximizing your RRSP contribution, investing in non-registered investments using borrowed funds, investing in stocks that pay no dividends, and making contributions to charitable and/or political organizations.

You may enjoy getting a large tax refund each year, but in reality that is not an efficient use of your capital. If you have too much withheld in taxes, you are in effect making an interest-free loan to the government while forgoing the use of that cash to pay off credit cards or make investments. However, if withholding too much ensures that you do not have to scramble to make your tax payment on April 30, then consider doing so. Some taxpayers who lack the self-discipline to save use their tax refunds to pay for summer vacations or large consumer purchases.

Some actions you can take now will make tax filing easier in the future. For example, if you buy stock within the year but expect to retain it for several years, you should maintain a record of the purchase transaction so that you will be able to calculate the capital gain or loss when you eventually sell the stock.

While many tax preparers suggest that you retain copies of your completed tax forms along with receipts for a period of seven years, it is advisable to keep completed forms indefinitely. If you are audited by the CRA and an error is found, the government does have the right to review previous years' returns. Keep the files—they will not take up much room.

STEPHANIE SPRATT'S FINANCIAL PLAN: Application of Tax Concepts

GOALS FOR TAX PLANNING

1. Reduce taxable income (thereby reducing taxes paid) to the extent allowable by the CRA.
2. Reduce taxes paid by deferring income.

ANALYSIS

Present Situation

Annual Salary = $38 000	
Federal Income Taxes = $5032.50	
Average Tax Rate = 13.24%	

Reduce Taxes by:

Increasing deductions?	*I have maximized the deductions available to me, so this is not an option for me this year.*
Reducing total income?	*I did not contribute any portion of my income to an individual retirement plan; therefore, this option is not available.*
Total tax savings?	*$0 per year*

LONG-TERM TAX PLAN

Reduce Taxes by:

Increasing deductions?	*As my income increases, I will be able to put more money toward my RRSP. In addition, I will be able to find non-registered investments that earn capital gains, thereby allowing me to defer income until I sell the investments.*
Reducing total income?	*The changes above will reduce my total taxable income, thereby reducing my taxes payable.*
	Remember that some deductions mean you do not pay any tax on income used to pay these expenses, such as union dues. RRSP or RPP contributions, while deductible against current income, are really means to defer income. When you use the money in either the RRSP or the RPP, it will be taxed in your hands at then-current rates.
	Investments can provide tax deferral opportunities as well.

DECISIONS

Decisions Regarding Tax Savings for This Year

I currently qualify for no tax savings.

Discussion Questions

1. How would Stephanie's tax planning decisions differ if she were a single mother of two children?

2. How would Stephanie's tax planning decisions be affected if she were 35 years old? If she were 50 years old?

SUMMARY

Taxes are an integral part of our economy in that they are used to pay for a variety of governmental services and programs. Individual income taxes must be filed and paid by April 30 of the year following the tax year.

The first step in filing a federal income tax return is to determine your total income. This information can be found on your T4 slip and other information slips. Total income consists primarily of your salary, commissions, government benefits, pension income, investment income, and various taxable benefits.

Your taxable income is determined by subtracting the total value of your deductions from your total income. The most common deductions include deductions for contributions to an RPP, contributions to an RRSP, union/professional dues, child care expenses, support payments, carrying charges, moving expenses, and employment expenses. Your tax liability depends on your taxable income, and the tax rate applied depends on your income level and your province or territory of residence.

After determining your federal tax payable on Schedule 1, you may be eligible to claim certain non-refundable tax credits that can be used to reduce your tax liability. For students, the most common tax credits are the basic personal amount, CPP/QPP contributions, EI premiums, public transit passes amount, and the tuition, education, and textbook amount. Certain non-refundable tax credits can be transferred to another individual, while others may be carried forward to future tax years.

INTEGRATING THE KEY CONCEPTS

Tax planning can be applied to all parts of your financial plan. It is useful for financing decisions because some types of financing result in interest expenses that are tax-deductible. It is useful when making investment decisions because the income (for example, dividends and capital gains) earned on some types of investments is subject to a lower tax rate. Tax planning is especially useful for retirement planning because the amount and type of income you receive is easier to control. It is even useful for estate planning because some estates may be subject to no or low taxes if they are properly organized.

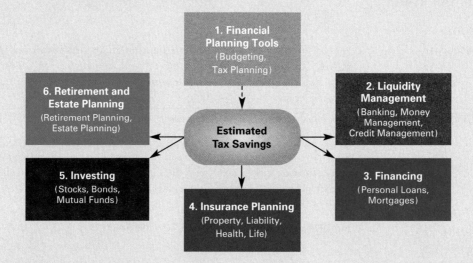

REVIEW QUESTIONS

1. What are taxes paid on?

2. With respect to taxation, what is the role of the federal government? What is the role of the provincial government?

3. When does the tax year end? By what date do taxpayers have to file their income tax returns?

4. What is the penalty if you do not pay taxes owing by the due date?

5. What are the eight steps to completing a T1 General?

6. Under what circumstances do you have to file a tax return?

7. Provide four reasons why students should file a tax return.

8. What is total income? List some types of income that are included in total income. What are some types of payments that you might receive that would not be included in total income?

9. What is the difference between a capital gain and a taxable capital gain?

10. What are deductions? Describe the most common types of deductions.

11. How is taxable income calculated?

12. What is meant by a progressive tax system? What is a marginal tax rate?

13. What is a non-refundable tax credit? What is the difference between a tax deduction and a tax credit? Which is more valuable?

14. List some common non-refundable tax credits.

15. List the non-refundable tax credits that are transferable. List the non-refundable tax credits that may be carried forward.

16. What is the difference between tax avoidance and tax planning?

FINANCIAL PLANNING PROBLEMS

1. Linda neglected to complete her T1 General in time for the filing deadline of April 30, 2007. This would not be a problem if she did not owe any tax. However, after completing her tax return, she realized that the amount of tax withheld by her employer was not enough to cover the amount of taxes she owed. In fact, Linda owed an additional $2000 of income tax. Linda completed her tax return and submitted it to the CRA by November 1, 2007. Calculate Linda's income tax penalty. How much will she have to pay in total?

2. Larry is in the 32 percent marginal tax bracket. Last year, he sold stock he had held for nine months for a gain of $1900. How much tax must he pay on this capital gain?

3. Stuart is in the 35 percent tax bracket. Recently, he sold stock he had held longer than a year for a loss of $20 000. What is Stuart's allowable capital loss?

4. Jim sold two stocks during the year. The capital gain on the sale of Alpha Corp. stock was $10 000. The capital loss on the sale of Gamma Inc. stock was $8000. What is the taxable capital gain Jim will record for the year?

5. Freda incurred a $20 000 capital gain during the year. She would like to reduce her capital gain by selling one of two stocks that are currently sitting at a capital loss. She purchased 10 000 shares in Sesame Inc. for $28 each. The shares are currently trading at $21. She also purchased 5000 shares in the Electric Co. for $33 each. These shares are currently trading at $25. Which shares should she sell? How many shares would she need to sell to reduce her taxable capital gain to zero?

6. Mohammed had total income for the year of $55 000. During the year, he contributed $5000 to an RRSP, $345 toward union dues, $4000 toward child support based on a written agreement established in 2005, and $180 toward a safety deposit box. Calculate his taxable income for the year.

7. Use the information in Exhibit 3.5 (see page 63) to determine the amount of federal tax payable for each of the following individuals. Non-refundable tax credits are not applicable.

   a. Brenda, who has taxable income of $28 000.

   b. Earl, who has taxable income of $70 000.

   c. Indira, who has taxable income of $200 000.

8. What is the average tax rate for each of the individuals in Problem 7?

9. Edna qualifies for the age amount; however, she had an earned income of $44 000 in 2006. As a result, her age amount is subject to a clawback of 15 percent for every dollar that her income is greater than the threshold of $30 270. Calculate Edna's age amount credit for 2006.

10. Carlos was enrolled in a qualifying full-time education program for six months of the year, and a qualifying part-time education program for the remaining six months of the year. What education amount is he eligible to claim on his income tax return for federal income tax purposes? What textbook amount is he eligible to claim?

ETHICAL DILEMMA

Kristal and Joe have been very active participants in their local real estate market. Two years ago, they completed a real estate deal with their neighbour Kevin. As a result of the deal, the couple earned a capital gain of $10 000. When the real estate transaction was completed, Kevin had assured the couple that they would receive their money very soon. Unfortunately, two months passed and Kristal and Joe, who had yet to receive their money, needed to complete their tax return. Since they were confident that they would receive their investment gain soon, they decided that the safe thing to do was to pay income tax on the $10 000 by reporting it on their tax return.

It is now two years later and the couple has yet to receive their $10 000 capital gain. Kevin has moved to another city. Joe is angry that he paid tax on money he never received. This year, the couple has earned another $10 000 in capital gains from selling real estate. They decide that in order to make up for what happened two years earlier, they will not report this gain on their tax return. If the CRA questions them about this in the future, they feel that they can justify their actions by explaining what happened with Kevin two years ago.

   a. Discuss whether you think Kristal and Joe are being ethical in not reporting the $10 000 they received this year.

b. Did the couple do the right thing by reporting the first $10 000 in capital gains on their income tax return two years ago? Explain.

c. Is there anything else the couple could do to clear up their tax mess?

FINANCIAL PLANNING ONLINE EXERCISES

1. Go to www.walterharder.ca/MarginalTaxRateCalculator .html.

   a. Using the Marginal Tax Rate Calculator for the current year, select your province of residence. Enter a taxable income amount of $50 000. What are the taxes payable? What is the average tax rate?

   b. Compare your province with the amount of taxes payable in other provinces on a taxable income of $50 000. Which province(s) display the lowest taxes payable? Which province(s) display the highest taxes payable?

2. Go to www.walterharder.ca/T1.html and input the following information:

   Province: Ontario

   Children: None

   Taxpayer/Spouse Age: 18 to 65

   Employment income: $50 000

   Capital gains: $5000

   RRSP deduction: $9000

   a. What is the taxable income? What is the net federal tax? What is the net provincial tax? What is the balance owing?

   b. The federal basic personal amount is $9600 for 2007. How does this compare to your province? (Change the province at the top of the page to see the impact on the provincial basic personal amount.) Which province(s) display the lowest basic personal amount? Which province(s) display the highest basic personal amount?

   c. Compare the deductions and tax credits on this website with those discussed in the chapter. Are there any differences? How would you incorporate any missing deductions and tax credits into the Income Tax Estimator on this website?

ON THE STUDENT CD-ROM FOR THIS CHAPTER YOU WILL FIND:

- Building Your Own Financial Plan exercise and worksheets
- The chapter-end Continuing Case about the Sampson family
- The first part-end Continuing Case about Brad Brooks
- Read through the Building Your Own Financial Plan exercise and use the worksheets to learn how to manage your income taxes.

- After reading the Sampson case study, use the Continuing Case worksheets to help the Sampsons estimate their federal income taxes.
- After reading the Brad Brooks case study, use the Continuing Case worksheets to help Brad prepare personal financial statements.

Study Guide

Circle the correct answer and then check the answers in the back of the book to chart your progress.

Multiple Choice

1. With respect to the federal tax system, the responsibilities of the CRA are:
   a. To draft and revise the *Income Tax Act*.

   b. To administer the *Income Tax Act*, whereas the provincial governments are responsible for distributing and collecting the forms and publications that taxpayers use to calculate their income taxes.

c. To administer the *Income Tax Act* and distribute and collect the forms and publications that taxpayers use to calculate their income taxes.

d. To distribute and collect the forms and publications that taxpayers use to calculate their income taxes, whereas the federal government is responsible for the administration of the *Income Tax Act*.

2. Individual income taxes must be filed and paid by _____ of the year following the tax year. Self-employed individuals have until _____ to file their income tax returns, and must pay any taxes payable by _____.
   a. April 30, June 15, June 15
   b. April 30, April 30, June 15
   c. April 30, June 15, April 30
   d. June 15, June 15, April 30

3. Under which of the following circumstances do you NOT have to file a tax return?
   a. You disposed of property in the calendar year
   b. You may be eligible for a refundable GST/HST credit
   c. You realized a taxable capital gain
   d. You do not have to pay tax for the calendar year

4. To be eligible for the GST/HST credit, you must meet which of the following criteria?
   a. You are 19 years of age or older
   b. You have, or previously had, a spouse or common-law partner
   c. You are, or previously were, a parent and live, or previously lived, with your child
   d. Any of the above

5. Some types of income are not taxed. Which of the following would not be included in taxable income?
   a. GST credits
   b. Canada Child Tax Benefit payments
   c. Lottery winnings
   d. All life insurance death benefits

6. The list of the most common deductions does NOT include:
   a. Spousal support payments made with respect to a court order made on or after May 1, 1997
   b. Child support payments made with respect to a court order made on or after May 1, 1997
   c. Carrying charges
   d. Contributions to an RPP or RRSP

7. Alison had a taxable income of $42 000 for the 2006 tax year. Using the information provided in Exhibit 3.5 (see page 63), calculate her federal tax liability and determine her average tax rate.

All numbers below have been rounded to the nearest whole number.
   a. $9240; 22 percent
   b. $9240; 16 percent
   c. $6785; 22 percent
   d. $6785; 16 percent

8. Which of the following tax credits are subject to a clawback based on income?
   a. Disability amount
   b. Spousal or common-law partner amount
   c. Pension income amount
   d. All of the above

9. Which of the following tax credits cannot be carried forward?
   a. Charitable contribution amount
   b. Tuition, education, and textbook amount
   c. Medical expenses amount
   d. None of the above; all of these tax credits can be carried forward

10. One of the most useful strategies to reduce taxes is to:
    a. Maximize your RRSP contributions
    b. Invest in stocks that pay no dividends
    c. Invest in stocks and/or bonds using borrowed funds
    d. All of the above

True/False

1. True or False? If you do not file a tax return by the deadline and you owe taxes, you will be charged 5 percent plus 1 percent for each additional full month that your return is late, to a maximum of six months.

2. True or False? The T1 General is used to determine your net federal income tax payable.

3. True or False? Generally, you should keep your tax returns and all supporting documents for seven years.

4. True or False? Total income consists of all reportable income from any source, including income from prizes and awards.

5. True or False? Capital gains income is always greater than taxable capital gains income.

6. True or False? Moving expenses incurred for the purpose of starting a new job are deductible if you move to within 40 kilometres of your new job location.

7. True or False? The income tax system in Canada is referred to as a progressive tax system because the

higher an individual's income, the higher the percentage of income taxes paid.

8. True or False? In general, it is better to have a tax credit than a tax deduction.

9. True or False? Interest that you pay on a student loan received from your parents is tax-deductible

as long as you use the proceeds of the loan for tuition and/or textbooks.

10. True or False? Tax avoidance occurs when taxpayers attempt to deceive the CRA by knowingly reporting less tax payable than what the law obligates them to pay.

PART 2

Managing Your Liquidity

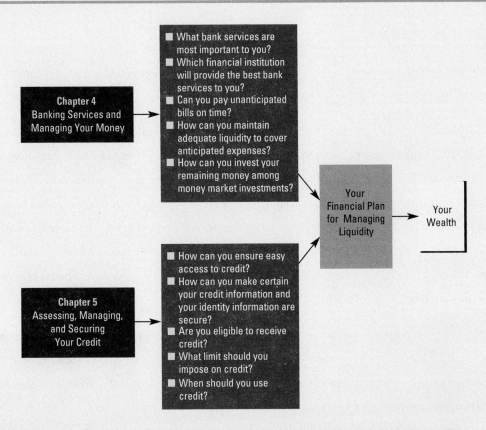

Chapter 4
Banking Services and Managing Your Money

- What bank services are most important to you?
- Which financial institution will provide the best bank services to you?
- Can you pay unanticipated bills on time?
- How can you maintain adequate liquidity to cover anticipated expenses?
- How can you invest your remaining money among money market investments?

Chapter 5
Assessing, Managing, and Securing Your Credit

- How can you ensure easy access to credit?
- How can you make certain your credit information and your identity information are secure?
- Are you eligible to receive credit?
- What limit should you impose on credit?
- When should you use credit?

Your Financial Plan for Managing Liquidity → Your Wealth

THE CHAPTERS IN THIS PART EXPLAIN THE KEY DECISIONS YOU CAN make to ensure adequate liquidity. Chapter 4 explains how to select a financial institution for your banking needs, and how you can manage your money to prepare for future expenses. Chapter 5 explains how you can assess, manage, and secure your credit situation. Your selection of a financial institution, your techniques for money management, and credit management will influence your liquidity and therefore affect your cash flows and wealth.

Chapter 4

Banking Services and Managing Your Money

W hen Shawna arrived on campus for her first year of college she relied on an Automated Banking Machine (ABM) to obtain cash for the many necessities of college life (food, movies, video rentals, and more food).

It was only on a weekend trip back home, when she reviewed her latest bank statement, that Shawna became aware of a problem. Her bank statement showed 34 separate charges for ABM fees. She had been charged $1.00 for each trip to an "out-of-network" ABM not owned by her bank. There was another $1.50 fee charged by the bank that owned the ABM, so each ABM visit created two charges. In addition, Shawna discovered that she had made five balance inquiries on "out-of-network" ABMs and her bank charged $0.50 for each of them. Altogether, for her 17 visits to the ABM, Shawna had accrued $42.50 in ABM fees and $2.50 in inquiry fees for a total of $45.00. Shocked by this discovery, Shawna found a bank that had a branch on campus and several convenient ABM locations.

This chapter explains how to manage your money. The money management process begins with the selection of a financial institution, such as a chartered bank, a credit union, or an online bank. A good bank is an essential ingredient of money management, whether you are depositing funds in a chequing account or a short-term savings vehicle. There are many types of short-term savings options. This chapter also explains how the use of cash management can lead to increased liquidity within your financial plan. Regardless of the bank you choose, it is important to know how well your money is secured.

The objectives of this chapter are to:

1. Provide a background on money management
2. Compare the types of financial institutions
3. Describe the banking services offered by financial institutions
4. Explain how to select a financial institution
5. Describe the savings alternatives offered by financial institutions

LO. 1 BACKGROUND ON MONEY MANAGEMENT

money management
A series of decisions made over a short-term period regarding income and expenses.

Money management describes the decisions you make over a short-term period regarding your income and expenses. It is separate from decisions on investing funds for a long-term period (such as several years) or borrowing funds for a long-term period. Instead, it focuses on maintaining short-term investments to achieve both liquidity and an adequate return on your investments, as explained next.

Liquidity

As discussed in Chapter 1, liquidity refers to your access to ready cash, including savings and credit, to cover short-term and unexpected expenses. Recall that the personal cash flow statement determines the amount of excess or deficient funds you have at the end of a period, such as one month from now. Money management is related to the personal cash flow statement because it determines how to use excess funds, or how to obtain funds if your income is insufficient. You should strive to maintain sufficient funds in liquid assets, such as a chequing account or a savings account, which you can draw on when your expenses exceed your income. In this way, you maintain adequate liquidity.

Some individuals rely on credit cards as a source of liquidity rather than maintaining liquid investments. Credit cards do provide temporary financing. This type of financing can be inexpensive if you pay the amount owing on your credit card before or on the due date. If you have insufficient funds to pay the entire credit card balance when the bill is due, you will pay only a portion of your balance and finance the rest. The interest rate on credit cards is usually quite high, commonly ranging from 8 to 20 percent. A line of credit (discussed in Chapter 5) also provides a source of liquidity when liquid assets are not available. The main advantage of a line of credit versus a credit card is that the interest rate on a line of credit is much lower. To avoid interest charges altogether, you can build an emergency fund that you can access easily when you need cash.

Liquidity is necessary because there will be periods when your income is not adequate to cover your expenses. In Chapter 2, Stephanie Spratt incurred a car maintenance expense that left her with a $270 cash shortage. If she had had sufficient money in an emergency fund, she could have covered the cost of her car maintenance without having to rely on credit.

There are opportunity costs when you maintain an excessive amount of liquid funds. The main opportunity cost is a loss of interest, dividend, or capital gain income. Because the assets in an emergency fund need to be accessed quickly, your rate of return is lower than it would be if you had invested the money in longer-term investments. Therefore, the amount of ready cash you may need access to for unexpected expenses should not be unlimited. A useful rule of thumb is that you should have between three and six months' worth of expenses in an emergency fund.

EXAMPLE

Stephanie Spratt's expenses total $1930 per month. She would like to maintain an emergency fund equal to three months of expenses, and calculates that she needs $5790 ($1930 × 3) in the fund. Her disposable income is normally about $2260 per month, leaving her with $330 in net cash flow each month, or $3960 per year. To build up her emergency fund as quickly as possible, Stephanie will deposit the entire $330 per month of excess cash into an emergency fund until she reaches her cash value objective. Based on her aggressive savings target, Stephanie should be able to reach her goal within 18 months, assuming that she does not need to access the emergency fund during the period she is building it up.

The money allocated to an emergency fund can be deposited in a number of different types of accounts, including chequing accounts, savings accounts, term deposits, guaranteed investment certificates (GICs), money market funds, and Canada Savings Bonds (CSBs). Before determining which of these accounts you should use to build an emergency fund, it is important to select a financial institution with which you will open the account. Most financial institutions offer many types of accounts where you can invest the net cash flows that you have allocated to short-term savings.

IN-CLASS NOTES

Background on Money Management
- Money management describes the decisions you make over a short-term period regarding income and expenses
- Liquidity refers to your access to ready cash to cover short-term and unexpected expenses:
  - Chequing and savings accounts
  - Credit cards and lines of credit
  - Emergency funds

_____

_____

_____

_____

_____

L.O. 2 TYPES OF FINANCIAL INSTITUTIONS

Individuals rely on many different financial institutions when they wish to invest or borrow funds. In this section, we'll examine the two major types of financial institutions: depository institutions and non-depository institutions.

Depository Institutions

depository institutions
Financial institutions that accept deposits from and provide loans to individuals and businesses.

Depository institutions are financial institutions that accept deposits from and provide loans to individuals and businesses. They pay interest on savings deposits and charge interest on loans. The interest rate charged on loans exceeds the interest rate paid on deposits. The institutions use this difference to cover expenses and to generate earnings for their stockholders.

Depository institutions are skilled in assessing the ability of prospective borrowers to repay loans. This is a critical part of their business since the interest collected on loans is a key source of their revenue.

There are three types of depository institutions: chartered banks, trust and loan companies, and credit unions and *caisses populaires.*

chartered banks
Financial institutions that accept deposits and use the funds to provide business and personal loans. These banks are federally incorporated.

Chartered Banks. Chartered banks are financial institutions that accept deposits in chequing and savings accounts and use the funds to provide business and personal loans. The chequing accounts may or may not pay interest. The savings accounts pay interest, while certain other accounts pay interest and can be used to write cheques. These accounts are described in more detail later in this chapter. Deposits at chartered banks are insured up to $100 000 per depositor by the Canada Deposit Insurance Corporation (CDIC), a federal Crown corporation that ensures the safety of bank deposits.

You can look to a chartered bank to provide a personal loan for the purchase of a car or other big-ticket items. They also offer mortgage loans for purchasing a home. Some chartered banks own other types of financial institutions (such as those described next) that provide additional services to individuals. Chartered banks can be distinguished by their ownership and size.

Schedule I Banks. Schedule I banks are domestic banks. There are 22 federally regulated domestic banks in Canada. The largest banks are the RBC Financial Group, Scotiabank, TD Canada Trust, CIBC, and BMO Financial Group.

Schedule II Banks. Schedule II banks are foreign banks that have subsidiaries operating in Canada. There are 24 federally regulated foreign bank subsidiaries in Canada. Schedule II banks are similar to Schedule I banks in that they are authorized to accept deposits. However, Schedule II banks are controlled by a foreign parent corporation while Schedule I banks are controlled domestically. Some of the more visible Schedule II banks are ING Bank of Canada and HSBC Bank Canada.

Schedule III Banks. Schedule III banks are subsidiaries of foreign banks that are restricted in their authority to accept deposits. Some of the more visible Schedule III banks are Capital One Bank and Citibank.

trust and loan companies
Financial institutions that, in addition to providing services similar to a bank, can provide financial planning services, such as administering estates and acting as trustee in the administration of trust accounts.

Trust and Loan Companies. Trust and loan companies are financial institutions that, in addition to providing services similar to a bank, can provide financial planning services, such as administering estates and acting as trustee in the administration of trust accounts. Most trust companies are subsidiaries of banks.

credit unions/caisses populaires
Provincially incorporated co-operative financial institutions that are owned and controlled by their members.

Credit Unions and *Caisses Populaires*. Credit unions and caisses populaires (as they are referred to in francophone regions of Canada) are provincially incorporated co-operative financial institutions that are owned and controlled by their members. Membership in a credit union involves the purchase of at least one share of the credit union. Credit unions were created to serve the financial needs of specific employee groups, such as those in hospitals, universities, and even some corporations. These groups were held together through a common bond that created a social obligation for borrowers, ensuring that loans were paid back promptly. In essence, the loan was extended by other members of the credit union or *caisse populaire*, and default rates were low. Today, this common bond may be residential, religious, employment-related, or cultural. Credit unions, which are not-for-profit financial organizations, offer their members deposit accounts, mortgages, personal loans, and other products similar to those offered by chartered banks and trust and loan companies. In addition, these accounts are eligible for deposit insurance protection through provincial deposit insurance agencies. In Ontario, deposit insurance is provided by the Deposit Insurance Corporation of Ontario (DICO). Credit unions and *caisses populaires* also differ in that they do not operate outside provincial boundaries.

Focus on Ethics: Special Rates on Deposits

As mentioned earlier, depository institutions pay interest on savings deposits. Some institutions have catchy advertisements stating that they will pay a higher annual interest rate on new deposits than other depository institutions. Are these offers a sure thing? Probably not. Before making any deposit, you need to check the fine print and ask important questions. How long does the rate apply? If it is for a short term only, what will be the renewal rate? How long must you maintain the deposit before you can withdraw your funds? Are there any additional fees? Is the deposit insured?

Usually the fine print in newspaper or Internet offers indicates that the rate will be lowered after the first month. The deposit is risky if it is not insured, and the rate may be lower than other banks' deposit rates after the first month. Either of these conditions could cause the return on this deposit to be less than that offered by other depository institutions. Carefully research advertised offers.

Non-depository Institutions

non-depository institutions
Financial institutions that do not offer federally insured deposit accounts but provide various other financial services.

Non-depository institutions are financial institutions that do not offer federally insured deposit accounts but provide various other financial services. The main types of non-depository institutions that serve individuals are finance and lease companies, mortgage companies, investment dealers, insurance companies, mutual fund companies, payday loan companies, cheque cashing outlets, and pawnshops.

finance and lease companies
Non-depository institutions that specialize in providing personal loans or leases to individuals.

Finance and Lease Companies. Finance and lease companies specialize in providing personal loans or leases to individuals. These loans may be used for various purposes such as purchasing a car or other consumer products or making renovations to a home. Many of the major car manufacturers have in-house finance and lease companies. For example, Ford Motor Company of Canada Ltd. allows customers to finance or lease vehicles using the services of Ford Credit. Finance and lease companies tend to charge relatively high rates on loans and leases because they lend to individuals whom they perceive to have a higher risk of defaulting on the loans. When the economy weakens, borrowers may have more difficulty repaying loans, causing finance and lease companies to be subject to higher levels of loan defaults.

mortgage companies
Non-depository institutions that specialize in providing mortgage loans to individuals.

Mortgage Companies. Mortgage companies specialize in providing mortgage loans to individuals. These companies are able to offer their clients competitive mortgage rates from a number of different financial institutions. This type of non-depository institution acts as a financial intermediary between depository institutions and the consumer.

investment dealers
Non-depository institutions that facilitate the purchase or sale of various investments by firms or individuals by providing investment banking and brokerage services.

Investment Dealers. Investment dealers facilitate the purchase or sale of various investments, such as stocks or bonds, by firms or individuals by providing investment banking and brokerage services. Investment banking services include assisting corporations and governments in obtaining financing for many activities, such as building projects and expansion plans. This financing advice helps both corporations and governments price their securities for sale and assists them in finding investors such as individuals, mutual funds, and other organizations willing to invest in their securities. Investment banking services also include advising and evaluating businesses with regard to mergers, acquisitions, and other similar corporate activities.

In addition to offering investment banking services, investment dealers provide brokerage services, which facilitate the trading of existing securities. That is, the firms execute trades in securities for their customers. One customer may want to sell a specific stock while another may want to buy that stock. Brokerage firms create a market for stocks and bonds by matching willing buyers and sellers.

insurance companies
Non-depository institutions that sell insurance to protect individuals or firms from risks that can incur financial loss.

Insurance Companies. Insurance companies sell insurance to protect individuals or firms from risks that can incur financial loss. Specifically, life and health insurance companies provide insurance in the event of a person's death, disability, or critical illness. Property and casualty companies provide insurance against damage to property, including automobiles and homes. Insurance serves a crucial function for individuals because it protects them (or their beneficiaries) from a significant loss of income and/or savings that may occur as a result of injury, illness, or death. Chapters 8 to 10 discuss insurance options in detail.

mutual fund companies
Non-depository institutions that sell units to individuals and use the proceeds to invest in securities to create mutual funds.

Mutual Fund Companies. Mutual fund companies sell units to individuals and use the proceeds to invest in securities to create mutual funds. The minimum amount an individual can invest in a mutual fund is typically between $500 and $5000. Since the investment company pools the money it receives from individuals and invests it in a portfolio of securities, an individual who invests in a mutual fund is a part owner of that portfolio. Thus, mutual funds provide a means by which investors with a small amount of money can invest in a portfolio of securities. More details on mutual funds are provided in Chapter 12.

Payday Loan Companies. Payday loan companies provide single-payment, short-term loans (usually for between 30 and 50 percent of an individual's biweekly salary) based on personal cheques held for future deposit (often postdated) or on electronic access to personal chequing accounts. Costs (interest and fees) are quite high.

Cheque Cashing Outlets. Cheque cashing outlets cash third-party cheques immediately, as long as you have adequate personal identification, and for a fee (usually a per-cheque fee plus a percentage of the face value of the cheque).

Pawnshops. Pawnshops provide small, secured loans for a fee and usually require a resaleable item worth more than the loan as a deposit (the security). If the loan is not repaid, the security is forfeited.

Financial Conglomerates

financial conglomerates Financial institutions that offer a diverse set of financial services to individuals or firms.

Financial conglomerates offer a diverse set of financial services to individuals or firms. Examples of financial conglomerates include RBC Financial, TD Canada Trust, Scotiabank, CIBC, and BMO Financial Group. In fact, most chartered banks are financial conglomerates. In addition to accepting deposits and providing personal loans, a financial conglomerate may also offer credit cards. It may have a brokerage subsidiary that can execute stock transactions for individuals. It also may have an insurance subsidiary that offers insurance services. It may even have an investment company subsidiary that offers mutual funds. Exhibit 4.1 shows the types of services offered by a typical financial conglomerate. By offering all types of financial services, the financial conglomerate aims to serve as a one-stop shop where individuals can conduct all of their financial services.

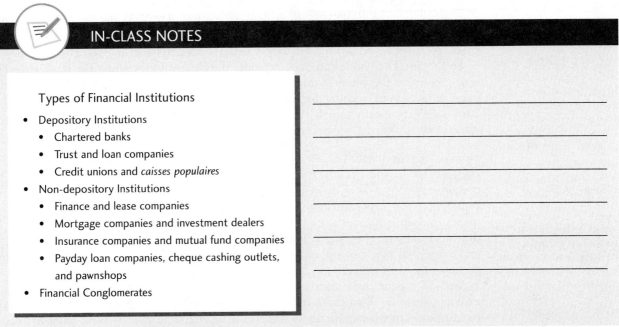

IN-CLASS NOTES

Types of Financial Institutions
- Depository Institutions
  - Chartered banks
  - Trust and loan companies
  - Credit unions and *caisses populaires*
- Non-depository Institutions
  - Finance and lease companies
  - Mortgage companies and investment dealers
  - Insurance companies and mutual fund companies
  - Payday loan companies, cheque cashing outlets, and pawnshops
- Financial Conglomerates

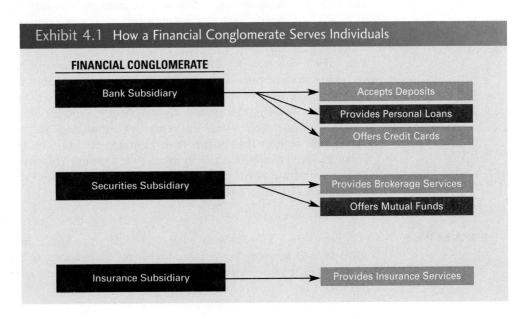

Exhibit 4.1 How a Financial Conglomerate Serves Individuals

FINANCIAL CONGLOMERATE

Bank Subsidiary → Accepts Deposits / Provides Personal Loans / Offers Credit Cards

Securities Subsidiary → Provides Brokerage Services / Offers Mutual Funds

Insurance Subsidiary → Provides Insurance Services

BANKING SERVICES OFFERED BY FINANCIAL INSTITUTIONS

A depository institution may offer you a wide variety of banking services. While a non-depository institution does not offer banking services, it may own a subsidiary that can. For example, Manulife Securities and Manulife Bank are both wholly owned subsidiaries of Manulife Financial. Manulife Securities is a large Canadian mutual fund company (that is, a non-depository institution), whereas Manulife Bank is a Schedule I, federally chartered bank (that is, a depository institution). A representative of Manulife Financial may be able to offer you services from both subsidiary companies. Some of the more important banking services offered to individuals are described here.

Chequing Services

You use a chequing account to draw on funds by writing cheques against your account. Most individuals maintain a chequing account so that they do not have to carry much cash when making purchases. In reality, as the popularity of electronic banking has increased, the use of debit and credit cards has made cheque writing obsolete in most cases. To illustrate how your chequing account works, assume that you pay a phone bill of $60 today. The phone company provides the cheque to its bank. The bank electronically increases the phone company's account balance by $60. At the same time, the bank reduces your account balance by $60 if your chequing account is at that same bank, or electronically signals your bank to reduce your balance by $60. This process is referred to as clearing or honouring.

Monitoring Your Account Balance. As you write cheques, you should record them in your chequebook so you can always determine how much money is in your account. The cheque register is a booklet in your chequebook where you record the details of each transaction you make, including deposits, cheque writing, withdrawals, and bill payments. A cheque register is most effective if you use it to record all deposits and withdrawals from your chequing account. By keeping track of your account balance, you can make sure that you stay within your limit when writing cheques. This is very important because you are charged fees when you write a cheque that is not honoured, referred to as an NSF cheque (NSF stands for not sufficient funds). These fees are not small. For example, one Canadian chartered bank charges a $40 fee for NSF cheques. The person or institution to whom you wrote the cheque may charge a fee as well, anywhere from $25 to $40 or more. In addition to the fees charged, you may lose some credibility when writing a bad cheque, even if it is unintentional. If you intentionally write a bad cheque, you are committing fraud.

Reconciling Your Account Balance. Financial institutions normally send you a chequing account statement once a month. Depending on the account you choose, you may also receive photocopies of the cheques you have written once they have cleared. When you receive your bank statement and cleared cheques, you should make sure that the statement reconciles (agrees) with the record of transactions in your cheque register. Mark off on your register the cheques that the statement indicates have cleared. The account balance changes from one month to another for three reasons: there have been deposits and/or withdrawals on the account, cheques have cleared through the account, and monthly fees have been withdrawn from the account.

cheque register
A booklet in your chequebook where you record the details of each transaction you make, including deposits, cheque writing, withdrawals, and bill payments.

EXAMPLE   Last month the balance in your chequing account was $600. This month you deposited $100 to your account. You wrote four cheques that cleared, totalling $400. You did not withdraw any funds from your account. No fees were charged this month. Your balance for this month is:

Last Month's Balance	$600
+ Deposits	+ $100
− Cheques That Cleared	− $400
= New Balance	= $300

In a month in which you had no fees, no deposits, and no withdrawals, the balance from the statement should be the same as the balance on your register as long as all cheques that you wrote cleared. However, if some cheques have not yet cleared, the balance on your statement will exceed the balance on your register by the amount of the cheques that have not yet cleared. If you write additional cheques, you may have a negative balance once all cheques clear. For this reason, you should not rely on the monthly statement to determine your balance.

EXAMPLE

Your most recent chequing account statement shows that you have a balance of $300. However, yesterday you wrote cheques totalling $250 to pay bills. When these cheques clear, your balance will be $50. Today you received a credit card bill for $200. Even though this amount is less than the balance shown on your most recent statement, you do not have sufficient funds in your chequing account to pay this bill.

If you write a cheque to cover the credit card bill, it will not be honoured, because you really only have a $50 account balance. By using the register to keep track of the cheques you write, you will know the amount of funds available in your account.

Many banks provide a worksheet that can be used to reconcile your cheque register balance with the bank's statement of your account. An example of a reconciliation worksheet is shown in Exhibit 4.2. Based on the cleared cheques, deposits, and withdrawals, the balance on your cheque register should be $500. This balance can be compared to the balance shown on the bank statement. If there is a discrepancy, your balance may be wrong or the bank's statement could be incorrect. The first step is to verify the math in your cheque register and then double-check the math on the bank statement. One common mistake is the omission of banking fees from your cheque register. Make sure you carefully review the bank statement for all fees, especially those for the use of ABMs at other financial institutions. If you still cannot resolve the discrepancy, contact the bank.

Accessing Your Account Balance. Many financial institutions allow you to verify your chequing account balance by calling an automated phone service or by going to the institution's website and logging in with a password. The advantage to this service is that the information you get should be up to date. Although managing a chequing account has been a prudent practice in the past, online banking is more common in today's fast-paced world. Online banking will be discussed later in this chapter.

Overdraft Protection. Some depository institutions offer **overdraft protection**, which protects a customer who writes a cheque for an amount that exceeds the chequing account balance. It is essentially a short-term loan from the depository institution where the chequing account is maintained. For example, if you write a cheque for $300 but have a chequing account balance of only $100, the depository institution will provide overdraft protection by making a loan of $200 to cover the difference. Without overdraft protection, cheques written against an insufficient account balance bounce, meaning that they are not honoured by the depository institution. Overdraft protection carries a fee every time you use the service. As well, a high interest rate (as much as 21 percent per year) will be charged on the loan. Some banks also charge a monthly fee simply for having overdraft protection available on your account

overdraft protection
An arrangement that protects a customer who writes a cheque for an amount that exceeds their chequing account balance; it is a short-term loan from the depository institution where the chequing account is maintained.

Exhibit 4.2 Example of a Worksheet to Reconcile Your Bank Statement

Beginning balance			**= $1000**
Deposits	$100		
	$400		
	$500	→	+ $500
Withdrawals	$50		
	$150		
	$200	→	− $200
Cheques that have cleared	$25		
	$75		
	$700		
	$800	→	− $800
Bank fees	$0		− $0
Balance Shown on Bank Statement			**$500**
Cheques that have not yet cleared	$100		
	$60		
	$40		
	$200	→	− $200
Adjusted bank balance (your prevailing bank balance)			**$300**

stop payment
A financial institution's notice that it will not honour a cheque if someone tries to cash it; usually occurs in response to a request by the writer of the cheque.

Stop Payment. If you write a cheque but believe that it was lost and never received by the payee, you may request that the financial institution stop payment, which means that the institution will not honour the cheque if someone tries to cash it. In some cases, a customer may even stop payment to prevent the recipient from cashing a cheque. For example, if you write a cheque to pay for home repairs, but the job is not completed, you may decide to stop payment on the cheque. To create a stop payment, you must provide accurate information, such as the date of the cheque and the name of the payee, to the financial institution. Normally, a fee is charged for stop payment service.

No Interest. A disadvantage of keeping funds in a chequing account is that interest does not accrue on these funds. For this reason, you should keep only enough funds in your chequing account to cover anticipated expenses and a small excess amount for unanticipated expenses that may arise. You should not deposit more funds in your chequing account than you think you may need because you can earn interest by putting your money in other investments. Because of this disadvantage, many financial institutions have introduced accounts that both earn interest and provide chequing services. It is important to check what account options are available at your financial institution.

Go to
www.fcac-acfc.gc.ca/eng/consumers/ITools/CreditCards/

This website provides a useful step-by-step guide to selecting a credit card that meets your specific needs.

Cheque Float

When you write a cheque, your chequing account balance is not reduced until the cheque is cashed by the recipient and clears. The time between writing a cheque and

debit card
A card that is not only used for identification for your bank, but also allows you to make purchases that are charged against an existing chequing account.

safety deposit box
A box at a financial institution in which a customer can store documents, jewellery, and other valuables. It is secure because it is stored in the bank's vault.

automated banking machine (ABM)
A machine individuals can use to deposit and withdraw funds at any time of day.

Go to
www.fcac-acfc.gc.ca/eng/consumers/BankInsurance/ABMFees/ABMFeesInfo_1_e.asp

This website provides examples of the costs incurred by using an ABM at your own financial institution, an ABM of a financial institution other than your own, and a privately owned ABM.

when your chequing account balance is reduced is referred to as the float. The float is partially due to the time it takes for the bank where the cheque was deposited to contact your bank. Some individuals know they do not have sufficient funds in their account when they write a cheque but they expect that the float will take a few days. This allows them time to deposit enough funds in their chequing account before the cheque clears. It is very important that you do not write a cheque if you anticipate that there will not be enough money in your account to clear it. The float period is neither standard nor predictable.

Credit Card Financing

Individuals use credit cards to purchase products and services on credit. At the end of each billing cycle, you receive a bill for the credit you used over that period. MasterCard and Visa cards allow you to finance your purchases through various financial institutions. Thus, if you are able to pay only the minimum balance on your card, the financial institution will finance the outstanding balance and charge interest for the credit, or loan, that it provides to you.

Debit Cards

You can use a debit card to make purchases that are charged against an existing chequing account. If you use a debit card to pay $100 for a car repair, your chequing account balance is reduced by $100. Thus, using a debit card has the same result as writing a cheque. Many financial institutions offer debit cards for individuals who find them more convenient than carrying their chequebook. In addition, some merchants will accept a debit card but not a cheque because they are concerned that the cheque may bounce. Debit transactions are cleared every day, so there is no float time. Therefore, there is no risk of NSF with debit transactions.

A debit card differs from a credit card in that it does not provide credit. When using a debit card, individuals cannot spend more than they have in their chequing account.

Safety Deposit Boxes

Many financial institutions offer access to a safety deposit box, in which a customer can store documents, jewellery, and other valuables. Customers are charged an annual fee, which depends on the size of the box, for access to a safety deposit box.

Automated Banking Machines (ABMs)

Bank customers can deposit and withdraw funds at an automated banking machine (ABM) by using their ABM or debit card and entering their personal identification number (PIN). Located in numerous convenient locations, these machines allow customers access to their funds 24 hours a day, any day of the year. The major chartered banks have ABMs throughout Canada and in many foreign countries. You can usually use ABMs from financial institutions other than your own, but you may be charged a service fee, such as $1 per transaction. In addition to ABMs owned by financial institutions, many ABMs are privately owned. These machines are often located in areas where someone may need access to cash. For example, privately owned ABMs can be found in malls, restaurants, pubs, and even at your post-secondary institution. Unfortunately, these ABMs charge service fees above and beyond the fees you would pay for using an ABM of a financial institution other than your own. According to the Financial Consumer Agency of Canada, it can cost more than $6 to use an ABM that is not owned by your financial institution.

"It says, all our accounts have been frozen!"

www.cartoonstock.com.

Certified Cheques

certified cheque
A cheque that can be cashed immediately by the payee without the payee having to wait for the bank to process and clear it.

A certified cheque can be cashed immediately by the payee without the payee having to wait for the bank to process and clear it. When a cheque is certified, it means that the cheque writer's bank has already withdrawn the money from the cheque writer's account. Therefore, the bank is able to guarantee that the money will be available to the payee.

EXAMPLE

You want to buy a used car for $2000 from Rod Simpkins, who is concerned that you may not have sufficient funds in your account. So you go to Lakeside Bank, where you have your chequing account. You overcome Rod's concern by obtaining a certified cheque made out to Rod (the payee). After verifying your account balance, the bank complies with your request and reduces the balance of your chequing account by $2000. It also will likely charge you a small fee, such as $10 or $15, for this service. Rod accepts the certified cheque from you because he knows that it is backed by Lakeside Bank and will not bounce.

Money Orders and Drafts

money orders and drafts
Products that direct your bank to pay a specified amount to the person named on them.

Money orders and drafts are products that direct your bank to pay a specified amount to the person named on them. You pay for a money order or draft at the time of purchase. They are similar to certified cheques in that the bank guarantees the amount indicated on the money order or draft. The difference is that money orders and drafts tend to be used for smaller amounts of money.

Traveller's Cheques

traveller's cheque
A cheque written on behalf of an individual that will be charged against a large, well-known financial institution or credit card sponsor's account.

A traveller's cheque is a cheque written on behalf of an individual that will be charged against a large, well-known financial institution or credit card sponsor's account. It is similar to a certified cheque, except that no payee is designated on the cheque. Traveller's cheques are accepted around the world. If they are lost or stolen, the issuer usually will replace them without charge. The fee for a traveller's cheque varies among financial institutions. It is considered to be much safer to carry traveller's cheques than cash when out of the country.

IN-CLASS NOTES

Banking Services Offered by Financial Institutions

- Chequing services
- Cheque float
- Credit card financing
- Debit cards
- Safety deposit boxes
- Automated banking machines (ABMs)
- Certified cheques
- Money orders and drafts
- Traveller's cheques

_____

_____

_____

_____

_____

_____

L.O. 4   SELECTING A FINANCIAL INSTITUTION

Your choice of a financial institution should be based on convenience, deposit rates, deposit insurance, and fees.

Convenience

You should be able to deposit and withdraw funds easily, which means that the financial institution should be located close to where you live or work. You also may benefit if it has ABMs in convenient locations. In addition, a financial institution should offer most or all of the services you might need. Many financial institutions offer Internet banking, which allows you to keep track of your deposit accounts and even to apply for loans online.

Many financial institutions also allow online bill payments. You indicate the payee and amount and the financial institution transfers the funds electronically. There is usually a small fee for this service, but it may be less than the cost of a stamp.

ING Direct (www.ingdirect.ca/en/) is an example of a web-based bank. While web-based banks allow you to keep track of your deposits online, they may not be appropriate for customers who prefer to deposit funds directly at a branch. For customers who prefer to make deposits at a branch but also want easy online access to their account information, the most convenient financial institutions are those with multiple branches and online access. Some web-based banks do not offer chequing accounts per se and so you may be required to maintain a chequing account at another institution.

Deposit Rates and Insurance

The interest rates offered on deposits vary among financial institutions. You should comparison shop by checking the rates on the types of deposits you might make. Financial institutions also vary on the minimum required balance needed to earn interest. For example, assume that Bank A pays 2 percent interest on a savings account without taking into consideration a minimum required balance. This means that every dollar you deposit earns interest. In contrast, Bank B requires you to have at least $1000 on deposit throughout the entire month in order to earn 2 percent interest. In this case, a lower minimum required balance is preferable because it gives you more flexibility if you do not want to tie up the entire $1000. Make sure that any deposits are insured by the CDIC or the credit union/ *caisses populaires* deposit insurance corporation for the province in which you live.

Web-based financial institutions tend to pay a higher interest rate on deposits than institutions with physical branches because they have lower overhead (fewer expenses). Customers must weigh these higher interest rates against the lack of access to branches. Those who prefer to make deposits through the mail may want to capitalize on the higher rates at web-based financial institutions.

Fees

Many financial institutions charge fees for various services. The amount of fees you will be charged depends on your banking habits and the number of services you use. If you tend to use the ABM on a daily basis, you will need an account that is suited for people with high ABM withdrawal habits. If you plan to write a number of cheques every month, you will want to look for an account that has cheque writing privileges. The number of bank accounts and options available to you is truly unlimited. Avoid financial institutions that charge high fees on services you will use frequently, even if they offer relatively high rates on deposits.

Go to
www.fiscalagents.com/
rates/index.shtml

Click on
Daily/Monthly Interest
Saving, under Savings
Accounts

This website provides
the daily and/or monthly
rates of interest available
at various financial
institutions.

Go to
www.fcac-acfc.gc.ca/eng/
consumers/ITools/CoB/
default.asp

Click on
Find the right banking
package for your needs

This website provides
an online tool to help you
find the banking package
that fits your needs.

IN-CLASS NOTES

Selecting a Financial Institution

Select your financial institution based on:
- Convenience
- Deposit rates and insurance
- Fees

_____

_____

_____

_____

_____

L.O. 5 ## SAVINGS ALTERNATIVES OFFERED BY FINANCIAL INSTITUTIONS

"Your pot o' gold is doing nothing for you sitting at the end of the rainbow. At the very least, you should put it in a no—risk interest-bearing account."

Savings Deposits

Traditional savings accounts offered by a depository institution pay interest on deposits. Depositing funds to a savings account is one option for money that is not needed to cover anticipated expenses. Funds can normally be withdrawn from a savings account at any time. A traditional savings account does not provide chequing services. However, a savings account is just as convenient as a chequing account because you can use an ABM to access funds. The interest rate offered on savings deposits varies among depository institutions. Many institutions quote their rates on their websites.

Term Deposits

Term deposits are offered as short-term or long-term investments. These investments offer slightly lower returns than GICs because they are cashable. They are designed for individuals who do not know when they will need access to their funds, but who would like an interest rate higher than that offered by savings accounts.

EXAMPLE

Stephanie Spratt wants to determine the amount of interest she would earn over one year if she deposits $1000 in a savings account that pays 4 percent interest annually.

Interest Earned = Deposit Amount × Interest Rate

= $1000 × 4.0%

= $40

Although the interest income is attractive, Stephanie cannot write cheques on a savings account. As she expects to need the funds in her chequing account to pay bills in the near future, she decides not to switch those funds to a savings account at this time.

Guranteed Investment Certificates

guaranteed investment certificate (GIC)
An instrument issued by a depository institution that specifies a minimum investment, an interest rate, and a maturity date.

Most depository institutions issue guaranteed investment certificates (GICs), which specify a minimum investment, an interest rate, and a maturity date. For example, a bank may require a $500 minimum investment on all of the GICs it offers. The maturity dates may include one month, three months, six months, one year, and five years. The money invested in a GIC usually cannot be withdrawn until the maturity date, or it will be subject to a penalty for early withdrawal.

The term *guaranteed* here refers to the coverage of the principal investment. Recall that some depository institutions are covered by the CDIC. Their deposits in bank accounts, including GICs, are protected against loss in the event of bankruptcy. Ensure that your investments and deposits are covered by the CDIC. Any deposits not covered should earn a much higher interest rate because of the additional risk.

Return. Depository institutions offer higher interest rates on GICs than on savings deposits and term deposits. This higher return is compensation for being willing to maintain the investment until the maturity date. Interest rates are quoted on an annualized (yearly) basis and vary according to maturity dates. The interest generated by your GIC is based on the annualized interest rate and the amount of time until maturity. For example, an annual interest rate of 6 percent on your deposit means that at the end of one year, you will receive interest equal to 6 percent of the amount you originally deposited.

EXAMPLE

A three-month (90-day) GIC offers an annualized interest rate of 6 percent and requires a $5000 minimum deposit. You want to determine the amount of interest you would earn if you invested $5000 in this GIC. Since the interest rate is annualized, you will receive only a fraction of the 6 percent rate because your investment is for a fraction of the year:

$$\text{Interest Earned} = \text{Deposit Amount} \times \text{Interest Rate} \times \text{Adjustment for Investment Period}$$
$$= \$5000 \times 0.06 \times 90/365$$

This calculation can be more easily understood by noting that the interest rate is applied for only 90 days, whereas the annual interest rate reflects 365 days. The interest rate that applies to your 90-day investment is for about one-fourth (90/365) of the year, so the applicable interest rate is:

$$\text{Interest Rate} = 0.06 \times 90/365 = 0.0148 \ (1.48\%)$$

The 1.48 percent interest rate represents the actual return on your investment.

Now the interest can be determined by simply applying this return to the deposit amount:

$$\text{Interest Earned} = \text{Deposit Amount} \times \text{Interest Rate}$$
$$= \$5000 \times 0.0148$$
$$= \$74.00$$

Liquidity. A penalty is imposed for early withdrawal from GICs, so these deposits are less liquid than funds deposited in a savings account or a term deposit. You should consider a GIC only if you are certain that you will not need the funds until after it matures. You may decide to invest some of your funds in a GIC and other funds in more liquid assets. Many financial institutions have introduced cashable GICs to make this investment more attractive. However, a cashable GIC does not offer the same interest rate as a regular GIC. If you are considering a cashable GIC, consider all of the savings alternatives that are available to you as well.

Choice among GIC Maturities. GICs with longer terms to maturity typically offer higher annualized interest rates. However, these GICs tie up your funds for a longer period of time and are therefore less liquid. Your choice of a maturity date for a GIC may depend on your need for liquidity. For example, if you know that you may need your funds in four months, you could invest in a three-month GIC and then place the funds in a more liquid asset (such as your chequing account or savings account) when the GIC matures. If you do not expect to need the funds for one year, you may consider a one-year GIC.

Focus on Ethics: Risky Deposits

Consider the case of a financial institution that promises depositors an annual rate of interest that is 4 percent higher than GIC rates offered by local banks.

While this certificate sounds appealing, it is probably much riskier than you think. A firm is not going to offer an interest rate that is 4 percent higher than other interest-bearing investments unless it needs to pay such a high return to compensate for risk. Ask whether the deposit is insured by the CDIC. While you could possibly earn 4 percent more on this investment, you also could lose 100 percent of your money if the financial institution goes bankrupt. There are many investment companies that prey on individuals (especially the elderly) who presume that because an investment sounds like a bank deposit, it is insured and safe. If an investment sounds too good to be true, it probably is.

Canada Savings Bonds (CSBs)

Canada Savings Bonds (CSBs)
Short-term to medium-term, high-quality debt securities issued by the Government of Canada.

Canada Savings Bonds (CSBs) are short-term to medium-term, high-quality debt securities issued by the Government of Canada. These bonds are virtually risk-free because they are issued by the federal government. In addition, they are highly liquid because they are cashable at any bank or financial institution. CSBs are available for purchase from early October through April 1 each year. You can choose either a CSB, which is cashable at any time, or a Canada Premium Bond (CPB). CPBs offer a more competitive interest rate and are cashable once a year. Both types of bonds can be purchased for as little as $100. In either case, you also have the option of purchasing either a regular or a compound interest bond. A regular interest bond pays out the interest earned every year, while a compound interest bond reinvests the interest earned. However, the interest income earned each year is taxable, even if it is reinvested in the bond.

Money Market Funds (MMFs)

money market funds (MMFs)
Accounts that pool money from individuals and invest in securities that have short-term maturities, such as one year or less.

Money market funds (MMFs) pool money from individuals and invest in securities that have short-term maturities, such as one year or less. In fact, the average term of debt securities held in a MMF is typically less than 90 days. Many MMFs invest in short-term Treasury securities or in wholesale GICs (valued at $100 000 or more). MMFs are not insured, but most invest in very safe investments and have a very low risk of default. Similar to bonds, the interest income earned each year from an MMF is taxable.

Determining the Optimal Allocation of Short-Term Investments

In general, your money management should be guided by the following steps:

1. Anticipate your upcoming bills and ensure that you have sufficient funds in your chequing account to cover all of these expenses.

2. Estimate the additional funds you might need in the near future and consider investing them in an instrument that offers sufficient liquidity (such as an MMF). You may even keep a little extra in reserve for unanticipated expenses.

3. Use the remaining funds in a manner that will earn you a higher return, within your level of risk tolerance.

Your optimal allocation likely will be different than the optimal allocation for another individual. If your future net cash flows will be far short of upcoming expenses, you will need to keep a relatively large proportion of funds in a liquid investment. Another person who has sufficient cash flows to cover expenses will not need much liquidity. This difference is illustrated in Exhibit 4.3. Even though the two individuals have the same level of net cash flows, one person must maintain more liquidity than the other.

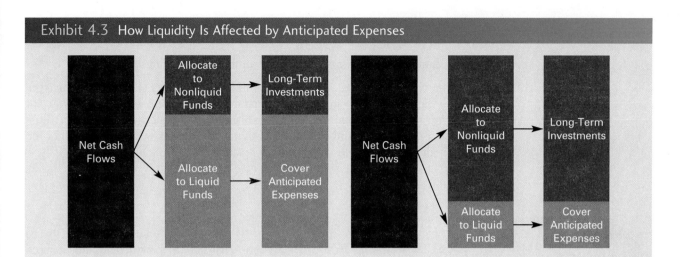

Exhibit 4.3 How Liquidity Is Affected by Anticipated Expenses

Your decision on how to invest your short-term funds (after determining how much money to maintain in your chequing account) should account for your willingness to tolerate risk. If you want to minimize all forms of risk, you may consider investing all of your funds in an MMF that focuses on Treasury securities maturing within a month or less. However, you will likely improve the yield if you are willing to accept some degree of risk. For example, if you know that you will not need your funds for at least six months and do not expect interest rates to rise substantially over that period, you might consider investing your funds in a six-month GIC. A compromise would be to invest a portion of your short-term funds in the six-month GIC and the remaining funds in the MMF that focuses on Treasury securities. The GIC offers you a higher expected return (although less liquidity) while the MMF offers you liquidity in case you need funds immediately.

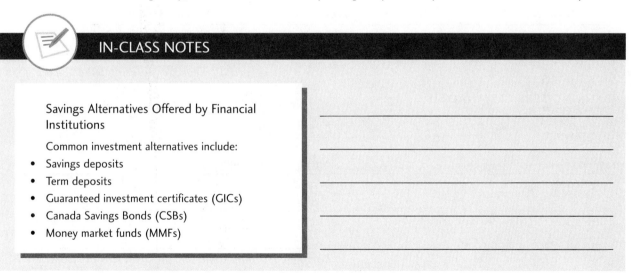

IN-CLASS NOTES

Savings Alternatives Offered by Financial Institutions

Common investment alternatives include:
- Savings deposits
- Term deposits
- Guaranteed investment certificates (GICs)
- Canada Savings Bonds (CSBs)
- Money market funds (MMFs)

HOW MONEY MANAGEMENT FITS WITHIN YOUR FINANCIAL PLAN

The key money management decisions for your financial plan are:

- How can you ensure that you can pay your anticipated bills on time?
- How can you maintain adequate liquidity in case you incur unanticipated expenses?
- What banking service characteristics are most important to you?

- What financial institution provides the best banking service characteristics in the most cost-effective manner?

- How should you invest any remaining funds among savings alternatives?

By making proper decisions, you can minimize your use of credit and maximize the return on your liquid assets. By making informed money management decisions, you can ensure that you receive the banking services you need to conduct your financial transactions at a reasonable cost and as conveniently as you desire, while at the same time providing a high return on your short-term deposits.

STEPHANIE SPRATT'S FINANCIAL PLAN: Money Management

GOALS FOR MONEY MANAGEMENT

1. *Maintain sufficient liquidity to ensure that all anticipated bills are paid on time.*

2. *Maintain sufficient liquidity in case I incur unanticipated expenses.*

3. *Identify the most important banking services for me.*

4. *Determine which financial institution will provide me with the best banking services.*

5. *Invest any excess funds in deposits that offer the highest return while ensuring adequate liquidity.*

MONEY MANAGEMENT ANALYSIS

	Amount	Payment Method
Monthly income	$2260	*Directly deposited into chequing account.*
Typical monthly expenses	$1330	*Write cheques to pay these bills.*
Other expenses for clothing or recreation	$600	*Use credit cards and then pay the credit card balance in full using online banking.*

BANKING SERVICES ANALYSIS

Characteristic	How It Affects Me
Interest rate offered on deposits	*This will affect the amount of interest income I earn on emergency fund deposits.*
Interest rate charged on mortgages	*I could use the same financial institution if I buy a home in the future.*
Interest rate charged on personal loans	*I could use the same financial institution if I obtain a personal loan in the future.*
Fees charged for chequing services	*I will be writing some cheques, so fees are somewhat important.*
Location	*The ideal financial institution would have a branch near my apartment building and near where I work.*
Online services available	*This would make my banking more convenient. Check fees for this service.*
ABMs	*Check locations for convenience and whether any fees are charged for using ABMs.*

DECISIONS

Decision on How to Ensure Adequate Liquidity to Cover Anticipated Expenses

The two paycheques I receive each month amounting to $2260 after taxes are directly deposited into my chequing account. I can use this account to cover the $1330 in anticipated bills each month. I can also go online to transfer money from this account to my credit card for the monthly bill of $600 for clothing and recreation. I will attempt to leave about $330 extra in the chequing account because my expenses may vary from month to month.

Decision on How to Ensure Liquidity to Cover Unanticipated Expenses

I will attempt to maintain about $5790, or three months' worth of expenses, in a money market fund in case I need additional funds. I can earn interest on this money while ensuring liquidity.

Decision Regarding Important Characteristics of a Financial Institution

My most important banking characteristic is the fee associated with using the bank's ABM machines. I prefer a bank that offers an account where I have access to low-cost withdrawals that I make each month. I also value the convenience of the location of the financial institution's branches, and its online services. I would prefer a financial institution that offers reasonable rates on its deposit accounts, but convenience is more important to me than the deposit rate.

Decision Regarding the Optimal Financial Institution

After screening financial institutions according to my criteria, I found three that are desirable. I selected Quality Savings, Inc. because it does not charge for ABM withdrawals, has branches in convenient locations, and offers online banking. It also pays relatively high interest rates on its deposits and charges relatively low interest rates (compared to other financial institutions) on its loans. I may consider obtaining a mortgage there someday if I buy a home, as mortgage rates were comparable to those of other financial institutions.

Decision on How to Invest Remaining Funds to Achieve the Highest Return While Enhancing Liquidity

As I accumulate additional savings, I will invest in guaranteed investment certificates with varying maturity dates. This money will not be as liquid as the MMF, but it will be accessible when the GIC matures. The interest rate on the GIC will be higher than the interest I can earn on my MMF.

Discussion Questions

1. How would Stephanie's money management decisions be different if she were a single mother of two children?

2. How would Stephanie's money management decisions be affected if she were 35 years old? If she were 50 years old?

SUMMARY

When applying money management techniques, you should first anticipate your expenses in the next month and maintain enough funds in your chequing account to cover those expenses. In addition, you should estimate the potential level of unanticipated expenses (such as possible car repairs) and maintain enough funds in a short-term investment, such as a money market fund, to cover these expenses. Finally, invest the remaining funds to earn a high return within your level of risk tolerance.

Depository institutions (chartered banks, trust and loan companies, and credit unions and *caisses populaires*) accept deposits and provide loans. Non-depository institutions include finance and lease companies (which provide financing and leasing options for assets, such as a car), mortgage companies (which provide mortgage brokerage services), investment dealers (which provide brokerage and other services), insurance companies (which provide insurance), mutual fund companies (which offer mutual funds), payday loan companies (which provide short-term loans), cheque cashing outlets (which cash cheques for a fee), and pawnshops (which provide small secured loans). Financial conglomerates offer a wide variety of these services so that individuals can obtain all of their financial services from a single firm.

Money management involves the selection of short-term investments that satisfy your liquidity needs and also provide you with an adequate return on your investment. It is challenging because the short-term investments that offer relatively high returns tend to have less liquidity.

Popular short-term investments considered for money management include savings deposits, term deposits, GICs, Canada Savings Bonds, and money market funds. Savings deposits offer the most liquidity, while GICs and money market funds offer the highest return.

INTEGRATING THE KEY CONCEPTS

Your money management decisions determine your level of liquidity and also affect other parts of your financial plan. If your investments have a high degree of liquidity, you have more funds available that you can use. The amount of liquidity you maintain is partly determined by your budgeting decisions (Part 1) because you will need more liquidity if your expenses are expected to exceed your income. The

decision to maintain a high degree of liquidity can affect your financing decisions (Part 3) because the greater amount of your cash you can use, the less you will need to rely on loans. Your money management will also affect your investment decisions (Part 5) because you can focus on investments that are not liquid if you already have sufficient liquidity in your short-term investments.

A financial institution can serve your liquidity needs (Part 2) by offering an account for your deposits. In addition, money management may also satisfy your financing needs (Part 3) by providing you with necessary cash or a personal loan or mortgage loan so that you can purchase a car or a home. A financial institution may have an insurance subsidiary that can provide you with insurance services (Part 4). It may be able to advise you on your investments (Part 5) or even sell you the types of investments you desire. It also may be able to offer you a retirement account (Part 6).

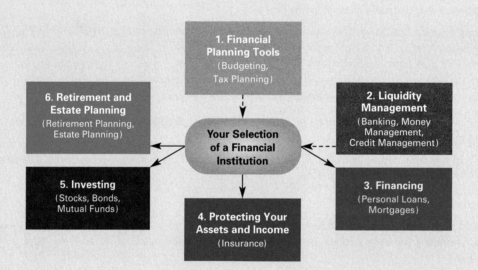

REVIEW QUESTIONS

1. Define money management. How does it differ from long-term investment or long-term borrowing decisions?

2. What is liquidity? How is your personal cash flow statement used to help manage your liquidity? How does money management relate to the cash flow statement?

3. Name some ways in which an individual might handle a cash flow deficiency. Which would be preferable? Why?

4. What is the opportunity cost of having excessive amounts of liquid funds?

5. Describe and compare the three types of depository institutions.

6. List and describe the eight types of non-depository financial institutions.

7. What is a financial conglomerate? List some services that financial conglomerates provide. Give some examples of financial conglomerates.

8. List and describe some of the banking services offered by financial institutions.

9. Why do individuals use chequing accounts? What is the disadvantage of having funds in a chequing account? Explain overdraft protection. Are all bank fee structures the same?

10. What is the difference between a debit card and a credit card?

11. Name some special services that banks provide. How might you make use of them?

12. Steve just received his first paycheque and wants to open a chequing account. There are five banks in his hometown. What factors should Steve consider when choosing a bank?

13. What terms does a financial institution specify for guaranteed investment certificates? Why are rates on GICs higher than those on savings accounts? What factor would most affect your choice of maturity date on a GIC?

14. Who issues Canada Savings Bonds? What are the two types of CSBs? What is a regular interest bond? What is a compound interest bond?

15. What are money market funds? What types of securities do they invest in? Are MMFs risky investments? Are they liquid?

16. Compare the return and liquidity of the various money market investments. Give specific examples.

17. What steps should you take to determine the best allocation of your money market investments? What factors should you consider in determining your allocation?

FINANCIAL PLANNING PROBLEMS

Refer to the chart below when answering Problems 1 through 4.

1. Stuart wants to open a chequing account with a $100 deposit. Stuart believes he will write 15 cheques per month and use other banks' ABMs eight times a month. He will not be able to maintain a minimum balance. Which bank should Stuart choose?

2. Julie wants to open a bank account with $75. Julie estimates that she will write 20 cheques per month and use her ABM card at the home bank. She will

maintain a $200 balance. Which bank should Julie choose?

3. Veronica plans to open a chequing account with her $1200 tax refund. She believes she can maintain a $500 minimum balance. Also, she estimates that she will write 10 cheques per month and will use other banks' ABMs as many as 15 times per month. Which bank should Veronica choose?

4. Randy, a student, has $500 to deposit in a new chequing account, but he knows he will not be able to maintain a minimum balance. He will not use an ABM card, but will write a large number of cheques. Randy is trying to choose between the unlimited cheque writing offered by West Trust and the low per-cheque fee offered by East Coast. How many cheques would Randy have to write each month for the account at West Trust to be the better option?

5. Paul has an account at ICBC Bank. He does not track his chequing account balance in a cheque register. Yesterday evening, he placed two cheques in the mail, for $156.66 and $238.94. Paul accesses his account online and finds that his balance is $568.40, and that all of the cheques he has written except for the two mailed yesterday have cleared. Based on his balance, Paul writes a cheque for a new stereo for $241. He has no intention of making a deposit in the near future. What are the consequences of his actions?

6. Mary's previous bank statement showed an ending balance of $168.51. This month, she deposited $600 in her account and withdrew a total of $239. Furthermore, she wrote a total of five cheques, two of which have cleared. These two cheques total $143. The three outstanding cheques total $106.09. Mary

	Winnipeg Bank	Canadian National	West Trust Bank	East Coast Bank
ABM charges				
Home bank	Free	Free	Free	Free
Other bank	4 free, then $1 per use	$1.25	$1.25	$1.25
Chequing				
Minimum deposit	$100	$25	$1	$1
Minimum balance required to avoid fees	N/A	N/A	$500	N/A
Monthly fees	$6	$7	$11	$2.50
Cheque writing charges	12 free, then $1 per cheque	7 free, then $1 per cheque	Unlimited	Each cheque 50 cents

pays no fees at her bank. What is the balance shown this month on Mary's bank statement? What is the adjusted bank balance?

7. Nancy is depositing $2500 in a six-month GIC that pays 4.25 percent interest. How much interest will she accrue if she holds the GIC until maturity?

8. Travis has invested $3000 in a three-month GIC at 4 percent. How much will Travis have when the GIC matures?

9. Akida has invested $10 000 in an 18-month GIC that pays 6.25 percent. How much interest will Akida receive at maturity?

10. Bart is a college student who has never invested his funds. He has saved $1000 and has decided to invest in a money market fund with an expected return of 2 percent. Bart will need these funds in one year. The MMF imposes fees that will cost Bart $20 when he withdraws the funds in one year. How much money will Bart have in one year as a result of this investment?

ETHICAL DILEMMAS

1. Mike, a recent college graduate, opened a chequing account with a local bank. He asked numerous questions before deciding on this bank, including inquiring about chequing account fees and annual credit card fees. When Mike returns from his first international business trip he is surprised to see numerous fees on his credit card statement and his bank statement. When he calls the bank, he is informed that it recently added service charges on international transactions involving its chequing and credit card accounts. When Mike protests, the bank points out that his last statement included a flyer detailing these changes. Looking back, Mike realizes that he did, in fact, receive the information but had ignored it because it was included with considerable advertising about car loan rate specials and because the lengthy document was in very small print.

   a. Comment on the ethics of banks and other financial institutions' efforts to notify customers of fee changes. Should a letter specifically dealing with these changes be sent to ensure that customers are aware of the information?

   b. Is there a lesson to be learned from Mike's experience?

2. Ernie is in his mid-fifties and was raised by parents from the Depression era. As a result, he is very risk adverse. Ernie recently came into a very large amount of money and he wants to put it where it will be safe but also earn him some return. His banker tells him that he should put the money in a five-year GIC. Ernie asks if there is any way he can lose his money and he is told that the CDIC insures the deposit and the GIC will give him a higher return than a passbook savings account. Ernie purchases the GIC and goes home happy, knowing that his money is safe and available whenever he needs it. Four months later, the roof on Ernie's barn collapses. He needs the money in his GIC to make repairs but finds that he can only withdraw it at a substantial penalty.

   a. Comment on the ethics of the banker in not fully discussing all risks associated with GIC investments.

   b. Is Ernie correct in his thinking that he can find a totally risk-free investment?

FINANCIAL PLANNING ONLINE EXERCISES

1. Go to www.atb.com/Dev/calcs/calcs_savings.asp and click on Savings Planner.

   a. Enter "vacation" as your reason for saving. For how many years are savings being calculated? What is the current cost of the vacation you are saving for? What is the annual rate of return? According to this calculator, how much do you need to save on a monthly basis to reach your goal?

   b. Suppose that you have already saved $2000. Enter this amount in the Savings Details section (at Current Savings). Click on Calculate. What is the new amount you need to save on a monthly basis to reach your goal?

2. Go to www.fcac-acfc.gc.ca/eng/consumers/rights/default.asp.

   a. Do you have a right to open a personal bank account even if you do not have a job? Do you have to put money in the account right away? If you have been bankrupt in the past, can you still open an account?

   b. What are your rights if you are trying to cash a Government of Canada cheque?

3. Go to www.ingdirect.ca/en/aboutus/whoweare/index.html. How do the services of this web-based bank differ from the services offered by a "regular" bank? What is the savings account interest rate at this online bank? Would you bank at an online financial institution? Why or why not?

4. Go to www.gicdirect.com.

   a. What is today's best three-year GIC rate?

   b. How large is the difference between the one-year and five-year GIC rates?

5. Go to http://money.canoe.ca/rates/savings.html. Compare the savings account interest rate offered by the bank in Exercise 3 and the savings account interest rates offered at other financial institutions.

How do the rates compare? How many financial institutions offer a lower rate than that found in Exercise 3? How many financial institutions offer a higher rate than that found in Exercise 3?

6. Go to www.csb.gc.ca/eng/ and click on Rates.

   a. What is the current Year 1 rate for Canada Premium Bonds?

   b. What is the current Year 1 rate for Canada Savings Bonds?

   c. Is there a difference between these two Year 1 rates? If so, give some reasons as to why one would be higher than the other.

7. Go to www.bankrate.com/can/default.asp. Click on GICs and then on Check the rates in your area. Click on your province of residence and then the city you live in (or the one that is closest to you).

   a. What are the three best rates for a Basic Chequing account? A Basic Savings account? A five-year Term Deposit, also known as a five-year non-redeemable GIC?

   b. Compare the three best rates offered for a five-year non-redeemable GIC and a five-year redeemable GIC? Is there a difference? Why would these rates differ?

ON THE STUDENT CD-ROM FOR THIS CHAPTER YOU WILL FIND:

- Building Your Own Financial Plan exercise and worksheets
- The chapter-end Continuing Case about the Sampson family
- Read through the Building Your Own Financial Plan exercise and use the worksheets to evaluate

financial institutions and to assess your liquidity.

- After reading the Sampson case study, use the Continuing Case worksheets to help the Sampsons assess their liquidity and select a GIC.

Study Guide

Circle the correct answer and then check the answers in the back of the book to chart your progress.

Multiple Choice

1. Which of the following statements regarding liquidity is incorrect?

   a. Liquidity is necessary because there will be periods when your income is not adequate to cover your expenses.

   b. Alternative sources of liquidity include access to a credit card, a line of credit, or an emergency fund.

   c. Maintaining adequate liquidity is important for situations where your income exceeds your expenses.

   d. A useful rule of thumb is that you should have between three and six months' worth of expenses in an emergency fund.

2. Which of the following is a type of non-depository institution?

   a. Chartered banks
   b. Trust companies
   c. Credit unions
   d. Finance companies

3. The main types of non-depository institutions that serve individuals include finance and lease companies, pawnshops, investment dealers, and _____.

   a. Financial advisers
   b. Insurance companies
   c. Schedule III banks
   d. *Caisses populaires*

4. When you receive your bank statement and cleared cheques, you should perform all of the following actions except:

   a. Deposit any excess funds shown on your bank statement into a short-term savings account.

b. Check to ensure that the deposits reported on the bank statement reconcile with the transactions recorded in your cheque register.

c. Mark on your cheque register the cheques that the bank statement indicates have cleared.

d. Check to ensure that the withdrawals reported on the bank statement reconcile with the transactions recorded in your cheque register.

5. The primary advantage of calling an automated phone service or logging on to your financial institution's website in order to check your account balance is:

a. You do not have to talk to someone.

b. The information on your account balance should be up to date.

c. You can also conveniently check your email and/or chat with friends if you are already online.

d. You can transfer money from your savings account to your chequing account if you realize that you do not have enough money in your chequing account for upcoming expenses.

6. The advantage of overdraft protection is that it protects a customer who writes a cheque for an amount that exceeds the balance of the chequing account. The cost of this service may include all of the following, except:

a. A high interest rate charged on the overdraft balance

b. A limit to the number of banking services you can have with one financial institution

c. A one-time fee every time you need to use the protection

d. A monthly fee to your account simply for having the protection available

7. Rank the following ABM machines in order of cost to you, from least expensive to most expensive. ABM1 belongs to the bank with which you have a chequing account. ABM2 is owned privately. ABM3 is owned by a financial institution with which you do not have an account.

a. ABM1, ABM2, ABM3

b. ABM2, ABM1, ABM3

c. ABM3, ABM2, ABM1

d. ABM1, ABM3, ABM2

8. Which of the following banking products can be cashed immediately upon receipt?

a. Certified cheque

b. Traveller's cheque

c. Draft

d. All of the above

9. When are Canada Savings Bonds available for purchase?

a. From early January to April 1 each year

b. Throughout the entire year

c. From early October to April 1 each year

d. From early January to June 30 each year

10. Donald is considering how he should allocate the money he has in his emergency fund. He expects that interest rates will decrease sharply in the next six months. As a result, he is considering investing in a two-year GIC. He feels that when his investment matures, interest rates will have increased back to where they are right now. However, his current net cash flow is less than $100 and he is concerned that if he incurs any unexpected expenses, he will need access to his funds. Which of the following investments would be inappropriate given his circumstances?

a. Two-year GIC

b. Money market fund

c. One-month term deposit

d. A savings account paying 2 percent on all deposits

True/False

1. True or False? Money management focuses on maintaining long-term investments to achieve both liquidity and an adequate return on your investments.

2. True or False? Credit unions/*caisses populaires* are provincially incorporated co-operative financial institutions that are owned and controlled by their members.

3. True or False? Investment dealers use money provided by individuals to invest in securities to create mutual funds.

4. True or False? The time between writing a cheque and when your chequing account balance is increased is referred to as the float.

5. True or False? A debit card differs from a credit card in that it does not provide credit.

6. True or False? The annual fee for a safety deposit box at a branch of ABC Bank is the same for all boxes.

7. True or False? A lower minimum balance required on a savings account is preferable because it gives you more flexibility if you do not want to tie up your funds in a savings account.

8. True or False? Term deposits offer slightly higher returns than GICs because they are cashable.

9. True or False? A savings account is not as convenient as a chequing account because you cannot write cheques on a savings account.

10. True or False? The average maturity date of debt securities held in an MMF is typically less than 90 days.

Chapter 5

Assessing, Managing, and Securing Your Credit

K im and Tara are sisters who have very different perspectives on the use of credit. Kim avoids using credit. She has paid cash for everything, including her car. When she decided to buy a motorcycle, she wanted to finance part of the cost. After applying for credit, she received a rude awakening. The finance company used a three-tier credit rating system. An A-level credit rating was the best and received an 11 percent rate. A B-level buyer received a 13 percent rate. Kim only qualified for the C level, at a 15 percent rate. She was stunned. How could she have such a low rating when she had never been late paying any bills?

When Tara began her first year of college, she was on a tight budget. To cover her spending needs, she decided to apply for a credit card so that she would be able to make emergency purchases. Applying was easy, as a credit card company advertising on campus offered gifts to anyone who filled out an application. When Tara received her card with a credit limit of $1000 she promised herself she would use it only for emergency purchases between paycheques, and that she would pay the balance in full every month.

Three years and two additional credit cards later, Tara graduated with $4000 of debt. She had not realized that the interest charged on unpaid balances was 18.5 percent, or that there was a fee and substantially higher interest associated with cash advances, or that she would be charged $35 for every late payment.

The consequences of having no credit history or excessive credit card debt can be severe. Kim may have thought that not having had to borrow money would demonstrate fiscal responsibility. This is not so to a financial institution. Tara has developed a poor credit rating, which will affect her ability to obtain a loan for a large purchase such as a car. In addition, it may take several years for her to pay off her debt.

This chapter focuses on obtaining and effectively using credit. You will discover that a good credit history is built by the proper use and control of credit, not by its absence. The second half of the chapter discusses identity theft: how it can affect your credit rating and how you can protect yourself from it.

The objectives of this chapter are to:

1. Provide a background on credit
2. Describe the role of credit bureaus
3. Explain the key characteristics of credit cards
4. Offer tips on using credit cards
5. Provide a background on identity theft
6. Describe identity theft tactics
7. Explain how to avoid identity theft
8. Discuss how to respond to identity theft

L.O. 1 BACKGROUND ON CREDIT

credit
Funds provided by a creditor to a borrower that the borrower will repay with interest or fees in the future.

Credit represents funds provided by a creditor to a borrower that the borrower will repay with interest or fees in the future. The funds borrowed are sometimes referred to as the principal and we segment repayment of credit into principal payments and interest. Credit is frequently extended to borrowers as a loan with set terms such as the amount of funds provided and the maturity date when the funds will be repaid. For some types of loans, interest payments are made monthly and the principal payment is made at the maturity date, when the loan is terminated. In the case of instalment credit, the interest and principal payments are blended, meaning that each payment includes both principal and interest.

Types of Credit
Credit can be classified as instalment or revolving open-end.

instalment credit
Credit provided for specific purchases, with interest charged on the amount borrowed. It is repaid on a regular basis, generally with blended payments.

Instalment Credit. Instalment credit is provided for specific purchases, such as a car. Also referred to as an instalment loan, the amount borrowed is repaid on a regular basis over a period of time (usually a few years). The timing and amount of each payment depend on the terms of the loan. In general, loan repayments are made monthly with a portion of the payment being applied to the principal and the remainder representing interest paid to the lender.

Some types of instalment credit allow payments to be structured so that the borrower pays interest only until the maturity date, when the balance of the loan is due. The payment made at the maturity of the loan is referred to as a balloon payment.

revolving open-end credit
Credit provided up to a specified maximum amount based on income, debt level, and credit history; interest is charged each month on the outstanding balance.

Revolving Open-End Credit. Revolving open-end credit, such as a credit card or a line of credit, allows consumers to borrow to a specified maximum amount (such as $1000 or $10 000). The credit limit is determined by the borrower's income level, debt level, and credit history. The consumer can pay the entire amount borrowed at the end of the month or pay a portion of the balance and have interest charged on the remainder. Typically, there is a minimum payment due each month. The minimum payment on revolving credit is usually 3 percent of the outstanding amount as of the date specified in the terms of the credit agreement.

Advantages of Using Credit
The appropriate use of credit helps you build a good credit score. Only by using credit wisely can you create the capacity to access credit in the future for large purchases such as a home or a car. This credit capacity allows individuals and families to avoid deferring large purchases until savings can be accumulated to make such purchases. Credit is also convenient because it eliminates the need for carrying cash or writing cheques. Credit is useful in situations where cash may not be an option, for example, if you are

Go to

http://money.canoe.ca/
FinancialTools/
personalloan_calc.html

This website provides
a personal loan calculator
that will help you determine
how much you can borrow
if you already know the
interest rate, the number of
payments to be made, and
the frequency of your
payments.

Go to

www.oaccs.com/main.html

This website provides
information on how to
establish, use, and protect
credit.

in an emergency situation or want to make a purchase via the Internet. Also, many credit cards offer additional benefits to their members. Air miles and travel insurance are two of the more popular benefits available on credit cards.

Disadvantages of Using Credit

There can be a high cost to using credit. If you borrow too much money, you may have difficulty making your payments. It is easier to obtain credit than to pay it back, and having a line of credit can tempt you to make impulse purchases that you simply cannot afford. A 2003 study published by the Canada Millennium Scholarship Foundation found that 60 percent of college students expect to graduate with debt; one-quarter anticipate having debt of more than $10 000, and another quarter expect to have debt of more than $20 000. If you are unable to repay the credit you use, you may not be able to obtain credit again or will have to pay a very high interest rate to obtain it. Your ability to save money will also be reduced if you have large credit payments, as illustrated in Exhibit 5.1. If your spending and credit card payments exceed your net cash flows, you will need to withdraw savings to cover the deficiency.

Credit History

You receive credit when you apply for and are approved to use credit instruments such as credit cards, retail credit cards (for example, a Future Shop card), lines of credit, and personal loans and leases. When you have accounts with companies that offer credit, you develop a credit history that documents how timely you are in paying your bills. You can establish a favourable credit history by paying the monthly payment associated with these debt obligations on or before the due date. Doing so indicates to potential creditors that you may also repay other credit in a timely manner. This helps to establish your character for new creditors.

Credit Insurance

Because access to credit is essential these days, some consumers attempt to ensure that they will be able to keep making credit payments (and therefore maintain their credit standing) under adverse conditions. They purchase credit insurance, which represents a commitment to cover their credit repayments under various circumstances. For instance, credit accident and sickness insurance ensures that monthly credit payments are made when consumers cannot work due to an accident or illness. Credit unemployment insurance ensures that monthly payments are made for consumers when they are unemployed. It is important to read the fine print with respect to credit insurance because the

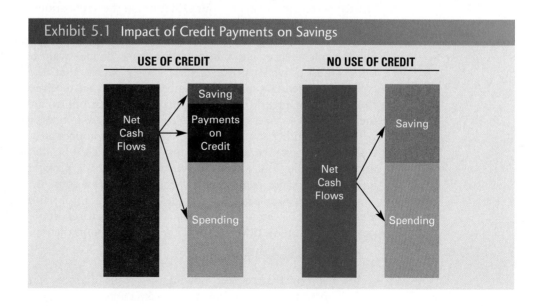

Exhibit 5.1 Impact of Credit Payments on Savings

payment period is usually limited to a short term. In some instances, your payments may only be covered for as little as three months. Credit insurance of this type is not a good substitute for the types of insurance coverage discussed in Chapters 8 through 10.

IN-CLASS NOTES

Background on Credit

- Types of credit: instalment and revolving open-end credit
- There are advantages and disadvantages to using credit
- Credit history: your history with credit instruments such as credit cards and lines of credit
- Credit insurance: a commitment to cover credit payments

_____

_____

_____

_____

_____

L.O. 2

CREDIT BUREAUS

credit reports
Reports provided by credit bureaus that document a person's credit payment history.

Credit bureaus provide credit reports that document your credit payment history to lenders and others. Your credit report shows every time you have applied for credit, whether you pay your bills on time, whether you maintain balances on your accounts, and whether you pay late fees. It may also contain information about public records such as bankruptcies and court judgments, and identify inquiries made by various companies and potential employers about your credit rating. Canada's three primary credit bureaus are Equifax Canada, TransUnion Canada, and Northern Credit Bureaus.

Focus on Ethics: Guarding Your Financial Information

The *Credit Reporting Act* limits the sharing of credit information to firms that certify that they have a purpose permitted by law to evaluate this information. For example, if the firms are evaluating your application for credit, insurance, or employment, they are eligible to request credit information from credit bureaus. In addition, you must give written permission (usually your signature on the application form) to allow these firms to access your credit report.

While the sharing of financial information may ease your application process, it also allows firms to access more information than you may want to disclose. Financial institutions must provide customers with privacy policies that detail what information they collect and intend to share. For example, a bank that receives a credit card application from you may intend to pass this financial information to an affiliate that can market their financial services to you. Don't overlook these notices, which are often tucked in with your monthly statement or bill. The privacy notices also give you the opportunity to limit some of that sharing by opting out, which typically involves calling a phone number or filling out a form to return to the service provider. No one can access the information in your credit report without your prior consent.

The *Credit Reporting Act* specifies the types of information that can be included in a credit report. Exhibit 5.2 displays a sample credit report along with useful consumer tips for each section of the report. The information in the report includes:

- your personal information
- a consumer statement showing the details of any explanation that you have submitted to the credit bureau regarding a particular account

Exhibit 5.2 Sample Credit Report

Check to see if your personal information is correct.

Personal Information

Name:	Audrey O'Dell	**Current Address:**	123 A ST
Also Known As:	Audrey T. O'Dell		HAMILTON, ON L8N 3L2
		Date Updated:	07/2000
Date of Birth:	04/30/1973		
Telephone #:	(123) 456-7890	**Previous Address:**	456 B ST
			CHARLOTTETOWN, PE C1A 2S8
Employer:	TransUnion	**Date Updated:**	01/1994
Date Updated:	09/1999		

If you gave the credit-reporting agency a statement to explain a particular situation, it will be included here.

Consumer Statement

None reported

Summary

Total Accounts:	5	**Balances:**	4430
Open Accounts:	0	**Payments:**	110
Closed Accounts:	5	**Public Records:**	0
Delinquent:	0	**Inquiries (2 years):**	3
Derogatory:	0		

This scale explains the symbols used to describe your payment history.

Account History

At-a-glance viewing of your payment history

			OK	30	60	90	120	150	PP	RF	CC
Not Open	Unknown	Current	30 days late	60 days late	90 days late	120 days late	150+ days late		Payment plan	Repossession Foreclosure	Collection Chargeoff

Revolving Accounts: Accounts with an open-end term

ZELLERS

Check to see if your credit card information and payment history are correct.

Account #:	1246****	**Type:**	Revolving account	**Opened:**	04/2002
Condition:	Open	**Pay status:**	Paid as Agreed	**Reported:**	06/09/2004
Balance:	$345	**Payment:**	$10 Monthly	**Responsibility:** Individual account	
High Balance:			(due every month)	**Past Due:**	
Terms:		**Limit:**	$1500		
Remarks					

Two Year Payment History:

OK	OK	OK	OK	OK	OK	OK	OK	OK	OK	OK	OK	OK	OK	OK	OK	OK	OK	OK	OK	OK	OK	OK	OK
jun	jul	aug	sep	oct	nov	dec	03	feb	mar	apr	may	jun	jul	aug	sep	oct	nov	dec	04	feb	mar	apr	may

Six Year Payment History:

30 days late:	0	60 days late:	0	90 days late:	0

TD/GM VISA

Check to see if all of your accounts are listed correctly. If you find an error, ask the credit-reporting agency about it to ensure you are not a victim of fraud.

Account #:		**Type:**	Revolving account	**Opened:**	11/2001
Condition:	Open	**Pay status:**	Paid as Agreed	**Reported:**	06/09/2004
Balance:	$1210	**Payment:**	$0 Monthly	**Responsibility:** Individual account	
High Balance:	$1500		(due every month)	**Past Due:**	
Terms:		**Limit:**	$1000		
Remarks					

Two Year Payment History:

OK	OK	OK	OK	OK	OK	OK	OK	OK	OK	OK	OK	OK	OK	OK	OK	OK	OK	OK	OK	OK	OK	OK	OK
jun	jul	aug	sep	oct	nov	dec	03	feb	mar	apr	may	jun	jul	aug	sep	oct	nov	dec	04	feb	mar	apr	may

Six Year Payment History:

30 days late:	0	60 days late:	0	90 days late:	0

Exhibit 5.2 continued

Check to see if the information about your installment loans, your car loan for example, and payment history are correct.

Installment Accounts: Accounts comprised of fixed terms with regular payments

ASSOCIATES FINANCIAL

Account #:	1465456****	**Type:**	Installment account	**Opened:**	04/2002
Condition:	Open	**Pay status:**	Paid as Agreed	**Reported:**	06/09/2004
Balance:	$2000	**Payment:**	$100 Monthly	**Responsibility:** Individual account	
High Balance:	$4000		(due every month)	**Past Due:**	
Terms:		**Limit:**			
Remarks					

Two Year Payment History:

OK	OK	OK	OK	OK	OK	OK	OK	OK	OK	OK	OK	OK	OK	OK	OK	OK	OK	OK	OK	OK	OK	OK	OK
jun	jul	aug	sep	oct	nov	dec	03	feb	mar	apr	may	jun	jul	aug	sep	oct	nov	dec	04	feb	mar	apr	may

Six Year Payment History:

30 days late: 0	**60 days late:** 0	**90 days late:** 0

Check to see that information about any collections is correct. Note the dates, since this information is usually removed from your credit report after 6 years.

Other: Accounts in which the exact category is unknown

None reported

Collection Accounts: Delinquent accounts sent for recovery

None reported

Bank Information

Bank accounts closed for derogatory reasons

None reported

Check to see if your banking information is correct.

Public Information

None reported

Check to see if the public information related to bankruptcies, judgments, and secured loans is correct. Check the date, since the information is usually removed from your credit report after 5 to 10 years, depending on the type of information and the laws of the province in which you live.

An unusual increase in the number of inquiries can have a negative influence on your credit score.

Your own inquiries do not have any effect on your credit score.

Make sure that you have given all of the companies listed here permission to see your credit report information.

Inquiries

Creditor Name	Date of Inquiry
CDN IMPERIAL BANK OF COM	03/20/2004
CITIBANK CANADA	12/04/2003
TCRS/COTTER	03/08/2003

Creditor Contacts

Creditor Name	Phone Number
None reported	

If there are companies listed here that you cannot remember doing business with, call them at the phone number listed.

Source: www.fcac-acfc.gc.ca/eng/publications/CreditReportScore/PDF/CreditReportScore_e.pdf (accessed June 19, 2007). Financial Consumer Agency of Canada, 2007. Reproduced with the permission of the Minister of Public Works and Government Services, 2008.

- a summary of your accounts
- your account history
- bank information regarding any accounts that were closed for derogatory reasons
- public information regarding bankruptcies, judgments, and secured loans
- the names of creditors who have made account inquiries
- a list of creditor contacts

Credit Score

A credit score is a rating that indicates a person's creditworthiness. It reflects the likelihood that an individual will be able to make payments for credit in a timely manner.

Lenders commonly assess the credit payment history provided by one or more credit bureaus when deciding whether to extend a personal loan or mortgage. For example, financial institutions may rely on this information when deciding whether to approve your credit card application, to provide you with a car loan, or to provide you with a home (mortgage) loan. Your credit score can also affect the interest rate quoted on the loan you request. A high credit score could reduce your interest rate substantially, which may translate into savings of thousands of dollars in interest expenses over time.

The credit bureaus rely on a credit scoring model created by the Fair Isaac Corporation (FICO). In Canada, this credit scoring model is referred to as your BEACON score. Exhibit 5.3 provides a chart of the factors that the credit bureaus consider important when calculating your score. The most important factor used in BEACON credit scoring is your credit payment history, which accounts for 35 percent of the score. If you have paid your bills on time over the last seven years, you will receive a high rating on that portion of your credit score.

Credit use, the amount of your available credit that you use each month, accounts for 30 percent of the score. If you continue to rely on most of the credit you were granted, you will receive a lower score. Put another way, if you have a high credit limit but do not rely much on that credit, you will receive a higher score. This second situation suggests that you have access to credit but have enough discipline not to use it.

Your score is also affected by the length of the relationship with your creditors. This factor accounts for 15 percent of the score. You will receive a higher score if you maintain longer relationships with creditors. A fourth factor is the type of credit that you establish, which accounts for 10 percent of the score. Everything else being equal, someone who uses only credit cards as a source of credit will have a lower score than someone who only uses personal loans as a source of credit.

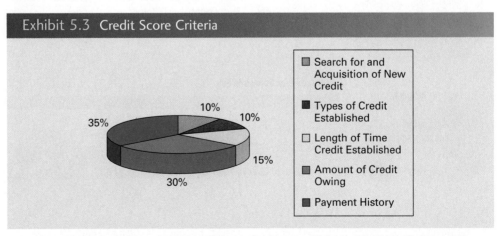

Exhibit 5.3 Credit Score Criteria

- Search for and Acquisition of New Credit
- Types of Credit Established
- Length of Time Credit Established
- Amount of Credit Owing
- Payment History

Source: www.alberta-mortgages.com/articles/credit-bureau.html (accessed February 20, 2007). Reprinted with permission of Alberta's Best Mortgages.

Finally, your score is affected by recent credit inquiries. A large number of credit inquiries may indicate that you are desperately seeking a creditor that will provide you with a loan. Therefore, you will receive a higher score if the number of inquiries is relatively low. This accounts for 10 percent of the score.

Overall, if you make your credit payments on time, maintain a low level of debt, and have demonstrated your ability to make timely credit payments over many years, you are likely to receive a very high credit score. The credit score is not allowed to reflect your sex, race, religion, natural origin, or marital status. Exhibit 5.4 displays a credit score based on the factors outlined above. It details the consumer's credit score, how this score compares to the rest of the Canadian population, and how this score is viewed by lenders. A detailed discussion on how to interpret the credit score scale is provided below.

Differing Scores among Bureaus. While the credit bureaus mentioned earlier rely on BEACON to determine your credit score, each bureau may give you a different score. The reason for differing scores is that the information each bureau receives about you is not exactly the same. Assume that Equifax received information from a utility company that you made a payment one month late, while that information was not made available to TransUnion. In this case, your credit score assigned by Equifax would likely be lower than that assigned by TransUnion. A difference in credit scores can easily be sufficient to cause you to be approved for a loan based on the credit bureau that provided the highest credit score, but to not receive approval for a loan based on the credit bureau that provided the lowest credit score. Keep in mind that some financial institutions may use more than one credit bureau for information about an applicant, so if any one of the bureaus assigns a low credit score, the lender may be more cautious in providing credit.

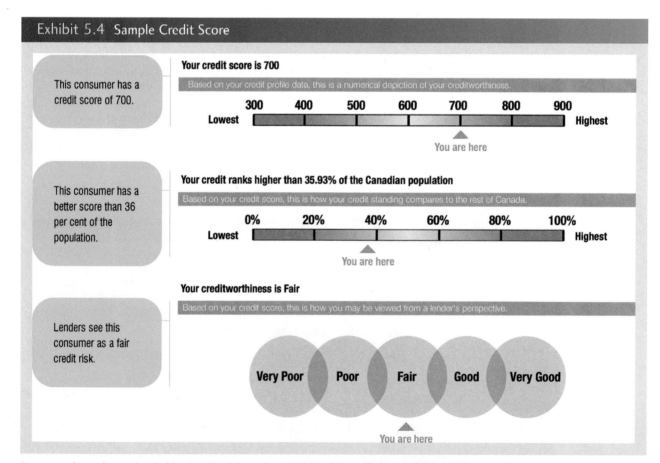

Exhibit 5.4 Sample Credit Score

This consumer has a credit score of 700.

Your credit score is 700

Based on your credit profile data, this is a numerical depiction of your creditworthiness.

300 400 500 600 700 800 900

Lowest   Highest

You are here

This consumer has a better score than 36 per cent of the population.

Your credit ranks higher than 35.93% of the Canadian population

Based on your credit score, this is how your credit standing compares to the rest of Canada.

0% 20% 40% 60% 80% 100%

Lowest   Highest

You are here

Lenders see this consumer as a fair credit risk.

Your creditworthiness is Fair

Based on your credit score, this is how you may be viewed from a lender's perspective.

Very Poor   Poor   Fair   Good   Very Good

You are here

Source: www.fcac-acfc.gc.ca/eng/publications/CreditReportScore/PDF/CreditReportScore_e.pdf (accessed June 19, 2007). Financial Consumer Agency of Canada, 2007. Reproduced with the permission of the Minister of Public Works and Government Services, 2008.

Interpreting Credit Scores. Exhibit 5.5 shows the percentage of the Canadian population that falls into each credit score range. Scores range from 399 to 862. A score of 600 or higher is considered good, and may indicate that you are worthy of credit. Bear in mind, though, that each financial institution sets its own criteria to determine whether to extend credit. Some may require a minimum score of 580, while others require a minimum of 620. Very high credit scores (such as 750 or higher) normally result in easy credit approval. Ratings in the 570–600 range may cause some creditors to reject your application. Other creditors may be willing to extend credit if you are in this range, but may charge a higher interest rate. The lower your score, the riskier lenders think you are. And risk to a lender means default or nonpayment.

The acceptable credit score may vary with the type of credit (credit card, car loan, home loan, and so forth) that you are seeking. While lenders commonly rely on credit information and a credit score from a credit bureau, they also consider other information not disclosed by credit bureaus, such as your income level. For example, a person with a high credit score may not be approved for a specific loan that would require very large payments each month. In this example, your income level may be the key factor that prevents a lender from giving you the loan.

Improving Your Credit Score. A low credit score is normally due to either missed payments or carrying an excessive amount of debt, both of which will be noted on your credit report. A poor credit history will appear on your credit report for three to ten years, depending on the type of information contained in the item reported. Filing for bankruptcy will remain on your credit record for six to seven years, depending on the province you lived in at the time of the bankruptcy.

You can begin to improve your score immediately by catching up on late payments, making at least the minimum payments on time, and reducing your debt. You might also consider:

- Reviewing your household budget and cutting back on all unnecessary expenditures, with an eye to increasing debt payments.

- Destroying or placing your credit cards in a safety deposit box, so that you will not be tempted to add to your debt. Keep your accounts open, however, because part of your credit rating is determined by how much credit you have and what percentage of it you use.

- Advising your creditors immediately if you will not be able to make your payments on time. Generally, creditors will work with you to establish an alternative payment schedule.

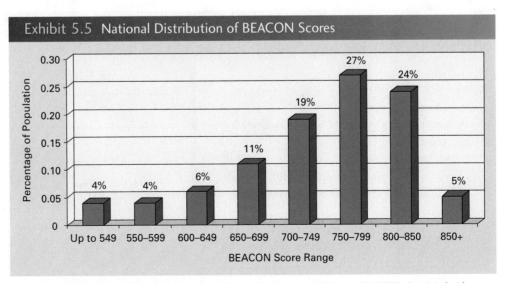

Exhibit 5.5 National Distribution of BEACON Scores

Source: www.alberta-mortgages.com/articles/credit-bureau.html (accessed February 20, 2007). Reprinted with permission of Alberta's Best Mortgages.

As you show a pattern of making payments on time and managing your credit responsibly, your credit score will improve. It might, however, take a few years before your credit is completely rebuilt.

Reviewing Your Credit Report

You should review your credit report from each of the credit bureaus at least once a year. A review of your credit report is beneficial for three reasons. First, you can ensure that the report is accurate. If there are any errors, you can contact each of the credit bureaus to inform them of those errors. Second, a review of the report will show you the types of information that lenders or credit card companies may consider when deciding whether to provide credit. Third, your credit report indicates what kind of information might lower your credit rating, so that you can attempt to eliminate these deficiencies and improve your credit rating prior to applying for additional credit.

The *Credit Reporting Act* requires credit bureaus and the institutions such as banks or credit card companies that provide information to credit bureaus to correct any information about consumers that is incorrect. Because each credit bureau has its own process for reporting credit information, you should check the accuracy of the credit report provided by each one. If you determine that any information is incorrect, you can contact the bureau through its website; there is a specific link that allows you to identify the errors on the credit report and to provide corrections. Upon receiving your information, the bureau will verify the corrections and then adjust the report accordingly. However, it is still your responsibility to follow up with the credit bureau to ensure that the changes were made.

EXAMPLE

Curious about her credit rating, last month Stephanie Spratt took advantage of her right to request a credit report from each of the credit bureaus. While the credit scores assigned by the three bureaus were all above 600, she was surprised to see that the scores varied. In addition, one of the bureaus recorded a late payment on a bill from a utility company about nine months earlier. This single late payment did not severely affect her credit rating, but Stephanie did not want it on her record, especially because she always pays her bills on time. She sent the credit bureau a letter with a copy of the cheque that proved her payment to the utility company was not late. The bureau removed the claim of a late payment from her record and her credit score was increased slightly. Stephanie learned from this experience that she should periodically check her credit rating, as it can affect her access to credit and the interest rate she may pay when obtaining credit.

IN-CLASS NOTES

Credit Bureaus

- Create credit reports
- Create credit scores, or BEACON scores, which record:
  - Your credit payment history (35%)
  - The amount of credit you use (30%)
  - The length of time you have had established credit (15%)
  - The types of credit you have established (10%)
  - The number of credit inquiries you make (10%)

L.O. 3 CREDIT CARDS

The easiest way to establish credit is to apply for a credit card. There is no shortage of credit card companies eager to extend credit to you. A credit card allows you to purchase products on credit wherever that card is honoured. You receive a monthly statement that identifies the purchases you made with the credit card during that period. Normally, credit cards are not used for very large expenditures such as cars or homes, but they are very convenient for smaller purchases, such as meals at restaurants, gasoline, clothing, car repairs, and groceries.

Credit cards offer three advantages. First, you can purchase products and services without carrying a large amount of cash or a chequebook. Second, as long as you pay off your balance each month, you receive free financing until the due date on your credit card statement. Third, you receive a monthly statement that contains a consolidated list of the purchases you made with the credit card, which enables you to keep track of your spending. In some cases, you can receive an annual statement as well, detailing expenses by category, which can be useful in preparing your income tax return if you can claim such expenses.

Applying for a Credit Card
When you apply for a credit card, potential creditors obtain information from you and from credit bureaus so that they can assess your ability to repay credit.

Personal Information. When you apply for credit, you are asked to complete an application that typically requests the following information.

- Revenues: What is your monthly income?

- Expenses: How much do you spend per month?

- Credit history: Have you borrowed funds in the past? Did you repay any previous credit in a timely manner?

- Capital: Do you have any funds in the form of savings or investments that can be used to cover future debt payments, if necessary?

- Collateral: Do you have any assets that can be used as collateral to secure the borrowed funds? (If you could not repay your debt, you could sell these assets to obtain the funds needed to repay it.)

Notice that the revenue and expense information requested by the lender can be quickly provided if you have already completed the cash flow statement outlined in Chapter 2. In addition, the net worth statement, also discussed in Chapter 2, will display the capital you have available to cover future debt payments. Creditors generally prefer that you have a high level of revenues, a low level of expenses, a large amount of capital and collateral, and a good credit history. Nevertheless, they commonly extend credit to individuals who do not have all of these attributes. For example, although creditors recognize that college students may not earn much income, they may still provide a limited amount of credit if they believe that the students are likely to repay it. Some creditors may also extend credit at higher interest rates to individuals who have a higher risk of default. The higher interest rates that creditors charge on these types of loans will offset the number of individuals who will not be able to repay their debt. The interest rate charged on a credit card is not only relatively high, but is also calculated on the daily outstanding balance. It is important to pay your credit card bill in full, every month, to avoid losing money by paying high interest charges.

Credit Check. When you apply for credit, a credit card issuer typically conducts a credit check as part of the application review process. It can obtain a credit report, discussed earlier, that indicates your creditworthiness. A credit report summarizes credit repayment with banks, retailers, credit card issuers, and other lenders. Recall that credit problems remain on a credit bureau's report for up to ten years.

Other Information That Creditors Evaluate. Some creditors also request that the applicant disclose income and existing debt level so that they can assess the existing debt level as a percentage of income. If an applicant's debt level is only a small fraction of his or her income, creditors are more willing to provide credit. Your existing debt level may be different than the amount of credit available to you, which can affect your application. For example, you may have a $10 000 line of credit that you never use. Lines of credit and credit cards are shown at their maximum limit, which may affect how your creditor perceives your credit risk. The creditor may question why you are applying for additional credit when you already have access to credit that you do not use. In addition, you may have existing debt, but your past payment history shows that you pay off this debt every month. You should make the lender aware that this debt is paid off every month so that it can take this into account when it assesses your application.

In addition to information about the applicant, creditors also consider existing economic conditions when they evaluate credit applications. If economic conditions weaken, and you lose your job, you may be unable to repay your loan. Thus, creditors are less willing to extend credit when the economy is weak.

Types of Credit Cards

The most popular credit cards are MasterCard, Visa, and American Express. These three types of cards are especially convenient because they are accepted by most merchants. The merchants honour credit cards because they recognize that many consumers will make purchases only if they can use their cards. A credit card company receives a percentage (commonly between 2 and 4 percent) of the payments made to merchants with its credit card. For example, when you use your MasterCard to pay for a $100 car repair at an Esso station, Esso will pay MasterCard a percentage of that amount, perhaps $3.

Many financial institutions issue MasterCard and Visa credit cards to individuals. Each financial institution makes its own arrangements with credit card companies to do the billing and financing when necessary. The institution provides financing for individuals who choose not to pay their balances in full when they receive a statement. The financial institutions benefit by providing financing because they typically earn a high rate of interest on the credit extended. Some universities and charitable organizations also issue MasterCard and Visa credit cards and provide financing if needed.

retail (or proprietary) credit card
A credit card that is honoured only by a specific retail establishment.

Retail Credit Cards. An alternative to MasterCard, Visa, and American Express credit cards is a retail (or proprietary) credit card, which is honoured only by a specific retail establishment. For example, many department stores (such as The Bay and Sears) and gas stations (such as Petro-Canada and Esso) issue their own credit cards. If you use an Esso credit card to pay for gas at an Esso station, Esso does not have to pay a small percentage of the proceeds to MasterCard or any other credit card company. You can usually obtain an application for a proprietary card when paying for products or services. In some cases, you may be given instant credit once you complete the application. With most retail credit cards, you can pay a small portion of the balance owed each month, which means that the merchant finances your purchase. The interest rate charged when financing with retail credit cards is normally higher than that charged on non-proprietary cards.

One disadvantage of a proprietary credit card is that it limits your purchases to a single merchant. You may find that the limit is an advantage if you are trying to restrict your use of credit so that you do not spend beyond your means. For example, you can use a Petro-Canada card to pay for gasoline and car repairs, but not to buy CDs, clothing, and many other products. Another disadvantage is that using many proprietary cards means that you will have several credit card bills to pay each month; using one card for all purchases allows you to make only one payment each month to cover all of your expenses.

Credit Limit

Credit card companies set a credit limit, which specifies the maximum amount of credit allowed. The credit limit varies among individuals. It may be a relatively small amount (such as $300) for individuals who have a low income. The credit limit usually can be increased for individuals who prove that they are creditworthy by paying their credit card bills on time. Some credit card companies may allow a large limit (such as $10 000 or more) to households that have made their payments consistently and have higher incomes.

Overdraft Protection

Some credit cards provide overdraft protection, which allows you to make purchases beyond your stated credit limit. This is similar to the overdraft protection provided on some chequing accounts at financial institutions, which honours cheques even if there are not enough funds in the chequing account. The overdraft protection on credit cards prevents your card being rejected because you are over your credit limit.

Fees are charged, however, whenever overdraft protection is needed. The fees vary among credit card issuers, but can be as high as $30 or more each time protection is needed. Thus, a person who made five transactions after reaching the credit limit in a particular month may incur overdraft protection fees of $150 (computed as five transactions × $30 per transaction) in that month.

Some people prefer to have overdraft protection to avoid the embarrassment of their credit card being rejected when making purchases, and to have flexibility to spend beyond the credit limit when necessary. Other people prefer no overdraft protection, so that they cannot spend beyond their credit limit and will not be charged overdraft protection fees.

Annual Fee

Some credit card companies charge an annual fee, such as $50 or $70, for the privilege of using their card. The fee is sometimes waived for individuals who use their credit cards frequently and pay their credit card bills in a timely manner.

Incentives to Use the Card

Some credit card companies offer a bonus to cardholders. For example, they may award a point toward a free airline ticket for every dollar spent. After accumulating 20 000 points, for example, you will receive a coupon for a free flight anywhere within Canada. Therefore, if you spend $20 000 over the year on purchases and use this particular credit card for all of them, you will accumulate enough points by the end of the year to earn this free flight. Some airlines issue their own credit cards, which provide similar benefits.

Prestige Cards

prestige cards
Credit cards, such as gold cards or platinum cards, issued by a financial institution to individuals who have an exceptional credit standing.

Financial institutions may issue prestige cards to individuals who have an exceptional credit standing. These cards, sometimes referred to as gold cards or platinum cards, provide extra benefits to cardholders. For example, the card may provide insurance on rental cars and special warranties on purchases. Many cardholders receive an upgrade to a gold card or platinum card after they prove that they are creditworthy by making their payments on time. Cardholders who carry prestige cards need to be careful because thieves may target these cards because of their higher credit limits. Prestige cards may charge an annual fee for the additional benefits they provide. You must carefully assess the usefulness of these benefits versus the cost of any annual fee.

Grace Period

Credit cards typically allow a grace period during which you are not charged any interest on your purchases. The grace period is usually about 20 days from the time the credit card statement is "closed" (any purchases after that date are put on the following month's bill) to the time the bill is due. The credit card issuer essentially provides you with free credit from the time you made the purchase until the bill is due, but only if you start the month with a zero balance.

EXAMPLE

On June 1, Stephanie Spratt paid a car repair bill of $200 with her credit card. The closing date for that month's billing statement is June 30, and the bill is due around July 20. In this case, Stephanie receives about 50 days of free credit. On June 20, she purchased some clothing with her credit card. For that purchase, which is on the same billing statement, she receives about 30 days of free credit. On July 10, she purchased concert tickets with her credit card. This purchase occurs after the closing date of the billing statement and therefore will be listed on the next billing statement, which is due around August 20. For this purchase, credit is extended for about 40 days only if Stephanie paid her bill in full by July 20.

Cash Advances

Many credit cards also allow cash advances at automated banking machines (ABMs). Since a cash advance represents credit extended by the sponsoring financial institution, interest is charged on this transaction from the date it is made. A transaction fee of 1 or 2 percent of the advance may also be charged. Credit card companies also provide cheques that can be used to make purchases that cannot be made by credit card. The interest rate applied to cash advances is often higher than that charged on credit extended for specific credit card purchases. The interest rate is applied at the time of the cash advance; therefore, the grace period that applies to purchases with a credit card does not apply to cash advances. So, although cash advances are convenient, they can also be extremely costly.

Financing

Some individuals use credit cards as a means of financing their purchases. That is, they pay only a portion of the credit card bill at the end of the month, and the sponsoring financial institution extends credit for the remainder and charges an interest rate on it. This interest rate is commonly between 15 and 20 percent on an annualized basis and does not vary much over time. Although financing is convenient for individuals who are short of funds, it is expensive and should be avoided if possible.

Credit cards can offer a variable rate, a fixed rate, or a tiered rate. A variable rate adjusts in response to a specified market interest rate, such as the prime rate. For example, the credit card interest rate could be based on the prime lending rate plus 6 percent. The bank that provides financing on a credit card can change the fixed interest rate it charges, but it must notify you if it does so.

Some banks offer a tiered interest rate on their credit cards, in which cardholders who make late payments are charged a higher rate. Banks that offer a tiered interest rate are expected to inform their cardholders of this practice.

Many credit cards advertise a very low "teaser" interest rate, which is normally applicable for the first three to six months. Some people transfer their balances from one credit card to another as soon as the period of low interest rates has ended. The issuer of one credit card may charge a fee when transferring the balance to another new credit card with the low teaser rate. Some credit card companies will also negotiate a lower interest rate if you are planning to switch cards.

finance charge
The interest and fees you must pay as a result of using credit.

The finance charge represents the interest and fees you must pay as a result of using credit. Purchases after the statement closing date are not normally considered when determining the finance charge because of the grace period, as they will appear on your next statement. The finance charge usually applies only to balances that were not paid in full before their due date in the current billing period. However, some credit card companies add in any new purchases when determining the average daily balance if there is an outstanding balance in the previous period. The finance charge is compounded daily, which means that interest is calculated every day. The following three methods are commonly used to calculate finance charges on outstanding credit card balances.

Previous Balance Method. With the previous balance method, interest is charged on the balance at the beginning of the new billing period. This method is the least favourable of the three to the cardholder because finance charges are applied even if part of the outstanding balance is paid off during the billing period.

Average Daily Balance Method. The most frequently used method is the average daily balance method. For each day in the billing period, the credit card company takes your beginning balance for the day and then subtracts any payments made by you on that day to determine your balance at the end of the day. Then, it determines the average daily balance at the end of the day for every day in the billing period. This method takes into account your paying any part of the outstanding balance. Thus, if you pay part of the outstanding balance during the billing period, your finance charges will be lower under this method than under the previous balance method. There are variations of this method. It may be adjusted to exclude any new purchases or to compute the average over two billing periods instead of one period.

Adjusted Balance Method. Under the adjusted balance method, interest is charged based on the balance at the end of the new billing period. This method is most favourable because it applies finance charges only to the outstanding balance that was not paid off during the billing period.

The following example illustrates the three methods used to determine finance charges.

EXAMPLE

Assume that as of June 10, you have an outstanding credit card balance of $700 due to purchases made over the previous month. The new billing period begins on June 11. Assume that your outstanding balance for the first 15 days of this new billing period (from June 11 to June 25) is $700. Then, on June 25, the financial institution receives a payment of $200 from you, reducing the balance to $500. This is the balance for the remaining 15 days of the billing period.

- Previous Balance Method. With this method, you will be subject to a finance charge that is calculated by applying the monthly interest rate, compounded daily, to the $700 outstanding at the beginning of the new billing period. Using an effective monthly interest rate of 1.5 percent, your finance charge is:

$$\$700 \times 0.015 = \$10.50$$

- Average Daily Balance Method. With this method, the effective monthly interest rate is applied to the average daily balance. Since your daily balance was $700 for the first 15 days and $500 for the last 15 days, your average daily balance was $600 for the 30-day billing period. Using an effective monthly interest rate of 1.5 percent, your finance charge is:

$$\$600 \times 0.015 = \$9.00$$

- Adjusted Balance Method. With this method, you will be subject to a finance charge that is calculated by applying the monthly interest rate to the $500 outstanding at the end of the new billing period. Using an effective monthly interest rate of 1.5 percent, your finance charge is:

$$\$500 \times 0.015 = \$7.50$$

Notice in the example that the finance charge is lowest if the credit card company uses the adjusted balance method. Individuals who frequently have financing charges can save a substantial amount of money over time by relying on a credit card that uses this method. The best way to reduce financing charges, however, is to pay the entire credit card bill before the due date every month.

Credit Card Statement

Individuals typically receive a credit card statement at the end of their billing cycle. It lists all purchases made with that credit card during that period, as well as any balance carried over from the previous statement.

A credit card statement includes the following information:

- Previous balance: the amount carried over from the previous credit card statement

- Purchases: the amount of credit used this month to make purchases

- Cash advances: the amount of credit used this month by writing cheques against the credit card or by making ABM withdrawals

- Payments: the payments you made to the sponsoring financial institution this billing cycle

- Finance charge: the finance charge applied to any credit that exceeds the grace period or to any cash advances

- New balance: the amount you owe the financial institution as of the statement date

- Minimum payment: the minimum amount you must pay by the due date

The credit card statement details why your new balance differs from the balance shown on your statement for the previous month. The difference between the previous balance and the new balance results from any new purchases, cash advances, or finance charges, which increase your balance, versus any payments, which reduce your balance. The statement also shows the method of calculating finance charges, typically explained in full on the reverse of the statement.

EXAMPLE

Suppose you have a credit card balance of $700 due to purchases made last month that you did not pay off. During that billing period, you pay $200 of your outstanding balance. You also use the credit card for $100 of new purchases. Since you relied on the sponsoring financial institution to pay $500 of last month's bill, you owe a finance charge. Assuming that the institution imposes a finance charge of 1.5 percent (effective interest) per month and uses the adjusted balance method to determine the finance charge (which results in a finance charge of $7.50), your credit card statement would be as follows:

Previous Balance	$700.00
+ New Purchases	100.00
+ Cash Advances	0
+ Finance Charges	7.50
− Payments	200.00
= New Balance	$607.50

If you had paid the full amount of the previous balance ($700) during the billing period, the statement would have been as follows:

Previous Balance	$700.00
+ New Purchases	100.00
+ Cash Advances	0

+ Finance Charges	0	
− Payments	700.00	
= New Balance	$100.00	

Thus, if you had paid $700 instead of $200, you would not have borrowed from the sponsoring financial institution and would not have incurred a finance charge. The new balance at the end of this billing period would simply be the amount of purchases that occurred over the period.

When you receive your account statement, you should always scrutinize it for errors. There may be a math error, a double charge for a purchase, or an incorrect amount on a purchase. Under consumer protection laws, you have the right to dispute possible errors. To prove that an error exists, you should always keep your credit card receipts and check them against your statement. Once you reconcile your statement, simply staple receipts to the statement for filing.

Comparing Credit Cards

Some individuals have numerous credit cards, which can complicate record keeping and increase the probability of losing one or more cards. You can consolidate your bills by using just one credit card to cover all purchases. If you decide to use only one credit card, the following criteria will help you determine which card is most desirable.

Acceptance by Merchants. You should ensure that your card is accepted by the types of merchants from whom you typically make purchases. MasterCard and Visa are accepted by more merchants than other credit cards.

Annual Fee. Shop around for a credit card that does not charge an annual fee or, if there is a fee, assess whether benefits are worth the additional cost. Will you actually use these benefits?

Interest Rate. Interest rates vary among financial institutions that provide financing on credit cards. Shop around for the lowest rate if you intend to carry a balance.

The interest rate may be a key factor that determines which credit card is appropriate for you if you plan to carry over part of your balance each month. A card with a higher interest rate can result in substantially higher interest expenses.

EXAMPLE

You plan to pursue credit card X because it has no annual fee, while credit card Y has an annual fee of $30. You typically have an outstanding credit balance of $3000 each month. Credit card X charges an annual interest rate of 18 percent on balances carried forward, while credit card Y charges an interest rate of 12 percent on balances carried forward. The difference in the expenses associated with each credit card are shown here.

	Credit Card X	Credit Card Y
Average monthly balance	$3000	$3000
Annual interest rate	18%	12%
Annual interest expenses	18% x $3000 = $540	12% x $3000 = $360
Annual fee	$0	$30
Total annual expenses	$540	$390

The annual interest expenses can be determined by knowing the average monthly balance over the year. The higher the average monthly balance, the higher your interest expenses because you will have to pay interest on the balance.

Notice that credit card X results in $540 in annual interest expenses, which is $180 more than the annual interest expenses from credit card Y. Thus, while credit card X does not charge an annual fee, your interest expenses from using credit card X could be very high. The high interest expenses more than offset the advantage of no annual fee.

If you always pay off your balance in the month that it occurs, you will not have any interest expenses. In this case, the interest rate on the credit card would not be important, and you may prefer credit card X because it does not have an annual fee. That is, you would benefit from no annual fee, and would not be adversely affected by the higher interest rate of credit card X.

Go to
www.fcac-acfc.gc.ca/eng/
publications/
CreditCardsYou/
CreditCardComparison
Tables_e.asp

This website provides
links to help you compare credit cards based on the type of card and/or the features of the individual cards.

As mentioned earlier, some credit cards offer a low "teaser rate" to entice you to apply for that card. Be aware, however, that this rate is likely to be available only for a short time. After the introductory period elapses, the normal interest rate is charged.

Maximum Limit. Some credit cards allow a higher maximum limit on monthly purchases than do others. A very high maximum limit may not be necessary, and may tempt you to spend excessively. Make sure that the maximum limit is high enough to cover any necessary monthly purchases, but not so high that it encourages you to spend more than you can afford.

Other Provisions. Some other important provisions that you should compare are:

- Does the credit card allow you to obtain a cash advance? Is this important to you? What fees (if any) and interest rates are charged for cash advances?
- What is the typical length of the grace period for the credit card?
- Is there a late-payment charge if your payment is made after the grace period?
- By how much is the interest rate increased (if at all) if your payment is made after the grace period?
- What is the fee if you access more credit than allowed by your credit limit?

IN-CLASS NOTES

Credit Cards

Owning a credit card involves:

- An application process
- A credit limit
- Fees and incentives
- Cash advances and financing, in some instances
- Keeping track of credit card statements

_____

_____

_____

_____

_____

L.O. 4   TIPS ON USING CREDIT CARDS

Since you are likely to have one or more credit cards, consider the following tips to enjoy their use without incurring excessive costs.

Use a Credit Card Only If You Can Cover the Bill

Treat a credit card as a means of convenience, not a source of funds. Use a credit card only if you will have the funds to make the payment when you receive your credit card statement. The use of this self-imposed credit limit is illustrated in Exhibit 5.6. The difference between your expected income and your expenses is the maximum amount of credit you can use and still ensure full payment of the credit card balance.

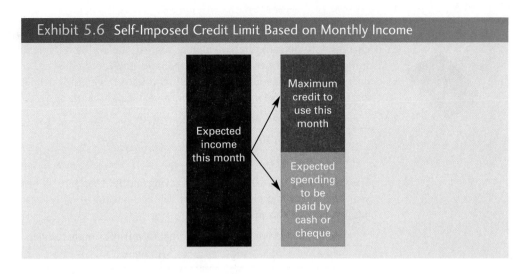

Exhibit 5.6 Self-Imposed Credit Limit Based on Monthly Income

Impose a Tight Credit Limit

You may consider imposing a tighter credit limit as part of your budgeting process so that you can save or invest a specific amount every month. This limit is illustrated in Exhibit 5.7. You determine the maximum amount of credit you can afford each month only after accounting for all spending to be paid by cheque or cash, as well as a specified amount of savings.

Pay Credit Card Bills before Investing Money

Go to
www.yourmoney.cba.ca/
tsam/en/tsam/credit_101

This website provides information about establishing, using, and protecting your credit.

In general, avoid carrying a balance on your credit cards when you have the money to pay the balance. The likely return that you might earn from investing your money is less than the financing rate you will be charged when you delay paying your credit card bills in full. Debit cards are a good alternative to credit cards because they offer the same convenience of not carrying cash.

Some individuals use their money to purchase risky investments (such as stocks) rather than pay off their credit card bills. They apparently believe that their return from the investments will be higher than the cost of financing. Although some investments have generated large returns in specific years, it is difficult to earn returns that consistently exceed the high costs of financing with credit cards. If the thrill of a good return on your investment makes you consider delaying your credit card payment, consider the following. When you use money to pay your credit card bill immediately, you are preventing a charge of about 20 percent interest, on an annual basis. Therefore, you have effectively increased your savings by 20 percent by using these funds to pay off the credit card debt.

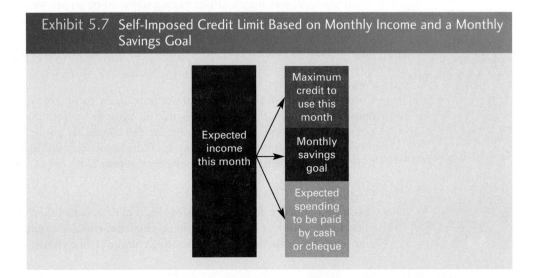

Exhibit 5.7 Self-Imposed Credit Limit Based on Monthly Income and a Monthly Savings Goal

EXAMPLE

Stephanie Spratt just received a credit card bill for $700. The sponsoring financial institution charges a 20 percent effective annual interest rate on the outstanding balance. Stephanie has sufficient funds in her chequing account to pay the credit card bill, but she is considering financing her payment. If she pays $100 toward the credit card bill and finances the remaining $600 for one year, she will incur interest expenses of:

Interest = Loan Amount × Interest Rate

= $600 × 0.20

= $120

She could use the $600 to invest in savings rather than pay off her credit card bill. After one year, the $600 in a savings account will accumulate to $618 based on a 3 percent annual interest rate, as shown here:

Interest Earned on Deposit = Initial Deposit × Interest Rate

= $600 × 0.03

= $18

Her interest owed on the credit card loan ($120) exceeds the interest earned on the deposit ($18) in one year by $102. Stephanie decides that she would be better off using her cash to pay off the credit card bill immediately. By using her money to cover the credit card bill, she gives up the opportunity to earn 3 percent on that money, but she also avoids the 20 percent rate that would be charged on the credit card loan. Thus, her wealth is $102 higher as a result of using funds to pay off the credit card bill rather than investing in a bank deposit. Although she could have used the funds to invest in a high-risk investment that might achieve a greater return, paying off the credit card guarantees that she can avoid a 20 percent financing rate.

Use Savings If Necessary to Pay the Credit Card Bill on Time

If your income is not sufficient to cover your credit card bill, you should pull funds from savings (if there is no penalty for withdrawal) to cover the payment.

If You Cannot Avoid Credit Card Debt, Pay It Off before Other Debt

Go to
www.free-financial-advice.net/time-to-pay-debt.html

This website provides a debt payment calculator that estimates how long it will take to pay off your credit card debt using different monthly payments.

If you cannot pay off your credit card balance in full each month with income or with savings, at least pay it off as soon as possible and decrease your discretionary spending. If you have other debt outstanding, you should pay off credit card debt first (assuming that the credit card debt has a higher interest rate). Even if you cannot pay your bill in full, you should still attempt to pay as much as possible to minimize finance charges.

If possible, you may consider taking out a home equity loan (discussed in Chapter 6) to pay any credit card bills so that you can avoid the high interest expenses. This strategy makes sense only if your credit card debt is substantial (such as several thousand dollars), and the interest rate on the home equity loan is less than that on your credit card.

Avoid Credit Repair Services

Companies that offer credit repair services claim to be able to solve your credit problems. For example, they may help you fix a mistake on your credit report. However, you can do this yourself, without paying for the service. If you have made late credit payments or have defaulted on a loan, a credit repair service does not have the power to remove such information from your credit report.

Dealing with Credit Debt

If you find yourself with an excessive credit card balance, there are several steps you can take. First, spend as little as possible. This could include reducing your entertainment and recreation expenses and/or choosing to take public transit instead of paying for fuel and insurance for your car. Then, consider how you can obtain funds to meet your monthly payments or to pay off your balance. Get a job if you don't have one, or work more hours at your current job. However, for students, additional work hours could disrupt their school schedule. An alternative solution is to borrow funds from a family member. You will now have monthly loan payments to a family member rather than credit card balances, but those payments may be lower. Another possible solution is a debt consolidation loan from a financial institution. The structured schedule for paying off the loan within a set time period will instill more discipline than meeting low minimum monthly payments on a credit card. If you choose not to get a loan, you should still discipline yourself to make more than the minimum payment on your credit card.

You also could consider selling some assets to obtain cash, such as trading in a relatively new car for an older model. Also consider ways to reduce your everyday expenses. For example, if you have large monthly payments because of your cellphone, you could stop using it. If you have your own apartment, you could consider getting a roommate.

consumer proposal
An offer made by a debtor to his or her creditors to modify his or her payments.

A last resort before filing for bankruptcy is to make a **consumer proposal**, which is an offer made by a debtor to his or her creditors to modify his or her payments. When a consumer files a proposal with a trustee in bankruptcy or an administrator of consumer proposals, creditors have up to 45 days to object; otherwise, the proposal is deemed to be accepted by the creditors. Under current legislation, a consumer proposal can be made as long as your debts are less than $75 000. Bill C-55 proposes to increase this threshold to $250 000. A consumer proposal will be removed from your credit bureau report once its terms have been met. Often, the entire debt is not completely paid off by the end of the proposal's term.

insolvent
A person who owes at least $1000 and is unable to pay his or her debts as they come due.

If all else fails, you may need to file for personal bankruptcy. Individuals can file for bankruptcy when they become **insolvent**. They may be deemed to be insolvent if they owe at least $1000 and are unable to pay their debts as they come due. When you declare bankruptcy, your property is given to a **trustee in bankruptcy**, a person licensed to administer consumer proposals and bankruptcies and manage assets held in trust. Your unsecured creditors will not be able to take legal steps to recover their debts from you, such as seizing property or garnishing wages. However, the trustee in bankruptcy will sell your assets and distribute the money obtained to your creditors on a pro rata basis. Certain assets are exempt from your bankruptcy (the amount and types of assets exempt differ among provinces). To determine the amount that is exempt from bankruptcy in the province in which you live, visit www.bankruptcycanada.com/question1.htm# bankruptcyexemptions. It is important to note that your spouse or common-law partner is not affected by your personal bankruptcy as long as he or she is not responsible for your debt. Bankruptcy should only be considered if there is no other option to deal with overwhelming debt.

trustee in bankruptcy
A person licensed to administer consumer proposals and bankruptcies and manage assets held in trust.

Go to
www.bankruptcycanada.com

This website provides useful bankruptcy tools, including video presentations, a bankruptcy predictor, and a bankruptcy trustee locator for the province in which you live.

IN-CLASS NOTES

Tips on Using Credit Cards and Dealing with Credit Debt

- Use a credit card only if you can cover the bill
- Impose a tight credit limit
- Pay your credit debts as promptly as possible
- Reduce your credit spending if necessary
- Avoid credit repair services
- File for bankruptcy if you become insolvent

_____

_____

_____

_____

_____

L.O. 5 # IDENTITY THEFT: A THREAT TO YOUR CREDIT

identity theft
Occurs when an individual uses personal, identifying information unique to you, such as your Social Insurance Number, without your permission for their personal gain.

Identity theft occurs when an individual uses personal, identifying information unique to you, such as your Social Insurance Number, driver's licence number, credit card account numbers, bank account numbers, or simply your name and date of birth, without your permission for their personal gain. Criminals use this stolen personal information to open accounts in your name. If you are a victim of identity theft, any purchases charged to the accounts appear under your name. When these accounts go unpaid, they appear on your credit report. Meanwhile, you are not even aware that these accounts exist. Your credit score may be reduced to the point that you no longer have access to credit. As well, you may be held responsible for the repayment of these fraudulent accounts. After all, these are your debts.

In some instances of identity theft, the criminal is not attempting to acquire money, goods, or services. Instead, the object is to obtain documents such as a driver's licence, birth certificate, Social Insurance Number, passport, visa, or other official government documents. These documents can then be used to establish a new identity unknown to the authorities to facilitate various criminal activities. Although these actions do not result in financial loss to the victim, embarrassing situations can occur. The victim may be arrested or detained by customs or immigration authorities as a result of the identity thief's actions.

In May 2006, more than 20 000 individual phishing complaints were reported, representing an increase of more than 34 percent from the previous year. Phishing is covered in detail later in this chapter. People of all ages and socio-economic classes are at risk from this increasingly common crime. Consider the following cases:

- In August 2006, a Florida man was indicted by a U.S. federal grand jury on charges of wire fraud related to a phishing scheme that included among its targets people seeking to donate to Hurricane Katrina disaster relief efforts.

- A former H&R Block employee allegedly victimized at least 27 customers by using their personal information to obtain credit cards that were used to steal thousands of dollars in cash from ABMs and make merchandise purchases.

- In March 2006, the RCMP uncovered an identity theft ring in Coquitlam, British Columbia. The items recovered included thousands of stolen house, car, and mailbox keys; manuals explaining how to reprogram bank machines; equipment to reset locks; and key-cutting equipment. Personal information, including credit cards, bank statements, birth certificates, social insurance cards, and medical cards, was also recovered.

- In November 2006, consumers were warned about a scam in which email recipients were asked to submit personal information and told that they would receive tickets to the Oprah Winfrey Show. The tickets would be sent once some personal financial information was verified and the email recipient wired money to an unknown third party.

In these instances alone, hundreds of individuals were affected and victimized financially by identity thieves.

The Scope of Identity Theft

The scope of identity theft may prove surprising to many people. PhoneBusters, a police task force set up to tackle telemarketing fraud in Canada, provides various statistics on identity theft including the cost of identity theft in other countries, the number of cases in other countries, the number of victims per province in Canada, and the total cost of identity theft in Canada. This information is available online at www.phonebusters.com/english/statistics.html. After reviewing the material on this website, you will discover that identity theft is a profitable business that affects Canadians in every province.

How big is the problem of identity theft? According to the findings of a 2003 Ipsos Reid survey, 9 percent of Canadians—or 2.7 million people—have fallen victim to identity theft at some point in their lives. In the United States, the FBI estimates identity theft costs American businesses and consumers $50 billion a year and affects some 10 million victims annually.

The Cost of Identity Theft

The personal cost of identity theft is difficult to measure but easy to imagine, beginning with the victim's feeling of being violated and the resulting insecurity. Identity theft victims have been turned down for employment because of incorrect information found in background checks. They have been hounded for back taxes on income they did not earn or receive, and have been referred to collection agencies for nonpayment of mortgages and student loans obtained by identity thieves. They have been refused loans for which they would normally have qualified, have had their driver's licences revoked for violations they did not commit, and have been enrolled for welfare benefits they didn't receive. One identity theft victim is even listed on a birth certificate as the mother of a child she didn't bear.

Calculating the financial costs of identity theft is an easier task. According to the Federal Trade Commission, the average individual loss due to identity theft is $1868.

Financial losses are not the only costs incurred by an identity theft victim. Time is lost as well. Recent estimates suggest that the average victim spends 600 hours dealing with damage control necessitated by identity theft. The cost of the actual losses incurred and the additional expenses of repairing the damage are substantial in both time and money to both individuals and businesses and, ultimately, to our economy.

L.O. 6 IDENTITY THEFT TACTICS

The identity thief has a wide variety of tactics at hand that can be used to obtain your personal data.

Shoulder Surfing

shoulder surfing
Occurs in public places where you can be readily seen or heard by someone standing close by.

Shoulder surfing occurs in public places where you can be readily seen or heard by someone standing close by. An example of shoulder surfing is someone standing close to you in a hotel or other business establishment and reading the number of your credit card. Shoulder surfing may also occur if you make a telephone call and someone is close enough to observe you entering your calling card number and personal identification number (PIN).

Dumpster Diving

dumpster diving
Occurs when an identity thief goes through your trash for discarded items that reveal personal information that can be used for fraudulent purposes.

As the name implies, dumpster diving occurs when an identity thief goes through your trash. The thief is looking for discarded items that reveal personal information that can be used for fraudulent purposes. Targets include information that might contain your Social Insurance Number, bank account numbers, or credit card numbers. As one example, if the thief finds something containing your credit card number, he or she can contact the credit card company to report a change of address and then obtain a card in your name.

The thief also may retrieve similar personal information from the dumpsters of places where you do business. Let us say that you complete a credit card application at a local store. If this credit card application, which contains substantial personal and financial information, is disposed of in the company's dumpster, it can be used by an identity thief. Other business dumpsters that could provide usable information are those of your health care providers, your broker, your accountant, and even your bank.

Skimming

skimming
Occurs when identity thieves steal your credit or debit card number by copying the information contained in the magnetic strip on the card.

Skimming occurs when identity thieves steal your credit or debit card number by copying the information contained in the magnetic strip on the card. Often, skimmers are the employees of stores and restaurants you patronize. When you are not looking, they swipe your card through a reader that captures and stores your data. Skimmers also attach card readers to ABMs that allow them to collect your information when you swipe your card for access. They then use the data to create fake debit and credit cards.

Pretexting, Phishing, and Pharming

pretexting
Occurs when individuals access personal information under false pretenses.

Another method of obtaining personal information is **pretexting**, which occurs when individuals access personal information under false pretenses. The pretexter may use information obtained from dumpster diving to identify the companies with which you do business. The pretexter then may pose as a survey taker or an employee of a financial institution, insurance company, or other firm with which you do business. You may be asked for information such as your Social Insurance Number; driver's licence number; or bank, brokerage, or credit card numbers. The pretexter will sound as if soliciting the information is part of routine business such as updating your file. Pretexters may use the information to steal your identity or they may sell it to others for illegal use.

phishing
Occurs when pretexting happens online.

When pretexting happens online, it is called **phishing**. A phisher sends an email message falsely claiming to be from a legitimate source that directs the recipient to a website where he or she is asked to update account information such as passwords, credit card numbers, bank account numbers, and Social Insurance Numbers. The website, in reality, is a fake.

pharming
Similar to phishing, but, targeted at larger audiences, it directs users to bogus websites to collect their personal information.

A practice similar to phishing, but that reaches many more targets with a single effort, is known as **pharming**. By manipulating email viruses and host files, pharmers redirect users, without their knowledge, from the legitimate commercial websites they thought they were visiting to bogus ones that look like the genuine sites. When users enter their login names and passwords, the pharmers collect the data.

Abusing Legitimate Access to Records

Employees at places where you work, bank, go to the doctor, and shop can steal your data. In many cases, these people have easy and legitimate access to personal information that can be used to steal your identity.

As well, anyone who has gone through a divorce has most, if not all, of their personal financial information, including Social Insurance Numbers, included in the court records. In most provinces, this information is considered part of the public record, making it easier to steal.

Crime Rings

In some cases, identity thieves may be part of a well-organized crime ring that has systematically infiltrated corporations and financial institutions for the sole purpose of obtaining information to facilitate large-scale identity thefts.

Violating Your Mailbox

A last source of information worth mentioning is your mailbox. Both incoming and outgoing mail may provide the necessary information to allow your identity to be stolen. Outgoing mail may provide credit card and bank information if you leave letters in your mailbox for the postal carrier to pick up. Incoming mail can also provide your credit card account numbers, bank information, driver's licence number, and Social Insurance Number.

IN-CLASS NOTES

Identity Theft and Identity Theft Tactics

- Identity theft occurs when someone uses personal, identifying information unique to you (e.g., your Social Insurance Number) without your permission for their personal gain.
- People can steal your identity by:
  - Shoulder surfing, dumpster diving, and skimming
  - Pretexting, phishing, and pharming
  - Abusing legitimate access to records
  - Participating in crime rings and mail theft

_____

_____

_____

_____

_____

L.O. 7 PROTECTING AGAINST IDENTITY THEFT

There are many ways to safeguard your personal information and make it harder for an identity thief to prey on you. Most of these safeguards are relatively easy and inexpensive.

- Personal information should only be provided over the phone, through email, or over the internet if you have initiated contact. In particular, avoid providing account numbers, your mother's maiden name, your date of birth, or your personal identification number (PIN).

- If possible, put a lock on your mailbox.

- Keep the amount of identification that you carry with you to a minimum. For example, you don't need to carry your birth certificate or social insurance card with you if you're just going shopping. In addition, you should also keep credit cards that you do not use on a regular basis in a safe place.

- Protect your personal information. Invest in a paper shredder. Items such as receipts, copies of credit applications, any items with your name or address on them, government forms, and credit card or other offers you receive in the mail should be shredded. Almost one in three people don't shred personal documents before tossing them in the garbage.

- Review the contents of the glove box in your car. Shred old vehicle registration and car licence renewal documents in a timely fashion. Remove any other documents that contain personal information that do not need to be in your vehicle.

- Make sure you are aware of when your regular bills arrive in your mail. If you stop receiving bills on time, or they appear later than you expect, notify the creditor.

- Do not give out your Social Insurance Number and do not carry it with you. According to recent Canadian surveys, nearly 6 in 10 Canadians carry their SIN card with them at all times. Many other forms of personal identification are acceptable at most retailers.

- Use common sense and be aware of potential security leaks. You would not give information to just anyone in the offline world. Apply the same discretion online.

- Check you credit report at least once a year. Report any discrepancies on your report to the credit agency.

- Change your passwords regularly, use hard-to-guess passwords (for example, a combination of letters and numbers), and never share your password with anyone.

- A reputable organization will never require you to provide information through email. If you recognize the organization that is emailing you, look up their phone number and call them. If you do not recognize the name of the organization, contact one of the organizations listed in Exhibit 5.8 on pages 127–128.

- Look for a company's privacy policy or link to its privacy statement when you visit its website. Pay attention to what information the company gathers, how it is used, and with whom it is shared.

- Always ensure that you are in a safe environment. Look for the closed-lock or unbroken-key icon in your web browser before entering your credit card number or other sensitive data. If you do not see these symbols, or if the key is broken or the padlock is open, your information is not being transmitted securely over the Internet. When you send messages insecurely, someone other than the organization you are sending to could intercept your information.

- Clear the cache of your browser after visiting secure sites. This will ensure that nobody else can view any confidential information you have transmitted.

- Be familiar with the encryption level of your web browser and what it means to your privacy. Many businesses require that you use 128-bit encryption to access secure websites. Update your web browser on a frequent basis to ensure that you are using the latest technology and the highest encryption level.

- Install and maintain a firewall to guard against unwanted access to your computer and ensure that you have the latest anti virus software installed.

- Be suspicious if you receive email from a business or person requesting personal information. Be particularly suspicious of emails that direct you to websites that request your password, Social Insurance Number, or other highly sensitive information. You may wish to call the organization to verify the legitimacy of the request.

- Be careful when downloading files from the Internet and installing programs. Also take care when reading email with attachments, as email is often used to transmit viruses.

- When your computer is not in use, make sure it is not connected to the internet.

- Review your financial history with your spouse or significant other on a regular basis. In a relationship, good communication will prevent, and sometimes uncover, fraudulent activity in your account.

L.O. 8 RESPONSE TO IDENTITY THEFT

If you are a victim of identity theft, you must take action immediately to clean up your credit report. The Office of the Privacy Commissioner of Canada, www.privcom.gc.ca/index_e.asp, has suggested a number of actions to take if you suspect that you are a victim of identity theft. The discussion below highlights the main features of their fact sheet on identity theft.

- Report the crime to the police immediately.

- Take steps to undo the damage. Avoid "credit repair" companies, as there is usually nothing they can do.

- Document the steps you take and the expenses you incur to clear your name and re-establish your credit.

- Cancel your credit cards and have new ones issued immediately.

- Have your credit report annotated to reflect the identity theft.

- Close your bank accounts and open new ones immediately.

- Obtain new ABM cards and telephone calling cards, with new passwords or PINs.

- In the case of passport theft, advise the Passport Office immediately.

- Contact Canada Post if you suspect that someone is diverting your mail.

- Advise your telephone, cable, and utilities providers that someone using your name could try to open new accounts fraudulently.

- Obtain a new driver's licence.

Go to
www.phonebusters.com

This website provides information on identity theft and the tools to report identity theft.

Notify the major credit reporting companies. Request that a fraud alert be placed in your file. An initial fraud alert will stay on your report for up to 90 days. An extended alert will remain on your credit report for seven years if you provide the credit bureau with an identity theft report. This report consists of a copy of the report filed with the police and any documentation beyond that verifying your identity to the satisfaction of the credit bureau. This alert will enable the bureau to contact you if there is any attempt to establish credit in your name. Also, request a credit report for your review to determine whether the identity theft has already affected your score.

Contact all of your creditors and any creditors with whom unauthorized accounts have been opened in your name. Many may request a copy of the police report. While contacting your credit card companies and financial institutions, take the opportunity to change all of your passwords. Do not use your mother's maiden name, the last three digits of your Social Insurance Number, your birthday, street address, wedding anniversary, or any other readily available information that the identity thief may have obtained.

If the identity thief has gained access to your bank accounts or created accounts in your name, you should also contact cheque verification companies. These companies maintain a database of individuals who have written bad cheques and of accounts in which there have been excessive or unusual transactions.

If you believe the identity thief has obtained your data or illegally used your personal information involving Canada Post in any way, you should contact your local post office. If the identity thief has compromised your Social Insurance Number, contact the authorities immediately. Exhibit 5.8 provides a list of contacts you can use if you are subjected to identity theft.

Exhibit 5.8 Contacts If You Are Subjected to Identity Theft

Major National Credit Bureaus

Equifax Canada
National Consumer Relations
P.O. Box 190, Station Jean-Talon
Montreal, QC H1S 2Z2
Tel. (toll-free): 1-800-465-7166
Fax: (514) 355-8502
Email: consumer.relations@equifax.com
https://www.econsumer.equifax.ca/ca/main?link=OPIEM&lang=en

(continued)

Exhibit 5.8 continued

TransUnion Canada
All provinces except Quebec:
TransUnion
Consumer Relations Centre
P.O. Box 338 LCD 1
Hamilton, ON L8L 7W2
Tel. (toll-free): 1-866-525-0262
Fax: (905) 527-0401
www.transunion.ca/

Quebec residents
TransUnion (Echo Group)
1 Place Laval, Suite 370
Laval, QC H7N 1A1
Tel. (toll-free): 1-877-713-3393
Fax: (905) 527-0401

Northern Credit Bureaus Inc.
336 Rideau Boulevard
Rouyn-Noranda, QC J9X 1P2
Fax (toll-free): 1-800-646-5876
www.creditbureau.ca/
Governmental Agencies

Office of the Privacy Commissioner of Canada
112 Kent Street
Ottawa, ON K1A 1H3
Email: info@privcom.gc.ca
www.privcom.gc.ca/

Competition Bureau Canada
Tel. (toll-free): 1-800-348-5358
Email: compbureau@cb-bc.gc.ca
www.cb-bc.gc.ca

PhoneBusters
Tel. (toll-free): 1-888-495-8501
Fax: (705) 494-4755
Fax (toll-free): 1-888-654-9426
Email: info@phonebusters.com
www.phonebusters.com/

Financial Consumer Agency of Canada
427 Laurier Avenue West, 6th Floor
Ottawa, ON K1R 1B9
For services in English:
Tel. (toll-free): 1-866-461-3222
For services in French:
Tel. (toll-free): 1-866-461-2232
www.fcac-acfc.gc.ca/

EXAMPLE

Recently, Stephanie Spratt was shocked to receive a statement from Visa indicating that her credit card had been charged to its $5000 limit. (The statement showed 18 unauthorized purchases, totalling $4903.88, all made within a two-day period.) Stephanie had paid the balance in full last month, and the only thing she bought with the card this month was a pair of running shoes. Thinking she must have lost her card, Stephanie quickly checked her wallet and found the card in its usual compartment.

Stephanie keeps a list of all of her credit card numbers and the toll-free phone numbers for the credit card companies in a fireproof box. She retrieves the information she needs and calls customer service at Visa to report the unauthorized charges, close the account, and request a new card. The customer service representative

1-26 © LaughingStock International Inc./dist. by United Media, 2004

"We were wondering if we could extend the maximum limit on our charge account."

explains that had Stephanie's card actually been stolen, she would have been liable under federal law for $50 of the $4903.88 in charges. However, because the thief stole Stephanie's credit card number, she is not liable for unauthorized use.

Stephanie is relieved that she will not be held accountable for the charges, but is puzzled about how the thief accessed her credit card number. Also, she is worried that perhaps the thief stole more than that. She recalls a recent email from a popular online store saying that her account would be terminated if she did not update her credit information. A quick email to the store confirms that no such message was sent—Stephanie is a victim of a phishing scam.

As best as Stephanie can recall, the information she provided to the phisher was her Visa account number, her name, and her address. To be safe, Stephanie's next step is to put an alert on her credit report. She decides to check her report in one month, and if there is fraudulent information, she will request corrections and fill out an identity theft report.

IN-CLASS NOTES

Protecting Against Identity Theft and Response to Identity Theft

- Know the party to whom you are giving personal information
- Carry a minimal amount of ID
- Keep personal information in a safe place
- Report identity theft to the police
- Cancel items such as your bank accounts, credit cards, and driver's licence
- Advise your utility companies and financial institutions of the theft

_____

_____

_____

_____

_____

_____

HOW CREDIT ASSESSMENT, MANAGEMENT, AND SECURITY FITS WITHIN YOUR FINANCIAL PLAN

The following are the key credit assessment, management, and security decisions that should be included within your financial plan:

1. Is your credit standing adequate so that you can use credit?

2. What limit should you impose on your credit card?

3. When should you use credit?

4. Is your credit and personal identity information secure?

By making proper decisions, you can ensure that you access credit only when your credit standing is adequate, avoid using credit when inappropriate to maximize the return on your liquid assets, and prevent others from using your credit or identity information.

STEPHANIE SPRATT'S FINANCIAL PLAN: Credit Standing, Decisions, and Security

GOALS

1. *Ensure that I always have easy access to credit so that I can obtain personal loans or use credit cards whenever I desire.*

2. *Set my own limit on credit card purchases to ensure that I will always be able to pay off the credit balance in the same month.*

3. *Set a policy to avoid incurring high interest expenses on credit cards.*

4. *Ensure that my credit and identity information is secure.*

ANALYSIS

Monthly Income	$2500	
− Typical Monthly Expenses	−1400	
= Amount of Funds Available	1100	
Liquid Assets	Balance	Annualized Interest Rate (%)
Cash	$100	0
Chequing account balance	800	0
Money market fund	330	3.0
One-month term deposit	1200	4.3
Credit card balance	600	20.0

Decision Regarding My Credit Report

Contact the credit bureaus to request a copy of my credit report and ensure that it is accurate. If any deficiencies are listed on my report, correct them so that I can ensure easy access to credit in the future.

Decision on Credit Limit

Given that I have $1100 each month left from my salary after paying typical expenses, I have $1100 remaining that can be used for credit card purchases, if necessary. I will impose a maximum limit of $1100 on my credit card spending. As my income rises over time, I may consider increasing my credit limit, but only up to a level that I can afford to pay off immediately when I receive the bill.

Decision on Paying Off Credit Balances

Given the interest rates that I can earn on deposit accounts versus the interest rate I would pay on a credit card balance, I will always pay off my credit card balance, even if I must withdraw funds from my savings account to do so.

Decision Regarding the Security of My Credit and Identity

Leave most of my personal information at home. Carry only my Visa, MasterCard, and driver's licence with me. Shred any documents that contain personal information I plan to discard.

Discussion Questions

1. How would Stephanie's credit management decisions be different if she were a single mother of two children?

2. How would Stephanie's credit management decisions be affected if she were 35 years old? If she were 50 years old?

SUMMARY

Credit, which is funds provided to a borrower that will be repaid in the future, has advantages and disadvantages. An advantage is the convenience that credit provides in making day-to-day purchases without carrying large amounts of cash. A disadvantage is that if not used properly, credit can result in bankruptcy or cause a significant reduction in the money you can save.

Instalment credit is provided for specific purchases and the borrower has a longer time (such as a few years) to repay the amount borrowed. Revolving open-end credit is used for credit cards. Consumers can repay the entire balance at the end of the month, or repay a portion of the balance and have interest charged on the remainder. The consumer may spend up to the credit limit at any time.

Good credit is easy to create by paying utility bills promptly and limiting the use of credit cards. A complete history of your credit transactions is maintained by credit bureaus that rate your credit score and report this information to interested parties.

Lenders commonly access the credit payment history provided by one or more credit bureaus when deciding whether to extend a personal loan. You can obtain a free credit report from any of the three credit bureaus to ensure that the report is accurate. The credit report contains potentially negative information from public records, such as bankruptcy filings. It also offers information on late payments, accounts in good standing,

inquiries made about your credit history, and personal information.

Another advantage of using credit is that it enables you to obtain products and services you cannot afford otherwise. A disadvantage of credit is that it is easier to obtain it than to pay it back. Some individuals use too much credit and are unable to make their payments, which may prevent them from obtaining credit in the future. When individuals apply for credit, they provide information about their cash inflows (income), cash outflows (spending habits), and collateral. Creditors also evaluate your credit report, which contains information on your credit history collected by a credit bureau.

Credit cards are distinguished by whether the sponsor is Visa, MasterCard, American Express, a proprietary merchant (such as Zellers), or some other firm. They are also distinguished by credit limit, annual fee, interest rate charged on balances not paid by the due date, and whether they provide cash advances.

Credit cards should be used with discipline. You should impose your own credit limits rather than spend to the limit granted by the card issuer. You should attempt to avoid financing costs, either by using income to cover the amount owing or by withdrawing money from savings, if necessary, to ensure that the balance is paid in full each month.

Not all threats to your credit score are the result of your actions. Identity theft, which involves the use of your personal, identifying information without your permission, is

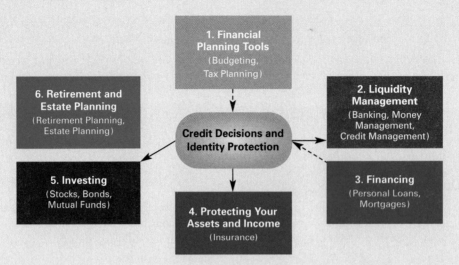

one of the fastest growing crimes in Canada. An identity thief may use your personal information to obtain goods, services, and money, or to create a new identity. All of these actions can have a negative effect on your credit history. Protecting your identity against actions such as shoulder surfing, dumpster diving, skimming, and pretexting is your responsibility.

Obtain a copy of your credit report at least once a year. Carefully review your credit report for unusual account activity and the existence of accounts of which you are not aware.

Should your identity be stolen, notify the police and request a copy of the police report. Notify credit bureaus, credit card companies, financial institutions, and, when appropriate, CSIS and the RCMP.

INTEGRATING THE KEY CONCEPTS

Your credit decisions affect not only your liquidity, but also other parts of your financial plan. If you have borrowed a large amount of funds through credit cards, you will be more restricted when obtaining additional financing (Part 3) because lenders are less willing to lend to you if you already have substantial debt. Lenders may also be less willing to lend funds if you have a large amount of credit available to you, even if you have not used it. Your credit decisions may affect your insurance planning (Part 4), because you might need more life insurance to cover your debt. You will also restrict your ability to invest (Part 5) because you would probably be better off avoiding investments until you pay off any credit card balances. Alternatively, you may need to sell some of your investments to obtain sufficient cash to pay off any credit card balances. Protecting your identity is crucial to protecting your assets and income (Part 4) and financing because if your credit history has been damaged by identity theft, it may be difficult to borrow money in the future.

REVIEW QUESTIONS

1. Explain the two types of credit. Under what conditions might a consumer find each type useful?

2. What are the advantages and disadvantages of using credit?

3. Name the three major credit bureaus. How do they score your credit rating? Will all three bureaus always produce the same credit score?

4. What eight major areas of information may be included on your credit report?

5. What five factors determine your credit score, and how are these factors weighted by BEACON?

6. What is the range for credit scores?

7. How can you improve your credit score, and how long can it take to erase a poor credit history?

8. How often should you review your credit report from each of the three major credit bureaus? Why is this review beneficial?

9. What are three advantages of using a credit card? What are the disadvantages?

10. What information will you need to supply when applying for credit? How does the cash flow and net worth statement help you when applying for credit? What kinds of attributes are creditors looking for? Do you need to have all of these attributes to get credit?

11. Describe the differences between a credit card like MasterCard or Visa and a retail (or proprietary) card. How do credit and retail cards generate revenue? What is the biggest disadvantage of a retail credit card?

12. What is a credit limit? How can you increase your credit limit?

13. How might you eliminate the annual fees charged by some credit cards?

14. Discuss how credit card companies offer incentives to use their cards. How else might credit card companies reward cardholders with excellent credit ratings?

15. What is a grace period? How can you use it to your advantage?

16. What is a cash advance? How is it commonly obtained? Discuss interest rates and grace periods with regard to cash advances.

17. When is a finance charge applied to credit purchases? What are teaser rates? What is the common range of interest rates on credit cards?

18. What are the three methods used by financial institutions to calculate finance charges on outstanding credit card balances? Briefly describe how interest is computed under each method.

19. List some items that appear on the credit card statement. What accounts for the difference between your previous balance and your new balance?

20. What should you consider when comparing credit cards?

21. List five tips for using credit cards wisely.

22. Why is paying your credit card balance in full so important? What should you do if you cannot avoid credit card debt? Explain.

23. What is a consumer proposal? When should you use a consumer proposal?

24. Under what circumstances may you be deemed insolvent? What amount is exempt from bankruptcy in your province? How is your spouse affected by your personal bankruptcy?

25. What constitutes identity theft?

26. Is identity theft only perpetrated to acquire money, goods, or services?

27. Aside from the financial losses, what other negative impacts might a victim of identity theft encounter?

28. Name and explain at least three tactics used by identity thieves to obtain information.

29. Can identity theft occur through legitimate access to your personal information? Explain.

30. Discuss the steps you can take to safeguard your personal information, both while you are "offline" and on the Internet.

31. What steps should you take if you become a victim of identity theft?

FINANCIAL PLANNING PROBLEMS

These problems may require a review of Appendix A, Applying Time Value Concepts, for those of you who are not familiar with time value of money problems.

1. You just borrowed $7500 and are charged an interest rate of 8 percent. How much interest do you pay each year?

2. Jarrod has narrowed his choice to two credit cards that may meet his needs. Card A has an interest rate of 21 percent. Card B has an interest rate of 14 percent, but also charges a $25 annual fee. Jarrod will not pay off his balance each month, but will carry forward a balance of about $400 each month. Which credit card should he choose?

3. Paul's credit card closes on the ninth of the month and his payment is due on the thirtieth. If Paul purchases a stereo for $300 on June 12, how many interest-free days will he have? When will he have to pay for the stereo in full in order to avoid finance charges?

4. Chrissy currently has a credit card that charges 15 percent interest. She usually carries a balance of about $500. Chrissy has received an offer for a new credit card with a teaser rate of 3 percent for the first three months; after that, the rate increases to 19.5 percent. What will her total annual interest be with her current card? What will her interest be the first year after she switches? Should she switch?

5. Margie has had a tough month. First, she had dental work that cost $700. Then, she had major car repairs, which cost $1400. She put both of these unexpected expenses on her credit card. If she does not pay her balance when due, she will be charged 15 percent interest. Margie has $15 000 in a money market account that pays 5 percent interest. How much interest would she pay (annualized) if she does not pay off her credit card balance? How much interest will she lose if she transfers the money from her money market account? Should she transfer the money from her money market account?

6. Troy has a credit card that charges 18 percent on outstanding balances and on cash advances. The closing date on the credit card is the first of each month. Last month Troy left a balance of $200 on his credit card. This month he took out a cash advance of $150 and made $325 in purchases. He also made a payment of $220. What will be Troy's new balance on his next credit card statement, taking into account finance charges?

7. Eileen is a college student who consistently uses her credit card as a source of funds. She has maxed out her card at its $6000 limit. She does not plan to

increase her credit card balance any further, but has already been declined for a car loan on a badly needed vehicle due to her existing debt. Her credit card charges 20 percent annually on outstanding balances. If Eileen does not reduce her debt, how much will she pay annually to her credit card company?

Problem 8 requires a financial calculator.

8. Eileen (from Problem 7) wants to purchase a car that costs $12 000. How long would it have taken Eileen to save for the outright purchase of the car if she did not have any credit card debt and used her credit card payments to save for the purchase of the car? Eileen can invest funds in an account paying 8 percent interest.

ETHICAL DILEMMA

Chen recently graduated from college and accepted a job in a new city. Furnishing his apartment has proven more costly than he anticipated. To assist him in making purchases, he applied for and received a credit card with a $5000 limit. Chen planned to pay off the balance over six months.

Six months later, Chen finds that other expenses incurred in starting his career have restricted him to making only minimum payments on his credit card. As well, he has borrowed to the full extent of its credit limit. Upon returning from work today, Chen finds a letter from the credit card company offering to increase his limit to $10 000 because he has been a good customer and has not missed a payment.

a. Discuss the ethics of credit card companies that offer to increase credit limits for individuals who make only minimum payments and who have maxed out their cards.

b. Should Chen accept the credit card company's offer?

FINANCIAL PLANNING ONLINE EXERCISES

1. Go to http://yourmoney.cba.ca/tsam/en/tsam/ credit_101/real_cost/.

   a. Choose the items that you want to buy. Choose to pay using your student credit card and indicate that it will take you six months to pay off the items. How much would you save in interest costs if you had saved for the purchase instead of buying it now with credit?

   b. Go back to the site and purchase everything that you think you could buy from an electronics store using a store credit card. If you took six months to pay, how much extra would you pay? What if you took 12 months to pay? Remember, the answers you get do not include any administration fees or other charges you may pay up front.

2. Go to http://yourmoney.cba.ca/tsam/en/tsam/ credit_101/credit_wise/. Complete the quiz and determine your Credit IQ.

3. Go to www.truecredit.com/help/learnCenter/ welcome/scoreSimulator.jsp?cb=TransUnion.

   a. Adjust credit score scenarios to see the impact that various factors have on your credit score.

   b. What is the impact of a $500 increase in debt? What is the impact of a $500 decrease in debt?

   c. Does your credit score increase or decrease if you obtain a new credit card?

   d. What is the impact of missing the most recent payment on one account?

4. Go to www.fcac-acfc.gc.ca/eng/consumers/ CreditLoanDebt/CreditChargeCards/ CreditChargeCards_e.asp.

   a. Complete the Credit Card Quiz.

   b. Click on Credit Card Comparison Tables, and then on Student Credit Cards. What is the range of annual interest rates? Is the grace period the same for all cards? Is there an annual fee for any of the cards? Which cards offer a rewards program? What other rewards and benefits are available?

   c. Go back to the website and click on Retail Credit Cards. How does the interest rate compare to the student credit cards you just looked at?

5. Go to www.cba.ca/en/viewdocument.asp?fl=3&sl= 65&tl=136&docid=259&pg=1#hologram.

   a. What are the embossing features you find on Visa and MasterCard?

   b. What are the signature panel features you find on Visa and MasterCard?

   c. How can you detect hologram tampering on a Visa or MasterCard?

6. Go to www.abcfraud.ca. Complete the Online Fraud Quiz by clicking on each of the five links located on this page.

ON THE STUDENT CD-ROM FOR THIS CHAPTER YOU WILL FIND:

- Building Your Own Financial Plan exercise and worksheets

- The chapter-end Continuing Case about the Sampson family

- The second part-end Continuing Case about Brad Brooks

   Read through the Building Your Own Financial Plan exercise and use the worksheets to help you determine how to use and select credit.

After reading the Sampson case study, use the Continuing Case worksheets to help the Sampsons make decisions on how to assess, manage, and secure their credit.

After reading the Brad Brooks case study, use the Continuing Case worksheets to provide Brad with some financial planning advice.

Study Guide

Circle the correct answer and then check the answers in the back of the book to chart your progress.

Multiple Choice

1. Which of the following most likely would not be considered an advantage of using credit?
   a. Credit helps you build a good credit score.
   b. Credit is inexpensive to use.
   c. Credit is convenient to use.
   d. Credit sometimes offers added benefits, such as Air Miles and/or travel insurance.

2. Which of the following statements accurately describes the information contained in a credit report?
   a. Public information regarding bankruptcies, judgments, and unsecured loans.
   b. The names of creditors who have made account inquiries with respect to a credit application completed by you and/or your spouse.
   c. A consumer statement showing the details of any explanation you have submitted to the credit bureau regarding a particular account.
   d. Banking information regarding any bank accounts that were opened during the reporting period.

3. The most important factor used in BEACON credit scoring is:
   a. Your credit payment history.
   b. The amount of credit owing.
   c. The length of time that credit has been established.
   d. The types of credit you have established.

4. The president of Warehouse Distributors Inc. is considering the introduction of a retail credit card for use by its customers. Which of the following factors would not be considered an advantage when evaluating whether a retail credit card should be considered?
   a. Warehouse Distributors does not have to pay a small percentage of the proceeds of retail credit card sales to another credit card company.
   b. Customers are able to make larger purchases because they only have to pay a small portion of the balance owed each month.
   c. Customers will be restricted to making purchases at Warehouse Distributors, which restricts their use of credit.
   d. Customers will save on interest costs because the interest rate charged when financing with a retail credit card is normally lower than that charged on non-proprietary cards.

5. Credit cards typically allow a grace period during which you are not charged any interest on your purchases. The grace period is usually about _____ days from the time the credit card statement is "closed" until the bill is due.
   a. 15
   b. 20
   c. 21
   d. 25

6. Which of the following methods for calculating the finance charge takes into account when you pay any part of the outstanding balance?
   a. Average daily balance method
   b. Adjusted balance method
   c. Add-on interest method
   d. Previous balance method

7. A credit card statement includes all of the following pieces of information, except:
   a. The amount you owe the financial institution based on an analysis of your spending pattern over the last 12 months.
   b. The minimum amount you must pay.
   c. The finance charge applied to any credit that exceeds the grace period or to any cash advances.
   d. The amount of credit used this month to make purchases.

8. Doug Bishop, CFP, is a financial adviser who specializes in helping clients get out of credit card debt. Most of his clients have large savings and investment portfolios. Which of the following tips does Doug most likely not provide to this particular client base?
   a. Pay credit card bills before investing money.
   b. Use savings if necessary to pay the credit card bill on time.
   c. If you cannot avoid credit card debt, pay it off before other debt.
   d. Use the services of a credit repair company.

9. Pretexting occurs:
   a. When online users are directed to bogus websites so that their personal information can be collected.
   b. When a store employee steals your credit card number by copying the information contained in the magnetic strip on the card.
   c. When an identity thief poses as an employee of a company with which you conduct business to solicit your personal information.
   d. None of the above.

10. Which of the following are ways in which you can protect yourself from identity theft?
    a. Install and maintain a firewall to guard against unwanted access to your computer and ensure that you have the latest anti-virus software installed.
    b. Be careful when downloading files from the Internet and installing programs. Also take care when reading email with attachments, as email is often used to transmit viruses.
    c. Always ensure you are in a safe online environment before transmitting personal data. Look for the closed-lock or unbroken-key icon on your web browser before entering your credit card number or other sensitive data. If you do not see the unbroken key or closed lock, or if the key is broken or the lock is open, your information is not being securely transmitted across the Internet.
    d. Do not give out your Social Insurance Number and do not carry it with you. Use other forms of identification when possible.
    e. All of the above.

True/False

1. True or False? Instalment credit allows consumers to borrow up to a specified maximum amount, such as $10 000.

2. True or False? Credit accident and sickness insurance ensures that monthly credit payments will continue until the debt is paid if a consumer is unable to work due to an accident or illness.

3. True or False? The primary credit bureaus in Canada will provide a different BEACON score for the same individual.

4. True or False? You should review your credit report from one of the major credit bureaus at least once per year.

5. True or False? Similar to the overdraft protection provided on some chequing accounts at financial institutions, overdraft protection on your credit card makes you aware that you may be over your credit limit before you make a purchase.

6. True or False? The interest rate charged on a cash advance is applied at the time of the cash advance. That is, there is no grace period during which you can pay off the cash advance with no interest charge.

7. True or False? Treat a credit card as a means of convenience, not a source of funds.

8. True or False? An insolvent person is someone who owes at least $10 000 and is unable to pay debts when they come due.

9. True or False? Identity theft is a profitable business that affects Canadians in every province except Manitoba.

10. True or False? When creating a password, it is important not to use your mother's maiden name, your birthday, or any other readily available piece of information.

PART 3

Personal Financing

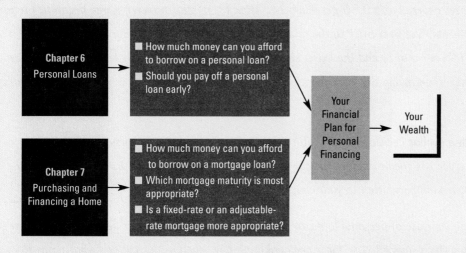

THE CHAPTERS IN THIS PART EXPLAIN HOW YOU CAN USE CREDIT TO obtain funds to support your lifestyle. Chapter 6 describes the process of obtaining a personal loan for a large purchase, such as a car, and the types of decisions you need to make when considering a personal loan. Chapter 7 describes the process of obtaining a mortgage and the types of decisions that you need to make when considering a mortgage loan. Your decisions regarding whether to borrow, how much to borrow, and how to borrow will affect your cash flows and wealth.

Chapter 6

Personal Loans

K aren realized that her car was facing some serious maintenance issues and decided to lease a new car. The monthly lease was $499.35 and she was allowed to drive 24 000 kilometres per year, with extra kilometres charged at $0.30 per kilometre. After 18 months, however, Karen began to tire of the large monthly payments. She went back to the auto dealer to explore the possibility of cancelling the lease. The dealership told her that to end the lease, she must pay $7350. Karen only had two real choices: buying the car outright or continuing the lease for its three-year term. Ending the lease was not a financially attractive option.

You may be faced with a similar decision in your future. The time to make a "lease versus buy" decision is before the lease is signed or before the car is purchased. Once committed to either action, you most likely will need to remain committed to your course.

This chapter focuses on your use of personal loans to finance large purchases. Proper decisions on whether to obtain a personal loan, which source to use for a personal loan, how much to borrow, and what terms to arrange can have a significant impact on your financial situation.

The objectives of this chapter are to:

1. Provide a background on personal loans
2. Outline the types of interest rates charged on personal loans
3. Describe home equity loans
4. Discuss car loans
5. Explain how to decide between financing the purchase of a car and leasing a car
6. Describe the key features of student loans

L.O. 1 BACKGROUND ON PERSONAL LOANS

Consumers commonly obtain a personal loan to finance a large purchase such as a car. A personal loan is different from access to credit (via a credit card) in that it is normally used to finance one large purchase and has a specific repayment schedule. The loan is provided at the time of purchase and is used along with your cash down payment to cover the entire purchase price. You can pay off the personal loan on an instalment basis, for example, by making a payment each month for the next 48 months.

The first step in obtaining a personal loan is to identify possible sources of financing and evaluate the possible loan terms.

Sources of Loans

The least expensive source of financing is usually one or more family members or friends. If they trust that you will repay the loan on time and in full, they may be willing to provide you with a loan that earns the same interest rate as their savings account. You could also offer to pay an interest rate that is a few percentage points above their savings account rate. By borrowing funds from family and friends, you can often get a more favourable rate than you would at a financial institution. Any loan agreement should be made in writing and signed by all parties to avoid possible misinterpretations.

The most common source of financing from a financial institution is a personal loan. Chartered banks, finance companies, and credit unions all provide personal loans. Some finance companies are subsidiaries of automobile manufacturers that finance car purchases. For example, GMAC Financial Services is owned by General Motors. Chartered banks are the primary lenders to individuals who need mortgage loans, the subject of Chapter 7.

The Personal Loan Process

The process of applying for a personal loan from a financial institution involves filling out the application, negotiating the interest rate, and negotiating the loan contract.

Application Process. When applying for a loan, you need to provide information from your personal balance sheet and personal cash flow statement to document your ability to repay the loan. You may need to provide proof of income using either a recent pay slip, T4 slip, or both.

- **Personal Balance Sheet.** Recall from Chapter 2 that your financial condition is partially measured by a personal balance sheet. The personal balance sheet indicates your assets, liabilities, and net worth at a specific point in time. The assets are relevant because they may serve as collateral to back a loan. The liabilities are relevant because they represent your existing debt.

- **Personal Cash Flow Statement.** Your financial condition is also represented by a personal cash flow statement, as discussed in Chapter 2. This statement indicates your income and expenses and therefore suggests how much free cash flow you have on a periodic basis. Lenders use this cash flow information to determine whether you qualify for a loan and, if so, the maximum size of the loan you can afford. An individual with existing loans or credit card debt may have insufficient cash flows to cover the payments on any additional loans.

The key component of most prospective borrowers' personal cash flow statements is their income. Lenders require income documentation, such as a T4 slip, which indicates annual earnings, or pay stubs, which indicate recent salary. Lenders may also require additional information depending on the amount of the loan.

Loan Contract. If the lender approves your loan application, it will work with you to develop a loan contract, which specifies the terms of the loan as agreed to by the borrower and the lender. Specifically, the loan contract identifies the amount of the loan, the interest rate, the repayment schedule, the maturity date, the collateral, and the lender's rights if payments are late or the loan is not repaid.

loan contract
A contract that specifies the terms of a loan as agreed to by the borrower and the lender.

- **Amount of the Loan.** The principal amount of the loan is based on how much the lender believes you can pay back in the future. You should borrow only the amount you will need because you will be charged interest on the entire amount you borrow. The lender may have self-interest when determining the amount of the loan, since it will be collecting interest from you.

- **Interest Rate.** The interest rate is critical because it determines the cost incurred on a personal loan. It must be specified in a loan contract. More information about interest rates is provided later in this chapter.

amortize
To repay the principal of a loan (the original amount borrowed) through a series of equal payments. A loan repaid in this manner is said to be amortized.

- **Loan Repayment Schedule.** Personal loans are usually amortized, which means that the principal of a loan is repaid through a series of equal payments. Each loan repayment includes both interest and a portion of the principal. As more of the principal is paid down, the amount of interest is reduced, and a larger portion of the payment is used to repay principal.

maturity or term
With respect to a loan, the life or duration of the loan.

- **Maturity or Term.** A loan contract specifies the maturity or term, the life or duration of the loan. A longer maturity for a loan results in lower monthly payments and therefore makes it easier to cover the payments each month. For example, the monthly payment on a five-year loan for $16 000 may be $100 less than the payment on a four-year loan for the same amount. With the five-year loan, however, you are in debt for an additional year, and you pay more interest over the life of the loan than you would on the four-year loan. In general, you should select a maturity that is as short as possible, as long as you allow yourself sufficient liquidity. If you find yourself with extra funds during the term of the loan, you should consider paying it off early for two reasons. First, you can reduce the total amount of interest. Second, you will be able to save the money that you would otherwise have used to make the loan payments.

  If you have a variable interest rate loan, the amount of interest you will pay and, therefore, the amount of money you will save on your loan depends on how interest rates change during the term of the loan. In general, you will reduce the total amount of interest you have to pay if interest rates stay the same or decrease. If interest rates increase during the term of the loan, you may end up paying more in interest—even if you decide to pay off the loan early.

- **Security.** Often lenders require borrowers to provide them with some kind of assurance that the borrower will pay back the debt. This assurance can take several forms. The first, and most common, is simply a promise to repay the debt as per the loan agreement. This is an important promise and should not be taken lightly. Other forms of security include assets, either cash that is kept on deposit at the financial institution or personal belongings of which ownership is transferred to the lender by way of a chattel mortgage until the debt is repaid. This is referred to as collateral, defined below.

collateral
Assets of a borrower that back a loan in the event that the borrower defaults. Collateral is a form of security for the lender.

- **Collateral.** A loan agreement also describes the collateral, or assets of a borrower (if any) that back or secure a loan in the event that the borrower defaults. When a loan is used to purchase a specific asset, that asset is commonly used as collateral. For example, if your purchase of a boat is partly financed, the boat would serve as collateral. That is, the lender could repossess the boat if you did not make the loan payments. Some loans are backed by assets other than those purchased with the loan. For example, a boat loan could be backed by investments that you own.

secured loan
A loan that is backed or secured by collateral.

unsecured loan
A loan that is not backed by collateral.

A loan that is backed or secured by collateral is referred to as a **secured loan**; a loan that is not backed by collateral is an **unsecured loan**. In general, you will receive more favourable terms (such as a lower interest rate) on a secured loan because the lender has less to lose in the event that the loan is not repaid. A credit card is one example of unsecured credit, while a car loan or home mortgage represents secured forms of credit.

A payday loan is a short-term loan provided to you if you need funds in advance of receiving your paycheque. To obtain a payday loan, you write a cheque to the lender for the amount of the loan plus interest and fees. You date the cheque for the day when you will receive your paycheque. The payday loan firm will hold the cheque until that time, and will cash it then because your chequing account will have sufficient funds. After you provide this cheque to the payday loan firm, it provides you with a loan in cash or by transmitting funds into your chequing account.

As an example, assume that you need $400 for some immediate purpose, but will not have any money until you receive your paycheque one week from today. You provide the payday loan firm with a cheque dated one week from today. Be aware that firms such as Money Mart, Rentcash, and Cash Money, which provide payday loans, may charge a high rate of interest on these short-term loans and/or fees such as administration costs. The payday loan firm may request that your payment be $440, which reflects the loan of $400 and $40 in interest and/or fees. You are paying $40 more than the loan you received, which reflects 10 percent of the loan amount. The cost of financing this payday loan is shown below.

Cost of Financing = 10 percent × (Number of Days in a Year/Number of Days in Which You Have the Loan)

= 10% × (365/7)

= 521%

While the federal government has usury laws that place a limit on the maximum interest rate that can be charged, the regulation of payday loan firms is shared between the federal and provincial governments. The result is that the payday loan industry has gone largely unregulated in Canada. Under section 347 of the Criminal Code, the maximum interest rate that can be charged on a consumer loan is 60 percent per annum.

There may be a number of reasons as to why people are willing to pay annual interest rates in excess of the maximum allowed by law. With respect to the example above, an individual may take into account the $40 cost of the loan without realizing what this works out to on an annual basis. Individuals also may prefer the convenience of obtaining loans at payday loan outlets. Finally, some people who need money quickly may not be creditworthy and therefore have difficulty obtaining funds from other sources.

You should avoid payday loans. By using your next paycheque to cover a loan payment, you may not have sufficient cash available to make normal purchases afterwards. Thus, you may need another loan to cover your purchases in that period, and this can create a continuous cycle in which your paycheque is always needed to repay short-term loans.

Many individuals may not realize that more affordable coverage is available if they make the effort to shop around. Consider how much you would have paid in interest on $400 if you were able to get a loan that charged you a more reasonable rate, such as 10 percent annually.

Interest Rate for a Seven-Day Period = 10% × (7/365)

= 0.192%

payday loan
A short-term loan provided in advance of receiving a paycheque.

Go to
www.fcac-acfc.gc.ca/eng/
publications/PaydayLoans/
PaydayLoans-6_e.asp

This website provides a comparison of payday loans with other types of short-term loans.

"A high-five isn't binding, sir. You still have to sign a loan agreement."

www.cartoonstock.com.

The interest to be paid is $400 × 0.192 percent, or $0.77. Thus, you would pay less than $1 in interest on a seven-day loan if you were charged a 10 percent annualized interest rate. This is substantially less than you would be charged by a payday loan firm. Often, the interest rate quoted is similar to the rate one would pay to other high-risk lenders. However, when fees are taken into account, the overall cost of the loan is astronomical. You may consider the fees as part of the interest costs, but the lender considers the fees as just that.

The simple solution is to avoid borrowing money until you have the funds to spend. But if you have to borrow, there are alternative methods of financing that are not as expensive. Perhaps you can borrow funds from a friend or family member for a week. Or you may be able to obtain credit through your credit card. While relying on credit card financing is not recommended, it is substantially wiser than financing through a payday loan. To illustrate, assume that you could have used a credit card to make your $400 purchase. Also assume that the interest rate on your credit card is 18 percent. Recall from Chapter 5 that credit cards charge interest on outstanding balances or cash advances on a daily basis. This means that the interest is compounded and therefore the actual interest rate paid would be higher than 18 percent. The interest you would pay on a daily basis if using the 18 percent annual rate amounts to 0.049 percent per day. In this case, your cost of financing would be $400 × 0.049 percent = $0.196 per day or $5.88 per month, assuming 30 days in the month. This financing cost for one month is much lower than the cost of financing when using a payday loan, and in this example the credit card financing lasts three weeks longer than the payday financing period. The website on page 141 also provides other alternatives that you should consider, including using overdraft protection on your bank account or borrowing from a line of credit. It is important to consider all of your options when shopping for emergency credit.

Co-signing. Some borrowers are only able to obtain a personal loan if someone with a stronger credit history co-signs the loan. The co-signer is responsible for any unpaid balance if the borrower does not repay the loan. If the borrower defaults and the co-signer does not repay the loan, the lender can sue the co-signer or try to seize the co-signer's assets, just as if the co-signer were the borrower. In addition, co-signing on a loan can restrict the amount that the co-signer is able to borrow. Co-signing a loan can have significant financial implications for the co-signer if he or she has to reduce some existing credit limits to satisfy the lender. For example, the lender may require the co-signer to reduce his or her credit card limit. Once the co-signer reduces the amount of credit available, he or she may not be able to get it back, even if the loan is paid off by the borrower. In general, co-signing a loan should be an action of last resort. You should never feel pressured or obligated to co-sign a loan.

Focus on Ethics: Predatory Lending

Watch out for dishonest predatory lenders who use illegal practices. Several of the more common predatory lending practices are listed here:

- A lender charges high loan fees, which cause the financing cost to be much higher than the quoted interest rate.

- A lender provides a secured loan with the expectation that the loan will not be repaid because the lender wants to take ownership of the collateral backing the loan.

- A lender stipulates that a loan will only be provided if the borrower purchases insurance or other financial services.

- A lender includes a large balloon payment at the end of a loan that will require additional financing to pay off.

- A loan agreement includes confusing information that does not clearly disclose the borrower's obligations.

Borrowers who accept these kinds of terms often think they have no alternatives, but shopping around for the best loan terms and interest rates is always the best option. You can take several other steps to protect yourself. Be wary of any lenders who pursue you with high-pressure tactics. Short-term offers and up-front application fees also indicate a disreputable lender. Always make sure you understand the loan terms before signing a loan agreement. If you cannot obtain reasonable loan terms, reconsider whether you truly need a loan at this time.

IN-CLASS NOTES

Background on Personal Loans

- Sources of Loans
  - Chartered banks, finance companies, credit unions, family and friends
- Contents of a Loan Contract
  - Amount of the loan
  - Interest rate
  - Loan repayment schedule
  - Maturity or term
  - Security
  - Collateral
  - Payday Loans
- Short-term loans at very high interest rates

_____

_____

_____

_____

_____

_____

_____

L.O. 2   INTEREST RATES ON PERSONAL LOANS

The three most common types of interest rates that financial institutions use to measure the interest due on personal loans are the annual percentage rate, simple interest, and add-on interest.

annual percentage rate (APR)
Measures the finance expenses (including interest and all other expenses) on a loan annually.

Annual Percentage Rate
The annual percentage rate (APR) measures the finance expenses (including interest and all other expenses) on a loan annually.

EXAMPLE

Suppose that you have a choice of borrowing $2000 over the next year from Bank A, Bank B, or Bank C. Bank A offers an interest rate of 10 percent on its loan. Bank B offers an interest rate of 8 percent, but also charges a fee of $100 at the time the loan is granted. Bank C offers an interest rate of 6 percent, but charges a fee of $200 at the time the loan is granted. Exhibit 6.1 shows the APRs.

Bank A offers the lowest APR for a one-year loan. Even though its interest rate is higher, its total financing costs are lower than those charged by the other banks because it does not have any fees. Thus, the APR on its loan is equal to the interest rate charged on the loan. In contrast, the APRs on the loans provided by Banks B and C are much higher than the interest rate charged on their loans because of the fees.

Exhibit 6.1 Measurement of the Annual Percentage Rate

	Interest Expenses	Other Finance Expenses	Total Finance Expenses	Number of Years	Average Annual Finance Expenses	Annual Percentage Rate (APR)*
Bank A	$200	$0	$200	1	$200	$200/$2000 = 10%
Bank B	160	100	260	1	260	$260/$2000 = 13%
Bank C	120	200	320	1	320	$320/$2000 = 16%

*The APR is calculated by dividing the average annual finance expenses by the average annual loan balance.

Simple Interest

simple interest
Interest on a loan computed as a percentage of the existing loan amount (or principal). Compounding is not taken into account.

Simple interest is interest on a loan computed as a percentage of the existing loan amount (or principal). It is measured using the principal, the interest rate applied to the principal, and the loan's time to maturity (in years). The loan repayment schedule is easily determined with a computer or calculator, or even using various websites. If you input the loan amount, the interest rate, and the maturity, the loan repayment schedule will provide you with the following information:

- The monthly payment

- The amount of each monthly payment applied to pay interest costs

- The amount of each monthly payment applied to pay down the loan principal

- The outstanding loan balance that remains after each monthly payment

The size of the monthly payment depends on the size of the loan, the interest rate, and the maturity. The larger the loan amount, the larger the monthly payment. The higher the interest rate, the larger the monthly payment. For a given loan amount and interest rate, the longer the period over which the loan is repaid (for example, 36 months versus 24 months), the smaller the monthly payment. As mentioned earlier, however, the longer the maturity, the more you will pay in interest expenses.

EXAMPLE

You obtain a loan of $2000 that is based on the simple interest method with an annual interest rate of 12 percent and 12 equal monthly payments. Given this information, a computer generates the loan repayment schedule shown in Exhibit 6.2. Notice at the top of the exhibit that each monthly payment is $177.70. Each payment consists of interest and a portion that pays down the loan principal. At the end of the first month, the interest owed on $2000 based on a monthly interest rate of 1 percent is:

$$\text{Interest Owed} = \text{Outstanding Loan Balance} \times \text{Interest Rate}$$

$$= \$2000 \times 0.01$$

$$= \$20$$

Since the total monthly payment is $177.70 and the interest portion is $20, the remainder ($157.70) is applied to pay down the principal. The outstanding loan balance after one month is:

$$\text{Outstanding Loan Balance} = \text{Previous Balance} - \text{Principal Payment}$$

$$= \$2000 - \$157.70$$

$$= \$1842.30$$

At the end of the second month, the monthly interest rate of 1 percent is applied to the outstanding balance to determine the interest payment:

	Interest Payment	Payment of Principal	Outstanding Loan Balance
Month			
			$2000.00
1	$20.00	$157.70	1842.30
2	18.42	159.28	1683.02
3	16.83	160.87	1522.16
4	15.22	162.48	1359.68
5	13.60	164.10	1195.58
6	11.96	165.74	1029.84
7	10.30	167.40	862.44
8	8.63	169.07	693.37
9	6.94	170.76	522.61
10	5.23	172.47	350.13
11	3.50	174.20	175.94
12	1.76	175.94	0

Exhibit 6.2 Example of Loan Repayment Schedule: One-Year Loan, 12 Percent Interest Rate (Monthly Payment = $177.70)

$$\text{Interest Owed} = \$1842.30 \times 0.01$$
$$= \$18.42$$

This same process is followed to determine the amount of interest paid each month. The remainder of each payment of $177.70 is applied to pay down the principal. As each month passes, the outstanding loan balance is reduced, so the interest payment in the following month is reduced. The total monthly payment remains the same for all months, so the principal payment increases over time.

add-on interest method
A method of determining the monthly payment on a loan; it involves calculating the interest that must be paid on the loan amount, adding together interest and loan principal, and dividing by the number of payments.

Add-On Interest

With the add-on interest method, the amount of the monthly payment is determined by calculating the interest that must be paid on the loan amount, adding together interest and loan principal, and dividing by the number of payments.

EXAMPLE

Reconsider the example in which you receive a loan of $2000 to be repaid over one year, but assume that you are charged 12 percent interest based on the add-on method. You first determine the amount of interest owed by applying the annual interest rate to the loan amount:

$$\text{Interest Owed} = \$2000 \times 0.12$$
$$= \$240$$

Next, determine the total payment owed by adding the interest to the loan amount:

Total Payment = $2000 + $240

= $2240

Finally, divide the total payment by the number of monthly payments:

Monthly payment = $2240/12

= $186.67

Notice that your monthly payment with the add-on method is about $9 per month greater than your payment with the simple interest method. Even though the same interest rate is used for both methods, the add-on method is more costly because the interest payment is not reduced over time as you pay down the loan.

IN-CLASS NOTES

Interest Rates on Personal Loans

- **Annual Percentage Rate:** measures the finance expenses, including interest and all other expenses, on a loan annually.
- **Simple Interest:** calculates interest payable as a percentage of the existing loan amount (or principal).
- **Add-on Interest:** calculates monthly loan payments after adding together interest and loan principal.

_____

_____

_____

_____

_____

L.O. 3

HOME EQUITY LOAN

home equity loan
A loan in which the equity in a home serves as collateral.

equity
The market value of your home less any outstanding mortgage balance and/or debts held by others that are secured against your property.

equity of a home
The market value of a home minus the debt owed on the home.

Another type of personal loan is a home equity loan, in which a home serves as collateral. This allows homeowners to borrow against the equity in their homes. In this context, equity refers to the market value of your home less any outstanding mortgage balance and/or debts held by others that are secured against your property. A home equity loan allows homeowners to borrow, within certain limits, any remaining equity in their homes after taking into account their mortgage balance, debts, and other secured obligations. The borrowed funds can be used for any purpose, including a vacation, home renovation expenses, or tuition payments.

The equity of a home is determined by subtracting the amount owed on the home from its market value. If a home has a market value of $100 000 and the homeowner has a mortgage loan (discussed in Chapter 7) with a balance of $60 000, the equity value is $40 000. A home equity loan essentially provides you with a line of credit. That is, it allows you to borrow the amount you need up to a specific credit limit. You pay interest only on the funds that you borrow. You can typically pay the interest owed per month on the amount you borrow and then pay the principal at a specified maturity date. You also may be allowed to pay off the principal at any point prior to maturity and still have access to the funds if you need them in the future. Many financial institutions refer to a home equity loan as a home equity line of credit, or HELOC.

Credit Limit on a Home Equity Loan

Financial institutions provide home equity loans of up to 75 percent (or more in some cases) of the market value of your home minus any outstanding mortgage balance. When the market value of a home increases, they are willing to provide more credit than when the market value remains the same.

If you default on a home equity loan, the lender can claim your home, use a portion of the proceeds to pay off the mortgage, and use the remainder to cover your home equity loan. If the market price of the home declines, the equity you invested is reduced. For this reason, lenders do not like to lend the full amount of the equity when extending a home equity loan.

second mortgage
A secured mortgage loan that is subordinate (or secondary) to another loan.

Since the credit limit calculation for a home equity loan usually takes into account an existing mortgage, a home equity loan can also be considered a second mortgage. A second mortgage is a secured mortgage loan that is subordinate (or secondary) to another loan. In the case of a home equity loan, the primary lender is the financial institution that provided the first mortgage. The secondary lender is the financial institution that provided the home equity loan, or second mortgage. Although you can get a home equity loan from the same institution that provided you with your mortgage, this does not have to be the case. When researching a home equity loan, make sure you shop around.

The following example illustrates how to determine the maximum amount of credit that can be provided on a home equity loan.

EXAMPLE

Suppose that you own a home worth $300 000 that you purchased five years ago. You initially made a down payment of $100 000 and took out a $200 000 mortgage. Over the last five years, your mortgage payments have added $25 000 in equity. Thus, you have invested $125 000 in the home, including your $100 000 down payment. At the same time, your mortgage has decreased to $175 000. Assume that the home's market value has not changed. Also assume that a creditor is willing to provide you with a home equity loan of 75 percent based on the current market value of your home minus the outstanding mortgage balance.

Maximum Amount of Credit That Can Be Provided or Extended

= Market Value of Your Home × 0.75 − Mortgage Balance

= $300 000 × 0.75 − $175 000

= $50 000

EXAMPLE

Using the information provided in the previous example, assume that the market value of your home has risen from $300 000 to $400 000 since you purchased it. Recall that you paid off $25 000 of the $200 000 mortgage loan, so your mortgage balance is $175 000. The credit limit based on the increased market value of your home is:

Maximum Amount of Credit That Can Be Provided or Extended

= Market Value of Your Home × 0.75 − Mortgage Balance

= $400 000 × 0.75 − $175 000

= $125 000

Interest Rate

A home equity loan typically uses a variable interest rate that is tied to a specified interest rate index that changes periodically. The loan contract specifies how the interest rate will be determined. For example, it may be set at the prime rate plus 3 percentage points. The **prime rate** is the interest rate a bank charges its best customers. Because the home

prime rate
The interest rate a bank charges its best customers.

serves as collateral for a home equity loan, the lender faces less risk than with an unsecured loan, thus the interest rate is lower.

As mentioned earlier, the borrower may have to pay only the interest portion on the amount borrowed with a home equity loan. Since the borrower is being charged a variable interest rate, there is always risk that the monthly payment on the loan will increase as interest rates increase. Interest-only payments and variable interest rates may create two problems for the borrower. First, the borrower may never get around to paying down the principal of the loan. Second, interest rates may rise to a point where the borrower is no longer able to afford the minimum interest-only payments. Although home equity loans provide a convenient source of funds for expenses such as vacations, home renovations, and tuition, you should apply for and use this source of credit with caution. Always have a plan for the repayment of the home equity loan. Having a home equity loan is convenient, as you get to decide how much of the credit to use and how and when to pay off the debt. However, you must consider the borrowing costs. Often, home equity lines of credit have variable or floating interest costs. Rates that are steady or even decreasing work in favour of the borrower. However, sometimes rates rise and they may rise dramatically, increasing the costs of borrowing beyond comfort levels. The borrower should monitor interest rates; if rates are expected to rise, the borrower should consider locking in current rates instead of being at risk.

IN-CLASS NOTES

Home Equity Loan

- Allows homeowners to borrow against the equity in their homes
- Home equity = Market value of home − Mortgage balance
- Maximum credit limit = (Market value of home × 75%) − Mortgage balance
- Risks
  - Borrower may never get around to paying down the principal of the loan
  - Interest rates may rise to a point where the borrower is no longer able to afford the minimum interest-only payments

---

Go to
http://ca.autos.yahoo.com

This website provides estimates of what you should pay for any new car based on the features and options you specify.

L.O. 4 CAR LOANS

Another common type of personal loan is a car loan. When you decide to buy a car, you must select the car, negotiate the price, and determine whether to finance the purchase of the car or lease it.

Selecting the Car

Before making any car-buying decisions, you should take into account the following criteria.

Personal Preference. First, determine the type of car you need. Keep in mind that the car you want may be different than the car you need. Reduce the list of available cars by deciding on the size of the car you need. Do you want a small car that is easy to park and gets good gas mileage? Or do you need a minivan to accommodate your children and their sports equipment? You can always screen the cars on your list further by deciding on the size of the engine. Do you want a car with a large engine that has fast acceleration or a car with a small engine that is less expensive?

Price. Stay within your budget. Avoid purchasing a car that will require you to obtain a second job or establish an unrealistic monthly budget to afford the car payments. You should also consider the cost of insurance, maintenance, and gas.

Some college students are on a tight budget, and only have sufficient funds to purchase a very inexpensive car that is likely to require more maintenance in the near future. Newer cars require less maintenance but are much more expensive to purchase. A compromise is a car that is a few years old. While its price may exceed the amount of cash that many students have, financing can be arranged. No matter what your budget is, you should not consider purchasing the most expensive car that financing will allow because the payments will absorb much of your income for the next several years.

Condition. When buying a used car, be sure to assess its condition, beginning with the exterior. Has some of the paint worn off? Is there rust? Are the tires in good shape? Are the tires worn on one side (which may indicate that a wheel alignment is needed)? Next, check the interior. Are the seats worn? Do the electric devices work? Now look under the hood. Is there any sign of leaks? If you are still seriously considering the vehicle, ask the car owner for repair and maintenance records. Has the car been properly maintained and serviced over time? Has the oil been changed periodically?

All of these checks can help you assess a car's condition, but none replaces the expertise of a qualified mechanic. The cost of having a mechanic evaluate the car is worthwhile, because it may enable you to avoid buying a car that will ultimately need expensive repairs.

Insurance. Some cars are subject to significantly higher insurance costs because they are more difficult to repair after accidents, are more expensive, or are common targets of theft. Obtain insurance estimates on any car before making a purchase.

Resale Value. Some cars have a much higher resale value than others. For example, you can expect an Acura to have a higher resale value than a Hyundai. Although you cannot predict the future resale value of a car, you can look at today's resale value of similar cars that were sold years ago. Numerous sites on the Internet, such as http://autos.canada.com, provide information on the current selling price of different makes and models of used cars across Canada. You can use this information to estimate the resale value as a proportion of the original sales price.

Go to
http://money.canoe.ca/rates/

Click on
Car Loans

This website provides
car loan interest rate quotations from various lenders based on the term of the loan and the loan amount.

Repair Expenses. Some cars are subject to much higher repair bills than others. To compare potential repair expenses, review *Consumer Reports* magazine, which frequently estimates the typical repair expenses for various cars.

Financing Rate. If you plan to finance your car purchase through the car dealer, you should compare financing rates among dealers. One dealer may charge a lower price for the car but higher financing costs for the loan. Other dealers may offer an unusually low financing rate, but charge a higher price on the car. When financing through a car dealer, beware the dealer's markup. This occurs when the dealer arranges the loan and then marks up the lender's interest rate without disclosing that markup to the customer. For example, a dealer may obtain financing for your car at 10 percent, but charge you 12 percent. If you obtain financing from a financial institution rather than the dealer, you can easily compare financing rates of various financial institutions on the Internet.

In some cases, you may wish to determine how much you can borrow before you decide which car to purchase. You can use auto loan Internet sites to estimate the maximum amount you can borrow, based on financial information you provide.

EXAMPLE

Stephanie Spratt has been working full-time for about a year and has saved enough money to afford a down payment on a new car. She considers which car to buy based on the following criteria:

- Price. Stephanie's favourite cars are priced in the $35 000 to $45 000 range, but she does not want to borrow such a large amount. She hopes to buy a home within a few years (which will require another loan) and therefore wants to limit the amount she borrows now.

  Stephanie reviews her current assets to determine her down payment amount. She can sell her existing car for $1000. She has accumulated about $4000 in savings, which she would like to maintain for liquidity. She also still has her stock investment, which is worth about $3000 at this time. She would prefer to keep her investment rather than sell it. She decides to use the $1000 from the sale of her used car to make the down payment.

  Stephanie wants to borrow no more than $17 000 to buy a car, so she considers cars in the $16 000 to $20 000 price range. She identifies eight cars within that range, but she does not like three of them and therefore focuses on the remaining five cars. Next, she obtains more detailed information on the prices of the five cars online.

- Resale Value, Repair Expenses, and Insurance. Stephanie also uses the Internet to obtain estimates of the resale value, repair expenses, and insurance rates for each of the five cars. She recognizes that some dealers attempt to attract customers by offering unusually low financing rates, but then price the car higher to offset these low rates. To avoid having to negotiate with the dealership on both the car purchase and the financing arrangement, Stephanie plans to determine her financing costs using a bank website. She inputs information about her salary and loan history and is quickly able to determine the financing rate she would pay.

  Using the Internet, Stephanie obtains the information shown in Exhibit 6.3. Car A has a relatively low resale value after two years. Car D has relatively high repair expenses and service maintenance. Cars A and C have relatively high insurance rates. Therefore, she eliminates Cars A, C, and D. She will choose between Cars B and E.

Exhibit 6.3 Stephanie Spratt's Car Analysis

Car	Expected Resale Value after Two Years (as a proportion of original sales price)	Repair Expenses and Service Maintenance	Insurance
A	Low	Moderate	High
B	Moderate	Low	Low
C	Moderate	Moderate	High
D	Moderate	High	Moderate
E	Moderate	Low	Moderate

Negotiating the Price

When shopping for a car, you have a choice between dealers that negotiate price and dealers that offer a set price for a specific car to all customers. Any dealer that negotiates will purposely price its cars well above the amount for which it is willing to sell the car. For example, the dealer initially may quote the manufacturer's suggested retail price (MSRP). This is also referred to as the sticker price. The strategy of some dealers is to make you think that you are getting a great deal as a result of the negotiations. If any customer is naive enough to pay the full price, the car dealer earns a much larger profit at the customer's expense.

Salespeople are trained to act as if they are almost giving the car away to the customer by reducing the price by 5 to 20 percent. During negotiations, they will say that they must discuss the price you offer with their sales manager. They already know the price at which they can sell the car, but this creates the appearance that they are pleading with the sales manager. During negotiations, the dealer may offer you "free" rust-proofing, a CD system, floor mats, or other features. These features are usually priced very high to make you believe you are getting a good deal.

Negotiating by Phone or Fax. When purchasing a new car, it may be beneficial to negotiate by phone or fax. After deciding on the type of car you want, call or fax a dealer and describe the car and options you desire. Explain that you plan to call or fax other local car dealers, and that you will select the dealer that offers the lowest price. You may also want to emphasize that you will only call or fax each dealer once.

Some dealers may not have the exact car you want, so you may still have to compare features. For example, one dealer may quote a price that is $200 lower than the next-lowest quote, but that car may not be the specific colour you requested. Nevertheless, the process described here can at least shorten the negotiation process. To meet monthly sales quotas, dealers may be more willing to give you a deal toward the end of a month. Therefore, the phone or fax negotiation tactic is most effective when it is used then.

Trade-in Tactics. If you are trading in a car, some dealers will pay a relatively high price for your trade-in, but also charge a high price for the new car. For example, they may pay you $500 more than your used car is worth, but then charge you at least $500 more than they would have charged for the new car if you did not have a trade-in. Attempt to negotiate the price on the new car first, before mentioning that you have a car to trade in.

If you purchase a car from a typical dealer, many of the salespeople will congratulate you as if you have just won the lottery. This is also part of their strategy to make you feel that you got a great deal.

No-Haggle Dealers. Recently, many car dealerships that do not haggle on the price have been established. Buying a car from these dealers is not only less stressful but far less time-consuming. They set one price for a car, so you do not have to prepare for a negotiating battle. Some of these car dealerships still negotiate, however, so before you buy the car you should ensure that the price is no higher than that quoted by other dealers.

The Value of Information. Some car dealers attempt to make higher profit from customers who are not well informed about the price they should pay for a car. To avoid being taken advantage of when purchasing a car, you should become informed. Shop around and make sure that you know the typical sales price for your car. You can obtain this information from *Consumer Reports* and other consumer magazines. Some websites will provide you with a quote based on the car model and features you want. You can do all of your research through your computer. For example, you may be able to obtain the dealer invoice price, which represents the price the dealer pays the manufacturer for the car. The difference between the price quoted by the dealer and the invoice price represents the dealer markup. Be aware that manufacturers commonly provide dealers with a rebate (referred to as a holdback), but dealers normally do not provide this information to their customers. A dealer could charge a price that is only $200 above its dealer invoice, but if it received an $800 rebate from the manufacturer, the price is really marked up $1000.

Purchasing a Car Online. You can buy a car online directly from some car manufacturers or from car referral services such as AutoNet or Driving.ca. Car referral services forward your price request to specific dealerships, which then respond by sending you a quote. In other words, the referral service acts as the intermediary between you and the dealership. If a customer agrees to a price, the car-buying service informs the dealership to deliver the car. Reviews of online buying sites can be found at www.where-can-i-buy-a-car-online.com/data/ca/.

Buying a new car online is not as efficient as buying an airline ticket or a book online. A car is not as standardized as a book, and the personal options can make online correspondence more difficult. At a dealership, a customer can see the difference in the designs of two models of a particular car. It is not as easy to detect this difference on a website. Unlike a website, a dealership can anticipate your questions and arrange a test drive. It is also more difficult to force an online service to honour its delivery promise to you. An online car seller may guarantee you a price for a specific car, but not necessarily meet the delivery date. You have limited ability to enforce the deal because you may only be able to reach the dealer by email or voice mail. You can place more pressure on a local dealership to meet its promise by showing up in person and expressing your concerns.

You can also buy used cars online, through eBay. The purchase of a used car online is subject to the same limitations as the purchase of a new car online. Given the limitations of buying a car online, many customers still prefer to buy a car at a dealership.

EXAMPLE

Stephanie Spratt has decided to use the Internet to shop for her car. Several websites state prices for each of the two new cars she is considering (Cars B and E from the previous example). She reviews specific details of each car, including which has more value relative to its price, the options, available colours, and the delivery dates. She believes that while Car B is cheaper, its value will depreciate more quickly than Car E's. In addition, she can get the exact options and colour she desires with Car E, and it can be delivered soon. She is almost ready to purchase Car E, which is priced at $18 000 including taxes. But first, she wants to consider the financing costs per month and whether to lease the car or purchase it.

Financing Decisions

If you consider purchasing a new car and plan to finance the purchase, you should estimate the amount of the monthly payments. By evaluating your typical monthly income and expenses, you can determine whether you can afford to make the required payments to finance the car. You should conduct this estimate before shopping for a car so that you know how much you can afford. The more money needed to cover the car payments, the less you can add to your savings or other investments.

EXAMPLE

Stephanie Spratt wants to compare her monthly car payments if she borrows $15 000 versus $17 000 to buy a car. She must also decide whether to repay the loan over three, four, or five years. The larger the down payment she makes, the less she will need to borrow. However, she wants to retain some of her savings to maintain liquidity and to use for a future down payment on a house.

Stephanie goes to a bank website where she is asked to input the approximate amount she will borrow. The website then provides the available interest rate and shows the payments for each loan amount and repayment period, as shown in Exhibit 6.4. The interest rate of 7.6 percent at the top of the exhibit is a fixed rate that Stephanie can lock in for the loan period. The possible loan amounts are shown at the top of the columns and each row shows a different repayment period.

Notice that the payments decrease if Stephanie extends the loan period. If she borrows $17 000, her monthly payment would be $530 for a three-year loan, $412 for a four-year

Exhibit 6.4	Stephanie's Possible Monthly Loan Payments (7.6 Percent Interest Rate)	
	Loan Amount	
Loan Maturity	**$15 000**	**$17 000**
36 months (3 years)	$467	$530
48 months (4 years)	363	412
60 months (5 years)	301	341

loan, or $341 for a five-year loan. Alternatively, she can lower her monthly payments by reducing her loan amount from $17 000 to $15 000. Notice that if she takes out a four-year loan for $15 000, her monthly payment is less than if she borrows $17 000.

Stephanie selects the $17 000 loan with a four-year term and a $412 monthly payment. The four-year term is preferable because the monthly payment for a three-year term is higher than she wants to pay. Since the purchase price of the car is $18 000, she will use the proceeds from selling her old car to cover the $1000 down payment.

L.O. 5 PURCHASE VERSUS LEASE DECISION

Go to
www.canadiandriver.com/
tools/index.htm

Click on
Loan Calculator

This website provides a comparison of what your car loan payments would be depending on the term of the loan.

A popular alternative to buying a car is leasing one instead. An advantage of leasing is that you do not need a substantial down payment. In addition, you return the car to the dealer at the end of the lease period, so you do not need to worry about finding a buyer for the car. Leasing will also result in lower monthly car payments since you only have to pay for the portion of the car that you use over the term of the lease.

Leasing a car also has disadvantages. Since you do not own the car, you have no equity investment in it, even though the car still has value. You are also responsible for maintenance costs while leasing it. Keep in mind that you will be charged for any damage to the car over the lease period. Damage may include customizing the car with aftermarket car accessories. Remember, you have no equity investment in the car, and therefore you do not own it.

Some dealers impose additional charges beyond the monthly lease payments. You will be charged if you drive more than the maximum number of kilometres specified in the lease agreement. You may be assessed a fee if you end the lease before the period specified in the contract. You also may have to purchase more car insurance than you already have. Be aware that some of these charges may be hidden within the lease agreement. Hundreds of customers have filed legal claims, alleging that they were not informed of all possible charges before they leased a car. If you ever seriously consider leasing, make sure you read and understand the entire lease agreement.

EXAMPLE

Stephanie Spratt wonders whether she should lease the car she selected, rather than purchasing it for $18 000. If she purchases the car, she can invest $1000 as a down payment, and the remaining $17 000 will be financed by a car loan. She will pay $412 per month over four years to cover the financing. She expects that the car will be worth $10 000 at the end of four years. By purchasing instead of leasing, she forgoes interest that she could have earned by investing the $1000 down payment over the next four years. If she invests the funds in a bank, she would earn 4 percent annually after considering taxes paid on the interest income.

Alternatively, she could lease the same car for $300 per month over the four-year period. The lease would require an $800 security deposit, which would be refunded at the end of the four-year period. She would forgo interest she could have earned if she had invested the $800 instead. At the end of the lease, she would have no equity and no car.

Stephanie's comparison of the cost of purchasing versus leasing is shown in Exhibit 6.5. She estimates the total cost of purchasing the car to be $10 936 (after resale is accounted for) while the total cost of leasing is $14 528. Therefore, she decides to purchase the car.

Exhibit 6.5 Stephanie's Comparison of the Cost of Purchasing versus Leasing

Cost of Purchasing the Car

	Cost
1. Down payment	$1000
2. Down payment of $1000 results in forgone interest income:	
Forgone Interest	
Income per Year = Down Payment × Annual Interest Rate	
= $1000 × 0.04	
= $40	
Forgone Interest over Four Years = $40 × 4	
= $160	160
3. Total monthly payments are:	
Total Monthly Payments = Monthly Payment × Number of Months	
= $412 × 48	
= $19 776	19 776
Total	$20 936
Minus: Expected amount to be received when car is sold in four years	– 10 000
Total cost	**$10 936**

Cost of Leasing the Car for Four Years

	Cost
1. Security deposit of $800 results in forgone interest income (although she will receive her deposit back in four years):	
Forgone Interest	
Income per Year = Down Payment × Annual Interest Rate	
= $800 × 0.04	
= $32	
Forgone Interest over Four Years = $32 × 4	
= $128	$128
2. Total monthly payments are:	
Total Monthly Payments = Monthly Payment × Number of Months	
= $300 × 48	
= $14 400	14 400
Total cost	**$14 528**

Go to
http://strategis.ic.gc.ca/ epic/site/oca-bc.nsf/en/ ca01851e.html

This website provides a comparison of the cost of leasing versus purchasing a car.

The decision to purchase versus lease a car depends greatly on the estimated market value of the car at the end of the lease period. If the expected value of the car in the previous example had been $6000 instead of $10 000 after four years, the total cost of purchasing the car would have been $4000 more. Substitute $6000 for $10 000 in Exhibit 6.5 and recalculate the cost of purchasing to verify this. With an expected market value of $6000, the total cost of purchasing the car would have been higher than the total cost of leasing, so leasing would have been preferable. Remember that some dealers may impose additional charges for leasing, such as a fee for driving more than the maximum kilometres allowed. Include any of these charges in your estimate of the leasing expenses.

IN-CLASS NOTES

Car Loans and Purchase versus Lease Decision

- Selecting a car means considering:
  - Personal preference, price, condition, insurance, resale value, repair expenses, and financing rate
- Negotiate the price
- Make sound financing decisions
- Decide whether to buy or lease

_____

_____

_____

_____

_____

L.O. 6   STUDENT LOANS

student loan
A loan provided to finance a portion of a student's expenses while pursuing post-secondary education.

Another popular type of personal loan is a **student loan**, which is a loan provided to finance a portion of a student's expenses while pursuing a post-secondary education. One of the best sources of information about student loans is the Canada Student Loans and Grants website at www.hrsdc.gc.ca/en/gateways/nav/top_nav/program/ cslp.shtml.

The lender may be the federal government or one of many financial institutions that participate in student loan programs. There are set limits on how much a student can borrow each year, based on the student's assessed need. Provincial programs can be used to cover the difference between the cost of education and what is provided through the federal Canada Student Loans Program. Loan limits are lower for students who are dependants. The repayment schedule is deferred, so full-time students do not begin repaying the loans until they have completed their education and entered the workforce. Part-time students must make interest payments while studying.

Even if you do not complete your education, you still have to pay back your student loans. Failure to do so will damage your credit history. In the event that you declare bankruptcy _within_ 10 years of ceasing to be a student, you must still pay back your student loan. In other words, if you finished your post-secondary education on May 31, 2007, any bankruptcies that you declare after May 31, 2017, will result in your Canada Student Loan being discharged. If you declare bankruptcy before May 31, 2017, you are still responsible for your Canada Student Loan.

IN-CLASS NOTES

Student Loans

- Obtained through the Canada Student Loans Program
- Set limit on how much students can borrow each year, based on assessed need
- Full-time students
  - Loan repayment begins after education is completed
- Part-time students
  - Must make interest payments while studying
- Student loans must still be paid back if you declare bankruptcy within 10 years of ceasing to be a student

_____

_____

_____

_____

_____

_____

HOW PERSONAL LOANS FIT WITHIN YOUR FINANCIAL PLAN

The following are the key personal loan decisions that should be included within your financial plan:

1. How much money can you afford to borrow through a personal loan?

2. If you obtain a personal loan, should you pay it off early?

By making sound decisions, you can avoid accumulating an excessive amount of debt.

STEPHANIE SPRATT'S FINANCIAL PLAN: Personal Loan Management

GOALS FOR PERSONAL FINANCING

1. _Limit the amount of financing to a level and maturity that I can pay back comfortably and on a timely basis._

2. _For any personal loan, I will consider paying off the loan balance as soon as possible._

ANALYSIS

Monthly Income	$2500
– Typical Monthly Expenses	1400
– Monthly Car Loan Payment	412
= Amount of Funds Available	$688

DECISIONS

Decision on Affording a Personal Loan

The financing of my new car requires a payment of $412 per month. This leaves me with $688 per month after paying typical monthly expenses. I can afford to make the payments. I will not need additional personal loans for any other purpose.

Decision on Paying Off Personal Loan Balances

The car loan has an interest rate of 7.6 percent. I expect that my investments will earn a higher rate of return than this interest rate. Once I have accumulated more savings, however, I will seriously consider using my savings and invested funds to pay off the balance of the loan earlier.

Discussion Questions

1. How would Stephanie's personal loan decisions be different if she were a single mother of two children?

2. How would Stephanie's personal loan decisions be affected if she were 35 years old? If she were 50 years old?

SUMMARY

When applying for a personal loan, you need to disclose your personal balance sheet and cash flow statement so that the lender can evaluate your ability to repay a loan. A loan contract specifies the amount of the loan, interest rate, maturity date, and collateral.

The common types of interest rates charged on personal loans are the annual percentage rate (APR), simple interest, and add-on interest. The APR measures the interest and other fees as a percentage of the loan amount on an annualized basis. Simple interest measures the interest as a percentage of the existing loan amount. Add-on interest calculates interest on the loan amount, adds the interest and principal, and divides by the number of payments.

A home equity loan commonly has more favourable terms than other personal loans. It has a relatively low interest rate because of the collateral (the home) that backs the loan. In general, a home equity loan requires interest-only payments based on a variable rate of interest. However, the borrower should plan to repay the principal at some point.

Your decision to purchase a car may require financing. You can reduce your monthly payments on the car loan if you make a higher down payment, but doing this may reduce your liquidity. Alternatively, you can reduce your monthly payments by extending the loan period.

The decision either to purchase a car with a car loan or to lease a car requires you to estimate the total cost of each alternative. The total cost of purchasing a car consists of the down payment, the forgone interest income on the down payment, and the total monthly loan payments. The total cost of leasing consists of the forgone interest income from the security deposit and the total monthly lease payments.

INTEGRATING THE KEY CONCEPTS

Your personal loan decisions not only determine how much money you can spend, but also affect other parts of your financial plan. Your decision to obtain a personal loan can affect your liquidity management (Part 2) because an existing personal loan may reduce the amount of credit you can

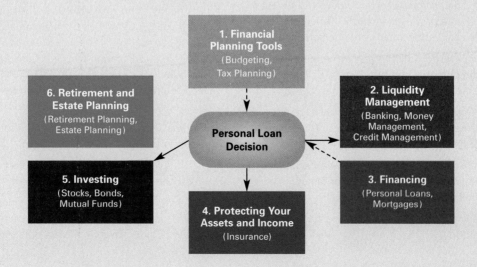

obtain with credit cards. A personal loan also places some pressure on your liquidity needs because you must ensure sufficient funds to cover your monthly loan payments. Personal loans can affect insurance planning (Part 4), as additional life insurance would be needed to cover these loans. If your personal loan decision results in the purchase of a new car, you will also have to obtain insurance (Part 4) because you will need to protect the value of the car and be insured against any liability resulting from it. Personal loans can also affect your investment decisions (Part 5) because it may be wise to avoid investments until the personal loan is paid off. Once you have a personal loan, the decision to invest makes sense only if the return on the investment will exceed the interest rate on the personal loan. Otherwise, you would benefit more from using your money to pay off the loan rather than make investments.

REVIEW QUESTIONS

1. List some possible sources of personal loans. What precautions should be taken with loans from family members or friends?

2. What does the personal loan process involve?

3. What does it mean if a loan is amortized? What do the loan payments represent?

4. What information must borrowers supply to lenders during the loan application process? Why is this information important to lenders?

5. What information is included in a loan contract? How is the amount of the loan determined?

6. Explain how collateral works. Do all loans have collateral? What is the relationship between collateral and interest rates?

7. How does the maturity date of a loan affect the monthly payments? What should you consider when selecting the maturity?

8. Explain the difference between a 10 percent interest rate charged on a payday loan and a 10 percent interest rate charged by a bank on a personal loan.

9. What are your responsibilities if you co-sign a loan? What are the potential consequences of failing to live up to your responsibilities as a co-signer?

10. What is the purpose of the annual percentage rate (APR) measurement? Could lenders with the same interest rates report different APRs?

11. What is simple interest? What information is needed to compute it? What information is contained in a loan repayment schedule?

12. How are payments calculated under the add-on interest method?

13. Why are loan payments under the simple interest method usually lower than those under the add-on interest method?

14. What is home equity? Describe how a home equity loan works. What happens if you default on a home equity loan?

15. How are interest rates calculated for home equity loans? Why may borrowers prefer home equity loans to other loans?

16. What is a second mortgage?

17. What are the potentially negative impacts a borrower may experience because of the interest-only payments and variable interest rates associated with a home equity loan?

18. List the steps in buying a car. What financial criteria should be considered? Discuss each briefly.

19. Why is purchasing a new car online not as efficient as buying a new car at a dealership?

20. Describe some techniques that car salespeople might use in negotiating the price of the car. What should you be aware of at "no-haggle" dealerships?

21. What should be the first step in financing a purchase? Aside from the interest rate, what two factors will have the largest impact on the size of your monthly payment?

22. What are the advantages and disadvantages of leasing? Give some advice to someone considering leasing.

23. Who extends student loans? What are the characteristics of student loans? If you declare personal bankruptcy, will your student loans be discharged?

FINANCIAL PLANNING PROBLEMS

1. Jack needs to borrow $1000 for the upcoming year. West Coast Bank will give him a loan at 9 percent. East Coast Bank will give him a loan at 7 percent with a $50 loan origination fee. First Canadian will give him a loan at 6 percent with a $25 loan origination fee. Determine the total interest and fees Jack will be charged in each case. Which loan should he choose?

2. Beth has just borrowed $5000 on a four-year loan at 8 percent simple interest.

   a. Complete the amortization table on the next page for the first five months of the loan.

   b. What if Beth had made the same loan under the add-on interest method? How would her payments differ? Why is there a difference?

Payment Number	Beginning Balance	Payment Amount	Applied to Interest	Applied to Principal	New Balance
1	$5000.00	$122	$33.33	$88.67	$4911.33
2	a	122	32.74	b	4822.07
3	4822.07	c	d	89.85	4732.22
4	4732.22	122	e	90.45	f
5	4641.77	122	30.95	g	h

3. Tracy is borrowing $8000 on a six-year, 11 percent, add-on interest loan. What will Tracy's monthly payments be?

4. Mary and Marty are interested in obtaining a home equity loan. They purchased their house five years ago for $125 000 and it now has a market value of $156 000. Originally, Mary and Marty made a $25 000 down payment on the house and took out a $100 000 mortgage. The current balance of their mortgage is $72 000. What will their credit limit be if the bank bases it on their equity investment and will lend them 70 percent of the equity?

5. Refer to Problem 4. What will Mary and Marty's credit limit be if the bank uses the market value of equity to determine it and will lend them 70 percent of the equity?

6. Sharon is considering the purchase of a car. After making the down payment, she will finance $15 500. She is offered three maturities. On a four-year loan, Sharon will pay $371.17 per month. On a five-year loan, her monthly payments will be $306.99. On a six-year loan, they will be $264.26. Sharon rejects the four-year loan, as it is not within her budget. How much interest will Sharon pay over the life of the loan on the five-year loan? On the six-year loan? Which should she choose if she bases her decision solely on total interest paid?

7. Refer to Problem 6. If Sharon had been able to afford the four-year loan, how much interest would she have saved compared to the five-year loan?

8. Bill wants to purchase a new car for $45 000. Bill has no savings, so he needs to finance the entire purchase amount. With no down payment, the interest rate on the loan is 13 percent and the maturity of the loan is six years. His monthly payments will be $903.33. Bill's monthly net cash flows are $583.00. Bill also has a credit card with a $10 000 limit and an interest rate of 18 percent. If Bill uses all of his net cash flows to make the monthly payments on the car, how much will he add each month to his credit card balance if he uses it to finance the remainder of the car? What will the finance charges on his credit card be for the first

two months that finance charges apply? (Assume that Bill makes no payments on his credit card.)

ETHICAL DILEMMA

Fritz and Helga work for a local manufacturing company. Since their marriage five years ago, they have been working extensive overtime, including Sundays and holidays. Fritz and Helga have established a lifestyle based on their overtime earnings. Recently, the company lost two major contracts and all overtime has been eliminated. As a result, Fritz and Helga are having difficulty paying their bills. Several months ago, they began using a local payday loan company to pay their bills on time. The first week, they borrowed only a small amount to cover some past due bills. The next week, however, in order to pay back the loan plus interest, they were left with an even smaller amount to pay bills, resulting in a higher payday loan that week. In paying back the second week's loan, their remaining available funds were further reduced. This cycle continued until they were no longer able to borrow because the repayment plus interest would have exceeded their paycheques. Fritz and Helga have had their cars repossessed, their home foreclosed on, and they are preparing to file for bankruptcy.

a. Was the payday loan company being ethical in continuing to lend more and more money to Fritz and Helga each week?

b. What could Fritz and Helga have done to avoid this financial mess?

FINANCIAL PLANNING ONLINE EXERCISES

1. Go to www.canadiandriver.com/tools/index.htm.

a. Click on Loan Calculator. In the fields provided, input 30 000 for Purchase price, 2500 for Down payment, 0 for Trade in, 36 months for Loan term, 6.0 for Interest rate (%), and Manitoba for Province. Click on CALCULATE. What is the monthly loan payment? What is the total interest paid?

b. Return to the link above. Click on Lease Calculator. In the fields provided, input 30 000 for Final negotiated price, 36 months for Total number of months leased, Manitoba for Province, 0 for Security deposit, 2500 for Capitalized cost of reduction, 15 000 for Residual value of car at lease end, and 6.0 for Interest rate. Click on CALCULATE. What is the monthly lease payment? Is the monthly lease payment lower than the monthly loan payment? By how much?

c. What happens to the monthly lease payment if the residual value is decreased? Increased? At the end of a lease, what does the residual value represent? Based on the information you have gathered, is it better to have a relatively high or a relatively low residual value?

2. a. Go to www.bankofcanada.ca/en/rates/ interest-look.html. In the Specific Dates and Rates section, enter January 1, 1997, as your start date and today's date as your end date. Under Quick date, scroll down to Prime business ("prime rate") and check off all boxes to its right. Click on GET RATES under section 1. What is the lowest prime rate in the last 10 years? When was this rate achieved? What is the highest prime rate in the last 10 years? When was this rate achieved? Based on your reading of this chapter, why is it important to understand the history of prime rates?

b. Go to www.bankofcanada.ca/pdf/ annual_page45_page46.pdf. The information displayed is the prime rate in Canada since 1935. In what month and year did the prime rate reach its highest point? During the year 1981, what was the month-over-month increase in the prime rate? Compare the changes in the prime rate during 1981 with the month-over-month changes for the period 1996 to 2006. How would changes in the prime rate in 1981 have affected a borrower with a variable interest rate home equity loan?

ON THE STUDENT CD-ROM FOR THIS CHAPTER YOU WILL FIND:

- Building Your Own Financial Plan exercise and worksheets
- The chapter-end Continuing Case about the Sampson family

Read through the Building Your Own Financial Plan exercise and use the worksheets to determine how best to finance the purchase of a home or a car with a personal loan.

After reading the Sampson case study, use the Continuing Case worksheets to advise the Sampsons on determining and assessing loan maturities.

Study Guide

Circle the correct answer and then check the answers in the back of the book to chart your progress.

Multiple Choice

1. Michelle Laroque has asked you to help her place the following three types of loans in order, highest to lowest, with regard to the cost of financing you would be charged on each.
    1. Secured Loans
    2. Unsecured Loans
    3. Payday Loans
    a. 1, 2, 3
    b. 3, 2, 1
    c. 2, 1, 3
    d. 3, 1, 2

2. You should avoid payday loans for all of the following reasons except:
    a. You may end up creating a continuous cycle in which your paycheque is always needed to repay short-term loans.
    b. If you shop around, you may find more affordable borrowing rates.
    c. You shouldn't spend money unless you have the money to spend.
    d. You may be able to obtain a temporary loan by using your credit card.

3. Which of the following is a predatory lending practice?
   a. A loan agreement includes confusing information that does not clearly disclose the borrower's obligations.
   b. A lender stipulates that a loan will be provided only if the borrower purchases life insurance on the loan.
   c. A lender provides a home equity loan with the expectation that the loan may not be repaid immediately. The borrower may decide to make interest payments only.
   d. A lender charges a loan fee that is higher than the competition.

4. Simple interest:
   a. Measures the finance expenses, including interest and other expenses, on a loan annually.
   b. Is the interest computed as a percentage of the existing loan amount.
   c. Involves calculating the interest that must be paid on the loan amount, adding the interest and loan principal together, and dividing by the number of payments.
   d. Is the interest computed as a percentage of the existing loan amount and finance expenses, including interest and other expenses.

5. Two years ago, Kristal and Joe purchased a home for $300 000. It has increased in value over the past two years and is currently worth $400 000. Their current mortgage balance is $150 000. Calculate the credit limit they would receive on a home equity loan. Assume that the financial institution they deal with will provide home equity loans of up to 75 percent of the market value of the home, less outstanding mortgages.
   a. $150 000
   b. $75 000
   c. $300 000
   d. $225 000

6. When you decide to buy a car, you must _____ the car, _____ the price, and determine whether to finance the purchase of the car or _____ the car.
   a. Select, negotiate, test drive
   b. Negotiate, select, lease
   c. Select, negotiate, lease
   d. Select, select, lease

7. Variable interest rates on a home equity loan may result in the following problem(s):
   a. The value of the home may decrease to the point where the loan is greater than the value of the house itself.
   b. If the borrower chooses a variable interest rate loan, it will become virtually impossible to convert the loan to a fixed interest rate loan.
   c. The borrower may never get around to paying down the principal on the loan.
   d. All of the above.

8. If you plan to finance your car purchase through the car dealer, you should compare financing rates among dealers because:
   a. Dealers may charge different prices for the same car.
   b. Dealers may charge different financing costs for the loan.
   c. Dealers may vary the price by using a markup if you decide to obtain financing from a financial institution that is not affiliated with the dealer.
   d. All of the above.

9. The best way to avoid being taken advantage of when shopping for a car is to:
   a. Only buy a from a no-haggle dealer.
   b. Be an informed buyer.
   c. Find a car dealership you can trust.
   d. Ask a friend for a referral to a reputable car dealership.

10. Which of the following is a disadvantage to leasing versus buying a car?
   a. You are not responsible for maintenance costs while you are leasing a car.
   b. You need a substantial down payment when you lease a car.
   c. You have no equity value in a leased car.
   d. You may need to find a buyer for the car once the lease term is up.

True/False

1. True or False? The least expensive source of financing is a personal loan from a financial institution.

2. True or False? All else being equal, a loan with a longer maturity will have lower monthly payments than a loan with a shorter maturity.

3. True or False? The maximum interest that can be charged on a consumer loan is 60 percent per annum.

4. True or False? The lender has the right to seize the assets of someone who has co-signed a loan. However, if the borrower has a spouse, the lender must first try to seize the assets of the spouse before attempting to seize the assets of the co-signer.

5. True or False? A home equity loan typically uses a variable interest rate that is tied to a specified interest rate index that changes periodically.

6. True or False? The phone/fax tactic for car shopping is most effective when it is used at the end of a month.

7. True or False? Buying an airline ticket online is not as efficient as buying a new car online.

8. True or False? When you lease a car, you will be charged if you drive more than the maximum number of kilometres specified in the lease agreement.

9. True or False? Full-time students do not begin repaying their student loans until they have completed their education.

10. True or False? In the event that you declare bankruptcy within 10 years of ceasing to be a student, you do not have to pay back your student loans.

Chapter 7

Purchasing and Financing a Home

Two years ago, Brian Menke purchased a small home that he could easily afford near the firm where he works. His co-worker Tim Remington also bought a home. Unlike Brian, Tim would need most of his paycheque to cover the mortgage and expenses of his home, but he thought the purchase would make a good investment.

Because his mortgage payment was relatively low, Brian was able to save money during the first year after buying his home. Tim, however, was unable to save any money, and also had large credit card bills on which he was paying only the minimum amount. Tim suddenly realized he could not afford his home. Because the demand for homes had weakened, housing prices had declined since Tim purchased his home. Tim sold his home, but for $20 000 less than he paid for it. He also had to pay the real estate broker a commission of $16 000. Thus, Tim received $36 000 less than the purchase price in the previous year from the sale of his home.

During the second year, the economy improved and home prices increased. Brian's home was now worth $12 000 more than he paid for it. However, the improved economy did not help Tim, who no longer owned a home and was still paying off the debt he had accumulated.

Financial planning made the difference. Brian's strategy was more conservative, which allowed for the possibility that the economy and market conditions could weaken temporarily. Conversely, Tim did not properly estimate how much money he would need to cover the expenses of a home, and also wrongly assumed that home prices would never decline.

Buying your first home is an important personal financial decision due to the long-term and costly nature of the investment. Your decision regarding how much to spend and how much to finance will affect your cash flows for years. This chapter describes the fundamentals of purchasing a home and will help you evaluate your first home purchase.

The objectives of this chapter are to:

1. Explain how to select a home to purchase

2. Explain how to conduct a valuation of a home

3. Describe the transaction costs of purchasing a home

4. Describe the characteristics of various mortgage options

5. Describe the characteristics of a fixed-rate mortgage

6. Describe the characteristics of a variable-rate mortgage

7. Show how to compare the costs of purchasing versus renting a home

8. Explain the mortgage refinancing decision

L.O. 1   SELECTING A HOME

Go to
www.atb.com/dev/calcs/
calcs_loan.asp

Click on
Rent Vs. Own Calculator

This website provides
access to a calculator that
will help you determine
whether it is in your best
interest to rent or own a
particular property.

Buying a home may be the single biggest investment you will ever make, so you should take the decision very seriously and carefully consider several factors. Evaluate the homes for sale in your target area to determine the typical price range and features. Once you decide on a realistic price range, identify a specific home that you desire. You can compare the cost of buying that home to the cost of renting. That way, you can weigh the extra costs against the benefits of home ownership.

An alternative to purchasing a house is to purchase a condominium. In a condominium, individuals own units of a housing complex, but jointly own the surrounding land and common areas (such as parking lots) and amenities (such as a swimming pool). The benefits of a condominium are somewhat different from those of a house. Whereas a house is generally detached, units in a condominium are typically attached, so there is less privacy. Condominium expenses are shared among unit owners, while the owners of a house pay for expenses on their own. Nevertheless, the factors to be considered when selecting or financing a house are also relevant when purchasing a condominium. Thus, the following discussion will use *home* rather than *house* to indicate that it also applies to a condominium.

Relying on a Realtor

Advice from a real estate broker can assist you when assessing homes, deciding whether to buy a home, or determining which home to purchase. Yet you should not rely completely on the advice of real estate agents or brokers because they have a vested interest: they earn a commission only if you purchase a home through them. You should consider their input, but make decisions that meet your needs and preferences. A good real estate agent will ask you about your preferences and suggest appropriate homes.

Using Online Realtor Services

Increasingly, online services are being used to facilitate home purchases. Websites such as www.mls.ca allow realtors to present detailed information about the homes they have available for sale in a database that is made accessible to other realtors. Multiple Listing Service (MLS) is an information database of homes available for sale through realtors who are members of the service. Essentially, MLS is a marketing service that allows you and your realtor to shop online for homes. By using this service, you can narrow down the homes you wish to view in person. The local real estate board administers and operates the local MLS system. The process of buying and selling a home is otherwise unchanged. You would still use the services of a realtor to complete the transaction.

Multiple Listing Service
(MLS)
An information database
of homes available for sale
through realtors who are
members of the service.

Other online services, such as ComFree, www.comfree.ca, allow sellers to list their homes in a database without providing real estate-related services through a realtor. Instead, the transaction would have to be completed by the buyer and seller without the help of a realtor. The advantage of this type of service is that it charges lower or no commissions. Usually, a flat one-time fee will give you a professional online listing, advertising exposure in a newsstand magazine, and access to professional services such as property appraisers, inspectors, and lawyers.

How Much Can You Afford?

When selecting a home, you should first determine how much you can afford to pay per month for a mortgage based on your budget. Once you remove homes that are too expensive from consideration, you should use various criteria to evaluate those you are still considering.

Most individuals pay for a home with a down payment (between 5 and 25 percent of the purchase price) and obtain a mortgage loan to finance the remaining cost. You then pay regular mortgage payments over the term of the loan. Mortgage lenders determine how much they will lend you based on your financial situation and credit history. Various websites can estimate the maximum mortgage you can afford based on your financial situation (such as your income and your net worth). Most financial institutions will issue a pre-approval certificate, which provides you with a guideline on how large a mortgage you can afford based on your financial situation. This certificate also provides you with a mortgage interest rate guarantee that is usually valid for 90 days. This guarantee means that the lender will apply the interest rate used for the calculations regarding the mortgage payment when you are approved for the mortgage. However, it does not guarantee that you will be approved for a mortgage. That is another process.

When you select a home and make an offer, you will usually put a financing condition on your offer to purchase. This tells the seller that you are interested in purchasing the home, but you must first get sufficient financing from a financial institution before you can actually buy it. Again, it is important to remember that the pre-approval certificate does not mean that you have a pre-approved mortgage; you must still apply for a mortgage when you have found the home you would like to purchase.

In most cases, financial institutions will provide you with a mortgage loan only if your gross debt service ratio (GDSR) is no more than 32 percent. Your gross debt service ratio (GDSR) is your mortgage-related debt payments—including mortgage loan repayments, heating costs, property taxes, and any condo fees—divided by your total monthly gross household income. In addition, financial institutions will normally require that your total debt service ratio (TDSR) be no more than 40 percent. Your total debt service ratio (TDSR) is your mortgage-related debt payments plus all other consumer debt payments divided by your total monthly gross household income. These generalizations do not apply to everyone, as other financial information and spending habits of the homeowners should also be considered. In addition, financial institutions base the mortgage on the property as well. The home must be worth the value of the mortgage, at the very least, as it does serve as security.

pre-approval certificate Provides you with a guideline on how large a mortgage you can afford based on your financial situation.

gross debt service ratio (GDSR) Your mortgage-related debt payments—including mortgage loan repayments, heating costs, property taxes, and any condo fees—divided by your total monthly gross household income.

total debt service ratio (TDSR) Your mortgage-related debt payments plus all other consumer debt payments divided by your total monthly gross household income.

EXAMPLE

Stephanie Spratt has asked her bank to help her determine whether she qualifies for a mortgage. As part of its initial assessment, the bank has to calculate her GDSR and TDSR. Based on its discussion with Stephanie, the bank gathers the following information:

Current monthly gross income = $3500	
Monthly mortgage payments = $900	
Monthly heating costs = $80	
Monthly property taxes = $100	
Monthly credit card payment = $200	
GDSR = ($900 + $80 + $100) ÷ $3500 = 0.3086 × 100 = 30.86%	
TDSR = ($900 + $80 + $100 + $200) ÷ $3500 = 0.3657 × 100 = 36.57%	

Stephanie's GDSR and TDSR are both below the allowable maximum. Based on this initial assessment, it appears that she is eligible for a mortgage.

"You see that dark, spooky image on the screen? That's your credit history coming back to haunt you."

Affordable Down Payment

You can determine your maximum down payment by estimating the market value of the assets you are willing to convert to cash for a down payment and for transaction costs (such as closing costs) incurred when obtaining a mortgage. Be sure to maintain some funds for liquidity purposes to cover unanticipated bills and closing costs.

Saving for the down payment on your first home is a daunting task. It takes planning and discipline. Currently, a federal program can help first-time home buyers reach their goals more quickly. The Home Buyers' Plan allows you to "borrow" up to $20 000 from your RRSP, interest-free. You then have 15 years to pay back this "loan." The advantage of using your RRSP to fund part of your down payment is the RRSP's tax-deferral feature.

This program will be discussed further in Chapter 15.

Go to
www.cmhc-schl.gc.ca/en/
co/buho/buho_005.cfm

This website provides an estimate of how much you could borrow to finance a home, based on your income and other financial information.

Affordable Monthly Mortgage Payments

How large a monthly mortgage payment can you afford? Refer to your cash flow statement to determine how much net cash flow you have to make a mortgage payment. If you purchase a home, you will no longer have a rent payment, so that money can be used as part of the mortgage payment. You should also be aware, however, that owning a home entails periodic expenses (such as property taxes, homeowner's insurance, and home maintenance repairs). You should not plan to purchase a home that will absorb all of your current excess income. The larger your mortgage payments, the less you can add to your savings or other investments, the lower your liquidity, and the greater your overall financial risk. You must consider possible "what ifs."

EXAMPLE

Stephanie Spratt just received an unexpected bonus and a promotion from her employer. After assessing her financial situation, she decides that she may want to purchase a home in the near future. She has about $41 250 in liquid assets for use toward a down payment and transaction costs. She evaluates her personal cash flows. Since she would no longer need to pay rent for her apartment, she can afford to allocate $900 a month to mortgage payments. She begins to look at homes for sale in the range of $160 000 to $180 000. Once she identifies a home she may want to purchase, she will obtain estimates of the required down payment, the transaction costs, and the mortgage payment, as well as an estimate of additional closing costs.

Criteria Used to Select a Home

The most important factors to consider when selecting a home are identified here.

- *Price.* Stay within your budget. Avoid purchasing a home you cannot afford. Although your favourite home may have ample space and a large yard, it may not be worth the stress of struggling to make the monthly mortgage payments. A pre-approval certificate is particularly useful in controlling the price you pay for a house. If you know in advance how large of a mortgage the bank is willing to provide, you can limit your search to homes within your price range. Be sure, though, to use the bank's information only as a starting point. Lenders have a vested interest in maximizing loan amounts. Therefore, the mortgage amount they suggest may end up cramping your lifestyle.

- *Convenient location.* Focus on homes in a convenient area so that you can minimize commuting time to work or travel time to other activities. You may save 10 or more hours of travel time a week through a convenient location. Remember, as well, that you must take into account additional commuting costs if you buy a home some distance from work.

- *Maintenance.* Newer homes tend to need fewer and less costly repairs than older homes. For example, replacing the hot water tank, a major appliance, or the shingles on the roof must be considered when buying an older home. This should not be as much of a concern with a newer home. A home with a large yard may require more maintenance depending on how you landscape the yard.

  In condominium buildings, residents share common areas, such as a swimming pool or tennis court. They normally pay a fixed monthly fee to cover the costs of maintaining these common areas. In addition, they may be assessed an extra cost to maintain the structure of the building, which can include a new roof or other repairs. These costs may be very costly and/or may result in an increase to your condo fee.

- *School system.* If you have children, the reputation of the local school system is very important. Even if you do not have children, the resale value of your house benefits from a good school system.

- *Insurance.* When you own a home, you need to purchase homeowner's insurance, which covers burglary, damage, or fire. The cost of insurance varies among homes. It is higher for more expensive homes and homes in high-risk areas (such as flood zones) because the replacement value of an expensive home is higher and homes in high-risk areas are exposed to a higher probability of claims.

- *Taxes.* Taxes are imposed on homes to pay for local services, such as the local school system, the local park system, and garbage collection. Taxes vary substantially among locations.

- *Resale value.* The resale value of a home depends greatly on its location. Most homes with similar features within a specific subdivision or neighbourhood are in the same range. Although home prices in a given subdivision tend to move in the same direction, price movements can vary substantially among homes. For example, homes in a subdivision that is within walking distance of a school may be worth more than comparable homes several kilometres from the school.

  You cannot accurately predict the future resale value of a home, but you can evaluate today's resale value of similar homes that were sold years ago in the same location. Information about home prices is provided on numerous websites. Be aware, however, that the rate of increase in home prices in previous years does not necessarily serve as a good predictor of the future.

  The rate of increase in home prices is difficult to predict because of the number of factors involved in determining resale value. Home prices are very dependent on economic and market conditions—in particular, positive economic growth is associated with an increase in real GDP. Over the last few years, the combination of increasing real GDP, low mortgage rates, net migration, and strong consumer confidence in the Canadian economy has fuelled increasing prices for homes throughout Canada.

  Keep in mind that when you use a realtor to sell a home (as most people do), you will pay the realtor a commission that is usually about 7 percent of the selling price on the first $100 000, and 3 percent on the remaining price. Thus, if you resell your home for $200 000, you will probably pay a commission of about $7000 on the first $100 000 and $3000 on the next $100 000. As a result, you will receive about $190 000, minus closing costs, which are discussed below. The buyer of a home does not pay a commission.

- *Personal preferences.* In addition to the general criteria described above, you will have your own personal preferences regarding features such as the number of bedrooms, size of the kitchen, and size of the yard.

Focus on Ethics: Disclosing Defects

For both the buyer and the seller, the sale of a home is stressful due to the large amount of money involved. Concerns about unethical behaviour only add to the tension. For example, there are many cases of sellers who did not disclose problems (such as a leaky roof or cracked foundation) with their homes.

As a seller, the law requires that you fully disclose any defect that may affect the value of the home. In addition to being the legal thing to do, disclosure is the moral thing to do. You would hope that a seller would be completely honest with you, so you should treat a potential buyer in the manner that you would wish to be treated. As well, if any problem arises shortly after you sell a house, the buyer can sue you for any misrepresentations.

IN-CLASS NOTES

Selecting a Home and How Much Can You Afford?

- Decide on the type of home you would like:
  - House or condominium
- Consider the input of a realtor
- Consider using online realtor services
  - Multiple Listing Service (MLS), ComFree
- Decide how much you can afford for a down payment and monthly mortgage payments
- Determine your criteria for selecting a home

_____

_____

_____

_____

_____

L.O. 2 VALUATION OF A HOME

You should use the criteria described earlier to screen your list of desirable homes so that you can spend time analyzing the advantages and disadvantages of three or four particular homes. You will probably find some homes that meet all of your criteria but are simply overpriced and therefore should not be considered. Keeping an objective stance is essential, as an emotional stance could lead to overspending.

Market Analysis

market analysis
An estimate of the price of a home based on the prices of similar homes in the area.

You can conduct a market analysis, in which you estimate the price of a home based on the prices of similar homes in the area. The market value can be estimated by multiplying the number of square feet in a home by the average price per square foot of similar homes in the area. A real estate broker or appraiser may also provide you with a valuation.

EXAMPLE

Stephanie Spratt finds the selling prices of three other homes in the same area, with a similar lot size, and of about the same age as the home she wants to purchase. The purchase prices are shown in the second column of Exhibit 7.1.

She recognizes that homes in an area vary in price due to their size. She determines the price per square foot by dividing each home's price by its square footage, as shown in the third column. Then she determines that the average price per square foot of the three homes is $139, as shown at the bottom of the exhibit.

Exhibit 7.1 Using a Market Analysis to Purchase a Home		
House Size	**Price**	**Price per Square Foot**
1250 square feet	$170 000	$170 000/1250 = $136
1275 square feet	$180 000	$180 000/1275 = $141
1150 square feet	$160 000	$160 000/1150 = $139
Average price per square foot = ($136 + $141 + $139)/3 = $139		

Since the home that Stephanie wants to purchase is 1300 square feet, she estimates its market value to be:

$$\text{Market Value of Home} = \text{Average Price per Square Foot} \times \text{Square Feet of Home}$$
$$= \$139 \times 1300$$
$$= \$180\ 700$$

She estimates the price of this home at $180 700. Although she will consider other factors, this initial analysis gives her some insight into what the home is worth. For example, the real estate broker told her that the owner of the home has already moved and wants to sell it quickly. Stephanie considers making an offer of $165 000, but she first needs to determine the costs she will incur as a result of purchasing the home.

Effects of Business Activity and Zoning Laws

The value of a home also depends on the demand for homes in that area or subdivision, which can vary in response to business activity and/or zoning laws.

Business Activity Nearby. When a large firm moves into an area, people hired for jobs at that firm search for homes nearby. As a result, demand for homes in the area increases, and home prices may rise as well. Conversely, when a large firm closes its facilities, home prices in that area may decline as homeowners who worked there attempt to sell their homes. The large supply of homes for sale relative to demand may cause homeowners to lower their prices to find willing buyers.

Zoning Laws. Locations are zoned for industrial use or residential use. When zoning laws for a location change, its desirability may be affected. Homes near areas that have just been zoned for industrial use become less desirable. Therefore, the demand for homes in these areas may decline, causing prices of homes to decline as well.

Zoning laws also change for school systems. The value of a subdivision can change substantially in response to a change in the public schools that the resident children attend. Proximity to schools can increase home values, while increased distance from schools often lowers home values.

Obtaining a Second Opinion on Your Valuation

If your valuation leads you to believe that a particular home is undervalued, you may want to get a second opinion before you try to purchase that home. If you are using a real estate broker to help you find a home, that broker may conduct a valuation of the home and offer suggestions about the price you should be willing to offer. Be aware, however, that although brokers are experienced at valuing homes, some brokers provide a valuation that is intended to serve the seller rather than the buyer. That is, they may overestimate the value so that potential buyers are convinced that the home is worth buying. In this way, the brokers can ensure that a home will sell and that they will receive a commission. Although many real estate brokers are honest and will provide an unbiased estimate, you should always conduct your own valuation and carefully assess the broker's valuation.

Negotiating a Price

Once you have finished your valuation and are convinced that you should buy a particular home, you need to negotiate a price with the seller by making an offer. Some homes are initially priced above the amount the seller will accept. As with any investment, you want to make sure that you do not pay more than you have to for a home.

You may consider the advice of your real estate broker on the offer you should make. Most sellers are willing to accept less than their original asking price, depending on local market conditions. Once you decide on an offering price, you can submit an offer in the form of a contract to buy the home, which must be approved by the seller. Your real estate broker takes the contract to the seller and serves as the intermediary between you and the seller during the negotiation process.

The seller may accept your offer, reject it, or suggest that you revise it. If the asking price is $200 000 and you offer $190 000, the seller may reject that offer but indicate a willingness to accept an offer of, say, $196 000. Then the decision reverts to you. You can agree, reject that offer, or revise the contract again. For example, you may counter by offering $192 000. The contract can go back and forth until the buyer and seller either come to an agreement or decide that it is no longer worthwhile to pursue an agreement. The contract stipulates not only the price, but also other conditions requested by the buyer, such as the completion of a home inspection, the date on which the buyer will be able to move into the home (known as the possession date), and the approval of a mortgage by the bank.

IN-CLASS NOTES

Valuation of a Home

- Conduct a market analysis
- Evaluate the effects of business activity and zoning laws on valuation
- Obtain a second opinion if your analysis suggests the home is undervalued
- Negotiate a price
  - Consider the advice of a realtor on the offer you should make
  - Most sellers will accept less than the asking price

_____

_____

_____

_____

_____

L.O. 3 TRANSACTION COSTS OF PURCHASING A HOME

Once you start the offer process, you should apply for a mortgage from a financial institution. As discussed earlier, this process is different than the pre-approval certificate process in that it requires the completion of a detailed loan application. The loan application process requires that you summarize your financial condition, including your income, assets, and liabilities. You will need to provide proof of income, such as a T4 slip, an employment letter, or a recent paycheque. The lender will sometimes check your financial condition by contacting your employer to verify both your employment and your present salary. The lender will pull a credit report as well.

In addition to applying for a mortgage, you need to plan to cover the transaction costs of purchasing the home. These include the down payment and closing costs.

Exhibit 7.2 CMHC Mortgage Loan Insurance Premiums

Financing Required	Premium % of Loan Amount
Up to and including 65%	0.50%
Up to and including 75%	0.65%
Up to and including 80%	1.00%
Up to and including 85%	1.75%
Up to and including 90%	2.00%
Up to and including 95%	2.75% to 2.90%
Up to and including 100%	3.10%

Source: www.cmhc.ca/en/co/moloin/moloin_005.cfm (accessed June 21, 2007). Canada Mortgage and Housing Corporation (CMHC). Table of CMHC Mortgage Loan Insurance Premiums, www.cmhc.ca, 2007. All rights reserved. Reproduced with the consent of CMHC. All other uses and reproductions of this material are expressly prohibited.

Down Payment

When you purchase a home, you use your money to make a down payment and pay the remaining amount with financing. Your down payment represents your equity investment in the home.

conventional mortgage A mortgage where the down payment is at least 25 percent of the home's appraised value.

A conventional mortgage refers to a mortgage where the down payment is at least 25 percent of the home's appraised value. The lender expects you to cover a portion of the purchase price with your own money because the home serves as collateral to back the loan. The lending institution bears the risk that you may default on the loan. If you are unable to make your mortgage payments, the lender can repossess the home by applying for foreclosure through the legal system. Foreclosure allows the lender to take possession and sell the home with the permission of the courts.

If the home's value declines over time, however, a creditor may not obtain all of the funds it initially loaned. Your down payment provides a cushion in case the value of the home declines. The lender could sell the home for less than the original purchase price and still recover the full amount of the mortgage loan. If you are unable to make a down payment of at least 25 percent, the lender will still give you a mortgage. This type of mortgage is referred to as a high ratio mortgage. A high ratio mortgage refers to a mortgage where the down payment is less than 25 percent of the home's appraised value.

high ratio mortgage A mortgage where the down payment is less than 25 percent of the home's appraised value.

Since the cushion provided by the down payment is much smaller with a high ratio mortgage, the lender will require that your mortgage be insured. Mortgage insurance can be purchased from the Canada Mortgage and Housing Corporation (CMHC), www.cmhc.ca, or Genworth Financial Canada, www.genworth.ca. With insured mortgages, a traditional lender extends the loan, but the mortgage insurer insures it in the event of default, thereby protecting the lender's investment. The mortgage insurer will charge the lender a mortgage loan insurance premium. The lender will add this premium to the cost of your mortgage. Exhibit 7.2 displays the premium charged by CMHC based on the amount of financing required.

EXAMPLE

Stephanie Spratt makes a $15 500 down payment on a $220 000 home. Her lender determines that she will need a mortgage for the remaining balance of the purchase price. In addition, since the mortgage is a high ratio mortgage, the lender will need to purchase mortgage loan insurance. The lender will pass on the mortgage loan insurance premium to Stephanie by adding it to her mortgage. Stephanie's mortgage payments will be calculated based on the adjusted mortgage balance.

Mortgage Required = $220 000 − $15 500 = $204 500

Mortgage Size as a Percentage of Lending Value = $204 500 ÷ $220 000 = 0.9295 × 100 = 92.95%

Stephanie has used her own money to make the $15 500 down payment. As a result, the mortgage loan insurance premium is calculated using a rate of 2.75 percent. If Stephanie had borrowed any portion of the down payment from a bank and/or another source, or if she had received a cash-back incentive from the lender, the mortgage loan insurance premium rate would be 2.90 percent.

Mortgage Loan Insurance Premium = $204 500 × 2.75% = $5623.75

Adjusted Mortgage Balance = $204 500 + $5623.75 = $210 123.75

In rare situations, the lender may require mortgage insurance even though the down payment is greater than 25 percent. For example, the lender may determine that there is a high probability that the borrower may default on the mortgage based on his or her financial history. In this case, CMHC will provide mortgage loan insurance at a premium of 0.5 percent on mortgage amounts up to and including 65 percent of the home's selling price.

vendor take-back mortgage
A mortgage where the lender is the seller of the property.

An alternative to a high ratio mortgage is a vendor take-back mortgage. A vendor take-back mortgage is a mortgage where the lender is the seller of the property. In this case, the buyer will make mortgage payments directly to the seller. The title of the property transfers to the buyer. If the buyer defaults on the mortgage payments, the property transfers back to the seller.

EXAMPLE

As in the previous example, Stephanie Spratt has a $15 500 down payment. Instead of applying for a mortgage for the balance through her bank, Stephanie could arrange a vendor take-back mortgage with the seller. If the seller has a mortgage of $160 000 on the property at the time of sale, the seller could arrange a second mortgage with Stephanie for the balance she needs to purchase the home. Using the amounts in the previous example, a second mortgage for the amount of $44 500 would be arranged between Stephanie and the seller.

Second Mortgage Required = $220 000 − ($160 000 + $15 500) = $44 500.

Stephanie's monthly mortgage payments will cover the existing mortgage payment currently paid by the seller plus the payments associated with the second mortgage.

This financing arrangement may be better for the buyer than a high ratio mortgage because total interest costs for the first and second mortgages may be lower than those associated with a high ratio mortgage. The incentive for the seller to set up a vendor take-back mortgage is that the interest earned by providing a second mortgage to the buyer is usually higher than what the seller could earn from other investments. It is important for the buyer to read carefully any contract about a vendor take-back mortgage, as legal obligations may be more restrictive and less flexible.

Closing Costs

A borrower incurs various fees when purchasing a home. These fees are often referred to as closing costs. The most important fees are identified here.

home inspection
A report on the condition of the home.

Home Inspection Fee. A home inspection is a report on the condition of the home. It should be a condition in your offer to purchase whenever you are not the original owner of the home. Home inspectors will evaluate the structure and systems of the home on which you have made an offer. If the home requires any major repairs, you can re-evaluate your decision to purchase. Any conditions in your offer to purchase that are not met to your satisfaction will allow you to take back your offer and have your deposit refunded. A home inspection commonly costs around $300.

Appraisal Fee. An appraisal is used to estimate the value of the home and thus protects the financial institution's interests. If you are unable to make your monthly mortgage payments, the financial institution can sell the home to recoup the loan it provided. The appraisal fee commonly ranges between $150 and $250. The appraisal value is used to calculate the mortgage size and should be no less than the purchase price, if not more.

Real Property Report. A real property report, also known as a land survey, is a legal document that clearly illustrates the location of significant visible improvements relative to property boundaries. You should ask for a real property report to ensure that any improvements, such as a deck, are in conformance with municipal property improvement guidelines. A real property report commonly ranges between $700 and $1000.

Land Transfer Tax. Some provinces charge a land transfer tax that must be paid by the purchaser. This tax is levied when property is sold. For example, in Ontario the land transfer tax for a $300 000 home is 1.5 percent. In addition to the tax, a registration fee may be applied. Land transfer tax is also charged in British Columbia, Manitoba, Nova Scotia, and Quebec.

Legal Fees and Disbursements. The purchase of a home should be completed using the services of a lawyer. If you are obtaining a mortgage on a property, the bank will require that the mortgage loan be disbursed in accordance with the mortgage loan agreement. In addition, a lawyer will ensure that a property is registered correctly with your local land titles office. In some provinces, property can be transferred without the services of a lawyer if no mortgage is involved. This type of property transfer is not recommended since property transactions require a good understanding of real estate law. Legal fees and disbursements commonly range between $1000 and $2500.

GST. You are normally required to pay GST on the purchase of a brand new home.

Title Insurance. Title insurance protects the insured against loss resulting from title defects and defects that would have been revealed by an up-to-date survey/real property report or building location certificate. Sometimes the real property report might be outdated or non-existent. Title insurance protects you if it is later determined that the real property report is inaccurate. If the seller does not provide you with a current real property report, you should purchase title insurance. Title insurance commonly ranges between $300 and $400.

interest adjustment
Occurs when there is a difference between the date you take possession of your home and the date from which your lender calculates your first mortgage payment.

Interest Adjustment. An interest adjustment occurs when there is a difference between the date you take possession of your home and the date from which your lender calculates your first mortgage payment. For example, Surj and Pam have purchased a home and received a mortgage from their bank in the amount of $200 000. They will take possession of their new home on April 15. On the possession date, the bank will advance the mortgage proceeds to the couple's lawyer. Surj and Pam will be charged interest starting on April 15. The mortgage documents indicate that the couple will make monthly mortgage payments on the first of each month. As a result, the bank will calculate the first mortgage payments starting on May 1. The interest adjustment will be calculated as the amount of interest that accumulates between April 15 and May 1. The bank will withdraw the accumulated interest for this period from the bank account that Surj and Pam specified when they took out the mortgage. As per the mortgage documents, regular mortgage payments will begin on the first of each month, starting with May 1.

Prepaid Property Tax and Utility Adjustments. If the seller has prepaid some bills before the closing date, you must reimburse the seller for the payments made. For example, if the seller has prepaid property tax for the entire calendar year on a home the buyer takes possession of on July 1, the buyer must reimburse the seller for six months' worth of taxes paid. In contrast, the buyer may end up in a position where the taxes and/or utility bills are in default. In this case, the buyer may be forced to cover these taxes and/or bills. The end result is that the adjustment for property tax and utilities may be higher than the buyer expected. Any unexpected bills may result in immediate financial difficulties for the buyer, therefore it is important to be aware of the status of bills that should have been paid before finalizing the purchase of a home.

Homeowner's Insurance. Homeowner's insurance protects you against financial loss that may result from damage to your home or its contents. It is discussed in more detail in Chapter 8. The cost of homeowner's insurance primarily depends on the size of the home and commonly ranges between $300 and $500 per year. The lender normally will require you to purchase property or homeowner's insurance before the mortgage proceeds are advanced to your lawyer. As part of the mortgage process, the lender will request proof that you have purchased this insurance.

Loan Protection Life and Disability Insurance. Loan protection life and disability insurance protects the lender against financial loss as a result of injury, illness, or death to you, the borrower. It is commonly referred to as creditor insurance. Creditor insurance is discussed in more detail in Chapter 10. The cost of this type of insurance varies based on the age of the applicant(s) and the size of the mortgage.

Exhibit 7.3 displays examples of closing costs and their approximate cost. Both the closing costs and the down payment are due after the offer for the home has been accepted at the time of the closing. During the closing, the title for the home is transferred to the buyer, the seller is paid in full, and the buyer takes possession of the home.

Exhibit 7.3 Examples of Closing Costs and Their Approximate Cost	
Cost	**Approximate Cost**
Home inspection fee	$300
Appraisal fee	$150 to $250
Real property report/land survey	$700 to $1000
Legal fees and disbursements	$1000 to $2500
GST	6%
Title insurance	$300 to $400
Interest adjustment	$100 to $1000
Prepaid property tax and utility adjustments	$300 to $500
Homeowner's insurance	$300 to $500
Loan protection life and disability insurance	Costs vary based on age of applicant(s)

Source: Adapted from *Gimme' Shelter* Brochure, ATB Financial. Reprinted with permission of ATB Financial.

EXAMPLE

Recall that Stephanie Spratt is considering making an offer of $165 000 on a house. She wants to determine what her transaction costs would be. She is planning to make a down payment of $41 250 and borrow $123 750. She contacted her financial institution for information about obtaining a mortgage loan and learned that if she applied for a $123 750 mortgage, her financial institution would charge the following:

- $200 for an appraisal
- $150 application fee (the bank has indicated that it would waive this fee)

In addition to her down payment, Stephanie has estimated her closing costs to be:

- $1265 for the provincial land transfer tax, including registration fee
- $300 for a home inspection

- $1200 for legal fees and disbursements
- $400 for title insurance
- $300 for homeowner's insurance
- $200 for other fees

Thus, the total closing costs would be:

Home Inspection	$ 300
Appraisal Fee	200
Provincial Land Transfer Tax	1265
Legal Fees and Disbursements	1200
Title Insurance	400
Homeowner's Insurance	300
Other Fees	200
Total	$3865

Stephanie will need a down payment of $41 250 and $3865 for closing costs to purchase the home.

IN-CLASS NOTES

Transaction Costs of Purchasing a Home

When you apply for a mortgage you will:

- Make a down payment
- Incur closing costs:
    - Home inspection and appraisal fee
    - Real property report
    - Land transfer tax
    - Legal fees and disbursements
    - GST
    - Title insurance
    - Interest adjustment
    - Prepaid property tax and utility adjustments
    - Homeowner's insurance
    - Loan protection life and disability insurance

_____
_____
_____
_____
_____
_____

L.O. 4 MORTGAGE OPTIONS

The amount of your monthly mortgage payment and how quickly you will be able to pay off your mortgage loan depends on the mortgage options you choose. First, you will have to decide over what period of time you would like to amortize your mortgage loan. This is known as **amortization**, which is the expected number of years it will take a borrower to pay off the entire mortgage loan balance. Amortization is usually expressed in number of years. For example, if you choose an amortization period of 30 years, your monthly mortgage payment will be calculated based on your mortgage being paid off

amortization
The expected number of years it will take a borrower to pay off the entire mortgage loan balance.

during the next 360 months. The maximum amortization period is different among financial institutions, but will be no more than 40 years, or 480 months. A longer amortization period results in lower monthly mortgage payments and a higher amount of mortgage interest payable over the life of the mortgage.

mortgage term
The period of time over which the mortgage interest rate and other terms of the mortgage contract will not change.

Second, you will need to determine the mortgage term you need. The mortgage term represents the period of time over which the mortgage interest rate and other terms of the mortgage contract will not change. The mortgage term will always be less than or equal to the amortization period. If you decide on a five-year mortgage term and a 25-year amortization, you will probably have to renegotiate the mortgage interest rate five times during the life of the mortgage. Typical mortgage terms include six months and one, two, three, four, five, and 10 years.

closed mortgage
Restricts your ability to pay off the mortgage balance during the mortgage term unless you are willing to pay a financial penalty.

open mortgage
Allows you to pay off the mortgage balance at any time during the mortgage term.

Third, you will have to make a decision as to the type of mortgage you would like to have. There are two basic types: closed and open. A closed mortgage restricts your ability to pay off the mortgage balance during the mortgage term unless you are willing to pay a financial penalty. An open mortgage allows you to pay off the mortgage balance at any time during the mortgage term. Closed mortgages are more popular than open mortgages because interest rates are lower. The lower interest rate offered by a closed mortgage needs to be weighed against the ability to prepay, without penalty, the entire balance of an open mortgage at any time.

Financial institutions have made closed mortgages more attractive by offering features that allow borrowers to increase their monthly mortgage payment and pay off a lump sum of the original mortgage balance during the course of each mortgage year. These accelerated payment features will be different among financial institutions, so it is in your best interest to shop around.

EXAMPLE

Blake and Donna Braithwaite decide to purchase a home using a $50 000 down payment and $200 000 of mortgage financing from their bank. They obtain a closed mortgage with a five-year mortgage term that is amortized over 25 years at an interest rate of 6 percent. The monthly mortgage payments are $1279.61. The Braithwaites will not be able to pay off the balance during the mortgage term since it is a closed mortgage. However, the bank will allow them to increase their mortgage payments by up to 20 percent of the regular monthly amount. In addition, the couple can pay off up to 20 percent of the original mortgage balance at any time during each year of the mortgage term.

Although closed mortgages are not as flexible as open mortgages, the accelerated payment features are usually sufficient to meet the needs of most borrowers. At the end of a mortgage term, you are able to pay off a closed or open mortgage without any financial penalty. You can also renegotiate new mortgage terms for an additional period of time. The borrower should read the terms of the mortgage contract to fully understand the options and penalties the lender is offering.

L.O. 5

CHARACTERISTICS OF A FIXED-RATE MORTGAGE

fixed-rate mortgage
A mortgage in which a fixed interest rate is specified for the term of the mortgage.

A mortgage loan is most likely the biggest loan you will ever obtain in your lifetime. In addition to the mortgage options above, you will need to decide whether to obtain a fixed-rate or variable-rate mortgage. A fixed-rate mortgage specifies a fixed interest rate for the term of the mortgage. When homeowners expect that interest rates will rise, they tend to prefer fixed-rate mortgages because their mortgage payments will be sheltered from the rising interest rates during the term of the mortgage. You can access various websites to obtain a general summary of prevailing mortgage rates. Although posted rates are similar among financial institutions, rates will vary based on your ability to negotiate with different lenders. It pays to shop around, as the mortgage industry is very competitive. Lenders are usually willing to decrease their posted rates if they know you are considering several

Go to
http://money.canoe.ca/
rates

Click on
Closed Mortgages

This website provides
national closed mortgage
rates by financial
institution.

institutions to get the best mortgage rate you can get. If you sell a home before the mortgage is paid off, you can use a portion of the proceeds to pay off the mortgage. Alternatively, it may be possible for the buyer to assume your mortgage under some conditions.

Amortization Table

Your monthly mortgage payments for a fixed-rate mortgage are based on an amortization schedule. This schedule discloses the monthly payments you will make based on a specific mortgage amount, a fixed interest rate level, and an amortization period.

Allocation of the Mortgage Payment. Each monthly mortgage payment represents a partial equity payment that includes a portion of the principal of the loan and an interest payment.

EXAMPLE

Stephanie Spratt decides to review mortgage websites to estimate her monthly mortgage payments. One website asks her to input the mortgage amount she desires and the interest rate she expects to pay over the life of the mortgage She inputs $123 750 as the mortgage amount and 7 percent as the interest rate. The website then provides her with an amortization schedule, which is summarized in Exhibit 7.4. This exhibit shows how her mortgage payments would be allocated to paying off principal versus interest. Notice that the initial payments are allocated mostly to

Exhibit 7.4 Amortization Schedule for a Fixed-Rate Mortgage Amortized over 40 Years for $123 750 at a 7 Percent Interest Rate				
Month	**Payment**	**Principal**	**Interest**	**Balance**
1	$760	$48	$712	$123 702
2	760	49	711	123 653
10 • • •	760	51	709	123 252
25 • • •	760	56	704	122 450
49 • • •	760	64	696	121 014
100 • • •	760	85	675	117 221
240 • • •	760	191	569	98 793
360 • • • • • •	760	380	380	65 744
480	760	756	4	0

Note: Numbers are rounded to the nearest dollar.

Exhibit 7.5 Allocation of Principal versus Interest Paid per Year on a $123 750 Mortgage

Year	Principal Paid in That Year	Interest Paid in That Year
1	$601	$8520
2	643	8477
3	689	8431
4	738	8382
6	847	8273
8	972	8148
10	1116	8005
12	1280	7840
15	1574	7547
17	1806	7315
20	2220	6901
24	2923	6197
28	3850	5271
32	5069	4052
36	6675	2446
40	8773	331

interest, with a relatively small amount used to pay off the principal. For example, for month 2, $49 of her payment is applied to the principal while $711 goes to pay the interest expense. Initially, when the amount of principal is large, most of each payment is needed to cover the interest owed. As time passes, the proportion of the payment allocated to equity increases. Notice that by month 480, $756 of the payment is applied to principal and only $4 to interest.

Notice, too, that her balance after 100 months is $117 221. This means that over a period of more than eight years, Stephanie would pay off less than $7000 of the loan outstanding on her home, or less than 10 percent of the original mortgage amount. After 240 months (half of the life of the mortgage), her mortgage balance would be almost $98 793, which means she would have paid off about $25 000 of the $123 750 mortgage. Finally, notice that it takes 360 months (30 years) of mortgage payments before at least half of the monthly payment is being used to pay down the principal.

The amount of Stephanie's annual mortgage payments that would be allocated to paying off the principal is shown in Exhibit 7.5. In the first year, she would pay off only $601 of the principal, while the rest of her mortgage payments ($8520) would be used to pay interest. This information is very surprising to Stephanie, so she reviews the mortgage situation further to determine whether it is possible to build equity more quickly.

Impact of the Mortgage Amount on Monthly Payments

The larger the mortgage amount, the larger your monthly payments will be for a given interest rate and maturity. Exhibit 7.6 shows the monthly payment based on a 40-year amortization and a 7 percent interest rate for different mortgage amounts. Notice the change in the mortgage payment for larger mortgage amounts. For example, the monthly mortgage payment for a $160 000 mortgage is $983, while the monthly payment for a $170 000 mortgage is $1044.

Exhibit 7.6 Monthly Mortgage Payments Based on Different Mortgage Amounts (Fixed-Rate Mortgage Amortized over 40 Years; 7 Percent Interest Rate)	
Mortgage Amount	**Monthly Mortgage Payment**
$120 000	$737
130 000	798
140 000	860
150 000	921
160 000	983
170 000	1044
180 000	1106
190 000	1167
200 000	1228

Interest and Principal Payments ($)

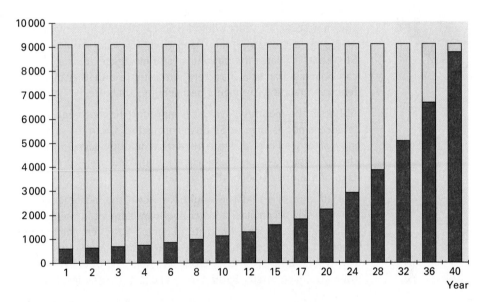

Impact of the Interest Rate on Monthly Payments

Given the large amount of funds you may borrow to finance a home, you should make every effort to obtain a mortgage loan that has a low interest rate. The lower the interest rate, the smaller the monthly mortgage payments. Even a slight increase (such as 0.5 percent) in the interest rate increases your monthly mortgage payments.

Over the last decade, mortgage rates have been decreasing steadily. This has been to the advantage of borrowers who selected a variable-rate mortgage. If you expect interest rates to continue to decrease, a variable-rate mortgage may be in your best interest. Homeowners seek a fixed-rate mortgage when they believe that interest rates will rise in the future. When negotiating the mortgage rate with your lender, you should be aware of economic conditions. In some circumstances, lenders are very aggressive and will negotiate better interest rates to get your business. You should be able to take advantage of market conditions to improve your interest rate. However, sometimes market conditions are such that negotiation is impossible.

Impact of the Amortization Period on Monthly Payments

The amortization period of the mortgage indicates how long you will take to complete your financing payments and pay off the mortgage in full. As discussed earlier, a longer amortization period will result in lower monthly mortgage payments and a higher

Go to
http://finance.sympatico.
msn.ca/Banking/
Mortgages/
mortgage_calculator.aspx

This website provides a Mortgage Calculator to determine the monthly payments on a mortgage based on the principal amount, mortgage term, interest rate, and amortization.

amount of mortgage interest payable over the life of the mortgage. If you increase your monthly payments by decreasing your amortization, you will pay your mortgage off at a faster pace and reduce the total amount of interest paid over the life of the mortgage. For example, you will have paid off your mortgage after 25 years if your amortization period is 25 years and interest rates do not change, whereas a 40-year amortization period will require mortgage payments for an additional 15 years.

You may be able to accelerate your mortgage payments according to your mortgage contract. This means that you may be able to double up your monthly mortgage payments. These additional payments go directly to pay off principal and can reduce your overall amortization period by years.

Estimating Monthly Mortgage Payments

You can use mortgage loan websites to obtain estimates of your monthly payments based on a specific mortgage amount and amortization periods.

EXAMPLE

Stephanie Spratt wants to estimate her monthly mortgage payment on a $123 750 fixed-rate mortgage, based on several interest rate scenarios for 25- and 40-year amortization periods, as shown in Exhibit 7.7. At an interest rate of 6 percent, the monthly payments on a mortgage amortized over 40 years would be $675. At an interest rate of 8 percent, the monthly payments on a mortgage amortized over 40 years would be $848, or $173 more. Next, Stephanie evaluates the payments for a mortgage amortized over 25 years. She believes she can obtain a loan at a 7 percent interest rate on either maturity, so she focuses on the difference in monthly payments pertaining to that rate.

Although the monthly payment is more for the mortgage amortized over 25 years, the difference is not as large as Stephanie expected. Given the interest rate of 7 percent, the mortgage amortized over 25 years requires a monthly payment of $867, which is $107 more than the $760 payment on the mortgage amortized over 40 years. This is the obvious disadvantage of a shorter amortization period.

The advantage is that she would pay down the mortgage sooner, meaning that she would more quickly accumulate a larger equity investment in the home. To gain more insight on this advantage, she reviews a website to compare the remaining loan balance for each of the two amortization periods on a year-by-year basis. This comparison is summarized in Exhibit 7.8. Notice that after six years, Stephanie would still owe $119 440 on the mortgage amortized over 40 years, versus $109 955 (almost $10 000 less) on the mortgage amortized over

Exhibit 7.7 Comparison of Monthly Payments for a 40-Year versus a 25-Year Amortization Period on a $123 750 Mortgage Based on Different Interest Rates

	Monthly Payment on a:	
Interest Rate	**40-Year Mortgage**	**25-Year Mortgage**
6.0%	$675	$792
6.5	717	829
7.0	760	867
7.5	804	905
8.0	848	944
8.5	893	984
9.0	939	1025

Note: Payments are rounded to the nearest dollar.

Exhibit 7.8 Comparison of Mortgage Balance for a 40-Year versus a 25-Year Amortization Period ($123 750 Initial Mortgage Amount; 7 Percent Interest Rate)

End of Year	Balance on 40-Year Mortgage	Balance on 25-Year Mortgage
1	$123 149	$121 828
2	122 506	119 768
3	121 817	117 562
4	121 078	115 199
5	120 287	112 667
6	119 439	109 955
7	118 532	107 050
8	117 560	103 939
9	116 518	100 605
10	115 403	97 034
11	114 207	93 209
12	112 927	89 111
13	111 556	84 721
14	110 086	80 019
15	108 513	74 982
16	106 827	69 586
17	105 021	63 805
18	103 086	57 613
19	101 013	50 980
20	98 793	43 875
21	96 415	36 263
22	93 867	28 110
23	91 138	19 375
24	88 215	10 019
25	85 083	0

Note: Balances are rounded to the nearest dollar.

25 years. After 15 years, she would owe almost $34 000 more on the 40-year mortgage than on the 25-year mortgage. After 25 years, she would still owe about $85 000 on the 40-year mortgage, while the 25-year mortgage would be paid off.

The website also shows the total payments over the life of the mortgage for both amortization periods if the mortgage is not paid off until maturity.

	40-Year Amortization	25-Year Amortization
Total Principal Payments	$123 750	$123 750
Total Interest Payments	241 062	136 277
Total Payments	$364 812	$260 027

Stephanie would pay about $105 000 more in interest with the mortgage amortized over 40 years. The total interest payments on the mortgage amortized over 40 years is considerably greater than the total interest payments that would be made over the life of the mortgage amortized over 25 years.

Weighing the advantages of the shorter amortization period against the disadvantage of paying an extra $107 per month, Stephanie decides she prefers the 25-year amortization period. Even if she decides to sell this home before she pays off the mortgage, she will have paid down a larger amount of the mortgage at the time of the sale. Since she will have a larger equity investment (from paying off more of the principal), she will increase her net worth to a greater degree in a shorter period of time.

L.O. 6   CHARACTERISTICS OF A VARIABLE-RATE MORTGAGE

variable-rate mortgage (VRM)
A mortgage where the interest charged on the loan changes in response to movements in a specific market-determined interest rate. The rate used is usually referred to as prime. Lenders will add a percentage to prime for the total mortgage rate.

Go to
www.invis.ca/article/articleItem.
cfm?cms_article_id=1

This website provides valuable information regarding variable-rate and fixed-rate mortgages that may be useful when deciding whether to finance your home with a variable- or fixed-rate mortgage.

An alternative to a fixed-rate mortgage is a variable-rate mortgage (VRM), in which the interest charged on the loan changes in response to movements in a specific market-determined interest rate. A VRM is sometimes referred to as an adjustable-rate mortgage. VRMs definitely should be considered along with fixed-rate mortgages. Like a fixed-rate mortgage, a VRM can be obtained for a 25-year or a 40-year maturity. VRMs have various characteristics that must be stated in the mortgage contract.

Initial Rate
Many VRMs specify a relatively low initial mortgage rate over the first year or so. This initial rate is beneficial to homeowners in that it results in a low monthly mortgage payment over the first year. Recognize, however, that this rate is only temporary, as it will be adjusted.

Interest Rate Index
The initial mortgage rate will be adjusted after a period (such as one year) in line with the prime rate of interest. Many VRMs use this rate because it is tied to the average cost of deposits of financial institutions. For example, the interest rate charged on a VRM might be set at 3 percentage points above the prime rate. Thus, if the benchmark is 4 percent in a given year, the VRM will apply an interest rate of 7 percent (computed as 4 percent plus 3 percent). If the interest rate index has risen to 5 percent by the time of the next mortgage rate adjustment, the new mortgage rate will be 8 percent (computed as 5 percent plus 3 percent).

IN-CLASS NOTES

Mortgage Options
- Fixed-rate mortgage
  - Specifies an interest rate for the mortgage term
  - Monthly mortgage payments pay a portion of the principal on your loan
- Variable-rate mortgage
  - The interest you owe changes in response to the market prime rate
  - Initial rates are generally low but will be adjusted after a short period (such as one year)

_____

_____

_____

_____

_____

Chapter 7 Purchasing and Financing a Home

L.O. 7   DECISION TO OWN VERSUS RENT A HOME

When considering the purchase (and therefore ownership) of a home, you should compare the costs of purchasing and renting. People attribute different advantages and disadvantages to owning a home versus renting because preferences are subjective. Some individuals value the privacy of a home, while others value the flexibility of an apartment, which allows them to move without much cost or difficulty. The financial assessment of owning a home versus renting can be performed objectively. Once the financial assessment is conducted, personal preferences can also be considered.

Estimating the Total Cost of Renting and Owning

The main cost of renting a home is the monthly rent payments. There is also an opportunity cost of tying up funds in a security deposit. Those funds could have been invested if they were not needed for the security deposit. Another possible cost of renting is the purchase of renter's insurance.

The primary costs of purchasing a home are the down payment and the monthly mortgage payments. The down payment has an opportunity cost because the funds could have been invested if they were not tied up in the purchase of the home. As well, closing costs are incurred at the time the home is purchased. Owning a home also involves some additional costs, such as maintenance and repair. Property taxes are assessed annually as a percentage of the home's value. Homeowner's insurance is paid monthly or annually and is primarily based on the value of the home and its contents.

EXAMPLE

Stephanie Spratt has found a home she desires and has researched the financing she needs. Before making a final decision, she wants to compare the cost of the home to the cost of remaining in her apartment. Although she would prefer a home, she wants to determine how much more expensive the home is compared to the apartment. If she purchases the home, she expects to live in it for at least three years. Therefore, she decides to compare the cost of owning a home to the cost of renting for the next three years. First, Stephanie calculates the cost of renting:

- Cost of Rent. Her estimated cost of renting is shown in the top panel of Exhibit 7.9. Her rent is currently $750 per month, so her annual rent is $9000 (computed as $750 × 12). She does not expect a rent increase over the next three years and therefore estimates her cost of renting over this period to be $9000 × 3 = $27 000. (If she had expected a rent increase, she simply would have added the extra cost to the estimated rent over the next three years.)

- Cost of Tenant's Insurance. She does not have tenant's insurance at this time, as the value of her household assets is low.

- Opportunity Cost of Security Deposit. She provided a security deposit of $750 to the apartment complex. While she expects to be refunded this deposit when she stops renting, there is an opportunity cost associated with it. She could have invested those funds in a money market fund earning 2.8 percent after-tax annually, which would have generated annual interest of $21, assuming a tax rate of 30 percent (computed as ($750 × 0.04) × (1 − 0.3)). The opportunity cost over three years is three times the annual cost, or $63.

- Total Cost of Renting. Stephanie estimates the total cost of renting as $9021 per year and $27 063 over the next three years, as shown in Exhibit 7.9.

Stephanie determines the total cost of purchasing a home by adding up expenses and subtracting the value of the equity:

- Mortgage Payment. The primary cost of buying a home is the mortgage payment, which she expects to be $867 per month, or $10 404 per year (not including payments for property taxes or home insurance).

- Down Payment. Stephanie would make a down payment of $41 250 to buy the home.

Exhibit 7.9 Comparing the Total Cost of Renting versus Buying a Home over a Three-Year Period

Cost of Renting

	Amount per Year	Total over Next Three Years
Rent ($750 per month)	$9 000	$27 000
Tenant's insurance	0	0
Opportunity cost of security deposit	21	63
Total cost of renting	$9 021	$27 063

Cost of Purchasing

	Amount per Year	Total over Next Three Years
Mortgage payment ($867 per month)	$10 404	$31 212
Down payment	41 250	41 250 (first year only)
Opportunity cost of down payment	1 155	3 465
Property taxes	2 500	7 500
Home insurance	600	1 800
Closing costs	3 865	3 865 (first year only)
Maintenance costs	1 000	3 000
Total costs		**$92 092**
Value of equity		**$63 938**
Cost of purchasing home over three years		**$28 154**

- Opportunity Cost of the Down Payment. If Stephanie did not buy a house, she could have invested the $41 250 in an investment and earned 2.8 percent per year, after-tax. Therefore, the annual opportunity cost (what she could have earned if she had invested the funds) is $1155, assuming a tax rate of 30 percent (computed as ($41 250 × 0.04) × (1 − 0.3)).

- Property Taxes. Stephanie assumes that the annual property tax will be $2500 based on last year's property tax paid by the current owner of the home.

- Home Insurance. Insurance on this home will cost $600 per year (this estimate is based on the insurance premium paid by the current owner of the home).

- Closing Costs. Closing costs (transaction costs) associated with buying a home must be included, although those costs are incurred only in the first year. The closing costs are estimated to be $3865, as shown on page 175.

- Maintenance Costs. Stephanie expects maintenance costs on the home to be $1000 per year.

- Utilities. She will pay for utilities such as water and electricity and will incur a cable TV bill if she buys the home. She already incurs those costs while renting an apartment, so she does not need to include them in her analysis.

- Value of the Equity Investment. Another advantage of owning a home is that Stephanie will have an equity investment in it. Her down payment will be $41 250, and she will pay about $6188 in principal on her mortgage over the three-year period.

- The value of this equity investment could be higher in three years if the market value of the home increases. As a conservative estimate, Stephanie expects the home to increase 10 percent in value over the next three years. Based on this assumption, the increase in the value of the home will be $16 500 ($165 000 × 10 percent). The value of the equity investment will be $63 938 (computed as $41 250 + $16 500 + $6188).

- Total Cost of Purchasing a Home. The total cost of purchasing a home is determined by adding all expenses, and then subtracting the equity investment. As shown in Exhibit 7.9, Stephanie estimates that the total cost of purchasing the home over the three-year period will be $28 154.

The total cost of purchasing a home over three years is about $1091 more than the cost of renting. Stephanie decides that she wants to buy the home. Aside from the fact that she would rather live in a home than an apartment, Stephanie realizes that building equity in a home will put her further ahead, in the long term, than renting.

Now that Stephanie has decided that she wants to purchase a home and can afford it, she submits her offer of $165 000, which is accepted by the seller.

IN-CLASS NOTES

Decision to Own versus Rent a Home
- Compare the costs of renting and owning a home
- Costs of renting
  - Rent, tenant's insurance, opportunity cost of security deposit
- Costs of owning
  - Mortgage payment, down payment, opportunity cost of down payment, property taxes, home insurance, closing costs, maintenance costs, utility costs
- Home ownership offers the opportunity to build equity

_____

_____

_____

_____

_____

_____

L.O. 8

MORTGAGE REFINANCING

mortgage refinancing
Paying off an existing mortgage with a new mortgage that has a lower interest rate.

Mortgage refinancing involves paying off an existing mortgage with a new mortgage that has a lower interest rate. You may use mortgage refinancing to obtain a new mortgage if market interest rates (and therefore mortgage rates) decline. One disadvantage of mortgage refinancing is that you will incur closing costs again. In addition, you will be charged prepayment penalties if you have a closed mortgage and choose to refinance your mortgage before the end of the term. Nevertheless, it may still be advantageous to refinance because the savings on your monthly mortgage payments may exceed the new closing costs and any prepayment penalties. Mortgage refinancing is more likely to be worthwhile when the prevailing mortgage interest rate is substantially below the rate on your existing mortgage. It is also more likely to be worthwhile when you expect to be living in the home for a long time because you will reap greater benefits from the lower monthly mortgage payments that result from refinancing.

Rate Modification

When interest rates decline, some mortgage lenders may be willing to allow a "rate modification" to existing mortgage holders who have fixed-rate mortgages. They may charge a one-time fee for this, which is typically between $500 and $1500. Your fixed-rate mortgage may be revised to reflect the prevailing mortgage rate. You can benefit from receiving the lower interest rate and you would not need to go through the process of mortgage refinancing or incur costs associated with a new mortgage application. Some mortgage lenders are willing to allow rate modifications because they realize that if they do not provide you with an opportunity to pay the lower interest rate, you will likely obtain a new mortgage from another lender and will pay off your existing mortgage. In this case, you would no longer make payments at the high interest rate and your existing mortgage lender would lose you as a customer. By allowing a rate modification, your existing mortgage lender retains you as a customer by offering you a mortgage that is similar to what it is currently offering to new customers. The lender also earns a one-time fee from you for modifying the mortgage rate you are charged.

Refinancing Analysis

To determine whether you should refinance, you can compare the advantage of monthly savings of interest expenses to the cost of refinancing. If the benefits from reducing your interest expenses exceed the prepayment penalties incurred from refinancing, the refinancing is feasible.

The advantages of refinancing (lower interest payments) occur each year, while the disadvantage (prepayment penalties) occurs only at the time of refinancing. Therefore, refinancing tends to be more beneficial when a homeowner plans to own the home for a longer period. The savings from a lower interest payment can accumulate over each additional year the mortgage exists.

HOW A MORTGAGE FITS WITHIN YOUR FINANCIAL PLAN

The following are the key mortgage loan decisions that should be included within your financial plan:

- What mortgage amount can you afford?

- What maturity should you select?

- Should you consider a fixed-rate mortgage or a variable-rate mortgage?

By making informed decisions, you can avoid accumulating an excessive amount of debt.

STEPHANIE SPRATT'S FINANCIAL PLAN: Mortgage Financing

GOALS FOR MORTGAGE FINANCING

1. *Limit the amount of mortgage financing to a level that is affordable.*

2. *Select the amortization period that is affordable without unduly increasing overall interest costs. Select the term that is most appropriate to your interest rate forecast. If rates are expected to rise, lock in for an extended period of time. If rates are expected to fall, shorten the term.*

3. *Select the type of mortgage loan (fixed- or variable-rate) that is more likely to result in lower interest expenses without increasing risk.*

DECISIONS

Decision on Affording a Mortgage

The monthly payment on a $123 750 mortgage loan with a 25-year maturity is $867. My rent is $750 per month, so the difference is $117 per month. Since my monthly cash flows (from my salary) exceed my typical monthly expenses (including my car loan payment) and my purchases of clothes by almost $600, I can afford that difference. I will not save as much money right now if I buy a home, but I will be building equity in the long run.

Decision on the Mortgage Maturity

I prefer the 25-year mortgage because I will pay off a larger portion of the principal each year.

Decision on the Type of Mortgage Loan

I prefer a fixed-rate mortgage because I know with certainty that the monthly payments will not increase. I am worried that interest rates may increase in the future, which would cause interest expenses to be higher on the adjustable-rate mortgage.

Discussion Questions

1. How would Stephanie's mortgage financing decisions be different if she were a single mother of two children?

2. How would Stephanie's mortgage financing decisions be affected if she were 35 years old? If she were 50 years old?

SUMMARY

When considering the purchase of a home, you should evaluate your financial situation to determine how much you can afford. Some of the key criteria used in the selection process are price, convenience of the location, condition of the home (taking into account maintenance and potential repairs), the school system, and the potential resale value.

You can conduct a valuation of a home with a market analysis. Homes in the same area that were recently sold can be used to determine the average price per square foot. This price per square foot can then be applied to the square footage of the home you wish to value.

The transaction costs of purchasing a home include the down payment and closing costs. Some of the important closing costs include the home inspection fee, the appraisal fee, legal fees, and title insurance.

A fixed-rate mortgage specifies a fixed interest rate to be paid over the term of the mortgage. Since most of the monthly mortgage payments on a mortgage amortized over 40 years are allocated to cover the interest expense in the early years, a relatively small amount of principal is paid off in those years. A shorter amortization period, such as 25 years, should be considered to reduce the time it takes to pay off the mortgage. It requires a larger monthly payment, but a larger proportion of the payment is allocated to principal in the early years.

A variable-rate mortgage (VRM) ties the interest rate to the prime rate, so the mortgage interest rate changes over time with the change in this prime rate. Homeowners who expect interest rates to decline in the future are especially likely to choose VRMs.

Before making a final decision to buy a home, you can compare the total cost of owning a home versus renting over a particular period to determine which choice will enhance your financial position. The total cost of owning a home is estimated by adding up the expenses associated with the home and subtracting the expected value of the equity of the home at the end of the period.

You may consider mortgage refinancing when quoted interest rates on new mortgages decline. When refinancing, you will incur closing costs. Thus, you should consider refinancing only if the benefits (expected reduction in interest expenses over time) exceed the closing costs.

INTEGRATING THE KEY CONCEPTS

Your mortgage decision affects your ability to purchase a home, as well as other parts of your financial plan. You will need to maintain more liquidity (Part 2) than before to ensure that you will have sufficient funds each month to make your mortgage payment. Your decision to buy a home means that you will have to obtain insurance (Part 4) to protect the home and be insured against any liability resulting from the home. You will likely have fewer funds for investments (Part 5) and may even have to sell some of your investments to have sufficient cash to make a down payment or monthly mortgage payments.

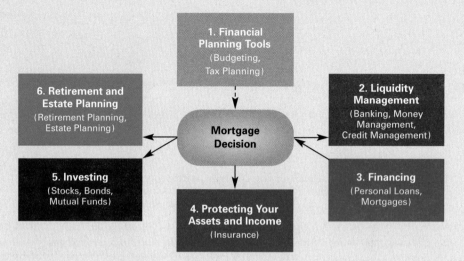

The following table can be considered as the typical process one may go through when considering the purchase of a home.

Do I want to buy or do I want to rent?	If I want to buy, I must save the down payment. I will ask friends and family for references for the professionals I will require for this purchase (that is, lawyer, surveyor, home inspector, mortgage broker, appraiser, real estate broker, or agent).
Once I have the down payment, I need to see what my money can buy.	I will apply for pre-approval with my financial institution before I look for a home. Once I am pre-approved I will prepare a budget to ensure that I can afford the mortgage and maintain my lifestyle. I plan to build in some room for possible interest rate increases and increases in living costs.
The pre-approval allows me to set a price for my home search.	I choose a location or neighbourhood and with the help of a real estate agent, I narrow down the choices to one home.
	After conducting a market analysis, I set a price for the home I am interested in purchasing. I make an offer and after some negotiation it is accepted, conditional on financing and a home inspection. When I make the offer, I will be required to put down a good-faith deposit to represent my seriousness about purchasing the home. I want to keep the deposit very small and the vendor wants a large deposit. Because I can lose the deposit if the purchase does not close, I offer a deposit of $500. In addition, I will ask for one more viewing of the home two weeks before closing to ensure that there is no damage and that what I purchased with the house is still there. As part of the offer I will include the closing date for the home (typically, closing is three months from the purchase date). That is the day I will get possession.
Once the offer is accepted, I need to arrange financing, a home inspection, home insurance, a property survey, and utilities.	In looking for financing, I approach several institutions to negotiate a better mortgage rate. I will shop around until I find an institution that will give me the best rate. I may use the services of a mortgage broker. I also arrange for movers. I will continue to save money, as I know there will be expenses that I have not planned for, such as window coverings, etc.
Before the closing date, my lawyer will contact me to advise on the down payment.	On the closing date, I will arrange to pick up the keys to my new home. While I would like to move in on that date, I have planned for some delay. Besides, I can use some time to clean or paint before I move in.
Finally, I have my own home.	

REVIEW QUESTIONS

1. What is your first task when considering buying a home? Why is this step important? How can a real estate broker help you?

2. What is the purpose of a pre-approval certificate? Does a pre-approval certificate indicate that you will get a mortgage? What does GDSR stand for? What does TDSR stand for? How do financial institutions use these ratios?

3. What should you consider when determining an affordable down payment and monthly mortgage payments?

4. List the criteria you should use when selecting a home.

5. How do price, convenience of the location, and maintenance affect your homebuying decisions?

6. Why is the reputation of the school system in the area of the home you are buying important?

7. Why do insurance costs and taxes vary among homes?

8. What is the main factor in determining a home's resale value? How can you predict a home's resale value? What factors are home prices dependent on? Who pays commissions when a home is sold?

9. Once you have reduced your list of three or four homes down to one home, what is your next step? Should you offer the price the seller is asking? Describe how you would conduct a market analysis of the home.

10. Why does the value of a home depend on the demand for homes? What factors influence the demand for homes?

11. What is the difference between a conventional mortgage and a high ratio mortgage? What is a vendor take-back mortgage? How does it work?

12. What are closing costs? List and briefly describe the different closing costs you might incur when applying for a mortgage.

13. What is the difference between amortization and the mortgage term? What is a closed mortgage? What is an open mortgage? Which type is more popular? Why?

14. Describe the characteristics of a fixed-rate mortgage. Why do certain homeowners prefer a fixed-rate mortgage to a variable-rate mortgage?

15. What is an amortization table? What does each mortgage payment represent?

16. List the three things that determine the amount of the monthly mortgage payments. Explain how each affects the payments.

17. Discuss the characteristics of a variable-rate mortgage. What influences your choice of a fixed- or variable-rate mortgage?

18. What are the costs of renting a home?

19. Describe some of the costs of buying a home.

20. What is mortgage refinancing? Are there any disadvantages to refinancing?

FINANCIAL PLANNING PROBLEMS

1. Isabella and Raphael are interested in buying a home. They have completed the initial steps in the home buying process, including contacting a realtor and obtaining a pre-approval certificate from their bank. During the process of determining an affordable down payment, they have asked you to determine whether their GDSR and TDSR ratios are within the guidelines set by their bank. They have provided you with the following information. Isabella earns $35 000 per year, while Raphael earns $30 000 per year. They believe that they could afford a mortgage payment of about $1000 per month. The annual property taxes in the area where they would like to purchase a home average about $1600. Heating costs should be about $125 per month. The couple have an outstanding balance on their line of credit of $15 000. In addition, Raphael has an outstanding balance on his student loan of $10 000. Currently, the couple are making a monthly payment of $450 on their line of credit and $300 on the student loan. Their bank requires that the GDSR be no more than 32 percent, and the TDSR be no more than 40 percent. Do Isabella and Raphael meet these requirements?

2. Dorothy and Matt are ready to purchase their first home. Their current monthly income is $4900, and their current monthly expenses are $3650. Their rent makes up $650 of their cash flow. They would like to put 10 percent of their income in savings every month and leave another $200 per month in their chequing account for emergencies. How much of a mortgage payment, including taxes and utilities, can they manage under these conditions?

3. Denise and Kenny are ready to make an offer on an 1800-square-foot home that is priced at $235 000. They investigate other homes on lots of similar size and find the following information:

   - 2400-square-foot home sold for $268 000
   - 1500-square-foot home sold for $206 500
   - 1100-square-foot home sold for $179 000

   All else being equal, what offer should they make on the home?

4. Larry and Laurie have found a home and made a $125 000 offer that has been accepted. They agreed to make a down payment of 10 percent. The CMHC mortgage loan insurance premium is 2 percent of the mortgage amount required. Larry and Laurie have decided to pay this fee at the time of closing instead of having it added to the mortgage. Other fees include a $175 loan application fee, a $250 appraisal fee, a $300 home inspection fee, $540 in legal fees, and $350 for title search and insurance. How much cash will Larry and Laurie need at closing?

5. Lloyd and Jean are considering purchasing a home requiring a $275 000 mortgage. The monthly payment on a mortgage amortized over 40 years at a fixed rate of 7 percent for this amount is $1689.01. The monthly payment on a mortgage amortized over 25 years at a fixed rate of 7 percent for this amount is $1926.15. What is the difference in the total interest paid between the two different maturities?

6. Teresa rents her apartment for $850 per month, utilities not included. When she moved in, she paid a $700 security deposit using money from her savings account that was paying 3 percent interest, after tax. Her tenant's insurance costs her $60 per year. What are Teresa's total annual costs of renting?

7. Matt has found a condominium in an area where he would enjoy living. He would need a $10 000 down payment from his savings and would have to pay closing costs of $2500 to purchase the condo. His monthly mortgage payments would be $850, including property taxes and insurance. The condominium's homeowner's association charges maintenance fees of $400 per month. Calculate the cost of Matt's condo during the first year if he currently has the $10 000 down payment invested in an account earning 5 percent interest, after tax.

Questions 8 and 9 require a financial calculator.

8. Paul really wants to purchase his own condo. He currently lives in an apartment, and his rent is being paid by his parents. Paul's parents have informed him that they would not pay his mortgage payments. Paul has no savings, but can save $700 per month. The condo he desires costs $120 000, and his real estate broker informs him that a down payment of 10 percent would be required. If Paul can earn 6 percent on his savings, after tax, how long will it take him to accumulate the required down payment?

9. For this problem, assume that the CMHC mortgage loan insurance premium of 2 percent will be added to the mortgage. Paul (from Problem 8) will be able to save $700 per month (which can be used for mortgage payments) for the indefinite future. If Paul finances the remaining cost of the home (after

making the $12 000 down payment) at a rate of 7 percent over a 25-year amortization period, what are his resulting monthly mortgage payments? Can he afford the mortgage? If not, over what period of time must the mortgage be amortized to make the mortgage payment affordable for Paul?

ETHICAL DILEMMA

Sarah and Joe own a small home that they would like to sell in order to build their dream home. Their current home has a mortgage and needs extensive repairs to make it marketable. A local loan company is offering home equity loans equal to 125 percent of a home's value. Since Sarah and Joe have good jobs and can make the additional home equity loan payments, they easily qualify for the 125 percent equity home loan. The entire home equity loan is required to complete the repairs and upgrades to the home. To their shock, they find that even after the upgrades they are unable to sell the home for enough to repay the mortgage and the home equity loan. In other words, they have negative equity in the home.

a. Comment on the finance company's ethics in making loans in excess of a home's appraised value.

b. What are Sarah and Joe's options in their current situation? Is there a way they can proceed with building their dream home?

FINANCIAL PLANNING ONLINE EXERCISES

1. Go to www.fcac-acfc.gc.ca/Tools/Mortgage/Qualifier/ MortgageQualifier_e.asp.

   a. Select "condo" at Type of home you are considering. Input a $150 000 estimated value. Enter a down payment of 5 percent. What is the dollar value of the CMHC premium?

   b. On the right-hand side, enter an anticipated annual interest rate of 7 percent, and an amortization period of 40 years. What are the monthly mortgage payments?

   c. Click on the Next arrow located in the bottom right-hand corner. Enter a gross income of $40 000 per year. Heating costs, property taxes, and condo fees are $80, $100, and $60, respectively. What is the GDS ratio?

   d. You are considering leasing a car. The lease would result in a $400 car payment. If you take on this car payment, will your TDS ratio remain below 40 percent? You have no other debt. What is the maximum car payment you can afford such that your TDS ratio remains below 40 percent?

2. Go to www.cmhc-schl.gc.ca/en/co/buho/buho_005.cfm.

   a. Click on Mortgage Calculator and then input:

      $5000 for gross monthly household income before taxes

      $25 000 for down payment.

      7 percent for mortgage interest rate

      30 years for amortization

      $200 for monthly property taxes

      $110 for monthly heating costs

      $0 for monthly condominium fees

      $200 for monthly debt payments

   b. What is the estimate for the maximum affordable home price? What are the estimated monthly mortgage payments?

3. Go to www.canadamortgage.com/RatesShow/ShowRates.cfm.

   a. What is the most common closed-term rate over six months? One year? Two years? Three years? Four years? Five years?

   b. What is the best 10-year closed-term mortgage rate? Do all banks offer 10-year mortgage rates? Why do you think this is the case?

   c. What is the maximum open-term rate? Why do you think this is the case?

4. Go to http://strategis.ic.gc.ca/epic/site/oca-bc.nsf/en/ca01821e.html.

   a. This website compares the impact on your wealth (net worth) of renting versus buying a home. Based on the information provided, which of the two options, renting or buying, increases your wealth the most?

   b. Is the difference in wealth between renting and buying higher or lower if you reinvest your savings? Why?

   c. What is the impact on the difference in wealth if you make the following changes? Before each change, make sure you reset the data by clicking on Reset.

      Amortization decreases to 240 months

      Your down payment decreases to $10 000

      Your return on real estate is 0 percent

ON THE STUDENT CD-ROM FOR THIS CHAPTER YOU WILL FIND:

- Building Your Own Financial Plan exercise and worksheets
- The chapter-end Continuing Case about the Sampson family
- The third part-end Continuing Case about Brad Brooks

  Read through the Building Your Own Financial Plan exercise and use the worksheets to determine whether home ownership or renting would be the best option given your financial situation.

- After reading the Sampson case study, use the Continuing Case worksheets to help the Sampsons lower their monthly payments by refinancing.
- After reading the Brad Brooks case study, use the Continuing Case worksheets to help Brad upgrade his car and housing situations.

Study Guide

Circle the correct answer and then check the answers in the back of the book to chart your progress.

Multiple Choice

1. When selecting a home, you should first determine how much money you can afford to pay per month for a mortgage based on your budget. Which of the following is an appropriate method you could use to help you determine how much of a monthly mortgage payment you can afford?

   a. Compare your financial situation to that of your friends/colleagues, and purchase a house that is similar in value to friends/colleagues who have the same income level as you do.

b. Obtain a pre-approval certificate from your financial institution.

c. Look at your cash flow statement and determine what you think you can afford based on the net cash flow you have available.

d. All of the above.

2. Financial institutions normally will require that your total debt service ratio (TDSR) is no more than _____ percent.

a. 40
b. 32
c. 38
d. 36

3. What would be the gross debt service ratio (GDSR) based on the following information?
Current monthly gross income = $4000
Current monthly after-tax income = $2800
Monthly mortgage payments = $950
Monthly heating costs = $90
Monthly garbage/recycling pickup costs = $20
Monthly property taxes = $100
Monthly credit card payment = $200

a. 28.50%
b. 40.71%
c. 34.00%
d. 48.57%

4. Which of the following is the least important factor to consider when selecting a home?

a. If you are concerned about excessive maintenance costs, you should consider newer homes, or renovated older homes that have received upgrades to costly items, such as a new hot water tank, furnace, or roof.

b. You should consider the school system in the area you are looking at. A good school system near your home will increase its resale value and provide your children with a good school nearby.

c. You should consider the cost of insurance. Insurance is more expensive for larger homes and/or homes in and around high-risk areas, such as an area prone to flooding.

d. You should consider who your neighbours will be. It is important to walk around the area and talk to those who would live near you. The sooner you can identify "troublemakers," the sooner you can move on in your search for a home.

5. Which of the following is not a method of conducting a market analysis?

a. Use the services of a mortgage underwriter.
b. Use the services of a real estate broker.
c. Use the services of an appraiser.

d. Find the selling prices for various homes in the area in which you would like to conduct a market analysis. Determine the average price per square foot for these homes. Multiply average price per square foot by the number of square feet in the home you are considering.

6. Which of the following statements regarding insured mortgages is true?

a. With insured mortgages, a mortgage insurance company, such as CMHC, extends the loan, but the mortgage insurer insures it in the event of default, thereby protecting the lender's investment.

b. With insured mortgages, a traditional lender extends the loan, but the mortgage insurer insures it in the event of default, thereby protecting the buyer from losing their home.

c. With insured mortgages, a traditional lender extends the loan, but the mortgage insurer insures it in the event of default, thereby protecting the lender's investment.

d. With insured mortgages, a mortgage insurance company, such as CMHC, extends the loan, but the mortgage insurer insures it in the event of default, thereby protecting the buyer from losing their home.

7. Title insurance:

a. Protects the insured against financial loss that may result from damage to their home or its contents.

b. Protects the insured in situations where someone else has claimed title to the home.

c. Protects the lender if the homeowner defaults on the mortgage payments by guaranteeing that title will pass back to the lender.

d. Protects the insured against loss resulting from defects that would otherwise have been detected by an up-to-date real property report or land survey.

8. Which one of the following provinces does not charge a land transfer tax?

a. Manitoba
b. British Columbia
c. Alberta
d. Ontario

9. A longer amortization period will result in _____ monthly mortgage payments and a _____ amount of mortgage interest payable over the life of the mortgage.

a. Lower; higher
b. Lower; lower
c. Higher; lower
d. Higher; higher

10. Which of the following is not considered one of the primary costs of purchasing a home?
    a. The cost of the mortgage payment.
    b. The opportunity cost of the security deposit.
    c. The opportunity cost of the down payment.
    d. None of the above. All of these primary costs need to be considered when purchasing a home.

True/False

1. True or False? Multiple Listing Service (MLS) is a marketing service that allows you and your realtor to shop online for homes.

2. True or False? Your gross debt service ratio (GDSR) is the ratio of your mortgage-related debt payments plus all other consumer debt payments divided by your total monthly gross household income.

3. True or False? Once you have determined your net cash flows, you should go ahead and purchase a home that will absorb all of your current excess cash flows.

4. True or False? When it comes to resale value, the rate of increase in home prices in previous years does not necessarily serve as a good predictor of the future.

5. True or False? Most sellers are willing to accept less than their original asking price.

6. True or False? A conventional mortgage is a mortgage where the down payment is less than 25 percent of the home's selling price.

7. True or False? In the case of a vendor take-back mortgage, the buyer will make mortgage payments directly to the seller, and the seller will maintain ownership of the property until the buyer has paid off the mortgage.

8. True or False? If property taxes have been prepaid for the entire calendar year, and possession of the home is transferred to the buyer on July 1, the seller will have to reimburse the buyer for six months' worth of taxes paid.

9. True or False? When comparing the cost of renting to the cost of home ownership, the value of the equity investment does not need to be considered if the properties are located in the same geographic area. If this is the case, the economic conditions that affect the increase in value of the rental property and home are the same.

10. True or False? Individuals will normally refinance their mortgage if market interest rates have decreased.

PART 4

Protecting Your Wealth

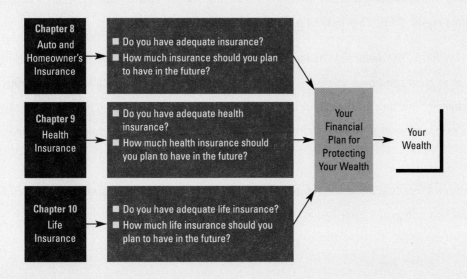

THE CHAPTERS IN THIS PART FOCUS ON INSURANCE, WHICH IS critical to protect you and your personal assets against damages and liability. Chapter 8 focuses on decisions about auto and homeowner's insurance. Chapter 9 presents key considerations regarding health, disability, critical illness, and long-term care insurance. Chapter 10 explains the provisions of life insurance.

Auto and Homeowner's Insurance

M att was recently in a major car accident that caused extensive damage to his eight-year-old sedan. When his insurance company asked Matt to get an estimate of the cost of repairs, he took it to a well-respected repair shop. They quoted a total repair bill of $5250.

Matt was prepared to pay his $250 deductible as long as the insurance company paid the rest. Since the book value of Matt's car, in good condition, was only $3240, the insurance company "totalled" it, declaring it a total loss and reimbursing him only to the extent of the book value. Matt must either repair the car using the insurance company reimbursement plus more than $2000 out of his own pocket or accept the loss and buy another car.

Understanding your insurance needs is important in determining the type and amount of coverage you need to shield you from financial loss and protect you against liability.

The objectives of this chapter are to:

1. Explain the role of risk management
2. Outline typical provisions of auto insurance
3. Describe financial coverage provided by homeowner's insurance

BACKGROUND ON INSURANCE

Property insurance ensures that any damages to your auto and home are covered, and that your personal assets are protected from any liability. In the context of insurance, the term *liability* is used to mean that you may be required to pay someone for damages you caused. Health insurance can ensure that most of your health care needs, such as physician, dental, and vision care will be covered. Disability insurance can ensure that your monthly income will continue in the event that you are unable to work as a result of an injury or illness. Critical illness insurance can ensure that you have access to lump-sum benefits in the event that you suffer a critical illness, such as a heart attack, stroke, or life-threatening cancer. Long-term care insurance can ensure that you have access to benefits that will help cover added living costs, such as in-home nursing care, when you are unable to take care of yourself as a result of an injury or illness. Life insurance can ensure financial support for your dependants, other individuals, or charities when you die.

The primary function of insurance is to maintain your existing level of wealth by protecting you against potential financial losses or liability as a result of unexpected events. It can ensure that your income continues if an accident or illness prevents you from working, or it can prevent others from taking away your personal assets.

You benefit from having insurance even when you do not receive any payments from the insurance company because you have the peace of mind of knowing that your assets are protected should you suffer a loss. Insurance may seem costly, but it is well worth the cost to ensure that your wealth will not be taken away from you.

L.O. 1   MANAGING RISK

As described in Chapter 1, risk management represents decisions about whether and how to protect against risk. The first step in risk management is to recognize the risks to which you are exposed. Then you must decide whether to protect against those risks. Once you decide whether to obtain a particular type of insurance, you must decide on the amount of coverage you need and the policy provisions you require. When deciding whether to protect against risk, your alternatives include avoiding, reducing, accepting, and sharing risk.

Avoid Risk

One method of managing risk is simply to avoid it. Consider your actions that expose you to a financial loss. Owners are exposed to a financial loss if their property is improperly maintained. You can avoid the risk of property damage if you do not own any property. However, you cannot completely avoid risk by avoiding ownership of property. If you lease a car, you are still exposed to liability and financial loss if the car is in an accident. Other types of risk are unrelated to property. For example, you are exposed to a financial loss if you require medical attention or become disabled.

Reduce Risk

Another method of managing risk is to reduce your exposure to financial loss. For example, you can purchase a small home rather than a large one to reduce the maximum possible financial loss due to property damage. You can purchase an inexpensive car to limit the possible financial loss due to property damage. You may be able to reduce your exposure to an illness or a disability by getting periodic health checkups.

Yet these steps do not fully block your exposure to financial loss. If you drive a car, you are subject not only to property damage, but also to liability. Your financial loss could be large even if the car you drive has little value.

Accept Risk

A third alternative when managing risk is to accept risk by not seeking to limit your exposure to a financial loss. This alternative may be feasible when the likelihood of an event that could cause a financial loss is very low and the potential financial loss due to the event is small. For example, if you seldom drive your car and live in a town with little traffic, you are relatively unlikely to get into an accident. You are also more likely to accept risk when the possible financial loss resulting from the event is limited. For example, if you drive an inexpensive and old car, you may be willing to accept your exposure to financial loss due to property damage by removing collision coverage from your auto insurance policy. However, you are still subject to liability, which could put all of your personal assets in jeopardy.

Share Risk

A final alternative is to share risk. If you cannot avoid a specific type of risk, you cannot reduce that risk, and you do not wish to be exposed to financial loss as a result of the risk, you should consider insurance. The concept of risk sharing is covered later in this chapter.

premium
The cost of obtaining insurance.

The decision to obtain insurance is determined by weighing its costs and benefits. The cost of obtaining insurance is the premium that is paid for a policy each year. The benefit of obtaining insurance is that it can protect your assets or income from events that otherwise might cause financial loss. Consequently, you protect your existing net worth and also increase the likelihood that you will be able to increase your net worth in the future. Without insurance, you could lose all of your assets if you are involved in an accident that causes major damages and/or liability as a result of an injury to others.

You cannot insure against all types of risk, as some types of insurance are either unavailable or too expensive. Your risk management strategy will determine which types of risk you wish to insure against. When there is a high likelihood that an event will cause a financial loss and the potential financial loss from that event is large, insurance should be considered. You may choose to accept the types of risk that might result in only small financial losses. In this chapter and the following two, you will learn the key provisions of auto, homeowner's, health, disability, critical illness, long-term care, and life insurance. With this background, you can create your own risk management plan.

Your risk management decisions are also affected by your degree of risk tolerance. For example, you and your neighbour could be in the same financial position and have the same exposure to various types of risk. Yet, you may obtain more insurance than your neighbour because you are more concerned about exposure to financial loss. While you incur annual insurance expenses from insurance premiums, you are protected from

peril
A hazard or risk you face.

financial losses resulting from covered perils (hazards or risks you face).

IN-CLASS NOTES

Background on Insurance and Managing Risks

- Types of insurance
  - Property insurance (auto and home insurance)
  - Health insurance (physician, dental, and vision care)
  - Disability insurance (provides income continuation)
  - Critical illness insurance (provides lump sum benefits)
  - Long-term care insurance (covers added cost of living)
  - Life insurance (provides financial support to dependants)
- Risk management options
  - Avoid, reduce, accept, and/or share risk

ROLE OF INSURANCE COMPANIES

Insurance companies offer insurance policies that can protect you against financial loss. Since there are many different types of risk that could cause financial losses, there are many different types of insurance that can protect you from those risks. Exhibit 8.1 describes some common events that can cause major financial loss and the related types of insurance that can protect you from these events. The most popular forms of insurance for individuals are property and casualty insurance, life insurance, and health insurance.

Property and casualty insurance is used to insure property and therefore consists of auto insurance and home insurance. Some insurance companies specialize in a particular type of insurance, while others offer all types of insurance for individuals. Companies that offer the same type of insurance vary in terms of the specific policies they offer.

In recent years, chartered banks and other types of financial institutions have established insurance businesses. Some financial institutions have an insurance centre within their branches. This enables customers to take care of their insurance needs where they receive other financial services.

Insurance Company Operations

When an insurance company sells an insurance policy to you, it is obliged to cover claims as described in the insurance policy. For example, if your car is insured by a policy, the insurance company is obliged to protect you from financial loss due to an accident up to the policy limits. If you are in a car accident while driving that car, the insurance company provides payments (subject to limits specified in the contract) to cover any liability to passengers and others and to repair property damage resulting from the accident.

As mentioned earlier, one method of protecting against risk is to share it with others. Insurance companies help policy owners share risk by pooling together a number of insurance policies based on the type of insurance purchased and the characteristics of a group of policy owners. The insurance company is able to generate a profit because it

Exhibit 8.1 Common Events That Could Cause a Financial Loss

Event	Financial loss	Protection
You have a car accident and damage your car	Car repairs	Auto insurance (collision)
You have a car accident in which another person in your car is injured	Medical bills and liability	Auto insurance (accident benefits)
You have a car accident in which another person in the other driver's car is injured	Medical bills and liability	Auto insurance (liability)
Your home is damaged by a fire	Home repairs	Homeowner's insurance
Your neighbour is injured while in your home	Medical bills and liability	Homeowner's insurance (liability)
You become ill and need medical attention	Prescription drugs	Health insurance
You develop an illness that requires long-term care	Nursing care	Long-term care insurance
You become disabled	Loss of income	Disability insurance
You die while family members rely on your income	Loss of income	Life insurance

knows that the majority of policy owners will not need to file claims during the coverage period. Consider a policy owner who pays $1000 in auto insurance for the year. Assume that he is in an accident, and that the insurance company has to pay $20 000 to cover liability and repair the car. The payout by the insurance company is 20 times the premium received. In other words, it would take 20 auto insurance policy premiums to generate enough revenue to cover the cost of this one claim. To generate sufficient revenue, the insurance company will sell a number of auto insurance policies. Based on historical claims information, it can estimate the number of policies it must sell and the price at which to sell these policies to ensure a profit for the company. In general, insurance companies generate their revenue by receiving payments for policies and by earning a return from investing the proceeds until the funds are needed to cover claims. They incur costs by making payments to cover policy owner claims. When an insurance company makes payments on a claim, these payments are commonly less than the total annual premium received from the group of policy owners. The difference between the amount of premiums collected from all policy owners plus the investment income earned by investing these premiums, and the total value of claims and other business expenses, represents the amount of profit the insurance company generates.

$$\text{Profit} = (\text{Premiums} + \text{Investment Earnings}) - (\text{Claims} + \text{Business Expenses})$$

Relationship between Insurance Company Claims and Premiums. Since insurance companies rely mostly on their premiums to cover claims, they price their insurance policies to reflect the probability of a claim and the size of that claim. For an event that is very unlikely and could cause minor damage, the premium would be relatively low. For an event that is more likely and could cause major damage, the insurance premium would be relatively high. In a sense, a high insurance premium indicates that there is a greater probability that you may use the insurance coverage provided.

underwriters
Employees of an insurance company who determine the risk of specific insurance policies and decide what policies to offer and what premiums to charge.

Insurance Underwriters. An insurance company relies on underwriters, who calculate the risk of specific insurance policies and decide what policies to offer and what premiums to charge. Underwriters recognize that their insurance company must generate revenue that is greater than its expenses to be profitable, so they set premiums that are aligned with anticipated claims.

Go to
www3.ambest.com/ratings/
default.asp

This website provides
information on how insurance companies are rated.

Insurance Company Credit Ratings and Service

An initial step in finding the right insurance policy is to contact several insurance companies to determine the types of policies that are offered. Also, check with your employer. Some employers obtain discounts on insurance for their employees, especially for life insurance and disability insurance.

It is important to select an insurance company that is in good financial condition, as you are relying on it to provide you with adequate coverage over the policy period. There are several services that rate insurance companies, including A.M. Best (www.ambest.com), Moody's Investor Services (www.moodys.com), and Standard & Poor's Corporation (www.standardandpoors.com).

insurance agent
Represents one or more insurance companies and recommends insurance policies that fit customers' needs.

captive (or exclusive) insurance agent
Works for one particular insurance company.

independent insurance agent
Represents many different insurance companies.

The level of service among insurance companies varies. The best insurance companies provide quick and thorough claims service. Sources of information on level of service by insurance companies include the Better Business Bureau and *Consumer Reports* magazine.

Role of Insurance Agents and Brokers

When contacting an insurance company, you will probably communicate with an insurance agent or broker. An insurance agent represents one or more insurance companies and recommends insurance policies that fit customers' needs. Captive (or exclusive) insurance agents work for one particular insurance company, whereas independent insurance agents (also called insurance brokers) represent many different insurance companies. These independent agents are linked to various insurance companies online and therefore can quickly obtain quotations for different policies from different vendors. In addition to helping customers with various types of insurance, insurance agents may offer financial planning services, such as retirement planning and estate planning. Some insurance agents are also licensed to serve as a sales representative for mutual funds or other financial products.

L.O. 2   AUTO INSURANCE

Auto insurance insures against the legal liability that may arise from causing death or injury to others; the expense associated with providing medical care to you, your passengers, and other persons outside your vehicle; and the costs associated with damage to your automobile. In this way, it limits your potential liabilities (expenses due to an accident) and also protects one of your main assets (your car). If you own or drive a car, you are required to have a minimum level of auto insurance. Auto insurance is provided by a government agency in British Columbia, Saskatchewan, and Manitoba. In Quebec, the expense associated with providing medical care to you, your passengers, and pedestrians is covered through a government agency. In all other provinces, auto insurance is purchased through private property and casualty insurance companies. Your policy specifies the amount of coverage if you are legally liable for bodily injury, if you and your passengers incur medical bills, or if your car is damaged as the result of an accident or some other event (such as a tree falling on it).

The estimated average automobile insurance premium by province, in 2005, is shown in Exhibit 8.2. Premiums vary among provinces. Recent reforms in the way private insurers are able to charge premiums have resulted in a significant decrease in the cost of auto insurance. As a result, Exhibit 8.2 shows that three of the four most expensive average auto insurance premiums in 2005 were in provinces that provide auto insurance through a government agency.

Auto Insurance Policy Provisions

An insurance policy is a contract between an insurance company and the policy owner. An auto insurance policy specifies the coverage (including dollar limits) provided by an insurance company for a particular individual and vehicle. The contract identifies the policy owner and family members who are also insured if they use the vehicle. You should have

insurance policy
Contract between an insurance company and the policy owner.

auto insurance policy
Specifies the coverage provided by an insurance company for a particular individual and vehicle.

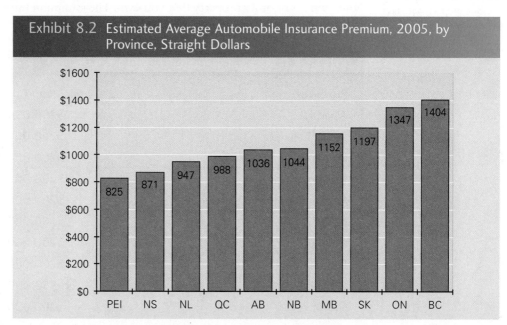

Exhibit 8.2 Estimated Average Automobile Insurance Premium, 2005, by Province, Straight Dollars

Source: Skinner, Brent J., *The False Promise of Government Auto Insurance: Estimating Average Auto Insurance Premiums in Ten Provinces*, The Fraser Institute: 2007. Reprinted with permission of the Fraser Institute.

insurance information such as your policy number and the name of a contact person at the insurance company with you when you drive. If you are in an accident, exchange your insurance information with that of the other driver and also fill out a police report.

Every auto insurance policy explains what is covered in detail. Generally, auto insurance policies contain three sections: third party liability coverage, accident benefits, and loss or damage to insured automobile. If you have one, review your own auto insurance policy as you read on, so that you understand your coverage.

Section A: Third Party Liability Coverage

third party liability
A legal term that describes the person(s) who have experienced loss because of the insured.

Third party liability is a legal term that describes the person(s) who have experienced loss because of the insured. Third party liability coverage consists of two key components: bodily injury liability and property damage liability. Bodily injury liability coverage protects you against liability associated with injuries you (or family members listed on the policy) cause to others. You or your family members are also covered if you cause injuries to others while driving someone else's car with their permission. Bodily injury expenses include medical bills and lost wages as a result of an accident you cause. The coverage is designed to protect you if you cause an accident and the driver of the other car sues you.

bodily injury liability coverage
Protects you against liability associated with injuries you cause to others.

It is critical to have adequate liability coverage. Exhibit 8.3 outlines the minimum required liability coverage by province. Third party liability coverage is mandatory in all provinces. Any legal expenses incurred by an insurance company while defending you against a lawsuit are not considered when determining the limits on liability coverage. For example, if a person sues you and is awarded an amount that is less than the liability limit in your contract, it is covered by your policy regardless of the legal expenses incurred by the insurance company. However, if the award granted in a lawsuit against you exceeds the limit on your policy's liability coverage, you will be required to pay the difference and therefore could lose your assets. The financial loss to you and your family from a lawsuit resulting from a car accident could be devastating. Therefore, you should always purchase more than the minimum required third party liability listed in Exhibit 8.3. You should have coverage of at least $1 million for third party liability. As your net worth increases, you should review your liability coverage with an eye to increasing it.

property damage liability coverage
Protects against losses that result when the policy owner damages another person's property with his or her car.

Property damage liability coverage protects against losses that result when the policy owner damages another person's property with his or her car. Examples include damage to a car, fence, lamppost, or building. Note that property damage liability does not cover your own car or other property that you own. The minimum third party liability amounts listed in Exhibit 8.3 also apply to property damage liability. However, check with your

Exhibit 8.3 Minimum Required Third Party Liability Coverage

Province	Minimum Coverage
Alberta	$200 000
British Columbia	$200 000
Manitoba	$200 000
New Brunswick	$200 000
Newfoundland and Labrador	$200 000
Nova Scotia	$500 000
Ontario	$200 000
Prince Edward Island	$200 000
Quebec	$50 000
Saskatchewan	$200 000

Source: Insurance Bureau of Canada, www.ibc.ca/en, 2007. Reprinted with permission of Insurance Bureau of Canada.

insurance agent on the impact that total claims in excess of the provincial minimum will have on your property damage coverage. In most provinces, there is a cap on the amount of property damage coverage if a total claim against you exceeds the provincial minimum. You should always purchase additional property damage liability coverage.

Section B: Accident Benefits

Accident benefits coverage insures against the cost of medical care for you and other passengers in your car. In addition to coverage for medical payments, such as the cost of rehabilitation, accident benefits generally include coverage for funeral costs, loss of income as a result of death or total disability, and uninsured motorist coverage. Accident benefits coverage is mandatory in all provinces except Newfoundland and Labrador. The medical coverage applies only to the passengers, including the driver of the insured car. If you were driving someone else's car at the time of the accident, the owner of that car would be responsible for the medical coverage for passengers.

No-Fault Auto Insurance. All provinces in Canada provide some accident benefits under what is known as a "no-fault" system. No-fault auto insurance does not mean that nobody is at fault when an accident occurs. However, determining who is at fault may take some time. To ensure that all insured individuals receive immediate medical treatment for their injuries, no-fault accident benefits allow policy owners in all provinces to receive immediate medical payments through their own insurance policy. The rationale is that the sooner you receive treatment, the sooner you will get better.

The amount of accident benefits you receive under your province's no-fault system is directly linked to your ability to sue the at-fault driver. The government agencies in Saskatchewan, Manitoba, and Quebec operate pure no-fault auto insurance systems. Under a pure no-fault system, you are unable to sue the at-fault driver for bodily injury or damage to personal property. As a result, the accident benefits in these three provinces tend to be higher than in the other provinces.

uninsured motorist coverage
Insures against the cost of bodily injury when an accident is caused by another driver who is not insured.

underinsured motorist coverage
Insures against the additional cost of bodily injury when an accident is caused by a driver who has insufficient coverage.

Uninsured motorist coverage insures against the cost of bodily injury when an accident is caused by another driver who is not insured. The coverage also applies if you are in an accident caused by a hit-and-run driver or by a driver who is at fault but whose insurance company goes bankrupt. This coverage applies to bodily injury when you are not at fault, while the third party liability coverage from Section A applies to bodily injury when you are at fault. Like the third party liability insurance, there are policy limits that you specify, such as $200 000. The higher the limits, the higher the insurance premium. Underinsured motorist coverage insures against the additional cost of bodily injury when an accident is caused by a driver who has insufficient coverage. Suppose that you suffer bodily injury as a result of an accident caused by an underinsured driver. If the damages to you are $40 000 and the insurance policy of the underinsured driver only covers $30 000, your insurance company will provide the difference of $10 000.

Section C: Loss of or Damage to Insured Automobile

collision insurance
Insures against costs of damage to your car resulting from an accident in which the driver of your car is at fault.

comprehensive coverage
Insures you against damage to your car that results from something other than a collision, such as floods, theft, fire, hail, explosions, riots, vandalism, and various other perils.

Collision insurance and comprehensive coverage insure against damage to your car. Both types of coverage are optional in all provinces. If you drive an old car that is not worth very much, you may decide not to carry this type of insurance. Collision insurance insures against costs of damage to your car resulting from an accident in which the driver of your car is at fault. Comprehensive coverage insures you against damage to your car that results from something other than a collision, such as floods, theft, fire, hail, explosions, riots, vandalism, and various other perils.

Although collision insurance and comprehensive coverage is optional, car loan providers may require the borrower to maintain insurance that will cover any property damage to the car to protect the lender in the event that the car owner has an accident and stops making loan payments. The car that serves as collateral on the loan may be worthless if it is damaged in an accident. In this event, the insurance company may pay the lender up to the book value of the car.

Collision insurance and comprehensive coverage is especially valuable if you have a new car that you would likely repair if it were damaged. Some insurance companies offer a new-car rider or clause that can protect you from the loss that occurs from the depreciation when you "drive the new car off the lot." The coverage may not be as valuable if you have an old car because you may not feel the need to repair damage as long as the car can still be driven. Note that the coverage is limited to the cash value of the car. For example, if your car was worth $2000 before the accident and is worth $1200 after the accident, your insurance company will pay no more than $800. The insurance company will not incur extremely high repair expenses to fix cars that have little value.

Collision coverage can be valuable even if you do not believe you were at fault in an accident. If the other driver claims that you were at fault, you and your insurance company may need to take the matter to court. Meanwhile, you can use the collision coverage to have the car repaired. If your insurance company wins the lawsuit, the other driver's insurance company will be required to pay the expenses associated with repairing your car.

Collision coverage is normally limited to the car itself and not to items that were damaged while in the car. For example, if you were transporting a new computer at the time of an accident, the damage to the computer would not be protected by comprehensive coverage. The computer may be covered by your homeowner's insurance, which is discussed later in this chapter.

deductible
A set dollar amount that you are responsible for paying before any coverage is provided by your insurer.

Deductible. The **deductible** is a set dollar amount that you are responsible for paying before any coverage is provided by your insurer. For example, a deductible of $250 means that you must pay the first $250 in damages due to an accident. The insurance company pays any additional expenses beyond the deductible, which is normally between $250 and $1000. This deductible should be an amount you can easily afford (part of your emergency fund or liquidity needs). However, the higher the deductible, the lower the insurance premium.

Facility Association

Facility Association
Ensures that drivers unable to obtain insurance with an individual company are able to obtain the coverage they need to operate their vehicles legally.

Facility Association is a not-for-profit organization made up of all auto insurance providers operating in every province and territory except British Columbia, Manitoba, Saskatchewan, and Quebec. Facility Association ensures that drivers unable to obtain insurance with an individual company are able to obtain the coverage they need to operate their vehicles legally. Higher-risk drivers may have difficulty obtaining insurance for many reasons: a poor driving record or claims history, the type of vehicle, and location or area of residence. Additional information on Facility Association coverage can be found at www.facilityassociation.com/brochures.asp.

Other Provisions

You can elect to have coverage for expenses not included in the standard policy. For example, a policy can cover the cost of a rental car while your car is being repaired after an accident. You can also elect to have coverage for towing, even if the problems are not the result of an accident. Your premium will increase slightly for these provisions.

You can also include a provision in your auto insurance policy to cover any car you rent. If you do not have such a provision, the rental car agency will typically offer to sell you collision damage coverage, liability insurance, medical coverage, and even coverage for theft of personal belongings from the car. If rental car insurance is not covered by your policy, some credit cards provide you with collision and comprehensive insurance benefits when you use that card to pay for the rental services.

exclusion
A term appearing in insurance contracts or policies that describes items or circumstances that are specifically excluded from insurance coverage.

An auto insurance policy also specifies exclusions (items or circumstances that are specifically excluded from insurance coverage) and limitations of the coverage. For example, coverage may not apply if you intentionally damage a car, if you drive a car that is not yours without the permission of the owner, or if you drive a car that you own but that is not listed on your insurance policy. It also explains how you should comply with procedures if you are in an accident.

Summary of Auto Insurance Provisions

The most important types of coverage identified above are included in a standard insurance policy. They are summarized in Exhibit 8.4. Notice that the exhibit classifies the potential financial damages as being related to:

- your car in an accident
- the other car or other property in an accident
- your car when not in an accident

FACTORS THAT AFFECT YOUR AUTO INSURANCE PREMIUMS

Your insurance premium is influenced by the likelihood that you will submit claims to the insurance company and the estimated cost to the insurance company for covering those claims. As explained earlier, your auto insurance premium will be higher for a policy that specifies a greater amount of liability coverage and a lower deductible. In provinces where insurance is provided by a government agency (British Columbia, Saskatchewan, and Manitoba), personal characteristics such as your age are not considered when determining auto insurance rates. Factors that are common to all provinces include the following.

How You Use Your Vehicle. People who use their cars to go to and from work are more likely to be involved in auto accidents than those who only drive their cars on weekends. Commuting distance is also considered.

Value of Car. Insurance premiums are high when the potential financial loss is high. Collision and comprehensive insurance premiums are higher for new cars. In addition, the premium is normally higher for an expensive car than an inexpensive car of the same age. For example, the insurance on a new Mercedes is higher than that on a new Saturn.

Exhibit 8.4 Summary of Auto Insurance Provisions

Financial Damages Related to Your Car in an Accident	Auto Insurance Provision
Liability due to passengers in your car when you are at fault	Bodily injury liability
Liability due to passengers in your car when you are not at fault but driver of other car is uninsured or underinsured	Uninsured/underinsured motorist coverage
Damage to your own car	Collision
Treatment of injuries to driver and passengers of your car	Accident benefits

Financial Damages Related to the Other Car or Other Property in an Accident	
Liability due to passengers in the other car	Bodily injury liability
Liability due to damage to the other car	Property damage liability
Liability due to damage to other property	Property damage liability

Financial Damages Related to Your Car When Not in an Accident	
Damage to your car as a result of theft, fire, vandalism, or other non-accident events	Comprehensive

Repair Record of Your Car. Some car models require more repair work for the same type of damage. For example, replacing a door on a Ford may be easier than on some other cars, which reduces the repair bill. When a car can be repaired easily and inexpensively, its insurance premium is lower.

Your Location. Auto insurance is more expensive in large cities, where the probability of being involved in an accident is higher. In contrast, auto insurance is less expensive in rural areas, where the probability of being involved in an accident is lower because there will be fewer cars on the road. In Saskatchewan, your location is not taken into consideration when determining auto insurance premiums.

Your Driver Training. Insurance companies recognize that driver training can improve driver performance, and therefore can reduce the likelihood of accidents in the future. They encourage drivers to enrol in driver training programs. If you have completed a driver training program, you may qualify for a discount.

Your Driving Record. If you have an excellent driving record, including no accidents and no moving violations for a year or longer, you may be charged a lower premium than other drivers. For example, drivers in Manitoba receive merit discounts depending on the number of years that they do not have any at-fault claims. No one purposely creates a bad driving record, but some drivers do not realize how much their insurance premium will increase if their record is poor. In provinces with private auto insurance, these drivers cannot comparison shop effectively. In many cases, they will have to rely on Facility Association coverage to have any auto insurance at all. Once drivers are labelled as high risk, it takes several years of safe driving to prove that they have improved their driving habits. Thus, they will pay very expensive insurance premiums for several years. After all, all drivers in the Facility Association are high risk and claims will be higher and greater in number.

In addition to the factors listed above, provinces that offer auto insurance through private property and casualty insurers may take into consideration the following factors.

Your Age and Sex. Insurance companies often base their premiums on personal profiles and age is one of the most important characteristics. Younger drivers are more likely to get into accidents, and therefore they pay higher insurance premiums. In particular, drivers between the ages of 16 and 25 are considered to be high risk. Insurance companies incur higher expenses from covering their claims and offset these higher expenses by charging higher premiums. Another important characteristic is sex, as male drivers tend to get into more serious or expensive accidents than female drivers. For these reasons, male teenagers are charged higher auto insurance premiums.

Your Driving Distance. You are more likely to get into an accident the more kilometres you drive. Thus, your premium will be higher if you drive more kilometres. Many insurance companies classify drivers into two or more driving distance groups. For example, if you drive fewer than 16 000 kilometres per year, you may qualify for the low driving distance group, which entitles you to a lower premium.

Comparing Premiums among Insurance Companies

One final factor that affects your auto insurance premium is the insurance company you select. Premiums can vary substantially among insurance companies, so always obtain several quotes before you select a company. The opportunity to shop around for auto insurance is only available in provinces where auto insurance is offered through private property and casualty insurers. Several websites (such as www.kanetix.ca/auto-insurance and www.insurancehotline.com) provide auto insurance quotes online.

If you have specific questions about the coverage offered and want to speak to an insurance salesperson, you can call some insurance companies directly. A comparison of quotes online might at least help you determine which companies to call for more information. Alternatively, you can call an independent insurance agent, who can help you purchase insurance from one of several companies.

When comparing premiums, recognize that the premium may vary with the type of policy desired. For example, an insurance company may have relatively low premiums compared to its competitors for a policy involving substantial coverage for bodily injury liability, but relatively high premiums for a policy involving collision coverage. Therefore, you should not select a company based on advice you receive from friends or family members. If their policies are different from the one you desire, another company may offer better coverage. In addition, companies change their premiums over time, so they may charge relatively low premiums in one period but relatively high premiums in the following period for the same policy because of their claims experience (the number and monetary values of claims the company has paid out over a recent period).

Comparing Prices at the Time of Renewal. Once an auto insurance policy has been in effect for 60 days, an insurance company can only cancel your policy if you provided fraudulent information on your application, if your driver's licence is suspended, or if you do not pay your premiums. However, it may decide not to renew your policy when it expires if you had a poor driving record over the recent policy period. For example, it is unlikely you will be able to renew your policy if you caused an accident as a result of drunk driving.

If an insurance company is willing to renew your policy, it may raise the premium in the renewal period even if your driving record has been good. You can switch to a different insurance company when the policy expires if you are not satisfied with your present one or think that the premium is too high. You should compare auto insurance prices among companies before renewing your policy. However, recognize that your driving record will follow you. If you recently caused one or more accidents, you will likely be charged a higher premium whether you continue with your existing company or switch to a new one. Some insurance companies also offer teaser rates. Soon after you switch, premiums are raised. Switching policies frequently can also raise your premiums.

IN-CLASS NOTES

Auto Insurance and Factors That Affect Your Auto Insurance Premiums

- Auto insurance features
  - Third party liability coverage (bodily injury and property damage liability)
  - Accident benefits (medical care)
  - Loss of or damage to insured automobile (collision and comprehensive coverage)
- Factors that affect auto insurance premiums
  - How you use your vehicle
  - Value and repair record of your car
  - Your location (except in Saskatchewan)
  - Your driver training and driving record
  - Your age, sex, and driving distance (in some provinces)

IF YOU ARE IN AN AUTO ACCIDENT

If you are in an auto accident, contact the police immediately if:

- someone is hurt

- you think the other driver may be guilty of a Criminal Code offence, such as drunk driving

- there is significant property damage

If it is safe to move your car, try to move it out of traffic. If you are unable to move your vehicle, use your hazard lights and any other warning devices, such as flares, you may have. Request information from the other drivers in the accident, including their names, addresses, phone numbers, driver's licence numbers, plate numbers, and insurance information. You may also obtain contact information (including licence plate numbers) from witnesses, in case they leave before the police arrive. Make sure that you can validate whatever information other drivers provide. Some drivers who believe they are at fault and without insurance may attempt to give you false names and leave before police arrive. Take pictures of any evidence that may prove you were not at fault. Write down the details of how the accident happened, including the time, date, location, speed of all cars, and road and weather conditions, while they are fresh in your mind. You should also sketch the accident scene, including the position and direction of all the vehicles involved in the accident. You should keep some paper and a pen or pencil in your glove compartment for such occasions. Finally, make sure you ask for a copy of the police report once the accident is reported.

File a claim with your insurance company immediately. It will review the police report and may contact witnesses. It will also verify that your insurance policy is still in effect, and determine whether repairs and medical treatment will be covered based on your policy's provisions. The insurance policy may specify guidelines for having your car repaired, such as obtaining at least two estimates before you have repairs done. A claims adjuster employed by the insurance company may investigate the accident details and attempt to determine how much you should be paid.

Once you incur expenses, such as car repairs or medical expenses, send this information along with receipts to the insurance company. It will respond by reimbursing you for a portion of the expenses based on your policy. It may provide full or partial reimbursement. Alternatively, it may state that some or all of your expenses are not covered by your policy. Keep copies of all correspondence and receipts sent to your insurance company.

If your insurance company believes that the other driver is at fault, it should seek damages from the other driver's insurance company. If the other driver is not insured, your insurance company will pay your claim if you have uninsured or underinsured motorist insurance. If your claim is denied by your insurance company and you still believe that the other driver is at fault, you may need to file a claim against the other driver or the other driver's insurance company. This is also the case when an injured party seeks damages greater than those offered by his or her policy. You must pay your deductible while you await the results of your claim against the other driver. If your claim is successful, you can request that your deductible be refunded by the other driver's insurance company.

<table>
<tr><td>L.O. 3</td></tr>
</table>

HOMEOWNER'S INSURANCE

homeowner's insurance
Provides insurance in the event of property damage, theft, or personal and third party liability relating to home ownership.

Homeowner's insurance provides insurance in the event of property damage, theft, or personal and third party liability relating to home ownership. It not only protects many individuals' most valuable asset, but also limits their potential liabilities (expenses) associated with the home. Premiums on homeowner's insurance are commonly paid either monthly or yearly.

all perils coverage
Protects the home and any other structures on the property against all events except those that are specifically excluded by the policy.

named perils coverage
Protects the home and any other structures on the property against only those events named in the policy.

Types of Perils Covered by Homeowner's Insurance

As discussed earlier, risk can be defined as exposure to events (or perils) that can cause a financial loss. Financial loss due to the ownership of a home could occur as a result of a wide variety of adverse events, such as flood, theft, burglary, fire, earthquake, or tornado. Homeowner's insurance can be structured to cover a few or all of these and similar perils. All perils coverage protects the home and any other structures on the property against all events except those that are specifically excluded by the policy. Named perils coverage protects the home and any other structures on the property against only those events named in the policy. To reduce premiums, a homeowner can apply coverage differently to the home and to the contents of the home.

HOMEOWNER'S INSURANCE POLICY PROVISIONS

A homeowner's insurance policy typically provides coverage for the building, its contents, and the liability of the homeowner. As shown in Exhibit 8.5, the specific details regarding the coverage vary among policies. Comprehensive coverage provides full coverage for all causes of financial loss. At the other end, basic coverage only covers losses for named perils. Although the premium for a basic policy will be lower than for a comprehensive policy, the potential to lose your home to an uncovered peril should not be ignored. Broad coverage will allow the homeowner to save on the cost of homeowner's insurance while maintaining full coverage for all causes of financial loss related to the house. Most homeowner's insurance policies focus on the following types of coverage.

Building (Property Damage)

cash value policy
Pays you the value of the damaged property after considering its depreciation.

replacement cost policy
Pays you the actual cost of replacing the damaged property.

The homeowner's policy covers damage to the home. The specific provisions of the policy explain the degree of coverage. A cash value policy pays you the value of the damaged property after considering its depreciation (wear and tear). A replacement cost policy pays you the actual cost of replacing the damaged property. A replacement cost policy is preferable because the actual cost of replacing damaged property is normally higher than the depreciated or assessed value of property. For example, assume that a home is completely destroyed and was valued at $90 000 just before that happened. A cash value policy would provide insurance coverage of $90 000, even though the cost of rebuilding (replacing) the home could be $100 000 or more. In contrast, the replacement cost policy would insure the home for its replacement cost, and therefore would cover the entire cost of repairing the damage up to a limit specified in the homeowner's policy. A policy typically specifies a deductible, or an amount that you must pay for damage before the insurance coverage is applied.

Minimum Limit. Many insurers require that your homeowner's insurance policy cover at least 80 percent of the full replacement cost. The financial institution that provides your mortgage loan likely will require homeowner's insurance that would at least

Exhibit 8.5 Types of Perils Protected by Various Types of Homeowner's Insurance Polices

	Level of Coverage	
Policy Type	Building	Contents
Comprehensive Coverage	all perils	all perils
Basic Coverage	named perils	named perils
Broad Coverage	all perils	named perils

cover your mortgage. In most cases, you want more insurance than is required by the mortgage lender. You should have sufficient insurance not only to cover the mortgage loan balance, but also to replace the property and all personal assets that are damaged.

Other Structures on Property

The homeowner's insurance policy also specifies whether separate structures such as a garage, shed, or swimming pool are covered, and the maximum amount of coverage for these structures. Trees and shrubs are usually included, with a specified maximum amount of coverage. A deductible may be applied to these other structures.

Contents (Personal Property)

A policy normally covers personal assets such as furniture, computers, or clothing up to a specified maximum amount. For example, a policy may specify that all personal assets such as furniture and clothing are covered up to $40 000. Standard homeowner's insurance policies limit the coverage of personal property to no more than half of the coverage on the dwelling. A deductible may be applied to the personal property.

home inventory
Contains detailed information about your personal property that can be used when filing a claim.

A home inventory contains detailed information about your personal property that can be used when filing a claim. Create a list of all of your personal assets and estimate the market value of each item. Use a video camera to film your personal assets in your home for proof of their existence. Keep the list and the video in a safe place outside of your home, so that you have access to them if your home is destroyed.

Policy Limits and Exclusions

The policy you purchase is not open ended, meaning that the insurance company will only reimburse you up to a certain maximum amount as stated in the policy. Exclusions are things or perils that are not specifically covered by the policy.

Personal Property Replacement Cost Coverage. Many homeowner's insurance policies cover personal property for their cash value. For example, if a home entertainment system priced at $2500 three years ago is assumed to have a life of five years, it has used up three-fifths of its life. Based on this amount of depreciation, the insurer will pay you the cash value of $1000. However, if this home entertainment system is destroyed in a fire, you might need to spend $3000 to replace it.

Just as the dwelling can be insured at replacement cost rather than cash value, so can personal assets. This provision will increase your premium slightly, but it may be worthwhile if you have personal assets that have high replacement costs.

personal property floater
An extension of the homeowner's insurance policy that allows you to itemize your valuables.

Personal Property Floater. Some personal assets are very valuable and are not fully covered by your homeowner's policy. You may need to obtain a personal property floater (also called supplementary insurance), which is an extension of the homeowner's insurance policy that allows you to itemize your valuables. For example, if you have very expensive computer equipment or jewellery in your home, you may purchase this additional insurance to protect those specific assets. An alternative is an unscheduled personal property floater, which provides protection for all of your personal property.

Home Office Provision. Assets in a home office, such as a personal computer, are not covered in many standard homeowner's policies. You can request a home office provision, which will require a higher premium. Alternatively, you could purchase a separate policy to cover the home office.

Liability

A homeowner's policy specifies coverage in the event that you are sued as the result of something that occurs in your home or on your property. Normally, you are responsible for an injury to another person while they are on your property. For example, if a neighbour falls down the steps of your home and sues you, your policy would likely cover you. In most cases, liability coverage purchased through your homeowner's insurance policy also extends to events that occur away from your home. For example, if you are skiing at Mont Tremblant and you run over someone on the slopes and cause injury, your homeowner's insurance liability coverage will protect you.

Your exposure to liability is not tied to the value of your home. Even if you have a small home of modest value, you need to protect against liability. Some insurance companies provide minimum coverage of $100 000 against liability. However, a higher level of coverage, such as $300 000, is commonly recommended. If you have uncommon risks, such as certain breeds of dogs or a pool, you may want to consider a much higher liability amount. Coverage includes court costs and any awards granted as a result of lawsuits against you due to injuries on your property.

Medical payments and voluntary property damage are also covered under the liability portion of homeowner's insurance. The medical payments provision covers the costs of medical care if someone is accidentally injured on your property. The voluntary damage provision provides coverage to you in the event that you accidentally damage the property of others (for example, if your child inadvertently throws a ball through your neighbour's window while playing catch). This event would be covered under the voluntary property damage provision of your liability coverage. Medical payments and voluntary property damage are designed to cover costs that are incurred before a lawsuit occurs.

Other Types of Expenses

Many other possible provisions could be included in a policy to cover a wide variety of circumstances. For example, if an event such as a fire forces you to live away from home, you will incur additional living expenses. A loss-of-use provision specifies whether your policy covers these expenses and the maximum amount of coverage.

Expenses Incurred by Homeowner's Insurance Companies

The allocation of expenses incurred by homeowner's insurance companies is shown in Exhibit 8.6. Overall, claims paid represent 62 percent of total expenses. The cost of settling claims represents 11 percent of total expenses.

IN-CLASS NOTES

Homeowner's Insurance and Policy Provisions
- Peril
  - The cause of a financial loss (e.g., flood)
- Types of coverage
  - All perils coverage
  - Named perils coverage
- Policy provisions
  - What is covered? (e.g., building, contents, liability of homeowner)
  - Types of policies (comprehensive, basic, broad)
  - Cash value policy vs. replacement cost policy

_____

_____

_____

_____

_____

_____

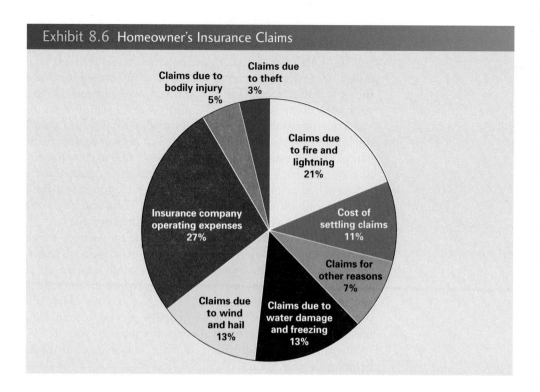

Exhibit 8.6 Homeowner's Insurance Claims

HOMEOWNER'S INSURANCE PREMIUMS

The annual cost of insuring a home can be substantial over time, as shown in Exhibit 8.7. Premiums have risen in recent years and are expected to rise in the future. This section describes the factors that influence the premium charged, and explains how you can reduce your premium. Your homeowner's insurance premium is influenced by the likelihood that you will submit claims to the insurance company and by the cost to the insurance company of covering those claims.

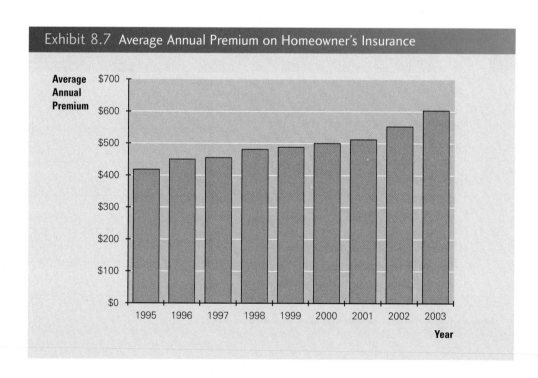

Exhibit 8.7 Average Annual Premium on Homeowner's Insurance

Factors That Affect Homeowner's Insurance Premiums

The premium you pay for homeowner's insurance primarily depends on the following factors.

- **Value of Insured Home.** Insurance premiums reflect the value of the insured home and therefore are higher for more expensive homes.

- **Deductible.** A higher deductible reduces the amount of coverage provided by the homeowner's insurance, and therefore results in a lower insurance premium.

- **Location.** The potential for damage is greater in some areas, and therefore the premiums are higher. For example, homes in Atlantic Canada are more likely to be damaged by severe weather than homes located in Saskatchewan. Home insurance rates are therefore much higher along the coast. Similarly, premiums will be higher for homes in locations prone to tornadoes, floods, or earthquakes.

- **Degree of Protection.** If you want protection against an earthquake on a home in Vancouver, you must pay a higher premium. If you want protection against a flood, you may need to buy an additional insurance policy.

- **Discounts.** You may obtain discounts on your insurance by maintaining an alarm system or a household fire extinguisher in your home, paying for your insurance in one lump sum, or purchasing multiple types of insurance (such as auto, health, and life) from the same insurer.

Reducing Your Homeowner's Insurance Premium

Consider the following actions you can take to reduce your homeowner's insurance premium.

Go to
www.kanetix.ca/home-insurance

This website provides answers to many important questions concerning homeowner's insurance.

Increase Your Deductible. If you are willing to pay a higher deductible, you can reduce your premium. For example, if you use a deductible of $1000 instead of $100, you may be able to reduce your premium by about 20 percent or more. Keep in mind that you must have access to $1000 in cash in the event of a claim.

Improve Protection. If you improve the protection of your home, your insurance premium will decline. For example, you could install storm shutters to protect against bad weather or a monitored security system to protect against robbery.

Use One Insurer for All Types of Insurance. Some insurance companies offer lower premiums to customers who purchase more than one type of insurance from them.

Stay with the Same Insurance Company. When you stay with the same insurance company, you may be rewarded with a lower insurance premium in future years.

Shop Around. As with auto insurance, you may be able to reduce your premium by obtaining quotations from various insurance companies. Premiums can vary substantially among insurers. Remember to compare policies and coverage, not just premiums.

EXAMPLE

Stephanie Spratt is reviewing her homeowner's insurance policy, shown in Exhibit 8.8, to determine whether she should change her policy once her existing policy expires. She is considering increasing her deductible from $500 to $1000 and using the same insurance company that insures her car. She calls an agent at her current homeowner's insurer to request a quote based on a $1000 deductible. Then she calls her auto insurer to request a quote on homeowner's insurance with the same coverage and deductibles. Her current homeowner's insurer quotes a premium of $300, which is $30 less than her present premium. Her current auto insurer quotes a homeowner's premium of $280, which includes a discount reflecting multiple policies with the same insurance company. Stephanie decides to switch companies to gain a package discount once her present homeowner's policy expires.

Exhibit 8.8 Stephanie Spratt's Homeowner's Insurance Policy

Existing Policy Coverages and Limits	
Deductible	$500
Dwelling	$250 000
Personal Property ($500 deductible)	$31 000
Personal Liability	$1 000 000
Damage to Property of Others	$500
Medical Payments to Others (per person)	$5 000
Discounts	$25 for House Alarm
Annual Premium	$330

FILING A CLAIM

If your property is damaged, you should contact your insurance company immediately. A claims adjuster will come to estimate the damage. Present your home inventory to the adjuster. The adjuster's estimate will include the cost of repairing the damage done to your home and compensation for damaged property. The insurance company may be willing to issue a cheque so that you can hire someone to make repairs. You should consider obtaining an independent estimate of the repairs to ensure that the amount the insurance company offers you is sufficient. If the insurance company's estimate is too low, you can appeal it.

IN-CLASS NOTES

Homeowner's Insurance Premiums and Filing a Claim

- Factors that affect premiums
  - Value and location of insured home
  - Deductible
  - Degree of protection desired
  - Discounts offered
- Reduce your premiums
  - Increase deductible
  - Improve protection (security system, fire extinguisher)
  - Use one company for all insurance and establish a long-term relationship with it
  - Shop around
- Filing a claim
  - Contact your insurance company immediately
  - Provide claims adjuster with your home inventory
  - Obtain an independent estimate of repair costs

_____

_____

_____

_____

_____

_____

_____

_____

_____

TENANT'S INSURANCE

tenant's insurance
An insurance policy that protects your possessions within a house, condominium, or apartment that you are renting.

Tenant's insurance protects your possessions within a house, condominium, or apartment that you are renting. It does not insure the structure itself because the insurance is for the tenant only, not the owner of the property. It covers personal assets such as furniture, a television, computer equipment, and stereo equipment. The insurance protects against damage due to weather or the loss of personal assets due to burglary. It can cover living expenses while the rental property is being repaired. It also covers liability in the event that a friend or neighbour is injured while on the rental property.

Tenants whose personal assets have a high market value need tenant's insurance to protect those assets. Even tenants without valuable personal assets may desire tenant's insurance to protect against liability.

Tenant's Insurance Policy Provisions

Go to
www.101apartments.com/
moving-services/renters-
insurance.asp

This website provides online quotes for tenant's insurance.

Tenant's insurance specifies the maximum amount of coverage for your personal assets. It may also specify maximum coverage for specific items such as jewellery. The premium depends on the amount of coverage you desire. Your tenant's insurance may also cover liability resulting from injury to a person while on your premises. For example, if your pet injures a neighbour in your yard, your tenant's insurance may cover your liability up to a limit. Because tenant's insurance policies vary, you should closely review any policy to ensure that the insurance coverage is appropriate for you.

UMBRELLA PERSONAL LIABILITY POLICY

umbrella personal liability policy
A supplement to auto and homeowner's insurance that provides additional personal liability coverage.

You can supplement your auto and homeowner's insurance with an umbrella personal liability policy, which provides additional personal liability coverage. This type of policy is intended to provide additional insurance, not to replace those other policies. In fact, the insurance will not be provided unless you show proof of existing coverage. Umbrella policies are especially useful when you have personal assets beyond a car and home that you wish to protect from liability. You may be able to purchase an umbrella policy for about $200 per year for coverage of $1 million.

IN-CLASS NOTES

Tenant's Insurance and Umbrella Personal Liability Policy

- Tenant's insurance
  - Does not insure the structure
  - Covers personal assets
  - Can cover living expenses
- Umbrella personal liability policy
  - Provides additional personal liability insurance beyond the coverage available in your homeowner's insurance or renter's insurance policy
  - Useful when you have a desire to protect additional assets from personal liability

_____

_____

_____

_____

_____

_____

_____

HOW HOME AND AUTO INSURANCE FIT WITHIN YOUR FINANCIAL PLAN

The following are the key decisions about car and homeowner's insurance that should be included within your financial plan:

- Do you have adequate insurance to protect your wealth?

- How much insurance should you plan to have in the future?

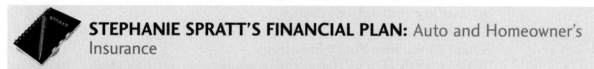

STEPHANIE SPRATT'S FINANCIAL PLAN: Auto and Homeowner's Insurance

GOALS FOR AUTO AND HOMEOWNER'S INSURANCE PLANNING

1. Maintain adequate insurance for my car and my home.

2. Determine whether I should increase my auto and homeowner's insurance levels in the future.

ANALYSIS

Type of Insurance	Protection	Status
Auto	*Protects one of my main assets and limits my potential liabilities.*	*Already have insurance but I'm considering more liability coverage.*
Homeowner's	*Protects my largest asset and limits my potential liabilities.*	*Recently purchased homeowner's insurance as a result of buying a home.*

DECISIONS

Decision on Whether My Present Insurance Coverage Is Adequate

I will increase my auto insurance liability coverage to $1 million. While more costly, the increased coverage is worthwhile. I will also raise my deductible from $500 to $1000, which will reduce the insurance premium.

I currently have sufficient homeowner's insurance, but I will switch my policy to my auto insurance company when the present policy expires. I will receive a discount on the premium as a result of having multiple insurance contracts with the same company. In the meantime, I will create a home inventory.

Decision on Insurance Coverage in the Future

If I buy a more expensive car, I will need additional insurance. However, I will not be buying a new car in the near future. If I buy a more expensive home or if the value of my existing home rises substantially, I will need more insurance.

I plan to review my policies each year to ensure that I have adequate coverage for personal belongings, increases in property values and wealth, and third party liability.

Discussion Questions

1. How would Stephanie's auto and homeowner's insurance purchasing decisions be different if she were a single mother of two children?

2. How would Stephanie's auto and homeowner's insurance purchasing decisions be affected if she were 35 years old? If she were 50 years old?

SUMMARY

Your risk management decisions determine whether and how to protect against risk. Your alternatives are to avoid, reduce, accept, or share risk. Some types of risk are difficult to avoid and dangerous to accept. For these types of risk, insurance is needed. Once you decide whether to obtain a particular type of insurance, you must decide on the amount of coverage and on where to purchase the insurance.

Automobile insurance insures against the legal liability that may arise if your property (car) causes death or injury to others, as well as the expense associated with providing medical care to you, your passengers, and pedestrians, and the costs associated with damage to your automobile. The premium paid for auto insurance depends on how you use the vehicle, the vehicle's value and repair record, where you live, your driving record, your age and sex, as well as the features of the policy you choose, including the insurance deductible.

Homeowner's insurance provides insurance in the event of property damage or personal liability. The premium paid for homeowner's insurance depends on the home's value, the deductible, and the likelihood of damage to the home.

INTEGRATING THE KEY CONCEPTS

Your decisions regarding auto and homeowner's insurance affect other parts of your financial plan. Auto and homeowner's insurance not only protect specific assets, but also cover some if not all of your liability. Such protection gives you more flexibility in your other financial planning decisions. For example, it allows you to maintain a smaller amount of liquidity (Part 2) because you do not have to accumulate the large amount of funds that would be needed to insure yourself. Insurance makes purchasing a home possible because financing (Part 3) is available only if you insure your home. It also allows you to maintain a smaller amount of investments (Part 5) because you do not have to accumulate a large amount of investments to insure yourself. Finally, it allows you to contribute extra savings toward retirement (Part 6) rather than maintain the funds to cover any liability due to an accident or other unexpected event.

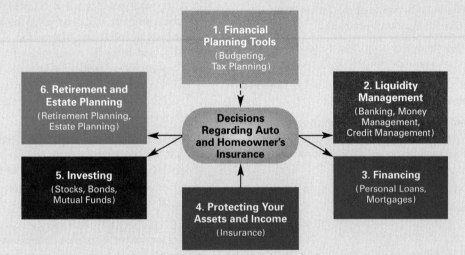

REVIEW QUESTIONS

1. What is the purpose of insurance? What is meant by the term *liability*? How can individuals benefit from insurance?

2. What is risk management? How does insurance fit into risk management?

3. What is the responsibility of the insurance company that sells you a policy? How do insurance companies determine their profits? What is the relationship between insurance company claims and premiums paid by policy owners?

4. What is the role of insurance underwriters? What is the role of insurance agents? Define the two different types of insurance agents.

5. Describe the two components of liability coverage in an auto insurance policy.

6. How does accident benefits coverage under an auto insurance policy work?

7. What is the intent of no-fault insurance? How does no-fault insurance generally work? What is a disadvantage of no-fault insurance?

8. What is the difference between uninsured and underinsured motorist coverage?

9. Describe collision insurance and comprehensive coverage. Is this type of coverage required by most provinces? Who may require this type of coverage?

10. What is the purpose of Facility Association? Is it available in all provinces? Why or why not?

11. List and briefly discuss factors that will affect your auto insurance premium. What factors may not apply in provinces where auto insurance is provided by a provincial government agency?

12. What steps should you take if you are in a car accident?

13. What is homeowner's insurance? How are the premiums normally paid?

14. What is the difference between all perils coverage and named perils coverage?

15. What is a cash value homeowner's policy? What is a replacement cost homeowner's policy?

16. Is personal property typically insured under a homeowner's insurance policy? If so, are there limits to the coverage of personal property? What is a home inventory?

17. What is a personal property floater? What is the difference between scheduled and unscheduled floaters?

18. How does homeowner's liability coverage work? What does the medical payments provision cover? What does the voluntary property damage provision cover?

19. List and briefly describe some of the factors that affect homeowner's insurance premiums.

20. What are some steps you could take to reduce your homeowner's insurance premium?

21. Describe the steps you would take to file a claim on your homeowner's insurance.

22. How is tenant's insurance different from homeowner's insurance? Who should consider purchasing tenant's insurance? Briefly describe some of the provisions of a tenant's insurance policy.

23. What is the purpose of an umbrella personal liability policy? Who might need one?

ETHICAL DILEMMA

You teach Personal Finance at a local community college. The province in which you teach requires proof of auto insurance to renew your licence plates.

During the discussion of this topic in class, several students admit that they obtain auto insurance policies just prior to the renewal of their licence plates and then cancel them immediately thereafter. They do this because they know that the province has no system for following up on the cancellation of the auto insurance policies once the licence plates are issued. These students, who are out of work as a result of a local plant shutdown, indicate that they cannot afford to maintain their insurance but must have access to cars for transportation.

a. Discuss whether you consider the conduct of the students to be unethical.

b. How does the conduct of these students potentially affect other members of the class who maintain auto insurance on their vehicles?

FINANCIAL PLANNING ONLINE EXERCISES

1. Go to www.kanetix.ca/auto-insurance.

a. Enter your postal code and select the city in which you live. Click on Next Step and enter the requested driver information. Click on Next Step and enter the requested vehicle details. Click on Next Step and select "No" for discounts. Click on Get Quotes. The screen will display quotes for coverage from various auto insurance companies.

b. Scroll down to Coverage details. Select a $500 deductible for both comprehensive and collision coverage. What is Loss of use? What is Legal liability for damage to non-owned automobiles? How much liability coverage can you purchase?

c. Do any of the insurance companies offer any discounts? If so, what types of discounts do they offer? What are the credit ratings for the various insurance companies? Which company has the highest credit rating?

ON THE STUDENT CD-ROM FOR THIS CHAPTER YOU WILL FIND:

- Building Your Own Financial Plan exercise and worksheets
- The chapter-end Continuing Case about the Sampson family

Read through the Building Your Own Financial Plan exercise and use the worksheets to identify assets that would require insurance coverage from an auto or homeowner's policy.

After reading the Sampson case study, use the Continuing Case worksheets to assist the Sampsons in taking stock of their vehicles and home.

Study Guide

Circle the correct answer and then check the answers in the back of the book to chart your progress.

Multiple Choice

1. Critical illness insurance can ensure that you have access to _____ in the event that you suffer a critical illness, such as a heart attack, stroke, or life-threatening cancer.
   a. a cure
   b. monthly income
   c. lump-sum benefits
   d. in-home nursing care

2. The alternatives available to you if you decide to protect against risk include all of the following except:
   a. Avoiding risk
   b. Reducing risk
   c. Sharing risk
   d. Accepting risk

3. Consider a policy owner who pays $1000 in auto insurance premiums for the year. Assume that he is in an accident, and the insurance company has to pay $25 000 to cover liability and repair the car. The insurance company expects to pay a total of $500 000 in claims for the year with respect to the group of policy owners of which this individual is a member. Business expenses for the year are $50 000. Investment earnings on premiums received are $25 000. How many insurance policies must the insurance company sell to break even (that is, earn $0 in profit)? Assume that all policies are sold for a $1000 premium.
   a. 500
   b. 525
   c. 550
   d. 575

4. Generally, auto insurance policies contain three sections:
   a. Third party liability coverage, accident benefits, and loss or damage to insured automobile
   b. Third party liability coverage, accident and sickness benefits, and loss or damage to insured automobile
   c. Third party liability coverage, accident benefits, and loss or damage to insured/uninsured automobile
   d. Third party liability coverage, accident and sickness benefits, and loss or damage to insured/uninsured automobile

5. Which of the following is not normally included as a covered expense in the accident benefits section of an auto insurance policy?
   a. Funeral costs
   b. Loss of income as a result of total disability
   c. Uninsured motorist coverage
   d. Liability arising from injuries you have caused

6. No-fault accident benefits allow policy owners in all provinces to receive immediate medical payments through:
   a. The insurance policy of the at-fault driver
   b. Their own insurance policy
   c. Their provincial government plan
   d. The federal government auto insurance reserve fund program

7. Facility Association ensures that drivers unable to obtain insurance with an individual company are able to obtain the coverage they need to operate their vehicles legally. In which of the following provinces would this coverage be valuable?
   a. Manitoba
   b. Ontario
   c. British Columbia
   d. Quebec

8. Which of the following factors that affect your auto insurance premiums is not considered in provinces in which auto insurance is offered through a government agency?
   a. Your age
   b. The repair record of your car
   c. Your location
   d. Your driving record

9. With respect to a homeowner's insurance policy, a personal property floater would be useful if you wish to insure which of the following assets?
   a. Your personal clothing
   b. Furniture
   c. Jewellery that you keep in your home
   d. All of the above

10. Which of the following actions would not be considered an effective method to help you reduce your homeowner's insurance premium?
    a. Increase your deductible
    b. Install storm shutters

c. Purchase all your insurance from one company

d. Purchase a larger fire extinguisher than the one you currently have

True/False

1. True or False? The primary function of insurance is to maintain your existing level of wealth by protecting you against potential financial losses or liability as a result of unexpected events.

2. True or False? Assuming that you have enough money, you should be able to insure against all types of risks.

3. True or False? A high insurance premium may indicate that there is a greater probability you may use the insurance coverage provided.

4. True or False? Insurance brokers work for one particular insurance company.

5. True or False? Third party liability protects you against liability associated with injuries that you cause and losses that result when you damage another person's property.

6. True or False? Accident benefits are mandatory in all provinces.

7. True or False? Collision coverage is especially valuable because it provides coverage not only for the car, but for items that were damaged in the car during the accident.

8. True or False? All perils coverage protects the home and any other structures on the property against all events except those that are specifically excluded by the homeowner's policy.

9. True or False? When purchasing a homeowner's insurance policy, you should consider a cash value policy because the actual cash value of replacing damaged property is normally higher than the assessed value of property.

10. True or False? Renter's insurance covers personal assets such as furniture, a television, computer equipment, and stereo equipment. It does not insure the structure itself.

Chapter 9

Health Insurance

G reg couldn't wait to embark on his new career. As the former Director of Technology Development for a major technology firm, Greg felt that he had the right skill set to become a self-employed consultant to the industry. Before starting out on his own, Greg decided to consult his insurance broker. Now that Greg would no longer have group insurance benefits from work, he thought it might be a good idea to see if he should transfer some of these group benefits to himself.

The meeting with his insurance broker was a real eye-opener for Greg. Greg was surprised to learn that none of his group insurance benefits were portable. Furthermore, although the health care system provides coverage for essential services, Greg did not realize that coverage for the cost of prescription drugs and dental care was provided for at the discretion of the province in which he lived. Greg also realized that he would need to purchase a private dental plan to look after the future needs of his two children.

In addition to the benefits he would lose, Greg was surprised to learn that his group disability insurance plan contained a definition of disability based on "any occupation," the most restrictive definition (discussed later in this chapter). After discussing this with his insurance broker, Greg realized that he wasn't protected nearly as well as he thought. Furthermore, Greg did not realize that he could purchase an insurance policy to protect against the costs associated with critical illnesses. This type of coverage wasn't available in his group insurance plan.

This chapter explains the features of the Canadian health care system. Although Canada is known for its universal health care program, a number of services must be provided for through provincial and/or private plans. An understanding of the benefits and protection offered by health care insurance plans will help you protect your net worth.

The objectives of this chapter are to:

1. Provide a background on health insurance

2. Outline the five criteria of the *Canada Health Act*

3. Describe the role of private health insurers

4. Explain the benefits of disability insurance

5. Describe critical illness insurance

6. Describe long-term care insurance

L.O. 1 BACKGROUND ON HEALTH INSURANCE

health insurance
A group of insurance benefits provided to a living individual as a result of sickness or injury.

Health insurance refers to a group of insurance benefits provided to a living individual as a result of sickness or injury. Health insurance is unique because the benefit is payable to the insured or to a health care professional who is working with the insured. In contrast, life insurance benefits, discussed in Chapter 10, are payable to the insured's beneficiary. Health insurance includes medicare, private health care, disability, critical illness, and long-term care insurance. Without health insurance, the high expenses of returning to good health and the loss of income as a result of sickness or injury could quickly eliminate most of your wealth. Therefore, health insurance is a critical component of your financial planning.

medicare
An interlocking system of ten provincial and three territorial health insurance plans provided by the governments, including the federal government.

Medicare is an interlocking system of ten provincial and three territorial health insurance plans provided by the governments, including the federal government. In Canada, our health care system is predominantly publicly financed. Public sector funding represents about 72.7 percent of total health care expenditures. The remaining 27.3 percent is financed privately through private health care plans, such as supplementary insurance and employer-sponsored benefits, or directly out-of-pocket. Health insurance has received much attention in recent years because it has become so expensive. The need for health care is greater for individuals who are older, and the average age of the population has increased in recent years. Since older individuals require more health care, the cost of providing it is rising. People are living longer, partly due to effective health care, and therefore require medical attention for a longer period of time.

Role of the Federal Government

With respect to the delivery of health care, the fundamental role of the federal government is to ensure that universal coverage for medically necessary services is provided to eligible residents on the basis of individual need, rather than on the ability of the individual to pay. If you ask a Canadian for a defining characteristic unique to Canada, the country's publicly funded, universally accessible health care system will be at or near the top of the list. Although the federal government sets and administers our health care system using the *Canada Health Act*, the provincial and territorial governments have most of the responsibility for delivering health care and other social services.

L.O. 2 CANADA HEALTH ACT

Canada Health Act
Establishes the criteria and conditions related to insured health care services that provinces and territories must meet in order to receive money from the federal government for health care.

The *Canada Health Act* is Canada's federal health insurance legislation. It establishes the criteria and conditions related to insured health care services that provinces and territories must meet in order to receive money from the federal government for health care. Insured health care services are medically necessary hospital, physician, and surgical–dental services provided to insured persons. An insured person is an eligible resident of a province, but does not include someone who may be covered by other federal or provincial legislation.

insured health care services
Medically necessary hospital, physician, and surgical–dental services provided to insured persons.

insured person
An eligible resident of a province. Does not include someone who may be covered by other federal or provincial legislation.

Canada Health and Social Transfer (CHST)
The largest federal transfer of money to the provinces and territories, providing them with cash payments and tax transfers in support of health care, post-secondary education, social assistance, and social services, including early childhood development.

Principles of the *Canada Health Act*

The provinces and territories must meet five principles in order to qualify for the full Canada Health and Social Transfer (CHST). The CHST is the largest federal transfer of money to the provinces and territories, providing them with cash payments and tax transfers in support of health care, post-secondary education, social assistance, and social services, including early childhood development. Provinces and territories that violate the five principles of the *Canada Health Act* may be subject to a reduction in the amount of CHST they receive. The five principles are:

- **Public Administration.** Plans must be administered and operated on a non-profit basis by a public authority accountable to the provincial or territorial government.

- **Comprehensiveness.** Plans must insure all medically necessary services provided by hospitals, medical practitioners, and dentists working within a hospital setting.

- **Universality.** Plans must entitle all insured persons to health insurance coverage on uniform terms and conditions.

- **Portability.** Plans must cover all insured persons when they move to another province or territory within Canada and when they travel abroad. The provinces and territories have some limits on coverage for services provided outside Canada, and may require prior approval for non-emergency services delivered outside their jurisdiction.

- **Accessibility.** Plans must provide all insured persons reasonable access to medically necessary hospital and physician services without financial or other barriers.

 IN-CLASS NOTES

Background on Health Insurance and *Canada Health Act*

- Health insurance includes:
  - Medicare, private health care, disability insurance, critical illness insurance, and long-term care insurance
- Role of the federal government
  - To ensure that universal coverage for medically necessary services is provided to eligible residents on the basis of individual need, rather than on the ability of the individual to pay.
- Principles of the *Canada Health Act*
  1. Public administration
  2. Comprehensiveness
  3. Universality
  4. Portability
  5. Accessibility

_____

_____

_____

_____

_____

_____

_____

_____

_____

ROLE OF THE PROVINCIAL AND TERRITORIAL GOVERNMENTS

As mentioned previously, Canada's publicly funded health care system is best described as an interlocking set of ten provincial and three territorial health insurance plans. The provinces and territories are constitutionally responsible for the administration and delivery of insured health care services. They decide where their hospitals will be located, how many physicians they will need, and how much money they will spend on their health care systems.

However, insured health care services provided by the *Canada Health Act* cover only basic medical needs, such as a trip to your doctor or in-patient/out-patient hospital care. As a result, most provincial and territorial governments offer and fund supplementary benefits for certain groups (for example, seniors, children, and social assistance recipients). These supplementary benefits include coverage for drugs prescribed outside hospitals, ambulance costs, hearing aids, vision care, medical equipment and appliances (prostheses, wheelchairs), home care and nursing, and the services of other health professionals, such as podiatrists and chiropractors. It is important to emphasize that the level of coverage for these supplementary benefits varies across the country. Medical expenses that are not covered by the provincial plan either must be paid in full by the individual or can be partially paid by a supplemental health insurance plan. This is the main reason why supplemental health insurance is necessary to cover the health care needs that provincial and territorial plans do not.

Health care is a significant expense for the provinces and territories. For example, in Alberta, health care costs as a percentage of government revenue increased from 24 percent in 1991–1992 to 33 percent in 2000–2001. Health care costs as a percentage of Alberta government revenue is projected to rise to 50 percent by 2008. Many people feel that the rising cost of health care will be the greatest challenge facing Canadians in the next 50 years.

L.O. 3   ROLE OF PRIVATE HEALTH INSURANCE

Private health insurance companies provide additional medical coverage through either group or individual supplemental health insurance plans. If you are not part of a group plan with your work, or if the company you work for does not offer sufficient coverage, you should consider an individual plan. It may be wise to purchase private health insurance if the coverage offered through the *Canada Health Act* and the supplemental coverage offered through your province or territory is not sufficient.

Group Health Insurance

Because employees are the most essential part of any business, many business owners offer group health insurance to their employees. Grouping individuals together under a policy generates savings for everyone when compared to individual coverage. The coverage in a group benefit plan will vary significantly among private health insurers. Coverage may include, but would not be limited to, dental care, vision care, medical care, life and disability insurance, and travel insurance for employees and/or their families. Offering a group plan to employees has a number of benefits. From the employee's perspective, group plans provide added protection beyond what is available from government plans. In addition, the employee may save money on provincial premiums or the cost of having to purchase individual insurance. Some employees may be uninsurable on an individual basis, but they may be able to get coverage as part of a group. From the employer's perspective, group plans:

- Provide owners with the opportunity to write off premiums as business expenses
- Encourage loyalty and trust among employees
- Enable better staff retention because of the security employees feel

To determine what is covered under your group plan, ask your human resources department what, if any, group health insurance plans the company provides. Exhibit 9.1 provides a general overview of the items covered in many basic supplemental group health insurance plans. This is not a reflection of all plans offering health insurance, as details may vary for individual companies. Depending on your annual contribution, your basic supplemental health insurance plan will cover anywhere from 40 to 80 percent of the health care benefits shown in Exhibit 9.1.

Individual Health Insurance

A family with health care needs beyond those covered by an employer's group plan might wish to buy additional supplemental health insurance. To obtain individual health insurance, you can contact an insurance agent. In exchange for paying a premium to an insurance company, you will be provided with specific health insurance coverage for an agreed-upon period. Individual health insurance plans provide coverage for drug, dental, and paramedical costs for you and your family if you do not have coverage through a group plan. Disability insurance provides an income benefit to replace a portion of your earnings if you become ill or are injured and cannot work. Critical illness insurance provides a lump-sum benefit if you are diagnosed with a covered illness such as cancer, heart attack, or stroke. Long-term care insurance provides an income if you lose the ability to care for yourself as a result of illness or injury. Unlike disability insurance, this final benefit is not linked to employment.

Exhibit 9.1 Possible Benefits Covered in Group Health Insurance Plans

Benefit	Description
Dental Care	■ Coverage: 90% of basic services and 50% of major services ■ Basic services: examinations, scaling and polishing, x-rays, cleanings; major services: inlays, onlays, crowns ■ Maximum: $2,000 per year (all coverage types)
Vision Care	■ Optometrist fees: maximum $50 per visit per year ■ Prescription lenses and frames: maximum $250 per year
Prescription Drugs	■ 80% coverage for any and all prescribed medications ■ Maximum: $5,000 per year
Life Insurance	■ Minimum employer-paid coverage: 1 times salary ■ Optional coverages: 2 to 5 times salary; spousal life insurance
Disability Insurance	■ General illness: coverage for 100 per cent of income for the first 10 consecutive days of missed employment due to illness or injury ■ Short-term and long-term disability insurance: 70 per cent of your income up to 2 years, and coverage beyond two years to age 65 or death, respectively. ■ Definition of disability: general illness and short-term—regular occupation; long-term—any occupation
Employee Assistance Program (EAP)	■ A counseling and referral service for personal and/or job stress, relationship issues, eldercare and childcare, addictions and related issues

IN-CLASS NOTES

Role of the Governments and Role of Private
Health Insurance

- Provincial/territorial governments
  - Responsible for the administration and delivery
    of insured health care services
  - May offer and fund supplementary benefits for
    certain groups (seniors, children, social
    assistance recipients)
  - Supplementary benefits may include drugs
    prescribed outside hospitals, ambulance costs,
    hearing aids, vision care, home care, and
    chiropractic services
- Private health insurance
  - Provides additional coverage beyond what is
    available under the *Canada Health Act* and provin-
    cial/territorial plans
  - Provides coverage for individuals who may not
    otherwise be insurable

_____

_____

_____

_____

_____

_____

_____

_____

_____

_____

CONTENTS OF HEALTH CARE INSURANCE POLICIES

Health care insurance policies contain the following information.

Identification of Insured Persons
A health insurance contract identifies the persons who are covered. It may be an individual or a family.

Location
Some Canadian insurance companies provide coverage for health care in Canada only,
while others provide coverage in foreign countries. Typically, full health insurance benefits are confined to the local area of the beneficiary. Benefits are
reduced or eliminated for non-emergency health care received outside of that area.

"Isn't it nice to find out right away
if insurance will cover the procedure?"

www.cartoonresource.com

Pre-existing Conditions
A policy may exclude coverage for pre-existing conditions, which
are health conditions that existed before your policy was granted.
For example, if you had torn ligaments when you applied for the
policy, you may not be allowed coverage for surgery to repair them.
The pre-existing conditions clause prevents people from buying
insurance just to treat existing illnesses or injuries.

Cancellation Options
A health insurance contract may allow the insurance company to
cancel the contract at any time. Other contracts guarantee continuous coverage as long as the policy owners pay the premiums on time.

Determinants of Non-reimbursed Medical Expenses

For a given health care service, the insurance policy specifies the means by which you can determine the amount of the bill you must pay. This amount is determined by the deductible, coinsurance, and coordination of benefits, as explained next.

Deductible. A deductible requires that the insured bear the cost of the health care up to a level specified in the policy. If a policy specifies a deductible of $500 for specific health care, and the bill is $475, you must pay the entire amount. If the bill is $900, you will pay the first $500, and the policy will cover the remaining $400. The deductible in health care is similar to the deductible in auto insurance, in that it reduces the potential liability to the insurance company. Therefore, premiums charged for a particular policy are generally lower when the deductible is higher.

Coinsurance. A coinsurance clause specifies the proportion of health care expenses that will be paid by the insurance company. For example, for a $1000 bill that is subject to a 20 percent copayment, you will pay $200 (20 percent of $1000) and the policy will cover the remaining $800.

Coordination of Benefits. When a policy has a coordination of benefits provision, it means that the benefits depend on the benefits that would be paid by other policies you have. The benefits that would be paid by multiple policies could overlap, but this provision limits the total reimbursement to no more than your expenses. This provision can be beneficial to you because your insurance premiums and coinsurance will be lower if the insurance benefits are coordinated among policies to limit the reimbursement amount. Coordination of benefits is usually required when you have a policy at work and your spouse has you listed as a beneficiary on his or her policy at work as well. In this case, it is important for you and your spouse to sit down and review the benefits both of you have. It may be beneficial for you to split your coverage between plans to avoid overlap.

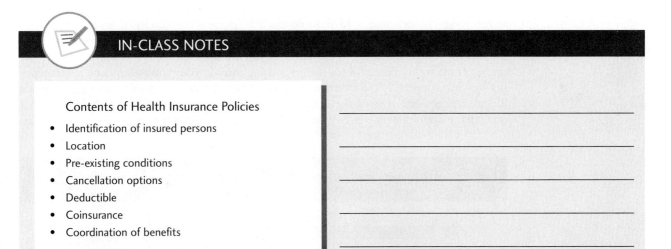

IN-CLASS NOTES

Contents of Health Insurance Policies

- Identification of insured persons
- Location
- Pre-existing conditions
- Cancellation options
- Deductible
- Coinsurance
- Coordination of benefits

L.O. 4   DISABILITY INSURANCE

When people consider the value of their assets, many think of their automobile or home as their most valuable asset. This statement could not be further from the truth. Your most valuable asset is your ability to earn an income. For example, if Jeff earns $40 000 per year from ages 30 to 60 with no increase in pay, he will earn $1.2 million during the course of his career. Jeff's lifetime earned income would be even higher if you consider increases in pay due to inflation and promotions.

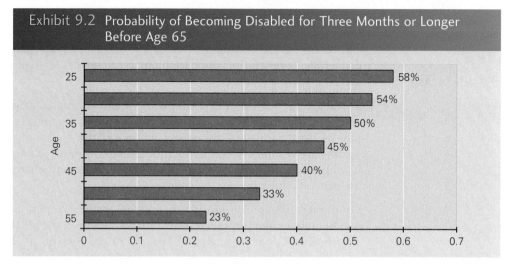

Source: "Probability of Becoming Disabled for 3 Months or Longer" from *1985 Commissioner's Disability Table, Society of Actuaries*. Reprinted with permission of Society of Actuaries.

disability income insurance
A monthly insurance benefit paid to you in the event that you are unable to work as a result of an injury or an illness.

In the event of an injury or illness, most people recognize that it is important to have adequate disability insurance to provide income for their family. Disability income insurance is a monthly insurance benefit paid to you in the event that you are unable to work as a result of an injury or an illness. Although you receive the benefit, the ultimate purpose of this income stream is to ensure that you are still able to provide for your family adequately even though you are unable to work. What is the possibility of this happening? Exhibit 9.2 displays the probability of becoming disabled for three months or longer before age 65. Exhibit 9.3 displays the average duration of a disability lasting more than three months.

Exhibits 9.2 and 9.3 show that disabilities are relatively probable and can become relatively long. For example, a 35-year-old has a 50 percent probability of being disabled for three months or longer, and the average length of a disability lasting more than three months for someone this age is 2.9 years. If you are disabled for 2.9 years, where will the money come from? Potential sources of income include your spouse's income, emergency savings, investments, RRSPs, borrowing against your home equity, or borrowing against a life insurance policy. If you review your personal circumstances, you will probably find that none of the options listed above would be adequate for 2.9 years. If your personal resources

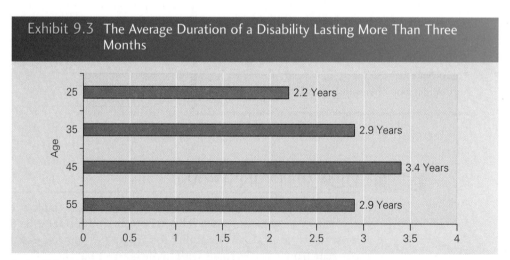

Source: "What is the Average Duration of a Disability Lasting Over 3 Months" from *1985 Commissioner's Disability Table, Society of Actuaries*. Reprinted with permission of the Society of Actuaries.

Exhibit 9.4 Sources of Disability Income

Benefit Source	What to Watch For
Workers' Compensation	■ You may not be covered since workers' compensation may not be provided at your place of work. ■ This benefit is only available for work-related injuries or illnesses. What if you are injured or become ill while away from work? ■ In general, the benefit amount, within a prescribed maximum, is up to 90 percent of your net income, which is your gross income less your income tax payable and your CPP and EI contributions.
Group Insurance	■ In addition to health insurance, many group plans provide benefits for long-term disability. ■ Although most plans will cover your full after-tax income, the most important issue you should consider is the definition of disability in your group plan. ■ In general, the benefit amount is 60 to 70 percent of your gross salary.
Canada Pension Plan	■ The definition of disability requires that you be totally disabled, and that your disability be severe and prolonged in nature. ■ *Severe* means that a person is incapable of regularly pursuing any substantially gainful occupation. ■ *Prolonged* means that the disability will prevent the individual from returning to work in the next 12 months, or is likely to result in death. ■ For 2007, the maximum disability benefit amount is $1053.77 per month.
Employment Insurance (EI)	■ The disability benefit under EI is only payable for 15 weeks. ■ For 2007, the benefit amount is 55 percent of your employment income to a maximum weekly benefit of $423.

Sources: Workers' Compensation Board, www.wcb.ab.ca/workers/benefits_wage_loss.asp (accessed October 7, 2006); Service Canada, "Canada Pension Plan (CPP) — Payment Rates," www1.servicecanada.gc.ca/en/isp/pub/factsheets/rates.shtml, and "Employment Insurance (EI) and Paternity, Parental and Sickness Benefits," www1.servicecanada.gc.ca/en/ei/types/special.shtml, (accessed October 7, 2006).

are inadequate, what are your other options? Exhibit 9.4 outlines potential sources of income in the event of an injury or illness and the problems associated with each.

Exhibit 9.4 shows that although benefits are available from many sources, those benefits may be unavailable to you or may be difficult to qualify for. Workers' compensation benefits are only payable for injuries and illnesses that occur while you are at work. This is like buying auto insurance that provides coverage only between 8 a.m. and 4 p.m. What about injuries and illnesses that occur when you are not at work? Most disabilities result from illnesses that cannot be linked to employment circumstances. Workers' compensation benefits do not provide comprehensive coverage and should be viewed as supplemental to other types of disability income benefits.

With respect to group disability insurance, the most important aspect is the definition of disability. Benefits are paid to you only if you meet the definition of disability as defined by your policy. The most liberal definition of disability is the "own occupation" definition. It means that the policy will provide benefits if you are unable to do the duties required of your occupation, and will also allow you to find employment elsewhere without a reduction in benefits. This definition of disability is particularly important to people who work in a professional occupation, such as surgeons or accountants. Surgeons may be unable to perform surgery if they develop arthritis in their hands; however, they would still be able to teach surgery to others. Similarly, accountants may be unable to sit for prolonged periods of time because they have back problems, but they may be able to work in other jobs where they are able to stand more often. The "own occupation" definition is attractive to these professionals because they are able to use their knowledge elsewhere without losing their benefits. Since "own occupation" provides additional flexibility to disabled policy owners, this definition is also the most expensive to purchase.

A more basic definition of disability is the "regular occupation" definition. It means that the policy will provide benefits if you are unable to perform the duties required by your occupation. However, your benefits will be reduced if you find employment elsewhere. This may be advantageous for people who would like to return to the workforce in another job at some later date. Although it seems as if a disabled individual is being penalized for working after a disability, it is important to remember that insurance is based on the principle of indemnification. Indemnification refers to the concept of putting an insured individual back into the same position he or she was in prior to the event that resulted in insurance benefits being paid. Payment of insurance benefits normally should not result in an improvement in your lifestyle.

indemnification
The concept of putting an insured individual back into the same position he or she was in prior to the event that resulted in insurance benefits being paid.

A more restrictive definition of disability is the "any occupation" definition. This means that the policy will provide benefits only if you cannot perform the duties of any job that fits your education and experience. Since the coverage provided by this type of policy is more restrictive, it has a lower premium than "own occupation" and "regular occupation" policies. In general, group insurance policies offer coverage if you are unable to do your job in your regular occupation for an initial period, such as two years. After that point, they generally offer coverage only if you are unable to perform the duties of any job that fits your education and experience. A group disability insurance plan is not owned by the members of the plan. Therefore, if you leave your employer, your group disability benefits will stop. If you become self-employed or your new employer does not offer coverage as a part of its employee benefits, you will be without disability insurance.

Canada Pension Plan (CPP) disability benefits are payable if you are totally disabled and your disability is severe and prolonged in nature. Severe means that a person is incapable of regularly pursuing any substantially gainful occupation. Prolonged means that the disability will prevent the individual from returning to work in the next 12 months, or is likely to result in death. Relative to other types of disability insurance, CPP disability benefits are difficult to qualify for. However, individuals who make CPP contributions must apply for CPP disability benefits, even if they believe they will not qualify.

Employment Insurance (EI) benefits provide sickness-related benefits for a 15-week period. As a result, this benefit does not provide adequate coverage for a long-term disability.

Individual disability insurance may provide the best source of protection. The policy owner is able to select the definition of disability; most choose a "regular occupation to age 65" definition or an "own occupation" definition. In addition, benefits may be payable in the event of a total or partial disability. Individual disability insurance policies may contain provisions that allow benefits to be paid for the insured's lifetime. Finally, these types of policies are portable. This means that you will have the insurance regardless of where you are working at the time of the disability.

Disability Insurance Provisions

The specific characteristics of disability insurance vary among insurance companies, as explained here.

Amount of Coverage. The disability insurance policy specifies the amount of income that will be provided if you become disabled. This amount may be specified as a maximum dollar amount or as a percentage of the income you were earning before becoming disabled. The higher your coverage, the more you will pay for disability insurance.

You should have enough coverage to maintain your lifestyle and continue to support your dependants if you become disabled. You can determine the disposable (after-tax) income you would normally need to support your lifestyle and your dependants.

EXAMPLE

Stephanie Spratt receives some disability insurance coverage from her employer, but she is considering purchasing additional disability insurance. She wants to determine how much more coverage she would need to cover her typical monthly expenses of about $2100. Approximately $100 of her monthly expenses are attributed to work, such as clothing and commuting expenses. Since Stephanie would not be going to work if she were disabled, she need not consider those expenses. Therefore, her typical monthly expenses when excluding work-related expenses are $2000, as shown in Panel A of Exhibit 9.5. This is the amount of disability coverage she would need.

Her next step is to determine how much disability coverage she already has. To be conservative, she assumes that there will be no Canada Pension Plan benefits, as she may have a disability that is not covered by its guidelines. Her employer-provided group disability coverage is $800 per month. She presumes that any disability she might have someday will not result from her work, so assumes that workers' compensation will not apply.

Her final step is to compare the coverage she needs (Panel A of Exhibit 9.5) with the coverage she has from sources other than individual disability insurance. In this example, the difference is $2000 − $800 = $1200. If she buys additional disability insurance, she will purchase coverage of $1200 per month. Since her present salary is $38 000, the amount of extra coverage needed reflects about 38 percent of her salary ($1200/$3167 = 0.38). The disability income that she would receive is normally not subject to tax.

Stephanie decides that she will buy the extra $1200 monthly disability insurance coverage through her employer.

Exhibit 9.5 Determining Stephanie Spratt's Disability Insurance Needs

Panel A: Total Coverage Needed

Typical monthly expenses	$2100
− Expenses related to work	−100
= Typical monthly expenses after excluding work expenses	$2000

Panel B: Coverage That You Expect to Receive from:

Employer Disability Insurance	$800
Canada Pension Plan	$0
Workers' Compensation	$0
Total	$800
Amount Needed from Individual Disability Insurance	$1200

waiting period
The period from the time you become disabled until you begin to receive disability income benefits.

Waiting Period. The disability insurance contract should specify whether there is a waiting period (such as three or six months) from when you become disabled until you begin to receive disability income benefits. Ideally, your emergency fund should comprise enough funds for all household expenses for the duration of the waiting period. Chapter 2 discussed how to create a cash flow statement to identify net cash flows that may be used for short-term or long-term savings. A successful short-term savings plan will help you cover your expenses during any waiting period. For example, if you become disabled today, and your policy specifies a three-month waiting period, you will receive benefits only if your disability lasts beyond that three-month period. Waiting periods eliminate many claims that would occur if people could receive benefits if they were disabled for just a few days or weeks because of a sore neck or back. The premiums for disability insurance would be higher if there was no waiting period or a very short waiting period.

Benefit Period. Disability benefits may be limited to a few years or may last for the policy owner's lifetime. The longer the period over which your policy provides disability income, the more you will pay for disability insurance. The most common length of time is to age 65.

Non-cancellable Provision. A non-cancellable provision gives you the right to renew the policy each year at the same premium, with no change in the benefits. In exchange, you pay a higher premium now to ensure that it will not be increased in the future.

Renewable Provision. A renewable provision gives you the right to renew the policy, with the same benefits. The insurance company can increase your premium if it is increasing the premium for all of its insured customers with the same profile.

Deciding on Disability Insurance

You can contact insurance companies about disability insurance rates or ask your employer's human resources department whether the insurance is available.

Taxation of Disability Insurance

Refer back to Exhibit 9.4 on page 229. Since the calculation for workers' compensation benefits uses your net income figure, these benefits are tax-free. Group insurance benefits are tax-free if the employee pays the entire premium for the coverage. If the employer pays any part of the premium, a substantial portion of any benefits paid would be taxable to the employee. CPP and EI benefits are taxable as ordinary income. In general, individual disability insurance benefits are tax-free because, in most cases, the premium is paid directly by the insured.

IN-CLASS NOTES

Disability Insurance
- Purpose
  - Ensures that you are still able to provide for your family adequately, even though you are unable to work
- Understand your definition of disability
  - Own occupation
  - Regular occupation
  - Any occupation
- Terminology
  - Waiting period, benefit period, non-cancellable provision, renewable provision

_____

_____

_____

_____

_____

_____

L.O. 5 CRITICAL ILLNESS INSURANCE

Critical illness insurance provides a lump-sum benefit in the event that you suffer a life-altering illness listed in the policy. The amount of the benefit usually is between $25 000 and $1 million. There are two main differences between critical illness insurance and disability insurance. First, critical illness insurance benefits are paid in one lump sum whereas disability insurance is a monthly benefit that may be paid for a long period of time. Many people consider critical illness insurance to be living life insurance since it generally pays a benefit only if you are able to survive a covered life-altering illness for at least 30 days. Second, critical illness insurance provides coverage for insured conditions. If your life-altering illness is not listed in the insurance policy as an insured illness, you are not covered for it. In contrast, disability insurance provides coverage for any injury or illness that prevents you from working.

Most group plans will not provide a lump-sum benefit for a critical illness. Although you will be covered for many of the treatments required when you suffer a critical illness, such as a stroke, the coverage may be limited or restricted to your province of residence. Critical illness insurance may be valuable if you would like to obtain a second medical opinion or would like to receive treatment outside of Canada. The lump-sum benefit you receive from a critical illness policy can be used in whatever manner you choose.

Critical illness insurance is purchased from health and life insurance companies. The three major critical illnesses include stroke, life-threatening cancer, and heart disease. With advances in medicine and treatments, more people than ever are surviving these illnesses. For example, the Heart and Stroke Foundation of Canada estimates that 85 percent of people who have a stroke survive the initial event. Unfortunately, more than 50 percent of individuals who survive a stroke are left with moderate to severe impairment or are severely disabled. Critical illness benefits can be used to cover the costs that stroke victims incur while having to live with their impairment or disability. Critical illness insurance provides protection by allowing you to choose how you will meet your health care needs, while preserving your savings or investments. It can be considered as both health insurance and a component of an overall financial plan.

The number of life-altering illnesses covered by critical illness insurance policies is not restricted to the three major illnesses listed above, and will vary among health and life insurance companies. In addition, a similar life-altering illness will be defined differently among companies. Some companies will offer additional features not offered by their competitors. As a result, it is important to shop around if you are considering this type of coverage.

L.O. 6 LONG-TERM CARE INSURANCE

Many people who are elderly or who have long-term illnesses need some assistance with everyday tasks such as eating or dressing. Others need around-the-clock medical assistance. Seven percent of Canadians age 65 and over reside in health care institutions. An additional 28 percent receive care due to a long-term health problem, although they do not live in health care institutions. Long-term care can be very expensive. The cost of having an aide provide basic care, such as feeding or dressing, at home each day can easily exceed $1000 per week. The cost of care by a nurse is higher. The cost of a nursing home is about $55 000 per year on average.

long-term care insurance Covers expenses associated with long-term health conditions that cause individuals to need help with everyday tasks.

Long-term care insurance covers expenses associated with long-term health conditions that cause individuals to need help with everyday tasks. It is provided by many private insurance companies, and typically covers nursing care, rehabilitation and therapy, personal care, homemaking services, and supervision by another person. However, given the high costs associated with long-term care, the premiums for this type of insurance can be very high.

Long-Term Care Insurance Provisions

Like other insurance policies, you can design a long-term care policy that fits your needs. Some of the more common provisions are listed here.

Eligibility to Receive Benefits. Policies include the range of benefits for which policy owners can file claims. For example, a policy may specify that the long-term care be restricted to medical health care services, while a more flexible policy also may allow other care such as feeding or dressing.

Types of Services. Policies specify the types of medical care services that are covered. A policy that covers nursing home care or assisted living will have higher premiums than a policy that only covers nursing home care. For individuals who prefer a more flexible long-term care policy that covers the cost of home health aides, premiums will be higher.

Amount of Coverage. Policies also specify the maximum amount of coverage provided per day. If you want the maximum amount of coverage a company will provide, you will pay a high premium. If you are willing to accept a lower maximum amount of daily coverage, your premium can be reduced. A policy with less coverage may not completely cover the daily costs you could incur. In that case, you would need to cover a portion of your expenses.

A policy can contain a coinsurance provision that requires the policy owner to incur a portion of the health care expense. For example, a policy owner can select a policy in which the insurance company pays 80 percent of the specified health care expenses, while the policy owner pays the remaining 20 percent. Since the potential expense to the insurance company is lower as a result of the coinsurance provision, the premium will be lower.

Elimination Period to Receive Benefits. A policy may specify an elimination (or waiting) period before policy owners are eligible to have their long-term care costs covered. An elimination period of between 60 and 90 days is common. The policy owner is responsible for covering expenses until the elimination period is completed. If the health care is needed over a period shorter than the elimination period, it will not be covered by the long-term care insurance.

Maximum Period to Receive Benefits. You can choose to receive insurance benefits for the entire period in which you need long-term care, even if the period is 30 years or longer. If you choose to receive insurance benefits for a limited period, you will be charged a lower premium. For example, your long-term care could be covered for up to three years.

Continued Coverage. A policy may contain a waiver of policy premium provision that allows you to stop paying premiums once you need long-term care. Some alternative provisions may also allow a limited amount of coverage after you have a policy for a specified number of years, without having to pay any more premiums. In general, any provision that provides additional benefits in the future will require higher premiums today.

Inflation Adjustment. Some policies allow for the coverage to increase in line with inflation over time. Thus, the maximum benefits will rise each year with the increase in an inflation index. You will pay a higher premium for a long-term health care policy that contains this provision.

Other Factors That Affect Long-Term Care Insurance Premiums

The premium charged for long-term care insurance is influenced by the likelihood that the insurance company will have to cover claims, and the size of those claims. Since the long-term care policy provisions described above affect the likelihood and size of claims, they affect the premiums on long-term care insurance. In addition to the provisions of the policy, the following characteristics of the policy owner also affect the premiums on long-term care insurance.

Age. Individuals who are older are more likely to need long-term care insurance, so they are charged higher premiums. Policy premiums are especially high for individuals who are 60 years of age or older.

Health Condition. Individuals who have an existing long-term illness are more likely to need to file a claim, so they are charged higher premiums.

Reducing Your Cost of Long-Term Care Insurance

When comparing long-term care insurance offered by insurance companies, recognize that a higher premium will be charged for various provisions that offer more comprehensive coverage. You can save money by selecting a policy that is flexible only on the provisions that are most important to you. For example, if you can tolerate a longer elimination period before the policy goes into effect, you can reduce your premium. If you think the continued coverage or the inflation-adjustment provisions are not very beneficial to you, select a policy that does not contain these provisions.

Insurance companies charge varying premiums for long-term care insurance policies, so you should shop around. Internet quotes are one option when researching policies. Also, review how insurance premiums have changed over time, since this may serve as an indication of future premiums.

Determining the Amount of Coverage

To determine whether you need long-term care insurance, consider your family's health history. If there is a history of long-term illnesses, you are more likely to need coverage. In addition, consider your financial situation. If you can afford substantial coverage for long-term care insurance, it may be worthwhile. Individuals who are under age 60 and have no serious illnesses can obtain long-term care insurance at reasonable rates.

IN-CLASS NOTES

Critical Illness Insurance and Long-Term Care Insurance

- Critical illness
  - Provides a lump-sum benefit in the event that you suffer a life-altering illness listed in the policy
  - Benefits received may be used in whatever manner you choose
  - Three major critical illnesses: stroke, life-threatening cancer, heart disease
- Long-term care
  - Helps cover expenses associated with long-term health conditions that cause individuals to need help with everyday tasks
  - Benefits may include nursing care, rehabilitation and therapy, personal care, homemaking services, and supervision by another person

_____

_____

_____

_____

_____

_____

_____

_____

HOW HEALTH INSURANCE FITS WITHIN YOUR FINANCIAL PLAN

The following are the key decisions about health insurance that should be included within your financial plan:

- Do you have adequate insurance to protect your wealth?
- How much insurance should you plan to have in the future?

STEPHANIE SPRATT'S FINANCIAL PLAN: Health Insurance

GOALS FOR HEALTH INSURANCE PLANNING

1. *Ensure that my exposure to health-related issues, disability, critical illness, and long-term care is covered by insurance.*

2. *Determine whether I should increase my health, disability, critical illness, and long-term care insurance in the future.*

ANALYSIS

Type of Insurance	Protection	Status
Health Insurance	*Protects my assets and wealth.*	*I have a good health insurance plan through work.*
Disability Insurance	*Protects my income if I become disabled.*	*My employer-provided disability policy offers some coverage, but I am buying a policy that offers additional coverage.*
Critical Illness	*Offers lump-sum benefits that I can spend as I choose.*	*My personally-owned critical illness policy offers adequate coverage.*
Long-Term Care	*Protects my assets if I need nursing care or other types of assistance*	*I am going to investigate whether I should buy this type of policy at this time.*

DECISIONS

Decision on Whether My Present Health Insurance Coverage Is Adequate

I presently rely on the group plan offered through my employer for any additional coverage I need outside of medicare. My group plan offers adequate insurance at an affordable premium. Because I am in my twenties and in good health, I do not need long-term care insurance at this time.

I currently have $800 of disability insurance coverage per month that is provided by my employer. I have decided to purchase a policy specifying an additional $1200 of coverage per month to cover my monthly expenses of $2000 if I become disabled.

Decision on Health Insurance Coverage for the Future

I will consider long-term care insurance in the future. I will also increase my disability insurance and/or my critical illness insurance if my income or expenses increase over time.

Discussion Questions

1. How would Stephanie's health insurance purchasing decisions be different if she were a single mother of two children?

2. How would Stephanie's health insurance purchasing decisions be affected if she were 35 years old? If she were 50 years old?

SUMMARY

The backbone of Canada's health care system is the *Canada Health Act*, which ensures adequate medically necessary coverage for all Canadians. The medicare program provides health insurance to individuals who are residents of Canada. There are also provincial government health plans. These health care plans supplement the coverage provided for medically necessary health issues. Provincial health care plans provide coverage for things such as drugs prescribed outside hospitals and vision care on a very limited, selected basis only. Group health insurance covers health care expenses incurred by policy owners. These health care plans can be classified as private plans that provide additional coverage and flexibility in the choice of the health care provisions you want for you and your family.

Disability insurance provides income to you if you become disabled. It can replace a portion of the income you would have received had you been able to continue working. This type of insurance is available from a number of federal, provincial, and private sources. In general, private disability insurance is the most comprehensive and the most expensive form of coverage.

Critical illness insurance provides a lump-sum benefit that will allow you to cover additional living expenses after a critical illness. You also may use the money to seek additional medical advice.

Long-term care insurance covers expenses associated with long-term illnesses, including care by a nursing home, by an assisted-living facility, or at home. The premium for long-term care insurance is very high but can be reduced by accepting a longer elimination period.

INTEGRATING THE KEY CONCEPTS

Your decisions regarding health insurance affect the other parts of your financial plan. With health insurance, you may not need to rely on your savings or other assets to cover health care expenses. In addition, you should not need to borrow funds to cover insurance expenses. The decision to purchase adequate health insurance can affect other financial decisions. If you do not purchase health insurance, you may be able to save more money (Part 2), have more capacity to finance the purchase of a car or a home (Part 3), and be more capable of investing in stocks (Part 5) and in your retirement fund (Part 6).

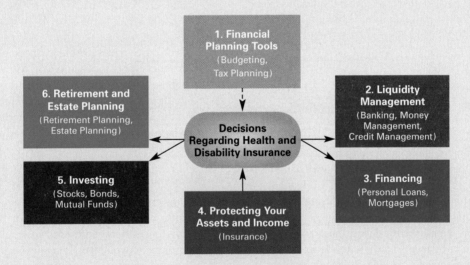

REVIEW QUESTIONS

1. How do individuals benefit from having health insurance? Why has health insurance received a lot of attention recently? What is the role of the federal government in the provision of health care?

2. Describe the features and principles of the *Canada Health Act*.

3. What is the role of the provincial and territorial governments in the provision of health care?

4. What is private health insurance? Briefly describe group health insurance. What do individual health insurance plans provide coverage for?

5. Describe the content of health care insurance policies.

6. What is the purpose of disability income insurance? Why might younger individuals consider purchasing it?

7. Briefly describe some of the sources of disability income insurance.

8. What is the difference between the "own occupation," "regular occupation," and "any occupation" definitions of disability?

9. What is the definition of disability under the Canada Pension Plan?

10. Briefly describe some of the provisions of disability income insurance.

11. Describe the tax implications of the various sources of disability insurance.

12. What is the purpose of critical illness insurance? What types of life-altering illness may be covered by a critical illness policy?

13. What is the purpose of long-term care insurance? What factors influence premiums? What factors should be considered when purchasing this insurance?

14. What are some other types of health insurance that might be offered by an employer?

FINANCIAL PLANNING PROBLEMS

1. Pete's group insurance policy specifies that he pays 30 percent of expenses associated with orthodontic treatment for his children. If Pete incurs expenses of $5000, how much would he owe?

2. Christine's monthly expenses typically amount to $1800. About $50 of these expenses are work-related. Christine's employer provides disability insurance coverage of $500 per month. How much individual disability insurance should Christine purchase?

ETHICAL DILEMMA

Abdel is a self-employed convenience store owner. An insurance agent has approached him about his need for critical illness insurance. Abdel is very interested and would like to purchase as much protection as he can. Unfortunately, his family health history is very poor. His father had a heart attack at age 40 and his mother had a stroke in her mid-thirties. Abdel understands that he may have difficulty qualifying for coverage based on his family health history. While filling out the application for critical illness insurance, Abdel tells the insurance agent that he was adopted and does not have any information on his biological parents that would indicate any family health concerns.

a. Assuming that Abdel is otherwise healthy, do you think that the insurance company would issue a policy? Why or why not?

b. If Abdel makes a claim, what are the potential problems he has created for himself?

c. If you were the insurance agent, what could you do to minimize the risk that someone may provide you with fraudulent information?

FINANCIAL PLANNING ONLINE EXERCISES

1. Go to www.healthquotes.ca/Individual.

a. Click on Instant Quotes. Obtain a personal health insurance estimate for yourself from Sun Life Financial. What features are available in the basic plan? How are the standard and enhanced plans different from the basic plan? What, if any, options are available?

b. Select the standard plan. What is the monthly premium quoted? Complete this step for the basic and enhanced plans. What is the difference in premiums? Which plan do you find most attractive? Why?

2. Go to www.rbcinsurance.com/healthinsurance/index.html and click on Calculators & Tools.

a. Click on Compare Disability Income Protection Products. This tool allows you to compare two different types of disability insurance policies. In the first column, click on The Foundation Series. In the second column, click on Bridge Series. What are the differences between these two types of disability insurance? Based on your career goals, which type of policy would be appropriate for you?

b. Now compare The Professional Series to the policy you selected in step a. What are the differences between these two types of disability insurance? Would you change your mind as to the type of insurance that is appropriate for you based on this new information? Why or why not?

ON THE STUDENT CD-ROM FOR THIS CHAPTER YOU WILL FIND:

- Building Your Own Financial Plan exercise and worksheets
- The chapter-end Continuing Case about the Sampson family

Read through the Building Your Own Financial Plan exercise and use the worksheets to determine what kind of health insurance you will need.

After reading the Sampson case study, use the Continuing Case worksheets to help the Sampsons determine the degree of health insurance coverage they need.

Study Guide

Circle the correct answer and then check the answers in the back of the book to chart your progress.

Multiple Choice

1. Why is health insurance unique?
   a. Benefits are payable to the insured or to a health care professional who is working with the insured.
   b. Benefits are payable to the insured's beneficiary or to a health care professional who is working with the insured.
   c. Benefits are payable to the insured or to the insured's beneficiary.
   d. Benefits are payable to the insured's spouse or to a health care professional who is working with the insured.

2. Which of the following is not a contributing factor to the escalating costs of health care?
   a. The average age of the population has increased in recent years.
   b. People are living longer.
   c. The health insurance industry relies on technology for improvements.
   d. The use of herbal medicines has reduced the reliance on more traditional practices.

3. Which of the following would not qualify as an insured health care service?
   a. Jackson has been diagnosed with appendicitis and will require an appendectomy.
   b. Tarlochan has been wearing glasses since he was nine years old. Now that he is in his early twenties, he has decided to have laser surgery on his eyes so that he will no longer have to wear glasses.
   c. Johanna has a fever. She visited her family physician, who diagnosed her with a cold and prescribed two days of bed rest before she returns to work.
   d. Tanya needs to have medically necessary dental surgery. The surgery can only be completed in a hospital.

4. Which of the following is not one of the five principles of the *Canada Health Act*?
   a. Public administration
   b. Comprehensiveness
   c. Accountability
   d. Universality

5. Most provincial and territorial governments offer and fund supplementary benefits for certain groups because:
   a. Plans must ensure that all medically necessary services are available to all residents of the province.
   b. Insured health care services provided by the *Canada Health Act* cover only basic medical needs.
   c. Plans cannot create situations in which there would be financial or other barriers.
   d. They will not be re-elected if they do not meet the needs of the groups that have voting power.

6. Many business owners offer group health insurance to their employees because group plans:
   a. Provide owners with the opportunity to write off premiums as business expenses.
   b. Encourage loyalty and trust among employees.
   c. Enable better staff retention because of the security employees feel.
   d. All of the above.

7. As a part of the process of determining the amount of an insurance bill you must pay, the coinsurance clause:
   a. Specifies the type of health care expenses that will be paid by the insurance company.
   b. Indicates that the benefits depend on what benefits are paid by other policies you have.
   c. Requires that the insured bear the cost of the health care up to a level specified in the policy.
   d. Indicates that the benefits depend on what benefits are paid by other policies that your spouse has.

8. Which of the following is not one of the features of the "own occupation" definition of disability?
   a. This definition of disability is particularly important to people who would like to return to the workforce in another job at some later date.
   b. The policy will provide benefits if you are unable to do the duties required of your occupation.
   c. The policy will allow you to find employment elsewhere without a reduction in benefits.
   d. This definition of disability is particularly important to people who work in a professional occupation.

9. There are two main differences between critical illness insurance and disability insurance. First, critical illness insurance is a _____ benefit, whereas disability insurance is a _____ benefit. Second, critical illness insurance provides coverage for _____ condition(s), whereas disability insurance provides coverage for _____ condition(s).
   a. Lump-sum, monthly, any, insured
   b. Lump-sum, monthly, insured, any
   c. Monthly, lump-sum, insured, any
   d. Monthly, lump-sum, any, insured

10. Which of the following long-term care insurance provisions is likely to increase the premium charged?
    a. Coverage of medical health care services only.
    b. A benefit period of one year instead of three years.
    c. The minimum amount of coverage that an insurance company will provide.
    d. An elimination period of 90 days instead of 60 days.

True/False

1. True or False? Medicare refers to that portion of Canada's health care system that is privately funded.

2. True or False? With respect to portability, the provinces and territories may require prior approval for emergency services delivered outside their jurisdiction.

3. True or False? One advantage of group health insurance is that some employees may be uninsurable on an individual basis, but may be able to get coverage as part of a group.

4. True or False? Critical illness insurance provides an income benefit to replace a portion of your earnings if you become ill or are injured and cannot work.

5. True or False? A pre-existing conditions clause allows individuals to buy insurance that will cover existing illnesses and injuries.

6. True or False? Your most valuable asset is your ability to earn an income.

7. True or False? A non-cancellable provision gives you the right to renew the policy each year at the same premium, with no change in the benefits.

8. True or False? The three major critical illnesses are stroke, life-threatening cancer, and heart disease.

9. True or False? With respect to long-term care insurance, if the health care is needed for a period shorter than the elimination period, it will not be covered by the policy.

10. True or False? If your spouse's family has a history of long-term illnesses, you are more likely to need long-term care insurance.

Chapter 10

Life Insurance

Maria quit her job to care for her young children. Shortly after she stopped working, her husband, Diego, was killed in an automobile accident. It was only then that Maria fully appreciated the benefit of a $400 000 life insurance policy. Shortly after their first child was born, their neighbour, an insurance agent, had approached Maria and Diego. The agent had convinced them that because Diego was the sole provider for the family, he needed a sizable insurance policy to replace his income in the event of his death. The insurance benefits are enough to cover expenses until well after the children are in school and Maria re-enters the workforce.

Without life insurance, the death of a breadwinner eliminates some or all of the household's employment income forever. Life insurance can provide financial protection for members of a household.

The objectives of this chapter are to:

1. Describe the types of life insurance that are available

2. Review the factors that affect life insurance premiums

3. Examine the decision of how much life insurance to purchase

4. Describe the contents of a life insurance policy

5. Explain the settlement options that are available for beneficiary payments

BACKGROUND ON LIFE INSURANCE

life insurance
Insurance that provides a payment to a specified beneficiary when the insured dies.

face amount
The amount stated on the face of the policy that will be paid on the death of the insured.

beneficiary
The named individual who receives life insurance payments upon the death of the insured.

life insured
The individual who is covered in the life insurance policy.

policy owner
The individual who owns all rights and obligations to the policy.

Life insurance provides a payment to a specified beneficiary when the insured dies. The payment is usually referred to as the face amount, which is the amount stated on the face of the policy that will be paid on the death of the insured. The beneficiary is the named individual who receives life insurance payments upon the death of the insured. The amount received by the beneficiary is not taxed. The life insured is the individual who is covered in the life insurance policy. Life insurance contracts represent an agreement between a life and health insurance company and the policy owner, the individual who owns all rights and obligations to the policy.

In most cases, the policy owner and the life insured are the same person. For example, Susan may purchase a $100 000 life insurance policy such that in the event of her death, her husband, Gordon, and their two children will receive $100 000 tax-free. In this example, Susan is the policy owner and the life insured, while Gordon is the beneficiary. However, there can be situations in which the policy owner and the life insured are two different parties. For example, Catherine and Manuel each own a 50 percent interest in a flower shop. If Catherine dies, her husband, Patrick, will inherit her share of the business and become a 50–50 partner with Manuel. Patrick has no interest in running a flower shop and would prefer to receive a cash payment in exchange for his inherited interest in the business. Therefore, in the event of Catherine's death, Manuel has agreed to buy out Catherine's share of the business using the payment received from a life insurance policy he has purchased. Manuel is the policy owner and beneficiary, while Catherine is the life insured. In the event that Catherine dies, Manuel will give the insurance payment to Patrick, who will surrender his inherited interest in the flower shop to Manuel. For the remainder of this chapter, however, we will assume that the policy owner and the life insured are the same person.

As of 2004, there were 105 life and health insurance companies operating in Canada, down from 163 companies in 1990. Almost 24 million Canadians are protected by life and health insurance products and services, 116 100 Canadians work in the life and health insurance industry in Canada, and Canadians receive $48.1 billion in payments from life and health insurance companies each year.

Role of Life Insurance

Before deciding whether to buy life insurance or how much life insurance to buy, you need to consider your financial goals. The most common financial goal related to life insurance is to maintain financial support for your dependants. Life insurance is critical to protect a family's financial situation in the event that a breadwinner dies. It provides the family with financial support to cover burial expenses or medical expenses not covered by health insurance. It can also maintain the family's future lifestyle even without the breadwinner's income. In addition, life insurance may help dependants pay off any accumulated debt. If you are the breadwinner and others rely on your income, you should have life insurance.

If no one else relies on your income, life insurance may not be necessary. For example, if you and your spouse both work full-time and your spouse could be self-sufficient without your income, life insurance is not as important. If you are single and not providing financial support to anyone, life insurance may not be needed.

However, many individuals without dependants still want to leave money to their heirs. For example, you may decide that you want to finance your nephew's post-secondary education. If you die before he attends college or university, a life insurance policy can achieve your goal. Alternatively, you may want to provide financial support for your parents. In this case, you can designate your parents as the beneficiaries of a life insurance policy. You can even set up a life insurance policy that designates your favourite charity as the beneficiary.

As time passes, rethink your life insurance decisions. Even if you decide not to purchase life insurance now, you may require it in the future. If you already have a life insurance policy, you may need to increase the coverage or add a beneficiary at a future point in time.

Role of Life Insurance Companies

Many insurance companies can provide you with life insurance coverage. They can explain the different types of life insurance available and help you determine which type would satisfy your needs. They can also help you determine the amount of coverage you need. Many people who purchase life insurance will be alive for another 40 or more years, and they rely on the life insurance company to provide benefits upon their death sometime in the future. Thus, it is important that the life insurance company be financially sound so that it will continue to exist and to fulfill its insurance contracts in the distant future.

Role of Canada Revenue Agency

Some types of life insurance, referred to as permanent insurance later in this chapter, allow policy owners to save money within the policy. The Canada Revenue Agency (CRA), a federal government agency that administers tax laws for the Government of Canada and most provinces and territories, provides detailed guidelines on how much can be saved inside a life insurance policy and how these funds can be used by the policy owner. A universal life insurance policy (discussed later in this chapter) is the most complex type from a tax perspective; therefore, the CRA has created numerous guidelines for regulating this form of insurance.

L.O. 1

TYPES OF LIFE INSURANCE

While the need for life insurance is straightforward, there are many options available. Policies belong to one of two main categories: term insurance is a common form of temporary or short-term insurance, while whole life and universal life insurance are common forms of permanent insurance.

Term Insurance

term insurance
Life insurance that is provided over a specified time period and does not build a cash value.

Term insurance is life insurance that is provided over a specified time period and does not build a cash value. The term is typically from 10 to 20 years. Term insurance is intended strictly to provide insurance to a beneficiary in the event of death. If the insured person remains alive over the term, the policy expires at the end of the term and has no cash value.

Consider the case of a single mother with three young children. She plans to provide financial support for her children until they complete their post-secondary education. While her income is sufficient to provide that support, she wants backup support in case she dies. She decides to purchase a 20-year term insurance policy. If she dies during this period, her children will receive the face amount specified in the policy. If she is still living at the end of the term, the policy will expire. Even under these conditions, the policy would have served its purpose, giving her peace of mind over the period by ensuring sufficient financial support for her children. When the term expires, the children will be old enough to support themselves financially.

Renewability of Term Insurance. At the end of the term, and depending on the age of the policy owner, a term life insurance policy can be renewed at a higher premium. Consider the example above of the single mother who has purchased Term20 insurance. Assume that she has decided to keep the policy at the end of the first 20-year period. If the policy contains a renewability option (discussed later in this chapter), she will be able to renew the policy at a higher premium. The higher premium reflects the fact that she is 20 years older at each renewal. At some point, she will not be able to renew the policy for 20 years. For example, assume that the insurance company will not continue a term life insurance policy beyond age 80 (a common cut-off age). If the single mother purchased the Term20 policy at age 26, she will have the option to renew the policy at age 46 for an additional 20 years. However, at age 66, she will only be able to renew the policy for an additional 14 years because the life insurance policy will expire at age 80.

grace period
The period the insurance company extends to the policy owner before the policy will lapse due to nonpayment.

Premiums on Term Insurance. Insurance companies may require that the premiums on term insurance be paid monthly, quarterly, semi-annually, or annually. If the premium is not paid by the due date, the policy owner is given a grace period, usually 30 days, before the policy will lapse due to nonpayment. If the premium is not paid during the grace period, the policy will be terminated.

Reviewing Premiums on Term Insurance Using the Internet. Some life insurance companies provide quotes for term insurance on their websites. You need to provide information such as your date of birth, your province or territory of residence, the amount of coverage desired, and the length of the term, and answer some general questions about your health. Within a minute of providing this information, you will receive quotes. You can even adjust the amount of insurance coverage if you want to determine how the premium is affected by alternative levels of coverage.

Some websites such as Kanetix (www.kanetix.ca) and Term4Sale (www.termforsale. net/canterm4sale.htm) provide quotes from various life insurance companies based on your specific needs, and may link you directly to those companies. They first request some information as described above, and then list various quotes on term insurance by different companies. This allows you to select the company you believe would best accommodate your needs. You can click on a link to the policy contract of that company and may be able to access the name and phone number of a company representative. The value of this type of website is that it may help you obtain quotes without being subjected to a sales pitch. Yet, once you have screened the list of possible insurance companies, you can speak to an insurance agent before selecting a company. Of course, you should also assess the financial soundness of the company you select.

L.O. 2

Why Premiums for Term Insurance Vary. The annual insurance premiums for term insurance vary for several reasons. First, the longer the term of the policy, the longer the period that the insurance company must provide coverage and thus the higher the annual premiums.

Second, the older the policy owner, the higher the premiums. Older people have a higher probability of dying during a given term. Exhibit 10.1 provides a sample of quoted annual premiums (based on no unusual medical problems of the policy owner).

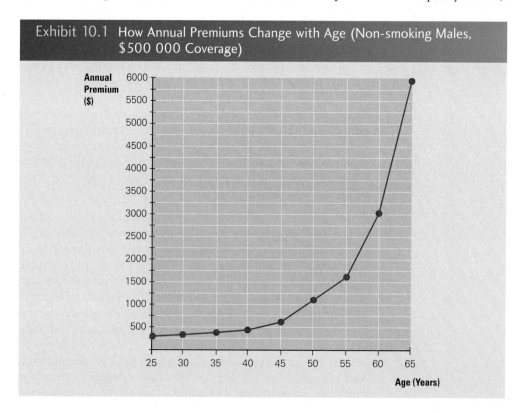

Exhibit 10.1 How Annual Premiums Change with Age (Non-smoking Males, $500 000 Coverage)

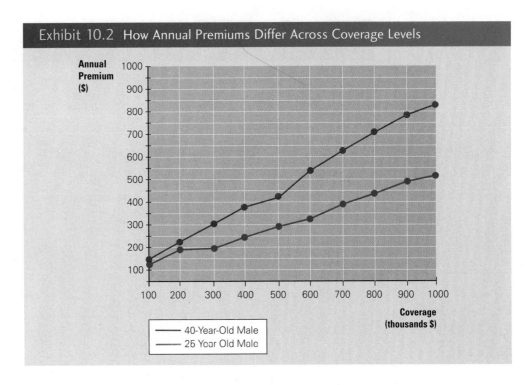

Exhibit 10.2   How Annual Premiums Differ Across Coverage Levels

The actual premiums will vary among life insurance companies, but the general comparison described here still holds. Notice that the annual premium for a 45-year-old is more than twice that for a 25-year-old. In addition, the annual premium for a 60-year-old is more than four times that for a 45-year-old.

Third, the greater the insurance coverage (benefits upon death), the higher the premiums. Exhibit 10.2 illustrates the annual premiums for two profiles based on various coverage levels. Notice that the annual premium for a $500 000 policy is more than twice that for a $100 000 policy.

Fourth, the annual premium is higher for a male than for a female of the same age. Because females tend to live longer than males, the probability of a male dying during a specified term is higher than that of a female of the same age. Exhibit 10.3 shows the difference in quoted annual premiums between males and females for various levels of coverage. In general, the quoted annual premiums for males are between 10 and 25 percent higher than those for females.

Fifth, the annual premium is substantially larger for smokers than for non-smokers. Exhibit 10.4 shows the difference in annual premiums of male smokers versus male non-smokers for various coverage levels. The annual premiums for smokers are more than twice that of non-smokers, regardless of the coverage level. This general relationship holds regardless of the age or gender of the applicant.

Sixth, the annual premium may be much larger for policy owners whose family members have a history of medical problems. For example, the annual premium quoted may be more than doubled if members of the applicant's immediate family have or had diabetes, heart disease, or kidney disease prior to age 60.

Finally, a better understanding of the causes of the number of deaths in a population or in a subgroup of the population, referred to as the mortality rate, has allowed the life insurance industry to develop preferred underwriting criteria. Underwriting is the process all life insurance companies undertake to evaluate an insurance application based on the applicant's age, sex, smoking status, driving record, and other health and lifestyle considerations and then issue insurance policies based on the responses. If you were to apply for a life insurance policy, the insurance company may request that you take a medical exam. Your physician or a physician of the company's choice would be asked to evaluate your blood pressure, your cholesterol level, your weight-to-height

mortality rate
The number of deaths in a population or in a subgroup of the population.

underwriting
The process of evaluating an insurance application based on the applicant's age, sex, smoking status, driving record, and other health and lifestyle considerations and then issuing insurance policies based on the responses.

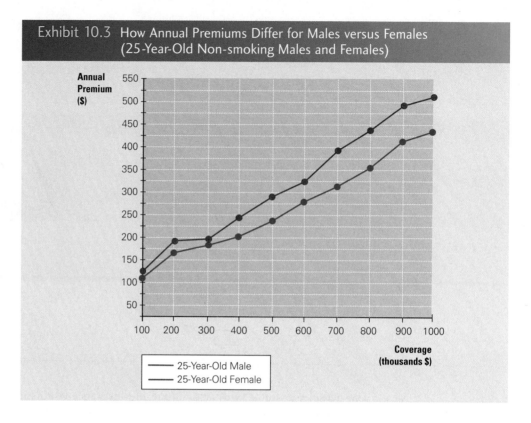

Exhibit 10.3 How Annual Premiums Differ for Males versus Females (25-Year-Old Non-smoking Males and Females)

ratio, whether you have a history of alcohol or drug abuse, or whether you participate in any dangerous sports. A high weight-to-height ratio may be indicative of a greater likelihood of developing diseases such as heart disease and adult-onset diabetes.

All life insurance companies implement underwriting criteria based on an applicant's health and lifestyle considerations. Some companies go even further by offering multiple premium categories to address these diverse considerations. It is important to look for a policy that best suits your lifestyle and the premium you are willing to pay.

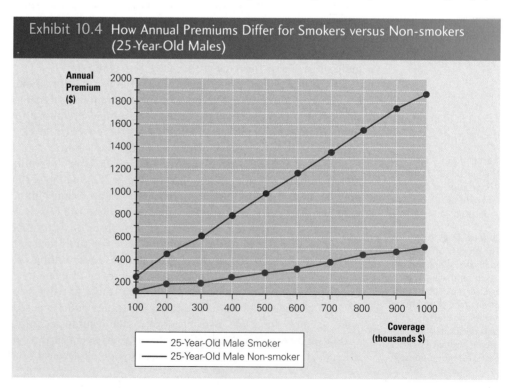

Exhibit 10.4 How Annual Premiums Differ for Smokers versus Non-smokers (25-Year-Old Males)

EXAMPLE

Identical twin brothers Kenyon and James Burris, both 32-year-old non-smokers, have each applied for a $100 000 life insurance policy with Lighthouse Life Insurance Company. Lighthouse Life offers three different premium levels to male non-smokers: gold, silver, and bronze. The policy type both brothers have applied for contains the same features and benefits. Based on the criteria of age, sex, smoking status, and family medical history alone, both men expect to qualify for the silver premium level, which represents the average premium charged to a 32-year-old male non-smoker. However, Lighthouse Life has determined that Kenyon and James do not fall into the silver level.

The company received Kenyon's driving record from his car insurance company, which indicated that he has received two speeding tickets in the last year. In addition, Kenyon is a licensed scuba diver who likes to dive at the Broken Group Islands off the coast of Pacific Rim National Park in British Columbia at least twice a year. Based on these lifestyle considerations, Kenyon would have to pay a higher-than-average premium at the bronze level.

The company received the results of James's physical and has determined that his blood pressure, cholesterol levels, and weight-to-height ratio are better than average for a 32-year-old male non-smoker. Furthermore, his clean driving record, combined with no history of alcohol or drug abuse and no participation in any hazardous sports, means that James would pay a lower-than-average premium at the gold level.

Focus on Ethics: Applying for Life Insurance

When applying for life insurance, you fill out a detailed form on which you provide information about your medical history and lifestyle that is used to determine your eligibility and premium. If you suffer from a chronic illness such as diabetes or heart disease or are a smoker, your premium will be higher. You may be tempted to omit some information in the hopes that you can pay a lower premium. As part of the application process, however, you will most likely undergo a medical exam. Between the exam results and information available from the Medical Information Bureau, a clearinghouse of medical information that insurers share, the insurance company will most likely uncover any inaccuracies in your application.

If your application does slip through with inaccuracies, your insurance benefits could be eliminated at a later date if the company discovers them. The policy is a legal contract between you and the insurance company, so you must be truthful. It is not worth jeopardizing the peace of mind that life insurance provides by trying to save a relatively small amount on premiums.

creditor insurance
Term life insurance where the beneficiary of the policy is a creditor.

creditor
An individual or company to whom you owe money.

Creditor Insurance. Creditor insurance is a type of term life insurance where the beneficiary of the policy is a creditor. A creditor is an individual or company to whom you owe money. For example, when you apply for a credit card, the credit card company may offer you creditor insurance. If you have an outstanding credit balance on your card when you die, the credit card company, who in this case is the beneficiary, would receive the face amount of your creditor insurance policy. The face amount is based on the outstanding credit balance at your death. Since credit card balances fluctuate, the monthly premium you pay and the potential face amount will change. As a rule of thumb, the higher your credit card balance at any point in time, the higher the monthly premium you will pay and the higher the face amount in the event of your death. Another common form of creditor insurance is mortgage life insurance. Mortgage life insurance pays off a policy owner's mortgage in the event of his or her death. In this case, the beneficiary is the financial institution with whom the policy owner set up his or her mortgage life insurance. People purchase mortgage life insurance to ensure that their families can afford to continue living in the home in the event of the death of one or more income earners.

Creditor Insurance versus Personally Owned Term Insurance. As discussed earlier in this chapter, the most common financial goal people have when they acquire life insurance is to ensure financial stability for their dependants in the event of their death. Although this financial goal can be met by owning a combination of creditor and personally owned insurance, people generally purchase one or the other. Creditor insurance ensures financial stability because it pays off a specific debt, and only that debt, that the policy owner owes. Alternatively, a policy owner of a personally owned term insurance policy can specify that the face amount of the policy be used to pay off a credit debt. Since both creditor and personally owned term insurance can be used to accomplish the same goal, individuals have to decide which type or types are appropriate for their circumstances.

Generally, an applicant chooses creditor insurance over personally owned term insurance because of the convenience of the purchase. For example, when you are approved for a mortgage, the bank representative will offer you the opportunity to buy mortgage life insurance. If you do not already have personally owned term insurance, it makes sense to purchase mortgage life insurance. A first-time homebuyer is often a first-time life insurance buyer. Before making such an important financial decision, it is important to understand the difference between mortgage life insurance and personally owned term insurance. The discussion below and the comparison shown in Exhibit 10.5 will help you assess the difference between mortgage life insurance and personally owned term insurance.

Before deciding to purchase mortgage life insurance, an applicant should consider the advantages of personally owned term insurance over creditor insurance. As discussed in Chapter 7, your mortgage balance decreases each time you make a mortgage payment. The face amount under mortgage life insurance decreases to match the balance outstanding on your mortgage. Although the face amount decreases over time, the premium you are paying on the mortgage life insurance policy does not. Mortgage life insurance is also known as decreasing term insurance. Decreasing term insurance is a type

decreasing term insurance A type of creditor insurance, such as mortgage life insurance, where the life insurance face amount decreases each time a regular payment is made on debt that is amortized over a period of time.

Exhibit 10.5 Comparison of Creditor Insurance and Personally Owned Term Insurance

Creditor Insurance	Personally Owned Term Insurance
The policy is owned and controlled by a creditor, for example, a bank, trust company, or credit union.	The policy owner owns the policy.
In the event of the death of the life insured, benefits are payable directly to the creditor.	In the event of the death of the life insured, the policy owner determines who the beneficiary will be.
Benefits are used to pay off the remaining credit balance, for example, the mortgage balance.	Beneficiaries determine whether they wish to pay off the mortgage balance or would like to use the benefits for another purpose.
As the credit balance decreases, the insurance coverage decreases. However, premiums do not decrease.	The policy owner determines whether insurance coverage should be decreased. If coverage is reduced, premiums may decrease.
If the credit balance is paid off, life insurance coverage will terminate. If credit is reapplied for with another creditor, life insurance will have to be reapplied for, possibly resulting in increased premiums.	The life insurance policy exists independent of any credit facility. Therefore, the policy is cancelled only if the policy owner decides to cancel it.

of creditor insurance where the life insurance face amount decreases each time a regular payment is made on debt that is amortized over a period of time.

With personally owned term insurance, the face amount does not decrease. As a result, if you purchase personally owned term insurance instead of mortgage life insurance from your financial institution, there will be money left over if you die and the remaining mortgage balance is paid off using the life insurance benefit. After paying off the mortgage balance, the remaining life insurance benefit can be used for other purposes.

As discussed in Chapter 7, you may decide to switch your mortgage to another lender at the end of your mortgage term because the new lender offers a better interest rate or provides better services. Since the bank is not the beneficiary of a personally owned term insurance policy, you can switch your mortgage and still maintain your insurance policy. However, if you applied for mortgage life insurance when you were first approved for the mortgage, you would now have to reapply for mortgage life insurance at the new financial institution. Your premiums would be higher, based on your age, and you also run the risk of not being insurable depending on your health and lifestyle at the time of reapplication.

Since personally owned term insurance offers some advantages to the policy owner relative to creditor insurance, you should expect it to be a little more expensive. This may or may not be the case depending on the financial institutions from which you are obtaining quotes. As a home buyer, it is in your best interest to understand the benefits and costs of each type of policy so that you can make an informed decision when the time comes. It is important to note that you cannot be denied a loan based on the fact that you have decided not to purchase creditor insurance from the financial institution. Therefore, you should know that it is within your rights to shop around for the coverage that is appropriate for you and your family.

group term insurance
Term insurance provided to a designated group of people with a common bond that generally has lower-than-typical premiums.

Group Term Insurance. **Group term insurance** is term insurance provided to a designated group of people with a common bond, such as the same employer. Group term premiums are usually lower than the typical premiums an individual would pay because the policy owner receives a group discount. Some companies that have a group plan may provide term insurance to their employees as a benefit.

IN-CLASS NOTES

Background on Life Insurance and Types of Life Insurance

- Parties to a life insurance contract
  - Beneficiary, life insured, policy owner
  - Life and health insurance company
- Types of temporary life insurance
  - Term insurance
    - Consider the implications of owning Term10 versus Term20
    - Renewability
  - Creditor insurance
    - Who is the beneficiary?
    - Should I buy creditor insurance or personally owned term insurance?
  - Group life insurance

_____

_____

_____

_____

_____

_____

_____

Permanent Insurance

permanent insurance
Life insurance that continues to provide insurance for as long as premiums are paid.

Permanent insurance is life insurance that continues to provide insurance for as long as premiums are paid. For most permanent insurance policies, life insurance companies divide premium payments into two portions. One portion is used to cover the costs associated with managing your policy, which include the cost of insurance and company expenses such as administrative, management, and other overhead costs. The cost of insurance represents the insurance-related expenses incurred by a life insurance company to provide the actual death benefit. The remainder of the premium goes into a savings account and is referred to as the cash value of the policy. The cash value is the portion of the premium in excess of insurance-related and company expenses that is invested by the insurance company on your behalf. In the event of your death, the death benefit, which may include a cash value, would be available to the beneficiary to cover things such as capital gains taxes payable at death, gifts to charity, or provision of an income stream for mentally and/or physically incapacitated loved ones. The death benefit is the total amount paid tax-free to the beneficiary on the death of the policy owner. As mentioned earlier, the death benefit may include the cash value of the policy. Policy owners often assume that the cash value is automatically a part of the death benefit. This is only true if the policy owner has set up the policy to include it. Otherwise, the cash value represents a prepayment of future premiums or a forced savings account that can be used in the future by the policy owner.

cost of insurance
The insurance-related expenses incurred by a life insurance company to provide the actual death benefit, sometimes referred to as the pure cost of dying.

cash value
The portion of the premium in excess of insurance-related and company expenses that is invested by the insurance company on behalf of the policy owner.

death benefit
The total amount paid tax-free to the beneficiary upon the death of the policy owner.

The cash value is available to the policy owner prior to his or her death. For example, the policy owner may decide to use the cash value for some specific purpose, such as paying for a child's tuition or purchasing a car. It is important to note that if you withdraw a cash amount, the amount by which the cash value exceeds the premiums that were paid is subject to tax.

As mentioned earlier in this chapter, the use of permanent insurance is regulated by the Canada Revenue Agency. We will discuss three forms of permanent insurance: whole life, universal life, and term to 100.

whole life insurance
A form of permanent life insurance that builds cash value based on a fixed premium that is payable for the life of the insured.

Whole Life Insurance. Whole life insurance is a form of permanent life insurance that builds cash value based on a fixed premium that is payable for the life of the insured. The cash value is typically specified on a schedule. The long-term growth rate of the cash value in the savings account depends on the types of investments the life insurance company selects. For example, if the company invests the cash value in term deposits, the long-term growth rate will be lower than if it had invested the cash value in long-term bonds. Based on historical investment returns for various asset classes, the life insurance company is able to make long-term predictions for the growth rate. As a result, the company will guarantee cash values based on very conservative estimates of long-term investment return. In addition, the life insurance company will provide estimates of the growth in cash value based on alternative investment returns. The guaranteed and non-guaranteed cash values are specified in the schedule.

A whole life insurance policy can serve as a source of liquidity. You can borrow against the cash value at an interest rate specified in the policy. However, recognize that this type of loan reduces the cash value of your insurance policy.

Whole Life Premiums. The premium on whole life insurance is constant for the duration of the policy. In the earlier years of the policy, the portion of the premium dedicated to paying for the cost of insurance is low. At the same time, company expenses, including sales commissions, can be quite high. As discussed earlier, the remainder is invested by the insurance company in the savings account. The portion of the premium dedicated to savings is high in the earlier years, when the policy owner is young, because the portion of the premium needed to insure against the possibility of death is relatively low. In the later years of the policy, the opposite is true: the cost of insurance increases as the policy owner ages. As a result, the portion of the premium required to insure against possible death is relatively high. Because the insurance premium remains constant, it is not sufficient to cover the amount needed to insure against the higher cost of insurance in the later years. Thus, a portion of the policy's cash value is used to supplement the premium paid in these later years. The main purpose of the cash value in a whole life policy is to pay for the cost of insurance in the later years.

If you fail to pay a premium on a whole life policy, the insurance company will (with your consent) draw from the cash value of your policy to cover the premium. This will continue until the cash value is nil. At that time, the policy will lapse (become null and void).

The premiums among whole life policies can vary substantially. Because a whole life policy provides coverage for life, the annual premiums are influenced by the same factors that affect term insurance premiums. In particular, the quoted annual premiums are higher when the applicant is a male smoker, over 60 years old, who requires a larger amount of insurance coverage.

limited payment policy
Allows you to pay premiums over a specified period but remain insured for life.

Forms of Whole Life Insurance. Many forms of whole life insurance are available, so you can structure the premium payments in a manner that suits your needs. One such policy is a **limited payment policy**, which allows you to pay premiums over a specified period but remain insured for life. For example, you could make payments until you retire, but continue to be insured after retirement. If you are 45 years old and plan to retire at age 65, this means you would request a payment period of 20 years. The insurance premiums are larger than if you were required to pay premiums continuously, but you build a large cash value during the payment period. Once the payment period ends, your savings accumulated within the whole life policy are used to cover future premiums.

Alternatively, a whole life policy can be structured to provide a higher level of death benefits to the beneficiaries in the earlier years of the policy. For example, it may specify coverage of $300 000 over the next 10 years, and coverage of $100 000 after 10 years. This type of policy may be useful for policyholders who have young children. The coverage is higher in the years when the children are young and unable to take care of themselves. In this case, the policy may be a combination of whole life and term.

EXAMPLE

Stephanie Spratt has a close relationship with her two young nieces, who come from a single-parent home. While Stephanie is currently focused on building her own wealth, she hopes that someday she will have sufficient funds to pay for her nieces' post-secondary educations. She is considering purchasing life insurance that would provide benefits of $100 000, and naming her nieces as beneficiaries. She will invest in either a 20-year term life insurance policy for $120 per year or a whole life policy for $500 per year.

The whole life premium is higher, but the policy builds a cash value over time. If she buys a term insurance policy for $120 per year, she could invest the difference in the premiums on her own. If she invests the money in a manner similar to the whole life policy, she will likely be able to accumulate savings more quickly on her own. A whole life policy typically generates low returns on the cash that is invested because part of the premium is used to cover administrative fees. Stephanie decides to purchase the term life policy. This is a good decision for her, as she has the self-discipline to save the difference in the two premiums.

universal life insurance
A form of permanent life insurance for which you do not pay a fixed premium and in which you can invest the cash value portion in a variety of investments.

Universal Life Insurance. **Universal life insurance** is a form of permanent life insurance for which you do not pay a fixed premium and in which you can invest the cash value portion in a variety of investments. As discussed, permanent life insurance premiums are usually divided such that a portion of the premium covers the cost of insurance-related and company expenses and the remainder goes into an investment account.

When you make a premium payment to a universal life insurance policy, the money is deposited directly into the investment account portion of the policy. The life insurance company will then withdraw from that account the amount of premium required to cover the cost of insurance-related and company expenses. The amount of money withdrawn depends on which cost of insurance option the policy owner has selected. A universal life insurance policy has two costs of insurance options: level term and yearly renewable term (YRT). If the policy owner selects the level term option, the amount withdrawn from the savings account to cover the cost of insurance is the same every year. A more conservative policy owner would choose this option. The cash value does not increase as quickly, but the cost of insurance will remain stable for the life of the policy. If the policy owner selects the YRT option, the cash value would grow more quickly for a given level of premium. This happens because, during the early years of the policy, the amount withdrawn to cover the cost of insurance under the YRT option is lower relative to the premium cost of the level term option. Therefore, a policy owner focused on increasing the cash value of the policy would choose the yearly renewable term option for the early years of the policy. During the later years of the policy, the policy owner can switch to the level term option so that the cost of insurance will remain the same every year for future years. The level term cost of insurance will be based on the age of the policy owner at the time of the switch.

Universal Life Insurance Premiums. The minimum premium payment required in a universal life insurance policy is designed to cover the cost of insurance-related and company expenses and to provide for a modest savings account that will result in very low cash values during the life of the policy. Policy owners might choose to pay the minimum premium for any number of reasons: they cannot afford to pay more than the minimum, they have purchased universal life insurance with the intention of building the cash value account in the future, or they decided that they had a financial need for permanent insurance but were not interested in building cash values. As mentioned earlier, the Canada Revenue Agency provides detailed guidelines on how much money can be saved inside a universal life insurance policy. These guidelines were created because the accumulated growth of savings inside a universal life policy is tax-sheltered until it is withdrawn. Without a maximum premium guideline, there would be an incentive for policy owners to put as much money as possible toward the cash value portion of their universal life policies. Therefore, to prevent excessive tax deferral, the CRA has set guidelines that deter investors from investing in a universal life insurance policy as a heavily capitalized investment tax shelter. A detailed discussion of these guidelines is beyond the scope of this textbook.

Why Buy Universal Life Insurance. Tax-sheltered growth inside a universal life insurance policy is advantageous to policy owners who have already maximized their contributions to other tax-sheltered plans, such as RRSPs. You can build additional tax-sheltered savings for retirement by purchasing a universal life insurance policy. The tax-sheltered growth inside a universal life insurance policy is particularly useful when building an estate plan. The cash value can be used to provide for long-term care or home care in your later years. The insurance benefits can be used to pay final expenses and estate taxes and/or to fund charitable contributions at death. A detailed discussion of the application of universal life insurance policies in estate planning is provided in Chapter 16.

Differences between Whole Life and Universal Life. Whole life and universal life are both permanent insurance policies that provide an opportunity to build cash value inside a savings account. However, there are key differences between these two forms of insurance that should be considered when evaluating which is right for you. First, the premium you pay for a whole life insurance policy is fixed for the life of the policy. Many people consider whole life insurance as a form of forced savings. In a universal life insurance policy, the premium is flexible between a minimum and a maximum range. Second, in a whole life policy, the insurance company selects the investments for the cash value. Since it is able to determine the investment choices, it is also able to guarantee a conservative amount of cash value. Life insurance companies invest the cash value in fixed-income investments. In a universal life policy, the policy owner controls the investment choices. The cash value generated in the investment account is determined by how successfully the policy owner chooses investments. As a result, the size of the investment account is not guaranteed by the life insurance company. The investment choices offered in a universal life insurance policy will differ among companies, but common options include term deposits, GICs, and segregated funds that invest in index-linked accounts, equities, and fixed-income securities. Segregated funds are discussed in more detail in Chapter 12.

Non-forfeiture Options. If the policy owner decides to terminate the policy prior to death, the remaining cash value can be used in a variety of ways, referred to as non-forfeiture options. **Non-forfeiture options** represent the options available to a policy owner who would like to discontinue or cancel a policy that has cash value. A policy owner may decide to discontinue a policy for several reasons: the life insurance is no longer needed, the policy is too expensive, or the type of policy is inappropriate for the needs of the policy owner and his or her family. In the event that the policy owner decides to cancel a policy that has accumulated cash value, the life insurance company will provide four non-forfeiture options with respect to the cash value. You may cancel the policy and keep the cash value, use the cash value to pay the policy premium until the cash value runs out and the policy subsequently terminates, use the cash value as a one-time premium payment to purchase term insurance, or use the cash value as a one-time premium payment to purchase permanent paid-up insurance.

Paid-up insurance is a permanent life insurance policy that results from exercising a non-forfeiture option on a policy that has accumulated cash value. The cash value is used to make a one-time premium payment, which means that the amount of paid-up insurance is relatively small compared to the terminated policy.

Term to 100 Insurance. **Term to 100 insurance** is a form of permanent life insurance designed for the sole purpose of providing a benefit at death. In most cases, the policy owner does not need to pay premiums if he or she lives beyond the age of 100. This form of insurance is more expensive than term insurance, but is less expensive than whole life or universal life insurance. The main advantage of term to 100 is that it provides life insurance for your entire life without the added expense of a savings component. The main disadvantage of term to 100 is that the cost of insurance is averaged over the entire life of the insurance policy, which is the number of years from the age at which you establish the policy to 100. As a result, you pay quite a bit more in the early years of the policy compared to other types of term life insurance.

If you go to www.termforsale.net/canterm4sale.php and create a quote for term to 100 life insurance, you will find results for approximately 14 companies. However, 105 life and health insurance companies were operating in Canada as of 2004. So, although term to 100 insurance is available, you will likely have to ask for a quote before an agent or broker will provide an illustration for this type of policy. Exhibit 10.6 provides an overview of the types of life insurance that have been discussed to this point.

Classifying Life Insurance. Life insurance policies can be classified as either participating or non-participating. A **participating policy** is a life insurance policy that is eligible to receive policy dividends, whereas a **non-participating policy** is a life insurance policy that is not eligible to receive policy dividends. All life insurance policies, with the exception of whole life insurance, are non-participating. A participating whole life insurance policy is eligible to receive policy dividends. A **policy dividend** is a refund of premiums that occurs when the long-term assumptions the insurance company made with respect to the cost of insurance, company expenses, and investment returns have changed.

As discussed earlier, whole life premiums remain level over the life of the insurance policy. To make this possible, the life insurance company has to make long-term assumptions with respect to the cost of insurance, company expenses, and investment returns. If these assumptions turn out to be incorrect, as outlined below, the policy owner essentially will have overpaid for the insurance. A policy dividend represents a repayment of

---

non-forfeiture options
The options available to a policy owner who would like to discontinue or cancel a policy that has cash value.

paid-up insurance
A permanent life insurance policy that results from exercising a non-forfeiture option on a policy that has accumulated cash value.

term to 100 insurance
A form of permanent life insurance designed for the sole purpose of providing a benefit at death.

participating policy
A life insurance policy that is eligible to receive policy dividends.

non-participating policy
A life insurance policy that is not eligible to receive policy dividends.

policy dividend
A refund of premiums that occurs when the long-term assumptions the insurance company made with respect to the cost of insurance, company expenses, and investment returns have changed.

Exhibit 10.6 Types of Life Insurance

	Term	Permanent		
Policy Type	Term	Whole Life	Universal Life	Term to 100
Period of Coverage	Depends on term in contract. Often renewable for additional terms but usually not past age 70 or 75.	Life	Life	To age 100 or life, depending on contract.
Premiums	Guaranteed in contract.	Guaranteed. Usually remain level.	Flexible. Can be increased or decreased by policyholder within certain limits.	Guaranteed. Usually remain level.
Death Benefits	Guaranteed in contract.	Guaranteed in contract. Remain level. Dividends may be used to enhance death benefits in participating policies.	Flexible. May increase or decrease according to fluctuations in cash value.	Guaranteed in contract. Remain level.
Cash Value	Usually none. (Some long-term policies have a small cash value or other non-forfeiture value.)	Guaranteed in contract.	Flexible. May increase or decrease according to investment returns and level of policyholder deposits.	Usually none. (Some policies have a small cash value or other non-forfeiture value after a long period, say, 20 years.)
Other Non-forfeiture Options	See above.	Guaranteed in contract.	Guaranteed in contract.	See above.
Dividends	Most policies do not pay dividends.	Payable on "participating" policies. Not guaranteed.	Most policies do not pay dividends.	Most policies do not pay dividends.
Advantages	■ Suitable for short-term insurance needs, or specific liabilities such as a mortgage. ■ Provides more immediate protection because, initially, it is less expensive than permanent insurance. ■ Can be converted to permanent insurance without medical evidence (if it has a convertibility option), often up to ages 65 or 70.	■ Provides protection for your entire lifetime, if kept in force. ■ Premiums usually stay level, regardless of age or health problems. ■ Has cash value that can be borrowed, used to are continue protection if premiums missed, or withdrawn if the policy is no longer required. ■ Other non-forfeiture options allow the policyholder various possibilities of continuing coverage if premiums are missed or discontinued. ■ If the policy is participating, it receives dividends that can be taken in cash, left to accumulate with interest, or used to purchase additional insurance.		■ Provides protection to age 100, if kept in force. ■ Premiums usually stay level, regardless of age or health problems. ■ Premiums are lower relative to traditional permanent policies.

Exhibit 10.6	(continued)		
Disadvantages	■ If renewed, premiums increase with age and at some point higher premiums may make it difficult or impossible to continue coverage. ■ Renewability of coverage will terminate at some point, commonly age 65 or 75. ■ If premiums are not paid, the policy terminates after 30 days and may not be reinstated if health is poor. ■ Usually no cash value and no non-forfeiture options.	■ Initial cost may be too high for a sufficient amount of protection for your current needs. ■ May not be an efficient means of covering short-term needs. ■ Cash value tends to be small in the early years. You have to hold the policy for a long time (say, over 10 years) before the cash value becomes sizable.	■ Usually no cash value and no or limited non-forfeiture options.

Source: Adapted from Canadian Life and Health Insurance Association Inc., *A Guide to Buying Life Insurance,* 1996, from www.clhia.ca/download/Life_Brochure_EN.pdf (pp. 6–7). Reprinted with permission of Canadian Life and Health Insurance Association Inc. (2206).

this excess premium. A policy dividend should not be confused with the dividend a company pays to its shareholders when it makes a net profit at the end of its fiscal year. A life insurance policy dividend does not represent growth in a company. Specifically, for a policy dividend to be paid, one of three things must occur: the cost of insurance was lower than expected, the insurance company's investment earnings with respect to the cash value in the savings account were higher than expected, or company expenses were lower than expected. Payment of a policy dividend is made at the discretion of the life insurance company. When policy owners receive policy dividends, the insurance company gives them a number of options, including the opportunity to buy more insurance. Policy owners often use policy dividends to increase the death benefit of a whole life insurance policy.

Comparison of Life Insurance Premiums. With respect to term insurance policies, the length of the term determines the premium to be paid for the insurance. Exhibit 10.7 illustrates the relative cost of the types of life insurance. Term insurance is the least expensive form for two reasons: it will expire earlier than permanent insurance policies and it does not build cash value. In Exhibit 10.7, the policy with a shorter term (Term10) is less expensive than the policy with a longer term (Term20). With respect to permanent insurance policies, the amount of the premiums deposited to the savings account portion of the policy determines the premium to be paid. Term to 100 is the least expensive form of permanent insurance because the policy owner is not contributing toward a cash value portion of the policy. The cost of insurance for whole life and universal life policies is similar to that for term to 100. The difference in premiums among types of permanent insurance is mainly a result of the amount you choose to deposit to the savings or investment account portion of each policy. A minimum premium payment universal life insurance policy is less expensive than whole life insurance because the minimum premium amount is generally lower than most whole life policy premiums. A maximum premium payment universal life insurance policy provides the greatest opportunity for tax-deferred growth.

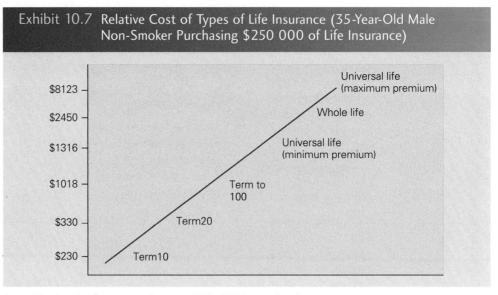

Exhibit 10.7 Relative Cost of Types of Life Insurance (35-Year-Old Male Non-Smoker Purchasing $250 000 of Life Insurance)

Source: The Canada Life Assurance Company, 1999–2004, example only.

IN-CLASS NOTES

Types of Permanent Life Insurance

- Whole life
  - Fixed premiums
  - Source of liquidity (you can borrow from the cash value)
  - Limited payment policies available
  - Investments made at the discretion of the life insurance company
- Universal life
  - Flexible premiums
  - Cost of insurance options
    - Level term
    - Yearly renewable term (YRT)
  - Company expenses will vary
  - Investment returns are based on the performance of the investments selected by the policy owner
- Term to 100
  - No cash value

L.O. 3

DETERMINING THE AMOUNT OF LIFE INSURANCE NEEDED

Once you identify the type of policy that best suits your needs, your next decision is the policy amount. You can determine the amount of life insurance you need by applying the income method or the budget method.

Income Method

income method
Determines how much life insurance is needed based on the policyholder's annual income.

The income method is a general formula that determines how much life insurance is needed based on your annual income. This method normally specifies the life insurance amount as a multiple of your annual income, such as 10 times your income. For example, if you have an annual income of $40 000, this formula suggests that you need $400 000 in life insurance. This method is very easy to use. The disadvantage is that it does not consider your age or household situation (including annual household expenses). Thus, it does not differentiate between a household with no children and one with children, which will likely need more life insurance because its expenses are higher.

EXAMPLE

The Trent household earns $50 000 per year. The Carlin household also earns $50 000 per year. Both households seek the advice of a neighbour who sells insurance, and are told that they should have coverage of 10 times their annual income. However, the Trent household's financial situation is completely different than that of the Carlin household.

The Trents are in their early thirties and have two very young children. Darren Trent is the sole breadwinner and Rita Trent plans to stay at home for several more years. They have even discussed having more children. They have large credit card balances, two car loans, and a mortgage loan. Their $50 000 annual income barely covers their existing expenses and they have very little savings. They tend to overspend on their children, and will likely continue to do so. They want to send their children to college or university and they would like to purchase a bigger home in the future.

The Carlins do not have any children. They are in their late fifties and both work part-time. They have established a very large amount of savings and a substantial retirement account, so they could retire now if they had to. They have completely paid off their mortgage, and do not have any other debt.

Given the distinct differences in financial conditions, insurance coverage should not be the same for both households. The Trents should apply a higher multiple of their annual income, while the Carlins should apply a lower multiple. Some insurance agents would likely suggest that the Trents use a multiple of 20, so that their life insurance would be 20 × $50 000 = $1 million. The Carlins may use a much smaller multiple, such as 6, so that their life insurance coverage would be 6 × $50 000 = $300 000.

The difference in the appropriate amount of coverage in the example above is due to the difference in future funds needed in the event of death. However, the adjustments here are arbitrary and may not provide proper coverage. Thus, the income method is limited, even if it allows for some adjustments to account for differences in financial situations.

Budget Method

budget method (or needs method)
A method that determines how much life insurance is needed based on the household's future expected expenses and current financial situation.

An alternative method is the budget method (also referred to as the needs method), which determines how much life insurance is needed based on your future expected expenses and current financial situation. This method requires a little more effort than the income method, but it provides a better estimate of necessary coverage. The main reason for having life insurance is to ensure that a household's needs are covered in the event of death, not simply to replace lost income. The budget method estimates the amount of future funds that will be needed, so that the insurance coverage will be adequate. Some important factors that should be considered when determining household needs are:

- **Annual living expenses.** You should have sufficient insurance so that your family can live comfortably without your income. Your family's future expenses will be higher if you have children and younger children will need financial support for a longer period of time.

- **Special future expenses.** If you want to ensure college or university educations for your children, you need adequate life insurance to cover the existing or future expenses.

- **Debt.** If your family relies on your income to cover debt, you may want to ensure that your life insurance can pay off credit card bills and even a mortgage.

- **Job marketability of spouse.** If your spouse has very limited job marketability, you may need more life insurance so that he or she can receive job training.

- **Value of existing savings.** If you have accumulated a large amount of savings, your family may draw interest or dividends from these savings to cover a portion of their periodic expenses. The more savings your household has accumulated, the less life insurance you need.

EXAMPLE

Calculators in the margin will alert you when it is necessary to use one to perform a particular financial function.

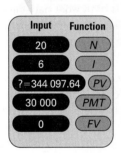

Input	Function
20	N
6	I
?=344 097.64	PV
30 000	PMT
0	FV

You wish to purchase a life insurance policy that generates a pre-tax income of at least $30 000 per year for the next 20 years to cover living expenses (excluding the mortgage payment) for your spouse and two children in the event that you die. You have just enough savings to cover burial expenses, and you anticipate no unusual expenses for the household in the future.

To determine your insurance needs, you must estimate the amount of insurance today that will cover your household's living expenses in the future. You can use the time value of money concepts in Appendix A to determine the amount of funds that can provide an annuity equal to $30 000 over each of the next 20 years. First, assume that your spouse will be able to earn at least 6 percent annually by investing the money received from the life insurance policy. Next, estimate the present value of an annuity that can provide your household with a $30 000 annuity over 20 years if it generates an annual return of 6 percent:

Amount of Insurance Needed = Annuity Amount × PVIFA ($i = 6\%, n = 20$)

$$= \$30\ 000 \times 11.47$$

$$= \$344\ 100$$

Based on the following additional information about your household, you then adjust the amount of insurance needed.

- *Special future expense.* You also want to allocate an extra $50 000 in life insurance to pay for your two children's college or university expenses. Although these expenses will rise in the future, the money set aside will accumulate interest over time, and therefore should be sufficient.

- *Job training.* You want to have additional insurance of $20 000 to ensure that your spouse can pay for job training in the event of your death.

- *Debt.* You have a $60 000 mortgage and no other loans or credit card debt. You decide to increase the life insurance amount so that the mortgage can be paid off in the event of your death. Therefore, you specify an extra $60 000 in life insurance.

By summing your preferences, you determine that you need a total of $474 100 in life insurance. You round off the number and obtain quotes for policies with coverages of $475 000 or $500 000.

Using a Life Insurance Agent to Determine Your Insurance Coverage. As discussed, the income method is very easy to use and does not require the assistance of a life insurance agent or a software program. However, the budget method does require an understanding of your household's future expected expenses in the event that you die. Although you may be able to anticipate most of these expenses on your own, an experienced life insurance agent may be able to point out expenses that you have not considered. For example, you may wish to leave a gift to a favourite charity in addition to providing for future household expenses.

Using the Internet to Determine Your Insurance Coverage. There are numerous websites that contain life insurance calculations that would be useful in determining your beneficiaries' needs. The websites ask you to provide basic information such as your total amount of debt, how much annual income you want your family to receive upon your death, and how many years you want that income to last. They may even allow you to specify the amount of funds you wish to provide for the education of your family members. An example of a life insurance needs calculator that uses the budget method can be found at www.kanetix.ca/life_cov_calc.

Limitations in Estimating Needs. When using the budget method to determine needs, keep in mind that the amount of funds you will need is subject to much uncertainty. Here are some common reasons why you may underestimate the coverage you need:

- Someone within your household could experience an unanticipated major illness or disability.

- The income level of your household may not rise over time as expected. It could even decline due to layoffs.

- Inflation could cause you to underestimate the cost of some needs. For example, you may have identified a home as one of your future needs and estimated that it would cost $120 000, based on existing home prices. However, the price of a home could double within 10 to 20 years. If the insurance policy only allowed $120 000 for a home, this amount might not be sufficient to purchase the kind of home you desire.

- The insurance policy you purchase today may not provide coverage until many years from now. For households that save money between the time a policy is purchased and the death of the policyholder, the funding needed from an insurance policy is reduced. However, for households that accumulate more debt every year, the funding needed from an insurance policy increases. Households should consider the potential change in their debt level over time so that they can more accurately estimate the insurance coverage they will need.

As you attempt to determine your needs, account for uncertainty by recognizing that the values of these needs may be higher under some conditions. For example, allow for the possibility of higher home prices or tuition when you estimate the values of these needs. When you review your financial plan, you should include your insurance as well.

Overestimating your future needs means that you will have more insurance benefits than you really need. You may pay only an extra $50 or so in annual premiums for this extra coverage. Underestimating your future needs means that you will have less insurance than you really need. The insurance benefits would not be adequate to provide the desired standard of living for your family. When accounting for uncertainty about your family's future needs, it is better to overestimate future needs than to underestimate them.

Distinguishing between Needs and Dreams. Before you estimate your needs, distinguish between needs and dreams. To illustrate, consider a young couple that presently has no savings but has dreams that the breadwinner's career path will generate a substantial amount of income and savings over time, so that they can retire by age 55 and live in a large home in the mountain resort town of Canmore, Alberta. To achieve their dream, they will likely need about $3 million by the time they are 55 years old. However, if the breadwinner dies, the spouse's life and aspirations may change completely. The idea of a large home in Canmore may no longer be appealing if the couple cannot live there together. The needs to be covered by life insurance should be separated from dreams.

Go to
www.kanetix.ca/
life_cov_calc

This website provides
a life insurance needs calculator that uses the budget method.

To determine your needs, apply the following logic. First, decide what necessities must be covered for your household to survive and continue its normal standard of living if you die. This exercise can help determine the minimal life insurance coverage you will need to live comfortably.

Second, you may wish to consider some additional preferences beyond necessities, such as having enough money to ensure that your children's post-secondary education is covered. There is an obvious tradeoff. The greater the total value of needs if you die, the greater the necessary life insurance coverage and the higher the life insurance premiums. A higher level of life insurance premiums today results in a smaller amount of funds that could be used for other purposes. In general, people attempt to strike a compromise when identifying their life insurance needs. The breadwinner may desire that the family enjoy an even higher standard of living than is possible today. However, life insurance is not normally viewed as a means by which surviving family members can suddenly become rich. Ideally, life insurance provides financial support so that family members can continue with their lives and pursue their goals, just as if the breadwinner were still alive.

IN-CLASS NOTES

Determining the Amount of Life Insurance Needed

- Income method
  - Multiple of your annual income
  - Does not consider age or household circumstances (children vs. no children)
- Budget method
  - Allows you to consider your household's future expected expenses
  - Does not account for unexpected expenses

_____

_____

_____

_____

_____

L.O. 4 CONTENTS OF A LIFE INSURANCE POLICY

A basic life insurance policy contains a number of standard features. Some of the more common policy contents include the beneficiary, grace period, reinstatement, living benefits, premium schedule, loans, suicide clause, incontestability date, and misstatement of age or sex. Although most of these features are common to both term life insurance and permanent insurance, a premium schedule is usually found in a term life policy, while living benefits and a loan clause are found in a permanent insurance policy.

Beneficiary

When naming a beneficiary on your life insurance policy, keep the following points in mind. You can name multiple beneficiaries and specify how you want the death benefits to be divided. You can also name a contingent beneficiary who would receive the benefits in the event that your primary beneficiary is no longer living at the time of your death. You can change the beneficiary any time you wish, but until you do, the existing contract will be enforced. If you name a person rather than your estate as beneficiary, the benefits can be paid to the person directly and avoid probate and related expenses.

Grace Period

The insurance policy specifies the grace period allowed beyond the date when payment is due. As mentioned earlier, the typical grace period is 30 days. During this period, benefits are payable even though the premium amount is due. A policy is said to be in lapse status after this 30-day period.

Reinstatement

After a policy has gone into lapse status, it may be reinstated within two years. Reinstatement is the process of completing a reinstatement application to restore a policy that is in lapse status. In addition to completing a reinstatement application, the policy owner must provide evidence of insurability (good health) and make all overdue payments. The advantage of reinstatement is that it allows the policy owner to maintain the premiums determined when the original policy was issued. This premium figure is likely to be lower than any new premium that would be calculated (due to the policy owner now being older).

reinstatement
The process of completing a reinstatement application to restore a policy that is in lapse status.

Living Benefits

Some whole life insurance policies allow living benefits (also referred to as accelerated death benefits), in which policyholders can receive a portion of the death benefits prior to death. Certain special circumstances must exist, such as terminal illness or long-term care needs of the insured.

living benefits (accelerated death benefits)
Benefits that allow the policyholder to receive a portion of death benefits prior to death.

Premium Schedule

A term life insurance policy includes a schedule of premiums that indicates what the new annual premium will be when the policy is renewed. For example, a Term10 policy will contain a premium schedule that indicates the new annual premium every 10 years. The premiums in the schedule are guaranteed. Therefore, the policy owner can shop around at the renewal date to see whether he or she could buy life insurance at a lower cost from another company. However, care should be taken when switching policies since some benefits may be lost. If you are considering a switch, consult an insurance agent.

Loans

You can borrow cash from your policy only if it can accumulate cash value. For example, a whole life policy accumulates cash value. The loan rates may be lower than those offered on personal loans, and interest is paid back into the cash value of the policy.

Suicide Clause

Life insurance benefits are not payable if the policy owner commits suicide within two years of the policy's effective date. After two years, benefits are payable in the event of a suicide. Some life insurance companies offer a suicide clause in which the restriction on benefit payments is only one year.

Incontestability Date

Policies specify a date, usually two years from the effective date, after which the policy provisions are incontestable. Until that date, an insurance company can cancel a policy if it determines that some of the information provided by the policy owner is misstated. The policy can be cancelled even if the information was misstated accidentally. Once the policy has passed the incontestability date, it cannot be cancelled because of an accidental misstatement of information. The misstatement must be proven to be intentional (fraudulent) for the life insurance company to cancel the policy. Misstating your age or sex is the one exception to this provision.

Misstatement of Age or Sex

If you misstate your age or sex on your application form and the life insurance company discovers this discrepancy, it will adjust your benefits to reflect what you are entitled to based on the existing premium you are paying. For example, if you indicated that you are 32 years old but you are really 34 years old, the benefit amount would be decreased. It is your responsibility to ensure that the correct age and sex is entered on your application form. If the insurance agent enters your age or sex incorrectly, you will still be held responsible for this error. Always review your entire application before signing it.

Renewability and Conversion Options

renewability option
Allows you to renew your policy for another term once the existing term expires.

A **renewability option** allows you to renew your policy for another term (up to an age limit specified in the policy) once the existing term expires. The premium for the next term will be higher than for the current term, since you will be older. In addition, the premium charged in the next term may increase to reflect changes in your health.

conversion option
Allows you to convert your term insurance policy into a whole life policy that will be in effect for the rest of your life.

A **conversion option** allows you to convert your term insurance policy into a whole life policy that will be in effect for the rest of your life. A policy with a conversion option specifies the period during which the conversion can occur. At the time of this conversion, the premium will be increased, but it will then stay constant for the rest of your life.

The renewability and conversion options apply only to term life insurance. If you are considering term life insurance, it is very important to ensure that these options are available in your policy. The two major drawbacks of term life insurance are that the policy will expire at the end of the term, and that it will not be available beyond a certain age. The advantage of the renewability option is that your renewal is guaranteed at the end of each term, up to a specified age limit. Without this option, you may not be able to renew your insurance if your health has deteriorated. If you decide that a permanent life insurance policy better suits your needs, the conversion option will allow you to convert your term insurance to permanent insurance.

If you are covered by group life insurance, it may be possible to convert this type of insurance into a personally owned policy. If you leave your employer and still require insurance, this conversion privilege can be useful.

Riders

riders
Options that allow you to customize a life insurance policy to your specific needs.

Riders are options that allow you to customize a life insurance policy to your specific needs. Riders are available on both term and permanent life insurance policies at an additional cost to you. Some of the more common riders and their specific features are discussed below.

Waiver of Premium. The waiver of premium rider provides a benefit in the case of the policy owner becoming totally disabled. Total disability often leads to a decrease in income, which may force the policy owner to stop making premium payments on the life insurance. This rider waives the obligation of premium payments by the policy owner for the period during which they are totally disabled. If the disability is permanent, the coverage will continue for the duration of the policy.

Guaranteed Insurability. The guaranteed insurability rider allows you to purchase additional life insurance without having to resubmit evidence of medical insurability, which you would otherwise need to do. If you no longer qualify for additional insurance because your health has deteriorated, this rider guarantees that you can purchase additional life insurance nonetheless. You may decide to purchase additional life insurance for two reasons: you did not purchase adequate insurance at the time of initial application, or you anticipate that you will require additional insurance in the future but are unsure of the amount. You may not have purchased an adequate amount of insurance because you could not afford the premium at the time of the application. The need for additional insurance also arises when your financial responsibilities increase. For example, the birth of a child or purchase of a cottage with a mortgage will increase your financial responsibilities.

Accidental Death. In the event of accidental death of the policy owner, this rider increases the death benefit payout of the policy. The death benefit is usually doubled if accidental death occurs. For example, if you purchase $250 000 of term life insurance and add the accidental death rider as an option, the death benefit will increase to $500 000 if you die as a result of an accident.

Child Term Coverage. The child term rider provides cash benefits in the event that a child of the policy owner dies. The benefit is usually limited to between $5000 and $25 000. The policy continues even if this benefit is paid.

Term Insurance Coverage. You can purchase term insurance coverage as a rider on permanent life insurance policies to help finance temporary needs. This rider is ideal for individuals who wish to purchase permanent insurance but also require affordable protection for temporary needs.

EXAMPLE

The Cheung household determines that they need $500 000 of life insurance. They would prefer to purchase whole life insurance so that they will be able to build cash value inside their policy. However, the premium for $500 000 of whole life insurance is more than the Cheungs can afford to pay. To meet their budget, the family decides to purchase $150 000 of whole life insurance with a $350 000 Term10 rider. This alternative meets both their budget and their life insurance needs. After 10 years, the Cheungs can renew their Term10 rider or let it expire.

Riders provide benefits that may be of value to you. However, you should first determine the amount of coverage you need and the type of policy that will provide this level of coverage within your budget. In the example above, assume that the Cheungs cannot afford a $150 000 whole life insurance policy with a $350 000 Term10 rider. Although they would prefer to purchase whole life insurance, their need for $500 000 of affordable insurance is more important. They should look at options that meet this need. Riders should only be considered once the insurance goal is accomplished and if you have money left in your budget.

Settlement Options

settlement options
The ways in which a beneficiary can receive life insurance benefits in the event that the policyholder dies.

Settlement options are the ways in which a beneficiary can receive life insurance benefits in the event that the policyholder dies. Normally, these benefits are not taxed, although there are some exceptions (the discussion of which is beyond the scope of this text). When you purchase a life insurance policy, you select the settlement option that is most appropriate for your beneficiaries. The most appropriate option depends on the needs and other characteristics of the beneficiaries.

lump sum settlement
A single payment of all benefits owed to a beneficiary upon the death of the policyholder.

Lump Sum. A lump sum settlement provides a single payment of all benefits owed to a beneficiary upon the death of the policyholder. A $250 000 life insurance policy would provide $250 000 to the beneficiary in a lump sum. This settlement option is often chosen if the beneficiary is disciplined and will use the payment wisely. If the beneficiary lacks sufficient discipline, however, an alternative settlement option may be more appropriate.

instalment payments settlement
The payment of life insurance benefits owed to a beneficiary as a stream of equal payments over a specified number of years.

Instalment Payments. The policy owner can elect to use an instalment payments settlement, which provides the payment of life insurance benefits owed to a beneficiary as a stream of equal payments over a specified number of years. For example, instead of paying $300 000 to the beneficiary in a lump sum, the policy may specify that the beneficiary receive annual payments starting at the time of the policy owner's death and lasting for 10 years. By spreading the amount over time, this settlement option ensures that the beneficiary will not spend the total amount immediately.

interest payments settlement
A method of paying life insurance benefits in which the insurance company retains the amount owed to the beneficiary for a specified number of years and pays interest to the beneficiary.

Interest Payments. The policy owner can also elect to use an interest payments settlement, which means that the insurance company retains the amount owed to the beneficiary for a specified number of years. Until the amount is distributed, the beneficiary will receive periodic interest payments on the amount. As with the instalment payments option, this settlement option prevents the beneficiary from spending all of the policy payments quickly.

IN-CLASS NOTES

Contents of a Life Insurance Policy
- Features
  - Beneficiary
  - Grace period
  - Reinstatement
  - Living benefits
  - Premium schedule
  - Loans
  - Suicide clause
  - Incontestability date
  - Misstatement of age or sex
  - Renewability and conversion options
- Riders
  - Waiver of premium
  - Guaranteed insurability
  - Accidental death
  - Child term coverage
  - Term insurance coverage

SELECTING A LIFE INSURANCE COMPANY

All life insurance companies are not the same. For this reason, you should research multiple insurance companies before you select one. Keep the following criteria in mind when you choose a company.

Other Types of Insurance Offered

Some life insurance companies offer all types of insurance, including group insurance and living benefits such as disability, critical illness, and long-term care insurance. You may want to select a life insurance company that can also provide these other types of insurance, assuming that it satisfies all other criteria. It is more convenient to have all types of insurance at one company. In addition, you may receive a discount on your life insurance premium if you purchase other types of insurance from the same company.

The Specific Policy You Want

While all life insurance companies offer some forms of term insurance and permanent insurance, make sure the company you choose offers the specific policy you want. For example, you may want a 10-year term policy with a settlement option that provides instalment payments.

Services Available

Make sure that the insurance company will provide you with the type of service you expect. For example, you may want to ensure that the company can supply convenient online services. If you want to discuss possible changes to your policy in person, you may consider choosing an insurance company that has an office close to your residence.

Relatively Low Insurance Premiums

The cost of insurance is an important factor to consider when selecting a particular life insurance policy. As you compare the premiums across insurance companies, make sure that the quotes you receive are for comparable policies.

Strong Financial Condition

As mentioned earlier, policy owners rely on a life insurance company to survive in the long run so that it can serve their beneficiaries upon their deaths. If an insurance company fails, it will not pay the benefits of its policy owners in the future. People who have paid life insurance premiums will not receive the benefits they deserve. Thus, it is important to assess the financial condition of the life insurance company before you purchase a policy. As discussed in Chapter 8, there are several services that rate insurance companies (see page 200). Many people who are not qualified to judge the financial condition of a company rely on ratings assigned by these services. Only consider insurance companies that are rated highly.

IN-CLASS NOTES

Selecting a Life Insurance Company
- Other types of insurance offered?
  - Group insurance
  - Living benefits
- Provides the specific policy desired?
  - Settlement options available?
- Services available?
  - Online services
  - Convenient office location
- Relatively low premiums?
- Financial condition?
  - What rating is assigned by services such as A.M. Best, Moody's, and Standard & Poor's?

_____

_____

_____

_____

_____

_____

HOW LIFE INSURANCE FITS WITHIN YOUR FINANCIAL PLAN

The following are the key decisions about life insurance that should be included within your financial plan:

- Do you need life insurance?

- What type of life insurance is most appropriate for you?

- How much life insurance should you plan for in the future?

STEPHANIE SPRATT'S FINANCIAL PLAN: Life Insurance

GOALS FOR LIFE INSURANCE PLANNING

1. *Determine whether I need to purchase life insurance.*
2. *Determine whether I should purchase or add to my life insurance in the future.*

ANALYSIS

Type of Insurance Plan	Benefits	Status
Term insurance	*Insurance benefits provided to beneficiary.*	*I have sufficient coverage through my employer for my last expenses. Not needed at this time since I do not have a spouse or dependants*
Whole life insurance	*Insurance benefits provided to beneficiary and policy may build cash value over time.*	*Not needed at this time.*
Universal life insurance	*Insurance benefits provided to beneficiary and policy may build cash value over time.*	*Not needed at this time.*
Term to 100 insurance	*Insurance benefits provided to beneficiary.*	*Not needed at this time.*

DECISIONS

Decision on Whether I Need Life Insurance

I decided to purchase term life insurance to provide my two nieces with a post-secondary education if I die. My reason for buying life insurance is simply to have insurance, not to build a cash value. Term insurance serves my purpose and is much cheaper than permanent insurance policies.

Decision on Insurance Coverage in the Future

In the future, I will need to ensure proper life insurance coverage if I have a family. I would want to ensure that my children have sufficient funds to support themselves and possibly even pay for their post-secondary education if I die. If I have a child, I will obtain a Term20 life insurance policy for $300 000, or whatever amount is appropriate at that time.

Discussion Questions

1. How would Stephanie's decisions regarding purchasing life insurance be different if she were a single mother of two children?

2. How would Stephanie's decisions regarding purchasing life insurance be affected if she were 35 years old? If she were 50 years old?

SUMMARY

Life insurance provides payments to specified beneficiaries if the policy owner dies. Term insurance is strictly intended to provide insurance in the event of the death of the insured, while whole life insurance and universal life insurance use a portion of the premium to build a cash value. The premiums for whole life and universal life insurance are higher to account for the portion distributed into a savings plan and for the administrative fees.

A number of factors are used to determine the premium that should be paid by the policy owner on a life insurance policy. For example, age, sex, and health considerations are used to calculate mortality rates. Company expenses tend to be different across the industry. Investment returns affect premiums in the case of participating whole life policies. These different factors result in different premiums being charged by different companies for similar coverage.

The amount of life insurance you need can be measured by the income method, in which you attempt to replace the income that would be discontinued due to death. However, this amount can be more precisely measured by the budget method, which considers factors such as your household's future expected expenses and existing debt.

Although the basic contents of a life insurance policy are similar across the industry, a number of riders can be used to customize the policy to the needs of the individual. These riders provide additional benefits, but should only be considered once the insurance goal is accomplished and if you still have money left in your budget.

A life insurance policy can be set up to pay beneficiaries a lump sum payment, instalment payments over a specified period, or interest payments over a specified period with a lump sum at the end of the period. The instalment option or interest payment option may be most appropriate to ensure that beneficiaries do not use the death benefit unwisely.

The decision to purchase life insurance partially depends on whether family members are currently relying on your income. If you decide to purchase insurance, a related decision is the choice of insurance company. Since the payment from the insurance company to your beneficiaries may not occur until the distant future, you should select a company that you believe will definitely be in business at that time. You can review life insurance company ratings to assess their financial condition, which may indicate whether they will survive over time.

INTEGRATING THE KEY CONCEPTS

Your decisions regarding life insurance affect other parts of your financial plan. Because life insurance provides income to your beneficiaries in the event of your death, you are not forced to create a level of wealth that will support your dependants. Instead, you can make investment and borrowing decisions without focusing on the future support of your dependants. This allows you to use a more conservative and long-term approach for your investing and borrowing decisions. You may maintain a larger amount of liquidity (Part 2) because there is no pressure to achieve the very highest returns on your money. You can finance a car or a home if you wish (Part 3) because you can more easily afford to make periodic loan payments. Finally, you can contribute extra savings to retirement (Part 6).

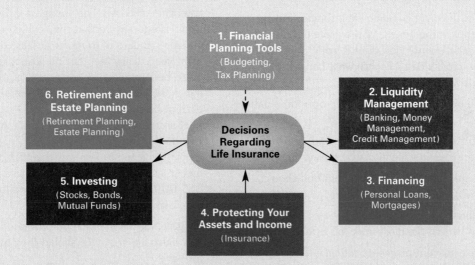

REVIEW QUESTIONS

1. What is the purpose of life insurance? Define the terms *face amount*, *beneficiary*, *life insured*, and *policy* owner.

2. Do you think that everyone needs life insurance? Explain.

3. What is term insurance? What factors determine the premium for term insurance?

4. What is creditor insurance? How is it different from personally owned term insurance?

5. What is mortgage life insurance? What is another name for it? Is mortgage life insurance a good buy? Why or why not?

6. What is permanent insurance? Define the terms *cost of insurance* and *cash value*. What are the benefits of building cash value inside a permanent life insurance policy?

7. What is whole life insurance? What is the main purpose of cash value inside a whole life policy? Describe the feature(s) of a limited payment policy.

8. What is universal life insurance? What are the two cost of insurance options in a universal life insurance policy? What is the impact on the growth of the savings account portion of the policy under each of these options?

9. Describe the features of universal life insurance premiums. Why would you buy universal life insurance? What are the differences between whole life and universal life?

10. Describe the non-forfeiture options of permanent insurance policies.

11. What is term to 100 insurance?

12. What are the two classifications of life insurance policies? What is a policy dividend? Under what circumstances is it paid?

13. Compare and contrast life insurance policy premiums.

14. Describe the income method of determining the amount of life insurance needed. What is the disadvantage of this method?

15. Discuss why life insurance needs should not be based on a family's dreams for the future.

16. Describe the budget method of determining the amount of life insurance needed. What elements must be considered in making this calculation?

17. List some of the more common life insurance policy contents. Explain the benefit of the grace period. What is reinstatement? How does it work? What is the incontestability date? Explain what happens if you misstate your age or sex.

18. What is the benefit of the renewability option? What is the benefit of the conversion option?

19. What is a rider? Describe the features and/or benefits of the major riders in a life insurance policy.

20. What are settlement options? Which option should you choose?

21. What is a lump sum settlement? What kind of beneficiary would benefit the most from this option?

22. What is an instalment payments settlement? When would an insured individual choose this option?

23. What is the interest payments option? How does it differ from the instalment payments option?

FINANCIAL PLANNING PROBLEMS

1. Ingrid is a widow with two teenage children. Her total income is $3000 per month and taxes take about 30 percent of this income. Using the income method, Ingrid calculates she will need to purchase about eight times her after-tax income in life insurance to meet her needs. How much insurance should she purchase?

2. Ingrid's employer provides her with two times her annual gross salary in life insurance. How much additional insurance should she purchase based on the information provided in Problem 1?

3. Roberto is married and has two children. He wants to be sure that he has sufficient life insurance to take care of his family if he dies. Roberto's wife is a homemaker but attends college part-time, pursuing a finance diploma. It will cost approximately $40 000 for her to finish her education. Since their children are teenagers, Roberto feels he will only need to provide the family with income for the next 10 years. He further calculates that the household expenses run approximately $35 000 per year. The balance on the home mortgage is $30 000. Roberto set up an education fund for his children when they were babies and it currently contains a sufficient amount for them to attend college or university. Assuming that Roberto's wife can invest the insurance payments at 8 percent, calculate the amount of insurance Roberto needs to purchase.

4. Naresh and Vani both have jobs and contribute to household expenses according to their income. Naresh contributes 75 percent of the expenses and Vani contributes 25 percent. Currently, their household expenses are $30 000 per year. They have three children. The youngest is 12, so they would like to ensure that they could maintain their current standard of living for at least the next eight years. They feel that the insurance payments could be invested at 6 percent. In addition to covering annual expenses, they would like to ensure that each of their children has $25 000 available for post-secondary education. If Naresh were to die, Vani would return to school part-time to upgrade her training as a nurse. This would cost $20 000. They have a mortgage on their home with a balance of $55 000. How much life insurance should they purchase for Naresh?

5. Considering the information provided in Problem 4, how much life insurance should they purchase for Vani?

6. Bart is a college student. He plans to get a job immediately after graduation and determines that he will need about $250 000 in life insurance to provide for his future wife (he is not yet married) and children (he does not yet have any children). Bart has obtained a quote over the Internet that would require him to pay $200 in life insurance premiums annually. As a student, this is a significant expense, and Bart would likely need to borrow money to pay for the insurance premiums. Advise Bart on the timing of his life insurance purchase.

ETHICAL DILEMMA

Shortly after Steve graduated from college, he purchased a whole life insurance policy that would provide $10 000 in life insurance protection and accumulate a cash value of twice his annual income by age 65. Two years later, after getting married, Steve bought a second policy. Through his working years, he paid the $280 annual premium per policy. Steve kept in mind what the agent had told him many years before about each policy having a cash value of double his annual income.

Steve was nearing age 65 and dug out the policies from his safety deposit box so that he could begin to put numbers together to plan his retirement. As he opened the two policies, he was appalled to see that the cash value on the older policy was $17 000 and on the newer policy was only $15 000. The two policies together amounted to only one-third his current annual earnings, far from the figure promised by the agent.

a. Was the agent unethical in not showing Steve the potential impact of inflation on the policies' cash values?

b. Considering just the first policy, would Steve have been better off investing the $280 annual premium in a mutual fund that would have given an annual return of 8 percent (assume a 30-year investment period)?

FINANCIAL PLANNING ONLINE EXERCISES

1. Go to www.kanetix.ca/life_cov_calc.

a. Determine the amount of life insurance you need by entering the following information:

Cost of your funeral arrangements	$10 000
Total amount owing on your mortgage	$150 000
Total amount of your outstanding debts	$20 000
Estimate the total of your children's future education	$30 000
How much income would your family need every month if you passed away?	$3000
How many years would your family need to rely on this monthly insurance income?	15

Click on Submit. How much life insurance will you need?

b. How will the answer in part a change if you have other investments and/or life insurance policies?

c. Increase the Estimated inflation rate to 3.0 and click on Submit. What happens to the amount of life insurance required? Why does this happen? Reset the Estimated inflation rate to 2.0 and click on Submit. This will bring you back to your original answer in part a. Now, increase After-tax investment yield to 5.0 and click on Submit. What happens to the amount of life insurance required? Why does this happen?

2. Go to www.termforsale.net/canterm4sale.php. Using the answer obtained in part a of Exercise 1, complete a term life insurance comparison. Set your health as Regular (Average), and premiums to be paid as Monthly. Click on Compare Now to see your results.

a. What is the range of premiums for the 10 Year Guaranteed Term option? What is the range of premiums for the 20 Year Guaranteed Term option?

b. Click on Health Analyzer. What factors are being considered in this health questionnaire? Complete the questionnaire. What is the impact on the premium comparison for the 10 Year Guaranteed Term and 20 Year Guaranteed Term options after completing the questionnaire?

c. Return to the first webpage. Change the initial level term option to Guaranteed Whole Life. All other information should be entered as in part a. Click on Compare Now. What is the monthly premium? What is the difference among the monthly premiums for Guaranteed Whole Life, 10 Year Guaranteed Term, and 20 Year Guaranteed Term?

3. Go to www.bank-banque-canada.ca/en/inflation/index.html.

a. What is the inflation-control target range? Click on Inflation Calculator and then on Calculate. What is the average annual rate of inflation?

b. Based on the information obtained from this website and the inflation calculator, what inflation rate should you have used when determining the amount of life insurance you need in Exercise 1?

ON THE STUDENT CD-ROM FOR THIS CHAPTER YOU WILL FIND:

- Building Your Own Financial Plan exercise and worksheets
- The chapter-end Continuing Case about the Sampson family
- The fourth part-end Continuing Case about Brad Brooks

  Read through the Building Your Own Financial Plan exercise and use the worksheets to complete a life insurance needs-analysis and determine the kind of life insurance that would best suit your needs.

After reading the Sampson case study, use the Continuing Case worksheets to help the Sampsons select an appropriate life insurance policy.

After reading the Brad Brooks case study, use the Continuing Case worksheets to provide Brad with information to help him make the right decisions regarding his automobile, tenant, disability, and life insurance needs.

Study Guide

Circle the correct answer and then check the answers in the back of the book to chart your progress.

Multiple Choice

1. With respect to life insurance, the policy owner is:
   a. The named individual who receives life insurance payments upon the death of the life insured.
   b. The individual who is covered by the life insurance policy.
   c. The life insurance company.
   d. The individual who owns all rights and obligations to the policy.

2. Which of the following is not one of the reasons why premiums for term insurance vary?
   a. The annual premium is higher for a male than a female of the same age because males tend to live longer than females.
   b. The annual premium is higher for policies of a longer term.
   c. The older the policy owner, the higher the premium.
   d. Some policy owners may have a family history of medical problems, resulting in higher premiums.

3. Mortgage life insurance purchased from a bank representative is also known as:
   a. Personally owned term insurance.
   b. Decreasing term insurance.
   c. Credit insurance.
   d. All of the above.

4. With respect to the borrower, which of the following is one of the potential advantages of creditor insurance over personally owned term insurance?

a. In the event of the death of the life insured, benefits are payable directly to the creditor.
b. Creditor insurance may be a little less expensive than personally owned term insurance.
c. In the event of the death of the life insured, the policy owner determines who will be the beneficiary.
d. If credit is reapplied for with another creditor, life insurance must be reapplied for, possibly resulting in increased premiums.

5. Which of the following statements regarding the cash value in a life insurance policy is true?
   a. Cash value can only be used to cover taxes payable at death on registered and tax-deferred non-registered investments, provide gifts to charity, or provide an income stream for mentally and/or physically incapacitated loved ones.
   b. Cash value is automatically part of the death benefit.
   c. Cash value often represents a prepayment of future premiums or a forced savings account that can be used in the future by the policy owner.
   d. Cash value is not normally available to the policy owner prior to his or her death.

6. Which of the following statements does not apply when discussing universal life insurance?
   a. The long-term growth rate of the cash value in the investment account depends on the types of investments the life insurance company selects.

b. It is a form of permanent life insurance for which you do not pay a fixed premium.

c. Premium payments are deposited directly into the savings account portion of the policy.

d. The cash value under the YRT option grows more quickly because the money the insurance company withdraws to cover the cost of insurance is lower relative to the premium cost of the level term option.

7. Which of the following is not one of the non-forfeiture options available to a policy owner who would like to discontinue or cancel a policy that has cash value?

a. Cancel the policy and forfeit the cash value.

b. Use the cash value to pay the policy premium until the cash value runs out and the policy subsequently terminates.

c. Use the cash value as a one-time premium payment to purchase term insurance.

d. Use the cash value as a one-time premium payment to purchase permanent paid-up insurance.

8. The calculation for the amount of life insurance you need is subject to much uncertainty for all the following reasons, except:

a. Someone within your household could experience an unanticipated major illness or disability.

b. The income level of your household may not rise over time as expected, and may even decline due to layoffs.

c. Inflation could cause you to underestimate the cost of some needs.

d. The insurance policy you purchase today may not provide coverage until many years from now. As a result, the funding needed from an insurance policy is likely to decrease for households that are spenders.

9. Which of the following is not a standard feature of a life insurance policy?

a. Suicide clause

b. Guaranteed insurability

c. Incontestability date

d. Misstatement of age or sex

10. Lucky Luke loves to gamble. His great-uncle Larry Luke has recently passed away and made Lucky the beneficiary of his life insurance benefits. Which of the following settlement options would be inappropriate for Lucky?

a. Instalment payments settlement

b. Interest payments settlement

c. Lump sum settlement

d. All of the above

True/False

1. True or False? A term life insurance policy can be renewed as often as necessary during the lifetime of the life insured.

2. True or False? The mortality rate refers to the number of deaths in a population or in a subgroup of the population in one year.

3. True or False? One of the main advantages of creditor insurance is the ability to name a minor as a beneficiary of the policy.

4. True or False? Cash value represents the portion of the premium in excess of insurance-related and company expenses that is invested by the insurance company on behalf of the beneficiary.

5. True or False? Three forms of permanent insurance include whole life, universal life, and term to 100.

6. True or False? All else being equal, to receive a policy dividend the life insurance company's investment earnings with respect to the cash value in the savings account must have been higher than expected.

7. True or False? For a household composed of two adult income earners and three children, the budget method of determining the amount of life insurance needed is probably most appropriate.

8. True or False? Life insurance benefits are not payable during the typical grace period of 30 days.

9. True or False? The renewability and conversion options apply only to term life insurance.

10. True or False? The term insurance coverage rider is ideal for individuals who want to purchase permanent insurance but also require affordable protection for temporary needs.

PART 5

Personal Investing

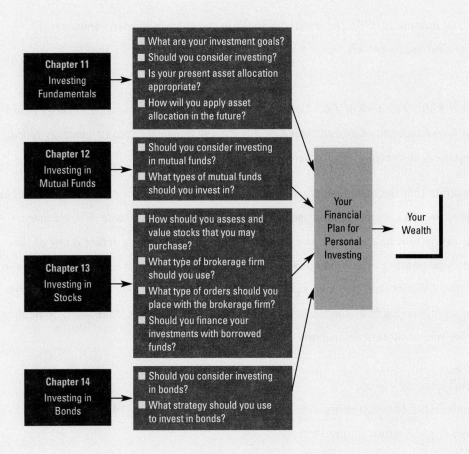

Chapter 11
Investing
Fundamentals

- What are your investment goals?
- Should you consider investing?
- Is your present asset allocation appropriate?
- How will you apply asset allocation in the future?

Chapter 12
Investing in
Mutual Funds

- Should you consider investing in mutual funds?
- What types of mutual funds should you invest in?

Chapter 13
Investing in
Stocks

- How should you assess and value stocks that you may purchase?
- What type of brokerage firm should you use?
- What type of orders should you place with the brokerage firm?
- Should you finance your investments with borrowed funds?

Chapter 14
Investing in
Bonds

- Should you consider investing in bonds?
- What strategy should you use to invest in bonds?

Your Financial Plan for Personal Investing → Your Wealth

THE CHAPTERS IN THIS PART EXPLAIN THE VARIOUS TYPES OF investments that are available, how to value investments, and how to determine which investments to select. Chapter 11 provides a background on investing. Chapter 12, on mutual funds, explains the advantages and disadvantages of investing in a portfolio of securities rather than individual stocks and bonds. Chapter 13 explains how to decide which stocks to buy, and Chapter 14 focuses on investing in bonds. Your decisions regarding whether to invest, how much to invest, and what to invest in will affect your cash flows and wealth.

Chapter 11

Investing Fundamentals

A nita is a patient investor. In 1995 she invested $3000 in stocks of well-known companies. By 2006, her original investment was worth $8000.

Meanwhile, Lisa invested $3000 in stock of Zyko Co. because the company suggested its technology would change the world. Lisa hoped that this investment would be a quick way to wealth. Zyko's technology failed, and in 2006 the company went bankrupt. Consequently, Lisa's stock was worthless.

These examples demonstrate that the same type of investment can have entirely different outcomes. As will be discussed in this chapter, there is a variety of investments and the risk and return of these different investments vary widely. The ability to reduce your risk while achieving an acceptable rate of return is one of the main principles of successful investing. If Lisa had understood that one of the benefits of diversification, also known as asset allocation, includes lower portfolio risk, she may have decided that this benefit far outweighed the potential gain she might have made by concentrating her investment in one stock. Your ability to analyze investments can enhance your investment income and increase your net worth.

The objectives of this chapter are to:

1. Describe the common types of investments
2. Explain how to measure the return on investments
3. Identify the risks of investments
4. Explain the trade-off between the return and risk of investments
5. Explain how diversification among asset classes can reduce risk
6. Describe strategies that can be used to diversify among stocks
7. Explain asset allocation strategies
8. Identify factors that affect your asset allocation decisions
9. Describe common investment mistakes that can be avoided

L.O. 1   TYPES OF INVESTMENTS

If you have money to invest, your first priority should be to ensure adequate liquidity. As discussed in Chapter 4, you can satisfy your liquidity needs by placing deposits in financial institutions or by investing in short-term securities such as term deposits. Since these types of investments primarily focus on providing liquidity, they offer a relatively low return. However, if you have additional funds beyond your liquidity needs, you must consider other types of investments that can offer better returns.

Money Market Securities

Recall from Chapter 4 that there are several different savings alternatives available, including term deposits, guaranteed investment certificates (GICs), Canada Savings Bonds (CSBs), and money market funds. Most money market securities provide interest income. Even if your liquidity needs are covered, you may invest in these securities to maintain a low level of risk. Yet, you can also consider some alternative securities that typically provide a higher rate of return but are more risky.

Mutual Funds

Recall that mutual funds sell units to individuals and invest the proceeds in a portfolio of investments such as bonds and stocks. They are managed by experienced portfolio managers and are attractive to investors who have limited funds and want to invest in a diversified portfolio. Because a stock mutual fund typically invests in numerous stocks, it enables investors to achieve broad diversification with an investment as low as $500. There are thousands of mutual funds to choose from.

Return from Investing in Mutual Funds. The income and/or capital gains generated by the mutual fund's portfolio of securities are passed on to the individual investor. Since a mutual fund represents a portfolio of securities, its value changes over time in response to changes in the values of those securities. Therefore, the price at which an investor purchases units of a mutual fund changes over time. A mutual fund can generate a capital gain for individual investors, since the price at which investors sell their units of the fund may be higher than the price at which they purchased the shares. However, the price of the mutual fund's shares may also decline over time, which would result in a capital loss. Mutual funds are discussed in more detail in Chapter 12.

Exchange Traded Funds. Another option for investors who want a diversified portfolio of stocks is to invest in **exchange traded funds (ETFs)**, a portfolio of securities whose value moves in tandem with a particular stock index. In Canada, exchange traded funds are commonly referred to as iShares.

exchange traded fund (ETF)
A portfolio of securities whose value moves in tandem with a particular stock index. Unlike a mutual fund, these funds trade on an exchange or stock market.

Go to
www.ishares.ca/index.do

This website provides an introduction to iShares ETFs and product information on most of the iShares available in Canada.

Much research has shown that sophisticated investors (such as well-paid portfolio managers) are unable to outperform various stock indexes on average over longer periods of time. Thus, by investing in an index, individual investors can ensure that their performance will match that index.

One of the most popular publicly traded iShares is the CDN LargeCap 60 Index Fund, which is an ETF designed to match the performance of the 60 largest and most liquid securities on the Toronto Stock Exchange (TSX). Similar to other stocks, iShares trade through the exchange using a ticker symbol. The ticker symbol for the CDN LargeCap 60 Index Fund is XIU. You can buy iShares through a broker, just like stocks. When investors expect that the large Canadian stocks represented by the CDN LargeCap 60 Index Fund will experience strong performance, they can capitalize on their expectations by purchasing shares of this ETF. iShares provide investors with not only a return in the form of potential share price appreciation, but also dividends in the form of additional shares to the investors. Any expenses incurred by the iShares from creating the index are deducted from the dividends.

Investors can also invest in specific sector indexes as well as in market indexes. Some exchange traded funds represent a variety of specific sectors, including the Internet, energy, technology, and financial sectors. Because an index represents several stocks, you can achieve some degree of diversification by investing in an index.

Stocks

As defined in Chapter 2, stocks are certificates that represent partial ownership of a firm. Firms issue shares to obtain funds to expand their business operations. Investors buy shares when they believe that they may earn a higher return than those offered on alternative investments. Since shares are a popular type of investment, they are the focus of Chapter 13.

Primary and Secondary Stock Markets. Shares can be traded in a primary or a secondary market. The primary market is a market in which newly issued securities are traded. Firms can raise funds by issuing new shares in the primary market. The first offering of a firm's shares to the public is referred to as an initial public offering (IPO). A secondary market facilitates the trading of existing securities such as debt securities, enabling investors to sell their shares at any time. These shares are purchased by other investors who wish to invest in that company. Thus, even if a firm is not issuing new shares, investors can easily obtain that firm's shares by purchasing them in the secondary market. On a typical day, more than 1 million shares of any large firm are traded in the secondary market. The price of the shares changes each day in response to fluctuations in supply and demand.

Types of Stock Investors. Stock investors can be classified as institutional investors or individual investors. Institutional investors are professionals employed by a financial institution who are responsible for managing large pools of money on behalf of their clients. A pension fund, such as the Ontario Teachers' Pension Plan, is an example of a pool of money managed on behalf of clients. Institutional investors, also known as portfolio managers, attempt to select stocks or other securities that will provide a reasonable return on investment. More than half of all trading in financial markets is attributable to institutional investors.

Individual investors commonly invest a portion of their income in stocks. Like institutional investors, they invest in stocks to earn a potentially better or higher return on their investment. In this way, their money can grow by the time they want to use it. The number of individual investors has increased substantially in the last 20 years.

Many individual investors hold their stocks for periods beyond one year. In contrast, some individual investors called day traders buy stocks and then sell them on the same day. They hope to capitalize on very short-term movements in security prices. In many cases, their investments may last for only a few minutes. Many day traders conduct their investing as a career, relying on their returns as their main source of income. This type of investing is very risky and requires skill, nerves, and capital. Day trading is not recommended for most investors.

Return from Investing in Stocks. Stocks can offer a return on investment through dividends and/or stock price appreciation. Some firms distribute quarterly income to their shareholders in the form of dividends rather than reinvest the earnings in their operations. They tend to keep the dollar amount of the dividends per share fixed from one quarter to the next, but may periodically increase the amount. They rarely reduce the dividend amount unless they experience relatively weak performance and cannot afford to make their dividend payments. The amount of dividends paid out per year is usually between 1 and 3 percent of the stock's price.

A firm's decision to distribute earnings as dividends may depend on the opportunities available to it. In general, firms that pay high dividends tend to be older, established firms that have less chance of substantial growth. Conversely, firms that pay low dividends tend to be younger firms that have more growth opportunities. The shares of firms with substantial growth opportunities are often referred to as growth stocks. An investment in these younger firms offers the prospect of a very large capital gain because

primary market
A market in which newly issued securities are traded.

initial public offering (IPO)
The first offering of a firm's shares to the public.

secondary market
A market in which existing securities such as debt securities are traded.

institutional investors
Professionals responsible for managing large pools of money, such as pension funds, on behalf of their clients.

individual investors
Individuals who invest funds in securities.

day traders
Investors who buy stocks and then sell them on the same day.

Go to
http://ipo.investcom.com

This website provides
Canadian IPO search capabilities by underwriters, offering size, stock exchange, industry, and other parameters.

growth stocks
Shares of firms with substantial growth opportunities.

they have not yet reached their full potential. At the same time, investment in these firms is exposed to much higher uncertainty because young firms are more likely than mature firms to fail or experience very weak performance.

Value stocks are another type of stock investment that offers the prospect of a substantial return. However, the returns on these stocks may not be based on the growth opportunities available to the firm. Instead, value stocks represent the stocks of firms that are currently undervalued by the market for reasons other than the performance of the businesses themselves. Value stocks are usually not newsworthy because they are often not associated with up-and-coming younger firms. As a result, the assets of value stocks are often underappreciated, and undervalued by the market. A knowledgeable investor will recognize the hidden value in these stocks and purchase shares in the hope that the stock will eventually be recognized for its true potential by other investors.

The higher the dividend paid by a firm, the lower its potential stock price appreciation. When a firm distributes a large proportion of its earnings to investors as dividends, it limits its potential growth and the potential degree to which its value (and stock price) may increase. Stocks that provide investors with periodic income in the form of large dividends are referred to as income stocks.

The market price of a stock depends on the number of investors willing to purchase the stock (the demand) and the number of investors wanting to sell their stock (the supply). There is no limit to how high a stock's price can rise. The demand for the stock and the supply of stock for sale are influenced by the respective firm's business performance, as measured by its earnings and other characteristics. When the firm performs well, its stock becomes more desirable to investors, who demand more shares. In addition, investors holding shares of this stock are less willing to sell it. The increase in the demand for the shares and the reduction in the number of shares for sale results in a higher stock price.

Conversely, when a firm performs poorly (has low or negative earnings), its market value declines. The demand for shares of its stock also declines. In addition, some investors who had been holding the stock will decide to sell their shares, thereby increasing the supply of stock for sale and resulting in a lower price. The performance of the firm depends on how well it is managed.

Investors benefit when they invest in a well-managed firm because the firm's earnings usually will increase, and so will its stock price. Under these conditions, investors may generate a capital gain, which represents the difference between their selling price and their purchase price. In contrast, a poorly managed firm may have lower earnings than expected, which could cause its stock price to decline.

Common versus Preferred Stocks. Stocks can be classified as common stock or preferred stock. Common stock is a certificate issued by a firm to raise funds that represents partial ownership in the firm. Investors who hold common stock normally have the right to vote on key issues such as the sale of the company. They elect the board of directors, which is responsible for ensuring that the firm's managers serve the interests of its shareholders. Preferred stock is a certificate issued by a firm to raise funds that entitles shareholders to first priority (ahead of common stockholders) to receive dividends. Corporations issue common stock more frequently than preferred stock. The price of preferred stock is not as volatile as the price of common stock and does not have as much potential to increase substantially. For this reason, investors who strive for high returns typically invest in common stock, while those interested in income purchase preferred shares.

Bonds

Recall that bonds are long-term debt securities issued by government agencies or corporations. Government bonds are issued by the Bank of Canada on behalf of the federal government and backed by the Canadian government. Corporate bonds are issued by corporations.

---

value stocks
Stocks of firms that are currently undervalued by the market for reasons other than the performance of the businesses themselves.

income stocks
Stocks that provide investors with periodic income in the form of large dividends.

Go to
http://ca.finance.yahoo.com/investing

Click on
Get Quotes after you type in the symbol for your stock and select Canadian Markets in the drop-down menu. To view charts showing the stock's price movements over time, click the links under the chart shown. Using these charts, you can assess the price movements of the stock you specify for today, the last year, or even the last five years.

This website provides
historical price movements for stocks that you specify.

common stock
A certificate issued by a firm to raise funds that represents partial ownership in the firm.

preferred stock
A certificate issued by a firm to raise funds that entitles shareholders to first priority to receive dividends.

Return from Investing in Bonds. Bonds offer a return to investors in the form of interest payments and bond price appreciation. They pay periodic interest (coupon) payments, and therefore can provide a fixed amount of interest income per year. Thus, they are desirable for investors who want their investments to generate a specific amount of income each year.

A bond's price can increase over time and therefore may provide investors with a capital gain, representing the difference between the price at which it was purchased and the price at which it was sold by an investor. However, a bond's price may decline, which could cause investors to experience a capital loss. More details about bonds are provided in Chapter 14.

Real Estate

One way of investing in real estate is by buying a home. The value of a home changes over time in response to supply and demand. When the demand for homes in your area increases, home values tend to rise. The return that you earn on your home is difficult to measure because you must take into account the financing costs and real estate agent commissions. However, a few generalizations are worth mentioning. For a given amount invested in the home, your return depends on how the value of your home changes over the time you own it. Your return also depends on your original down payment on the home. The return will be lower if you made a smaller down payment when purchasing the home because interest and other costs will be higher. Since the value of a home can decline over time, there is the risk of a loss (a negative return) on your investment. If you are in a hurry to sell your home, you may have to lower your selling price to attract potential buyers, which will result in a lower return on your investment.

You can also invest in real estate by purchasing rental property or land. The price of land is based on supply and demand. There is little open land and dense populations in southern Ontario, so open land in this region typically has a high price.

Return from Investing in Real Estate. Real estate (such as office buildings and apartments) can be rented to generate income in the form of rent payments. In addition, investors may earn a capital gain if they sell the property for a higher price than they paid for it. Alternatively, they may sustain a capital loss if they sell the property for a lower price than they paid for it.

The price of land changes over time in response to real estate development. Many individuals may purchase land as an investment, hoping that they will be able to sell it in the future for a higher price.

IN-CLASS NOTES

Types of Investments

- Mutual funds
- Exchange traded funds
- Stocks
    - Primary versus secondary market
    - Types of investors: institutional, individual, day traders
    - Growth, value, and income stocks
    - Common versus preferred stocks
- Bonds
- Real estate

INVESTMENT RETURN AND RISK

When individuals consider any particular investment, they must attempt to assess two characteristics: the potential return that will be earned on the investment and the risk of the investment.

Measuring the Return on Your Investment

For investments that do not provide any periodic income (such as dividends or interest payments), the return can be measured as the percentage change in the price (P) from the time the investment was purchased (time $t-1$) until the time at which it is sold (time t):

$$R = \frac{P_t - P_{t-1}}{P_{t-1}}$$

For example, if you pay $1000 to make an investment and receive $1100 when you sell the investment one year later, you earn a return of:

$$R = \frac{\$1100 - \$1000}{\$1000}$$

$$= 0.10, \text{ or } 10\%$$

Incorporating Dividend or Coupon Payments. If you also earned dividend or interest payments over this period, your return would be even higher. For a short-term period such as one year or less, the return on a security that pays dividends or interest can be estimated by adjusting the equation above. Add the dividend or interest amount to the numerator. The return on your investment accounts for any dividends or interest payments you received as well as the change in the investment value over your investment period. For stocks that pay dividends, the return is:

$$R = \frac{(P_t - P_{t-1}) + D}{P_{t-1}}$$

where R is the return, P_{t-1} is the price of the stock at the time of the investment, P_t is the price of the stock at the end of the investment horizon, and D is the dividends earned over the investment horizon.

EXAMPLE

You purchased 100 shares of Wax Inc. stock for $50 per share one year ago. The firm experienced strong earnings during the year. It paid dividends of $1 per share over the year and you sold the stock for $58 per share at the end of the year. Your return on your investment was:

$$R = \frac{(P_t - P_{t-1}) + D}{P_{t-1}}$$

$$= \frac{(\$58 - \$50) + \$1}{\$50}$$

$$= 0.18, \text{ or } 18\%$$

Differing Tax Rates on Returns. Income received as a result of interest payments is classified as ordinary income for tax purposes. Dividend income is subject to a dividend gross up and tax credit. The dividend adjustment involves grossing up the dividend

Monies Earned/Received	Salary Income	Interest Income	Dividend Income	Capital Income
	$1000	$1000	$1000	$1000
Federal Tax Rate	29%	29%	29%	29%
Gross-up Dividends 45%	–	–	450	–
Capital Gains Taxed at 50% of Gain	–	–	–	500
Taxable Income	1000	1000	1450	500
Federal Tax	290	290	420.50	145
Less: Dividend Tax Credit 27.5% of actual dividend	–	–	275	–
Total Federal Tax Owing	290	290	145.50	145

Exhibit 11.1 Impact of Taxes on $1000 of Income (Federal Tax Rate = 29%)

Source: www.taxtips.ca/marginaltaxrates.htm#Canada; www.taxtips.ca/divtaxcredits.htm#DTCDescription.

paid to the taxpayer by 45 percent and applying a dividend tax credit of 27.5 percent to the actual dividend paid. The net effect of the dividend adjustment is to reduce the amount of income tax payable by the individual taxpayer. Dividend income is recorded on line 120 of your T1 General. In addition, capital gains resulting from the sale of investments are subject to capital gains tax. A taxable capital gain is equal to 50 percent of a capital gain. Similarly, an allowable capital loss is equal to 50 percent of a capital loss.

Exhibit 11.1 highlights the impact of taxes on $1000 of income. The income received is in the form of salary, interest, dividend, or capital gain. Interest income is taxed in the same way and to the same extent as salary income. Dividend and capital gain income result in less taxes being paid by the taxpayer. The tax savings of dividend and capital gains indicates that the federal government strongly encourages investment in either common or preferred stocks. Remember, though, that there is more risk in such investments.

How Wealth Is Influenced by Your Return on Investment

When an investment provides income to you, any portion of that income that you save will increase the value of your assets. For example, if you receive an interest payment of $100 this month as a result of holding a debt security and deposit the cheque in your savings account, your assets will increase by $100. If the value of your investments increases and your liabilities do not increase, your wealth increases.

The degree to which you can accumulate wealth partially depends on your investment decisions. You can estimate the amount by which your wealth will increase from an investment based on some assumed rate of return. If you invest the same amount at the end of each year, the future value (*FV*) of this investment can be measured by applying the time value of money to the future value interest factor (*FVIF*) for an annuity:

$$FV \text{ of Investment} = \text{Investment} \times FVIF_{i,n}$$

where *i* is the annual return on the investment and *n* is the number of years until the end of the investment period.

EXAMPLE

Stephanie Spratt hopes to invest $4000 at the end of the year. If her investments appreciate by 6 percent annually, the value of her investments will be $7163 in 10 years. If she earns an annual return of 10 percent, the value of those investments will be $10 375 in 10 years. If she can earn an annual return of 20 percent, the value of her investment will be $24 767 in 10 years. The higher the rate of return, the higher the future value interest factor, and the larger the amount of funds that she will accumulate.

If you can invest a specific amount in the stock market every year, the future value of these annual investments can be estimated as:

$$FV \text{ of Annual Stock Investments} = \text{Annual Investment} \times FVIFA_{i,n}$$

where *FVIFA* represents the future value interest factor of an annuity.

The following example shows how your investment decisions and the performance of your investments can affect your future wealth.

EXAMPLE

Stephanie Spratt believes that she can save $4000 to invest in stocks at the end of each year for the next 10 years. If she expects the investment value to increase by 10 percent annually, she can use the future value interest factor of an annuity at 10 percent over 10 years, which is 15.937 (see Appendix A). Based on her annual investment of $4000 and the future value interest factor of an annuity, she will accumulate:

$$FV \text{ of Annual Stock Investments} = \text{Annual Investment} \times FVIFA_{i,n}$$
$$= \$4000 \times 15.937$$
$$= \$63\ 748$$

The input for the financial calculator is shown at the left.

If Stephanie's investment value increases by 20 percent per year, the *FVIFA* is 25.959, and the value of her annual investments in 10 years will be:

$$FV \text{ of Annual Stock Investments} = \text{Annual Investment} \times FVIFA_{i,n}$$
$$= \$4000 \times 25.959$$
$$= \$103\ 836$$

The input for the financial calculator is shown at the left.

Notice how the increase in Stephanie's wealth is sensitive to the rate of return earned on her annual investment. An annual increase in investment value of 20 percent would allow her to accumulate $40 088 more than if the annual increase is 10 percent.

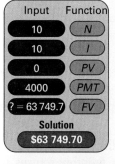

Input	Function
10	N
10	I
0	PV
4000	PMT
? = 63 749.7	FV
Solution	
$63 749.70	

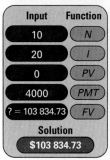

Input	Function
10	N
20	I
0	PV
4000	PMT
? = 103 834.73	FV
Solution	
$103 834.73	

L.O. 3 Risk of Investing

The risk of an investment comes from the uncertainty surrounding its return. The return you will earn on a specific stock is uncertain because its future dividend payments are not guaranteed and its future price (when you sell the stock) is uncertain. The return you will earn on a bond is uncertain because its interest payments are not guaranteed and its future price (when you sell the bond) is uncertain. The return you will earn from investing in real estate is uncertain because its value when you sell it is uncertain. Chapters 12, 13, and 14 discuss specific risks that mutual fund, stock, and bond investments are subject to.

The future values of investments depend on the demand by investors. When economic conditions are favourable, the income levels of investors are high, the earnings levels of corporations are high, and there is a strong demand for most types of investments. When economic conditions are weak, the income levels of investors are low, the earnings levels of firms are low, and there is a weak demand for most types of investments. However, future economic conditions are uncertain, so it is difficult to predict the level of demand for various investments, and therefore the future values of those investments.

EXAMPLE

You are considering purchasing the stock of Cerro Inc. The future value of Cerro's stock depends on the future performance of the company. If the economy strengthens, Cerro Inc. should perform well, and the value of its stock may increase by more than 9 percent. However, if the economy weakens, Cerro Inc. will perform poorly, and the stock could decline by 30 percent or more.

It is easy to find examples to illustrate the risk of investing. Many firms went bankrupt in the 2001–2002 period, including large ones such as Enron, Global Crossing, and WorldCom. Numerous investors who invested in these stocks lost 100 percent of their investments. Even firms that have normally performed well over time can experience weak performance in particular periods. Thus, it is not unusual for the stock or bond prices of even the most well-known firms to decline by more than 10 percent within a particular month or year. Stocks and bonds of smaller firms tend to be even more risky since their earnings are more volatile. Some firms are more stable than others and are therefore less likely to experience a major decline in their market value. Nevertheless, some investors prefer investments that have a higher growth potential, and they tolerate the higher level of risk. Before you select an investment, you should assess the risk of the investment and weigh this risk against your own risk tolerance.

Measuring an Investment's Risk. Investors measure the risk of investments to determine the degree of uncertainty surrounding their future returns. Two common measures of an investment's risk are its range of returns and the standard deviation of its returns. These measures can be applied to investments whose prices are frequently quoted over time.

range of returns
Returns of a specific investment over a given period.

Range of Returns. By reviewing the monthly returns of a specific investment over a given period, you can determine the range of returns, from the smallest (most negative) to the largest return. Compare an investment that has a range of monthly returns from 0.2 percent to 1.4 percent over the last year with an investment that has a range of 23.0 percent to –4.3 percent. The first investment is less risky because its range of returns is smaller and therefore it is more stable. Investments with a wide range have more risk because they have a higher probability of experiencing a large decline in price.

standard deviation
The degree of volatility in the stock's returns over time.

Standard Deviation of Returns. A second measure of risk is the standard deviation of an investment's monthly returns, which measures the degree of volatility in the investment's returns over time. A large standard deviation means that the returns deviate substantially from the mean over time. The more volatile the returns, the greater the chance that the stock could deviate far from its mean in a given period. Thus, an investment with a high standard deviation is more likely to experience a large gain or loss in a given period. The investment's return is subject to greater uncertainty, and for this reason it is perceived as more risky.

Although these two measures differ, they tend to rank the risk levels of investments rather consistently. That is, a very risky investment will normally have a relatively wide range of returns and a high standard deviation of returns.

Subjective Measures of Risk. The use of the range and standard deviation of returns is limited because these measures of risk are not always accurate predictors of the future changes in an investment's price. For example, an investment that had stable returns in the past could experience a substantial decline in price in the future in response to poor economic conditions or poor management. Because of this limitation, the risk of some investments is commonly measured subjectively. For example, the risk of a bond may be measured by a subjective assessment of the issuing firm's ability to repay its debt. The assessment may include an estimate of the firm's future monthly revenue to determine whether it will have sufficient funds to cover its interest and other expenses. Investors may rely on experts to offer their risk assessment of a particular type of investment. Bond rating agencies offer risk assessments of various bonds, as explained in Chapter 14.

L.O. 4 TRADE-OFF BETWEEN RETURN AND RISK

Every individual investor would like investments that offer a very high return and have no risk. However, such investments do not exist. Investors must weigh the trade-off between the potential return of an investment and the risk. If you want an investment that may generate a higher return, you have to tolerate the higher degree of uncertainty (risk) associated with that investment.

Investors expect a higher return for taking on additional risk. As a result, any investment that is not risk-free contains a **risk premium**, an additional return beyond the risk-free rate you could earn from an investment. The higher the potential risk of an investment, the higher the risk premium you should expect.

risk premium
An additional return beyond the risk-free rate you could earn from an investment.

If a particular risky deposit is supposed to offer a specific return (R) over a period and you know the risk-free rate (R_f) offered on a deposit backed by the government, you can determine the risk premium (RP) offered on the risky deposit:

$$RP = R - R_f$$

EXAMPLE

Stephanie Spratt has $1000 that she could invest for the next three months in a three-month bank GIC or in a stock. The bank GIC offers a return of 2 percent over the three-month period. Alternatively, she thinks that the price of the stock will rise by 5 percent over the next three months. However, since the future price of the stock is uncertain, her return from investing in this stock is also uncertain. The return could be less than 5 percent, and might even be negative. Stephanie decides to invest in the GIC rather than the stock because the 3 percent risk premium offered by the stock is not enough to entice Stephanie to take on the additional risk.

The example above illustrates the trade-off between a risk-free investment and a risky investment. There are also trade-offs between assets with varying degrees of risk, as explained below for each type of investment.

Return–Risk Trade-Off among Mutual Funds

When you invest in a mutual fund composed of stocks, you earn a return from the dividend payments and the increase in the prices of the stocks held by the mutual fund. The risk of a stock mutual fund is that the prices of the stocks can decline in any particular period. Since the mutual fund is composed of numerous stocks, the adverse impact caused by any single stock is reduced. However, when economic conditions weaken, most stocks tend to perform poorly. Just as the shares of smaller companies (in terms of capital) tend to be more risky than those of companies with larger capitalization, mutual funds that hold mostly small capitalization (small-cap) companies will be more risky than those that hold the larger capitalization companies. Yet, some investors still prefer mutual funds that contain small stocks because they expect a higher return from these stocks.

default
Occurs when a company borrows money through the issuance of debt securities and does not pay either the interest or the principal.

When you invest in a mutual fund composed of bonds, your primary risk is that the bonds held by the mutual fund could **default**, which occurs when a company borrows money through the issuance of debt securities and does not pay either the interest or the principal. Since a bond mutual fund contains numerous bonds, the adverse effect of a single bond default within a mutual fund is reduced. However, when economic conditions deteriorate, many firms that issued bonds could experience financial problems and have difficulty making their interest payments. Some bond mutual funds are not highly exposed to risk because they invest only in corporate bonds issued by the most creditworthy corporations. Others are highly exposed because they invest in bonds issued by relatively weak corporations that pay higher interest rates. Investors who prefer risky bond mutual funds because of their potential to offer a high return must tolerate the higher level of risk. There is another risk with debt securities: interest-rate risk. This will be discussed in Chapter 14.

Return–Risk Trade-Off among Stocks

Some firms have the potential to achieve a much higher performance level than others. But to do so, they take on more risk than other firms. That is, they may try to operate with less funding and pursue riskier opportunities. Investors who invest in one of these firms may earn very high returns if the firm's strategies are successful. However, they could lose most or all of their investment if the firm's strategies fail.

In general, smaller firms have more potential for faster growth and their stocks have the potential to increase in value to a greater degree. However, their stocks are risky because many small firms never reach their potential. The more mature firms that have already achieved high growth have less potential for future growth. However, these firms tend to be less risky because their businesses are more stable.

Initial public offerings (IPOs) are another stock investment option. You may have heard that IPO returns may exceed 20 percent over the first day. However, there is much risk with this type of investment. Individual investors rarely have access to these IPOs at the initial price. Institutional investors (such as mutual funds or insurance companies with large amounts of money to invest) normally have the opportunity or chance to purchase shares of an IPO. Most individual investors can invest (if there are any shares left) after the institutional investors' needs have been satisfied. By the time individual investors are able to invest in a newly issued stock, the price will have already risen. Thus, individual investors commonly obtain the shares only after the price has reached its peak, and incur large losses as the stock price declines over the next several months.

Many IPOs have performed poorly. On average, the long-term return on IPOs is weak compared to typical returns of other stocks in aggregate. Many firms that engage in IPOs (such as pets.com) fail within a few years, causing investors to lose all of their capital investment.

Return–Risk Trade-Off among Bonds

You may invest in a bond issued by a firm to earn the high interest payment. The risk of your investment is that the firm may be unable to make this payment if its financial condition deteriorates. If you purchase a bond of a large, well-known, and successful firm, there is minimal risk that the firm will default on its payments. If you purchase a bond issued by a firm that is struggling financially, there is more risk that this firm will default on its payments. If this firm defaults on the bond, your loss may be total.

High-risk bonds tend to offer higher interest payments. Thus, you must weigh the trade-off between the potential return and the risk. If you are willing to tolerate the higher risk, you may consider investing in a bond issued by a weak firm. Alternatively, if you prefer less risk, you can purchase

"Good news! I held my IPO at recess and now I'm the 12th richest man in America."

a bond issued by a successful and established firm, as long as you are willing to accept a lower return on your investment.

Return–Risk Trade-Off among Real Estate Investments

When you invest in real estate, your risk depends on your particular investment. If you buy rental property, it may not generate your anticipated periodic income if you cannot find renters or if your renters default on their rent payments. In addition, there is a risk that the property's value will decline over time. The degree of risk varies with the type of real estate investment. If you purchase an office building that is fully occupied, the risk is relatively low. Conversely, if you purchase a piece of open land in Saskatchewan because you hope you will someday discover oil on the land, the risk in your investment is high.

Comparing Different Types of Investments

As a prudent investor, you must choose investments that suit your personal objectives. If you want to achieve a fixed return over a short-term period without any risk, you should consider investing in a term deposit. The disadvantage of this type of investment is that it offers a relatively low return. If you want to achieve a stable return over a long-term period, you should consider a GIC or mutual funds that contain GICs. At the other extreme, if you desire a very high return, you could consider investing in land or in high-growth stocks.

Many investors fall in between these two extremes. They prefer a higher return than is offered by term deposits or GICs but want to limit their risk. There is no formula that can determine your ideal investment because the choice depends on how much risk you want to take, and on your financial situation.

To illustrate, consider the situations and possible solutions shown in Exhibit 11.2. In general, you are in a better position to take some risk when you know that you will not need to sell the investment in the near future. Even if the value of the investment declines, you have the flexibility to hold on to the investment until the value increases. Conversely, individuals investing for the short term should play it safe. Since the prices of risky investments fluctuate substantially, it is dangerous to invest in a risky investment when you know that you will be selling that investment in the near future. You could be forced to sell it when the investment has a low value. Investors who decide to pursue higher potential returns must be willing to accept the high risk associated with these investments.

Exhibit 11.2 How Investment Decisions Vary with Your Situation

Situation	Decision
You have $1000 to invest but will need the funds in one month to pay bills.	You need liquidity. You should only consider money market securities.
You have $3000 to invest but will need the funds in a year to make a tuition payment.	You should consider safe money market securities such as a 1-year GIC.
You have $5000 to invest, and will likely use the funds in about 3 years when you buy a home.	Consider a 3-year GIC, or stocks of relatively stable firms that have relatively low risk.
You have $10 000 to invest, and have no funds set aside for retirement in 20 years.	Consider investing in a diversified stock mutual fund.
You have $5000 to invest. You expect that you will be laid off from your job within the next year.	You should probably invest the funds in money market securities so that you will have easy access to the funds if you lose your job.

By having a variety of investments, you can find a tolerable risk level. You can diversify your investments among many different investments, thereby reducing your exposure to any particular investment. If you divide your money equally among five investments and one investment performs poorly, your exposure is limited.

Even if you diversify your portfolio among various investments, you are still exposed to general economic conditions since the values of all investments can decline during periods in which economic conditions are weak. For this reason, you should consider diversifying among various types of investments that are not equally sensitive to economic conditions. The strategy of diversification, also known as asset allocation, is crucial for investors.

IN-CLASS NOTES

Investment Return and Risk, and Trade-Off between Return and Risk

- Investment return (R)
  - $R = [(P_t - P_{t-1}) + D] \div P_{t-1}$
- Investment risk
  - Investment return is uncertain
  - Measurement → range of returns, standard deviation, subjective measurement
- Trade-off between return and risk
  - Risk premium (RP)
    - $RP = R - R_f$

_____

_____

_____

_____

_____

_____

L.O. 5   HOW DIVERSIFICATION REDUCES RISK

If you knew which investment would provide the highest return for a specific period, investment decisions would be easy. You would invest all of your money in that particular investment. In the real world, there is a trade-off between risk and return when investing. Although the return on some investments (such as a Canada Savings Bond or a GIC) is known for a specific investment period, these investments offer a relatively low rate of return. Many investments such as stocks, some types of bonds, and real estate, offer the prospect of higher rates of return.

Benefits of Portfolio Diversification
Because the returns from many types of investments are uncertain, it is wise to allocate your money across various types of investments so that you are not completely dependent on any one type. Asset allocation is the process of allocating money across financial assets (such as mutual funds, stocks, and bonds) with the objective of achieving a desired return while maintaining risk at a tolerable level.

asset allocation
The process of allocating money across financial assets (such as mutual funds, stocks, and bonds) with the objective of achieving a desired return while maintaining risk at a tolerable level.

portfolio
A set of multiple investments in different assets.

Building a Portfolio.   You can reduce your risk by investing in a **portfolio**, which is a set of multiple investments in different assets. For example, your portfolio may consist of various stocks, bonds, and real estate investments. By constructing a portfolio, you diversify across several investments rather than focus on a single investment. Investors who had all of their funds invested in Nortel Networks stock saw their investments fall from more than $200 per share in March 2000 to less than $1 per share by September 2002. Given the difficulty in anticipating when an investment might experience a major decline, you can at least reduce your exposure to any one stock by spreading your investments across several firms' stocks and bonds. A portfolio can reduce risk when its investments do not move in perfect tandem. Then, even if one investment experiences very poor performance, the other investments may perform well.

Focus on Ethics: The Risk of Insider Trading

It can be tempting to seek insider information (non-public information known by employees and other professionals that is not known by outsiders) when deciding how to invest your funds. For example, you might casually ask friends for tips about the firms that employ them, hoping that you can buy a company's stock before any significant news is released that will cause the stock price to rise. Investors are legally bound to use only information that is publicly available. When insider trading occurs, investors who play by the rules are at a disadvantage.

You can minimize your risk by using proper asset allocation. For example, if your assets are widely diversified among different types of mutual funds and other investments, you minimize your exposure to any one investment (such as a stock) that could experience a substantial decline in value once any negative news is released.

Determining Portfolio Benefits

To determine a portfolio's diversification benefits, you compare the return on the individual investments it consists of to the overall portfolio.

EXAMPLE

You are considering investing in a portfolio consisting of investments A and B. Exhibit 11.3 illustrates the portfolio diversification effect of using these two stocks. It shows the return per year for investments A and B, as well as for a portfolio with 50 percent of the investment allocated to A and 50 percent to B. The portfolio return in each year is simply the average return of A and B. Notice that the portfolio's range of returns is smaller than the range of returns of either stock. Also notice that the portfolio's returns are less volatile over time than the returns of the individual stocks. Since the portfolio return is an average of A and B, it has a smoother trend than either individual investment. The smoother trend demonstrates that investing in the portfolio is less risky than investing in either individual investment. You decide to create a partially diversified portfolio of both investments to reduce your risk.

insider information
Non-public information known by employees and other professionals that is not known by outsiders. It is illegal to use insider information.

As the previous example illustrates, the main benefit of diversification is that it reduces the exposure of your investments to the adverse effects of any individual investment. In Exhibit 11.3, notice that when investment A experienced a return of –20 percent in year 2, the portfolio return was –5 percent. The adverse effect on the portfolio was limited because B's return was 10 percent during that year. Investment A's poor performance still affected the portfolio's performance, but less than if it had been the only investment. When B experienced a weak return (such as –15 percent in year 5), its poor performance was partially offset because A's performance was 5 percent in that year.

Factors That Influence Diversification Benefits

A portfolio's risk is often measured by its degree of volatility because the more volatile the returns, the more uncertain the future return on the portfolio. By recognizing the factors that reduce a portfolio's risk, you can ensure that your portfolio exhibits these

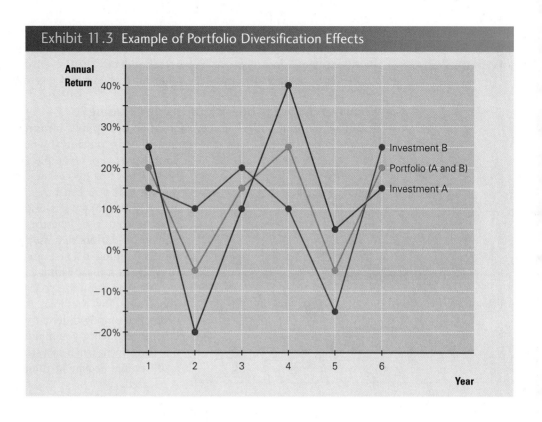

Exhibit 11.3 Example of Portfolio Diversification Effects

characteristics. The volatility of a portfolio's returns is influenced by the volatility of returns on each individual investment within the portfolio and by the correlation (a mathematical measure that describes how two securities' prices move in relation to one another) of the returns among investments.

correlation
A mathematical measure that describes how two securities' prices move in relation to one another.

Volatility of Each Individual Investment. As Exhibit 11.4 illustrates, the more volatile the returns of individual investments in a portfolio, the more volatile the portfolio's returns are over time (holding other factors constant). The left graph shows the returns of investment A (as in Exhibit 11.3), investment C, and an equally weighted portfolio of A

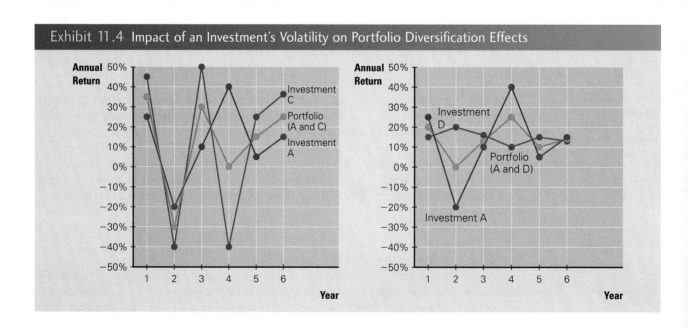

Exhibit 11.4 Impact of an Investment's Volatility on Portfolio Diversification Effects

and C; the right graph shows the individual returns of investments A and D, along with the return of an equally weighted portfolio of A and D. Comparing the returns of C on the left with the returns of D on the right, it is clear that C is much more volatile. For this reason, the portfolio of A and C (on the left) is more volatile than the portfolio of A and D (on the right).

Impact of Correlations among Investments. The more similar the returns of individual investments in a portfolio, the more volatile the portfolio's returns are over time. This point is illustrated in Exhibit 11.5. The left graph shows the returns of A, E, and an equally weighted portfolio of the two investments. Notice that the investments have very similar return patterns. When investment A performs well, so does E. When A performs poorly, so does E. This is referred to as positive correlation.

Consequently, the equally weighted portfolio of A and E has a return pattern that is almost identical to that of either A or E. Thus, this portfolio exhibits limited diversification benefits.

The middle graph in Exhibit 11.5 shows the returns of A, F, and an equally weighted portfolio of the two investments. Notice that the return patterns of the investments are opposite to one another. When A performs well, F performs relatively poorly. When A performs poorly, F performs well. The returns of A and F are therefore negatively correlated. Consequently, the equally weighted portfolio of A and F has a very stable return pattern because the returns of the stocks moved in opposite directions. Due to the negative correlation of returns, this portfolio offers substantial diversification benefits.

The right graph in Exhibit 11.5 shows the returns of A, G, and an equally weighted portfolio of the two investments. Notice that the return patterns of the two stocks are independent of each other. That is, A's performance is not related to G's performance. The return pattern of the equally weighted portfolio of A and G is more volatile than the returns of the portfolio of A and F (middle graph), but less volatile than the returns of the portfolio of A and E (left graph). Thus, the portfolio of investments A and G exhibits more diversification benefits than a portfolio of two investments that are positively related, but fewer diversification benefits than a portfolio of negatively correlated investments.

Go to
http://ca.finance.yahoo.com/investing

Click on
Basic Chart after inserting a stock symbol and selecting Get Quotes. Then enter the symbol for another stock in the box labelled Compare and perform your own comparison.

This website provides
a graph that shows the returns on two stocks so that you can compare their performance over time and determine their degree of correlation.

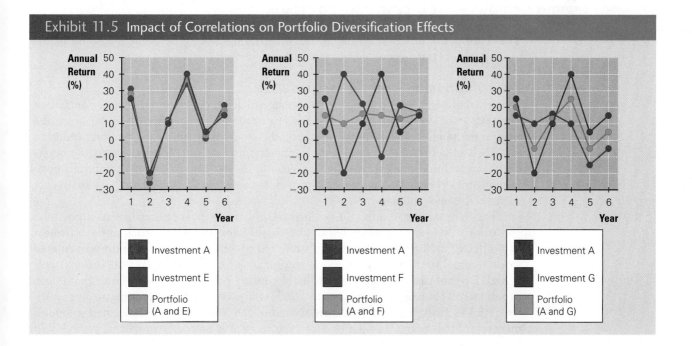

Exhibit 11.5 Impact of Correlations on Portfolio Diversification Effects

This discussion suggests that when you compile a portfolio you should avoid including investments that exhibit a high positive correlation. Although finding investments that are as negatively correlated as A and F may be difficult, you should at least consider investments whose values are not influenced by the same conditions. In reality, many investments are similarly influenced by economic conditions. If economic conditions deteriorate, most investments perform poorly. Nevertheless, some are influenced to a higher degree than others.

IN-CLASS NOTES

How Diversification Reduces Risk

- Asset allocation
  - The process of allocating money across financial assets (such as mutual funds, stocks, and bonds) with the objective of achieving a desired return while maintaining risk at a tolerable level
- Construct a portfolio
  - A portfolio can reduce risk when its investments do not move in step
- Factors that influence diversification benefits:
  - Volatility → the more volatile the returns of individual investments in a portfolio, the more volatile the portfolio's returns are over time
  - Correlation → the more similar the returns of individual investments in a portfolio, the more volatile the portfolio's returns are over time

L.O. 6 STRATEGIES FOR DIVERSIFYING

There are many different strategies for diversifying among investments. Some of the more popular strategies related to stocks are described here.

Diversification of Stocks across Industries

When you diversify your investments among stocks in different industries, you reduce your exposure to one particular industry. For example, you may invest in the stock of a firm in the publishing and music industry, the stock of a firm in the banking industry, the stock of a firm in the health care industry, and so on. When demand for books declines, conditions may still be favourable in the health care industry. Therefore, a portfolio of stocks diversified across industries is less risky than a portfolio of stocks that are all from the same industry.

The left graph in Exhibit 11.6 illustrates the diversification benefits of a portfolio consisting of two equally weighted stocks: Royal Bank and Alcan. Each of these firms is in a different industry and therefore is subjected to different industry conditions. Annual stock returns are shown for a recent period in which stock market conditions were mixed. Diversification is especially valuable during poor conditions. Notice that Alcan experienced very poor performance in 2002, while Royal Bank's stock return was positive. Alcan's stock price performance soared in 2003, while Royal Bank had a modest increase for that year. Overall, the poor performance of one stock in specific periods was

Exhibit 11.6 Benefits from Diversification across Industries

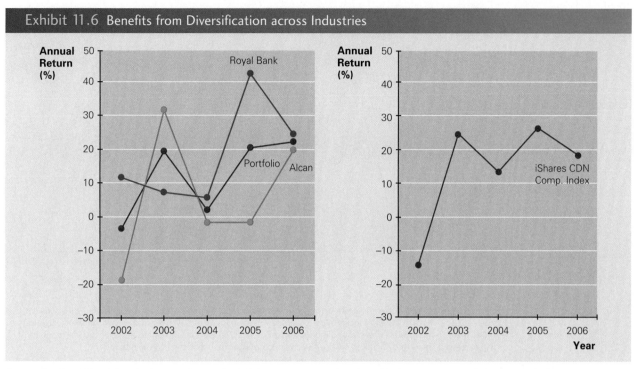

Sources: data from Yahoo! Canada, "Historical Prices for S&P/TSX Composite Index," http://ca.finance.yahoo.com/q/hp?s=%5EGSPTSE (accessed June 21, 2007). Reproduced with permission of Yahoo! Inc.® 2007 by Yahoo! Inc. YAHOO! and the YAHOO! logo are trademarks of Yahoo!; and Globefund, "Fund Filder," http://globefunddb.theglobeandmail.com/gishome/plsql/gis.fund_filter?pi_type=B (accessed June 21, 2007).

partially offset by the other stock within the portfolio. Notice how the returns of the two-stock portfolio are less volatile than those of either individual stock.

When adding more stocks to the portfolio, the diversification benefits are even greater because the proportional investment in any stock is smaller. Thus, the portfolio is less exposed to poor performance by any single stock.

To illustrate how diversification benefits would be even stronger for a more diversified portfolio, the returns from investing in the iShares Canadian Composite Index are shown in the right graph of Exhibit 11.6. The performance of this iShares portfolio is a good proxy for the S&P TSX Composite Index. Notice that the overall trend is more stable than the trend of returns for the two-stock portfolio in the left graph. The diversification benefits realized from investing in a representation of the entire Canadian economy is not as obvious because almost 60 percent of the stocks that make up the S&P TSX Composite Index come from the energy and/or financial services sector of the economy. In general, a very diversified portfolio can reduce the potential for very large losses, but it can also reduce the potential for very large gains.

Although diversification among stocks in different industries is more effective than diversification within an industry, the portfolio can still be very susceptible to general economic conditions. Stocks exhibit market risk, or susceptibility to poor performance because of weak stock market conditions. A stock portfolio composed of stocks of Canadian firms based in different industries may perform poorly when economic conditions in Canada are weak. Thus, diversification will not necessarily prevent losses when economic conditions are poor, but it can limit the losses.

Diversification of Stocks across Countries

Because economic conditions (and therefore stock market conditions) vary among countries, you may achieve more favourable returns by diversifying your stock investments across countries. For example, you may wish to invest in a variety of Canadian stocks

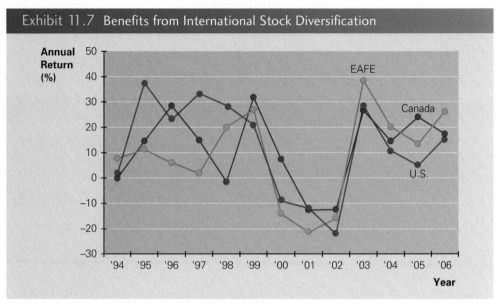

Exhibit 11.7 Benefits from International Stock Diversification

Sources: Adapted from Callan Associates, *The Callan Periodic Table of Investment Returns: Annual Returns for Key Indices, 1987–2006,* © 2007 Callan Associates Inc. Reprinted with permission of Callan Associates; and Franklin Templeton Investments, "Why Diversify," www.franklintempleton.ca/ca/retail/en/jsp_cm/education/life_planning/why_diversify.jsp (accessed June 21, 2007). Reprinted with permission of Franklin Templeton Investments.

across different industries, U.S. stocks, European stocks, and Asian stocks. Many investment advisers recommend that you invest about 20 to 30 percent of your money in Canadian stocks and allocate 70 to 80 percent to foreign countries.

Diversifying among stocks based in different countries makes you less vulnerable to economic conditions in any one country. Economic conditions in countries can be interrelated, however. In some periods, all countries may simultaneously experience weak economic conditions, causing stocks in all countries to perform poorly at the same time. When investing in stocks outside Canada, recognize that they are typically even more volatile than Canadian-based stocks, as they are subject to more volatile economic conditions. Therefore, you should diversify among stocks within each foreign country rather than rely on a single stock in any foreign country. Exhibit 11.7 illustrates the benefits of a diversified international portfolio over the 1994 to 2006 period, when market conditions were generally mixed. An equal investment is allocated to three regions: Canada, the United States, and EAFE (Europe, Australasia, and the Far East). EAFE is an international index that represents the performance of stock markets in developed countries outside North America. Notice that the United States generated more stable and higher returns during the mid to late 1990s. In the 2000 to 2002 period, all three markets were weak, reflecting general worldwide pessimism. In such periods, diversification is still beneficial if you include other assets, such as bonds, in your portfolio. In recent years, most major stock markets in the world have experienced positive growth. If you want to reduce risk though, you should not concentrate too heavily on the stock markets of developing countries because they commonly exhibit very volatile returns.

L.O. 7   ASSET ALLOCATION STRATEGIES

When investors make asset allocation decisions, they should not restrict their choices to stocks. All stocks can be affected by general stock market conditions, so diversification benefits are limited. Greater diversification benefits can be achieved by including other financial assets, such as bonds, income trusts, money market funds, and real estate. Your portfolio size and knowledge level will help determine the financial assets you should include in your portfolio.

Including Bonds in Your Portfolio

The returns from investing in stocks and from investing in bonds are not highly correlated. Stock prices are influenced by each firm's expected future performance and general stock market conditions. Bond prices are inversely related to interest rates and are not directly influenced by stock market conditions. Therefore, including bonds in your portfolio can reduce your susceptibility to stock market conditions. The expected return on bonds is usually less than the return on stocks, however, since bonds are often perceived as having less risk.

As you allocate more of your investment portfolio to bonds, you reduce your exposure to stock market risk but increase your exposure to interest rate risk. Your portfolio is more susceptible to a decline in value when interest rates rise because the market values of your bonds will decline. As will be discussed in Chapter 14, you can limit your exposure to interest rate risk by investing in bonds with relatively short maturities because the prices of those bonds are less affected by interest rate movements than the prices of long-term bonds.

In general, the larger the proportion of your portfolio that is allocated to bonds, the lower your portfolio's overall risk (as measured by the volatility of returns). The portfolio's value will be more stable over time, and it is less likely to generate a loss in any given period. Investors who are close to retirement commonly allocate much of their portfolio to bonds because they are relying on it to provide them with periodic income. Conversely, investors who are 30 to 50 years old tend to focus their allocation on stocks because they can afford to take risks in order to strive for a high return on their portfolio.

Including Income Trust Investments in Your Portfolio

As a result of the general weakness in world stock markets in the 2000 to 2002 period, many individuals who had become pessimistic about stocks began to include income trusts in their portfolio. An income trust is a flow-through investment vehicle that generates income and capital gains for investors. It is similar to a mutual fund in that many investors purchase units of the trust. This money is used by the trust to invest in income-producing assets.

In theory, one of the main benefits of an income trust is that almost 100 percent of the income generated by the trust assets is "flowed through" to the investors who have purchased units in the trust. Many investors have misinterpreted this steady cash flow as a reliable substitute for bonds and dividend-paying stocks. Although many income trusts have bond-like features, such as the regular distribution of income, an income trust is similar to a stock investment. A stock's price will decrease if a company cannot generate adequate earnings from its assets. Similarly, the unit price of an income trust will decrease if the assets in the trust are unable to generate adequate income. Income trust investors may earn income from the trust, but lose part of their capital if the value of the units decreases.

Until October 2006, the major difference between a stock and an income trust was that a stock company paid corporate income tax on earnings while an income trust was able to avoid paying any tax by flowing through all of its income to investors. Essentially, income trusts earned income tax-free, as long as this income was passed on to investors. Investors were happy because they received more cash flow than they would have if the trust had paid taxes. As a result of new rules that came into effect in 2007, income trusts are now taxed in the same manner as corporations. However, some real estate investment trusts (REITs) have been excluded from this treatment.

There are three major categories of income trusts: royalty income trusts, business investment trusts, and real estate investment trusts. Some REITs continue to benefit from the tax advantages available to income trusts. A real estate investment trust (REIT) is an income trust that pools funds from individuals and uses that money to invest in real estate. REITs commonly invest in commercial real estate such as office buildings and shopping centres.

REITs are similar to closed-end mutual funds in that their shares are traded on stock exchanges; the value of the shares is based on the supply of shares for sale (by investors) and investor demand for the shares. REITs are popular among individual investors because the shares can be purchased with a small amount of money. For example, an investor could purchase 100 shares of a REIT priced at $30 per share for a total of $3000 (computed as $30 × 100 shares). Another desirable characteristic of REITs is

income trust
A flow-through investment vehicle that generates income and capital gains for investors.

Go to
www.globeinvestor.com/v5/content/trusts/

This website provides news, ratings, and other information that will help you analyze income trusts.

real estate investment trusts (REITs)
Income trusts that pool investments from individuals and use the proceeds to invest in real estate.

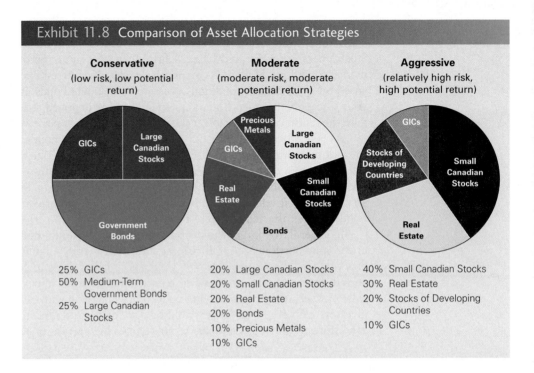

Exhibit 11.8 Comparison of Asset Allocation Strategies

Conservative
(low risk, low potential return)

25% GICs
50% Medium-Term Government Bonds
25% Large Canadian Stocks

Moderate
(moderate risk, moderate potential return)

20% Large Canadian Stocks
20% Small Canadian Stocks
20% Real Estate
20% Bonds
10% Precious Metals
10% GICs

Aggressive
(relatively high risk, high potential return)

40% Small Canadian Stocks
30% Real Estate
20% Stocks of Developing Countries
10% GICs

that they are managed by skilled real estate professionals who decide what properties to purchase and who will maintain the properties.

Role of REITs in Asset Allocation. Individual investors may invest in REITs to further diversify their investment portfolios. When stock market and/or bond market conditions are poor, real estate conditions may still be favourable. Thus, REITs could perform well in a period when stocks or bonds are performing poorly. Consequently, a portfolio that contains stocks, bonds, and REITs may be less susceptible to major declines because it is unlikely that all three types of investments will perform poorly simultaneously.

How Asset Allocation Affects Risk

Some asset allocation strategies reduce risk to a greater degree than others. To maintain a very low level of risk, an asset allocation may emphasize money market funds, Canadian government bonds, and the stocks of large, established Canadian firms. These types of investments tend to have low risk, but also offer a relatively low rate of return. To strive for a higher return, the asset allocation should include more real estate and stocks of developing countries. Exhibit 11.8 compares different asset allocation strategies in terms of risk and potential return. Even the most conservative asset allocation strategy shown here could result in a loss over a given period because some of the investments included in the portfolio are subject to losses.

Benefits of Asset Allocation

To illustrate the potential benefits of asset allocation, Exhibit 11.9 shows the one-year returns on a variety of investments over 2006. Investors who diversified only among Canadian sectors experienced good performance during this period because of the strength of the Canadian economy. However, some sectors, such as energy and bonds, were not as strong as other sectors. In addition, the U.S. stock market (S&P 500) and foreign markets (EAFE) also had good performance. Would you have been able to pick the winners in 2006? By having a diversified portfolio, you can always guarantee that you will have some of your money in markets that will reward you with above average returns.

An Affordable Way to Conduct Asset Allocation

When allocating money across a set of financial assets, you are subject to transaction fees on each investment you make. Thus, it can be costly to invest in a wide variety of

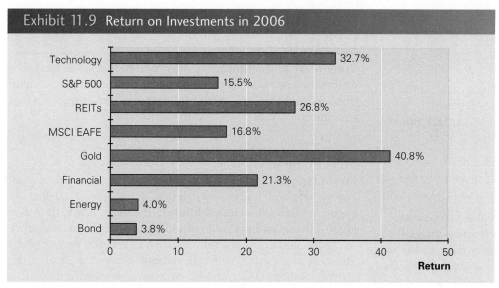

Exhibit 11.9 Return on Investments in 2006

Investment	Return
Technology	32.7%
S&P 500	15.5%
REITs	26.8%
MSCI EAFE	16.8%
Gold	40.8%
Financial	21.3%
Energy	4.0%
Bond	3.8%

Source: GLOBAL FUND REPORTS, UPDATED FUND LIST 2006 from theglobefund.com (http://globefunddb.
theglobeandmail.com) using data from the following benchmarks: iShares CDN Tech Sector Index; iShares CDN
S&P 500 Index ; iShares CDN REIT Sector Index; iShares CDN MSCI EAFE Index; iShares CDN Gold Sector Index;
iShares CDN Financial Sector Index; iShares CDN Energy Sector Index; iShares CDN Bond Index. Reprinted with
permission from The Globe and Mail.

investments. You can reduce your diversification costs by investing in mutual funds.
Since a typical stock mutual fund contains more than 50 stocks, you can broadly diversify by investing in a few stock mutual funds.

IN-CLASS NOTES

Strategies for Diversifying and Asset Allocation Strategies

- Industry diversification
  - A portfolio of stocks diversified across several industries is less risky than a portfolio of stocks in the same industry
  - Industry diversification is less effective when economic conditions in Canada are weak
- Country diversification
  - Diversifying with investments in other countries makes the portfolio less vulnerable to economic conditions in any one country
- Bonds
  - Not highly correlated to stocks
  - Prices are inverse to interest rates
- Income trusts
  - Types: royalty income trusts, business investment trusts, real estate investment trusts (REITs)
  - REITs could perform well in a period when stocks/ bonds are performing poorly

L.O. 8 FACTORS THAT AFFECT YOUR ASSET ALLOCATION DECISION

Go to
http://scotiabank.com/
cda/content/
0,1608,CID825_LIDen,00.
html

Click on
Complete the Scotia
Investment Selector today!

This website provides
a recommended asset allo-
cation that considers your
income, your stage in life,
and other characteristics
once you input some basic
information regarding your
desired return and your
degree of risk tolerance.

Your ideal asset allocation may not be appropriate for someone else because of differences in your personal characteristics and investment goals. The asset allocation decision hinges on several factors, including your stage in life and your risk tolerance.

Your Stage in Life

Investors in the early life stages need easy access to funds, so they should invest in relatively safe and liquid securities, such as money market investments. If they do not expect to need the invested funds in the near future, they may want to consider investing in a diversified portfolio of individual stocks, individual bonds, stock mutual funds, and bond mutual funds. Investors who expect to be working for many more years may invest in stocks of smaller firms and growth stock mutual funds, which have high growth potential. Conversely, investors nearing retirement age may allocate a larger proportion of money toward investments that will generate a fixed income, such as individual bonds, stock mutual funds containing high-dividend stocks, bond mutual funds, and some types of REITs. In any case, you must have enough money saved to invest wisely.

Although no single asset allocation formula is suitable for everyone, the common trends in asset allocation over a lifetime are shown in Exhibit 11.10. Notice the heavy emphasis on stocks at an early stage of life, as individuals take some risk in the hope that they can increase their wealth. Over time, they gradually shift toward bonds or to stocks of stable firms that pay high dividends. The portfolio becomes less risky as investments become more heavily weighted in bonds and stocks of stable firms. This portfolio is less likely to generate large returns, but it will provide periodic

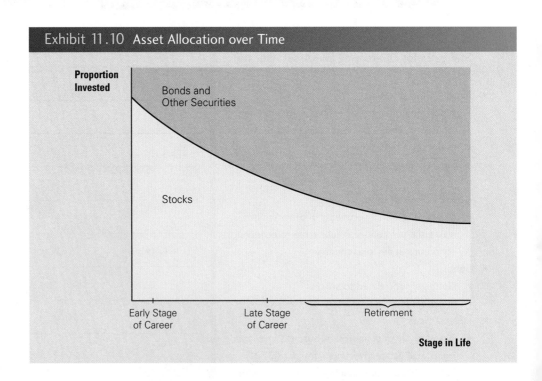

Exhibit 11.10 Asset Allocation over Time

income upon retirement. In fact, your portfolio will likely be your main source of income after you retire. (Chapter 15 discusses the role of savings in retirement planning in detail.)

Your Degree of Risk Tolerance

Investors also vary in their degree of risk tolerance. If you are unwilling to take much risk, you should focus on safe investments. For example, you could invest in government bonds with relatively short maturities. If you are willing to accept a moderate level of risk, you may consider a stock mutual fund that represents the S&P 500 stock index and/or large-cap stock mutual funds that invest in stocks of very large and stable firms. These investments offer more potential return than an investment in bonds, but they also may result in losses in some periods.

If you are willing to tolerate a higher degree of risk in order to strive for higher returns, you may consider individual stocks. Smaller stocks that are focused on technology tend to have potential for high returns, but they are also very risky. Even if you can tolerate a high level of risk, you should still diversify your investments. You might consider various mutual funds that have the potential to achieve a high return but contain a diversified set of stocks, so you are not overexposed to a single stock. Chapter 12 discusses some of the types of funds you could choose from, including various growth funds, capital appreciation funds, and even funds focused on sectors such as health care or financial firms. You may also consider bond mutual funds that invest in corporate bonds. You can increase your potential return (and therefore your risk) by focusing on high-yield (junk) bond mutual funds with long terms to maturity.

Your Expectations about Economic Conditions

Your expectations about economic conditions also influence your asset allocation. If you expect strong stock market conditions, you may shift a larger proportion of your money into your stock mutual funds. Conversely, if you expect a temporary weakness in the stock market, you may shift a larger proportion of your money to your bond mutual funds. If you expect interest rates to decrease, you may consider shifting money from a bond mutual fund containing bonds with short maturities to one containing bonds with long maturities. You can easily shift money among mutual funds if the funds are part of the same family.

If you anticipate favourable real estate conditions, you may allocate some of your money to REITs. As time passes, your expectations may change, causing some types of financial assets to become more desirable than others. You should change the composition of your investment portfolio in response to changes in your market expectations, investment goals, and life circumstances. While a review can take place when you conduct your overall financial plan review, investments need more attention. Despite the fact that mutual funds are considered long-term investments (except for money market mutual funds), investors should review portfolio performance and composition on a regular basis. If investors are investing in individual stocks and bonds, reviews must be done a great deal more frequently.

Because it is nearly impossible to predict economic conditions, it is difficult to determine which types of investments will perform best in a given period. Consequently, you may be better off basing your asset allocation decisions completely on your stage in life and degree of risk tolerance. Then, once you establish a diversified portfolio of investments, you will need to revise the portfolio only when you enter a different stage in life or change your degree of risk tolerance.

EXAMPLE

Stephanie Spratt wants to develop a long-term investment plan for allocating money to various financial assets. Specifically, she wants to set rough goals for the proportion of money she will invest in stocks, bonds, and REITs over the next 10 years. Since she started her career only recently and may be working for another 30 years, she does not feel it is necessary to allocate a large proportion of her money to bonds at this time. She recognizes that bonds are typically safer than stocks, but plans to consider bond and stock mutual funds in the future. She recognizes that stocks are risky, but is comfortable taking some risk at this stage in her life. She plans to consider some equity mutual funds, growth stock mutual funds, and international mutual funds.

As Stephanie accumulates more funds for investing over the next five years, she plans to invest in various stocks or stock mutual funds. She will invest in REITs only if her view of the real estate market throughout Canada becomes more favourable.

As she approaches retirement, she will still consider market conditions, but will adjust to a more conservative investment approach that reduces risk (and offers a lower potential return).

L.O. 9

LEARNING FROM THE INVESTMENT MISTAKES OF OTHERS

Many individual investors learn from their own mistakes or the mistakes of others. Consider the following investment mistakes, so that you can avoid them.

Making Decisions Based on Unrealistic Goals

One of the most common mistakes is letting unrealistic goals dictate your investment decisions. These goals may force you to take more risk than you should, and can result in major losses.

EXAMPLE

Laurie Chen has $4000, which should cover her school expenses next year. She is considering investing the money in a one-year GIC that would earn about 4 percent, or about $160, in interest before next year. However, she would like to earn a higher return within the next year so that she can buy a used car. She decides to invest in a small stock that earned a return of 50 percent last year. If the stock's value increases by 50 percent again over the next year, her investment would generate a gain of $2000, which would allow her to buy a used car. Unfortunately, the stock's value declines by 30 percent over the year. At the end of the year, her investment is worth $2800, a $1200 loss. She does not have sufficient funds to cover her school expenses or to buy the car. She did not view her investment as a gamble, as the money was invested in the stock of a firm. However, her investment in one small stock was just as risky as gambling, especially since she had no information to support her decision except that the stock performed well in the previous year.

Borrowing to Invest

Another common mistake is to invest money that could have been used to pay off an existing loan. The potential to earn a high return on an investment can tempt individuals to take on more risk than they should.

EXAMPLE

Charles Krenshaw recently took out a $5000 loan to cover this year's college expenses. His parents then gave him $5000 so that he could pay off the loan. Rather than doing that, Charles invested the $5000 in one stock. He had hoped that he could earn a large return on the $5000, so that he could sell the investment at the end of the year, pay off the loan, and have enough funds left over to travel through Europe during the summer. During the year, he had to make interest payments on the existing loan. The stock that he purchased declined in value by 90 percent, leaving him with just $500 at the end of the year. He now has insufficient funds to pay off the loan or to take a vacation.

Taking Risks to Recover Losses from Previous Investments

Another common mistake is taking excessive risks to recover your losses. This can lead to additional losses, and may even push individuals toward bankruptcy.

EXAMPLE   Sarah Barnes lost 10 percent of her investment over the last year in a diversified mutual fund. She needs the money before next winter to purchase a new furnace for her home. She wants to make up for her loss, so has shifted her money into a risky mutual fund that will likely generate a higher return if economic conditions are favourable but will perform poorly if economic conditions are unfavourable. She experiences a 20 percent loss on this investment because economic conditions weakened. She no longer has a sufficient amount of funds to pay for the furnace.

During the late 1990s, many investors bid up the prices of stocks because of their unrealistic expectations about how well these stocks would perform in the future. The media hype added to the investors' irrational exuberance. These actions created a so-called speculative bubble, meaning that once the prices are blown up to a certain level, the bubble will burst, and stock prices will decline to more realistic levels. One reason for the generally poor stock performance in 2000 to 2002 was that the speculative bubble burst. In addition, economic conditions weakened.

While there may someday be another period in which stocks or other investments earn abnormally high returns, you should be realistic when making investment decisions. An investment that has the potential to rise substantially in value also has the potential to decline substantially in value. If you cannot afford the possible loss, you should not make that investment.

Focus on Ethics: Falling Prey to Online Investment Fraud

The Internet is a remarkably easy and inexpensive means of obtaining investment advice and researching investment opportunities. Hundreds of online newsletters recommend investments, such as specific stocks or bonds. Investors can use online bulletin boards to share information. Advice is also distributed in the form of spam, or junk email.

With all of these sources at hand, it can be difficult to tell the difference between legitimate and fraudulent opportunities. The recommendations could be provided by unqualified individuals or people paid by the companies to recommend their stocks or bonds. In some cases, individuals send out millions of emails and set up websites to promote a particular firm's stock. Others push specific investments that they already own, hoping to create more demand to drive the price higher. For some small stocks that have less than 1000 shares traded per day, orders instigated by Internet rumours could easily push the stock price higher, at least temporarily.

To protect against this type of fraud, avoid making any investment decisions until you have the facts at hand. Obtain the annual report of the firm to review general background information. Check credible news sources such as the *Globe and Mail*. If you would rather not wait a day to read a financial newspaper, use trustworthy online services such as the Business News Network (www.bnn.ca). However, be careful how you interpret news about a rumour. The news source may repeat a rumour, but will not necessarily confirm that the rumour is true. Another option is to check with a trusted financial adviser. As a general rule, be wary of promises of quick profits, "guaranteed" or limited-time opportunities, or investments that are in foreign countries.

IN-CLASS NOTES

Factors That Affect Your Investment Decisions

- Your stage in life
- Your degree of risk tolerance
- Your expectations about economic conditions
- Learning from the mistakes of others
  - Making decisions based on unrealistic goals
  - Borrowing to invest
  - Taking risks to recover losses from previous investments

_____

_____

_____

_____

_____

HOW INVESTMENTS FIT WITHIN YOUR FINANCIAL PLAN

The following are the key investment decisions that should be included within your financial plan:

- What are your investment goals?
- Given your existing budget, should you make investments?
- Based on your risk tolerance, how should you invest funds?
- Is your present asset allocation of investments appropriate?
- How will you apply asset allocation in the future?

STEPHANIE SPRATT'S FINANCIAL PLAN: Investments

GOALS FOR INVESTING

1. Determine my investment goals.
2. Determine whether to make investments.
3. Determine the types of investments that would achieve my investment goals.
4. Ensure that my present asset allocation is appropriate.
5. Determine a plan for asset allocation in the future as I accumulate more money.

ANALYSIS OF FUNDING

Monthly Income	$2500
− Typical Monthly Expenses	1488
− Monthly Car Loan Payment	412
= Amount of Funds Available	$600

ANALYSIS OF POSSIBLE INVESTMENTS

Type of Investment	Assessment
1. GICs and other short-term securities	*Many money market securities provide good liquidity and are safe, but they typically offer low returns.*
2. Stock mutual funds	*Can provide high returns and offer more diversification than investing in individual stocks, but can generate losses if stock market conditions are weak.*
3. Bond mutual funds	*Offer more diversification than investing in individual bonds, but can generate losses if bond market conditions are weak.*
4. Stocks	*Can provide high returns, but are risky given the limited amount of funds I anticipate I will have for investing.*
5. Bonds	*Some bonds have low risk, but they offer lower potential returns than stocks.*
6. Real estate	*The value of my home may increase over time. Additional real estate investments can generate high returns but are risky.*

Investment	Market Value of Investment	Proportion of Invested Funds Allocated to This Investment
Common stock	*$3000*	*$3000/$5000 = 60%*
Stock mutual fund	*1000*	*$1000/$5000 = 20%*
Bond mutual fund	*1000*	*$1000/$5000 = 20%*
Total	*$5000*	

DECISIONS

My primary investment goal is to maintain sufficient liquidity in any funds that I invest to cover any unanticipated expenses. However, I would like to earn a return on any funds that I have until they are needed to cover expenses.

After paying for my typical monthly expenses (not including recreation), I have $600 left each month. I am not in a financial position to make long-term investments at this time because I will use some of these funds each month for recreation and will deposit the remaining funds in liquid accounts such as a money market fund. I need to increase my liquidity since I might incur unexpected home repair expenses periodically. Beyond maintaining liquidity, I hope to save enough money to pay off my car loan before maturity. Once I pay off that loan, I will reconsider whether to invest in riskier investments that have the potential to offer a higher return. My salary should also increase over time, which will make investments more affordable. When I start long-term investing, I will consider stock mutual funds and bond mutual funds rather than individual stocks or bonds. I can periodically invest in mutual funds with small amounts of money and achieve diversification benefits. Since I already own a home, I do not want to invest in additional real estate.

Decision on Whether My Present Asset Allocation Is Appropriate

My present asset allocation is too heavily concentrated on one stock. With just $5000 in investments, I should probably have all of my money invested in mutual funds so that my investments are more diversified. I will consider selling the stock and investing the proceeds in a stock mutual fund. I already own shares of a mutual fund focused on technology firms. I will invest the proceeds from selling my stock in a different type of stock mutual fund so that I can achieve diversification.

Decision on Asset Allocation in the Future

Once I revise my asset allocation as described above, I will have $4000 invested in stock mutual funds and $1000 in bond mutual funds. This revision will result in a balance of 80 percent invested in stock funds and 20 percent *invested in bond funds. The stock funds have a higher potential return than the bond funds. During the next few years, I will invest any extra money I have in stock or bond mutual funds, maintaining the same 80/20 ratio.*

Discussion Questions

1. How would Stephanie's investing decisions be different if she were a single mother of two children?

2. How would Stephanie's investing decisions be affected if she were 35 years old? If she were 50 years old?

SUMMARY

Common types of investments include money market securities, stocks, bonds, mutual funds, and income trusts. Each type of investment is unique in terms of how it provides a return to its investors.

The return on an investment is determined by the income the investment generates and the capital gain of the investment over the investment period. Some stocks offer periodic income in the form of dividends, while bonds offer periodic income in the form of interest payments.

The risk from making an investment varies among types of investments. In particular, money market securities tend to have low risk, while many stock and income trust investments have high risk. However, the risk also varies within a particular type of investment. Some money market securities have more risk than others. Some stocks have more risk than others.

Investors weigh the trade-off between risk and return when making investment decisions. When they select investments that have the potential to offer high returns, they must accept a higher degree of risk. Alternatively, they can select investments that have lower risk, but they must accept a relatively low return. The proper choice depends on the investor's willingness to accept risk, which is influenced by the investor's financial position and psychological attitude to loss of capital. Some investors are not in a financial position in which they can afford to take much risk, and should therefore select investments that have little or no risk. Some investors cannot abide loss of capital, regardless of potential return. Again, low-risk securities would be the best choice.

Asset allocation uses diversification to reduce your risk from investing. In general, a portfolio achieves more benefits when it is diversified among assets whose returns are less volatile and are not highly correlated with each other over time.

Common stock diversification strategies include diversifying among stocks across industries and among stocks across countries. You should consider using these two types of diversification so that you limit the exposure of your stock investments to any external forces that could affect their value.

Your asset allocation decision should not be restricted to stocks. Because bond returns are primarily influenced by interest rate movements rather than stock market conditions, they are not highly correlated with stock returns over time. Therefore, bonds can help reduce the risk of an investment portfolio. Real estate investment trusts (REITs) are primarily influenced by real estate conditions and can also be useful for diversifying an investment portfolio.

Your asset allocation decision should take into account your stage in life, your degree of risk tolerance, and your expectations of economic conditions. If you are young, you may be more willing to invest in riskier securities to build wealth. If you are near retirement, you should consider investing more of your money in investments that can provide you with a stable income (dividends and interest payments) over time. If you are more willing to tolerate risk, you would invest in riskier stocks and bonds. Your asset allocation is also influenced by your expectations about future economic conditions. These expectations affect the expected performance of stocks, bonds, and REITs and therefore should shape your decision of how to allocate your money across these financial assets.

You can learn from investment mistakes made by others. In particular, do not make investments that are driven by unrealistic goals. Do not invest when the funds could be more properly used to pay off existing debt. Do not attempt high-risk investments as a means of recovering recent losses. Finally, recognize the risk of investing when the market is inflated because of a speculative bubble.

INTEGRATING THE KEY CONCEPTS

Your investment decisions can affect your income (dividends and capital gains). As a result, these decisions may also affect your liquidity (Part 2). Investment decisions are related to financing (Part 3) because you should consider paying off any personal loans before you invest in other assets. The amount of insurance you need (Part 4) will change if your investment decisions are successful and you increase your net worth. You may need less insurance because you have personal access to ready cash instead. You may also need more insurance to protect the value of assets that may be subject to income tax upon your death. If, after considering your liquidity and financing situation, you decide to invest in securities or mutual funds, you need to decide whether the investment should be for your retirement account (Part 6). There are tax implications that may influence your decision.

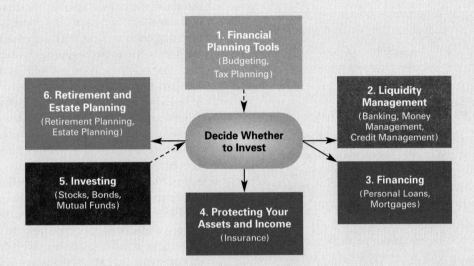

REVIEW QUESTIONS

1. What should your first priority be when investing? What is the disadvantage of investments that satisfy that priority?

2. How do mutual funds operate? Who manages mutual funds? How are interest or dividend payments handled by the mutual fund? Can investors incur capital losses with mutual funds?

3. What is an exchange traded fund (ETF)? Why would investors select these types of investments?

4. What are stocks? How are stocks beneficial to corporations? Why do investors invest in stocks?

5. How do shareholders earn returns from investing in stocks? What determines the market price of a stock?

6. What type of firm typically pays dividends? What are growth stocks? What are value stocks? What are income stocks?

7. What are dividends? Do all firms pay them?

8. Discuss the differences between common stock and preferred stock.

9. What are bonds? How do bonds provide a return to investors?

10. In what geographic areas would the land value be relatively high? What components make up the return from investing in real estate?

11. What is the formula for estimating returns on dividend-paying stocks? Describe each element of the formula. How do you calculate the dollar amount of your returns?

12. What is the difference in the tax treatment of different types of investment income?

13. How can investments in stock increase your wealth?

14. Define the risk of an investment. What types of firms are particularly risky? Why do investors measure risk? Describe the two common measures of risk.

15. What is the return–risk trade-off? Describe the return–risk trade-offs among mutual funds, stocks, bonds, and real estate investments.

16. How can you limit your risk through diversification? Why is it important to diversify your financial holdings across financial assets? How does asset allocation enable you to accomplish diversification?

17. What is a portfolio? How does a diverse portfolio help reduce risk? What factors influence a portfolio's risk? Explain.

18. Describe two strategies for diversifying a stock portfolio.

19. How can allocating some of your assets to bonds reduce the level of risk in your portfolio?

20. What is an income trust? What are the major categories of income trusts? What are real estate investment trusts (REITs)? What are some attractive characteristics of REITs?

21. Why can asset allocation be expensive? How can you reduce the costs?

22. Discuss the role that your stage in life plays in the asset allocation decision.

23. How does your risk tolerance affect the asset allocation decision?

24. How might your expectations of economic conditions influence your asset allocation? What is the problem with this strategy?

25. Describe common investment mistakes made by individuals.

FINANCIAL PLANNING PROBLEMS

1. Joel purchased 100 shares of stock for $20 per share. During the year, he received dividend cheques amounting to $150. Joel recently sold the stock for $32 per share. What was Joel's return on the stock? What is the dollar amount of Joel's return?

2. Emma bought a stock a year ago for $53 per share. She received no dividends on the stock and sold the stock today for $38 per share. What is Emma's return on the stock?

3. Tammy has $3500 that she wants to invest in stock. She believes she can earn a 12 percent annual return. What would be the value of Tammy's investment in 10 years if she is able to achieve her goal? (See Appendix A.)

4. Dawn decides to invest $2000 per year in stock at the end of each of the next five years. She believes she can earn a 9 percent return over that time period. How much will Dawn's investment be worth at the end of five years? (See Appendix A.)

5. Bob purchased a dot-com stock, which was heavily advertised on the Internet, for $40 per share shortly after the stock's IPO. Over the next three years, the stock price declined by 15 percent each year. What is the company's stock price after three years?

6. Morris will start investing $1500 a year in stocks. He feels he can average a 12 percent return. If he follows this plan, how much will he accumulate in five years? In 10 years? In 20 years?

7. Thomas purchased 400 shares of stock A for $23 per share and sold them more than a year later for $20 per share. He purchased 500 shares of stock B for $40 per share and sold them for $53 per share after holding them for the same time period. If Thomas is in a 25 percent tax bracket, what will his capital gains tax be for the year?

8. Charles just sold 500 shares of stock A for $12 000. He then sold 600 shares of stock A for $6000. Charles paid $20 per share for all of his shares of stock A. What amount of capital loss will he have?

ETHICAL DILEMMA

Mike has decided that it is time he put his money to work. He has accumulated a substantial nest egg in a savings account at a local bank but he realizes that with less than 3 percent interest, he will never reach his financial goals. After doing some research he withdraws the money, opens an account at a local brokerage firm, and buys 500 shares of a large manufacturing company and 600 shares of a well-known retail store. From the beginning, his broker emphasizes that his portfolio is not sufficiently diversified with just two stocks. Over time, the broker convinces Mike to sell these two stocks to purchase stock in other companies. Two years later Mike owns stock in 14 different companies and views his portfolio as well diversified. His cousin Ed, who has recently graduated from business school, looks at his portfolio and comments, "You are not very well diversified, as 10 of the stocks you own are considered technology stocks." Mike tells Ed that he followed his broker's recommendations and sold his original stocks to purchase the new stocks in order to attain a diversified portfolio. Ed comments that Mike's brokerage firm is noted as a specialist in technologies. Mike is disappointed because he thought he was getting good advice about building a well-diversified portfolio. After all, Mike followed his broker's advice to the letter, and why would his broker give him bad advice?

a. Comment on the broker's ethics in recommending the sale of the original stocks to purchase a portfolio weighted so heavily toward technologies. Include in your discussion reasons why the broker may have followed the course of action that he did.

b. To achieve diversification, what other course of action could Mike have taken that would not have involved buying individual stocks in a variety of companies?

FINANCIAL PLANNING ONLINE EXERCISES

1. Go to www.mackenziefinancial.com/en/pub/tools/calculators/index.shtml. Locate the Advantage of Early Investing calculator under the Investment and Saving heading. This calculator will help you understand the importance of early investing as a part of wealth accumulation.

a. Once you are in the calculator, click on Next. Make sure that you have not changed any of the default settings. Which scenario provides the greatest accumulated value?

b. Click on Back. Which scenario has the earliest start age? Which scenario has the largest initial deposit amount? Which scenario has the largest periodic deposit amount? Based on your answers, what was the most important variable in increasing the accumulated value under each scenario?

c. Increase the annual rate of return under Scenarios 2 and 3 by 1 percent. Click on Next. What is the impact of the change in the annual rate of return on accumulated value? Is the accumulated value under either scenario higher than the accumulated value under Scenario 1?

d. Increase the annual rate of return under Scenario 2 such that the accumulated value of Scenario 2 is equal to that of Scenario 1. What is the required annual rate of return for Scenario 2? Complete this procedure for Scenario 3. What is the required annual rate of return for Scenario 3? With respect to Scenario 3, what other options may be available to increase the accumulated value if the annual rate of return is the same as that calculated for Scenario 2?

2. Go to http://ca.finance.yahoo.com/etf. Click on ETF Education. Next, click on Asset Allocation with ETFs. Comment on the following statement: "Investors should spend most of their time on overall asset selection and ignore individual stocks for the most part." According to this article, why is stock picking unproductive? How can you use ETFs to build an asset allocation strategy?

3. Go to www.atb.com/Dev/investing/inv_compass.asp.

a. This website describes a variety of asset allocation portfolios. Click on Maximum Growth. What is the asset allocation range for each of the types of investments in this portfolio?

b. Create a table that will display the asset allocation range for each of the different types of Compass portfolios. Comment on the differences in the asset allocation ranges among the various portfolios. Why is there a difference?

ON THE STUDENT CD-ROM FOR THIS CHAPTER YOU WILL FIND:

- Building Your Own Financial Plan exercise and worksheets
- The chapter-end Continuing Case about the Sampson family

    Read through the Building Your Own Financial Plan exercise and use the worksheets to determine your risk tolerance towards investing and whether or not your current asset allocation is appropriate given your personal

risk tolerance. If you do not have an investment portfolio, consider what types and proportions of investments are appropriate for you.

    After reading the Sampsons case study, use the Continuing Case worksheets to help the Sampsons evaluate their investment decisions.

Study Guide

Circle the correct answer and then check the answers in the back of the book to chart your progress.

Multiple Choice

1. Which of the following statements is correct?
    a. Institutional investors are semi-professionals employed by a financial institution who are responsible for managing money on behalf of the clients they serve.
    b. Day traders are professionals who work on a day-to-day basis.
    c. Portfolio managers are the employees of financial institutions who make investment decisions.
    d. Institutional investors commonly invest a portion of the money earned from their jobs.

2. _____ stock is a certificate issued by a firm to raise funds that entitles shareholders to first priority to receive dividends.

    a. Dividend-paying
    b. Preferred
    c. Growth
    d. Common

3. Fernando purchased 1500 shares of Johnson Enterprises Inc. for $23 per share in 2006. During 2007, Johnson Enterprises paid a dividend of $1 per share. Fernando sold his shares in Johnson Enterprises for $26 per share at the end of 2007. What was his investment return during the holding period? Round your answer to one decimal place.
    a. 13.0%
    b. 11.5%
    c. 14.8%
    d. 17.4%

4. Calculate the federal tax owing on dividend income of $2000. Assume that the federal tax rate is 26%.
   a. $204
   b. $754
   c. $520
   d. $479

5. Which of the following statements regarding the trade-off between risk and return is incorrect?
   a. Since the prices of risky investments fluctuate substantially, it is dangerous to invest in a risky investment when you know that you will be selling that investment in the near future.
   b. A risk premium is an additional return beyond the risk-free rate you could earn from an investment.
   c. By the time individual investors are able to invest in a newly issued stock, the price has already risen.
   d. The risk of your investment is that the firm may be unable to make its dividend payment if its financial condition deteriorates.

6. With respect to investment return, the benefits of portfolio diversification include:
   a. A portfolio of investments will result in a smoother trend of returns since returns are averaged among the investments in the portfolio.
   b. On average, the range of returns of a portfolio of investments is less than the range of returns of any individual investment.
   c. An equally weighted portfolio of two stocks will have a rate of return that is equal to the average return of the two stocks combined.
   d. All of the above.

7. To diversify your portfolio against weak economic conditions in Canada, it is important to diversify your stocks across _____.
   a. the Atlantic Ocean
   b. industries
   c. countries
   d. sectors

8. Lee Ann would like to diversify her individual stock portfolio with other investments. Currently, she owns a portfolio of five stocks. Which of the following investments would you be least likely to recommend to Lee Ann in order to help her achieve her goal?
   a. A bond
   b. ETFs
   c. An income trust
   d. A stock-based mutual fund

9. Your current investment portfolio is equally diversified across stocks, bonds, and real estate. You have decided to reposition your portfolio based on your expectations about economic conditions. For the upcoming year, you expect stock market conditions to be weak, interest rates to decrease, and real estate conditions to be unfavourable. Which of the following investments would you most likely add to your portfolio?
   a. A bond mutual fund containing bonds with short maturities
   b. A stock mutual fund
   c. A bond mutual fund containing bonds with long maturities
   d. A real estate investment trust (REIT) fund

10. Which of the following is not a common investment mistake?
    a. Making decisions based on realistic goals
    b. Borrowing to invest
    c. Taking risks to recover losses from previous investments
    d. None of the above. All of these choices represent common investment mistakes.

True/False

1. True or False? The popularity of exchange traded funds (ETFs) is a result of research showing that sophisticated investors are able to outperform various stock indexes on average.

2. True or False? The secondary market facilitates the trading of existing securities by enabling investors to sell their shares at any time.

3. True or False? Real estate can be rented to generate income in the form of rent payments. In addition, investors may earn a capital gain if they sell the property for a higher price than they paid for it.

4. True or False? An investment with a high standard deviation is more likely to experience a large gain or a small loss in a given period.

5. True or False? When economic conditions weaken, most stocks tend to perform poorly.

6. True or False? Portfolio construction involves the selection of investments that exhibit positive correlation.

7. True or False? The returns on stocks and the returns on bonds are highly correlated.

8. True or False? To reduce your exposure to stock market risk, you could invest in either long-term debt securities or money market securities.

9. True or False? If you have aversion to risk, you should invest in small-cap mutual funds.

10. True or False? An investment that has the potential to rise substantially in value also has the potential to decline substantially in value.

Chapter 12

Investing in Mutual Funds

R ob bought 200 units of a mutual fund for $25 per unit in late September. By December, his mutual fund units were priced at $23.50. He was not terribly disappointed, as this was a long-term investment.

What surprised Rob, however, was the capital gains distribution he received in December. While the value of his investment was $300 less than the purchase price, the mutual fund distributed $3.95 per unit, a total distribution of $790 that Rob must report as taxable income. What Rob failed to realize at the time of his purchase was that the fund he had selected was sitting on accumulated capital gains from stocks it had purchased in previous years. After five years of good returns, the fund managers had sold some of the stocks within the fund to lock in gains. Rob, as a current unitholder, received his share of the gains. Too late, Rob realized that most mutual funds distribute their gains, as they are required to do by law, near the end of the year. Rob has more to learn about mutual funds and their tax implications.

This chapter explains how to invest in equity mutual funds and bond mutual funds to diversify your investment portfolio. An understanding of mutual funds can help you make proper investment decisions and can enhance your wealth.

The objectives of this chapter are to:

1. Describe the advantages and disadvantages of mutual funds
2. Identify the types of equity funds
3. Present the types of bond funds
4. Explain how to choose among mutual funds
5. Describe quotations of mutual funds
6. Explain how to diversify among mutual funds
7. Explain the differences between segregated funds and mutual funds

L.O. 1 BACKGROUND ON MUTUAL FUNDS

equity mutual funds
Funds that sell units to individuals and use this money to invest in stocks.

bond mutual funds
Funds that sell units to individuals and use this money to invest in bonds.

money market mutual funds
Funds that sell units to individuals and use this money to invest in cash and investments that can be converted to cash quickly (very liquid investments).

Mutual funds can be broadly distinguished according to the securities in which they invest. Equity mutual funds sell units to individuals and use this money to invest in stocks. Bond mutual funds sell units to individuals and use this money to invest in bonds. Money market mutual funds sell units to individuals and use this money to invest in cash and investments that can be converted to cash quickly (very liquid investments). Money market funds were discussed in Chapter 4. Mutual funds employ portfolio managers who decide what securities to purchase; the individual investors do not select the investments themselves. The minimum initial investment in a mutual fund is usually between $500 and $5000, depending on the fund. Many mutual funds are subsidiaries of other types of financial institutions.

Advantages of Investing in Mutual Funds

Mutual funds offer a number of advantages over other types of investments. First, by investing in a mutual fund, you can invest in a broadly diversified portfolio with a small initial investment. If you have $1000 to invest, you (along with other investors) can own a portfolio of 100 or more stocks through a mutual fund. If you had attempted to buy stocks directly with your $1000, you might not have had enough money to buy even 100 shares of a single stock. Second, mutual funds provide professional money management. Your investments reflect the decisions of experienced professionals who have access to the best research available. Third, after your minimum initial investment, subsequent investment deposits into a mutual fund may be as low as $25. This allows investors to set up a deposit plan where they can invest regularly into a number of different funds. Fourth, mutual funds offer **marketability**, which means that you can redeem them through the issuing company easily. Finally, mutual funds simplify the process of record keeping because the mutual fund company will send you a statement on a regular basis.

marketability
The ease with which an investor can convert an investment into cash.

Disadvantages of Investing in Mutual Funds

There are a number of potential disadvantages of investing in mutual funds. First, the management fees and other costs associated with a mutual fund vary substantially among funds. It is important to understand the fees charged by any fund you invest in. Mutual fund fees are discussed later in this chapter. Second, the investment decisions for a mutual fund are made by the portfolio manager. As a mutual fund investor, you will have no control over the investments that are purchased and/or sold within the mutual fund. Third, although they are professional money managers, portfolio managers are only human. It is possible that you could invest in a well-diversified mutual fund that is invested in a group of poorly performing investments. Finally, other than with money market funds, liquidity can be very low. Liquidity refers to the ease with which the investor can convert the investment into cash without a loss of capital. You may need to redeem your units when the market conditions are not favourable. Many investors buy and sell mutual funds as a short-term investment. With the exception of money market funds, mutual funds are designed to be medium- to long-term investments and should not be used as a part of your emergency fund or other short-term needs.

liquidity
The ease with which the investor can convert the investment into cash without a loss of capital.

Net Asset Value per Unit

Each mutual fund's value can be determined by its net asset value (NAV), which rep-resents the market value of the securities that it has purchased minus any liabilities and fees owed. For example, suppose that a mutual fund owns 100 different stocks, including 10 000 shares of Canadian National Railway Company (CNR) that

net asset value (NAV)
The market value of the securities that a mutual fund has purchased minus any liabilities and fees owed.

are currently worth $60 per share. This mutual fund's holdings of CNR are worth $600 000 (computed as $60 × 10 000 shares) as of today. The value of the other 99 stocks owned by the fund is determined in the same manner, and all values are totalled. Then, any liabilities, such as expenses owed to the mutual fund's managers, are subtracted to determine the NAV.

net asset value per unit (NAVPU)
Calculated by dividing the NAV by the number of units in the fund.

The NAV is commonly reported on a per-unit basis. The net asset value per unit (NAVPU) is calculated by dividing the NAV by the number of units in the fund. Each day, the market value of all of the mutual fund's assets is determined. Any interest or dividends earned by the fund are added to the market value of the assets, and any expenses (such as mailing, marketing, and portfolio management) that are charged to the fund and any dividends distributed to the fund's unitholders (investors) are deducted. As the value of the mutual fund's portfolio increases, so does the fund's NAVPU.

Exhibit 12.1 shows how a mutual fund works. In this exhibit, an equity mutual fund receives $5000 from new investors. The mutual fund manager uses this money to purchase shares of stock. To help them keep track of their investment, each investor is given units in the mutual fund. Assume that the mutual fund issues 500 total units. The NAVPU would be calculated as:

$$\text{NAVPU} = \text{Net Asset Value (NAV)} \div \text{Number of Units Outstanding}$$
$$= \$5000 \div 500$$
$$= \$10$$

Since one unit is worth $10 and Investor G invested $2000, this investor would receive 200 units. An increase in NAV will result in an increase in NAVPU. A decrease in NAV will result in a decrease in NAVPU.

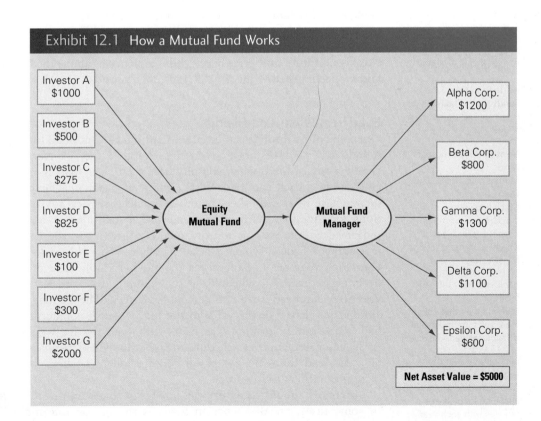

Exhibit 12.1   How a Mutual Fund Works

Open-End versus Closed-End Funds

Mutual funds are classified as either open-end funds or closed-end funds.

open-end mutual funds
Funds that sell units directly to investors and will redeem those units whenever investors wish to "cash" in.

Open-End Funds. Open-end mutual funds sell units directly to investors and will redeem those units whenever investors wish to "cash" in. The funds are managed by investment companies that are commonly subsidiaries of a larger financial conglomerate. CIBC, Royal Bank, Great-West Life, and many other financial institutions have investment company subsidiaries that operate open-end mutual funds. Many investment companies operate a family, or group, of separately managed open-end mutual funds. For example, Fidelity, AGF, and Altamira manage several different open-end funds, each of which has its own investment objective or purpose. By offering a diverse set of mutual funds, these investment companies satisfy investors with many different investment preferences.

Consider an open-end equity mutual fund that receives $5 million today as new investors purchase units of the fund. In addition, today some investors who had previously purchased units decide to redeem them, resulting in $3 million in redemptions in the fund. In this example, the equity mutual fund has a net difference of $2 million of new money that its portfolio managers will invest.

On some days, the value of redemptions may exceed the value of new units purchased. Mutual fund managers typically maintain a small portion of the fund's portfolio in the form of cash or liquid securities so that they have sufficient liquidity when redemptions exceed new unit purchases. Otherwise, they may be required to sell some stocks in their portfolio to obtain the necessary money for redemptions.

closed-end funds
Funds that sell units to investors but will not redeem these units; instead, the fund's units are traded on a stock exchange.

premium
The amount by which a closed-end fund's unit price in the secondary market is above the fund's NAVPU.

discount
The amount by which a closed-end fund's unit price in the secondary market is below the fund's NAVPU.

Closed-End Funds. Closed-end funds issue units to investors when the funds are first created, but do not redeem those units. Unlike an open-end fund, units of a closed-end fund are traded on a stock exchange. Thus, the fund does not sell new units upon demand to investors and does not allow investors to redeem units. The market price per unit is determined by the demand for units versus the supply of units that are being sold. The price per unit of a closed-end fund can differ from the fund's NAVPU. A closed-end fund's unit price may exhibit a premium (above the NAVPU) in some periods and a discount (below the NAVPU) in other periods.

no-load mutual funds
Funds that sell directly to investors and do not charge a fee.

front-end load mutual funds
Mutual funds that charge a fee at the time of purchase, which is paid to stockbrokers or other financial service advisers who execute transactions for investors.

back-end load mutual funds
Mutual funds that charge a fee if units are redeemed within a set period of time.

declining redemption schedule
A fee schedule where the back-end load charge reduces with each year an investor holds the fund.

Load versus No-Load Funds

Open-end mutual funds can be either load funds or no-load funds. No-load mutual funds sell directly to investors and do not charge a fee. Conversely, load mutual funds charge a fee (or load) when you purchase them. The load charge can be either a front-end load or a back-end load. With a front-end load mutual fund, a fee is paid at the time of purchase to stockbrokers or other financial service advisers who execute transactions for investors. With a back-end load mutual fund, a fee is charged if units are redeemed within a set period of time. The amount of the fee is based on a declining redemption schedule, which is a fee schedule where the back-end load charge reduces with each year an investor holds the fund. Exhibit 12.2 provides an example of a declining redemption schedule. In this exhibit, if a fund is redeemed within the first year after purchase, a fee of 6 percent is charged. The fee may be based on the original amount purchased or the value of the fund when it is redeemed. If this same investor had waited until the fund was in its fifth year, the fee would have been 2 percent. A declining redemption schedule may be anywhere from 5 to 10 years in length. Since no-load funds do not pay a commission to brokers, brokers are less likely to recommend them to investors.

Investors should recognize the impact of loads on their investment performance. In some cases, the difference in loads is the reason one mutual fund outperforms another.

Exhibit 12.2 Declining Redemption Schedule

Year Funds Are Redeemed	Deferred Sales Charge
Within the first year	6%
In the second year	5%
In the third year	4%
In the fourth year	3%
In the fifth year	2%
In the sixth year	1%
After the sixth year	0%

Source: The Canadian Securities Institute, *The Canadian Securities Course: Volume 2*, page 10-9, 2004. Reprinted with permission of CSI Global Education Inc.

EXAMPLE

You have $5000 to invest in a mutual fund. You have a choice of investing in a no-load fund by sending your investment directly to the fund, or purchasing a mutual fund that has a 4 percent front-end load and has been recommended by a broker. Each fund has an NAV of $20 per unit and their equity portfolios are very similar. You expect each fund's NAVPU will be $22 at the end of the year, which would represent a 10 percent return on the prevailing NAV of $20 per unit (assuming there are no dividends or capital gain distributions over the year). You plan to sell the mutual fund in one year. If the NAVPU for each fund changes as expected, your return for each fund will be as shown in Exhibit 12.3.

Exhibit 12.3 Comparison of Returns from a No-Load Fund and a Front-End Load Fund

No-Load Fund	
Invest $5000 in the mutual fund	$5000
Your investment converts to 250 shares	− $0
	$5000
	÷ $20
$5000/$20 per share = 250 shares	250 shares
End of Year 1: You redeem shares for $22 per share	× $22
Amount received = 250 shares × $22 = $5500	$5500
Return = ($5500 − $5000)/$5000 = 10%	10%
Front-End Load Fund	
Invest $5000; 4% of $5000 (or $200) goes to the broker	$5000
	− $200
The remaining 96% of $5000 (or $4800) is used to purchase 240 shares	$4800 ÷ $20
$4800/$20 per share = 240 shares	240 shares
You redeem shares for $22 per share	× $22
Amount received = 240 shares × $22 = $5280	$5280
Return = ($5280 − $5000)/$5000 = 5.6%	5.6%

Notice that you would earn a return of 10 percent on the no-load fund versus 5.6 percent on the front-end load fund. While the load fund's portfolio generated a 10 percent return, your return is less because of the load fee. Based on this analysis, you decide to purchase units of the no-load fund.

Studies on mutual funds have found that no-load funds perform at least as well as load funds on average, even when ignoring the commission paid on a load fund. When considering the commission, no-load funds have outperformed load funds on average.

Given this information, why do some investors purchase load funds? They may believe that specific load funds will generate high returns and outperform other no-load funds, even after considering the commission that is charged. Or, perhaps some investors who rely on their brokers for advice do not consider no-load funds. Some investors may purchase load funds because they do not realize that no-load funds exist or do not know how to invest in them. To invest in no-load funds, you can simply call a 1-800 number for an application or print the application off a fund's website. As with any funds, though, the investor should review the fee structure, as there are many differences in how no-load funds charge fees.

Management Expense Ratio (MER)

As mentioned earlier in this chapter, mutual funds incur expenses, including administrative, legal, and clerical expenses and portfolio management costs. Some mutual funds have much higher expenses than others. These expenses are incurred by the fund's unitholders because the fund's NAVPU (which is what investors receive when redeeming their units) accounts for the expenses incurred. Investors should review the annual expenses of any mutual funds in which they invest. In particular, they should focus on each fund's **management expense ratio (MER)**, which measures the annual expenses incurred by a fund on a percentage basis, calculated as annual expenses of the fund divided by the net asset value of the fund; the result of this calculation is then divided by the number of units outstanding. An expense ratio of 1 percent means that unitholders incur annual expenses amounting to 1 percent of the value of the fund. The higher the expense ratio, the lower the return for a given level of portfolio performance. Mutual funds that incur more expenses are worthwhile only if they offer a high enough return to offset the extra expenses. MERs for no-load funds can be higher than those for load funds.

On average, mutual funds have an MER of about 2.68 percent. The MERs of mutual funds can be found in various financial newspapers and on many financial websites.

management expense ratio (MER)
The annual expenses incurred by a fund on a percentage basis, calculated as annual expenses of the fund divided by the net asset value of the fund; the result of this calculation is then divided by the number of units outstanding.

Reported Components of MERs. The components of MERs include management expenses, dealer/adviser compensation, administrative costs, and GST. The management expenses represent the costs incurred for investment research, portfolio management, marketing costs, and profit. The dealer/adviser compensation includes, among other things, fees paid to advisers and salespeople. The third component of the expense ratio, administrative costs, includes general business expenses such as transaction processing, client reporting, and audit and legal fees. MERs do not include brokerage commissions and related expenses, as they are incurred with the purchase and sale of the investment of the portfolio and are already accounted for in the NAV.

Relationship between Expense Ratios and Performance. Research has shown that mutual funds with relatively low expenses tend to outperform other funds with similar objectives. This finding suggests that mutual funds with higher expenses cannot justify their MERs.

Some funds will have higher costs than others because of their objectives. An equity fund with the objective of aggressive growth will have higher costs than an equity fund with an income objective. Global and international funds are often the most expensive of all funds because of additional research costs and currency costs.

IN-CLASS NOTES

Background on Mutual Funds

- Advantages
  - Diversified portfolio
  - Professional management
  - Marketability
  - Simplified record keeping
- Disadvantages
  - Management fees
  - Lack of control
  - Portfolio manager performance may be poor
  - Liquidity may be low
- Open-end vs. closed-end funds
- Front-end load vs. back-end load vs. no-load
- Management expense ratio (MER)

_____

_____

_____

_____

_____

_____

TYPES OF MUTUAL FUNDS

Investors can select from a wide array of mutual funds, including equity mutual funds and bond mutual funds. Each category includes many types of funds to suit the preferences of individual investors.

Types of Equity Mutual Funds

Open-end equity mutual funds are commonly classified according to their investment objectives. If you consider investing in an equity mutual fund, you must decide on the type of fund in which you wish to invest. Some of the more common investment objectives are described here.

Growth Funds. Growth funds focus on stocks that have potential for above-average growth.

Small Capitalization (Small-Cap) Funds. Small capitalization (small-cap) funds focus on firms that are relatively small. Smaller firms tend to have more potential for growth than larger firms.

Mid-Size Capitalization (Mid-Cap) Funds. Mid-size capitalization (mid-cap) funds focus on medium-size firms. These firms tend to be more established than small-cap firms, but may have less growth potential. Mid-cap firms may have more growth potential than large-cap firms.

Dividend Funds. Dividend funds focus on firms that pay a high level of dividends. These firms tend to exhibit less growth because they use a relatively large portion of their earnings to pay dividends rather than reinvesting earnings for expansion. The firms normally have less potential for high capital gains and exhibit less risk. These large-cap firms represent mature industries.

Balanced Growth and Income Funds. Balanced growth and income funds contain both growth stocks and stocks that pay high dividends. This type of fund distributes dividends periodically, while offering more potential for an increase in the fund's value than a dividend fund.

sector funds
Mutual funds that focus on stocks in a specific industry or sector, such as technology stocks.

Sector Funds. Sector funds focus on stocks in a specific industry or sector, such as technology stocks. Investors who expect a specific industry to perform well may invest in a sector fund. Sector funds enable investors with a small amount of funds to invest in a diversified portfolio of stocks within a particular sector. Sector funds are more risky, as they are less diversified. Sector funds should be used with discretion.

An example of a sector fund is a technology fund, which focuses on stocks of Internet-based firms. Most of these firms are relatively young. They have potential for very high returns, but also exhibit a high degree of risk because they do not have a consistent record of earnings.

index funds
Mutual funds that attempt to mirror the movements of an existing equity index.

Index Funds. Index funds are mutual funds that attempt to mirror the movements of an existing equity index. Investors who invest in an index fund should earn returns similar to what they would receive if they actually invested in all stocks in the index. For example, CIBC offers a mutual fund containing a set of stocks that moves in the same manner as the S&P TSX Composite Index. It may not contain every stock in the index, but it is still able to mimic the index's movement.

Index funds have become very popular because of their performance relative to other mutual funds. They incur fewer expenses than a typical mutual fund because they are not actively managed. The index fund does not incur expenses for researching various stocks because it is intended simply to mimic an index. In addition, the fund's portfolio is not frequently revised. Consequently, index funds incur very low transaction costs, which can enhance performance. Index funds have relatively lower MERs when compared to other mutual funds. However, there can be tracking errors, and any fees or costs will affect the return of these funds.

Index funds can also offer tax advantages. Since they engage in less trading than most other mutual funds, they generate limited capital gains (which must be distributed to unitholders). Index funds composed of stocks that do not pay dividends are especially valuable because they do not have dividend income that must be distributed to unitholders.

Much research has found that the performance of portfolios managed by portfolio managers is frequently lower than the performance of an existing equity index. Thus, investors may be better off investing in an index fund rather than investing in an actively managed portfolio.

EXAMPLE

You consider investing in either a no-load mutual fund that focuses on growth stocks or an index mutual fund. When ignoring expenses incurred by the mutual funds, you expect that the growth fund will generate an annual return of 9 percent versus an annual return of 8 percent for the index fund. The growth fund has an MER of 2.5 percent, versus an MER of 0.85 percent for the index fund. Based on your expectations about the portfolio returns, your returns would be:

	Growth Fund	Index Fund
Fund's portfolio return (before expenses)	9.0%	8.0%
Expense ratio	2.5%	0.85%
Your annual return	**6.5%**	**7.15%**

The comparison shows that the index fund can generate a higher return for you than the other fund even if its portfolio return is lower. Based on this analysis, you should invest in the index fund.

International Equity Funds. International equity funds focus on firms that are based outside Canada. Some of these funds focus on firms in a specific country, while others focus on a specific region or continent. Funds with a country or regional concentration are attractive to investors who want to invest in a specific country, but prefer to rely on an experienced portfolio manager to select the stocks. The expenses associated with managing a portfolio are higher for international mutual funds than for other mutual funds because monitoring foreign firms from Canada is expensive. In addition, transaction costs associated with buying and selling stocks of foreign firms are higher.

Some mutual funds invest in stocks of both foreign firms and Canadian firms. These are called "global mutual funds" to distinguish them from international mutual funds. Any fund that invests outside of Canada incurs a special risk in foreign currency. While choice in investments may be spectacular, gains can be wiped out because of changes in the value of the Canadian dollar relative to those currencies.

Ethical Funds. Ethical funds screen out firms viewed as offensive by some investors. For example, they may not invest in firms that produce cigarettes or guns or that pollute the environment.

Other Types of Equity Funds. The types of mutual funds described here can be further subdivided, as funds have proliferated to satisfy the preferences of investors. As an example, some growth equity funds focus on small firms while others concentrate on large ones. Investors who desire stock in large firms that are expected to grow would consider investing in large-cap growth funds. Investors who desire stock in small firms that are expected to grow would consider investing in small-cap growth funds.

L.O. 3 Types of Bond Mutual Funds

Investors can also select a bond fund that satisfies their investment objectives. The more popular types of bond funds are identified here.

Canadian Bond Funds. Canadian bond funds focus on investments in Canadian bonds. The types of investments held within a Canadian bond fund vary significantly. Some bond funds focus on bonds issued by the federal government or a federal Crown corporation. Other bond funds will have a large portion of their portfolio invested in bonds issued by provincial governments or municipalities. Still other bond funds will focus on bonds issued by high-quality firms that tend to have a low degree of default risk, while others focus on high-risk bonds.

High-Yield Bond Funds. High-yield bond funds focus on relatively risky bonds issued by firms that may have a higher default risk. These bond funds tend to offer a higher expected return than Canadian bond funds because of the high yields offered to compensate for the higher potential default risk.

Index Bond Funds. Index bond funds are intended to mimic the performance of a specified bond index. For example, Barclays Global Investors offers six different Canadian bond index funds:

- a Canadian bond index fund that tracks an aggregate (broad) bond index,

- a Canadian corporate bond index fund that tracks a corporate bond index,

- a Canadian government bond index fund that tracks a government bond index,

- a Canadian short-term bond index fund that tracks an index representing bonds with one to five years until maturity,

- a Canadian real return bond index fund that tracks an index representing real return bonds, and

- a Canadian long-term bond fund that tracks an index representing bonds with more than 10 years until maturity.

global bond funds
Mutual funds that focus on bonds issued by non-Canadian firms or governments.

exchange rate risk
The risk that the value of a bond may drop if the currency denominating the bond weakens against the Canadian dollar.

Global Bond Funds. Global bond funds focus on bonds issued by non-Canadian firms or governments. Some global bonds are attractive to Canadian investors because they offer higher yields than Canadian bonds. They are subject to exchange rate risk along with the other risks associated with bonds. If the currency denominating a foreign bond weakens against the Canadian dollar, the value of the foreign bond is reduced and the global bond fund's performance is adversely affected. Also, expenses incurred by global bond funds tend to be higher than those of domestic bond funds because of costly international transactions. Although the emphasis in a global bond fund is to invest in bonds issued by non-Canadian firms and governments, most global bond funds invest a portion of their assets in Canadian bonds.

Like other bond funds, global bond funds are exposed to interest rate risk. Foreign bond prices are influenced by the interest rate of the country denominating the bond in the same way that Canadian bond prices are influenced by Canadian interest rate movements. When the interest rate of the country denominating the bonds increases, bond prices decline. Conversely, when the interest rate of the country decreases, prices of bonds denominated in that country increase.

Maturity Classifications. Each type of bond fund can be segmented further by the range of maturities held in the fund. For example, some Canadian bond funds are classified as short-term (one to five years), medium-term (five to 10 years), or long-term (10-plus years). Other bond funds may also be segmented in this manner.

IN-CLASS NOTES

Types of Mutual Funds	
Equity	**Bond**
Growth	Canadian
Small-cap and mid-cap	High-yield
Dividend	Index
Balanced growth and income	Global
Sector	
Index	
International	
Ethical	

RETURN AND RISK OF A MUTUAL FUND

Investors purchase units of a mutual fund so that they can receive a reasonable return on their investment. However, you must balance the expected return with the fund's risk, which reflects the uncertainty surrounding the expected return. Before you purchase a mutual fund you should set your objectives in terms of expected return and the risk you can tolerate.

Return from Investing in a Mutual Fund

A mutual fund can generate returns for its investors (unitholders) in four different ways: interest income distributions, dividend distributions, capital gain distributions, and capital gain distributions from redeeming units. A mutual fund that receives interest income, dividends, or capital gains must distribute these payments to its investors in the same year. However, investors are normally given the opportunity to choose whether to receive these distributions in the form of a cash payment or as additional units (which means that the distributions are reinvested to buy more units of the fund).

Go to
http://globefunddb.
theglobeandmail.com/
gishome/plsql/gis.
show_5star_rep

This website provides up-to-date information on mutual funds that have received a five-star rating from Globefund.

Capital Gain from Redeeming Units.   You earn a capital gain if you redeem units of a mutual fund when the price exceeds the price at which you purchased the units. For example, if you purchased 200 units of an equity mutual fund at a price of $25 per unit and sell them for $30 per unit, your capital gain will be:

Capital Gain = (Selling Price per Unit − Purchase Price per Unit) × Number of Units

$$= (\$30 - \$25) \times 200$$

$$= \$1000$$

Determining your capital gain is more difficult when you have reinvested distributions into the fund because each distribution results in the purchase of more units at the prevailing price on that day. The capital gain on the units purchased at the time of the distribution depends on the price you paid for them. Many investors rely on the mutual fund to report their capital gain after they redeem the units. Now that many mutual fund companies allow you to review your account online, finding price information is easy. Recall from Chapter 3 that only 50 percent of a capital gain is taxable.

Returns vary among equity mutual funds in any particular period. While they are normally affected by the general stock market conditions, equity mutual funds' returns could vary with the specific sector or industry in which the stocks are concentrated. For example, technology stocks performed better than other types of stocks in the late 1990s, so mutual funds focusing on technology stocks performed well at that time. In the 2001 to 2003 period, stocks as a group did not perform well. Because of the significant rise in price that technology stocks had experienced in the 1990s (resulting more from speculation than from actual increases in earnings), the price declines were even greater than for non-technology stocks. The same mutual funds whose performance was enhanced in the 1990s by focusing on technology stocks now suffered the greatest decline in performance.

Since the returns are highly dependent on the performance of the sector in which the equity mutual fund is concentrated, be careful when comparing mutual funds. The difference between the performances of two equity mutual funds during a particular period may be attributed to the sector rather than to the skill of the funds' managers. Some investors tend to invest in whatever equity mutual fund performed well recently because they presume that the fund has the best portfolio managers. However, if the fund performed well simply because its sector performed well, it would be a mistake to judge the management based on past performance.

Risk from Investing in an Equity Mutual Fund

market risk
The susceptibility of a mutual fund's performance to general market conditions.

Although different types of equity mutual funds experience different performance levels in a given time period, they are all influenced by general stock market conditions. The performance of an equity mutual fund depends on the general movements in stock prices. When the stock market is weak, prices of stocks held by an equity fund decrease and the NAVPU of the fund declines as well. This susceptibility of a mutual fund's performance to general market conditions is often referred to as market risk.

Focus on Ethics: Risk from Investing in Hedge Funds

hedge funds
Limited partnerships that manage portfolios of funds for wealthy individuals and financial institutions.

Hedge funds are limited partnerships that manage portfolios of funds for wealthy individuals and financial institutions. They sell units and use the proceeds to invest in various securities. In this way, they serve a similar purpose to mutual funds, yet they are often structured as limited partnerships in which investors have little or no control of the company's management. An investor must be classified as either an accredited investor or a sophisticated investor to invest in a hedge fund. The investor's income level, net worth, and investment knowledge are used to determine whether they fit one of these two classifications. Hedge funds are not regulated by a securities commission. While they strive to earn very high returns, they tend to make very risky investments that can lead to extremely poor returns. Hedge funds may invest not only in risky stocks, but also in a wide variety of investments, including silver or other metals. They may engage in short selling, the practice

of selling securities not currently owned and buying these securities back at a later date. This strategy is designed to take advantage of overvalued securities. If the security's price declines, the funds will earn a high return, but if the security's price rises, they will experience a large loss. Hedge funds also commonly buy stocks on margin by supporting their investment with borrowed funds. This strategy will increase the magnitude of the gain or the loss on the investment. The number of hedge fund strategies available to qualified investors is difficult to quantify. In general, hedge fund investing should not be a part of your core investment strategy.

Trade-Off between Expected Return and Risk of Equity Funds

Some investors are willing to tolerate risk from investing in an equity mutual fund when they expect that the mutual fund may offer a very high return. The trade-off between the expected return and the risk of an equity mutual fund is shown in Exhibit 12.4. On the conservative side, a dividend fund represents firms that pay a high level of dividends. As mentioned earlier, these firms tend to exhibit less growth because they use a relatively large portion of their earnings to pay dividends rather than reinvesting earnings for expansion. Thus, the fund's expected return is somewhat limited, but so is its risk. However, income funds such as dividend funds are subject to interest rate risk. A growth equity fund offers potential for higher returns than a dividend fund, but it also has more risk (more potential for a large decline in value). On the aggressive side, a fund that invests only in growth stocks of small firms has potential for a very high return, but it also exhibits high risk. A fund that invests within one sector (such as a technology fund) has even more potential return and risk.

Risk from Investing in a Bond Mutual Fund

Although different types of bond mutual funds will experience different performance levels in a given time period, they are all influenced by general bond market conditions. The performance of a bond mutual fund depends on the general movements in interest

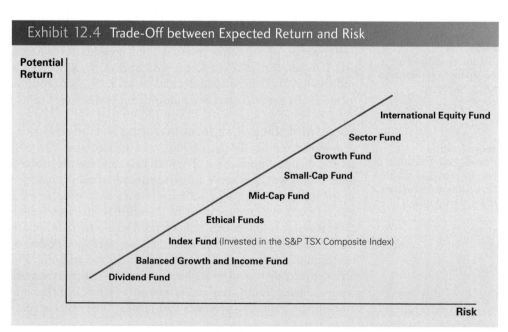

Exhibit 12.4 Trade-Off between Expected Return and Risk

Potential Return

International Equity Fund
Sector Fund
Growth Fund
Small-Cap Fund
Mid-Cap Fund
Ethical Funds
Index Fund (Invested in the S&P TSX Composite Index)
Balanced Growth and Income Fund
Dividend Fund

Risk

rates. When interest rates rise, prices of bonds held by a bond fund decrease, and the NAVPU of the fund declines. This susceptibility to interest rate movements is often referred to as interest rate risk.

interest rate risk
The risk that occurs because of changes in the interest rate. This risk affects funds that invest in debt securities and other income-oriented securities.

The prices of all bonds change in response to interest rate movements, but the prices of longer-term bonds are the most sensitive. Thus, investors who want to reduce exposure to interest rate movements can select a bond fund that focuses on bonds with short terms to maturity. Conversely, investors who want to capitalize on an expected decline in interest rate movements can select a bond fund that focuses on long-term bonds.

The performance of many bond mutual funds also depends on the default risk of the individual bond holdings. Bond funds that invest most of their money in bonds with a high degree of default risk tend to offer a higher potential return to investors, but also exhibit a high degree of risk. Under favourable economic conditions, the issuers of those bonds may be able to cover their payments, and the bond funds will consequently perform very well. If economic conditions are weak, however, some of the bond issuers may default on their payments, and these bond funds will provide relatively low or even negative returns to their unitholders.

Some bond funds, such as those that invest primarily in bonds issued and guaranteed by the federal government or a Crown corporation, have no (or low) default risk and a high level of interest rate risk. Other bond funds, such as short-term high-yield bond funds, have a low level of interest rate risk and a high level of default risk. Some bond funds, such as long-term high-yield bond funds, are highly exposed to both default risk and interest rate risk.

Trade-Off between Expected Return and Risk of Bond Funds

On the conservative side, a bond fund that holds Government of Canada bonds with a short term remaining until maturity has no exposure to default risk and limited exposure to interest rate risk. Thus, the prices of the bonds it holds are not very sensitive to external forces, so the NAVPU of the fund will not be very sensitive to these forces. The expected return on this fund is relatively low as compared to other funds. A high-yield bond fund that invests only in high-yield bonds with long terms to maturity has the potential for a very high return. Its value is subject to default risk, however, because the high-yield bonds could default. It is also subject to a high level of interest rate risk because of the long-term maturities. A bond fund that invests in bonds issued by risky firms in a small foreign country has even more potential return and risk.

IN-CLASS NOTES

Return and Risk of a Mutual Fund

- Return
  - Distributions: interest income, dividends, capital gain
  - Redemptions: capital gain
- Risk
  - All equity mutual funds are influenced by general stock market conditions
  - All bond mutual funds are influenced by interest rate risk
  - Most bond mutual funds are influenced by default risk

_____

_____

_____

_____

_____

_____

_____

L.O. 4   DECIDING AMONG MUTUAL FUNDS

Your decision to purchase a specific mutual fund should be made once you determine your investment objectives, evaluate your risk tolerance, and decide on the fund characteristics you want. The final step is to search for mutual funds that exhibit those desired characteristics.

Determining Your Preferred Mutual Fund Characteristics

When identifying the type of mutual fund you want, you will want to consider various fund characteristics.

Minimum Initial Investment. If you have a relatively small amount to invest (such as $1000), you should limit your choices to mutual funds whose initial investment is equal to or less than that amount. As mentioned earlier, many funds allow smaller subsequent investments if you decide to make regular contributions to your account.

Investment Objective (Type of Fund). You must identify your investment goals. First, determine whether you are interested in an equity mutual fund or a bond mutual fund. If you want your investment to have high potential for increasing value over time, you should consider growth funds. If you want periodic income, you should consider bond funds or other "income-oriented" funds. Then, once you select an equity fund or a bond fund, you should select the particular type of fund that will match your investment objective. Funds vary according to their potential return and their risk, as mentioned earlier.

Investment Company. Whatever your investment objective, there are probably many investment companies that offer a suitable fund. One way to choose an investment company is by assessing the past performance of the type of mutual funds you are considering. Past performance is not necessarily a good indicator of future performance, however. A better approach may be to compare fees and expenses on the funds you are considering along with returns and risks. In addition, you should compare the funds' MERs, since some investment companies charge much lower expenses than others.

Reviewing a Mutual Fund's Simplified Prospectus

simplified prospectus
A document that provides financial information about a mutual fund, including expenses and past performance.

For any mutual fund that you consider, you should obtain a simplified prospectus, which is a document that provides financial information about the fund, including expenses and past performance. When you initially purchase a mutual fund, a simplified prospectus must be provided to you within 48 hours of your purchase. In many cases, you may be able to download the prospectus from the Internet. The prospectus contains considerable information, as described below.

investment objective
In a prospectus, a brief statement about the general goal of the mutual fund.

Investment Objective. The investment objective is a brief statement about the general goal of the mutual fund, such as capital appreciation (increase in value) of stocks and achieving returns that exceed that of the S&P TSX Composite Index or some other index.

investment strategy
In a prospectus, a summary of the types of securities that are purchased by the mutual fund to achieve its objective.

Investment Strategy. The investment strategy (also called investment policy) summarizes the types of securities that are purchased by the mutual fund to achieve its objective. For example, a fund's investment strategy may be to focus on large stocks, technology stocks, stocks that have a high level of growth, foreign stocks, Government of Canada bonds, corporate bonds, or other securities.

Past Performance. The prospectus will include the return on the fund over recent periods (such as the previous year, three years, and five years). The performance is normally compared to a corresponding equity index (such as the S&P TSX Composite) or bond index, which is important since performance should be based on a comparison to general market movements. An equity mutual fund that earned a 15 percent annual return would normally be rated as a high performer, but during the late 1990s such a return would have been relatively low when compared to the stock market in general. Although the past performance offers some insight into the ability of the fund's managers to select stocks, it will not necessarily persist in the future.

Fees and Expenses. The prospectus will provide a breakdown of the following fees and expenses:

- The maximum front-end load imposed on purchases of the fund's units.

- The redemption fee or back-end load (if any) imposed when investors redeem units.

- Expenses incurred by the fund, including management fees resulting from monitoring the fund's portfolio, distribution fees resulting from the fund's advertising costs, and marketing costs that are paid to brokers who recommend the fund to investors. A fund can be classified as a no-load fund and still have substantial advertising and marketing fees.

The most important expense statistic mentioned in the prospectus is the management expense ratio. Since it adjusts for the size of the fund, you can compare the efficiency of various mutual funds. The MER may also be converted into the actual expenses you would be charged if you had invested a specified amount in the fund (such as $1000). The MER may be as low as 1 percent for some funds and more than 5 percent for others. MERs can change over time, so you should monitor them when investing in a mutual fund.

Risk. The prospectus of an equity fund typically states that the fund is subject to market risk, or the possibility of a general decline in the stock market, which can cause a decline in the value of the mutual fund. In addition, the prices of individual stocks within the fund may experience substantial declines in response to firm-specific problems. Bond funds normally mention their exposure to interest rate risk and default risk. These risks are stated so that investors understand that there is some uncertainty surrounding the future performance of the mutual fund and that the value of the mutual fund can decline over time.

Distribution of Interest Income, Dividends, and Capital Gains. The prospectus explains how frequently the mutual fund makes distributions to investors. Most funds distribute their interest income and dividends to their unitholders quarterly and distribute their capital gains once a year (usually in December). The prospectus also describes the means by which interest income, dividends, and capital gains are distributed.

Minimum Investment and Minimum Balance. The prospectus states the minimum investment that can be made in the fund. In addition, it may require you to maintain a minimum balance, as it is costly for a fund to maintain an account that has a very small balance.

How to Buy or Redeem Units. The prospectus explains that you can invest in the fund by sending a cheque along with a completed application form (which is normally attached to the prospectus). If the mutual fund is part of a family of funds operated by a single investment company, the prospectus explains that you can call the investment company to transfer money from one fund to another within the family. The prospectus also explains how you can redeem your units.

Making the Decision

Once you have narrowed your list to a small number of possible mutual funds, you can create a table to compare the important characteristics. This process will help you select the mutual fund that will best satisfy your preferences.

EXAMPLE

Stephanie Spratt has $2000 to invest. She is interested in investing in both stocks and bonds. Since she has limited funds to invest at this time, a mutual fund is an attractive option. She wants to invest in stocks, but also wants to keep her expenses low. She creates a list of possible mutual funds that focus on technology stocks and require a minimum investment of $1000 that would satisfy her preferences. Using a prospectus for each fund, which she downloaded online, she assesses the load fees, MERs, and past performances of the funds:

Mutual Fund	Load Status	MER	Recent Annual Performance
1	Back-end load	2.5%	13%
2	No-load	1.8%	12%
3	No-load	3.5%	14%
4	3% front-end load	3.2%	11%

Stephanie immediately eliminates #4 because of its front-end load and high MER. She then removes #1 because it is a back-end load fund. She also removes #3 from consideration because of its high MER. She selects #2 because it is a no-load fund and has a relatively low expense ratio. Stephanie then reviews returns earned by the funds over different periods of time to ensure consistency. A conservative fund should not have a wide variance in returns over a 3-month, 6-month, and 12-month period. Returns over greater time spans should be reviewed as well.

Stephanie also wants to invest $1000 in a bond mutual fund. She is considering bond funds that contain at least AA-rated government and corporate bonds. She is concerned about interest rate risk because she expects that interest rates may rise. She creates a list of possible bond funds that allow a very small minimum investment and evaluates information from the prospectuses.

Bond Fund	Load Status	MER	Typical Terms to Maturity
1	Back-end load	2.0%	6–8 years
2	No-load	2.0%	6–8 years
3	No-load	1.8%	5–7 years
4	No-load	2.2%	5–7 years

Stephanie eliminates #1 because it has a back-end load. She eliminates #2 because it focuses on bonds with long terms to maturity. She removes #4 from consideration because it has a relatively high MER in comparison with #3. She decides to invest in #3 because it is a no-load fund, has a low MER, and its bonds have a relatively short term to maturity, which reduces the amount of interest rate risk. She also prefers bond fund #3 because it is in the same family of mutual funds as the equity mutual fund she just selected. Thus, she can easily transfer money between these two mutual funds. Stephanie sends her completed application and a cheque for $2000 to the mutual fund company.

IN-CLASS NOTES

Deciding among Mutual Funds
- What is the minimum initial investment?
- What is the investment objective?
- What are the key characteristics of the investment company?
  - Past performance, MERs, and other fees
- Review the simplified prospectus
  - Investment objective
  - Investment strategy

L.O. 5   QUOTATIONS OF MUTUAL FUNDS

Go to
www.canadianbusiness.com/
my_money/index.jsp

Click on
Mutual Funds

This website provides
mutual fund information,
including articles, newsletters, testimonials, and much
more.

Financial newspapers such as the *National Post* publish price quotations of open-end mutual funds, as shown in Exhibit 12.5. As the Internet has grown in popularity, financial market data have found their way out of the printed page and onto newspaper websites. The *Financial Post* publishes the majority of its mutual fund data and related analysis tools on its website at www.financialpost.com/markets/market_data/index.html. In Exhibit 12.6, each fund's NAVPU is shown in the second column, the net dollar change in the NAVPU is shown in the third column, and the percent return over the year is shown in the fourth column. For example, MD Equity Fund has an NAVPU of $27.82. The net change in the NAVPU on the previous day was –0.09. The fund has generated a return of 5.7 percent since the calendar year started.

In any particular period, some types of mutual funds perform better than others. For example, in some years large-cap equities perform well while small-cap equities perform poorly. In other years, small-cap equities perform better than large-cap equities. When

Exhibit 12.5 Open-End Mutual Fund Price Quotations

Fund	NAVPS	$ ch	Yr % ch	Fund	NAVPS	$ ch	Yr % ch
GroPtA	7.28	+.04	+5.8	**GGOF Equity Funds-Mutual(n)**			
URDv A	27.49	+.19	−4.8	Div Growth	20.16	+.14	+6.8
Frnkln Tmpltn-Bissett-A(n)				**GGOF Income Funds-Mutual(n)**			
AlCdnFo A	17.78	+.12	+18.2	Hi Yld Bnd	9.79	+.04	+.2
Bond A	12.41	+.01	−2.3	Mthly Div	10.31	+.02	+2.9
Cdn Bal A	29.58	+.14	+1.2	Mthly Hiln	12.22	+.05	+11.0
Cdn Eq A	92.64	+.83	+9.3	Mthly Hinll	16.09	+.06	+11.1
Div Inc A	28.59	+.14	+2.0	**Great-West NL**			
Income A	16.77	+.06	+12.5	CdnRE 1 (G)7/12	197.47	+.04	+6.1
It Eq A	13.07	+.11	+1.7	**Highstreet**			
MMkCC A	10.00	−.06	−.2	Balanced	16.41	+.09	+5.2
SmlCapA	80.04	−.01	+5.7	Cdn Equity	32.12	+.37	+16.4
Frnkln Tmpltn-Franklin C$(n)				**HSBC Funds Inv Ser C$(n)**			
Stg IncA	7.64	+.01	−6.7	Balanced I	24.46	+.12	+2.9
Frnkln Tmpltn-MutualSer C$(n)				Div Inc I	32.92	+.21	+8.7
Beacon A	8.14	+.02	+5.9	MMF Inv	10.00	unch	+.2
Disc A	17.25	+.03	+10.2	**IA Clarington Invest C$(n)**			
frontier Alt Inv				Cdn Div CS	8.09	+.06	+7.5
Canada A	8.37	+.03	. . .	Cdn Income	7.31	+.03	+3.1
				Cdn SmCap	34.55	+.19	+15.3
World A	11.75	+.06	. . .	**IA Clarington Investments(n)**			
GBC Funds				R Div Inc	28.16	+.17	+10.2
GBCCdnGro7/10	56.29	. . .	. . .	**Ind Alllance-Cdn Equlty(n)**			
GGOF Diversified-Mutual(n)				CdnEqu val	43.85	+.32	+8.4
Div Mth In	13.10	+.04	+4.2	**Ind Alllance-Diversified(n)**			

(continued)

Exhibit 12.5 continued

Fund	NAVPS	$ ch	Yr % ch	Fund	NAVPS	$ ch	Yr % ch
Diversifi	30.18	+.13	+1.8	Japan Equ	9.88	+.09	−6.3
Ind Alllance-XN/A NewCont(n)				Merg & Acq	18.00	+.07	+6.8
Dividends	32.69	+.26	+8.5	Mtg&STInc	4.84	+.00	.0
Integra Funds				Mutual	19.57	+.11	+6.5
Divers7/12	40.45	+.12	. . .	N.A. Equ	23.63	+.21	+7.5
Inv Group/AGF(n)				PremiumMMF	10.00	+.01	. . .
Cdn Growth	21.99	+.18	+9.4	Real Prop	5.38	. . .	. . .
Inv Group/Alto Ser A(n)				Retire Gro	13.79	+.10	. . .
Moderate A	13.12	+.05	. . .	Retire Pl	8.51	+.04	. . .
Mthlyl&EGA	11.96	+.05	. . .	Summa	17.58	+.16	+13.1
Inv Group/FI(n)				Tact AA	7.13	+.04	. . .
FidCdnEqu	16.01	+.19	+14.6	USLgCapVal	63.94	+.45	−5.6
Inv Group/Mackenzle(n)				**Investors Group/Allegro (n)**			
Div Growth	20.09	+.15	+5.6	Mod Agg	11.82	+.06	. . .
Income	10.18	+.02	−2.0	ModAggCdFc	11.96	+.06	. . .
Investors Group(n)				Moderate	11.14	+.04	. . .
Cdn Bal	15.14	+.07	+7.7	**Legg Mason Funds I(n)**			
Cdn Bond	10.24	+.01	−2.1	Act Bond	23.38	+.04	−1.3
Cdn Equity	23.30	+.21	+10.6	Divers	189.97	+1.16	+4.8
Cdn HYI	9.71	+.01	+2.2	LM US Val	9.66	+.04	−2.9
Cdn LC Val	25.67	+.19	+10.7	**London Life Funds**			
Cdn MMF	1.00	unch	. . .	Adv Pr7/12	15.32	+.12	+3.1
Cdn NatRes	22.34	+.20	+13.5	Agg Pr	17.58	+.17	+5.1
Cdn SmlCap	28.69	+.09	+20.4	Bal Pr	14.94	+.08	+.6
Dividend	24.51	+.12	+2.4	Bond (LC)	265.21	−.81	−2.5
Euro Equ	17.08	−.02	+6.2	Cdn Equ(L)	691.92	+9.43	+10.5
Euro MC Eq	29.21	−.09	+8.2	CdnEqu (G)	20.83	+.34	+12.0
Glo Div C	11.37	+.03	−.7	Conserv Pr	14.36	+.01	−.3
Global	16.23	+.09	+5.9	Div (L)	28.09	+.33	+7.1
Govt Bond	5.01	+.01	−2.2	Divers (L)	250.44	+1.56	+1.8
Gro Plus	11.07	+.05	. . .	Equity (MF)	15.17	+.13	−1.4
Growth	14.49	+.10	. . .	Glo Eq (L)	9.73	+.10	−1.2
Inc Plus	7.85	+.02	. . .	Gr & Inc (MF)	15.37	+.10	−1.3
Income	5.57	+.01	. . .	Inc (L)	17.26	+.02	+.1

Source: National Post, April 10, 2007. Reprinted with permission of TSX Data Linx.

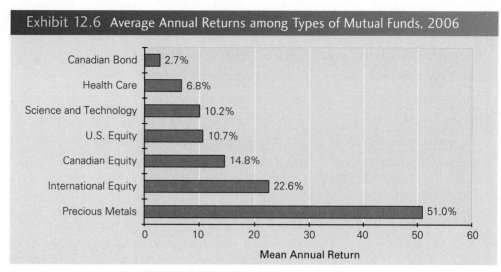

Exhibit 12.6   Average Annual Returns among Types of Mutual Funds, 2006

Source: theglobefund.com (http://globefunddb.theglobeandmail.com/) using data from the Mutual Funds, 2006 returns averaged from AGF Canadian Bond: Canadian Fixed Income; Altamira Health Sciences: Health Care Equity; AGF Global Technology Class: Science and Technology Equity; AGF American Growth Class: U.S. Equity; Acquity Canadian Equity Class: Canadian Equity; Acadian Core International Equity: International Equity; AGF Precious Metal: Precious Metals Equity. Reprinted with permission from The Globe and Mail.

investors want to assess the performance of a mutual fund, they compare the return on that fund to the average return for the same type of fund. In this way, investors can determine whether their mutual fund was managed effectively. Exhibit 12.5 shows the average annual return of various types of mutual funds. Notice that the average return varies substantially among types of mutual funds. Health care funds earned relatively low returns (5.6 percent) on average, while mutual funds focused on precious metals earned very high returns (44.1 percent) on average. Thus, if you owned a health care fund that earned a return of 10 percent in this period, the management of that fund was effective because the fund outperformed the average fund of that type. Conversely, if you owned a precious metals fund that earned a return of 30 percent in this period, your fund performed worse than the average fund in the category.

Various information sources indicate the benchmark performance levels you can use to evaluate your mutual funds. For example, the *Financial Post* indexes provide benchmark information on the performance of growth (FPX Growth), balanced (FPX Balanced), and income-oriented (FPX Income) portfolios. In addition, the newspaper's FP Markets section provides information on various North American and international indexes.

L.O. 6   DIVERSIFICATION AMONG MUTUAL FUNDS

If you plan to invest in more than one mutual fund, you may want to consider diversifying across several types of mutual funds to achieve a lower level of risk. When an equity mutual fund that contains large stocks is performing poorly, another equity mutual fund that contains small stocks may be performing well. Diversification benefits can be limited, though, since all equity funds are subject to stock market risk. Therefore, diversifying among equity mutual funds that invest in Canadian stocks has only limited effectiveness in reducing risk.

Diversification across bond mutual funds may result in less risk than investing in a bond fund that focuses only on long-term bonds. Virtually all bond funds are adversely affected by an increase in interest rates, however, so diversification among bond funds is not an effective means of reducing exposure to interest rate risk.

A more effective diversification strategy is to diversify across equity and bond mutual funds, as Stephanie Spratt chose to do earlier in this chapter. The returns of equity mutual funds and bond mutual funds are not highly correlated, so diversifying among equity and bond funds can be effective. When Canadian stock market conditions are poor, equity funds focused on Canadian stocks will perform poorly, but the bond

Exhibit 12.7   Diversifying among Mutual Funds That Are Primarily Affected by Different Factors

Your Return from Investing in:	Is Primarily Affected by:
Canadian growth equity fund	Canadian stock market
Canadian bond fund	Canadian interest rates
European equity fund	European stock markets and the value of the euro
Latin American equity fund	Latin American stock markets and the values of Latin American currencies
Australian bond fund	Australian interest rates and the value of the Australian dollar

funds may still perform well. If Canadian interest rates rise, the bond funds may perform poorly, but the equity funds may still perform well.

You may be able to reduce your overall risk further by diversifying among mutual funds that represent different countries. International equity funds tend to be susceptible to the market conditions of the countries (or regions) where the stocks are based and to the exchange rate movements of the currencies denominating those stocks against the Canadian dollar. Thus, the returns of international equity funds are less susceptible to Canadian stock market conditions but are susceptible to the market risk of their respective countries. International bonds are primarily influenced by the interest rates of their respective countries, so they are also less susceptible to Canadian interest rate movements.

Consider a strategy of investing in the portfolio of mutual funds listed in the first column of Exhibit 12.7. The primary factor that affects each mutual fund's return is shown in the second column. Notice that each fund is primarily affected by a different factor, so one adverse condition (such as a weak Canadian market) will have only a limited adverse effect on the overall portfolio of mutual funds. Any adverse conditions in a single country should affect only a mutual fund focused on that country.

L.O. 7   SEGREGATED FUNDS

Segregated funds are insurance products. However, the advantages and disadvantages of mutual funds that were discussed earlier in this chapter also hold true for segregated funds. In fact, it is very easy for an investor to mistake a segregated fund for a mutual fund. Since segregated funds are regulated through the insurance legislation of the province in which they are sold, there are a number of unique features that may make segregated funds an attractive alternative to mutual funds.

Principal Protection
Unlike mutual funds, segregated funds offer a guarantee on your deposits when the contract matures. A segregated fund contract usually matures 10 years after the date of purchase. At the time of maturity, the policy owner is guaranteed to receive at least 75 percent of his or her deposits back. In some cases, the deposit guarantee may be as high as 100 percent.

EXAMPLE   Carla invested $10 000 in a Canadian equity segregated fund on July 13, 1997. The maturity guarantee clause in her contract indicates that she will receive at least 100 percent of her deposits back at the end of the maturity period, which is 10 years. During these 10 years, the Canadian equity market fluctuated in value. At maturity, the market and the fund have decreased in value relative to where they were 10 years earlier. Carla's investment is now worth $8900. She will receive her remaining deposit of $8900 plus $1100 from the insurance company to cover the maturity guarantee. Notice that if Carla's maturity had been 75 percent, she would not receive any additional money from the insurance company unless her fund had decreased in value by more than $2500. If Carla leaves her money on deposit with the insurance company, a new 10-year guarantee period will start.

Death Benefit Guarantee

This feature of a segregated fund also offers principal protection. However, the determination of the value of the guarantee is made at the time of death of the policy owner instead of at the maturity date of the policy. The death benefit is usually between 75 and 100 percent of the amount invested. This benefit is particularly advantageous to older investors who still want to hold stocks in their portfolio. The segregated fund contract indicates the beneficiary of the policy. As a result, the death benefit can be paid directly to the beneficiary, thereby avoiding probate fees.

Creditor Protection

Since segregated fund contracts are legally considered insurance policies, they are normally exempt from seizure by creditors in the event that the policy owner declares bankruptcy. The money invested in a segregated fund is an asset of the insurance company, not of the policy owner. The policy owner owns a contract that outlines his or her rights with respect to the money that has been invested with the insurance company. Creditor protection can be a valuable benefit for business owners who deal with creditors on a regular basis.

Assessing the Value of Protection

On the surface, segregated funds offer investors the best of both worlds. Conservative investors can purchase an equity segregated fund with the knowledge that they will receive at least their deposit back at maturity. In the event of death, the segregated fund contract will contain a death benefit provision that may return up to 100 percent of the money invested to the policy owner's beneficiaries. In addition, business owners can protect their investment assets from creditors by investing their money in a segregated fund or a portfolio of segregated funds. Since a segregated fund is regulated by provincial insurance legislation, probate fees can be avoided. Exhibit 12.8 compares the effect of different guarantees on the MER for segregated funds and mutual funds. Although the fund names in Exhibit 12.8 are fictitious, the MERs reflect the actual costs that an investor would incur if they considered mutual and/or segregated fund investments offered by a leading Canadian manufacturer of investment funds. For example, the Canadian Value Segregated Fund that offers a 100 percent maturity and death benefit guarantee has an MER of 5.13 percent; whereas the same segregated fund with a 75 percent guarantee has an MER of only 4.11 percent. The Canadian Value Fund, which is the mutual fund equivalent for these segregated funds, has an MER of 2.50 percent. As mentioned, mutual funds with relatively low expenses tend to outperform other funds with similar objectives. Exhibit 12.8 clearly shows that any segregated fund will underperform its mutual fund equivalent as a result of the difference in MERs. It is up to the individual investor to determine whether the benefits of owning a segregated fund outweigh the added costs. In addition, the term of the contract can be a detriment, reducing liquidity.

Exhibit 12.8 Effect of Different Guarantees on Management Expense Ratios			
Investment Fund	100% Maturity and Death Benefit Guarantee Option MER	75% Maturity and Death Benefit Guarantee Option MER	Underlying Mutual Fund MER (No Guarantee)
International Equity Segregated Fund	5.46	4.18	2.75
US Equity Segregated Fund	5.26	4.40	2.76
Canadian Equity Segregated Fund	5.09	3.60	2.48
Canadian Value Segregated Fund	5.13	4.11	2.51
Money Market Segregated Fund	1.92	1.39	1.06

IN-CLASS NOTES

Segregated Funds
- Principal protection
  - Usually matures 10 years after the date of purchase
  - Deposit guarantee of between 75 and 100 percent
- Death benefit guarantee
  - Usually matures at death of policy owner
  - Deposit guarantee of between 75 and 100 percent
- Creditor protection
  - Money invested in a segregated fund is an asset of the insurance company, not of the policy owner
- Management expense ratio
  - Can be double that of its mutual fund equivalent

_____

_____

_____

_____

_____

_____

_____

HOW MUTUAL FUNDS FIT WITHIN YOUR FINANCIAL PLAN

The following are the key decisions about mutual funds that should be included within your financial plan:

- Should you consider investing in mutual funds?
- What types of mutual funds would you invest in?

STEPHANIE SPRATT'S FINANCIAL PLAN: Mutual Funds

GOALS FOR INVESTING IN MUTUAL FUNDS

1. _Determine whether and how I could benefit from investing in mutual funds._
2. _If I decide to invest in mutual funds, determine what types of mutual funds to invest in._

ANALYSIS

Characteristics of Mutual Funds	Opinion
I can invest small amounts over time.	_Necessary for me_
Each fund focuses on a specific type of investment (growth equities versus dividend-paying equities, etc.).	_Desirable_

Mutual fund managers decide how the money should be invested.	*Desirable*
Investment is well diversified.	*Desirable*
I can withdraw money if I need to.	*Necessary for me*

Type of Equity Mutual Fund	Opinion
Growth	*Some potential for an increase in value.*
Small-cap	*Much potential for an increase in value, but may have high risk.*
Mid-cap	*Good potential for an increase in value, with moderate risk.*
Dividend	*Provides dividend income, but my objective is appreciation in value.*
Balanced growth and income	*Not as much potential for an increase in value as some other types of funds.*
Sector	*May consider in some periods if I believe one sector will perform well. These funds have a high risk.*
Index	*Canadian index funds should have less risk than many other types of funds.*
International	*Too risky for me at this time.*
Ethical	*I am open to all types of firms.*

Type of Bond Mutual Fund	Opinion
Canadian bond	*Risk and return depend on the individual holdings of the mutual fund. A bond that focuses on high-quality firms should offer more return, at a higher risk than bonds that are based on federal government holdings.*
High-yield bond	*Higher risk, higher potential return.*
Index bond	*Low risk, low return.*
Global bond	*Higher risk, higher potential return.*

Risk and return assumptions are relative to other funds of the same type.

DECISIONS

Decision on Whether to Invest in Mutual Funds

Mutual funds would allow me to invest small amounts of money at a time, and I could rely on the fund managers to make the investment decisions. I will likely invest most of my excess money in mutual funds.

Decision on Which Mutual Funds to Consider

At this time, I would prefer equity mutual funds that offer potential for capital appreciation. In particular, I believe that an index fund should perform well because the Canadian economy has performed very well lately. I expect the Canadian economy to continue to perform well. I prefer to invest in an index fund because of the low fee structure and the fund's focus on the entire economy.

I prefer Canadian bond mutual funds that have a balanced focus on government and corporate bonds because they offer adequate returns and I think the risk is minimal right now. My financial situation and my preferences may change, so I may switch to other types of mutual funds. I will always select a specific mutual fund that achieves my investment objective and has a relatively low expense ratio.

Discussion Questions

1. How would Stephanie's mutual fund investing decisions be different if she were a single mother of two children?

2. How would Stephanie's mutual fund investing decisions be affected if she were 35 years old? If she were 50 years old?

SUMMARY

The common types of equity mutual funds include growth funds, small-cap funds, mid-cap funds, dividend funds, balanced growth and income funds, sector funds, index funds, and international equity funds. Income funds typically have a lower expected return than the other funds and a lower level of risk. Growth funds tend to have a higher potential return than the other funds and a higher level of risk.

The common types of bond mutual funds are Canadian bond funds, high-yield bond funds, index bond funds, and global bond funds. Canadian bond funds with short maturities have low potential return and low risk. High-yield bond funds have higher potential return and high risk (because some of their bonds may default). Any bond funds that invest in long-term bonds are subject to a high level of interest rate risk.

When choosing a mutual fund, you should select a fund with a required initial investment that you can afford, an investment objective that satisfies your needs, and a relatively low management expense ratio (MER). The prospectus of each fund provides information on these characteristics.

Mutual fund quotations are provided in the *Financial Post* and other business periodicals. These quotations can be used to review the prevailing prices, net asset value per unit (NAVPU), MERs, and other characteristics. The quotations can also be used to assess recent performance.

When diversifying among mutual funds, recognize that most equity funds are affected by general stock market conditions, while most bond funds are affected by bond market conditions. All types of mutual funds are affected by general economic conditions. You can achieve more

effective diversification by investing across equity and bond mutual funds. You may also consider including international equity and bond funds to achieve a greater degree of diversification.

A segregated fund is an insurance product that is often mistaken for a mutual fund because these types of funds share many of the same advantages and disadvantages. The features that distinguish a segregated fund from a mutual fund include principal protection, a death benefit guarantee, and creditor protection. When assessing the value of these features, it is important to consider the additional costs associated with them. In general, a segregated fund will underperform its mutual fund equivalent as a result of the difference in MERs.

INTEGRATING THE KEY CONCEPTS

Your decision to invest in mutual funds not only relates to your other investment decisions, but also affects other parts of your financial plan. Before investing in mutual funds, you should consider your liquidity situation (Part 2). While you can redeem a mutual fund when you need money, its value may decline in some periods and you may prefer to avoid selling it during those periods.

The decision to invest in mutual funds should take into account your financing situation (Part 3). Pay off any personal loans before you invest in mutual funds, unless the return on the fund will exceed the interest rate incurred on the debt. If after considering your liquidity and your financing situation you still decide to invest in mutual funds, you need to decide whether the investment should be for your retirement savings plan (Part 6).

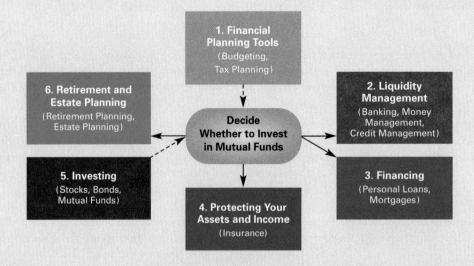

REVIEW QUESTIONS

1. What are mutual funds? What three broad categories of mutual funds exist, and how are they different? Do investors select the securities that the mutual fund invests in?

2. List four advantages of investing in mutual funds. List four disadvantages of investing in mutual funds.

3. What is a mutual fund's net asset value per unit (NAVPU)? How is the NAVPU calculated and reported?

4. What is an open-end mutual fund? What types of companies usually manage open-end funds? Describe how these funds work on a day-to-day basis.

5. What is a closed-end fund? Describe how closed-end funds function.

6. What is the difference between no-load, front-end load, and back-end load mutual funds? How do loads affect a fund's return? Why do some investors purchase load funds? How does an investor purchase a no-load fund?

7. What is a management expense ratio (MER)? What kinds of expenses do mutual funds incur? How are MERs calculated? Why should investors pay attention to MERs?

8. Describe the four components of the MER. How can a no-load fund compensate brokers?

9. List and briefly describe the different types of equity mutual funds.

10. Why do investors invest in index funds? Discuss the popularity of index fund investment as it relates to expenses. What tax advantage do index funds offer relative to other types of mutual funds?

11. List and briefly describe the types of bond mutual funds.

12. Describe the four ways in which a mutual fund can generate returns for investors.

13. Is an equity mutual fund's past performance necessarily an indicator of future performance? What type of risk affects all equity mutual funds? Describe the trade-off between the expected return and risk of equity funds.

14. Discuss return and risk as they relate to bond mutual funds. What type of risk are all bond funds subject to? What other risk is associated with some bond funds? Describe the trade-off between risk and the expected return of bond mutual funds.

15. What should investors consider when deciding whether to purchase a mutual fund? What characteristics of a mutual fund should be considered? Briefly discuss each characteristic.

16. What is a simplified prospectus? How does an investor obtain one? What information does a prospectus provide?

17. Where can an investor find price quotations for open-end funds? What information will be provided in a quotation for open-end funds?

18. Discuss diversification among mutual funds. Describe some strategies that make diversification more effective.

FINANCIAL PLANNING PROBLEMS

1. Hope invested $9000 in a mutual fund at a time when the price per unit was $30. The fund has a load fee of $300. How many units did she purchase?

2. If Hope (from Problem 1) had invested the same amount of money in a no-load fund with the same price, how many units could she have purchased?

3. Hope later sells her mutual fund for $37 per unit. What would her return be in each of the above cases (Problems 1 and 2)?

4. Hunter invested $7000 in a load mutual fund. The load is 7 percent. When Hunter purchased the units, the NAVPU was $70. A year later, Hunter sold at a NAVPU of $68. What is Hunter's return from selling his mutual fund?

5. Mark owns a mutual fund that has an NAVPU of $45.00 and expenses of $1.45 per unit. What is the management expense ratio for Mark's mutual fund?

6. Rena purchased 200 units of an equity mutual fund. During the year she received $3 per unit in dividend distributions, $2 per unit in capital gain distributions, and capital gains of $1100 when she sold the fund after owning it for eight months. What are the tax consequences of Rena's ownership of this equity fund? Rena is in a 40 percent marginal tax bracket.

ETHICAL DILEMMA

To obtain more business, mutual fund companies have made it easier for investors to switch between mutual funds within the same family. For example, if you buy the XYZ Equity Growth Fund, you are able to switch to the XYZ Equity Value Fund at no charge. This feature is particularly beneficial for investors who purchase funds that have a back-end load, since these funds normally charge a fee if you redeem the investment within a certain period of time. In many cases, the same fund may be redeemed as a no-load fund or as a back-end load fund. Investment advisers normally earn more commission for selling a back-end load fund. However, the regular annual service fee on a no-load fund is higher than it is on a back-end load fund. As a result of the free switching rule, some advisers have recommended a back-end load fund and then transferred a portion of the investment during the following year into an identical fund that has a no-load fee structure. By doing this, the adviser is able to maximize his or her commission at the beginning of the trade and during the period that the investor owns the investment.

a. Discuss the ethics of this practice.

b. As a consequence of this practice, what is the impact on the management expense ratio over the long term? Discuss fully.

FINANCIAL PLANNING ONLINE EXERCISES

1. Go to www.fundlibrary.com.

   a. Under Tools, click on Ratings Filter. This tool allows you to select the top-rated funds as determined by various fund-rating companies. Click on Top-Rated (by All Providers). The website will display only those funds that were top-rated by all of the fund-rating companies. Click through the various tabs located above the funds. What information is provided under each?

   b. Which fund has the most assets? Which fund has the lowest MER? Do any of the funds display a 20-year return? A 15-year return? Using standard deviation as a measure of risk, which fund offers the lowest risk?

   c. Record the name of one of the funds from the list. Under Tools, click on Chart Maker. Type in the full or partial name of the mutual fund you selected

and click on Search. Then click on Chart it beside your fund's name. A chart will be created comparing the performance of the fund you selected against a similar index benchmark and the average performance for all other similar funds. How does your fund compare? Change the chart period to five years. How does your fund compare in the last five years?

   d. Under Tools, click on Drawdown Charts. Type in the full or partial name of the mutual fund you selected and click on Search. Then click on Chart it beside your fund's name. What does this chart tell you? How can you use this information to determine whether you should invest in this fund?

2. Go to www.globefund.com.

   a. This website provides research tools to help you select among mutual funds. You can choose a fund based on any number of criteria. Under Research Tools, click on Fund Filter. Select mutual funds based on the following two criteria: Asset Class: Canadian Equity and MER <= 2.0%. Click on Get Results. How many funds match your criteria?

   b. Refine your search criteria. Return to the main page. After re-entering the above two criteria, add the following criterion: Load Type: No Load. Click on Get Results. How many funds match your criteria?

   c. Click on the Long-term tab. Put a check mark in the box beside those mutual funds that have a 15-year performance history. Click on Update Fundlist. Return to the main page. Under Tracking Tools, click on View Fundlist. A list of the funds you have selected for further analysis will be generated.

ON THE STUDENT CD-ROM FOR THIS CHAPTER YOU WILL FIND:

- Building Your Own Financial Plan exercise and worksheets
- The chapter-end Continuing Case about the Sampson family

Read through the Building Your Own Financial Plan exercise and use the worksheets to decide which mutual funds would suit your needs.

After reading the Sampson case study, use the Continuing Case worksheets to help the Sampsons decide which mutual funds to invest in to support their children's education.

Study Guide

Circle the correct answer and then check the answers in the back of the book to chart your progress.

Multiple Choice

1. All of the following are advantages of owning a mutual fund, except:
   a. You can invest in a broadly diversified portfolio with a small initial investment.
   b. Your investments reflect the decisions of experienced professionals who have access to the best research available.
   c. Mutual funds simplify the process of record keeping because the mutual fund company will send you a statement on a regular basis.
   d. Mutual funds are designed for sophisticated investors seeking short-term capital gains only.

2. A mutual fund that aggressively seeks capital growth:
   a. Will have an MER that is approximately the same as a T-Bill fund.
   b. Will have an MER that is higher than a global fund.
   c. Will have an MER similar to that of a fixed-income fund.
   d. Will have an MER that reflects the increased costs of research.

3. _____ mutual funds sell units directly to investors and redeem those units whenever investors wish to redeem them.
   a. Open-end
   b. Equity
   c. Bond
   d. Closed-end

4. Which of the following items is not a component of the management expense ratio (MER)?
   a. Management expenses
   b. Dealer/adviser compensation
   c. Brokerage commissions
   d. Administrative costs

5. "Since they engage in less trading than most other mutual funds, they generate a limited amount of capital gains that must be distributed to unitholders." This statement refers to which of the following types of funds?
   a. Bond funds
   b. Dividend funds
   c. Index funds
   d. Growth funds

6. Which of the following types of income received from a mutual fund may result from a mutual fund distribution?
   a. Interest income
   b. Capital gain
   c. Dividend
   d. All of the above

7. When you initially purchase a mutual fund, a simplified prospectus must be provided to you within _____ of your purchase.
   a. 24 hours
   b. 3 business days
   c. 7 days
   d. 48 hours

8. Given the following mutual fund price quotation, determine which of the following statements most accurately reflects the data.

Fund	$ NAVPU	$ Ch	Yr %Ch
ABC Health Care Fund	21.95	+0.11	−1.1

   a. ABC Health Care Fund has a net asset value per unit of $21.95. The net change in the NAVPU during the previous day was +0.11. The fund has generated a return of −1.1 percent since the start of the calendar year.
   b. ABC Health Care Fund has a net asset value of $21.95. The net change in the NAVPU during the previous day was +0.11. The fund has generated a return of −1.1 percent since the start of the calendar year.
   c. ABC Health Care Fund has a net asset value per unit of $21.95. The net change in the NAVPU during the previous week was +0.11. The fund has generated a return of −1.1 percent since the start of the calendar year.
   d. ABC Health Care Fund has a net asset value of $21.95. The net change in the NAVPU during the previous week was +0.11. The fund has generated a return of −1.1 percent since the start of the calendar year.

9. Your return from investing in _____ is primarily affected by _____.
   a. a Canadian equity fund, Canadian interest rates
   b. an Australian bond fund, Australian interest rates and the value of the Australian dollar

c. a European equity fund, European stock markets and the value of the Canadian dollar

d. a Canadian equity fund, Canadian money markets

10. The potential benefits of investing in a segregated fund include all of the following except:

a. Segregated funds offer a guarantee on your deposits when the contract matures.

b. Segregated funds offer a guarantee on your deposits when the policy owner dies.

c. Segregated fund contracts are normally exempt from seizure by creditors in the event that the policy owner declares bankruptcy.

d. Segregated funds are more expensive than similar mutual funds.

True/False

1. True or False? One disadvantage of mutual funds is that you could invest in a well-diversified mutual fund that is invested in a group of poorly-performing companies rather than good ones.

2. True or False? Unlike an open-end fund, units of a closed-end fund are purchased and sold on stock exchanges.

3. True or False? Recent studies on mutual funds have found that no-load funds outperform load funds on average, even when ignoring the fees paid on a load fund.

4. True or False? Exchange rate risk is the result of a decrease in the value of a foreign bond because the currency denominating the bond weakens against the Canadian dollar.

5. True or False? Short-term bonds are more sensitive to changes in interest rates than long-term bonds.

6. True or False? The most important expense statistic mentioned in the prospectus is the back-end load.

7. True or False? When investors want to assess the performance of a mutual fund, one technique is to compare the return on that mutual fund to the average return for the same type of mutual fund.

8. True or False? Diversification among bond funds is not an effective means of reducing exposure to interest rate risk.

9. True or False? With respect to segregated funds, the determination of the value of the death benefit guarantee is similar to that of the maturity guarantee.

10. True or False? Any segregated fund may underperform its mutual fund equivalent.

Chapter 13

Investing in Stocks

B lake thought he had a good strategy for investing. For any company in which he was interested, he carefully read the summary provided by the chief executive in the company's annual report. He also read research reports about those companies, which were provided by investment companies. His confidence in investing grew because each company in which he was interested also had a very optimistic outlook in its annual report. In addition, the research reports provided about these companies were always very positive. Blake was so confident, he purchased 500 shares of a particular stock at $40 per share. His research seemed to be paying off, as the price rose steadily over the course of several months to more than $48 per share. Blake felt that this stock had reached the upper limit of its price increase. He decided to implement a sell strategy that would take the uncertainty out of the sales transaction. He called his broker and placed a limit order to sell his stock if and when it reached $50 per share. A $50 per share price would allow Blake to earn at least a 25 percent return on his investment and would result in a $5000 gain before subtracting commissions.

Over the next few days, the price slipped to the mid-40s and then drifted lower still. Blake didn't sell because he was sure the dip in price was only temporary. Finally, when the price reached $30 per share, he called his broker and sold all of his shares. He ultimately suffered a $5000 loss on his investment.

Blake could not understand how this stock could decrease in value, since his own view of the stock was fully supported by the annual reports and other research reports.

Blake learned the hard way that most outlooks by chief executives and research reports by investment companies tend to be overly optimistic. If Blake had relied on a more objective method of stock analysis and valuation, he may have been able to make better investments.

This chapter explains how to make investment decisions with respect to stocks so that you can enhance your wealth.

The objectives of this chapter are to:

1. Describe how to interpret stock quotations
2. Illustrate how to conduct an analysis of a firm
3. Describe how to conduct an economic analysis of stocks
4. Show how to conduct an industry analysis of stocks
5. Explain how to value stocks
6. Identify the functions of stock exchanges
7. Explain how to execute the purchase or sale of stocks
8. Discuss buying stocks on margin
9. Explain how to assess your stock portfolio's performance

L.O. 1

STOCK QUOTATIONS

If you are considering investing in stocks, you will need to learn how to obtain and interpret stock price quotations. Fortunately, price quotations are readily available for actively traded stocks. The most up-to-date quotes can be obtained online. Price information is available from stockbrokers and is widely published by the news media. Popular sources of stock quotations are financial newspapers (such as the *Financial Post* and the *Globe and Mail*), business sections of many local newspapers, financial news television networks (such as BNN), and financial websites.

Stock quotations provide information about the price of each stock over the previous day or a recent period. An example of stock quotations provided by the *Financial Post* is shown in Exhibit 13.1. The first column contains the name of the stock. To the right is the ticker symbol (Ticker) associated with the stock. The next column shows the closing price (Close), which is the price at the end of the day when the stock market closed. The fourth column discloses the net change (Net ch) in the price of the stock, which is measured as the change in the closing price from the previous day. Investors review this column to determine how stock prices changed from one day to the next.

The fifth column shows the net change in the price of the stock as a percentage (% ch). The sixth column shows the volume of trading (in 00s). For some widely traded stocks, a million shares may trade per day, while 20 000 or fewer shares may trade per day for other stocks. The next two columns display the daily high (Day high) and the daily low (Day low) at which the stock was traded. The dividend yield (annual dividends as a percentage of the stock price) is shown in the ninth column. This represents the annual return you would receive solely from dividends if you purchased the stock today, and if the dividend payments remain unchanged for the entire year. In the tenth column is the price–earnings (P/E) ratio, which represents the stock price divided by the firm's earnings per share. Some investors closely monitor the P/E ratio when attempting to value stocks, as discussed in more detail later in this chapter.

The next two columns display the high (52wk high) and low (52wk low) price of the stock during the last year. Stocks that are subject to much more uncertainty tend to have a wider range in prices over time. Some investors use this range as a simple measure of the firm's risk. Finally, the last two columns show the percent change in the stock price during the last week (Wk %ch) and during the last year (52wk %ch).

Review the stock quotations of CN Rail in Exhibit 13.1. The ticker symbol for this stock is CNR. At the close of trading in the stock market, its stock price was $57.34. The net change in the price was up $0.61 per share from the day before. This translates into a percent change of +1.1. CN Rail's volume of trading for the day was 1 062 900 shares.

Go to
www.globeinvestor.com

This website provides stock quotations for the stocks you specify. It also provides a summary of financial market conditions and links to information about investments.

Exhibit 13.1 Daily Stock Quotations

Stock	Ticker	Close	Net ch	% ch	Vol 00s	Day high	Day low	% yield	P/E	52wk high	52wk low	Wk %ch	52wk %ch
ACE Aviatn B	ACE.B	27.60	+0.01	nil	1726	27.67	27.45	n.a.	12.8	40.01	25.50	+0.1	−8.9
AgnicoEag	AEM	45.17	+0.37	+0.8	9185	45.71	44.75	0.3	34.2	52.03	30.72	+5.6	+17.1
Agrium	AGU	47.92	+2.22	+4.9	5839	48.04	45.88	0.2	84.6	49.54	24.56	+1.6	+83.8
Alcan	AL	102.34	−0.41	−0.4	34992	102.69	102.00	0.8	19.0	104.60	41.78	+12.6	+100.0
BCE	BCE	41.20	+0.04	+0.1	32777	41.29	41.15	3.5	17.8	41.80	25.32	−1.3	+57.1
BkMtl	BMO	69.55	+0.23	+0.3	7906	69.72	69.12	3.9	14.6	72.75	60.81	+0.8	+13.2
BkofNS	BNS	52.09	+0.25	+0.5	15506	52.27	51.79	3.5	13.4	54.73	44.76	+1.1	+14.9
Barrick	ABX	33.59	+0.25	+0.7	16001	33.68	33.27	0.9	33.0	38.11	29.74	+4.4	+1.2
Blovail	BVF	27.49	+0.31	+1.1	4724	27.50	27.05	5.7	17.7	28.78	16.25	+3.2	+12.6
Bombrdr BSV	BBD.B	6.64	+0.04	+0.6	52360	6.69	6.58	n.a.	42.2	6.97	2.98	+2.6	+108.8
Brkfld ALV	BAM.A	43.06	+0.20	+0.5	6407	43.15	42.75	1.2	20.7	48.12	29.193	+2.1	+43.4
Cameco	CCO	53.25	+1.10	+2.1	10863	53.31	52.15	0.4	57.9	59.90	35.35	+1.0	+18.1
CIBC	CM	98.15	+1.25	+1.3	10496	98.20	97.06	3.1	11.4	107.45	76.00	+3.0	+26.5
CN Rail	CNR	57.34	+0.61	+1.1	10629	57.86	56.71	1.5	14.6	60.00	44.43	+3.7	+18.0
CdnNatRes	CNQ	74.18	+1.85	+2.6	12133	74.80	72.45	0.5	14.6	74.99	45.49	+4.2	+26.9
CdnOilSnd	COS.UN	33.65	+0.81	+2.5	17057	33.89	32.96	4.8	15.7	38.75	24.32	+5.5	+0.5
CdnPacRail	CP	77.37	+0.67	+0.9	2597	77.56	76.36	1.2	14.9	78.48	51.05	+4.0	+43.2
CdnTireA NV	CTC.A	87.50	+1.55	+1.8	1769	87.75	85.81	0.8	19.2	87.75	61.25	+3.5	+35.7
CelesticaSV	CLS	6.66	nil	nil	12528	6.73	6.62	n.a.	n.a.	13.90	6.62	−1.8	−33.4
Cognos	CSN	42.53	−0.61	−1.4	3640	43.22	42.28	n.a.	29.4	53.38	28.44	−0.2	+41.7
Cott	BCB	16.59	+0.41	+2.5	1632	16.65	16.08	n.a.	n.a.	20.35	13.55	+5.1	+20.6
Enbridge	ENB	37.25	+0.33	+0.9	4301	37.25	36.60	3.3	19.6	41.48	34.44	+2.3	+5.7
EnCana	ECA	67.29	+0.71	+1.1	15285	67.65	66.56	1.2	12.7	71.21	48.28	+2.6	+18.2
1stQuantm	FM	109.07	−3.65	−3.2	7150	112.94	109.07	0.6	15.7	114.18	45.39	+5.5	+102.8
FrdngCdnum	FDG.UN	36.39	−0.49	−1.3	3933	37.00	36.15	7.1	13.0	37.11	21.50	+1.4	+7.8
Goldcorp	G	27.82	−0.09	−0.3	25565	28.16	27.73	0.7	31.2	35.89	22.97	+3.2	−17.2
HuskyEnrg	HSE	44.90	+0.50	+1.1	4825	45.00	44.46	2.2	13.4	46.65	33.10	+2.8	+20.4
IPSCO	IPS	167.50	+0.68	+0.4	1447	167.90	166.99	0.5	12.5	179.35	90.00	+0.4	+70.1
ImpOll	IMO	51.16	+0.72	+1.4	8275	51.22	50.66	0.7	15.3	54.70	34.31	+2.3	+21.9
KinrossGld	K	14.14	+0.08	+0.6	26924	14.26	14.03	n.a.	22.5	17.00	11.78	+4.7	+14.3
Loblaw	L	51.67	-0.33	−0.6	7073	52.15	51.62	1.6	n.a.	55.00	44.92	−0.2	−0.1
Lundin	LUN	15.35	-0.07	−0.5	23619	15.42	15.04	n.a.	14.2	15.84	9.117	+7.0	+43.6
MDS	MDS	21.79	nil	nil	5534	21.90	21.63	0.3	n.a.	22.66	18.56	+1.1	+4.0
Magna A SV	MG.A	100.23	+2.12	+2.2	2121	100.50	97.71	1.0	19.5	100.50	76.69	+2.9	+24.5
Manulife	MFC	40.26	+0.38	+1.0	22594	40.40	39.51	2.2	15.7	41.49	34.39	+2.4	+12.7
NOVA Chem	NCX	40.70	+0.10	+0.2	2454	41.20	40.46	1.0	n.a.	42.43	31.05	−0.2	+27.9
NatlBk	NA	62.84	+0.69	+1.1	3993	62.88	62.15	3.8	11.4	66.80	57.18	+2.4	+10.2
Nexen	NXY	34.66	+0.61	+1.8	24155	34.71	34.13	0.3	23.8	37.60	26.065	+4.8	+12.3
Nortel	NT	24.70	−0.09	−0.4	7761	24.95	24.52	n.a.	n.a.	37.35	21.40	+0.8	+5.6

Source: National Post, July 11, 2007. Reprinted with permission of TSX Data Linx.

For the day, the stock price traded between $56.71 and $57.86. The annual dividend yield of 1.5 percent means that investors purchasing the stock at the time of this quotation would earn an annual dividend equal to 1.5 percent on their investment if the annual dividend remains unchanged. The price–earnings ratio is 14.6, which means that the prevailing stock price of CN Rail is approximately 15 times its annual earnings per share. Its stock has traded between $44.43 and $60.00 per share over the last year. In the last week, the stock price rose 3.7 percent. Furthermore, the stock price rose 18.0 percent over the last year.

L.O. 2 ANALYSIS OF A FIRM

One firm can outperform another in the same industry because its managers make better decisions about how to finance its business, market its products, and manage its employees. By conducting an analysis of a firm, you can assess its future performance.

Annual Report

Firms that are publicly traded create an annual report that contains standardized financial information. Among other things, the report includes a corporate profile, a message from the firm's chief executive officer (CEO), and a section summarizing recent performance and expected future performance. It also contains financial statements measuring the firm's financial condition that you can examine in the same manner that you evaluate your personal financial statements to determine your financial condition. Many annual reports can be downloaded online. Prospective investors typically focus on the balance sheet and the income statement.

balance sheet
A financial statement that indicates a firm's sources of funds and how it has invested those funds as of a particular point in time.

Balance Sheet. A firm's **balance sheet** indicates its sources of funds and how it has invested those funds as of a particular point in time. The balance sheet shown in Exhibit 13.2 is segmented into three parts: assets, liabilities, and shareholders' equity. Assets must equal the sum of liabilities and shareholders' equity.

The firm's assets indicate how it has invested its funds and what it owns. Assets are often classified as short-term and long-term assets. Short-term assets include cash, securities purchased by the firm, accounts receivable (money owed to the firm for previous sales), and inventories (materials used to produce products and finished products waiting to be sold). Long-term assets (sometimes called fixed assets) include machinery and buildings purchased by the firm.

Exhibit 13.2 Balance Sheet for Gurshinder Corporation (Numbers Are in Millions)

Assets		Liabilities and Shareholders' Equity	
Short-term (current) assets		Short-term liabilities	
Cash and marketable securities	$100	Accounts payable	$300
Accounts receivable	400	Short-term debt	0
Inventories	500	**Total short-term liabilities**	**$300**
Total short-term assets	**$1000**		
Fixed assets	$400	**Long-term debt**	**$200**
Less depreciation	−100		
Net fixed assets	**$300**	Shareholders' equity	800
Total assets	**$1300**	**Total liabilities and Shareholders' equity**	**$1300**

Exhibit 13.3 Income Statement for Gurshinder Corporation (Numbers Are in Millions)	
Revenue (Sales)	$3000
Cost of goods sold	1400
Gross profit	**$1600**
Operating expenses	1130
Earnings before interest and taxes	**$470**
Interest expense	20
Earnings before taxes	**$450**
Taxes	150
Earnings after taxes	**$300**

The liabilities and shareholders' equity indicate how the firm has obtained its funds. Liabilities represent the amount owed to creditors or suppliers and are classified as short-term or long-term debts. Shareholders' equity is the net worth of the firm. It represents the investment in the firm by equity investors. It also represents earnings retained by the company that have been reinvested in its inventory and assets.

income statement
A financial statement that measures a firm's revenues, expenses, and earnings over a particular period of time.

Income Statement. A firm's **income statement** measures its revenues, expenses, and earnings over a particular period of time. Investors use it to determine how much income (earnings) the firm generated over a particular period and what expenses the firm incurred. An annual report may include an income statement for the year of concern and for the four quarters within that year.

An example of an income statement is shown in Exhibit 13.3. It starts with revenues generated by the firm over the period of concern. Then the cost of goods sold (which includes the cost of materials used in production) is subtracted to derive gross profit. Operating expenses (such as salaries) are subtracted from the gross profit to determine earnings before interest and taxes (also referred to as operating profit). Finally, interest payments and taxes are subtracted to determine the earnings after taxes (also referred to as net profit).

Firm-Specific Characteristics

Investors use a firm's balance sheet and income statement to analyze the following characteristics:

- Liquidity
- Financial leverage
- Efficiency
- Profitability

Each of these characteristics is described below. Some popular ratios used to measure these characteristics are summarized in Exhibit 13.4 and applied to Gurshinder Corporation's financial statements.

Liquidity. A firm's assets and liabilities can be assessed to determine its liquidity, or its ability to cover expenses. A firm has a high degree of liquidity if it has a large

Exhibit 13.4 Ratios Used to Analyze Gurshinder Corporation

Measures of Liquidity

Gurshinder Corporation (numbers in millions)

$$\text{Current ratio} = \frac{\text{current assets}}{\text{current liabilities}}$$

$$\text{Current ratio} = \frac{\$1000}{\$300} = 3.33$$

Measures of Financial Leverage

$$\text{Debt ratio} = \frac{\text{total long-term debt}}{\text{total assets}}$$

$$\text{Debt ratio} = \frac{\$200}{\$1300} = 0.15$$

$$\text{Times interest earned ratio} = \frac{\text{earnings before interest and taxes}}{\text{interest payments}}$$

$$\text{Times interest earned ratio} = \frac{\$470}{\$20} = 23.5$$

Measures of Efficiency

$$\text{Inventory turnover} = \frac{\text{cost of goods sold}}{\text{average daily inventory}}$$

$$\text{Inventory turnover} = \frac{\$1400}{\$500^*} = 2.8$$

$$\text{Average collection period} = \frac{\text{average receivables}}{\text{average daily sales}}$$

$$\text{Average collection period} = \frac{\$400}{(\$3000/365)} = 48.67$$

$$\text{Asset turnover ratio} = \frac{\text{sales}}{\text{average total assets}}$$

$$\text{Asset turnover ratio} = \frac{\$3,000}{\$1300^\dagger} = 2.31$$

Profitability Ratios

$$\text{Net profit margin} = \frac{\text{earnings}}{\text{sales}}$$

$$\text{Net profit margin} = \frac{\$300}{\$3000} = 10\%$$

$$\text{Return on assets} = \frac{\text{earnings}}{\text{assets}}$$

$$\text{Return on assets} = \frac{\$300}{\$1300} = 23\%$$

$$\text{Return on equity} = \frac{\text{earnings}}{\text{equity}}$$

$$\text{Return on equity} = \frac{\$300}{\$800} = 37.5\%$$

*This assumes that the inventory level represents the average level during the year.
†This assumes that the prevailing asset level represents the average level.

current ratio
The ratio of a firm's short-term assets to its short-term liabilities.

amount of assets that can be easily converted to cash and has a relatively small amount of short-term liabilities. You can assess a firm's liquidity by computing its current ratio, which is the ratio of its short-term assets to its short-term liabilities. A high ratio relative to the industry norm represents a relatively high degree of liquidity.

Financial Leverage. Investors assess a firm's balance sheet to determine its ability to make debt payments. A firm obtains funds by borrowing from suppliers or creditors or by selling shares of its stock (equity) to investors. Many firms prefer to borrow funds rather than issue stock. An excessive amount of stock may spread the shareholder ownership of the firm too thin, placing downward pressure on the stock price. If a firm borrows too much money, however, it may have difficulty making its interest

financial leverage
A firm's reliance on debt to support its operations.

debt ratio
A measure of financial leverage that calculates the proportion of total assets financed with debt.

times interest earned ratio
A measure of financial leverage that indicates the ratio of the firm's earnings before interest and taxes to its total interest payments.

inventory turnover
A measure of efficiency; computed as the cost of goods sold divided by average daily inventory.

average collection period
A measure of efficiency; computed as accounts receivable divided by average daily sales.

asset turnover ratio
A measure of efficiency; computed as sales divided by average total assets.

operating profit margin
A firm's operating profit divided by sales.

net profit margin
A measure of profitability that measures net profit as a percentage of sales.

return on assets
A measure of profitability; computed as net profit divided by total assets.

return on equity
A measure of profitability; computed as net profit divided by the owners' investment in the firm (shareholders' equity).

payments on loans. A firm's financial leverage indicates its reliance on debt to support its operations.

A firm's financial leverage can be measured by its **debt ratio**, which calculates the proportion of total assets financed with debt. A firm with a high debt ratio relative to the industry norm has a high degree of financial leverage and therefore may have a relatively high risk of default on its future debt payments. Some firms with a relatively high degree of financial leverage can easily cover their debt payments if they generate stable cash inflows over time. The debt ratio focuses just on the firm's level of debt and does not account for its cash flows. Thus, a more appropriate measure of a firm's ability to repay its debt is the **times interest earned ratio**, which indicates the ratio of the firm's earnings before interest and taxes to its total interest payments. A high times interest earned ratio (relative to the industry norm) means that the firm should be more capable of covering its debt payments than an average firm. The earnings figure is before taxes, as all debt interest costs are paid before taxable income is calculated. Interest costs are thus categorized as a business expense.

Efficiency. The composition of assets can indicate how efficiently a firm uses its funds. If it generates a relatively low level of sales and earnings with a large amount of assets, it is not using its assets efficiently. A firm that invests in assets must obtain funds to support those assets. The fewer assets it uses to generate its sales, the fewer funds it needs to borrow or obtain by issuing stock.

You can use **inventory turnover** to measure how efficiently a firm manages its inventory. It is calculated as the cost of goods sold divided by average daily inventory. A higher number relative to the industry norm represents relatively high turnover, which is more efficient.

You can use a firm's **average collection period** to determine the average age of accounts receivable. It is measured as accounts receivable divided by average daily sales. A higher number relative to the industry norm means a longer collection period, which is less efficient.

You can use the **asset turnover ratio** to assess how efficiently a firm uses its assets. This ratio is measured as sales divided by average total assets. A higher number relative to the industry norm reflects higher efficiency.

Profitability. You can also use the income statement and the balance sheet to assess a firm's profitability. The **operating profit margin** is the operating profit divided by sales, and the **net profit margin** measures net profit as a percentage of sales. The **return on assets** is the net profit divided by total assets. The **return on equity** is measured as net profit divided by the owners' investment in the firm (or shareholders' equity). The higher the profitability ratios relative to the industry norm, the higher the firm's profitability.

Information Provided by Value Line Investment Survey

Firm-specific information is also available from Value Line Investment Survey. Each component of Exhibit 13.5 discussed here is designated with a letter code. The name of the firm is shown in the top left corner (a). Along the top of the page, notice the recent stock price (b), the price–earnings (P/E) ratio (c), the relative P/E ratio comparable to other firms in the industry (d), and the firm's dividend yield, equal to annual dividends divided by the price per share (e).

Just below the firm's name in the upper left corner are Value Line's ratings of the firm (f). The firm's beta (g), which measures the sensitivity of its stock price relative to a broad market index, is shown below those ratings. To the right of the beta is the firm's stock price trend over the last several years (h). The firm's stock trading volume information (i) appears below the stock price trend.

Exhibit 13.5 An Example from Value Line Investment Survey

a b c d e

GAP, INC. (THE) NYSE-GPS | **RECENT PRICE** 12.77 | **P/E RATIO** 44.0 (Trailing: NMF / Median: 24.0) | **RELATIVE P/E RATIO** 2.70 | **DIV'D YLD** 0.7% | **VALUE LINE** 1734

f

TIMELINESS **3** Raised 7/26/02
SAFETY **3** New 7/27/90
TECHNICAL **3** Lowered 10/25/02
BETA 1.55 (1.00 = Market)

g

2005-07 PROJECTIONS

	Price	Gain	Ann'l Total Return
High	30	(+135%)	24%
Low	19	(+50%)	11%

h

Insider Decisions

	D	J	F	M	A	M	J	J	A
to Buy	0	0	0	0	0	0	0	0	0
Options	0	0	0	3	0	0	0	0	0
to Sell	0	0	0	2	0	0	0	0	0

Institutional Decisions

	4Q2001	1Q2002	2Q2002
to Buy	205	210	180
to Sell	231	219	218
Hld's(000)	434704	472838	492551

Percent shares traded 15/10/5

i

% TOT. RETURN 10/02

	THIS STOCK	VL ARITH. INDEX
1 yr.	-9.3	-8.8
3 yr.	-67.0	-0.1
5 yr.	-21.6	13.1

Target Price Range 2005 | 2006 | 2007

1986	1987	1988	1989	1990	1991	1992	1993	1994	1995	1996	1997	1998	1999	2000	2001	2002	2003	© VALUE LINE PUB., INC. 05-07	
.88	1.10	1.32	1.67	2.03	2.62	3.04	3.36	3.81	4.53	5.70	7.36	10.55	13.68	16.01	16.00	15.85	16.30	Sales per sh A	21.20
.09	.10	.11	.15	.22	.32	.33	.41	.50	.57	.72	.91	1.34	1.84	1.72	1.09	1.15	1.50	"Cash Flow" per sh	2.25
.07	.07	.08	.11	.15	.24	.22	.26	.33	.36	.47	.58	.91	1.26	1.00	.15	.25	.55	Earnings per sh B	1.05
.01	.02	.02	.03	.03	.04	.05	.06	.07	.07	.09	.09	.09	.09	.09	.09	.09	.09	Div'ds Decl'd per sh C	.15
.22	.28	.29	.36	.49	.70	.91	1.15	1.41	1.69	1.79	1.79	1.83	2.63	3.43	3.48	3.75	4.20	Book Value per sh D	6.40
960.42	968.49	948.55	948.72	953.53	962.03	973.25	980.43	977.16	971.15	926.50	884.55	857.96	850.50	854.00	865.73	868.00	870.00	Common Shs Outst'g D	872.00
18.6	24.4	14.6	15.8	14.7	23.6	25.0	18.8	17.9	15.0	19.0	22.3	29.2	33.5	32.5	NMF	Bold figures are Value Line estimates		Avg Ann'l P/E Ratio	23.0
1.26	1.63	1.21	1.20	1.09	1.51	1.52	1.11	1.17	1.00	1.19	1.29	1.52	1.91	2.11	NMF			Relative P/E Ratio	1.55
.9%	1.1%	1.8%	1.5%	1.5%	.8%	.9%	1.1%	1.2%	1.3%	1.0%	.7%	.3%	.2%	.3%	.4%			Avg Ann'l Div'd Yield	Nil

j k l m

CAPITAL STRUCTURE as of 8/3/02
Total Debt $3373.1 mill. Due in 5 Yrs $1628 mill.
LT Debt $2873.1 mill.   LT Interest $260.0 mill.
(48% of Cap'l)
Leases, Uncapitalized Annual rentals $816.3 mill.

Pension Liability None—no defined benefit plan

Pfd Stock None

Common Stock 870,401,079 shs.   (52% of Cap'l)

MARKET CAP: $11.1 billion (Large Cap)

2960.4	3295.7	3722.9	4395.3	5284.4	6507.8	9054.5	11635	13673	13848	13750	14200	Sales ($mill) A	18500
37.8%	39.9%	41.4%	40.3%	41.9%	42.3%	44.9%	45.5%	41.4%	37.2%	38.5%	41.0%	Gross Margin	41.5%
15.5%	17.2%	18.4%	17.4%	17.9%	17.2%	18.3%	19.4%	14.9%	9.8%	10.5%	13.5%	Operating Margin	15.0%
1307	1307	1508	1680	1370	2130	2428	3018	3676	4171	4260	4350	Number of Stores	4600
210.7	258.4	320.2	354.0	452.9	533.9	824.5	1127.1	877.5	128.9	225	495	Net Profit ($mill)	920
38.0%	39.2%	39.5%	39.5%	39.5%	37.5%	37.5%	36.9%	36.5%	71.1%	49.0%	43.0%	Income Tax Rate	38.0%
7.1%	7.8%	8.6%	8.1%	8.6%	8.2%	9.1%	9.7%	6.4%	.9%	1.6%	3.5%	Net Profit Margin	5.0%
355.7	494.2	555.8	728.4	554.4	839.4	318.7	444.9	d151.0	988.4	1730	1820	Working Cap'l ($mill)	3120
75.0	75.0	--	--	--	496.0	496.5	784.9	780.3	1961.4	3000	2800	Long-Term Debt ($mill)	2200
887.8	1126.5	1375.2	1640.5	1654.5	1584.0	1573.7	2233.0	2928.2	3009.6	3245	3660	Shr. Equity ($mill)	5585
22.2%	21.5%	23.3%	21.6%	27.4%	25.9%	40.7%	38.1%	24.5%	3.4%	5.5%	9.5%	Return on Total Cap'l	13.5%
23.7%	22.9%	23.3%	21.6%	27.4%	33.7%	52.4%	50.5%	30.0%	4.3%	7.0%	13.5%	Return on Shr. Equity	16.5%
18.8%	18.2%	18.6%	17.5%	22.3%	28.7%	47.5%	47.1%	27.4%	1.7%	4.5%	11.5%	Retained to Com Eq	13.5%
21%	21%	20%	19%	19%	15%	9%	7%	9%	59%	35%	16%	All Div'ds to Net Prof	17%

o n

CURRENT POSITION ($MILL)

	2000	2001	8/3/02
Cash Assets	408.8	1035.7	2386.8
Receivables			
Inventory (FIFO)	1904.1	1677.1	1853.7
Other	335.2	331.8	342.7
Current Assets	2648.1	3044.6	4583.2
Accts Payable	1067.2	1105.1	882.1
Debt Due	1029.9	41.9	500.0
Other	702.0	909.2	1015.2
Current Liab.	2799.1	2056.2	2397.3

p

ANNUAL RATES

of change (per sh)	Past 10 Yrs.	Past 5 Yrs.	Est'd '99-'01 to '05-'07
Sales	22.0%	26.5%	5.5%
"Cash Flow"	21.0%	21.0%	6.5%
Earnings	17.0%	15.5%	4.5%
Dividends	10.0%	3.5%	9.0%
Book Value	20.0%	14.5%	13.0%

q

QUARTERLY SALES ($ mill.) A

Year Begins	Apr.Per	Jul.Per	Oct.Per	Jan.Per	Full Fiscal Year
1999	2278	2453	3045	3859	11635
2000	2732	2948	3414	4579	13673
2001	3180	3245	3333	4090	13848
2002	2891	3268	3450	4141	13750
2003	2940	3370	3580	4310	14200

r

EARNINGS PER SHARE A B

Year Begins	Apr.Per	Jul.Per	Oct.Per	Jan.Per	Full Fiscal Year
1999	.22	.22	.35	.47	1.26
2000	.27	.21	.21	.31	1.00
2001	.13	.12	d.06	d.04	.15
2002	.04	.06	.06	.09	.25
2003	.08	.08	.13	.26	.55

s

QUARTERLY DIVIDENDS PAID C

Cal-endar	Mar.31	Jun.30	Sep.30	Dec.31	Full Year
1998	.022	.022	.022	.022	.09
1999	.022	.022	.022	.022	.09
2000	.022	.022	.022	.022	.09
2001	.022	.022	.022	.022	.09
2002	.022	.022	.022		

BUSINESS: The Gap, Inc. operated 4,171 casual apparel specialty stores with over 36 million sq. ft. of selling space as of 2/2/02. Gap and GapKids (2,298 U.S. and 634 foreign stores) sell jeans, sweatsuits, shirts, sweaters, and related apparel. Banana Republic (441 stores) sells upscale casual wear. Old Navy (798 stores) sells budget-priced clothing. Gap and Banana Republic have Internet sites. All merchandise is private label; 13% sourced from China. '01 deprec. rate: 12.2%; Has about 165,000 employees; 6,645 stockholders. Officers & dirs. own 29.0% of stock; other major investors, 6.0% (4/02 proxy). Chairman: D.G. Fisher. Pres. & CEO: Paul Pressler. Inc.: DE. Address: One Harrison St., San Francisco, CA 94105. Tel.: 415-952-4400. Internet: www.gap.com.

t u

The hunt is finally over for a new leader at The Gap . . . Following a comprehensive search to fill the shoes of the retired Millard Drexler, the company recently named Paul Pressler, former chairman of Disney's theme parks and resorts, to the positions of CEO and president.

. . . and the new CEO has his work cut out for him. The company has been struggling to reconnect with its customer base for some time, although we are encouraged by changes that have been implemented at the three core chains. The one-time industry leader is looking to recapture lost market share by returning to the classic styles that were the foundation behind The Gap's growth in earlier years. If the company can execute this strategic plan effectively, as we believe it will, shoppers will likely return to The Gap's stores. Indeed, we think merchandise assortments more in line with the traditional "Gap" signature style, coupled with a more-favorable U.S. economic backdrop ought to result in improved sales and earnings trends in fiscal 2003 (starts February 2nd). In the ensuing years, the return to its traditional roots should enable operations to strengthen further.

Disruptions related to western port closures will likely be a drag on The Gap's vital holiday selling season. The bottom line should suffer from higher distribution costs, and potentially from higher markdowns on delayed merchandise. All told, repercussions related to the work stoppages will likely shave about $0.07 a share off the bottom line in the fourth quarter. This, alongside our expectations of weak store traffic trends and heavy promotional activity, has caused us to lower our 2002 share-net estimate by a dime, to $0.25. Although this figure is much higher than last year's tally, it still remains well below The Gap's profit levels of only a few years ago.

Patient investors may want to take a look at The Gap shares. As depicted in our 2005-2007 projections, a successful implementation of the back-to-basics strategy should support significant annual profit and share-price growth over the period. We caution, however, that the road to recovery may not be a smooth one.
Carrie Galeotafiore   November 15, 2002

(A) Fiscal year ends Sat. closest to Jan. 31st.
(B) Diluted earnings. Excl. loss on discontinued operations/nonrecurrings: '89, 2¢.; '01, 16¢. Next earnings report due mid-Feb.
(C) Next dividend meeting late Nov. Next ex-date late Nov. Div'd payment dates: about Mar. 18th, June 12th, Oct. 2nd, Dec. 26th.
(D) In millions, adjusted for stock splits.

Company's Financial Strength	B++
Stock's Price Stability	30
Price Growth Persistence	65
Earnings Predictability	35

Source: © 2003 Value Line Publishing, Inc.

"Remember, the customer
always comes first in the billing department."

In the middle of the page is a spreadsheet that shows the trends of various financial statistics that are identified in the right margin. The top rows of the spreadsheet (j) show the financial statistics on a per share basis so that they can be compared with those of other firms.

In the middle of the spreadsheet is the trend of the P/E ratio (k), the relative P/E ratio (l), and the dividend yield (m). Also notice the trends of various profitability ratios, including the net profit margin (n).

The firm's long-term sources of funds are shown in the section called "capital structure" (o) to the left of the bottom part of the spreadsheet. Just below the capital structure is information that can be used to assess the firm's liquidity (p). Below that information are quarterly data on sales (q), earnings (r), and dividends (s). A general summary of the firm's business (t) appears below the right portion of the spreadsheet, and a general analysis of the business (u) appears below the business summary.

Focus on Ethics: Accounting Fraud

Motivation for Fraud. The top managers of a firm are commonly evaluated according to how the firm's value (as measured by stock price) changes over time. These managers may receive shares of the firm's stock as part of their compensation. Their goal is to increase the value of the firm so that they can sell their shares at a high price and earn a high level of compensation.

Consequently, they may seek an accounting method that will either inflate the firm's level of revenue or deflate the reported level of expenses, so that it can boost its reported earnings. Investors who use those reported earnings to derive the stock value will buy the stock when they believe that the firm's earnings have risen. Their actions push the value of the stock higher.

Some accounting methods may only inflate revenue or deflate expenses for a short-term period, which means that the managers cannot boost the firm's reported earnings indefinitely. At some point, investors will recognize that the estimates are misleading, and they will sell their holdings in the firm's stock.

Revenue-Inflating Techniques. The accounting methods used to measure revenue can vary substantially, which makes it difficult for investors to compare various financial ratios among firms. Several examples of accounting methods used to inflate revenue are listed here:

- A service firm may have a five-year contract with a client, in which the client can cancel the agreement after the first year. The firm records the expected revenue over the next five years in the first year of the contract, even though it only received payment for the first year.

- A publisher of a magazine receives three-year subscriptions, in which payment is made annually. It reports all of these sales as revenue even when the cash has not been received. The cash flow attributed to the sales will occur either in a future period or not at all.

- A firm uses a lenient policy that allows customers to cancel their orders. The firm counts all orders as revenue even though it is likely that many of these orders will be cancelled.

Go to
www.globeinvestor.com/v5/
content/filters

This website provides information on various industry groups and allows you to obtain financial information on firms you specify in any industry. By reviewing financial information for various firms within an industry, you can measure the industry norm.

Preventing Future Accounting Fraud. Publicly traded firms are required to have their financial statements audited by an independent auditor to ensure that the statements are accurate. Yet, auditors did not prevent Enron, Nortel Networks, or many other firms from issuing inaccurate financial statements. One reason for this type of negligence may be that the auditors want to retain these clients. They may worry that if they force a firm to report more accurate earnings, it will hire a different auditor in the future. Arthur Andersen was the accounting firm responsible for auditing Enron. In 2000, it received $25 million in auditing fees and $27 million in consulting fees from Enron. If it did not sign off on Enron's books, it would have risked losing annual fees of this scale in future years. Investors learned from the Enron scandal that they cannot necessarily trust that a firm or its auditor will provide reliable information about earnings.

Various provincial securities commissions, stock exchanges, and self-regulatory organizations (SROs) have introduced new rules intended to ensure more accurate disclosure by firms.

IN-CLASS NOTES

Stock Quotations and Analysis of a Firm

- Where can you find stock quotes?
    - Stockbrokers, financial newspapers, business sections of local newspapers, financial news television networks, financial websites
- Examples of information obtained from a stock quote
    - Ticker symbol, closing price, net change in price, volume traded, highs and lows, dividend yield, price–earnings ratio
- Firm analysis
    - Annual report, balance sheet, income statement, firm-specific characteristics, Value Line Investment Survey

---

L.O. 3 ECONOMIC ANALYSIS OF STOCKS

A firm's future revenue and earnings are influenced by demand for its products, which is typically influenced by economic and industry conditions. In addition, firm-specific conditions (such as managerial expertise) can influence the firm's revenue or earnings.

An economic analysis involves assessing any economic conditions that can affect a firm's stock price, including economic growth, interest rates, and inflation.

Economic Growth

economic growth
The growth in a country's economy over a particular period.

gross domestic product (GDP)
The total market value of all products and services produced in a country.

Economic growth is the growth in a country's economy over a particular period. It is commonly measured by the amount of production in a country, or the **gross domestic product (GDP)**, which reflects the total market value of all products and services produced in the country. The production level of products and services is closely related to the aggregate (overall) demand for products and services. When aggregate demand by consumers rises, firms produce more products to accommodate the increased demand. This higher level of production results in more jobs and higher incomes. Consumers then have more money to spend, which results in additional aggregate demand for products and services. The firms that provide products and services experience higher sales (revenue) and earnings, and their stock prices may rise.

Weak Economic Conditions.   When economic conditions are weak, the aggregate demand for products and services declines. Firms experience lower sales levels and earnings, and their stock prices may decline as a result. Some firms may lay off employees and reduce their operations overall. Some may even fail if conditions weaken substantially. Consumers have less income and therefore less money to spend. This may cause an additional decline in the aggregate demand for products and services, and firms' earnings and stock prices may decrease further.

Fiscal Policy Effects.   Given the potential impact of economic growth on stock prices, Canadian investors also monitor the federal government's fiscal policy, or how the government imposes taxes on individuals and corporations and how it spends tax revenues. When corporate tax rates are increased, the after-tax earnings of corporations are reduced, which means that there is less money for shareholders. When individual tax rates are increased, individuals have less money to spend and therefore consume fewer products. As a result, the demand for products and services declines and firms' earnings are reduced. However, if taxpayers/consumers demand more government services, such as health care, taxes must increase.

fiscal policy
How the government imposes taxes on individuals and corporations and how it spends tax revenues.

Interest Rates

Interest rates can affect economic growth and therefore have an indirect impact on stock prices. In general, stocks perform better when interest rates are low because firms can obtain financing at relatively low rates. Firms tend to be more willing to expand when interest rates are low, and their expansions stimulate the economy. When interest rates are low, investors also tend to shift more of their funds into stock because the interest earned on fixed-income securities is relatively low. The general shift into stocks increases the demand for stocks, which places upward pressure on stock prices.

Lower interest rates may enable more consumers to afford cars or homes. Car manufacturers and home builders then experience higher earnings, and their stock prices tend to increase as well.

Financial publications often refer to the Bank of Canada when discussing interest rates because it uses monetary policy (techniques used to affect the economy of a country) to influence interest rates. Through its interest rate policies, the Bank of Canada affects the amount of spending by consumers with borrowed funds and therefore influences economic growth.

In addition to influencing interest rates, the Bank of Canada can use other techniques to affect the economy, including managing the money supply (how much currency is available) and trading currency on the international markets.

Go to
www.oecd.org/canada

Click on
Economic Survey of Canada 2006

This website provides information about economic conditions that can affect the value of investments.

monetary policy
Techniques used by the Bank of Canada (central bank) to affect the economy of the country.

Inflation

Stock prices are also affected by inflation, or the increase in the general level of prices of products and services over a specified period. One of the most common measures of inflation is the consumer price index (CPI), which represents the increase in the prices of consumer products such as groceries, household products, housing, and gasoline over time. Inflation can cause an increase in the prices that firms pay for materials or equipment. These firms may then pass on these price increases to the consumer in the form of higher selling prices for their products. Thus, inflation, in the form of increased prices of inputs such as materials or equipment, may lead to more inflation, in the form of increased prices of outputs such as products available for sale to consumers. In this situation, the Bank of Canada may use monetary policy to control inflation so that its effect on stock prices and the general economy is not too negative. The main publications providing information about inflation and other economic conditions are listed in Exhibit 13.6. These publications commonly provide historical data for inflation, economic growth, interest rates, and many other economic indicators.

inflation
The increase in the general level of prices of products and services over a specified period.

consumer price index (CPI)
A measure of inflation that represents the increase in the prices of consumer products such as groceries, household products, housing, and gasoline over time.

Exhibit 13.6 Sources of Economic Information

Published Sources

- **Bank of Canada Weekly Financial Statistics:** provides key banking and money market statistics.
- **The Daily:** issues news releases on current social and economic conditions and announces new products. It provides a comprehensive one-stop overview of new information available from Statistics Canada.
- **Bank of Canada Monetary Policy Report and Update:** provides a detailed summary of the Bank's policies and strategies, and of the economic climate and its implications for inflation.

Online Sources

- **Bank of Canada (www.bank-banque-canada.ca):** provides reports on interest rates, other economic conditions, and news announcements about various economic indicators.
- **Statistics Canada (www.statcan.ca/menu-en.htm):** provides information and news about economic conditions by subject area.
- **Department of Finance Canada (www.fin.gc.ca/access/ecfisce.html):** provides detailed information on economic and fiscal conditions.
- **Government of Canada (www.canadianeconomy.gc.ca):** provides a one-stop guide to the national economy, and tools to learn more about various economic concepts and events.

L.O. 4 INDUSTRY ANALYSIS OF STOCKS

A firm's stock price is also susceptible to industry conditions. The demand for products or services within an industry changes over time. For example, the popularity of the Internet increased the demand for computers, disks, printers, and Internet guides in the 1990s. Producers of these products initially benefited from the increased demand. However, as other firms notice increased demand in a particular industry, they will often enter that industry and cause increased competition. Competition is another industry factor that frequently affects sales and earnings, and therefore the stock price of a firm. Competition has intensified for many industries as a result of the Internet, which has reduced the costs of marketing and delivering products for some firms.

Industry Indicators
Investors can obtain information about firms and their corresponding industry from various sources, as summarized in Exhibit 13.7. Numerous financial websites also provide information on specific industries. Another indicator of industry performance is the industry stock index, which measures how the market value of the firms within the industry has changed over a specific period. The prevailing sector stock index for a particular industry indicates the general expectations of investors about that industry.

L.O. 5 STOCK VALUATION

Some stocks of high-performing firms are priced high, and therefore may not be good investments for the future. Before investing in a stock, you should estimate its market value just as you would estimate the market value of a car or a home. A stock is different from a car or a home, however, in that it does not serve a physical function such as transportation or housing. A stock is simply intended to generate a return on the money invested.

> ### Exhibit 13.7 Sources of Industry Information
>
> **Published Sources**
>
> Although some government publications offer industry information, the most popular sources are provided by the private sector.
>
> - **Value Line Industry Survey:** provides an industry outlook, performance levels of various industries, and financial statistics for firms in each industry over time.
>
> - **Report on Canada's Industrial Performance:** provides a semi-annual analysis of the current economic and financial performance of Canadian industries.
>
> - **Standard & Poor's Analysts Handbook:** provides financial statistics for various industries over time.
>
> **Online Sources**
>
> - **Investcom (www.investcom.com):** identifies the performance of various industry sectors on a daily basis.
>
> - **Report on Business (www.reportonbusiness.com):** contains news articles related to specific industries.
>
> - **Yahoo! Canada (http://ca.yahoo.com):** provides financial news and statistics for each industry.
>
> - **TSX Group (www.tsx.com):** provides equity and bond market indices for various industry sectors.

The price of a stock is based on the demand for that stock versus the supply of stock available for purchase. The demand for shares is determined by the number of investors who wish to purchase shares of the stock. The supply of stock is determined by the number of investors who want to sell their shares. (Remember, too, that the firm itself may be either a buyer or a seller of its own stock.)

The valuation process involves identifying a firm that you think may perform well in the future and determining whether its stock is overvalued, undervalued, or on target. You buy a stock when you think that it is undervalued so that you can therefore achieve a high return from investing in it. Yet your purchase of the stock means that some other investor was willing to sell it. So, while you believe the stock is undervalued, others apparently think it is overvalued. This difference in opinion is what causes a high volume of trading. With some stocks, more than a million shares are traded each day as a result of these divergent views of the stock's true value. Investors who use specific methods to value a stock may be able to achieve higher returns than others.

technical analysis
The valuation of stocks based on historical price patterns using various charting techniques.

When valuing stocks, investors can use technical analysis or fundamental analysis. **Technical analysis** is the valuation of stocks based on historical price patterns using various charting techniques. For example, you might purchase a stock whenever its price rises on three consecutive days because you expect that a trend in prices indicates future price movements. Alternatively, you may decide to sell a stock if its price declines on several consecutive days, because you expect that the trend will continue. There are many different chart techniques using price and time elements.

fundamental analysis
The valuation of stocks based on an examination of fundamental characteristics such as revenue, earnings, and/or the sensitivity of the firm's performance to economic conditions.

Fundamental analysis is the valuation of stocks based on an examination of fundamental characteristics such as revenue, earnings, and/or the sensitivity of the firm's performance to economic conditions. There are many different ways to apply fundamental analysis when valuing stocks, including the two popular methods discussed below. Although both methods can easily be applied to value a stock, they are subject to limitations (addressed below).

Price–Earnings (P/E) Method

One method used to determine the value of a stock is based on the value of the firm's earnings. The higher the earnings, the more funds the firm has to pay in dividends to its shareholders or to reinvest for further expansion (which will ultimately generate additional earnings). The most common method of using earnings to value stocks is the price–earnings (P/E) method, in which a firm's earnings per share are multiplied by the mean industry P/E ratio. A stock's P/E ratio is its stock price per share (P) divided by its annual earnings per share (E):

> **price–earnings (P/E) method**
> A method of valuing stocks in which a firm's earnings per share are multiplied by the mean industry price–earnings (P/E) ratio.

$$\text{Price–Earnings (P/E) Ratio} = P/E.$$

You can find the P/E ratio of any firm in stock quotations published in financial newspapers, such as the *National Post*, and on many financial websites. A P/E ratio of 10 means that the firm's stock price is 10 times the firm's earnings per share. You can use the P/E method to value a firm as follows:

1. Look up the P/E ratios of stocks in the firm's industry.

2. Multiply the average industry P/E ratio by the firm's earnings per share.

3. Compare your estimated value of the firm's stock to its market value to determine whether the stock is currently undervalued or overvalued.

EXAMPLE

Stephanie Spratt is impressed with Trail.com, an online clothing firm that focuses on the 18 to 22 age bracket. Its prices are much lower than its competitors' and the quality of its products is high. After reading about the firm on its website and in various financial newspapers, Stephanie has learned that it plans to expand its clothing lines. The prevailing price of Trail.com stock is $61 per share.

Stephanie decides to apply the P/E method to value Trail.com stock, which has had recent annual earnings of $5 per share. Only three other corporations have very similar businesses to Trail.com and have stock that is traded. Stephanie uses the Stock Quotes section of the Yahoo! Canada website to determine the P/E ratios of these firms. One firm has a P/E ratio of 10, the second a ratio of 12, and the third a ratio of 14.

Stephanie derives a value for Trail.com's stock by multiplying its recent annual earnings per share by the average industry P/E ratio:

1. Mean P/E Ratio of Industry = (10 + 12 + 14) ÷ 3
= 12
2. Valuation of Stock = Firm's Earnings per Share × Mean Industry P/E Ratio
= $5 × 12
= $60

This valuation of $60 is below the prevailing stock price ($61) of Trail.com, indicating that the stock is slightly overvalued. Given this valuation, Stephanie decides not to purchase Trail.com stock at this time.

Deriving an Estimate of Earnings. Because the stock price of a firm is influenced by expected earnings, investors may prefer to use expected earnings rather than past earnings to value a firm and its corresponding industry. Many investors rely on Value Line and other investment services for earnings forecasts. Some earnings forecasts can be obtained from publications and websites. If investors expect no change in earnings from last year to this year, last year's earnings can be used.

Limitations of the P/E Method. Forecasting earnings is difficult. Therefore, valuations of a stock that are based on expected earnings may be unreliable. Investors who overestimate future earnings risk overpaying for a stock.

Go to
www.globeinvestor.com

Click on
Earnings Estimates under
Tracking Tools

This website provides
recent earnings-per-share
estimates of a firm that you
specify, which you can use
when applying the P/E
method of valuing stocks.

price–sales (P/S) method
A method of valuing stocks
in which the revenue per
share of a specific firm is
multiplied by the mean
industry ratio of share price
to revenue.

Even if the forecast of earnings is accurate, there is still the question of the proper P/E multiple that should be used to value a stock. The firm that you are valuing may deserve to have a lower P/E ratio than other firms if its future performance is subject to more uncertainty. For example, perhaps the firm is using less advanced technology than its competitors, which could adversely affect its performance in a few years. Consequently, its lower P/E ratio may not necessarily mean that the firm's stock is undervalued by the market.

Another limitation of the P/E method is that results will vary depending on the firms selected to derive a mean industry P/E ratio. Should this ratio be derived from the three closest competitors (as in the example above) or from the 10 closest competitors? For firms that conduct several types of business, it is difficult to determine who the closest competitors are. Investors who apply the wrong industry P/E ratio will derive an inaccurate valuation, which may cause them to buy stocks that are not really undervalued.

Price–Sales (P/S) Method

A second common valuation method is the price–sales (P/S) method, in which the revenue per share of a specific firm is multiplied by the mean industry ratio of share price to revenue. When a firm sells its products, it generates revenue. The higher a firm's revenues, the higher its valuation within a specific industry. Since stock prices reflect expectations of future performance, investors should use recently reported revenues only if they believe that the reported revenues represent a reasonable forecast of the future. The P/S method is especially popular for valuing firms (such as some Internet firms) that cannot be valued with the P/E method because they have negative earnings.

EXAMPLE

Stephanie Spratt applies the P/S method to value Trail.com's stock. A financial website discloses that Trail.com has expected revenues of $29 per share and that the other firms in the same industry have a price-to-sales (P/S) ratio of 2.0, on average. Based on this information, Stephanie estimates the value of Trail.com to be:

Valuation of Stock = Expected Revenues of Firm per Share × Mean Industry P/S Ratio

= $29 × 2.0

= $58

Since Trail.com stock is currently priced at $61, she decides that the stock is overpriced and she will not buy it at this time.

Limitations of the P/S Method. The P/S method is subject to error if it is based on an overestimate of revenues or on a set of firms whose operations are not very similar to those of the firm being valued. As well, revenues do not indicate how well a firm is managed. If two firms in the same industry have the same revenues, the firm with the lower costs will normally be valued higher. Yet the P/S method will give these two firms the same value because it ignores costs incurred by the firms. For this reason, the P/E method may be a more appropriate valuation method.

Integrating Your Analyses. By conducting an analysis of the firm itself, the economy, and the industry, you can assess a firm's possible future performance. This process enables you to determine whether to purchase the firm's stock. Exhibit 13.8 summarizes the potential impact of economic, industry, and firm-specific conditions on a firm's stock price.

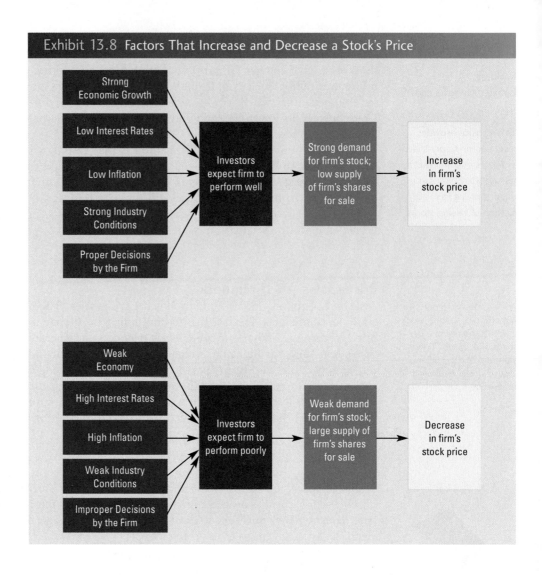

Exhibit 13.8 Factors That Increase and Decrease a Stock's Price

Go to
www.globeinvestor.com/v5/
content/filters

This website provides
a list of stocks that meet
criteria that you specify for
performance over the last
year, such as specific
price–earnings (P/E) ratios
and other characteristics.

EXAMPLE

Stephanie Spratt has been monitoring Trail.com, a firm that sells clothing to people in the 18 to 22 age bracket. Her valuations of the firm's stock indicated that it is overvalued. She decides to conduct an economic and industry analysis to make a more informed decision about whether to buy this stock.

First, Stephanie reviews various financial websites that provide information on future economic growth. Most of these websites suggest that economic growth will be strong and that the unemployment rate will be low. She expects that a strong economy will enhance Trail.com's future performance.

Then Stephanie reviews websites on the clothing industry for the 18 to 22 age bracket. She reads that several small clothing firms are expanding rapidly and will be establishing retail stores in malls throughout the country. All of these firms are also establishing websites so that they can sell their clothing directly to customers who wish to place orders online. Many of these firms are expected to compete directly with Trail.com because they also sell clothing to customers in the 18 to 22 age bracket. This industry analysis suggests that Trail.com will face much more competition in the near future.

As well, Stephanie learns from an online news source that Trail.com has announced plans to expand and has recently borrowed a substantial amount of funds to support its growth. Consequently, it has a high debt ratio. She believes that there is room for only a limited number of firms to achieve a successful growth strategy in this industry and that Trail.com may not generate sufficient revenue to meet its high debt payments in the future.

Overall, the economic outlook is favourable for Trail.com, but the industry outlook is very unfavourable, and the firm's high debt level is a concern. Stephanie decides not to invest in the stock unless industry conditions become more favourable and Trail.com proves that it can handle its large amount of debt without experiencing financial problems.

IN-CLASS NOTES

Economic and Industry Analysis of Stocks and Stock Valuation

- Economic analysis involves assessing:
  - Economic growth (GDP, fiscal policy)
  - Interest rates
  - Inflation (CPI)
- Industry analysis
  - Changes in consumer demand
  - Threat of new entrants and more competition
  - Industry indicators
- Stock valuation
  - Historical price patterns using technical analysis
  - Fundamental characteristics using fundamental analysis
  - P/E method: compare your estimated value of the firm's stock to its market value to determine whether the stock is currently undervalued or overvalued according to industry standards
  - P/S method: especially popular for valuing firms that have negative earnings

STOCK MARKET EFFICIENCY

Because investors use different methods to value and analyze stocks, they derive different valuations for a stock. Stock market efficiency is relevant for investors who are attempting to achieve abnormally high returns by analyzing financial information or relying on investment advisers. If stock prices fully reflect information that is available to investors, the stock market is said to be efficient.

Conversely, the stock market is referred to as inefficient if stock prices do not reflect all public information that is available to investors. In general, an efficient stock market implies that you and other investors will not be able to identify stocks that are undervalued because stocks are valued properly by the market.

The argument for efficiency is that demand for shares by investors should drive the equilibrium price of a stock toward its proper value. If a stock was really priced below its estimated value, the large institutional investors who have more access to information about the stock than individual investors would buy substantial

efficient stock market A market in which stock prices fully reflect information that is available to investors.

inefficient stock market A market in which stock prices do not reflect all public information that is available to investors.

amounts of it. The strong demand for shares would force the price of the stock higher, bringing the stock's price close to its estimated value. Thus, institutional investors capitalizing on the discrepancy would push the stock price back to its estimated value.

Reviewing historical stock prices, investors can identify several stocks that experienced very large returns. Some stocks have doubled in price in a single day. Some stocks will experience very large returns in the future. These performances do not mean that the stock market is inefficient, however, unless information that was available to investors should have justified higher valuations of those stocks before their prices increased. It is easy to look back and realize that you would have benefited from purchasing shares of Microsoft or Dell Computer when their stocks were first publicly traded. Yet who really knew that these stocks would perform so well at that time? An investor can achieve high returns from a hunch about a specific stock. The concept of market efficiency acknowledges that when you invest in stocks, some of those stocks may outperform the market in general. However, it implies that stock selections by an investor will not consistently beat the market.

L.O. 6 STOCK EXCHANGES

stock exchanges
Facilities that allow investors to purchase or sell existing stocks.

By understanding some very basic methods of evaluating stocks, you can start to make stock investments. Stock exchanges are facilities that allow investors to purchase or sell existing stocks. They facilitate trading in the secondary market so that investors can sell stocks that they previously purchased. An organized securities exchange occupies a physical or virtual location where trading occurs. A stock must be listed on a stock exchange to be traded there, meaning that it must fulfill specific requirements of the exchange. To be listed on the Toronto Stock Exchange, for example, a firm must meet minimum listing requirements in areas such as revenue, cash flow, net tangible assets, working capital, and cash. The exchange's requirements ensure that there will be an active market for stocks in which shares are commonly traded.

Canadian Stock Exchanges

TSX Group. Historically, stock exchanges have been referred to by their location. For example, until 1999, the exchange in Vancouver was known as the Vancouver Stock Exchange (VSE). However, since 1999, Canadian capital markets have gone through a major overhaul. Gone are the days when major exchanges were located throughout the country in Vancouver, Calgary, Winnipeg, Toronto, and Montreal. As a result of realignments and acquisitions, Canadian stocks are now traded on two markets: the Toronto Stock Exchange (TSX) and the TSX Venture Exchange. The TSX is where senior equities are traded while the TSX Venture Exchange serves the public venture capital market. (Venture capital refers to investors' funds destined for risky, generally new businesses with tremendous growth potential.) Both markets are owned and operated by a for-profit organization, the TSX Group. As of March 31, 2007, 3709 companies were listed on the TSX and the TSX Venture Exchange, representing 9.5 percent of all listings worldwide.

venture capital
Refers to investors' funds destined for risky, generally new businesses with tremendous growth potential.

Montreal Exchange. Canada's other stock exchange, located in Montreal, is a derivatives exchange. Investors interested in trading options and futures would use the services of the Montreal Exchange to meet their trading needs. On December 10, 2007, the TSX Group and the Montreal Exchange announced that they will merge their organizations to create TMX Group Inc.

Electronic Trading. The major exchanges in Canada offer trading services electronically. This has eliminated the open-outcry system, where floor traders would complete trades on behalf of their brokerage houses' customers. For example, on the TSX and TSX Venture Exchange, an integrated system of several order routing and terminal vendors allows electronic access to the exchange. Liquidity of an electronic trading system is enhanced by using **market makers**, securities dealers who are required to trade actively in the market so that liquidity is maintained when natural market forces cannot provide sufficient liquidity.

market makers
Securities dealers who are required to trade actively in the market so that liquidity is maintained when natural market forces cannot provide sufficient liquidity.

Other Stock Exchanges

NYSE Euronext. On April 4, 2007, NYSE Group, Inc. and Euronext N.V. merged to form the world's largest and most liquid exchange group. Euronext N.V. was created in 2000 as a result of the mergers of the Paris, Brussels, and Amsterdam stock exchanges. In 2002, the Lisbon Stock Exchange merged with Euronext. Prior to these mergers, a number of the stock exchanges that formed Euronext had consolidated their domestic derivatives markets into one national exchange. The subsequent merger with the NYSE Group, which itself was formed as a result of the consolidation of a number of exchanges, brought together seven stock exchanges and six derivatives markets from six countries. The result is a world leader for listings, stock market trading, derivatives, bonds, and the distribution of market data.

demutualization
Refers to the transformation of a firm from a member-owned organization to a publicly owned, for-profit organization.

The rapid consolidation that is occurring in global capital markets has been fuelled by the demutualization of stock exchanges. **Demutualization** refers to the transformation of a firm from a member-owned organization to a publicly owned, for-profit organization.

NASDAQ and AMEX. The NASDAQ, or the National Association of Securities Dealers Automated Quotation system, provides continual updated market price information on stocks that meet its requirements on size and trading volume. Similar to the TSX, it is an electronic exchange. The American Stock Exchange (AMEX) is a nationally organized exchange in the United States that lists about 800 stocks. These stocks are generally from smaller firms and are less actively traded than those on the NYSE Euronext. The NASDAQ and the AMEX merged in 1998, although they still perform separate functions.

Over-the-Counter (OTC) Market

over-the-counter (OTC) market
An electronic communications network that allows investors to buy or sell securities.

The **over-the-counter (OTC) market** is an electronic communications network that allows investors to buy or sell securities. It is not a transparent facility like the organized exchanges. Stock exchanges are considered to be transparent because you can see the trading taking place, even if only online, and you have access to the trade information as it occurs. The debt marketplace, however, is less transparent, as trade information is compiled at the end of the day rather than as it occurs. Some OTC markets are similar to the debt marketplace.

Trades made on the OTC market are communicated through a computer network by market makers who earn a profit on each trade based on the difference between the prices at which they buy and sell securities. The OTC market is less hindered by rules and regulations and can be driven more by supply and demand than organized stock exchanges. OTC markets are also characterized by trading methods. In an OTC market, you are transacting business with one person, principal to principal, at their price and their price alone. In contrast, an organized exchange market is an auction market and the price paid for a security is the best price at that time.

The Canadian OTC market was designed for companies that do not meet the listing requirements of the TSX or the TSX Venture Exchange. OTC stocks can be accessed using the NEX board on the TSX Venture Exchange. OTC markets also exist in other countries where companies do not meet the listing requirements of the exchanges in that particular country.

IN-CLASS NOTES

Stock Market Efficiency and Stock Exchanges

- Efficient stock market
  - A market in which stock prices fully reflect information that is available to investors
  - Stock selections by an investor will not consistently beat the market
- Inefficient stock market
  - A market in which stock prices do not reflect all public information that is available to investors
  - Stock selections by an investor may beat the market
- Canadian stock exchanges
  - Toronto Stock Exchange (TSX) – senior equity exchange
  - TSX Venture Exchange – public venture capital market
  - Montreal Exchange – derivatives exchange
- Other stock exchanges
  - NYSE Euronext
  - NASDAQ
  - American Stock Exchange (AMEX)

L.O. 7

PURCHASING OR SELLING STOCKS

The market for a stock is created from the flow of buy and sell orders from investors. Recall from Chapter 11 that orders to buy a stock are matched with orders to sell that stock at a price agreeable to both parties in each transaction. To buy or sell a stock, you establish an account at a brokerage firm.

Relying on Brokerage or Analyst Recommendations

When using a full-service broker, you can receive investment advice. In addition, you have access to stock ratings that are assigned by stock analysts employed by brokerage firms.

Evaluating Analyst Advice. Recommendations from brokers and analysts have limitations. Some advisers may suggest that you buy or sell securities frequently, rather than holding on to your investment portfolio over time. Keep in mind that you must pay a commission to that adviser for each transaction.

Many studies have shown that recommendations made by brokers or analysts do not lead to better performance than the stock market in general. Some advisers have very limited experience in analyzing and valuing securities. Even those who are very experienced will not necessarily be able to help you achieve unusually high performance.

Focus on Ethics: Relying on Analyst Recommendations

Brokers and analysts tend to be overly optimistic about stocks. They are generally unwilling to recommend that investors sell stocks because they do not want to offend any firms with which their own investment firm might do business in the future. In

1999, the firm First Call tracked 27 000 recommendations of stocks by analysts, and only 35 of these recommendations were to sell a specific stock. In other words, analysts made about 1 "sell" recommendation for every 770 "buy" recommendations.

In response to much criticism, some analysts recently have been more willing to offer "sell" recommendations on some stocks. However, there is still a tendency for them to be generally optimistic about most stocks and there may be some conflicts of interest. For example, analysts may own the stock they are recommending, so it is in their best interest to create a demand for the stock so that its price will rise. However, analysts must disclose ownership of stocks they recommend.

How Can You Review Your Broker's History? The Investment Dealers Association of Canada's website (www.ida.ca/IDAWebsite/English/Investors/MemberFirmEmployee Information/) allows you to perform a search for any disciplinary information against a broker by entering a broker's last name or the name of the brokerage firm. In addition, you can obtain a list of current IDA member firms and complete an online information request form detailing the specific information you are looking for. The website for your provincial securities commission will also provide a listing of enforcement proceedings on any brokers and/or firms that are registered within your province.

Brokerage Commissions. You can choose a discount or full-service brokerage firm. A **discount brokerage firm** executes transactions but does not offer investment advice. A **full-service brokerage firm** offers investment advice and executes transactions. Full-service brokerage firms tend to charge higher fees for their services than discount brokers. For example, a full-service brokerage firm may charge a commission of between 3 and 8 percent of a transaction, or between $150 and $400 for a $5000 transaction, whereas a discount brokerage firm would likely charge you between $8 and $60 for the same transaction.

> **discount brokerage firm**
> A brokerage firm that executes transactions but does not offer investment advice.
>
> **full-service brokerage firm**
> A brokerage firm that offers investment advice and executes transactions.

Buying or Selling Stock Online

Individuals who wish to buy or sell stocks are increasingly using online brokerage services such as Qtrade Investor and E*Trade Canada. One advantage of placing orders online is that the commission charged per transaction is very low, such as $8 or $20, regardless of the size of the transaction (up to a specified maximum level). A second advantage is convenience. In addition to accepting orders, online brokers provide real-time stock quotes and financial information. To establish an account with an online brokerage service, go to its website and follow the instructions to set up an account. Then send the online broker a cheque. Once the cheque has cleared, your account will show that you have funds you can use to invest online.

Recall from Chapter 4 that many online brokerage firms have a money market fund where your cash is deposited until it is used to make transactions. Consequently, you can earn some interest on your funds until you use them to purchase securities. Once you place an order, the online brokerage firm will use the money in your fund to pay for the transaction. You may even receive blank cheques so that you can write cheques against your money market account.

Because many investors have shifted to online brokerage services, financial conglomerates such as RBC offer online brokerage services in addition to traditional brokerage firm services. You can place an order from your computer in less than a minute and it usually will be executed within a minute. Timely execution depends on the liquidity of the security as well as the type of order entered.

Go to
www.canada.etrade.com/
pages/home/main.shtml

This website provides
information that you can
use when making investment
decisions. It also illustrates
how you can trade stocks
online through their
services, which typically
reduces your transaction
costs.

ticker symbol
The abbreviated term used
to identify a stock for
trading purposes.

board lot
Shares bought or sold in
multiples of typically 100
shares. The size of the
board lot depends on the
price of the security.

odd lot
Less than a board lot of
that particular stock.

market order
An order to buy or sell a
stock at its prevailing
market price.

Placing an Order

Whenever you place an order to buy or sell a stock, you must specify the following:

- Name and class of the stock
- Buy or sell
- Number of shares
- Market order or limit order

Name and Class of the Stock. It is important to know the ticker symbol for your stock. The ticker symbol is the abbreviated term used to identify a stock for trading purposes. For example, Celestica's symbol is CLS, and Enbridge's symbol is ENB. A symbol is shorter and simpler than the formal name of a firm and easily distinguishes between different firms with similar names. As well, the class of that stock is also included, reducing the risk of error when choosing different equities offered by the same firm.

Buy or Sell. Brokerage firms execute both buy and sell transactions. Therefore, it is necessary to specify whether you are buying or selling a security when you place an order. Once you place your order and it is executed, you are bound by the instructions you gave. You must indicate when selling whether you own the stock now or are selling borrowed stock.

Number of Shares. Shares are typically sold in multiples of 100, referred to as a board-lot transaction. An order to buy or sell fewer than 100 shares is referred to as an odd-lot transaction. Lower-priced stocks may sell in board lots of 1000 shares while higher-priced stocks may sell in board lots of 10.

Market Order or Limit Order. You can buy or sell a stock by placing a market order, which is an order to buy or sell a stock at its prevailing market price. The advantage of a market order is that you are assured that your order will be executed quickly. A disadvantage is that the stock price could change abruptly just before you place your order. Prevailing market prices are just that, and the market can change more rapidly than you expect.

EXAMPLE

You want to buy 100 shares of Trendy stock, which had a closing price of $40. You assume that you will pay about $40 per share when the market opens this morning, or $4000 ($40 × 100 shares) for the order ignoring the commission. However, your order is executed at $43, which means that you pay $4300 ($43 × 100 shares). Unfortunately, many other investors wanted to buy Trendy stock this morning, creating increased demand. The strong demand relative to the small number of shares available for sale caused the stock price to increase to $43 before your broker could find a willing seller of Trendy stock.

limit order
An order to buy or sell a
stock only if the price is
within limits that you
specify.

Alternatively, you can buy or sell stock by placing a limit order, which is an order to buy or sell a stock only if the price is within limits that you specify. A limit order sets a maximum price at which the stock can be purchased and can be for one day only or valid until cancelled (normally cancelled in six months if a transaction has not been executed by then). The limit order will specify whether you are willing to accept a portion of the shares desired (normally in board lots of 100); alternatively, you can specify that you want the full number of shares to be traded or none at all.

EXAMPLE

Using the information provided in the previous example, you place a limit order on Trendy stock, with a maximum price of $41, good for the day. When the stock opens at $43 this morning, your order is not executed because the market price exceeds your limit price. Later in the day, the stock price declines to $41, at which time your order is executed.

The example above illustrates the advantage of a limit order. However, the disadvantage is that you may miss out on a transaction you desire. If the price of Trendy stock had continued to rise throughout the day after opening at $43, your order would not have been executed at all.

Limit orders can also be used to sell stocks. In this case, a limit order specifies a minimum price at which the stock should be sold.

EXAMPLE

You own 100 shares of Zina stock, which is currently worth $18 per share. You do not have time to monitor the market price but would be willing to sell the stock at $20 per share. You place a limit order to sell 100 shares of Zina stock at a minimum price of $20, good until cancelled. A few months later, Zina's stock price rises to $20 per share. You soon receive confirmation from your brokerage firm that the transaction has been executed.

on-stop order
An order to execute a transaction when the stock price reaches a specified level; a special form of limit order.

Stop Orders. An on-stop order is a special form of limit order; it is an order to execute a transaction when the stock price reaches a specified level. A buy stop order is an order to buy a stock when the price rises to a specified level. Conversely, a sell stop order is an order to sell a stock when the price falls to a specified level. These are specialized types of orders that should only be used by experienced trader-investors who fully understand their implications (which are beyond the scope of this book).

L.O. 8 BUYING STOCK ON MARGIN

buy stop order
An order to buy a stock when the price rises to a specified level.

sell stop order
An order to sell a stock when the price falls to a specified level.

on margin
Purchasing a stock with a small amount of personal funds and a portion of the funds borrowed from a brokerage firm.

Some investors choose to purchase stock on margin, meaning that a portion of their purchase is funded with money borrowed from their brokerage firm. Buying a stock on margin enables you to purchase stocks using less of your own capital. As with any loan, you will pay interest costs and your capital risk remains the total cost of the purchase.

As shown in Exhibit 13.9, the margin requirement limits vary depending on the price of the stock that is being margined. For example, you decide to purchase 500 shares of a stock that is currently trading at $20. The margin requirement is calculated as:

500 shares × $20 per share × 30% margin rate = $3000

This is the amount of money you are required to have in order to purchase this stock. The brokerage firm is lending you the other 70 percent of the purchase price, or $7000. This amount is called the maximum loan value.

margin call
A request from a brokerage firm for the investor to increase the cash in the account in order to return the margin to the minimum level.

If the value of investments purchased on margin declines, you will receive a margin call from your brokerage firm, a request to increase the cash in your account in order to return the margin to the minimum level. For example, if the value of the stock discussed above decreases to $15, the maximum loan value is:

500 shares × $15 × 70% loan value = $5250.

Therefore, the brokerage firm is now willing to lend you $5250. Since your loan amount outstanding is $7000, the brokerage firm will make a margin call in the amount of $1750 ($7000 – $5250). Since a margin call may occur again if the stock price decreases further, many investors will maintain a cash balance in their margin account to cover any future decreases in stock price.

On the other hand, if the stock price increases, this will free up money that the investor can use to make additional investments. For example, if the value of the stock discussed above increases to $25, the maximum loan value would be:

500 shares × $25 × 70% loan value = $8750.

The brokerage firm is now willing to lend you $8750. Since your loan amount outstanding is $7000, you have excess margin of $1750 ($8750 – $7000).

Exhibit 13.9 Margin Requirements for Securities Listed on Various Exchanges

Category of Security	Margin Requirement	Concentration Guidelines
Canadian Securities		
TSX Listed/IDA Approved List for Reduced Margin ($5.00+)	30%	$1 million Loan Value
TSX Listed Securities ($3.00+)	50%	$500 000 Loan Value
TSX Venture ($3.00+) Listed Securities	75%	$25 000 Loan Value
Listed Securities under $3.00	100%	Not Applicable
Listed Warrants ($3.00+)	50%	$250 000 Loan Value
U.S. Securities (NYSE, NASDAQ, AMEX)		
Option Eligible Securities ($5.00+)	30%	US$1 million Loan Value
Listed Securities ($3.00+)	50%	US$500 000 Loan Value
Listed Securities under $3.00	100%	Not Applicable
OTC Bulletin Board	100%	Not Applicable

Source: TD Canada Trust, "How to Place a Trade: Margin Requirements and Concentration Guidelines," www.tdcanadatrust.com/planning/investing/margin.jsp (accessed July 13, 2007). Reprinted with permission of TD Canada Trust.

Impact of Margin on Returns

When you buy a stock on margin, the return on your investment is magnified. This effect is favourable if the stock's price increases sufficiently over the period you hold the stock. Remember that interest costs will accrue.

EXAMPLE

You want to buy 100 shares of Lynde Corporation, which is currently trading at $50 per share. Therefore, the total investment costs $5000. However, you plan to purchase on margin. This means that you will put some money in your account to purchase the stock and borrow the remainder from your brokerage firm at 12 percent annual interest. The brokerage firm will lend 50 percent of the market value of the stock.

After one year, you sell the stock for $60 per share, repaying the loan plus interest. Lynde Corporation paid dividends of $1 per share over the year. The return from buying on margin is:

$$\text{Return} = \frac{(SP + D) - (BP + I)}{\text{Margin Deposit per Share}}$$

where *SP* is the selling price, *D* is the dividends received over the time period, *BP* is the original purchase price, and *I* is the interest paid on the loan over the time period. The margin deposit per share is what the investment house required as a deposit on the trade. In this example, the loan value is calculated as 50 percent of the current market value. The margin deposit per share represents the balance owing.

In this example:

$$\text{Return} = \frac{(\$60 + \$1) - (\$50 + \$3)}{\$25} \times 100$$

$$= 0.32 \times 100$$

$$= 32\%$$

If you had purchased the stock for cash, the return would be:

$$\text{Return} = \frac{(SP + D) - BP}{BP} \times 100$$

$$= \frac{(\$60 + \$1) - \$50}{\$50} \times 100$$

$$= 0.22 \times 100$$

$$= 22\%$$

The return when purchasing on margin is 10 percent higher than when using the cash investment method.

Impact of Margin on Risk

Margin purchases will amplify the potential profit or potential loss. If the price of the stock you buy on margin declines, the negative return from buying on margin will be worse than if you had paid cash.

EXAMPLE   Suppose that Lynde Corporation stock declines to $40 per share by the end of the year.

$$\text{Return} = \frac{(SP + D) - (BP + I)}{\text{Margin Deposit per Share}} \times 100$$

$$= \frac{(\$40 + \$1) - (\$50 + \$3)}{\$25} \times 100$$

$$= -0.48 \times 100$$

$$= -48\%$$

If you had purchased the stock for cash, your return would be:

$$\text{Return} = \frac{(\$40 + \$1) - (\$50)}{\$50} \times 100$$

$$= -0.18 \times 100$$

$$= -18\%$$

Thus, your percentage loss when buying on margin is 30 percentage points worse than when buying with cash. Buying on margin changes the risk–return trade-off. The higher the percentage of funds borrowed, the higher both your potential risk and your potential return.

IN-CLASS NOTES

Purchasing or Selling Stocks and Buying Stock on Margin

- Analyst recommendations
  - Brokers and analysts tend to be overly optimistic about stocks
- Discount brokerage firm
  - Executes transactions but does not offer investment advice
- Online brokerage services
  - Very low commissions, convenient
- Placing an order
  - Name and class of the stock, buy or sell, number of shares (board lot vs. odd lot)
  - Market order, limit order, and stop orders
- Buying stock on margin
  - Involves completing a stock purchase with a small amount of personal funds and a portion of the funds borrowed from the brokerage firm
  - If the stock price declines substantially, the brokerage firm will make a margin call
  - Buying stocks on margin will magnify profits and/or losses

_____

_____

_____

_____

_____

_____

_____

_____

_____

_____

_____

L.O. 9 ASSESSING PERFORMANCE OF STOCK INVESTMENTS

How can you measure the performance of your stock investments? How can you distinguish between performance due to general market conditions and performance of the stock?

Comparing Returns to an Index

A convenient and effective method of measuring performance is to compare the return on your stock (or stock portfolio) to the return on a stock index representing similar types of stocks. Stock index returns are provided in most business periodicals and on numerous websites such as Yahoo! Canada.

EXAMPLE

Stephanie Spratt invested in one stock about one year (or four quarters) ago. The returns on her stock are shown in column 2 of Exhibit 13.10. Her return was lowest in the first quarter but increased in the following three quarters. Stephanie wants to compare her stock's return to the market in general to get a true assessment of its performance. This comparison will indicate whether her specific selection generated a higher return than she could have earned by simply investing in a stock index. In Exhibit 13.10, the return on a market index over the

Go to
http://ca.finance.yahoo.com

This website provides
a summary of recent stock
market performance and
other key indicators.

Exhibit 13.10 Stock Performance Evaluation

	Return on Stephanie's Stock	Return on a Canadian Stock Index	Excess Return of Stephanie's Stock (above the market)
Quarter 1	−1%	3%	−4%
Quarter 2	2%	3%	−1%
Quarter 3	2%	4%	−2%
Quarter 4	3%	4%	−1%

Note: The returns calculated above assume that Stephanie purchases the stock at the beginning of the first quarter and sells at the end of each subsequent quarter.

same period is shown in column 3. Given the information in columns 2 and 3, Stephanie determines the excess return on her stock as:

$$ER = R - R_i$$

where ER is excess return, R is the return on her stock, and R_i is the return on the stock index.

The excess return of the stock was negative in each of the four quarters. Stephanie is disappointed in its performance and decides to sell it in the near future if its performance does not improve. She intends to review her initial evaluation to ensure that her assumptions were correct when she conducted her analysis.

Price Quotations for Indexes Used to Measure Stock Performance

Market and sector indexes are reported in financial newspapers. For example, the *Financial Post* provides such quotations, as shown in Exhibit 13.11. The data provided by the *Financial Post* for stock indexes are similar to those for daily stock quotations (refer back to Exhibit 13.1 on page 337).

IN-CLASS NOTES

Assessing Performance of Stock Investments
- Compare returns to an index
- $ER = R - R_i$
  where

  ER = excess return

  R = the return on the stock

  R_i = the return on the stock index

Exhibit 13.11 An Example of Stock Index Information

NORTH AMERICAN INDEXES

TORONTO STOCK EXCHANGE

Index	Close	Net ch	%ch	Vol 00s	Day high	Day low	% Yield	P/E	52wk high	52wk low	Wk %ch	YTD %ch	52wk %ch
S&P/TSX Composite	14,131.93	-45.59	-0.3	1953359	14,207.07	14,131.93	2.36	17.46	14,216.21	11,407.27	+0.5	+9.5	+21.3
Capped Energy	360.71	+0.20	+0.1	355379	363.73	358.63	2.86	14.33	372.01	277.48	+0.2	+11.1	+6.4
Capped Materials	309.08	-1.50	-0.5	917277	311.71	308.22	0.88	19.67	311.71	205.30	+3.1	+17.9	+39.8
Capped Metal/Mining	902.21	-3.05	-0.3	440038	911.17	890.95	1.25	12.84	911.17	497.88	+4.9	+40.3	+73.8
Global Mining	107.85	-2.04	-1.9	1477935	110.34	107.83	n.a.	n.a.	110.34	98.62	+2.0	n.a.	n.a.
Global Gold	284.06	-0.52	-0.2	474970	287.16	283.43	0.46	46.43	347.66	254.04	+4.1	-12.7	-4.8
Capped Industrials	120.21	-0.44	-0.4	99459	120.69	119.95	1.65	18.43	121.85	85.75	+0.4	+21.9	+33.4
Capped Consumer Disc	126.59	-0.05	nil	71268	126.95	126.22	2.31	21.01	127.36	103.31	+0.9	+9.5	+21.3
Capped Consumer Stap	205.86	-0.02	nil	54442	206.28	205.06	1.52	31.75	210.97	176.81	+1.2	+5.1	+14.1
Capped Health Care	49.56	-0.51	-1.0	14476	50.10	49.45	2.61	61.57	54.62	45.14	-0.8	-6.0	-3.1
Capped Financials	217.23	-0.36	-0.2	161256	218.67	217.00	3.04	13.87	226.15	182.08	-1.1	+1.4	+16.2
Capped Real Estate	247.00	-2.13	-0.9	50009	249.41	246.97	3.71	32.05	282.77	199.77	-0.9	+2.7	+22.8
Capped Info Tech	35.83	-0.20	-0.6	31599	36.09	35.82	n.a.	53.09	37.35	22.89	-1.1	+4.9	+46.1
Capped Telecom	114.59	-0.97	-0.8	60475	116.15	114.47	3.53	23.57	116.22	77.50	+0.4	+24.6	+47.6
Capped Utilities	221.17	-0.03	nil	38303	221.76	220.46	4.30	22.49	225.26	190.51	+3.1	+1.9	+14.8
Capped Composite	16,372.88	-52.82	-0.3	1953359	16,459.93	16,372.88	2.36	17.46	16,470.52	13,216.16	+0.5	+9.5	+21.3
TSX Unweighted	268.22	-0.71	-0.3	1953359	n.a.	n.a.	2.54	20.77	269.12	215.94	+1.2	+10.7	+21.3
S&P/TSX 60	808.86	-2.65	-0.3	853048	813.79	808.57	1.97	16.48	815.70	644.38	+0.2	+8.9	+22.5
S&P/TSX 60 Capped	894.44	-2.93	-0.3	853048	899.88	894.11	1.97	16.48	901.99	712.55	+0.2	+8.9	+22.5
S&TSX Completion	958.28	-2.95	-0.3	1100310	961.66	957.76	3.39	20.76	969.97	770.11	+1.2	+10.8	+21.8
S&TSX SmallCap	820.21	+0.17	nil	890352	821.57	818.83	3.59	35.55	823.42	640.40	+1.9	+12.9	+16.8
Income Trust	157.76	+0.46	+0.3	240522	157.93	157.16	8.55	17.91	177.31	134.95	+0.6	+6.5	-5.9
Capped Energy Trust	181.94	+0.34	+0.2	137727	182.28	181.24	9.83	15.85	230.32	156.96	+0.1	+2.5	-13.9
Capped REIT	164.64	-0.06	nil	36769	165.32	164.52	5.31	41.05	177.99	137.26	+1.6	+3.2	+20.1

Source: National Post, April 10, 2007. Reprinted with permission of TSX Data Linx.

HOW STOCK DECISIONS FIT WITHIN YOUR FINANCIAL PLAN

The following key decisions about stock should be included within your financial plan:

- Should you consider buying stock? Is this in keeping with your financial circumstances and risk tolerance?

- How should you value stocks when determining whether to buy them?

- Which stocks should you purchase?

- What methods should you use for investing in stocks?

The first point was discussed in Chapter 11. If you consider buying stock, you need to determine which common stocks are undervalued and should be considered for purchase. This requires an analysis of stocks, as discussed in this chapter. Your final decision will be about how to conduct stock transactions.

STEPHANIE SPRATT'S FINANCIAL PLAN: Stock Valuation

GOALS FOR INVESTING IN STOCKS

1. Determine whether I could benefit from investing in stocks (discussed in Chapter 11).

2. If I consider investing in stocks, decide which stocks to purchase.

3. Determine how to execute stock transactions.

ANALYSIS

Method Used to Assess the Value of Trail.com Stock	Opinion
1. Assessment of the firm, economy, and industry	*These methods provide much valuable information but they are subjective and do not lead to a precise estimate of the firm's value.*
2. Price–earnings (P/E) method	*Can easily be used to value a stock but is limited because it assumes that the firm should have the same P/E ratio as its competitors.*
3. Price–sales (P/S) method	*Is more appropriate than the P/E method when the firm's earnings are negative. However, it is limited because it assumes the firm should have the same P/S ratio as its competitors.*

Type of Brokerage Firm	
Full-service	*Guidance on stock selection; higher commissions charged on transactions.*
Discount	*No guidance on stock selection; lower commissions charged on transactions.*

Type of Order When Purchasing Stock	
Market order	*An order is executed at the prevailing market price.*
Limit order	*A buy order is only executed if the price is at or below the price I specify. A sell order is only executed if the price is at or above a price I specify.*

Whether to Borrow	
Pay with cash	*Need cash to pay for the entire investment. My return will be equal to the return on the stock itself. My return can be easily calculated.*
Buy on margin	*Can make investment with less capital (by borrowing a portion of the funds needed). My return (whether a gain or a loss) is more pronounced if I borrow to buy the stock, which increases the risk of my investment.*

DECISIONS

Decision Regarding How to Value Stocks

Although all three methods can be used, each has limitations. I plan to use all three methods when valuing a stock. I will consider purchasing a stock only if all three methods indicate that the stock may be undervalued. I may still consider investing in a stock only if other sources of information (such as financial experts) agree with my views. Until I have more net income, I should limit the amount of money I invest in individual stocks.

Decision Regarding How to Execute Stock Transactions

In the future when I invest in stocks, I will probably use a discount broker instead of a full-service broker because I prefer to make my own investment decisions and the commissions charged by a discount broker are usually lower. However, I will first discuss my investment goals with a few full-service brokers to see how their services may help me reach my goals. Regardless of whether I use a discount broker or full-service broker, I will use only limit orders to buy stocks, so that I can set the maximum price I am willing to pay. I will only invest in a stock if I have sufficient funds to cover the entire investment because it is a less risky method of executing a stock transaction. Buying on margin magnifies the return (whether positive or negative) on the stock, and causes the investment to be more risky than I desire.

Discussion Questions

1. How would Stephanie's stock investing decisions be different if she were a single mother of two children?

2. How would Stephanie's stock investing decisions be affected if she were 35 years old? If she were 50 years old?

SUMMARY

Quotations for exchange traded stocks are provided in daily newspapers and online. These quotations should be considered when deciding whether to purchase a stock.

An analysis of a firm involves reviewing the firm's annual report and the financial statements (such as the balance sheet and the income statement), along with other financial reports. This analysis includes an assessment of the firm's liquidity, financial leverage, efficiency, and profitability. Be careful when interpreting financial statements, since accounting guidelines allow firms to use methods that may exaggerate or underestimate their performance.

An economic analysis involves assessing how a stock's price can be affected by economic conditions. The most closely monitored economic factors that can affect stock prices are economic growth, interest rates, and inflation. In general, stocks are favourably affected by economic growth, a decline in interest rates, and a decline in inflation.

An industry analysis involves assessing how a stock's price can be affected by industry conditions. Two closely monitored industry characteristics are consumer preferences within an industry and industry competition. Stocks are favourably affected when the firms recognize and take advantage of shifts in consumer preferences and/or when the firms face a relatively low degree of competition.

Stocks can be valued using several methods. The price–earnings (P/E) method estimates the stock's value by applying the mean industry P/E ratio to the firm's recent or expected annual earnings. The price–sales (P/S) method estimates the stock's value by applying the mean industry P/S ratio to the firm's sales per share.

Stock market efficiency implies that stock prices reflect all public information. If the stock market is efficient, there may be little or no benefits to trying to use public information to achieve unusually high returns. Many investors, however, believe that the stock market is not efficient and therefore attempt to determine whether a specific stock is undervalued. It is the interpretation of public information that can lead to higher returns.

Stocks are listed on stock exchanges, where they can be purchased or sold. Recently, stock exchanges have been demutualized. This has resulted in the consolidation of stock exchanges throughout North America and Europe. Unlisted stocks can be purchased on the over-the-counter (OTC) market. In Canada, this means using the NEX board on the TSX Venture Exchange.

Once you have decided which stocks to buy or sell, you contact a brokerage firm. You can also use an online brokerage firm, which may be more convenient and also less costly than a traditional full-service brokerage firm. Upon receiving your order, the brokerage firm sends it to the stock exchange where the trade is executed.

When buying a stock on margin, you borrow part of the purchase amount from the brokerage firm. This approach can magnify the returns you earn from investing in the stock. However, it also magnifies any losses and therefore increases your risk.

After you execute a stock transaction, you should monitor the performance of your investment over time. Compare the return on that stock with an index of stocks that represents similar firms or even the general market. Several stock market indexes and sector indexes are available to use as benchmarks when assessing a stock's performance.

INTEGRATING THE KEY CONCEPTS

Your decision to invest in specific stocks not only is related to your other investment decisions, but also affects other parts of your financial plan. When buying stocks, you should consider your liquidity (Part 2). Stocks are not liquid but they are marketable. Before investing in stocks, you should ensure that your emergency fund is appropriately invested in liquid investments such as money market instruments, Canada Savings Bonds, and similar investments. While some of your funds may be invested in less liquid investments, you may have to sell at a loss if you need to raise cash quickly.

Before investing in any stocks, you should reassess your financing (Part 3). Compare your expected return on any specific stock you may purchase with the interest rate incurred on any personal loan you have. Consider paying off any personal loans before you invest in stocks, unless the return on stocks will exceed the interest rate incurred on your personal loans. In addition, ensure that your insurance needs are covered (Part 4) before using funds to buy stocks. If your investments perform well and increase your wealth, you may need more insurance. If you decide to invest in stocks, you need to determine whether the investment should be for your retirement savings plan (Part 6) or held outside that type of plan. Your choice of stocks may be different if the investment is for your retirement savings plan because those stocks that typically result in more taxes (such as those that pay high dividends) may be more appropriate for a retirement plan where the dividend income can be tax-deferred. You may also need to save additional funds for retirement if the return on your investment is low.

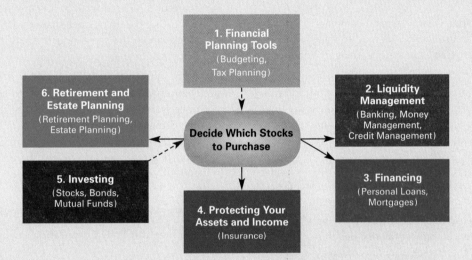

REVIEW QUESTIONS

1. What information about a stock are you able to obtain if you know how to read a stock quotation?

2. Why is it necessary to analyze a firm? What is an annual report? What information does it contain to aid in your analysis?

3. List the characteristics of a firm that investors analyze by using the balance sheet and the income statement.

4. What is liquidity? How is it measured?

5. What is financial leverage? Discuss two ways to measure financial leverage.

6. What is an indicator of the efficiency of a firm? How can efficiency be measured?

7. Where can you find the necessary information to determine a firm's profitability? Describe the financial ratios used to measure profitability.

8. List some sources of information about individual firms other than the annual report. Why should you carefully evaluate the information you use?

9. What information is provided by the Value Line Investment Survey?

10. Why may the top managers of a firm be tempted to use misleading estimates of revenues and expenses? How may managers be able to boost the reported earnings of their firm?

11. What are the limitations of measuring financial characteristics using financial ratios?

12. When performing an economic analysis of stocks, what three economic factors are most closely watched?

13. Explain how economic growth is measured. How does economic growth affect stock prices? What are some popular indicators of economic growth? How does the government's fiscal policy affect economic growth?

14. What is monetary policy? How do interest rates affect economic growth? Why do interest rates affect some stock prices more than others? Which federal agency influences interest rates?

15. What is inflation? How is inflation measured? How does inflation affect stock prices?

16. Why is an industry analysis of stocks important? List some sources of information about firms and their industry.

17. What two basic factors drive the price of a stock? What is the first step in the valuation process for a stock? What are you trying to determine through stock valuation? How do differences in stock valuation affect the volume of trading? Which investors may be able to achieve a high rate of return?

18. How is the price–earnings ratio computed? Describe how you can use the P/E method to value a firm. How can you derive an estimate of earnings? What are the limitations of using the P/E method?

19. When might you use the price–sales method rather than the P/E method to value a stock? How is the P/S ratio calculated? What are some limitations of the P/S method?

20. What is an efficient market? What is an inefficient market?

21. What is the argument for market efficiency?

22. Historically, some stocks that provide very high returns can be identified. Does this mean that the market is inefficient? Why or why not?

23. What are stock exchanges? How do they facilitate the trading of stocks?

24. What are the two major stock exchanges in Canada? What is the purpose of the Montreal Exchange? What are market makers? Describe some of the other stock exchanges. What is the over-the-counter market?

25. How is the market for a stock created? How do brokerage firms expedite this process? Compare the two types of brokerage services.

26. What are some advantages of using online brokerage services? Describe how an investor would set up and use an online brokerage account.

27. What information must you provide when placing an order to buy or sell stock? What is a ticker symbol, and why is it important?

28. What do the terms *board lot* and *odd lot* mean in stock transactions?

29. Discuss the differences between a market order and a limit order.

30. What is buying a stock on margin? What may happen if the value of the stock bought on margin declines? What are the advantages to investors and brokerage firms when stocks are bought on margin?

31. Discuss the impact of margin on risk and return.

32. Describe an effective method of measuring the performance of a stock.

33. How can market sectors be used to measure the performance of a stock? Give an example.

FINANCIAL PLANNING PROBLEMS

1. Denise has a choice between two stocks. Stock A has a current stock price of $33.50 and earnings per share of $2.23. Stock B has a current stock price of $30.50 and earnings per share of $2.79. Both stocks are in the same industry, and the average P/E ratio for the industry is 13. Using the P/E ratio, which stock is the better choice? Why?

2. Denise (from Problem 1) decides to use the price–sales method to value the firms. She determines that the industry P/S ratio is 1.5. Stock A is reporting revenues at $20 per share. Stock B is reporting revenues at $22 per share. Both stocks are currently trading for $32 per share. Which stock is the better choice?

The following information applies to Problems 3 through 6.

Balance Sheet for Polly Corporation (in millions)

Assets

Cash and marketable securities	$150
Accounts receivable	$320
Inventories	$430
Net fixed assets	$700
Total assets	$1600

Liabilities and Shareholders' Equity

Accounts payable	$350
Short-term debt	$100
Long-term debt	$300
Shareholders' equity	$850
Total liabilities and shareholders' equity	$1600

Income Statement for Polly Corporation (in millions)

Revenue	$4500
Cost of goods sold	$2800
Gross profit	$1700
Operating expenses	$1200
Earnings before interest costs and taxes (EBIT)	$500
Interest	$50
Earnings before taxes	$450
Taxes	$200
Earnings after taxes	$250

3. What is Polly Corporation's current ratio? If the current ratio averages 2.5 in Polly's industry, is Polly liquid?

4. Compute two measures of financial leverage for Polly Corporation and interpret them.

5. What is Polly Corporation's average collection period? Other firms in the industry collect their receivables in 25 days, on average. How does Polly compare to other firms in the industry?

6. Use ratios to assess Polly Corporation's profitability.

7. A year ago, Rebecca purchased 100 shares of Havad stock for $25 per share. Yesterday, she placed a limit order to sell her stock at a price of $30 per share before the market opened. The stock's price opened at $29 and slowly increased to $32 in the middle of the day, before declining to $28 by the end of the day. The stock did not pay any dividends over the period in which Rebecca held it. What was Rebecca's return on her investment?

8. Explain how the results in Problem 7 would be different if Rebecca had placed a limit order of $33.

9. Trey purchases 200 shares of Turner stock for $40 per share. Trey pays $4000 in cash and borrows $4000 from his broker at 11 percent interest to complete the purchase. One year later, Trey sells the stock for $50 per share. What is Trey's return if the stock paid no dividends during the year?

10. What return would Trey (from Problem 9) receive if he had purchased the stock for cash?

   Use the information provided in Exhibit 13.9 to answer Problems 11 and 12.

11. Kareem would like to purchase 200 shares of a stock listed on the TSX Venture Exchange. The stock is currently trading at $4.50. Using a loan value of 50 percent, what is Kareem's margin requirement?

12. The value of Kareem's stock decreases to $2.00. How much cash will Kareem have to deposit in his margin account to return the margin to the minimum level? What options would be available to Kareem if the price of the stock increased to $6.00?

ETHICAL DILEMMA

Nick, a recent college graduate, wishes to begin investing to meet some of his financial goals. His father recommends a stockbroker who he says has always given him good advice. Nick's grandfather has also begun doing business with the same stockbroker as a result of Nick's father's recommendation. Over the next several months, the broker recommends four stocks as a must for Nick's portfolio. Nick buys all four stocks based on this advice. During the family's annual reunion, Nick, his father, and his grandfather compare their experiences with the same broker. Nick is surprised to learn that the broker recommended the same four stocks to both his father and his grandfather. His father defends the broker by saying that if it is a good stock for Nick, why would it not be a good stock for all of them? Besides, his father says, since the broker's company does all of the investment banking for the four stocks he recommended, he undoubtedly knows everything there is to know about these four firms.

a. Discuss the ethical issues of the broker's recommending the same four stocks to Nick, his father, and his grandfather.

b. Why might these four stocks be a good investment for Nick, but not for his father or his grandfather? Why might all four stocks be a good investment for all three of them?

FINANCIAL PLANNING ONLINE EXERCISES

1. In this exercise, you will examine information on the financial condition of a stock. Go to www.stockhouse.ca.

a. Beside Quote Search, enter the stock symbol IMO and click on Go. From the list, select the stock that trades on the TSX. You will get information on Imperial Oil. Click on Profile. You will be provided with information on this company, including a description of its business, the head office address, a link to the company website, some financial numbers, the status of company shares, related companies, a list of board members, and officers of the company. How is this information useful to investors?

b. In the Financials section, review the Key Ratios. Do you think Imperial Oil shares are a good investment at the current share price?

c. Now enter the symbol BNS beside Quote Search and obtain information on Bank of Nova Scotia. In the Financials section, review the Key Ratios. Do you think Bank of Nova Scotia shares are a good investment at the current price? Why or why not?

d. How do Imperial Oil and Bank of Nova Scotia compare as investments based on the financial information available on this website?

2. Go to www.globeinvestor.com/v5/content/filters.

a. This exercise allows you to identify stocks that satisfy your criteria. For Industry, choose Food Processing; for Security, choose Common; for Country, choose Canada. Click on Get Results and then View Report. What information is displayed on the screen? Which stocks have a five-star rating? How has this rating changed over the last year? How does the return on the various stocks compare with the return in the industry? Do five-star stocks have higher returns than lower-ranked stocks? Why or why not?

b. You can also use this website to filter stocks based on their performance statistics. Return to www.globeinvestor.com/v5/content/filters. For Security, choose Common. Next, enter a minimum and maximum value for Price/Earnings per Share of 10 and 20, respectively. Enter a minimum and maximum value for the Dividend Yield of 3 and 10, respectively. Finally, enter a minimum and maximum value for the 3 Year % Revenue Growth of 5 and 20, respectively. Click on Get Results, and then View Report. In general, what types of companies have the performance statistics parameters you entered? Are these growth stocks or value stocks?

Of the stocks that are from the same industry, which would you select for your portfolio?

3. Go to www.investcom.com. This website provides a sector watch list showing the most recent performance of each of the major sectors of the TSX. In addition, you can access the opinion of various stock analysts with respect to any particular stock.

a. Click on Gold under Sector Watch, and then click on one of the stocks in that sector. Next, click on Analyst News. What is the opinion of the various stock analysts with respect to this stock? Do they all agree?

b. Compare stock analysts' opinions for four or five stocks from within the same sector. Do all of the analysts agree on each individual stock? In general, are there any stocks within the sector that are receiving a favourable opinion, while other stocks are not in favour?

ON THE STUDENT CD-ROM FOR THIS CHAPTER YOU WILL FIND:

- Building Your Own Financial Plan exercise and worksheets
- The chapter-end Continuing Case about the Sampson family

Read through the Building Your Own Financial Plan exercise and use the worksheets to decide how to value a stock and how best to invest in stocks.

After reading the Sampson case study, use the Continuing Case worksheets to help the Sampsons decide which stocks to invest in to support their children's education.

Study Guide

Circle the correct answer and then check the answers in the back of the book to chart your progress.

Multiple Choice

1. All of the following are pieces of information displayed in a stock quotation, except:
   a. The stock price divided by the firm's sales revenue (P/S).
   b. The price at the end of the day when the stock market closes (Close).
   c. The daily high at which the stock was traded (Day high).
   d. The ticker symbol associated with the stock (Ticker).

2. A firm has a high degree of _____ if it has a large amount of assets that can be easily converted to cash and has a relatively small amount of short-term liabilities.
   a. efficiency
   b. financial leverage
   c. liquidity
   d. profitability

3. Which of the following situations provides an example of how accounting methods can be used to inflate revenue?
   a. A firm uses a lenient policy that allows customers to cancel their orders. The firm does not count cancelled orders as revenue.

b. A publisher of a magazine receives three-year subscriptions, for which payment is made annually. It reports these sales as revenue in the year in which the magazine is delivered. The cash flow attributed to the sales will occur either in a future period or not at all.

c. A service firm has a five-year contract with a client, in which the client can cancel the agreement after the first year. The firm records the expected revenue over the next five years in each of the five years of the contract.

d. None of the above.

4. What is gross domestic product (GDP)?
a. A measure of the total market value of all products and services produced in Canada by Canadians.
b. A measure of the total market value of all products and services produced by Canadians.
c. A measure of the total market value of all products and services produced in Canada.
d. A measure of the total market value of all products and services produced in Canada by foreigners.

5. In general, stocks perform better when interest rates are low. This statement is true because low interest rates normally will result in all of the following, except:
a. Firms tend to be more willing to expand.
b. Investors tend to shift more of their funds into bonds to take advantage of interest rates before they decrease.
c. Consumers are able to afford cars or homes.
d. Investors tend to shift more of their funds into stock.

6. Which of the following methods represents an application of the technical analysis method for evaluating stocks?
a. You will purchase a stock if its price rises for three consecutive days.
b. You will purchase a stock if its P/E ratio is 15 or lower.
c. You will purchase a stock if you are able to determine that its exposure to a weakening economic condition is below average.
d. You will purchase a stock if its P/S ratio is 10 or lower.

7. Which of the following is not a limitation of the P/E method?
a. Forecasting earnings is difficult.
b. It is subject to error if it is based on an overestimate of revenues.
c. It is difficult to determine the proper multiple that should be used to value a stock.

d. The results will vary depending on the firms that are selected to derive a mean industry ratio.

8. Investors who wish to trade options and futures would place their orders through which of the following exchanges?
a. Toronto Stock Exchange
b. Winnipeg Stock Exchange
c. TSX Venture Exchange
d. Montreal Exchange

9. Whenever you place an order to buy or sell a stock, you must specify all of the following, except:
a. The number of shares you wish to purchase.
b. The name of the firm selling you the stock.
c. Whether you are buying or selling the stock.
d. The name of the stock.

10. The advantage of a market order is that:
a. You are assured that your order will be executed quickly.
b. You can control the price at which you are willing to purchase the stock.
c. You can specify that you want the full number of shares to be traded or none at all.
d. Your order will expire if it is not completed within three hours.

True/False

1. True or False? Among other things, a firm's annual report includes a message from the chief environmental officer (CEO).

2. True or False? Many firms prefer to borrow funds rather than issue stock to avoid placing upward pressure on the stock price.

3. True or False? The average collection period can be used to determine the average age of accounts payable. A higher number relative to the industry norm means a longer collection period, which is less efficient.

4. True or False? One of the reasons top managers may inflate the revenue of their firm is to be able to sell their shares at a higher price at some point in the future.

5. True or False? High-priced stocks of well-performing firms are a good investment for the future.

6. True or False? An efficient stock market is a market in which stock prices reflect most of the information available to investors.

7. True or False? The OTC market was designed for companies that do not meet the listing requirements of the TSX or the TSX Venture Exchange.

8. True or False? One of the advantages of relying on analyst recommendations is that many studies have shown that these recommendations often lead to better performance than the stock market in general.

9. True or False? An on-stop order, which is a special form of limit order, is an order to execute a transaction when the stock price reaches a specified level.

10. True or False? A convenient and effective method of measuring performance is to compare the return on your stock to the return on that stock in the past.

Chapter 14

Investing in Bonds

N eal wanted to invest in bonds because he knew that they could provide periodic interest payments that would serve as a source of income. He knew that he could buy bonds issued by the Government of Canada. However, these bonds offered a yield of only 5 percent. Neal wanted to earn a higher yield. His broker suggested that he invest in high-yield bonds, which are issued by companies whose financial condition is weak. Neal noticed that some of these bonds offer a yield of 10 percent, double that provided by Government of Canada bonds. He also noticed that these bonds provided very high returns to investors over the previous five years while the economy was strong, much higher than Government of Canada bonds. He decided to invest in high-yield bonds issued by one particular company that were presently offering a yield of 11 percent. During the following year, the Canadian economy weakened and this company could not afford to cover its debt. It filed for bankruptcy and Neal's bonds became worthless. While many other companies also had poor performance, their financial condition was strong enough to cover their debt payments. Neal realized the potentially adverse consequences of investing in risky bonds too late.

Like other investments, bonds have unique characteristics. As with stocks, the return and risk of bonds vary depending on their issuer as well as on current and expected economic conditions. Understanding the different types of bonds and various bond investment strategies can help you build your own investment portfolio and enhance your wealth.

The objectives of this chapter are to:

1. Identify the different types of bonds

2. Explain what affects the return from investing in a bond

3. Describe why some bonds are risky

4. Identify common bond investment strategies

BACKGROUND ON BONDS

bonds
Long-term debt securities issued by government agencies or corporations that are collateralized by assets.

par value
For a bond, its face value, or the amount returned to the investor at the maturity date when the bond is due.

debentures
Long-term debt securities issued by corporations that are secured only by the corporation's promise to pay.

Recall that investors commonly invest some of their funds in bonds, which are long-term debt securities issued by government agencies or corporations that are collateralized by assets. Bonds frequently offer more favourable returns than bank deposits. In addition, they typically provide fixed interest payments that represent additional income each year. The par value of a bond is its face value, or the amount returned to the investor at the maturity date when the bond is due. Debentures are similar to bonds, except that these long-term debt securities issued by corporations are secured only by the corporation's promise to pay. Debentures are therefore riskier than bonds issued by the same company. All other aspects of bonds discussed in this chapter also apply to debentures. For simplicity, the term *bond* will be used throughout this chapter.

Bond maturities may vary between 1 and 30 years. Investors provide the issuers of bonds with funds (credit). In return, the issuers are obligated to make interest (or coupon) payments and to pay the par value at maturity. When a bond has a par value of $1000, a coupon rate of 6 percent means that $60 (0.06 × $1000) is paid annually to investors. The coupon payments are normally paid semi-annually (in this example, $30 every six months). Initially, some bonds are issued by firms to investors at a price below par value; in this case, investors who hold the bonds until maturity will earn a return from the difference between par value and what they paid for the bond. This income is in addition to the coupon payments earned. The principal, or face value, of the bond will be paid back to the investor on the maturity date.

You should consider investing in bonds rather than stock if you wish to receive periodic income from your investments. As explained in Chapter 11, many investors diversify among stocks and bonds to achieve their desired return and risk preferences.

Bond Characteristics

Bonds that are issued by a particular type of issuer can offer various features, such as a call feature or convertibility.

call feature
A feature on a bond that allows the issuer to repurchase the bond from the investor before maturity.

Call Feature. A call feature on a bond allows the issuer to repurchase the bond from the investor before maturity. This feature is desirable for issuers because it allows them to retire existing bonds with coupon rates that are higher than the prevailing interest rates.

Investors are willing to purchase bonds with a call feature only if the bonds offer a slightly higher return than similar bonds without a call feature. This premium compensates the investors for the possibility that the bonds may be repurchased before maturity. Call features also may add to the feeling of security in the investment, as part of the debt is paid off prior to maturity. Investors should look at how the call feature is set up.

EXAMPLE

Five years ago, Cieplak Inc. issued 15-year callable bonds with a coupon rate of 9 percent. Interest rates have declined since then. Today, Cieplak could issue new bonds at a rate of 7 percent. It decides to retire the existing bonds by repurchasing them from investors and to issue new bonds at a 7 percent coupon rate. By calling the old bonds, Cieplak has reduced its cost of financing. However, call features do not usually allow the company to call all outstanding bonds at one time. In addition, there is usually a call premium to compensate investors for the call.

convertible bond
A bond that can be converted into a stated number of shares of the issuer's stock at a specified price.

Convertible Feature. A **convertible bond** allows the investor to convert the bond into a stated number of shares of the issuer's stock at a specified price. This feature enables bond investors to benefit when the issuer's stock price rises. Because convertibility is a desirable feature for investors, convertible bonds tend to offer a lower return than non-convertible bonds. Consequently, if the stock price does not rise to the specified trigger price, the convertible bond provides a lower return to investors than alternative bonds without a convertible feature. If the stock price does rise above the trigger price, however, investors can convert their bonds into shares of the issuer's stock, thereby earning a higher return than they would have earned on alternative non-convertible bonds. Convertible bonds offer investors a two-for-one investment suitable for those with a higher risk tolerance and reduced need for the income offered by this type of bond.

extendible bond
A short-term bond that allows the investor to extend the maturity date of the bond.

Extendible Feature. An **extendible bond** allows an investor to extend the maturity date of a short-term bond. This feature enables bond investors to benefit when interest rates are decreasing. If interest rates decrease, investors can extend the maturity of their bonds at a slightly higher rate than what is available in the bond market. Because extendibility is a desirable feature for investors, extendible bonds tend to offer a lower return than non-extendible bonds.

put feature
A feature on a bond that allows the investor to redeem the bond at its face value before it matures.

Put Feature. A **put feature** on a bond allows the investor to redeem the bond at its face value before it matures. This feature is desirable for investors who are unsure whether interest rates will increase. If interest rates increase, investors can redeem the bonds and invest their money at a higher rate elsewhere.

Investors who are willing to purchase bonds with a put feature will receive a slightly lower return than similar bonds without a put feature. This discount compensates the issuer for the possibility that the bonds may be redeemed before maturity. This type of bond is also known as a retractable bond.

Yield to Maturity

yield to maturity
The annualized return on a bond if it is held until maturity.

A bond's **yield to maturity** is the annualized return on the bond if it is held until maturity. Consider a bond that is priced at $1000 and has a par value of $1000, a maturity of 20 years, and a coupon rate of 10 percent. This bond has a yield to maturity of 10 percent, which is the same as its coupon rate, because the price paid for the bond equals the principal that will be received at maturity 20 years hence.

discount
A bond that is trading at a price below its par value.

As an alternative example, if this bond's price was lower than its par value, its yield to maturity would exceed the coupon rate of 10 percent. A bond that is trading at a price below its par value is said to be trading at a **discount**. The bond would also generate income in the form of a capital gain because the purchase price would be less than the principal amount to be received at maturity. Conversely, if this bond's price was higher than its par value, its yield to maturity would be less than the 10 percent coupon rate because the amount paid for the bond would exceed the principal amount to be received at maturity. A bond that is trading at a price above its par value is said to be trading at a **premium**.

premium
A bond that is trading at a price above its par value.

Go to
www.qtrade.ca/en/itools/calculators/bond_yield.jsp

This website provides an estimate of the yield to maturity of a bond based on its present price, its coupon rate, and its maturity. Thus, you can determine the rate of return the bond will generate from today until it matures.

Bond Trading in the Secondary Market

Investors can sell their bonds to other investors in the secondary market before the bonds reach maturity. Bond prices change in response to interest rate movements and other factors. Bonds are traded in an over-the-counter market. Many investors sell their bonds in the secondary market to raise funds to cover upcoming expenses or to invest in other, more attractive types of securities. Investors buy or sell bonds from a brokerage firm's bond inventory. If the firm does not own the bond that the investor would like to buy, it may purchase the bond from another firm and then sell it to the investor at a higher price.

IN-CLASS NOTES

Background on Bonds

- Bonds → long-term debt securities issued by government agencies or corporations that are collateralized by assets
- Par value → the amount returned to the investor at the maturity date when the bond is due
- Bond features
  - Callable, convertible, extendible, retractable
- Discount → bond price < par value
- Premium → bond price > par value

_____
_____
_____
_____
_____

L.O. 1   TYPES OF BONDS

Bonds can be classified according to the type of issuer as follows:

- Government of Canada bonds
- Federal Crown corporation bonds
- Provincial bonds
- Municipal bonds
- Corporate bonds

Government of Canada Bonds

Government of Canada bonds
Debt securities issued by the Canadian government.

Government of Canada bonds are debt securities issued by the Canadian government. Because the payments are guaranteed by the federal government, they are not exposed to the risk of default by the issuer. These bonds are issued with a term to maturity of between 1 and 30 years. Interest is paid semi-annually. Government of Canada bonds are a very safe investment and can be sold easily in the secondary market. Unlike corporate bonds that are backed by the corporation's assets, government bonds are backed by the ability to raise funds through taxation.

Federal Crown Corporation Bonds

Federal Crown corporation bonds
Debt securities issued by corporations established by the federal government.

Federal Crown corporation bonds are debt securities issued by corporations established by the government. The major Crown corporations that are active in the bond market are the Export Development Corporation (EDC), the Canada Mortgage and Housing Corporation (CMHC), the Farm Credit Corporation (FCC), and the Business Development Bank of Canada (BDBC). Because the payments are guaranteed by the federal government, they are not exposed to the risk of default by the issuer. These bonds are issued with a term to maturity of between 2 and 10 years. Interest is paid semi-annually. These bonds are a very safe investment and can be sold easily in the secondary market. These bonds offer a slightly higher return than Government of Canada bonds.

Provincial Bonds

provincial bonds
Debt securities issued by the various provincial governments.

Provincial bonds are debt securities issued by the various provincial governments. Interest and principal payments are guaranteed by the provincial government that issued the bonds. The risk of default by the issuer will differ depending on the province from which you purchased the bond. For example, the prosperity enjoyed in Alberta, mainly as a result of high oil prices, will likely result in a lower default risk for that province relative to other provinces. Since the risk of an Alberta bond is lower, the yield to maturity will also be lower. These bonds are issued with a term to maturity of between 1 and 30 years. Interest is paid semi-annually. Provincial bonds are a very safe investment and can be sold easily in the secondary market.

Municipal Bonds

municipal bonds
Long-term debt securities issued by local government agencies.

Municipal bonds are long-term debt securities issued by local government agencies, and provide the funds necessary for municipal projects such as parks or sewage plants. In some cases, municipal bonds are not free from the risk of default. Nevertheless, most municipal bonds have a very low default risk. To entice investors, municipal bonds that are issued by a local government with a relatively high level of risk offer a higher yield than other municipal bonds with a lower level of risk. Municipal bonds are uncommon investments in Canada for individuals and tend to suit the needs of certain institutional investors. The terms and conditions of a municipal bond will vary with the needs of the municipality.

Corporate Bonds

corporate bonds
Long-term debt securities issued by large firms.

high-yield bonds
Bonds issued by less stable corporations that are subject to a higher degree of default risk.

Corporate bonds are long-term debt securities issued by large firms. The repayment of debt by corporations is not backed by the federal government, so corporate bonds are subject to default risk. At one extreme, bonds issued by corporations such as Ontario Hydro and National Bank of Canada have very low default risk because of the companies' proven ability to generate sufficient cash flows for many years. At the other extreme, bonds issued by less stable corporations are subject to a higher degree of default risk. These bonds are referred to as high-yield bonds. Many investors are willing to invest in high-yield bonds because they offer a relatively high rate of return. However, they are more likely to default than other bonds, especially if economic conditions are poor. Given the potential to lose money in a high-yield bond, most individual investors should buy these higher-risk investments only through the purchase of a high-yield bond mutual fund. The terms and conditions of a corporate bond will vary with the needs of the corporation.

Go to
www.globeinvestor.com/servlet/Page/document/v5/data/bonds

This website provides quotations of yields offered by various types of bonds with various terms to maturity. Review this information when considering purchasing bonds.

OTHER FIXED-INCOME PRODUCTS

In addition to the bond classifications above, a number of other fixed-income products offer special features and/or are characterized by a short-term maturity. These investments include:

- T-Bills
- Banker's acceptances (BAs)
- Commercial paper
- Mortgage backed securities (MBSs)
- Strip bonds
- Real return bonds

Short-Term Debt Securities

T-Bills
Short-term debt securities issued by the Canadian government and sold at a discount.

T-Bills are short-term debt securities issued by the Canadian government and sold at a discount (less than the par value). T-Bills do not make coupon payments. Instead, the return an investor receives is based on the rise in the value of the investment as it reaches maturity. Similar to T-Bills, banker's acceptances and commercial paper are short-term

banker's acceptances (BAs)
Short-term debt securities issued by large firms that are guaranteed by a bank.

commercial paper
A short-term debt security issued by large firms that is guaranteed by the issuing firm.

debt securities issued by corporations that are sold at a discount. These investments can be differentiated by the issuer of the security and the entity that guarantees the investment. **Banker's acceptances (BAs)** are short-term debt securities issued by large firms that are guaranteed by a bank. **Commercial paper** is a short-term debt security issued by large firms that is guaranteed by the issuing firm.

As a result of their differences, these short-term investments have different risk and return characteristics. The yield to maturity will be lowest for T-Bills because they are issued and guaranteed by the Government of Canada. T-Bills are the safest investment available to Canadian investors. The yield to maturity of BAs will be higher than it is for T-Bills because BAs are riskier since they are issued by a firm. However, since BAs are guaranteed by a bank, commercial paper will have the highest yield to maturity because it is only guaranteed by the issuing corporation. Although no interest is paid, interest must be recognized every year. The recognition of interest may result in tax being payable even though no income has been received. As a result, tax planning is an important consideration when deciding whether to purchase these investments outside an RSP tax shelter.

Recall from Chapter 4 that money market funds (MMFs) invest in securities that have short-term maturities, such as one year or less. T-Bills, BAs, and commercial paper are important parts of an MMF's investment portfolio. Although some high-net-worth investors may purchase T-Bills, BAs, and commercial paper as individual securities, MMFs are ideal for most investors who want to invest in short-term debt securities.

Mortgage Backed Securities (MBSs)

mortgage backed securities (MBSs)
Represent a pool of CMHC-insured residential mortgages that are issued by banks and other financial institutions.

Mortgage backed securities (MBSs) represent a pool of CMHC-insured residential mortgages that are issued by banks and other financial institutions. The CMHC guarantees the mortgages in the pool in the event of default. An MBS is a guaranteed flow-through investment. The mortgage payments made on the pool of mortgages in an MBS represent principal and interest payments. The principal and interest are flowed-through to MBS investors. If mortgage payments are missed, CMHC guarantees the payment of principal and interest to the pool. This steady flow of interest and principal makes MBSs a secure and attractive investment for investors looking for debt securities that offer a slightly higher yield than Government of Canada bonds. They are particularly attractive to investors seeking income (for example, retirees). Similar to most other bonds, MBSs are marketable since they can be sold in the secondary market. MBSs are issued with a term to maturity of between 1 and 10 years. One unique risk with MBSs is that of prepayment. Mortgages are sometimes paid back before the end of the term because homeowners may refinance at a lower rate or sell their homes. Prepayment is more likely to occur when interest rates fall and/or there is an active real estate market.

Strip Bonds

strip bonds
Long-term debt securities issued by the Government of Canada that do not offer coupon payments.

Strip bonds are long-term debt securities issued by the Government of Canada that do not offer coupon payments. Instead, the coupon payments are stripped from the bond and sold separately. The strip bond is valued at the present value of the future principal amount. When the time to maturity is long, this present value can be very low. The strip bond is sold at a very deep discount. As it moves toward maturity, the present value should rise, assuming interest rates remain the same. However, rates are not static and movement in interest rates affects strip bonds to a greater extent than other bonds. The longer the term to maturity, the greater the price movement will be. The original bonds are issued with a term to maturity of 18 months to 30 years. Although no interest is paid, interest must be recognized every year. The recognition of interest may result in tax being payable even though no income has been received. As a result, tax planning is an important consideration when deciding whether to purchase these investments outside an RSP portfolio. Strip bonds are a very safe investment in terms of default risk and can be sold in the secondary market. However, they have a *very* high interest rate risk.

Real Return Bonds

real return bonds
Long-term debt securities issued by the Government of Canada that protect you from inflation risk.

Real return bonds are long-term debt securities issued by the Government of Canada that protect you from inflation risk. All other bonds are exposed to inflation risk. For example, if inflation is 4 percent in 2007 and your bond makes interest payments based on a 3 percent coupon rate, your inflation-adjusted return is –1 percent. Real return bonds eliminate inflation risk by adjusting the par value of the bond for changes in the inflation rate (as measured by the CPI). As a result, your par value at maturity will be higher and your coupon payments will increase with each increase in the face value if inflation has occurred.

EXAMPLE

You buy a $1000 real return bond that has a coupon rate of 5 percent. Assume that inflation increases by 2 percent in the next six months. Interest is paid semi-annually. The bond's par value and coupon payment will increase as follows:

Inflation-adjusted par value = $1000 × (1 + 0.02) = $1020

Inflation-adjusted semi-annual coupon payment = $1020 × (0.05 ÷ 2) = $25.50

The actual amount of interest paid during the year will be based on the initial par value. In the example above, the semi-annual interest payment will be calculated as $1000 × (0.05 ÷ 2) = $25. At maturity, the accumulated difference between the inflation-adjusted coupon payment and the regular coupon payment will be paid to the investor, along with the inflation-adjusted par value. These bonds are issued with a term to maturity of between 1 and 30 years. They are a very safe investment and can be sold easily in the secondary market.

IN-CLASS NOTES

Types of Bonds and Other Fixed-Income Products

- Types of bonds
  - Government of Canada bonds
  - Federal Crown corporation bonds
  - Provincial bonds
  - Municipal bonds
  - Corporate bonds
- Other fixed-income products
  - Short-term debt securities (T-Bills, banker's acceptances, commercial paper)
  - Mortgage backed securities (MBSs)
  - Strip bonds
  - Real return bonds

L.O. 2 RETURN FROM INVESTING IN BONDS

If you purchase a bond and hold it until maturity, you can earn the yield to maturity specified when you purchased it. As mentioned, however, many investors sell bonds in the secondary market before they reach maturity. Since a bond's price changes over time, your return from investing in a bond depends on the price at the time you sell it.

Another risk that investors must consider when investing in bonds is reinvestment risk. When the price of a bond is calculated, one of the assumptions is that all interest received through the years will be reinvested at the current interest rate. While it is believed that the yield quoted is what the investor will receive, the assumption that rates will remain static for any period of time is somewhat simplistic.

Impact of Interest Rate Movements on Bond Returns

Your return from investing in a bond can be highly influenced by interest rate movements over the period you hold the bond. To illustrate, suppose that you purchase a bond at par value that has a coupon rate of 8 percent. After one year, you decide to sell the bond. At this time, new bonds being sold at par value are offering a coupon rate of 9 percent. Since investors can purchase a new bond that offers higher coupon payments, they will not be willing to buy your bond unless you sell it to them for less than par value. In other words, you must offer a discount on the price to compensate for the bond's lower coupon rate.

If interest rates had declined over the year rather than increased, the opposite effect would occur. You could sell your bond for a premium above par value because the coupon rate of your bond would be higher than the coupon rate offered on newly issued bonds. Thus, interest rate movements and bond prices are inversely related. Your return from investing in bonds will be more favourable if interest rates decline over the period you hold the bonds.

Tax Implications of Investing in Bonds

When determining the return from investing in a bond, you need to account for tax effects. The interest income you receive from a bond is taxed as ordinary income for federal income tax purposes. Tax on interest income is the same as other forms of income and must be paid in the year it is earned. This may not coincide with the interest payments.

Selling bonds in the secondary market at a price different than what you originally paid for them results in a capital gain (or loss). The capital gain (or loss) is the difference between the price at which you sell the bond and the initial price you paid for it. Recall from Chapter 3 that only 50 percent of a capital gain is taxable as income. In addition, only 50 percent of a capital loss is deductible as an allowable capital loss.

EXAMPLE

You purchase $10 000 face value newly issued bonds for $9700. The bonds mature in 10 years and pay a coupon rate of 8 percent, or $800 (computed as 0.08 × $10 000) per year. The coupon payments are made every six months, so each payment is $400. Exhibit 14.1 shows your return and the tax implications for four different scenarios. Notice that taxes incurred from the investment in bonds depend on the change in the bond price over time and the length of time the bonds are held, as well as the reinvestment rate applied to the coupons received every six months.

Go to
www.canadianbusiness.com/
markets/bonds/index.jsp

This website provides a summary of recent financial news related to the bond market, which you may consider before selling or buying bonds.

VALUING A BOND

Before investing in a bond, you may wish to determine its value using a time value of money analysis. A bond's value is determined as the present value of the future cash flows to be received by the investor, which are the periodic coupon payments and the principal payment at maturity. The present value of a bond can be computed by discounting the future cash flows (coupon payments and principal payment) to be received from the bond. The discount rate used to value the cash flows should reflect your required rate of return. The value of a bond can be expressed as:

Exhibit 14.1 Potential Tax Implications from Investing in Bonds

Scenario	Implication
1. You sell the bonds after 8 months at a price of $9800.	You receive one $400 coupon payment 6 months after buying the bond, which is taxed at your marginal income tax rate; you also earn a capital gain of $100 and a taxable capital gain of $50, which is taxed at your marginal income tax rate.
2. You sell the bonds after 2 years at a price of $10 200.	You receive coupon payments (taxed at your marginal income tax rate) of $800 in the first year and in the second year; you also earn a capital gain of $500 in the second year and a taxable capital gain of $250, which is subject to capital gains tax in that year.
3. You sell the bonds after 2 years at a price of $9500.	You receive coupon payments (taxed at your marginal income tax rate) of $800 in the first year and in the second year; you also incur a capital loss of $200 and an allowable capital loss for capital gains deduction purposes of $100 in the second year.
4. You hold the bonds until maturity.	You receive coupon payments (taxed at your marginal income tax rate) in each year over the 10-year life of the bond. You also receive the bond's principal of $10 000 at the end of the 10-year period. This reflects a capital gain of $300 and a taxable capital gain of $150, which is subject to capital gains tax in the year you receive the gain.

$$\text{Value of Bond} = \sum_{t=1}^{n} [C_t/(1 + k)^t] + Prin/(1 + k)^n$$

where C_t represents the coupon payments in year t, $Prin$ is the principal payment at the end of year n when the bond matures, and k is the required rate of return. Thus, the value of a bond is composed of the present value of all future coupon payments, along with the present value of the principal payment. If you pay the price that is obtained by this valuation approach and hold the bond to maturity, you can earn the return that you require.

EXAMPLE

Victor is planning to purchase a bond that has seven years remaining until maturity, a par value of $1000, and a coupon rate of 6 percent (assume that the coupon payments are made annually, at the end of the year). He is willing to purchase this bond only if he can earn a return of 8 percent because he knows that he can earn 8 percent on alternative bonds.

The first step in valuing a bond is to identify the coupon payments, principal payment, and required rate of return:

- Future cash flows:

  Coupon payment (C) = 0.06 × $1000 = $60

  Principal payment ($Prin$) = $1000

- Discount rate:

  Required rate of return = 8 percent

Input	Function
7	N
8	I
? = 895.87	PV
60	PMT
1000	FV

The next step is to use this information to discount the future cash flows of the bond with the help of the present value tables in Appendix A.

Value of Bond = Present Value of Coupon Payments + Present Value of Principal

$= [C \times (PVIFA, 8\%, 7 \text{ yrs})] + [Prin \times (PVIF, 8\%, 7 \text{ yrs})]$

$= [\$60 \times 5.2064] + [\$1000 \times 0.5835]$

$= \$312.38 + \$583.50$

$= \$895.88$

When using a financial calculator to determine the value of the bond, the future value will be $1000 because this is the amount the bondholder will receive at maturity.

Based on this analysis, Victor is willing to pay $895.88 for this bond, which will provide his annualized return of 8 percent. If he can obtain the bond for a lower price, his return will exceed 8 percent. If the price exceeds $895.88, his return would be less than 8 percent, so he would not buy the bond.

The market price of any bond is based on investors' required rate of return, which is influenced by the interest rates that are available on alternative investments at the time. If bond investors require a rate of return of 8 percent, as Victor does, the bond will be priced in the bond market at the value derived by Victor. However, if the bond market participants use a different required rate of return than Victor, the market price of the bond will be different. For example, if most investors require a 9 percent return on this bond, it will have a market price below the value derived by Victor (conduct your own valuation using a 9 percent discount rate to verify this).

IN-CLASS NOTES

Return from Investing in Bonds and Valuing a Bond

- Impact of interest rate movements
  - Bond coupon rate < current coupon rate on similar bonds, sell bond at discount
  - Bond coupon rate > current coupon rate on similar bonds, sell bond at premium
- Tax implications
  - Interest income → results from coupon payments
  - Capital gain or loss → results from cost price being more or less than market price when sold
- Bond valuation
  - Present value of future cash flows, including coupon payments and principal payment at maturity

_____

_____

_____

_____

_____

_____

_____

L.O. 3   RISK FROM INVESTING IN BONDS

Bond investors are exposed to the risk that the bonds may not provide the expected return. The main sources of risk are default risk, call (prepayment) risk, and interest rate risk.

Exhibit 14.2 Bond Rating Classes

Risk Class	Standard & Poor's	Moody's
Highest quality (least risk)	AAA	Aaa
High quality	AA	Aa
High-medium quality	A	A
Medium quality	BBB	Baa
Medium-low quality	BB	Ba
Low quality	B	B
Poor quality	CCC	Caa
Very poor quality	CC	Ca
Lowest quality	DDD	C

Default Risk

risk premium
The extra yield required by investors to compensate for default risk.

default risk
Risk that the borrower of funds will not repay the creditors.

If the issuer of the bond (a firm) defaults on its payments, investors do not receive all of the coupon payments they are owed and may not receive all or any of the principal they are owed. Investors will invest in a risky bond only if it offers a higher yield than other bonds to compensate for this risk. The extra yield required by investors to compensate for default risk is referred to as a risk premium. Government of Canada bonds do not contain a risk premium because they are free from default risk.

Use of Risk Ratings to Measure the Default Risk. Investors can use ratings (provided by agencies such as Moody's Investor Service or Standard & Poor's) to assess the risk of corporate bonds. The ratings reflect the likelihood that the issuers will repay their debt over time and are classified as shown in Exhibit 14.2. Investors can select the corporate bonds that fit their degree of risk tolerance by weighing the higher potential return against the higher default risk of lower-quality debt securities.

Relationship of Risk Rating to Risk Premium. The lower (weaker) the risk rating, the higher the risk premium offered on a bond.

Impact of Economic Conditions. Bonds with a high degree of default risk are most susceptible to default when economic conditions are weak. Investors may lose all or most of their initial investment when a bond defaults. They can avoid default risk by investing in Government of Canada bonds or can at least keep the default risk to a minimum by investing in federal Crown corporation bonds or AAA-rated corporate bonds. However, they will receive lower yields on these bonds than investors who are willing to accept a higher degree of default risk.

EXAMPLE

Stephanie Spratt reviews today's bond yields for bonds with a 10-year maturity, as shown in the second column.

Type of Bond	Bond Yield Offered	Risk Premium Contained within Bond Yield
Government of Canada bonds	7.0%	0.0%
AAA-rated corporate bonds	7.5	0.5
A-rated corporate bonds	7.8	0.8
BB-rated corporate bonds	8.8	1.8
CCC-rated corporate bonds	9.5	2.5

Based on the bond yields, she derives the risk premium for each type of bond, shown in the third column. Notice that since Government of Canada bonds are risk-free, they have no risk premium. However, the other bonds do have a risk premium, which is the amount by which their annualized yield exceeds the Government of Canada bond yield. This premium can change over time because of economic conditions as well as industry conditions and specific corporate risk.

Stephanie decides that she prefers Government of Canada bonds or AAA-rated bonds to other types of bonds because she believes that the risk premiums are not enough compensation for the increased risks. However, at this time, she cannot afford to buy any type of bond. Some investors would select specific CCC-rated corporate bonds that they believe will not default. If these bonds do not default, they will provide a yield that is 2.0 percentage points above the yield offered on AAA-rated bonds and 2.5 percentage points above the yield offered on Government of Canada bonds.

Focus on Ethics: Accounting Fraud and Default Risk

Bond rating services are important not only for investors, but also for creditors. Just as the interest on a loan for an individual with a poor credit history will be higher than that for an individual with a great credit history, corporations are subject to similar risk premiums. Therefore, a higher rating, such as AAA, will allow a corporation to issue debt with a lower interest rate.

Rating companies are vigilant in monitoring the state of corporations and if they reduce a firm's rating the firm's bond price will fall. If the firm's rating has been reduced because of questionable financial statements, the price reduction on its bonds can be quite severe. Once a debt rating agency becomes aware that a firm's financial statements are misleading, it will lower the firm's bond rating and investors will in turn reduce their demand for the firm's bonds. Investors will lose confidence in the firm's ability to repay its debt. Even if a bond does not default, its price will decline if the perception of its risk is increased by credit rating agencies and investors.

The role of the various provincial and territorial securities commissions is to ensure that firms accurately disclose their financial condition. However, some firms still provide misleading financial statements. Some bondholders who invested in the bonds issued by Enron, WorldCom, and other firms that have gone bankrupt recently, lost most or all of their investments. Therefore, you need to recognize that a firm may default on its bonds even if its most recent financial statement was very optimistic.

Call Risk

call (prepayment) risk
The risk that a callable bond will be called.

Bonds with a call feature are subject to call risk (also called prepayment risk), which is the risk that the bond will be called. If issuers of callable bonds call these bonds, the bondholders must sell them back to the issuer.

EXAMPLE

Two years ago, Christine Ramirez purchased 10-year bonds that offered a yield to maturity of 9 percent. She planned to hold the bonds until maturity. Recently, interest rates declined and the issuer called the bonds. Christine could use the proceeds to buy other bonds, but the yield to maturity offered on new bonds is lower because interest rates have declined. The return that Christine will earn from investing in new bonds could be less than the return she would have earned if she could have retained the 10-year bonds until maturity.

Often, there is a call premium on callable bonds to account for at least a portion of the call risk. As well, callable bonds can offer a return higher than non-callable bonds, again to offset the call risk. Investors should be aware of the circumstances that would trigger a call.

Interest Rate Risk

interest rate risk
The risk that a bond's price will decline in response to an increase in interest rates.

All bonds are subject to **interest rate risk**, which is the risk that a bond's price will decline in response to an increase in interest rates. A bond is valued as the present value of its future expected cash flows. Most bonds pay fixed coupon payments. If interest rates rise, investors will require a higher return on a bond. Consequently, the discount rate applied to value the bond is increased and the market price of the bond will decline.

EXAMPLE

Three months ago, Rob Suerth paid $10 000 for a 20-year Government of Canada bond that has a par value of $10 000 and a 7 percent coupon rate. Since then, interest rates have increased. New 20-year Government of Canada bonds with a par value of $10 000 are priced at $10 000 and offer a coupon rate of 9 percent. Thus, Rob would earn 2 percentage points more in coupon payments from a new bond than he does from the bond he purchased three months ago. He decides to sell his bond and use the proceeds to invest in the new bonds. However, he quickly learns that no one in the secondary market is willing to purchase his bond for the price he paid. These investors avoid his bond for the same reason he wants to sell it; they would prefer to earn 9 percent on the new bonds rather than 7 percent on his bond. The only way that Rob can sell his bond is by lowering the price to compensate for the bond's lower coupon rate (compared to new bonds).

Impact of a Bond's Maturity on Its Interest Rate Risk. Bonds with longer terms to maturity are more sensitive to interest rate movements than bonds that have short terms remaining until maturity. To understand why, consider two bonds. Each has a par value of $1000 and offers a 9 percent coupon rate, but one bond has 20 years remaining until maturity while the other has only one year remaining until maturity. If market interest rates suddenly decline from 9 to 7 percent, which bond would you prefer to own? The bond with 20 years until maturity becomes very attractive because you would be able to receive coupon payments reflecting a 9 percent return for the next 20 years. Conversely, the bond with one year remaining until maturity will provide the 9 percent payment only over the next year. Although the market price of both bonds increases in response to the decline in interest rates, it increases more for the bond with the longer term to maturity.

Now assume that, instead of declining, interest rates have risen from their initial level of 9 percent to 11 percent. Which bond would you prefer? Each bond provides a 9 percent coupon rate, which is less than the prevailing interest rate. The bond with one year until maturity will mature soon, however, so you can reinvest the proceeds at the higher interest rates at that time (assuming the rates remain high). Conversely, you are stuck with the other bond for 20 more years. Although neither bond would be very desirable under these conditions, the bond with the longer term to maturity is less desirable. Therefore, its price in the secondary market will decline more than the price of the bond with a short term to maturity.

Selecting an Appropriate Bond Maturity. Since bond prices change in response to interest rate movements, you may wish to choose maturities on bonds that reflect your expectations of future interest rates. If you prefer to reduce your

"Interest rates gyrated wildly today, on rumors that the Federal Reserve Board would be replaced by the cast of 'Saturday Night Live.'"

exposure to interest rate risk, you may consider investing in bonds that have a maturity that matches the time when you will need the funds. If you expect that interest rates will decline over time, you may consider investing in bonds with longer maturities than the time when you will need the funds. In this way, you can sell the bonds in the secondary market at a relatively high price, assuming that your expectations were correct. However, if interest rates increase instead of declining over this period, your return will be reduced.

IN-CLASS NOTES

Risk from Investing in Bonds

- Default risk → the risk that the borrower of funds will not repay the creditors
- Call risk → the risk that a callable bond will be called
- Interest rate risk → the risk that a bond's price will decline in response to an increase in interest rates
- The longer the term to maturity, the greater the interest rate risk

_____

_____

_____

_____

_____

L.O. 4 BOND INVESTMENT STRATEGIES

If you decide to invest in bonds, you need to determine a strategy for selecting them. Most strategies involve investing in a diversified portfolio of bonds rather than in one bond. Diversification reduces your exposure to possible default by a single issuer but may not reduce your interest rate and reinvestment risks. If you cannot afford to invest in a diversified portfolio of bonds, you may consider investing in a bond mutual fund with a small minimum investment (such as $1000). Additional information on bond mutual funds is provided in Chapter 12. Whether you focus on individual bonds or bond mutual funds, the bond investment strategies summarized here apply.

Interest Rate Strategy

interest rate strategy
Selecting bonds based on interest rate expectations.

With an **interest rate strategy**, you select bonds based on interest rate expectations. When you expect interest rates to decline, you invest heavily in long-term bonds whose prices will increase the most if interest rates fall. Conversely, when you expect interest rates to increase, you shift most of your money to bonds with short terms to maturity to minimize the adverse impact of the higher interest rates.

Investors who use the interest rate strategy may experience poor performance if their guesses about the future direction of interest rate movements are incorrect. In addition, this strategy requires frequent trading to capitalize on shifts in expectations of interest rates. Some investors who follow this strategy frequently sell their entire portfolio of bonds so that they can shift to bonds with different maturities in response to shifts in interest rate expectations. This frequent trading results in high transaction costs but may generate more short-term capital gains. This is a strategy that should be attempted only by sophisticated and risk-tolerant investors.

Passive Strategy

passive strategy
Investing in a diversified portfolio of bonds that are held for a long period of time.

With a **passive strategy**, you invest in a diversified portfolio of bonds that are held for a long period of time. The portfolio is simply intended to generate periodic interest income in the form of coupon payments. The passive strategy is especially valuable for investors who want to generate stable interest income over time and do not want to incur costs associated with frequent trading.

A passive strategy does not need to focus on high-quality bonds that offer low returns; it may reflect a portfolio of bonds with diversified risk levels. The diversification is intended to reduce the exposure of default from a single issuer of bonds. To reduce exposure to interest rate risk, a portfolio may even attempt to diversify across a wide range of bond maturities. This passive strategy is known as bond laddering. Bond laddering will be discussed in Chapter 15.

One disadvantage of this strategy is that it does not capitalize on expectations of interest rate movements. Investors who use a passive strategy, however, are more comfortable matching general bond market movements than trying to beat the bond market and possibly failing.

Maturity Matching Strategy

maturity matching strategy
Investing in bonds that will generate payments to match future expenses.

The **maturity matching strategy** involves selecting bonds that will generate payments to match future expenses. For example, parents of an eight-year-old may consider investing in a 10-year bond so that the principal can be used to pay for the child's college education at maturity. Alternatively, an older couple may invest in a bond portfolio just before retirement so that they will receive annual income (coupon payments) to cover periodic expenses after retirement. The maturity matching strategy is conservative, in that it is intended simply to cover future expenses, rather than to beat the bond market in general.

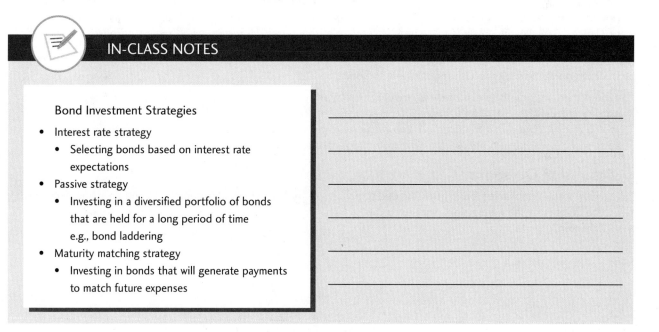

IN-CLASS NOTES

Bond Investment Strategies

- Interest rate strategy
  - Selecting bonds based on interest rate expectations
- Passive strategy
  - Investing in a diversified portfolio of bonds that are held for a long period of time e.g., bond laddering
- Maturity matching strategy
  - Investing in bonds that will generate payments to match future expenses

HOW BOND DECISIONS FIT WITHIN YOUR FINANCIAL PLAN

The following are the key decisions about bonds that should be included within your financial plan:

- Should you consider buying bonds?

- What strategy should you use for investing in bonds?

STEPHANIE SPRATT'S FINANCIAL PLAN: Bonds

GOALS FOR INVESTING IN BONDS

1. *Determine whether I could benefit from investing in bonds.*

2. *If I decide to invest in bonds, determine what strategy to use to invest in bonds.*

ANALYSIS

Strategy to Invest in Bonds	Opinion
Interest rate strategy	*I cannot forecast the direction of interest rates (even experts are commonly wrong on their interest rate forecasts), so this strategy could backfire. It is too risky for me at this time. This strategy would also complicate my tax return.*
Passive strategy	*May be appropriate for me in many situations, and the low transaction costs are appealing.*
Maturity matching strategy	*Not applicable to my situation since I am not trying to match coupon payments to future expenses.*

DECISIONS

Decision on Whether to Invest in Bonds

I cannot afford to buy bonds right now, but I will consider purchasing them in the future when my financial position improves. Bonds can generate a decent return, and some bonds are free from default risk. I find Government of Canada or AAA-rated bonds to be most attractive at this point. However, I will review all possibilities in the future, taking into account my risk tolerance at that time.

Decision on the Strategy to Use for Investing in Bonds

I am not attempting to match coupon payments with future anticipated expenses. I may consider expected interest rate movements according to financial experts when I decide which bond fund to invest in, but I will not shift in and out of bond funds frequently to capitalize on expected interest rate movements. I will likely use a passive strategy of investing in bonds and will retain bond investments for a long period of time.

Discussion Questions

1. How would Stephanie's bond investing decisions be different if she were a single mother of two children?

2. How would Stephanie's bond investing decisions be affected if she were 35 years old? If she were 50 years old?

SUMMARY

Bonds are long-term debt securities and can be classified by their issuer. The common issuers are the Government of Canada, federal Crown corporations, provinces, municipalities, and corporations. Other types of bonds include short-term debt securities (T-Bills, banker's acceptances, commercial paper), mortgage backed securities, strip bonds, and real return bonds.

A bond's yield to maturity is the annualized return that may be earned by an investor who holds the bond until maturity.

This yield is composed of interest (coupon) payments as well as the interest earned over time on that interest and the difference between the principal value and the price at which the bond was originally purchased.

Bonds can be exposed to default risk, which reflects the possibility that the issuer will default on the bond payments. Some bonds are exposed to call risk, which is the risk that the bond will be called before maturity. Bonds are also subject to interest rate risk, which is the risk of a decline in price in response to rising interest rates. This leads to reinvestment risk. Inflation, closely associated to interest rates, poses another risk for bond investors.

One bond investment strategy is the interest rate strategy, where the selection of bonds depends on the expectation of future interest rates. An alternative strategy is a passive strategy, in which a diversified portfolio of bonds is maintained. A third bond strategy is the maturity matching strategy, in which the investor selects bonds that will mature on future dates when funds will be needed. Strip bonds are an attractive alternative for investors with this purpose in mind.

INTEGRATING THE KEY CONCEPTS

Your decision to invest in bonds not only is related to your other investment decisions, but also affects other parts of your financial plan. Before investing in bonds, you should reassess your need for liquidity (Part 2). Bonds that provide periodic coupon payments offer some liquidity. However, the value of a bond is subject to an abrupt decline, and you may not want to sell the bond when its price is temporarily depressed. Bonds should be considered marketable. Their liquidity depends on their maturity, with short-term bonds having a higher liquidity than long-term bonds.

The bond decision is related to financing (Part 3) because you should consider paying off any personal loans before you invest in bonds. If, after considering your liquidity and your financing situation, you still decide to invest in bonds, you need to decide whether the investment should be for your retirement savings plan (Part 6). There are some tax advantages to that choice, but also some restrictions on when you have access to those funds (as explained in more detail in Chapter 15).

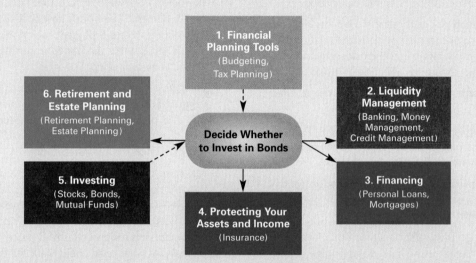

REVIEW QUESTIONS

1. What is a bond? What is a bond's par value? What are coupon payments and how often are they normally paid? What happens when investors buy a bond below par value? When should you consider investing in bonds?

2. What is a call feature on a bond? How will a call feature affect investor interest in purchasing the bond? How is this risk compensated for by issuers?

3. What is a convertible bond? How does a bond's convertibility feature affect its return?

4. What is an extendible bond? How does a bond's extendibility feature affect its return?

5. What is a put feature on a bond? How will a put feature affect investor interest in purchasing the bond?

6. What is a bond's yield to maturity? How does the price paid for a bond affect its yield to maturity?

7. Discuss how bonds are sold on the secondary market.

8. What are Government of Canada bonds? What characteristic makes these bonds especially attractive to investors?

9. What are federal Crown corporation bonds? Which major Crown corporations issue these types of bonds? What characteristic makes these bonds especially attractive to investors?

10. What are provincial bonds? Do all provincial bonds offer the same default risk? Why or why not?

11. What are municipal bonds? Why are they issued? Are all municipal bonds free from default risk?

12. What are corporate bonds? Are corporate bonds subject to default risk? What are high-yield bonds? Why would investors purchase high-yield bonds?

13. List and describe the three types of short-term debt securities. Why would most investors purchase these investments?

14. Describe the features and benefits of mortgage backed securities. Name a risk that is unique to this investment.

15. What is the unique feature of a strip bond? What are the tax implications of a strip bond?

16. How is a real return bond able to protect you from inflation?

17. When an investor sells a bond in the secondary market before the bond reaches maturity, what determines the return on the bond? How do interest rate movements affect bond returns in general?

18. Discuss the effect of taxes on bond returns.

19. How is the value of a bond determined? What information is needed to perform the calculation?

20. Discuss default risk as it relates to bonds. How may investors use risk ratings? What is the relationship between the risk rating and the risk premium? How do economic conditions affect default risk?

21. What is interest rate risk? How does a rise in interest rates affect a bond's price?

22. How is interest rate risk affected by a bond's maturity? How can investors use expectations of interest rate movements to their advantage?

23. Describe how the interest rate strategy for bond investment works. What are some of the potential problems with this strategy?

24. How does the passive strategy for bond investment work? What is the main disadvantage of this strategy?

25. Describe the maturity matching strategy of investing in bonds. Give an example. Why is this strategy considered conservative?

FINANCIAL PLANNING PROBLEMS

1. Bernie purchased 20 bonds with par values of $1000 each. The bonds carry a coupon rate of 9 percent payable semi-annually. How much will Bernie receive at his first interest payment?

2. Sandy has a choice between purchasing $5000 in Government of Canada bonds paying 5 percent interest or purchasing $5000 in BB-rated corporate bonds with a coupon rate of 7.2 percent. What is the risk premium on the BB-rated corporate bonds?

3. Bonnie paid $9500 for corporate bonds that have a par value of $10 000 and a coupon rate of 9 percent, payable annually. Bonnie received her first interest payment after holding the bonds for 12 months and then sold the bonds for $9700. If Bonnie is in a 35 percent marginal tax bracket for federal income tax purposes, what are the tax consequences of her ownership and sale of the bonds?

4. Katie paid $9400 for an Ontario Hydro bond with a par value of $10 000 and a coupon rate of 6.5 percent. Two years later, after having received the annual interest payments on the bond, Katie sold the bond for $9700. What are her total tax consequences if she is in a 25 percent marginal tax bracket?

5. Timothy has an opportunity to buy a $1000 par value municipal bond with a coupon rate of 7 percent and a maturity of five years. The bond pays interest quarterly. If Timothy requires a return of 8 percent, what should he pay for the bond?

6. Mia wants to invest in Government of Canada bonds that have a par value of $20 000 and a coupon rate of 4.5 percent. The bonds have a 10-year maturity and Mia requires a 6 percent return. How much should Mia pay for the bonds, assuming that interest is paid semi-annually?

7. Emma is considering purchasing bonds with a par value of $10 000. The bonds have an annual coupon rate of 8 percent and six years to maturity. They are priced at $9550. If Emma requires a 10 percent return, should she buy these bonds?

8. Mark has a Government of Canada bond that has a par value of $30 000 and a coupon rate of 6 percent, paid semi-annually. The bond has 15 years to maturity. Mark needs to sell the bond, and new bonds are currently carrying coupon rates of 8 percent, paid semi-annually. At what price could Mark sell the bond?

9. What if Mark's Government of Canada bond (from Problem 8) had a coupon rate of 9 percent, paid semi-annually, and new bonds still had interest rates of 8 percent, paid semi-annually? What price could Mark sell the bond for in this situation?

10. Melissa purchases a one-year $10 000 Government of Canada real return bond that has a coupon rate of 6 percent, paid semi-annually. Inflation increases 2 percent over the next six months, and then 1.5 percent for the following six-month period. Determine the value of the first semi-annual coupon payment. Then determine the final coupon payment and the par value of the bond at maturity.

ETHICAL DILEMMA

John is a relatively conservative investor. He has recently come into a large inheritance and wishes to invest the money where he can get a good return but

not worry about losing his principal. His broker recommends that he buy 20-year corporate bonds in
the country's largest automobile company, United
General. The broker assures him that the bonds are
secured by the assets of the company and the interest payments are contractually set. He explains that
although all investments carry some risk, the risk of
losing his investment with these bonds is minimal.
John buys the bonds and over the next two years
enjoys a steady stream of interest payments. During
the third year, United General posts the largest quarterly loss in its history. Although the company is far
from bankruptcy, the bond rating agencies down-
grade the company's bonds to high-yield status. John
is horrified to see the decline in the price in his
bonds, as he is considering selling a large portion of
them to buy a home. When he discusses his dissatis-
faction with his broker, the broker tells him that he is
still receiving interest payments and if he holds the
bonds until maturity he will not sustain a capital loss.
The broker reiterates that in their initial meeting
John's concerns were safety of principal and interest
payments, and the investment still offers both of
these features.

a. Was the broker being ethical by not informing
   John of the other risks involved in the purchase of
   bonds? Why or why not?

b. What could John have done differently with his
   bond investments if he anticipated buying a home
   in the next three to five years?

FINANCIAL PLANNING ONLINE EXERCISES

1. Go to http://personal.fidelity.com/products/
   fixedincome/ladders.shtml.

   a. This website describes three different bond build-
      ing strategies. Describe the impact of each strat-
      egy on default risk and interest rate risk. In your
      view, when would each strategy be appropriate?

   b. What is the risk inherent in each strategy? How
      can you overcome the risk involved with buying
      individual bonds?

2. Go to www.smartmoney.com/onebond/index.cfm?
   story=bondcalculator.

   a. This website allows you to calculate the change in
      the price of a bond based on changes in maturity
      and interest rates. Assume that your coupon rate
      is 6 percent for this exercise. What is the new
      price for the bond if your yield decreases by
      1 percent? What is the new price for the bond if
      your yield increases by 1 percent? Confirm the
      answers provided by the bond calculator using
      your financial calculator.

   b. Decrease the maturity by 10 years and repeat
      part a. What is the impact of a shorter maturity?

   c. Decrease the maturity by another 10 years and
      repeat part a. Compare these results with those
      from part b. Did decreasing the maturity by twice
      as much have twice as much impact on the price
      of the bond?

ON THE STUDENT CD-ROM FOR THIS CHAPTER YOU WILL FIND:

- Building Your Own Financial Plan exercise and worksheets
- The chapter-end Continuing Case about the Sampson family
- The fifth part-end Continuing Case about Brad Brooks

Read through the Building Your Own Financial Plan exercise and use the worksheets to determine whether you could benefit from investing in bonds.

After reading the Sampson case study, use the Continuing Case worksheets to help the Sampsons decide which bonds to invest in to support their children's education.

After reading the Brad Brooks case study, use the Continuing Case worksheets to provide Brad with feedback on his investment plan.

Study Guide

Circle the correct answer and then check the answers in the back of the book to chart your progress.

Multiple Choice

1. Which of the following is not a bond feature that is desirable for bond investors?
   a. Put feature
   b. Convertible feature
   c. Call feature
   d. Extendible feature

2. An investor may be interested in investing in a Government of Canada bond because:
   a. They are a safe investment.
   b. They are available with a term to maturity of anywhere between 1 and 30 years.
   c. They can be sold easily in the secondary market.
   d. All of the above.

3. Which of the following types of bonds is subject to the most default risk?
   a. Corporate bonds
   b. Federal Crown corporation bonds
   c. Municipal bonds
   d. Provincial bonds

4. Which of the following short-term debt securities is issued by the Government of Canada?
   a. Banker's acceptances
   b. Strip bonds
   c. Commercial paper
   d. T-Bills

5. Real return bonds protect you from inflation risk by:
   a. Increasing your coupon payments every six months.
   b. Adjusting the par value of the bond for changes in the inflation rate.
   c. Offering a term to maturity that will result in a very safe, low-risk investment.
   d. All of the above.

6. All of the following are types of investment income that can be earned from owning a bond, except:
   a. Capital gains
   b. Dividends
   c. Capital losses
   d. Interest

7. With respect to bond valuation, which of the following statements is true?
   a. A bond's value is determined as the future value of the future cash flows to be received by the investor, which are the periodic coupon payments and the principal payment at maturity.

   b. A bond's value is determined as the future value of the future cash flows to be received by the investor, which are the periodic coupon payments.
   c. A bond's value is determined as the present value of the future cash flows to be received by the investor, which are the periodic coupon payments and the principal payment at maturity.
   d. A bond's value is determined as the present value of the future cash flows to be received by the investor, which are the periodic coupon payments.

8. Calculate the value of a $1000 par value bond that has five years until maturity and a coupon rate of 8 percent, paid semi-annually. New $1000 par value bonds offer a coupon rate of 6 percent.
   a. $1085
   b. $915
   c. $1045
   d. $1084

9. To minimize the effects of default risk, an investor should choose which one of the following corporate bonds?
   a. AAA-rated corporate bonds with the shortest term to maturity
   b. AA-rated short-term corporate bonds with the shortest term to maturity
   c. AAA-rated long-term corporate bonds with the longest term to maturity
   d. AA-rated long-term corporate bonds with the longest term to maturity

10. Darvin and Kim would like to purchase a portfolio of bonds that will mature when their kids are ready to attend a post-secondary institution. What would be the most appropriate bond investment strategy given their objectives?
    a. Interest rate strategy
    b. Passive strategy
    c. Bond laddering strategy
    d. Maturity matching strategy

True/False

1. True or False? The coupon payments for a bond are normally paid quarterly.

2. True or False? A bond that is trading at a price below its par value is said to be trading at a discount.

3. True or False? Crown corporation bonds are guaranteed by the province in which they are issued.

4. True or False? The risk of default by the issuer of a provincial bond will vary depending on the province that issued the bond.

5. True or False? Banker's acceptances are short-term debt securities issued by large firms that are guaranteed by the issuing firm.

6. True or False? Strip bonds are always sold at a discount to their par value.

7. True or False? If you wish to sell a bond that has a coupon rate of 8 percent when new bonds being sold at par value are offering a coupon rate of 9 percent, you will have to sell your bond for less than par value in order to attract investors.

8. True or False? A bond is more likely to be exposed to call risk when interest rates are rising.

9. True or False? Bonds with longer terms to maturity are more sensitive to interest rate movements than bonds that have short terms remaining until maturity.

10. True or False? With respect to an interest rate strategy, you would select long-term bonds if you expect interest rates to increase.

PART 6

Retirement and Estate Planning

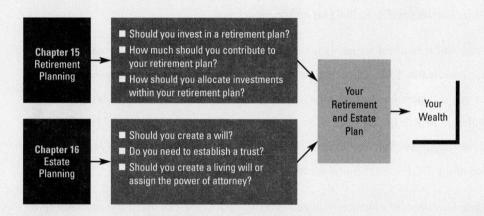

Chapter 15 Retirement Planning	■ Should you invest in a retirement plan? ■ How much should you contribute to your retirement plan? ■ How should you allocate investments within your retirement plan?
Chapter 16 Estate Planning	■ Should you create a will? ■ Do you need to establish a trust? ■ Should you create a living will or assign the power of attorney?

Your Retirement and Estate Plan → Your Wealth

THE CHAPTERS IN THIS PART EXPLAIN HOW YOU CAN PROTECT THE wealth you accumulate over time through effective financial planning. Chapter 15 explains how to plan effectively for your retirement so that you can maintain your wealth and live comfortably. Chapter 16 explains how you can pass on as much of your estate as possible to your heirs.

Retirement Planning

P atrick O'Toole, who is divorced, really wanted to retire at age 57. But, at 57, he was at least three years away from receiving Canada Pension Plan (CPP) benefits, and an additional eight years away from drawing Old Age Security (OAS). His mortgage still had 25 years of payments remaining, and after his divorce, he had only $225 000 accumulated in his RRSP. Even though he was unhappy in his present job, he needed to remain there as long as possible to build his retirement account.

Three years later, Patrick had refinanced his mortgage and had only 15 years of payments remaining. In addition, his RRSP had accumulated to $315 000. He was now in a position to begin withdrawing money from the CPP. However, this would require him to take an early retirement and reduce his CPP benefit by 30 percent, and he would still have to wait another five years before he would begin receiving OAS benefits. In five years' time, he would not only be eligible for OAS benefits, but also receive 100 percent of his CPP amount. The accumulated value of his RRSP might also be higher if he worked until age 65.

If you begin contributing to retirement plans early in your working years, you can avoid the situation that Patrick is in. The quality and timing of your retirement will depend largely on your own decisions, even if your employer has a retirement plan available. It will take sound planning and diligent preparation to be financially prepared for the retirement you would like to have. This chapter describes the process and details some of the tools available to you.

The objectives of this chapter are to:

1. Describe the role of Old Age Security
2. Describe the role of the Canada Pension Plan
3. Explain the difference between defined-benefit and defined-contribution retirement plans
4. Present the key decisions you must make regarding retirement plans
5. Describe types of individual retirement savings plans
6. Describe types of retirement income conversion options
7. Illustrate how to estimate the savings you will have in your retirement account at the time you retire
8. Show how to measure the tax benefits of contributing to a retirement account

L.O. 1   OLD AGE SECURITY

Recall from Chapter 3 that Social Security, more commonly known as Old Age Security (OAS), is a federal program funded by income tax and other tax revenues that makes payments to you upon retirement (subject to age and other requirements). In addition to this program, the federal government sponsors a contribution-based public pension system known as the Canada Pension Plan (CPP). Together, these federally sponsored programs are intended to ensure that you receive some income once you retire, and therefore form an important part of retirement planning. However, on their own, these programs do not provide sufficient income to support the lifestyles of most individuals. Therefore, additional retirement planning is necessary to ensure that you can live comfortably when you retire. Before discussing other means of retirement planning, we will describe how the public pension systems function.

Old Age Security (OAS) Program

Old Age Security (OAS) Pension. The first level of Canada's public retirement income system consists of a group of benefits that are funded by general tax revenues. The fact that these benefits are funded by general tax revenues, and not based on personal contributions, is an important distinction to make. Since you do not have to contribute to the Old Age Security (OAS) program, the only qualifying criteria are age and residency requirements. Essentially, if you have lived in Canada for at least 40 years since turning age 18, you will receive the full OAS pension. You may be eligible to receive a partial pension if you have lived in Canada for fewer than 40 years, but more than 10 years, since turning age 18. In general, the partial pension is equal to the number of years you have lived in Canada since turning 18 multiplied by 0.025 (or 1/40). To receive the OAS pension, a pensioner must have attained the age of 65. The OAS system, which was created in 1952, represents Canada's largest public pension system. Over time, the rules for the OAS pension have become more complex. However, the general rules outlined above provide a foundation on which you can reliably approximate how much OAS pension you will receive in the future. Exhibit 15.1 highlights the payment rates for the different benefits available under the OAS program. The maximum monthly OAS pension for the period July 2007 to September 2007 was $497.83. This translates to an annual OAS pension of $5973.96.

OAS Clawback. All of the benefits available under the OAS program are subject to a "means test." That is, if your income exceeds a certain amount, the benefits you will receive from the OAS program will be reduced. With respect to the OAS pension, this reduction in benefits is referred to as an OAS clawback. In 2007, the OAS pension was

Exhibit 15.1 Old Age Security Benefit Payment Rates (July to September 2007)

Type of Benefit	Maximum Recipient	Maximum Annual Monthly Benefit	Income
OAS Pension	All recipients	$497.83	See OAS clawback
GIS	Single person	$628.36	$15 096
	Spouse of pensioner	$414.96	$19 920
	Spouse of non-pensioner	$628.36	$36 192
	Spouse of allowance recipient	$414.96	$36 192
Allowance	All recipients	$912.79	$27 888
Allowance for survivor	All recipients	$1011.80	$20 304

Source: Service Canada, "Old Age Security (OAS) Payment Rates," www.hrsdc.gc.ca/en/isp/oas/oasrates.shtml (accessed July 26, 2007). Reproduced with the permission of the Minister of Public Works and Government Services Canada, 2008.

reduced by $0.15 for every dollar of income above $63 511 that an individual earned. If income exceeded $103 337.40 in 2007, the individual did not receive an OAS pension in that year.

Guaranteed Income Supplement (GIS). In addition to the OAS pension, low-income pensioners may qualify for supplemental benefits. In general, a single, divorced, or widowed pensioner who is at least 65 years of age, and whose sole source of income is the OAS pension, will also receive the full GIS benefit of $628.36 (see Exhibit 15.1). If a pensioner receives any income other than the OAS pension, the GIS benefit is reduced by $0.50 for every $1 of additional income. This is referred to as the GIS clawback. Exhibit 15.1 illustrates that the GIS benefit will be reduced to nothing if other income reaches $15 096. Otherwise, the combined OAS pension and GIS benefit would result in a monthly pension of $1126.19, or $13 514.28 on an annual basis.

For married couples, where both spouses are receiving OAS pensions, each spouse may be eligible for a maximum GIS benefit of $414.96.

EXAMPLE

Martha is a 66-year-old OAS pensioner married to Fred, who is a 65-year-old OAS pensioner. Both of them were born and raised in Canada. They have no other sources of income besides their respective OAS pensions. Martha's total income for the month would be $912.79 ($497.83 + $414.96). Similarly, Fred's total income for the month would be $912.79. As a result, their combined annual income from OAS and GIS would be $21 906.96 (calculated as ($912.79 × 12) × 2). The maximum annual income column in Exhibit 15.1 indicates that if either Martha or Fred has annual income other than OAS pension that is greater than $19 920, she or he would not be eligible to receive the GIS. This maximum annual income figure applies to each of them individually.

In Exhibit 15.1, "spouse of non-pensioner" refers to a situation in which both spouses are over age 65 but one spouse does not receive either an OAS pension or the GIS. "Spouse of allowance recipient" refers to a situation in which one spouse receives the OAS pension, while the other spouse is between the ages of 60 and 64 and receives the allowance benefit, which is discussed next.

Allowance Benefit. The allowance benefit is available to the spouse or common-law partner of a pensioner who is receiving, or is eligible to receive, the OAS pension and the GIS. To be eligible for the allowance benefit, the spouse or common-law partner must be between the ages of 60 and 64. In the previous example, if Fred was only 63, he would not be eligible to receive the OAS pension or the GIS. In this case, Martha and Fred would only receive half of the $21 906.96 benefit amount above, or $10 953.48. The allowance benefit was designed to reduce the financial burden that would result from only one low-income pensioner being eligible to receive OAS program benefits. Notice that if Fred is only 63, and is receiving the maximum monthly allowance benefit of $912.79, the total amount of income the couple receives is $21 906.96, the same amount they would have received if Fred was over age 65 and receiving both the OAS pension and the GIS.

Go to
www.cppib.ca

This website provides information on the CPP Investment Board and its policies and financial highlights of the performance of your federal pension plan.

Allowance for the Survivor Benefit. The allowance for the survivor benefit is available to the spouse or common-law partner of a deceased pensioner who was receiving the OAS pension. To be eligible for the allowance for the survivor benefit, the surviving spouse or common-law partner must be between the ages of 60 and 64. This benefit was designed to provide benefits to the surviving spouse of a low-income senior.

Applying for Benefits. OAS program benefits do not automatically start once you have attained the appropriate age to receive benefits. You must apply to receive these benefits.

Inflation Protection. The OAS pension, GIS, and the allowance benefits are adjusted for inflation every January, April, July, and October.

Taxation of Benefits. The OAS pension is a taxable benefit. The GIS, allowance, and allowance for the survivor benefits are tax-free.

L.O. 2   CANADA PENSION PLAN

Canada Pension Plan (CPP) Program

Canada Pension Plan. The second level of Canada's retirement income system consists of a contributory pension plan program called the Canada Pension Plan (CPP). The amount of CPP benefit you are eligible to receive is based on the dollar value of your contributions and the number of years you contribute to the plan. You may apply to receive benefits as early as age 60 and as late as age 70. Under the CPP, normal retirement is considered to be at age 65. If the amount of CPP you are eligible to receive is different than the amount your spouse is eligible to receive, you may benefit from a pension assignment. Finally, in addition to the CPP retirement benefit, the survivors of a CPP contributor who has passed away may be eligible to receive survivor benefits.

In general, individuals over the age of 18 who earn more than $3500 in a calendar year must contribute to the CPP. Under CPP rules, the first $3500 of annual income, also known as your year's basic exemption (YBE), is exempt from the CPP contribution calculation. Once your income rises above the YBE, the contribution rate is 9.9 percent of **pensionable earnings**. Pensionable earnings refers to the amount of income you earn between the year's basic exemption (YBE) and the year's maximum pensionable earnings (YMPE). For the 2007 calendar year, the YMPE was $43 700. The CPP contribution rate is split between employees and their employers. As a result, the CPP contribution rate for employees and employers is 4.95 percent each. Self-employed individuals must contribute to the CPP based on the full contribution rate of 9.9 percent. In recent years, the YBE has remained at $3500. The YMPE increases every year based on a formula that takes into account the growth in average income in Canada.

> **pensionable earnings**
> The amount of income you earn between the year's basic exemption (YBE) and the year's maximum pensionable earnings (YMPE).

EXAMPLE

Colleen works as an employee for Dynamex Industries. During 2007, she earned income of $50 000. Her spouse, Chris, is a self-employed carpenter. His earned income in 2007 was $38 000.

Colleen's CPP contribution amount would be calculated as follows:

(The Lesser of Annual Income or YMPE − YBE) × 4.95%

= ($43 700 − $3500) × 4.95%

= $1989.90

Chris's CPP contribution amount would be calculated as follows:

(The Lesser of Annual Income or YMPE − YBE) × 9.9%

= ($38 000 − $3500) × 9.9%

= $3415.50

> **Go to**
> www1.servicecanada.gc.ca/en/isp/cpp/soc/proceed.shtml
>
> **This website provides** an online form you can use to request your CPP Statement of Contributions.

CPP contributions are deducted by your employer at each pay period. Your employer sends your contribution along with its matching contribution to the CRA. Investment decisions with respect to the money deposited in the CPP are made by the CPP Investment Board.

CPP Benefit Amount. As mentioned, the amount of CPP benefit you are eligible to receive is based on the dollar value of your contributions and the number of years you contribute to the plan. Since the dollar value of your contributions will fluctuate during the course of your career, you are allowed to exclude 15 percent of your lowest earnings years from the final calculation. In addition, you are allowed to exclude those years of employment during which you were raising children under the age of seven. Individuals are also allowed to exclude any months during which they were collecting a CPP disability pension and/or any low earnings after the age of 65.

After taking into account these excluded periods, your CPP benefit is calculated. Although the CPP calculation is beyond the scope of this text, you can request a Statement of Contributions from the federal government. In addition to providing you with a history of your CPP contributions, this statement provides individuals who have reached age 30 with an estimate of their CPP retirement pension. For 2007, the maximum monthly CPP retirement pension was $863.75, or $10 365.00 per year.

Applying for Benefits. CPP retirement benefits do not automatically begin once you have attained the appropriate age to receive benefits. You must apply to receive these benefits. As mentioned, you may apply to receive benefits as early as age 60 and as late as age 70. The decision to apply for CPP retirement benefits should not be taken lightly. Depending on your personal circumstances, you may wish to apply early or to delay application to some point in the future. Exhibit 15.2 highlights the amount of total CPP benefits you would receive under three different scenarios.

EXAMPLE

Andy has decided to apply for early CPP benefit, Bill will apply for CPP at the normal retirement age, and Colin will apply for CPP at age 70. The annual CPP benefit amount is calculated using the 2007 maximum monthly CPP retirement pension of $863.75. Inflation is assumed to be 2 percent per year. Exhibit 15.2 illustrates that Bill will receive an annual CPP benefit of $10 365 when he turns age 65. This represents 100 percent of the amount he is eligible for, calculated as $863.75 × 12 = $10 365. Notice that Andy receives less than this amount ($7256) and that Colin receives more than this amount ($13 475). According to CPP legislation, benefits are reduced by 0.5 percent for every month that you take benefits early, and are increased by 0.5 percent for every month that you take benefits late, up to age 70. Andy is taking his CPP at age 60, which is 60 months earlier than the normal retirement age of 65. As a result, his CPP benefit is reduced by 30 percent, calculated as 0.5 × 60 months. Colin is taking his CPP at age 70, which is 60 months later than the normal retirement age of 65. As a result, his CPP benefit is increased by 30 percent.

Exhibit 15.2 shows that even though Bill and Colin start receiving CPP benefits later than Andy, the total CPP retirement pension received by both men will eventually be greater than the amount received by Andy. In Bill's case, his total CPP benefit will exceed that of Andy by age 79. Colin will exceed Andy's total CPP benefit by age 84, and he will pass Bill by age 91. The amount of CPP you will collect over a period of time should not be the only consideration as to when you apply for CPP benefits. Exhibit 15.2 implies that Andy, Bill, and Colin will each live until at least age 92. Although this may not be the case, Exhibit 15.2 does illustrate that if you have other retirement income options, you should carefully consider the timing of your CPP retirement pension application.

pension assignment
Occurs when a married or common-law couple decides to share their CPP retirement pensions in order to reduce their income taxes.

Pension Assignment. A **pension assignment** occurs when a married or common-law couple decides to share their CPP retirement pensions in order to reduce their income taxes. To apply for this, both individuals must be at least 60 years old and receiving a CPP pension. The amount of pension that may be assigned is the amount that was earned while they were in the relationship. As a result, the amount of CPP pension that each individual receives will be identical if they were together during the entire time they were contributing to the program. If either or both individuals contributed to CPP prior to the start of their relationship, a pension assignment will reduce the CPP pension amount of the high-income pensioner, and increase the CPP pension amount of the low-income pensioner by an equivalent amount. In this case, the CPP pension benefits will not be identical.

Exhibit 15.2 Accumulated CPP Retirement Pension

	ANDY	BILL	COLIN
Age	Early Retirement	Normal Retirement	Late Retirement
60	7 256	-	-
61	14 656	-	-
62	22 205	-	-
63	29 904	-	-
64	37 758	-	-
65	45 769	10 365	-
66	53 939	20 937	-
67	62 274	31 721	-
68	70 775	42 720	-
69	79 446	53 940	-
70	88 290	65 384	13 475
71	97 311	77 056	27 218
72	106 513	88 962	41 237
73	115 899	101 107	55 537
-	-	-	-
-	-	-	-
78	165 720	165 570	131 439
79	**176 290**	**179 246**	**147 542**
80	187 071	193 196	163 967
-	-	-	-
-	-	-	-
84	**232 396**	**251 842**	**233 020**
-	-	-	-
-	-	-	-
90	307 484	348 999	347 417
91	**320 889**	**366 344**	**367 840**
92	334 562	384 036	388 671

Source: Adapted from CCH Canadian Limited, *Financial Planning Fundamentals*, Third Edition, pages 4–20, CFP® Education Program, CCH Canadian Limited, 2006. Reprinted with permission of CCH Canadian Limited.

EXAMPLE

Alphonso and Luisa, both age 65, have been married for 15 years. Alphonso has been contributing to the CPP program for the past 25 years, and is eligible for a CPP pension of $700. Luisa has been contributing to the CPP program for the past 18 years, and is eligible for a CPP pension of $400. The couple has decided to complete an application for assignment. Assuming that their application is accepted, their CPP pension benefits will change based on the following calculation.

Alphonso can share the following portion of his pension:

CPP Pension × (Years of Marriage/Years of Contributions)

= $700 × (15/25)

= $420

Luisa can share the following portion of her pension:

CPP Pension × (Years of Marriage/Years of Contributions)

= $400 × (15/18)

= $333.33

Therefore,

Total Pension to be Shared = $420 + $333.33

= $753.33

Alphonso's CPP pension after assignment:

CPP remaining after assignment + 50% of pension to be shared

= ($700 − $420) + ($753.33 × 0.50)

= $280 + $376.67

= $656.67

Luisa's CPP pension after assignment:

CPP remaining after assignment + 50% of pension to be shared

= ($400 − $333.33) + ($753.33 × 0.50)

= $66.67 + $376.67

= $443.34

After assignment, Alphonso's pension has been reduced from $700 to $656.67, while Luisa's pension has been increased from $400.00 to $443.34.

Inflation Protection. CPP retirement pensions are adjusted for inflation every January.

Taxation of Benefits. The CPP retirement pension is a taxable benefit. Employee contributions to the CPP can be claimed as a non-refundable tax credit. Employer contributions are a deductible business expense, and are not considered a taxable benefit for the employee. Self-employed individuals can claim both the tax credit and the expense deduction.

Concern about Retirement Benefits in the Future

The ongoing success of Old Age Security and the CPP is critical to many Canadians. In 2005, it was estimated that nearly one-half of employed Canadians would rely solely on benefits from the OAS and CPP programs for their retirement. Based on 2007 benefit payout rates, a single pensioner who retires with no private savings will receive approximately $18 696.78 per year in retirement income. This calculation assumes that a single pensioner receives 100 percent of the OAS and CPP amounts and a portion of the GIS, which would be reduced as a result of having received CPP income. A June 2007 study completed by the University of Waterloo suggested that "two-thirds of Canadian households expecting to retire in 2030 are not saving at levels required to meet necessary living expenses." By themselves, the OAS and CPP programs provide only a modest income base and they are not intended to replace personal retirement savings.

The concern with respect to retirement benefits should be based on two important questions:

- Will government-sponsored benefits, such as the OAS and CPP programs, be available to future generations?

- What other retirement income options are available to Canadian employees?

Fortunately, any individual who has a savings ethic should be able to reach his or her retirement goals. First, given the expected reliance of so many Canadians on the OAS and CPP programs, it is hard to imagine a situation where either of these federally sponsored programs will cease to exist or substantially reduce benefits to retirees. In addition, reforms to the CPP over the last 10 years have provided this program with enhanced long-term stability. Specifically, an increase in the CPP contribution rate over the last 10 years, and the adoption of an independent CPP Investment Board has improved the future viability of the program. The more important question that needs to be addressed by today's employee is what other retirement income options are available? OAS and CPP do provide a base, but it would be difficult for most people to have the retirement lifestyle they would like on an income of less than $20 000 per year. For this reason, it is important to understand Canada's private pension system so that you can implement a savings program that will build on the benefits you receive from government-sponsored plans. Canada's private pension system is composed of two parts: employer-sponsored pension plans and individual retirement savings plans.

IN-CLASS NOTES

Old Age Security and Canada Pension Plan

- Old Age Security
  - Old Age Security (OAS) pension
  - Guaranteed Income Supplement (GIS)
  - Allowance and allowance for the survivor benefits
- Old Age Security benefits are subject to a "means test"
- Canada Pension Plan
  - Benefit reduction: 0.5% per month between age 60 and 65
  - Benefit increase: 0.5% per month between age 65 and 70
- You must apply to receive benefits
- Taxation of benefits
  - OAS and CPP are taxable
  - GIS, allowance, and allowance for the survivor are tax-free

_____

_____

_____

_____

_____

_____

_____

_____

EMPLOYER-SPONSORED RETIREMENT PLANS

Employer-sponsored retirement plans are designed to help you save for retirement. At each pay period, you and/or your employer contribute money to a retirement account. This money is not taxed until you withdraw it from the account. Any money you withdraw from the retirement account after you retire is taxed as ordinary income.

Employer-sponsored retirement plans are classified as defined-benefit or defined-contribution pension plans.

Defined-Benefit Pension Plans

defined-benefit pension plan
An employer-sponsored retirement plan that guarantees you a specific amount of income when you retire, based on your salary and years of employment.

Defined-benefit pension plans guarantee you a specific amount of income when you retire, based on your salary and years of employment. Unless you are in a contributory plan, your employer makes all contributions to the plan. The amount of employer contributions is based on actuarial values. Actuarial values are determined based on a set of assumptions, including that employees will retire at age 65, the retirement account will grow at 7 percent per year, and salaries will increase at 5.5 percent per year. These assumptions must be made in the case of a defined-benefit pension plan because the benefit at retirement is guaranteed. By making these assumptions, an actuary is able to work backwards and provide the employer with an assessment of how much it must contribute to fulfill its obligations to its employees. Since these assumptions are subject to change, an actuary reassesses the plan every three years. If there has been a substantial change in assumptions, the employer may have to increase its contributions. In a contributory plan, an employer is able to offset some of its contributions by having employees contribute as well. Even in this case, the employer is required to make at least 50 percent of the contributions.

At retirement, an employee will receive a pension benefit based on a specific formula. Exhibit 15.3 illustrates the specific formulas that are applied to defined-benefit pension plans. A flat benefit plan does not take into account the salary of the employee. Instead, a fixed benefit amount is earned by the employee based on the number of years of service. For example, an employee who earns a pension of $40 per month for each year of service would receive annual pension income of $14 400 if he or she works for that employer for 30 years. In general, the amount of pension income earned under a flat benefit plan is lower than the amount that may be earned under a unit benefit plan.

A unit benefit plan takes into account the earnings of an employee as well as their years of service. There are three types of unit benefit plans: final average earnings plans, best average plans, and career average plans. All three types provide a pension that is usually expressed as a fixed percentage of earnings. Pension legislation requires that an employee cannot earn an annual pension income of more than 2 percent of their current earnings. In addition, the amount of current earnings that can be used to calculate the maximum annual pension income is restricted. For 2007, the maximum annual earnings for this calculation was $111 100. For example, if your 2007 income is $120 000, the maximum amount of pension you can earn for this year of employment is $2222, calculated as $111 100 × 0.02. If you work for the same employer for 30 years without any additional increases in income or changes to the pension plan, you will receive an annual pension income of $66 660 at retirement, calculated as $111 100 × 0.02 × 30. This is an example of a career average plan because your annual income for each year of your career is used to determine your pension income.

In contrast, a final average earnings plan usually calculates your pension income based on your last three to five years of employment. Normally, your income will increase throughout your career. As a result, the final average earnings plan generally will result in a higher pension income than a career average plan. A variation of the final average earnings plan is the best average plan. Under this type of unit benefit plan, your employer will take into account your best three to five consecutive years of income when determining your pension benefit.

EXAMPLE

Bridgette is retiring after 30 years of employment with Barney, Smith, and Caulfield. Her employer-sponsored defined-benefit pension plan uses a best average earnings calculation to determine her benefit amount. For each year of service, Bridgette earns an annual pension income of 1.5 percent of her best average earnings. To calculate Bridgette's pension income, her best three consecutive years of income are taken into account. Bridgette's best earnings years occurred at the end of her career. The table below displays her income for the last five years of her career.

Exhibit 15.3 Registered Pension Plans

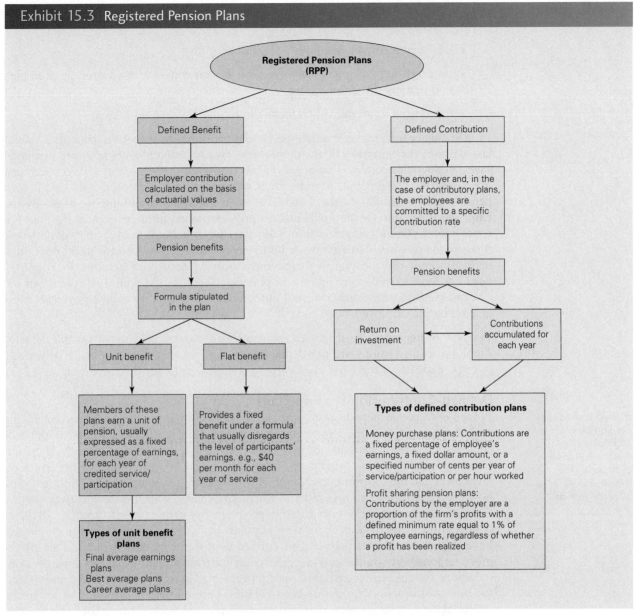

Source: *Canada's Pension Predicament: The widening gap between public and private sector retirement trends and pension plans*, p. 6, Canadian Federation of Independent Business Research, January 2007. Reprinted with permission of Canadian Federation of Independent Business.

	2003	2004	2005	2006	2007
Annual Earnings	$55 000	$70 000	$90 000	$100 000	$65 000

Bridgette's best earnings years were 2004, 2005, and 2006. Her average earnings for this period were $86 667, calculated as ($70 000 + $90 000 + $100 000) ÷ 3. Her annual pension income will be $86 667 × 0.015 × 30 = $39 000.

vested

Having a claim to the money in an employer-sponsored retirement account that has been reserved for you upon your retirement, even if you leave the company.

Pension legislation determines when employees are **vested, which means that they have a claim to the money that has been reserved for them upon retirement, even if they leave their company.** Contributions within an employer-sponsored retirement plan must be vested with the employee no later than two years after the employee has become a member of the pension plan. Once you are fully vested, the employer and employee contributions must be used to provide you with a retirement income at retirement. Vested pension benefits may be:

- left in your former employer's pension account

- transferred to your new employer, if it has an employer-sponsored pension plan that permits the transfer, or

- transferred to an individual locked-in retirement account (LIRA)

One major advantage of a defined-benefit pension plan is that the benefits accumulate without the initiation of the employees. This helps employees who are not good savers and would spend this money if they were given it in the form of salary. Therefore, it ensures that these people save for their retirement. In this respect, a defined-benefit pension plan is similar to the Canada Pension Plan. Contributions are made by the employer in an amount that will ensure a pre-determined future benefit. If the plan is a contributory plan, a deduction from your paycheque is made at every pay period. The funds in the pension plan are invested on your behalf. In its most basic interpretation, a defined-benefit pension plan is a retirement plan on auto pilot because the employee does not have to make any retirement planning decisions. As well, such plans put the risk on the employer, as any shortfall in the plan with regard to benefit payments must be paid by the employer.

Taxation of Benefits.   As discussed, pension plan income provides a taxable benefit. Employee contributions are tax-deductible. Employer contributions are a deductible business expense, and are not considered a taxable benefit for the employee.

Defined-Contribution Pension Plans

defined-contribution pension plan
An employer-sponsored retirement plan where the contribution rate, not the benefit amount, is based on a specific formula.

Defined-contribution pension plans are employer-sponsored retirement plans where the contribution rate, not the benefit amount, is based on a specific formula. A defined-contribution pension plan may or may not be set up as a contributory plan. As shown in Exhibit 15.3, the pension benefits you ultimately receive are determined by the return on investment and the contributions accumulated for each year. In most cases, you can decide how you want the money invested and whether to change your investments over time.

Since employers are not obligated to provide a pre-defined benefit amount, defined-contribution plans have become very popular. In the last 10 years, many employers have shifted from defined-benefit to defined-contribution pension plans. This places more responsibility on the employees to contribute money and to decide how the contributions should be invested until their retirement. Therefore, you need to understand the potential benefits of a defined-contribution pension plan and how to estimate the potential retirement savings that can be accumulated within this plan. The various aspects of retirement planning you must consider are covered in the next section of this chapter.

There are two types of defined-contribution pension plans: money purchase plans and profit sharing pension plans. In a money purchase plan, contributions are a fixed percentage of employee earnings, a fixed dollar amount, or a specified number of cents per year of service or per hour worked. In a profit sharing pension plan, contributions by the employer are a proportion of the firm's profits, with a defined minimum rate equal to 1 percent of employee earnings, regardless of whether a profit has been realized. Profit sharing defined-contribution pension plans are not very popular since contributions must be made even when the employer does not realize a profit during the year.

Benefits of a Defined-Contribution Pension Plan.   A defined-contribution pension plan provides you with many benefits. Any money contributed by your employer is like extra income paid to you above and beyond your salary. In addition, being involved in a defined-contribution pension plan can encourage you to save money at each pay period by directing a portion of your income to the pension account before you receive your

Go to
www.rbcroyalbank.com/
RBC:visa07junrvgke/cgi-
bin/retirement/ws_are.pl

This website provides
an annual retirement
expense worksheet that can
be used to estimate your
expenses at retirement
based on your current level
of expenses.

paycheque. Your contributions to the plan are tax-deductible. The income generated by your investments in a retirement account is not taxed until you withdraw the money after you retire. This tax benefit is very valuable because it provides you with more money that can be invested and accumulated. Finally, by the time you are taxed on the investments (at retirement), you will likely be in a lower tax bracket because you will have less income. However, because there is no guarantee with regard to the retirement benefit, the risk of shortfall rests on the employee's shoulders.

Investing Funds in Your Retirement Account. Most defined-contribution pension plans sponsored by employers allow some flexibility on how your retirement funds can be invested. You can typically select from a variety of stock mutual funds, bond mutual funds, or even money market funds. The amount of money you accumulate until retirement will depend on how your investments in the retirement account perform. In contrast, the accumulation of investment income inside a defined-benefit pension plan is not as much of a concern for each individual employee. Although you want the investments in the retirement account to perform well, the fact that you are guaranteed your final pension puts pressure on the employer to ensure that pension benefits are being managed well.

Pension Adjustment. To maintain fairness in the private pension system, the federal government restricts the ability of employees who are members of employer-sponsored pension plans from contributing to individual retirement savings plans. A pension adjustment calculates the remaining annual contribution room available to an individual after taking into account any employer-sponsored pension plan contributions. If an individual does not belong to an employer-sponsored pension plan, the pension adjustment is zero. With respect to a defined-contribution pension plan, the pension adjustment calculation is straightforward. Every dollar that you or your employer contributes to a defined-contribution pension plan reduces the amount you have available to contribute to an individual retirement savings plan by one dollar.

pension adjustment
Calculates the remaining
annual contribution room
available to an individual
after taking into account
any employer-sponsored
pension plan contributions.

EXAMPLE

Barney has a salary of $50 000. His company's defined-contribution pension plan allows him to contribute 5 percent of his annual salary to the plan. This contribution is matched by the company. Barney's pension adjustment would be calculated as:

$$\text{(Annual Salary} \times \text{Contribution Rate)} \times 2$$
$$= (\$50\ 000 \times 0.05) \times 2$$
$$= \$5000$$

As a result of this pension adjustment, the amount that Barney can contribute to an individual retirement savings plan for the following year is reduced by $5000.

With respect to a defined-benefit pension plan, the annual contribution amount is estimated using the pension earnings rate and the employee's pensionable earnings for the year. From the example above, if Barney was a member of a defined-benefit pension plan that provided a maximum annual pension income of 2 percent of his current earnings, the pension adjustment calculation would be:

$$(\$9 \times \text{Earnings Rate} \times \text{Pensionable Earnings)} - \$600$$
$$= (\$9 \times 0.02 \times \$50\ 000) - \$600$$
$$= \$8400$$

How do we interpret this number? Recall from the discussion of defined-benefit pension plans that the amount of pension Barney has earned would be calculated as $50 000 × 0.02 = $1000. In other words, at age 65, Barney would receive an annual pension of $1000 for this one year of service to the company. The next question to ask is approximately how much money would have to be contributed to a pension plan during Barney's working years to provide a $1000 annual pension at retirement? Using mathematical calculations and various retirement assumptions, the federal government determined that multiplying a pensioner's annual pension by $9 and then subtracting $600 gives a good estimate of the pension adjustment that results from a defined-benefit pension plan. In this example, the $8400 pension adjustment represents an estimate of the lump sum contribution required to provide a $1000 annual pension during Barney's retirement. The amount that Barney can contribute to an individual retirement savings plan for the following year is reduced by $8400.

Receiving Retirement Income from Your Employer-Sponsored Retirement Plan. Under pension legislation, every registered pension plan provides an age, referred to as the **normal retirement age**, by which employees are entitled to receive 100 percent of the pension income they are eligible for. In many plans, the normal retirement age is 65. Some plans use a combination of age and years of service to determine normal retirement age. As discussed earlier, the amount of pension income an employee will receive under a defined-benefit pension plan is based on factors such as salary and years of employment. At the normal retirement age, an employee will be offered several options with respect to pension income. Most provinces require that employer-sponsored retirement plans provide a pension income on a joint and survivor basis. As a result, if the pensioner should die before his or her spouse, the spouse will continue to receive a portion of the pension. With respect to a defined-contribution pension plan, the calculation for the amount of pension income an employee will receive is similar to the calculation used to determine the regular payment received when a registered life annuity is purchased. Registered life annuities are discussed later in this chapter. Defined-contribution pension plans tend to be more flexible in the retirement income options offered to employees. In many cases, a retiring employee may transfer the assets from a defined-contribution pension plan into an individual locked-in account, such as a LIRA.

Beginning with the 2007 taxation year, pensioners receiving income that is eligible for the pension income tax credit, discussed in Chapter 3, may split their pension income with their spouse or common-law partner. As a result, pensioners should be able to reduce their overall tax burden. For individuals aged 65 years and older, the major types of qualifying income that can be allocated to a spouse or common-law partner are:

- a pension from a registered pension plan (RPP)

- income from a registered retirement savings plan (RRSP) annuity

- payments from or under a registered retirement income fund (RRIF)

For individuals under 65 years of age, the major type of qualifying income that can be allocated to a spouse or common-law partner is a pension from an RPP. RRSPs and RRIFs are discussed later in this chapter.

normal retirement age
The age by which employees are entitled to receive 100 percent of the pension income they are eligible for.

EXAMPLE

Dominic, aged 65, has been a member of a defined-benefit pension plan for the past 35 years. Now that he has reached normal retirement age, Dominic would like to receive his regular pension income. His employer calculates his pension benefit to be $3000 per month. In addition, if Dominic dies before his spouse, Lisette, she will receive 60 percent of the pension that Dominic was receiving. Prior to 2007, Dominic's pension benefit of $36 000 per year would have been recorded as his pension income and taxed accordingly. Under the new guidelines for the taxation of pension income, half of the pension income received by Dominic may be deducted from his tax return and included on Lisette's tax return. Assuming that they have no other income, Dominic and Lisette will each pay tax based on an annual income of $18 000.

IN-CLASS NOTES

Employer-Sponsored Retirement Plans

- Defined-benefit pension plans
  - Guarantee you a specific amount of income when you retire
  - Flat, final average, best average, or career average benefit formula
  - Actuarial valuation required every three years
- Defined-contribution pension plans
  - Do not guarantee you a specific amount of income when you retire
  - Contribution rate is based on a specific formula particular to each plan
  - Two types: money purchase plans and profit sharing plans
- Plans may or may not be contributory
- Employer-sponsored retirement plans must be vested with the employee within two years of membership
- Taxation of benefits
  - Employer-sponsored retirement benefits are taxable to the employee
  - Employee contributions are tax-deductible

_____

_____

_____

_____

_____

_____

_____

_____

_____

_____

L.O. 4 YOUR RETIREMENT PLANNING DECISIONS

Your key retirement planning decisions involve choosing a retirement plan, determining how much to contribute, and allocating your contributions. Several websites provide useful calculators that can help you make these decisions, such as www.scotiabank.com/cda/content/0,1608,CID5239_LIDen,00.html and www.bmonesbittburns.com/retirementyourway/Tools.asp. Using these calculators can help you understand the trade-offs involved so that you can make the retirement planning decisions that fit your specific needs.

Which Retirement Plan Should You Pursue?

The retirement benefits from an employer-sponsored retirement plan vary among employers. Some employer-sponsored plans allow you to invest more money than others. If your employer offers a retirement plan, it should be the first plan you consider, because your employer will likely contribute to it.

How Much Should You Contribute?

Many defined-contribution pension plans allow you to determine how much money (up to a specified maximum level) to contribute to your retirement account. Although some individuals like this freedom, others are not comfortable making this decision. A first step is to determine your potential savings from contributing to your retirement plan. This requires assumptions about how much you could contribute per year, the return you will earn on your investments, and the number of years until your retirement, as illustrated in the following example.

EXAMPLE

Stephanie Spratt is considering whether she should start saving toward her retirement. Although her retirement is 40 years away, she wants to ensure that she can live comfortably at that time. She decides to contribute $2500 per year ($208.33 per month) to her retirement through her employer's defined-contribution pension plan. Her employer will provide a matching contribution of $2500 per year. Therefore, the total contribution to her retirement account will be $5000 per year. As a result of contributing to her retirement, Stephanie will have less spending money and will not have access to these savings until she retires in about 40 years. However, her annual contribution helps to reduce her taxes now because the money she contributes is not subject to income taxes until she withdraws it at retirement.

Stephanie wants to determine how much money she will have in 40 years based on the total contribution of $5000 per year. She expects to earn a return of 10 percent on her investment. She can use the future value of annuity tables (in Appendix A) to estimate the value of this annuity in 40 years. Her estimate of her savings at the time of her retirement is:

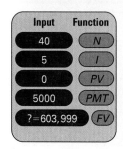

Input	Function
40	N
10	I
0	PV
5000	PMT
?=2 212 963	FV

Savings in Retirement Account = Annual Contribution × FVIFA (i = 10%, n = 40)

= $5000 × 442.59

= $2 212 950

Stephanie realizes that she may be overestimating her return, so she recalculates her savings based on a 5 percent return:

Input	Function
40	N
5	I
0	PV
5000	PMT
?=603,999	FV

Savings in Retirement Account = Annual Contribution × FVIFA (i = 5%, n = 40)

= $5000 × 120.797

= $603,985

Even with this more conservative estimate, Stephanie realizes that she will be able to accumulate more than $600 000 by the time she retires.

The amount that you try to save by the time you retire partially depends on the retirement income you will need to live comfortably. There are various methods of determining the amount you should save for your retirement. Among the important variables to consider are the levels of your existing assets and liabilities, whether you will be supporting anyone other than yourself at retirement, your personal needs, the expected price level of products at the time of your retirement, and the number of years you will live while retired. Various online calculators that take into consideration these factors are available.

Given the difficulty of estimating how much income you will need at retirement, a safe approach is to recognize that OAS and the CPP will not provide sufficient funds and to invest as much as you can on a consistent basis in your retirement plan. After maintaining enough funds for liquidity purposes, you should invest as much as possible in retirement accounts, especially when the contribution is matched by your employer. A common rule of thumb is to save at least 10 percent of your after-tax earnings in a combination of retirement accounts. If you are not able to invest this much in an employer-sponsored retirement plan, consider an individual retirement savings plan, such as an RRSP. RRSPs will be discussed in the next section of this chapter.

How Should You Invest Your Contributions?

When considering investment alternatives within a defined-contribution pension plan, you do not need to worry about tax effects. All of the money you withdraw from your retirement account at the time you retire will be taxed at your ordinary income tax rate, regardless of how it was earned. Most financial advisers suggest a diversified set of investments, such as investing most of your funds in one or more stock mutual funds and the remainder in one or more bond mutual funds.

Your retirement plan investment decision should take into account the number of years until your retirement, as shown in Exhibit 15.4. If you are far from retirement, you

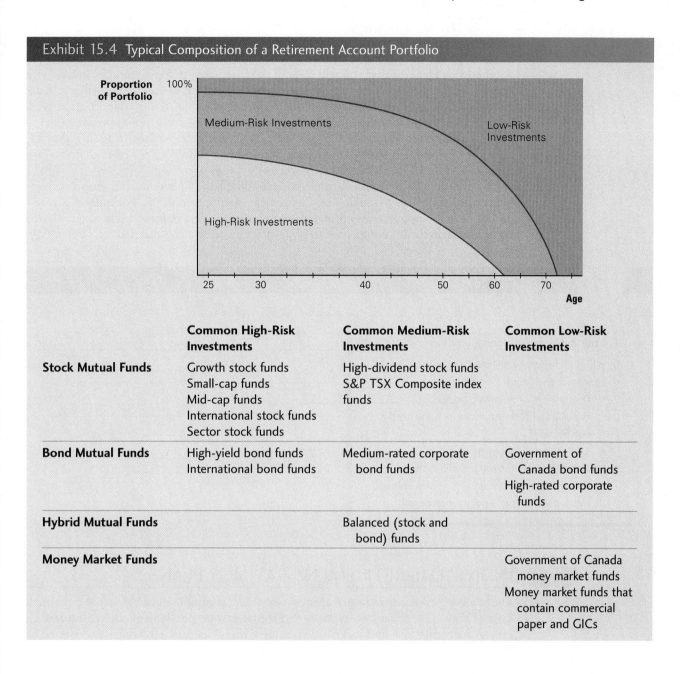

Exhibit 15.4 Typical Composition of a Retirement Account Portfolio

	Common High-Risk Investments	**Common Medium-Risk Investments**	**Common Low-Risk Investments**
Stock Mutual Funds	Growth stock funds Small-cap funds Mid-cap funds International stock funds Sector stock funds	High-dividend stock funds S&P TSX Composite index funds	
Bond Mutual Funds	High-yield bond funds International bond funds	Medium-rated corporate bond funds	Government of Canada bond funds High-rated corporate funds
Hybrid Mutual Funds		Balanced (stock and bond) funds	
Money Market Funds			Government of Canada money market funds Money market funds that contain commercial paper and GICs

might consider mutual funds that invest in stocks with high potential for growth (such as a growth fund, a sector fund, and perhaps an international stock or bond fund). If you are close to retirement, you might consider balanced growth and income funds, Canadian bond funds, and a large-cap stock that pays high dividends. Remember, however, that any investment is subject to a possible decline in value. Some investments (such as a money market fund focused on T-bills or bank GICs) are less risky, but also offer less potential return. Most retirement plans allow a wide variety of investment alternatives to suit various risk tolerances.

If you are young and far from retirement, you are in a position to take more risk with your investments. As you approach retirement, however, your investments should be more conservative. For example, you may shift some of your investments to Canadian bonds so that your retirement fund is less exposed to risk. Most people invest at least part of their retirement money in mutual funds. Regardless of the specific mutual funds in which you invest, one of the most important tips for accumulating more wealth by retirement is to avoid mutual funds with high management expense ratios (MERs).

If you start saving for your retirement by age 30, you can accumulate an extra $200 000 or more by the time of retirement simply by choosing low-expense mutual funds. Put another way, the odds that you will run out of retirement savings are much higher if you choose high-expense mutual funds because your retirement savings likely will not accumulate to the same degree. However, the return on the fund is very important as well. Buying a fund with low expenses is not very wise if the return is not appropriate to the fund's risk level. Investors should always look at historical returns to ensure that the fund's management is skilled. Sometimes, choosing a fund with a higher-than-average MER is warranted if management has performed well over time.

In addition to defined-contribution pension plans, individual retirement savings plans will require you to make sound retirement planning decisions. For individuals who do not have the opportunity to save through an employer-sponsored retirement plan, a registered retirement savings plan (RRSP) offers an equivalent alternative.

IN-CLASS NOTES

Your Retirement Planning Decision

- Which retirement plan should you pursue?
- How much should you contribute?
  - Determine your potential savings
  - How much retirement income will you need to live comfortably?
  - Compare your savings to your needs
- How should you invest your contributions?
  - Investment decisions should take into account the number of years until your retirement

_____

_____

_____

_____

_____

L.O. 5 INDIVIDUAL RETIREMENT SAVINGS PLANS

The second part of Canada's private pension system is composed of individual retirement savings plans. There are two types of individual private pensions: registered retirement savings plans (RRSPs) and locked-in retirement accounts (LIRAs), which are referred to as locked-in RRSPs in British Columbia and Nova Scotia.

Registered Retirement Savings Plans (RRSPs)

registered retirement savings plan (RRSP)
A type of private pension that enables you to save for your retirement on a tax-deferred basis.

A **registered retirement savings plan (RRSP)** is a type of private pension that enables you to save for your retirement on a tax-deferred basis. This type of plan, introduced in 1957, is registered with the CRA. As a result of registration, individuals who contribute to an RRSP receive a tax deduction for their contributions. In addition, the income earned on your investments within the RRSP is not taxed until you withdraw money at retirement. Although RRSP withdrawals can be made at any time, the purpose of an RRSP is to provide you with income at retirement. Any withdrawal you make is considered regular income and is subject to income tax. To assist you with tax payments, the RRSP plan sponsor will withhold some of the money you withdraw as a withholding tax. This should be considered a down payment on the total taxes payable. When you file your tax return, you claim the amount that is withheld as partial payment of the taxes you must pay on your RRSP withdrawal. Almost all financial institutions in Canada can act as an RRSP plan sponsor. As a result, many options are available to you when deciding which financial institution you want to use.

RRSP Account Types. There are three main types of RRSP accounts: an individual RRSP, a self-directed RRSP, and group RRSPs. When you open an individual RRSP account, you can invest your money in the investment instruments offered by the financial institution with which you opened the account. For example, if you open an individual RRSP with Alpha Investments mutual fund company, you can invest in any of the mutual funds offered by Alpha Investments. An individual RRSP is sufficient for the needs of investors who are opening their first account or have all of their RRSP assets in the mutual funds of a single company.

A self-directed RRSP allows you to hold a variety of investments within one plan. Within this type of RRSP, you may hold any number of investments that qualify under the rules set by the CRA (covered in the following section). Because of their nature, self-directed RRSP accounts are more costly to administer and will result in direct fees being charged to the individual investor. In general, self-directed RRSP accounts should be opened only by investors who own shares in a variety of mutual funds from different companies and/or investors who prefer to invest in an individual portfolio of stocks and/or bonds.

A group RRSP represents a series of individual RRSPs that are administered through one employer or association. Contributions to a group RRSP are normally made through payroll deductions. This type of plan provides employers with an opportunity to offer their employees another alternative to the employer-sponsored pension plans discussed earlier. Many employers prefer group RRSPs because they do not require employer contributions but still offer employees an opportunity to have a retirement savings plan through their employer. The costs to employers are substantially reduced and some companies will match the employee's contributions.

Qualified Investments. Investments that are qualified to be held within an RRSP account include:

- Cash, GICs, and other short-term deposits

- Individual stocks and bonds that are listed on an exchange

- Mutual and index funds

- Annuities

- Warrants, rights, and options

- Royalty and limited partnership units

- Mortgages (under specific circumstances)

- Investment-grade bullion, coins, bars, and certificates

How Much Can I Contribute? Exhibit 15.5 highlights the RRSP contribution limits for the most recent and upcoming years. If you were not a member of an employer-sponsored pension plan in 2006 or 2007, your maximum RRSP contribution limit for 2007 is $19 000. To determine the specific limit that applies to you for 2007, multiply your 2006 income by 18 percent. For example, Francesca has earned income of $35 000 for 2006. In addition, she has never been a member of an employer-sponsored pension plan. Her RRSP contribution limit for 2007 is $6300, calculated as $35 000 × 0.18. If you are, or were, a member of an employer-sponsored pension plan, you must take into account your pension adjustment in addition to some other factors.

If Francesca does not contribute the full amount she is eligible to contribute to her RRSP, she can carry forward the balance and contribute this amount in future years. The extent to which Canadians do not contribute to their RRSPs is surprising. According to Statistics Canada, only 31 percent of eligible Canadian tax filers made contributions to their RRSPs in 2005. Although Canadians contributed nearly $30.6 billion to their RRSPs in 2005, this figure only represents about 7 percent of the total contribution room available after taking into account the RRSP carry forward balance. Based on

Exhibit 15.5 Annual RRSP Contribution Limits

Year	Contribution Limit
2005	$16 500
2006	$18 000
2007	$19 000
2008	$20 000
2009	$21 000
2010	$22 000
2011	indexed

Source: Adapted from Taxtips.ca, "RRSP Contribution Limits," www.taxtips.ca/rrsp/rrspcontributionlimits.htm (accessed July 26, 2007), using Years 2005–2011 and Annual Contributions Limits. Reprinted with permission of Taxtips.ca.

these estimates, the total RRSP carry forward balance is more than $400 billion. This figure represents a significant amount of money that has not been invested in individual RRSP accounts. You can contribute to your RRSP up to and including the year in which you turn age 71.

spousal RRSP
A type of RRSP where one spouse contributes to the plan and the other spouse is the beneficiary, or annuitant.

Spousal RRSPs. A spousal RRSP is a type of RRSP where one spouse contributes to the plan and the other spouse is the beneficiary, or annuitant. A spousal RRSP offers a number of advantages. First, it allows the higher-income spouse to receive a tax deduction for contributions, which results in greater tax savings for the couple. Second, spousal RRSP contributions may provide a useful income splitting tool by allowing the couple to equalize their RRSP assets. In addition, since RRSP contributions can be made up to and including the year in which an individual turns age 71, a spouse who has passed age 71 can still contribute to a spousal RRSP for his or her younger spouse.

EXAMPLE

Pasquale is a 40-year-old self-employed accountant. His 2006 earned income was $100 000. Based on this income, Pasquale is eligible to contribute $18 000 to his RRSP. Pasquale's spouse, Roberta, is a 35-year-old stay-at-home mom. Prior to 2007, Roberta also worked as an accountant for a public firm. After the birth of their second child, the couple decided that Roberta should stay at home until this youngest child starts kindergarten. At present, they each have $200 000 in their RRSP plans and neither of them has any carry-forward room. To maintain similar-sized retirement plans, Pasquale has decided to open a spousal RRSP. He will split his 2007 contribution in half by contributing $9000 to his personal RRSP and $9000 to a spousal RRSP. Once he has completed this transaction, Pasquale will have $209 000 in his RRSP plan while Roberta will have $200 000 in her RRSP plan, plus an additional $9000 in a spousal RRSP. As a result of these transactions, Pasquale will have an $18 000 tax deduction and the couple will maintain RRSP accounts of similar size. They will continue to use this strategy until Roberta returns to the workforce. In the year that Pasquale turns age 72, he will still be able to make spousal RRSP contributions since Roberta will only be 67 years old.

Tax-Free Withdrawals from an RRSP

Home Buyers' Plan (HBP)
A tax-free RRSP withdrawal option that is available to Canadians who would like to buy their first home.

There are two circumstances under which money can be withdrawn tax-free from an RRSP. The Home Buyers' Plan (HBP) is a tax-free RRSP withdrawal option that is available to Canadians who would like to buy their first home. You are considered a first-time home buyer if you or your spouse or common-law partner have not owned a home as a principal residence in the four years preceding the year of withdrawal. The maximum withdrawal allowed is $20 000 per person. Although the withdrawal is tax-free, it must be paid back into the RRSP over a 15-year period, with payments beginning the second year after withdrawal at the latest. If you do not meet the minimum annual payment requirement of one-fifteenth of the amount withdrawn, this amount will be added to your taxable income for the year. You can also pay back all or a portion of the withdrawal before it is required by the CRA. In addition, this loan from your RRSP is interest-free. The HBP allows you to save more quickly because of the tax-sheltered RRSP environment and because by having a larger down payment on your home you may be able to negotiate a better mortgage rate.

A tax-free withdrawal from your RRSP may also be made under the **Lifelong Learning Plan (LLP)**, which is available to full-time students who temporarily would like to use an RRSP to finance their education. The withdrawal can be made from an RRSP owned by you and/or your spouse or common-law partner. The maximum annual withdrawal is $10 000. The total withdrawal allowed during the period you are participating in the LLP is $20 000. Although the withdrawal is tax-free, it must be paid back into the RRSP over a 10-year period, with payments beginning the fifth year after your first withdrawal at the latest.

Before using the withdrawal options available under the HBP and the LLP, it is important to consider carefully the long-term effect of withdrawing funds from your RRSP. Any funds withdrawn from an RRSP will no longer be earning tax-sheltered income. As you will see later in this chapter, the long-term growth that results from the compounding of interest inside an RRSP account can be quite significant. Recall that an RRSP is your personal pension plan. If you had a company pension plan with your employer, would you withdraw funds to purchase a home or go back to school? Every financial planning decision you make, or choose not to make, will have an opportunity cost that may affect you many years into the future.

Locked-in Retirement Accounts (LIRAs)

A **locked-in retirement account (LIRA)**, also known as a locked-in RRSP in some jurisdictions, is a private pension plan that is created when an individual transfers vested money from an employer-sponsored pension plan. The main purpose of a LIRA is to provide an opportunity for employees who leave a company pension plan to take the value of their pension plan assets with them. The characteristics of a LIRA are very similar to those of an RRSP. The plan can be established as an individual LIRA or as a self-directed LIRA. In addition, the qualified investments for a LIRA are similar to those for an RRSP. However, unlike RRSPs, LIRAs do not provide an opportunity to make regular contributions. In addition, the money in a LIRA is subject to the rules that govern pension plans, and therefore funds cannot be withdrawn at any time. At retirement, the money in a LIRA or locked-in RRSP must be used to provide a retirement income. In contrast, the money in an RRSP may be cashed in at any time.

L.O. 6 RETIREMENT INCOME CONVERSION OPTIONS

Retirement Income Conversion Options for an RRSP

As discussed earlier, you can contribute to your RRSP up to and including the year in which you turn age 71. By the end of the year in which you turn age 71, you must cash in your RRSP or transfer your RRSP assets into an income-producing plan. In general, cashing in your RRSP is a bad option because of the immediate tax consequences. Any money withdrawn from your RRSP, aside from money withdrawn as part of the HBP or LLP, is subject to income tax as regular income. If you cash in a $200 000 RRSP, the amount will be taxed as if you had earned a salary of $200 000 for that year.

A more commonly used alternative is to transfer all of your RRSP assets into a registered retirement income fund (RRIF). RRSPs and RRIFs are similar in many ways, including the types of investments that qualify to be held within each plan. As a result, transferring money from an RRSP into an RRIF is an exercise in paperwork. Assets do not have to be sold when moving from one plan to the other. Since an RRIF may hold

Lifelong Learning Plan (LLP)
A tax-free RRSP withdrawal that is available to full-time students who temporarily would like to use an RRSP to finance their education.

locked-in retirement account (LIRA)
A private pension plan that is created when an individual transfers vested money from an employer-sponsored pension plan.

similar investments to an RRSP, there is always the risk that you are investing in assets that may decrease in value. For example, if you own a portfolio of stock mutual funds in your RRSP, and subsequently transfer this portfolio into an RRIF, you are still exposed to the risks that come with investing in stocks. If your stock mutual funds decrease in value, your RRIF will decrease in value. This may have a negative impact on your retirement income. The main difference between an RRSP and an RRIF is that a certain percentage of the assets held within an RRIF must be taken into income each year after the year in which the RRIF was established, and any money so taken will be taxed at the prevailing income tax rates.

EXAMPLE

Vicky Zhao turns 71 in 2007. Before the end of the year, she must either collapse her RRSP for its cash value or transfer her RRSP assets into an income-producing plan. Vicky decides to transfer her RRSP to an RRIF on November 15, 2007. As a result of this transfer, Vicky will have to make a withdrawal from her RRIF before December 31, 2008.

The amount that must be withdrawn from an RRIF is prescribed by the CRA in an RRIF table. Exhibit 15.6 shows an RRIF table highlighting the amount that must be withdrawn from qualifying and non-qualifying RRIFs. A qualifying RRIF is one that was established on or before December 31, 1992, whereas a non-qualifying RRIF is one that was established after December 31, 1992. The only difference between these two types of RRIFs is that the withdrawal rate is higher for a non-qualifying RRIF between ages 71 and 77. Assuming that Vicky is age 71 on January 1, 2008, she will have to withdraw 7.38 percent of her non-qualifying RRIF assets during 2008. The amount she has to withdraw will be based on the value of her RRIF assets on January 1. The RRIF table represents only minimum withdrawal amounts. Vicky has the option to cash in her RRIF at any time.

term annuity
A financial contract that provides regular payments until a specified year.

life annuity
A financial contract that provides regular payments for one's lifetime.

registered annuities
Annuities that are created using assets from a registered plan, such as an RRSP.

In addition to cashing in your RRSP or transferring these assets to an RRIF, you can consider investing in an annuity. There are two types of annuities. A term annuity is a financial contract that provides regular payments until a specified year. A life annuity is a financial contract that provides regular payments for one's lifetime. Annuities that are created using assets from a registered plan, such as an RRSP, are referred to as registered annuities. The main advantage of a registered annuity over an RRIF is that you are no longer exposed to the risk that your investment may decrease in value. An annuity can also be designed such that the regular payment you receive is indexed to inflation.

EXAMPLE

Vicky could have used her RRSP assets to purchase an annuity. For example, if she expects to need income that would be produced by her RRSP until age 91, she could use her RRSP to purchase a 20-year registered term annuity. Of course, there is always the concern that Vicky may live past age 91. To avoid the risk that her annuity income will stop at age 91, she could use her RRSP to purchase a registered life annuity, which would guarantee her an income for life. On the other hand, what happens if Vicky dies the year after purchasing the life annuity? In this case, Vicky will lose most of her investment since the RRSP assets were used to purchase the annuity. To reduce this risk, Vicky could purchase a registered term certain annuity for 20 years. This type of annuity will guarantee an income payable to Vicky or her estate for 20 years.

Retirement Income Conversion Options for a LIRA

The retirement income conversion options for a LIRA are more limited than those for an RRSP since a LIRA is required to provide an income for life. As a result, the two main conversion options for a LIRA are a registered life annuity and a life income fund (LIF). A LIF is a restricted form of an RRIF. Unlike an RRIF, the annual withdrawal from a LIF is subject to a maximum amount, which means that the investments in a LIF cannot be cashed in. In addition, in the year that the owner of the LIF account reaches age 80, any remaining assets in a LIF must be used to purchase a registered life annuity. In some provinces, the assets from a LIRA or locked-in RRSP may be transferred to a locked-in

Exhibit 15.6 CRA-Prescribed Factors Expressed as a Percentage of the January 1 RRIF Value

Age of RRIF Owner or Spouse or Common-Law Partner at January 1	Qualifying RRIFs(%)	Non-Qualifying RRIFs(%)
65	4.00	4.00
66	4.17	4.17
67	4.35	4.35
68	4.55	4.55
69	4.76	4.76
70	5.00	5.00
71	**5.26**	**7.38**
72	**5.56**	**7.48**
73	**5.88**	**7.59**
74	**6.25**	**7.71**
75	**6.67**	**7.85**
76	**7.14**	**7.99**
77	**7.69**	**8.15**
78	8.33	8.33
79	8.53	8.53
80	8.75	8.75
81	8.99	8.99
82	9.27	9.27
83	9.58	9.58
84	9.93	9.93
85	10.33	10.33
86	10.79	10.79
87	11.33	11.33
88	11.96	11.96
89	12.71	12.71
90	13.62	13.62
91	14.73	14.73
92	16.12	16.12
93	17.92	17.92
94 or older	20.00	20.00

Source: Adapted from CCH Canadian Limited, *Comprehensive Practices in Risk and Retirement Planning*, Second Edition, pages 16–38, CFP® Education Program, CCH Canadian Limited, 2005. Reprinted with permission of CCH Canadian Limited.

retirement income fund (LRIF). In general, a LIF and an LRIF are identical retirement income options. However, there are two main differences between them: the formula used to calculate the maximum withdrawal from an LRIF is different, and an LRIF does not have to be converted to a life annuity at age 80. Exhibit 15.7 provides a summary of the retirement income conversion options available for RRSPs and LIRAs.

Exhibit 15.7 Retirement Income Conversion Options

Plan Type	Cash In	RRIF	LIF/LRIF	Registered Term Annuity	Registered Life Annuity
RRSP	Yes	Yes	No	Yes	Yes
LIRA/ Locked-in RRSP	No	No	Yes	No	Yes

Source: CCH Canadian Ltd., *Comprehensive Practices in Risk and Retirement Planning,* Third Edition, Module 12, CFP® Education Program, CCH Canadian Limited, 2006. Reprinted with permission of CCH Canadian Limited.

Reverse Mortgages

reverse mortgage
A secured loan that allows older Canadians to generate income using the equity in their homes without having to sell this asset.

According to a 2005 study by Statistics Canada, 69.2 percent of Canadians age 65 or older in 2005 owned a home, and 88 percent of them did not have a mortgage. In addition, a 2003 study by Statistics Canada revealed that 77 percent of a senior's net worth is home equity. These numbers reveal that, for many Canadians, the most important source of retirement income will be the equity they have in their homes. In many cases, the ideal solution for unlocking home equity is to use a reverse mortgage. A reverse mortgage is a secured loan that allows older Canadians to generate income using the equity in their homes without having to sell this asset. To apply for a reverse mortgage, an applicant must be 60 years of age or older. Depending on various criteria, a homeowner can borrow up to 40 percent of the value of their home or $500 000 using a reverse mortgage. The largest provider of reverse mortgages in Canada is the Canadian Home Income Plan (CHIP; www.chip.ca).

Even though it is a loan, a reverse mortgage does not have to be repaid immediately. Instead, a reverse mortgage provider, such as CHIP, allows the interest to accumulate during the period of the loan. In many cases, a reverse mortgage does not have to be paid back until the death of the borrower. The proceeds from a reverse mortgage may be paid in a single lump sum, set up as a line of credit, or used to purchase an annuity for the borrower.

There are two major drawbacks to a reverse mortgage. First, the setup costs, which include appraisal, legal, and closing costs, may be as high as $2000 to $2500. Second, the interest that accumulates on the reverse mortgage loan will reduce the value of your estate over time. As a result of these drawbacks, the decision to use a reverse mortgage should be considered carefully. It can be an ideal product for seniors who wish to remain in their home but do not have sufficient retirement income from the other income sources discussed in this chapter. However, a sound financial plan may reduce or eliminate the need for a reverse mortgage and its associated setup costs.

L.O. 7   ESTIMATING YOUR FUTURE RETIREMENT SAVINGS

To determine how much you will have accumulated by retirement, you can calculate the future value of the amount of money you save.

Estimating the Future Value of One Investment

Using the information available in Appendix A, the future value of a registered investment today can be computed by using the future value interest factor (*FVIF*) table. You need the following information:

- The amount of the investment
- The annual return you expect on the investment
- The term of the investment

IN-CLASS NOTES

Individual Retirement Savings Plans and Income Conversion Options

- Registered retirement savings plans (RRSPs)
  - Various types (individual, self-directed, group, spousal)
- Taxation of benefits
  - Withdrawals from an RRSP are taxable
  - Contributions are tax-deductible
- Locked-in retirement accounts (LIRAs)
  - Created from the lump-sum transfer of vested employer-sponsored pension benefits
  - Withdrawals are not permitted
- Retirement income conversion options
  - Cash in
  - Registered retirement income fund (RRIF)
  - Registered term annuity
  - Registered life annuity
  - Life income fund (LIF)
  - Locked-in retirement income fund (LRIF)
  - Reverse mortgage

EXAMPLE

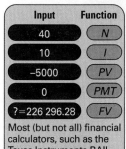

Input	Function
40	N
10	I
–5000	PV
0	PMT
?=226 296.28	FV

Most (but not all) financial calculators, such as the Texas Instruments BAII PLUS, require a negative present value (PV) input. You should consult your manual to determine the requirements of your financial calculator.

You consider investing $5000 this year, and this investment will remain in your account for 40 years until you retire. You believe that you can earn a return of 10 percent per year on your investment. Based on this information, you expect the value of your investment in 40 years to be:

$$\text{Value in 40 Years} = \text{Investment} \times FVIF\ (i = 10\%, n = 40)$$

$$= \$5000 \times 45.259$$

$$= \$226\ 295$$

It may surprise you that $5000 can grow into more than a quarter of a million dollars if it is invested over a 40-year period. This should motivate you to consider saving for your retirement as soon as possible.

Exhibit 15.8 Relationship between Savings Today and Amount of Money at Retirement (in 40 Years, Assuming a 10% Annual Return)

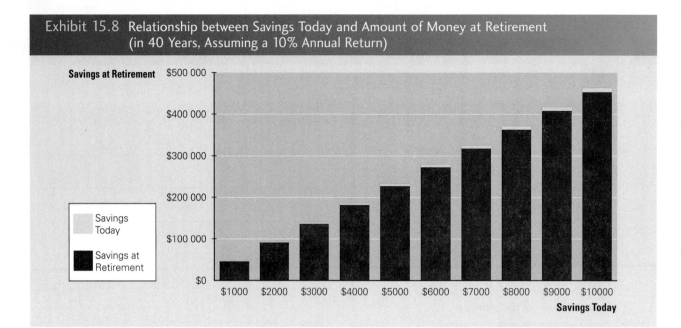

Relationship between Amount Saved Now and Retirement Savings. Consider how the amount you save now can affect your future savings. As Exhibit 15.8 shows, if you invested $10 000 instead of $5000 today, your savings would grow to $452 590 in 40 years. The more you save today, the more money you will have at the time of your retirement.

Relationship between Years of Saving and Your Retirement Savings. The amount of money you accumulate by the time you retire also depends on the number of years your savings are invested. As Exhibit 15.9 shows, the longer your savings are invested, the more they will be worth (assuming a positive rate of return) at retirement. If you invest $5000 for 25 years instead of 40 years, it will be worth only $54 175.

Relationship between Your Annual Return and Your Retirement Savings. The amount of money you accumulate by the time you retire also depends on your annual return, as

Exhibit 15.9 Relationship between the Investment Period and Your Savings at Retirement (Assuming a $5000 Investment and a 10% Annual Return)

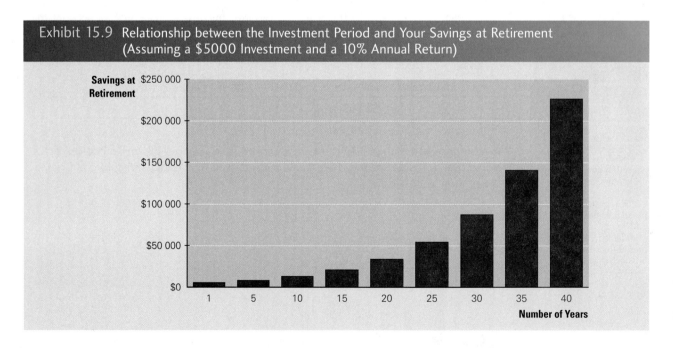

Exhibit 15.10 Relationship between the Annual Return on Your Investment and Your Savings at Retirement (in 40 Years, Assuming a $5000 Initial Investment)

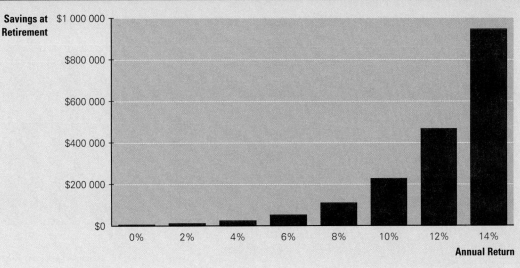

shown in Exhibit 15.10. Notice the sensitivity of your savings at retirement to the annual return. Two extra percentage points on the annual return can increase the savings from a single $5000 investment by hundreds of thousands of dollars. With a 12 percent return instead of 10 percent, your $5000 would be worth $465 200 in 40 years instead of $226 300. A decline in return rates would have a similar effect but, of course, on the negative side. Another consideration is the reinvestment rate. Return calculations assume that the interest earned through the time period can be reinvested at the same rate as the original investment, which may not be possible.

Estimating the Future Value of a Set of Annual Investments

If you plan to save a specified amount of money every year for retirement, you can easily determine the value of your savings by the time you retire. Recall that a set of annual payments is an annuity. The future value of an annuity can be computed by using the future value interest factor of an annuity (*FVIFA*) table in Appendix A. You need the following information:

- The amount of the annual payment (investment)
- The annual return you expect on the investment
- The term of the investment

EXAMPLE

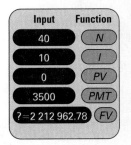

You consider investing $5000 at the end of each of the next 40 years to accumulate retirement savings. You anticipate that you can earn a return of 10 percent per year on your investments. Based on this information, you expect the value of your investments in 40 years to be:

Value in 40 Years = Annual Investment × *FVIFA* (*i* = 10%, *n* = 40)

= $5000 × 442.59

= $2 212 950

This is not a misprint. You will have more than $2 million in 40 years if you invest $5000 each year for the next 40 years and earn a 10 percent annual return. The compounding of interest is very powerful and allows you to accumulate a large amount of funds over time with relatively small investments. Set aside income for your retirement as soon as possible so that you can benefit from the power of compounding.

Exhibit 15.11   Relationship between Amount Saved per Year and Amount of Savings at Retirement (in 40 Years, Assuming a 10% Annual Return)

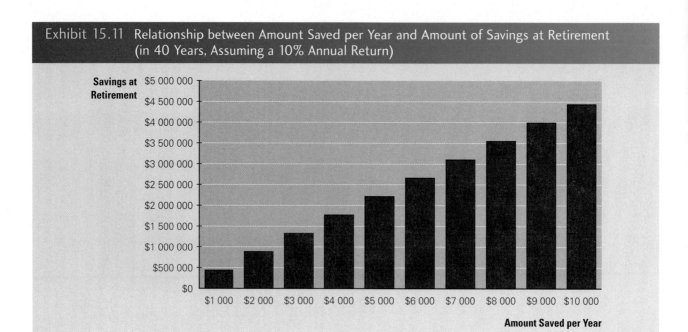

Relationship between Size of Annuity and Retirement Savings. Consider how the amount of your savings at retirement is affected by the amount that you save each year. As Exhibit 15.11 shows, for every extra $1000 that you can save by the end of each year, you will accumulate an additional $442 590 at retirement.

Relationship between Years of Saving and Retirement Savings. The amount of money you accumulate when saving money on an annual basis also depends on the number of years your investment remains in your retirement account. As Exhibit 15.12 shows, the longer your annual savings are invested, the more they will be worth at retirement. If you plan to retire at age 65, notice that if you start saving $5000 per year at age 25 (and therefore save for 40 years until retirement), you will save $857 850 more than if you wait until age 30 to start saving (and therefore save for 35 years until retirement).

Exhibit 15.12   Relationship between the Number of Years You Invest Annual Savings and Your Savings at Retirement (Assuming a $5000 Investment and a 10% Annual Return)

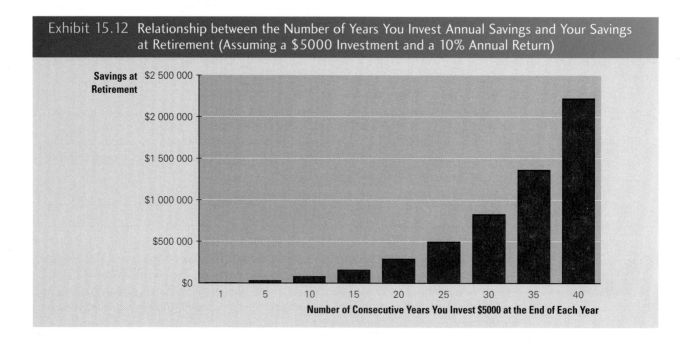

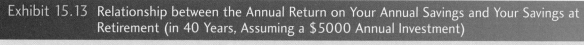

Exhibit 15.13 Relationship between the Annual Return on Your Annual Savings and Your Savings at Retirement (in 40 Years, Assuming a $5000 Annual Investment)

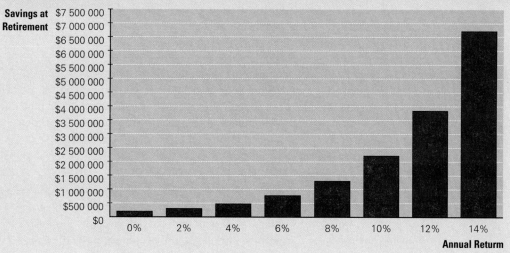

Relationship between Your Annual Return and Your Savings at Retirement. The amount you will have at retirement also depends on the return you earn on your annual savings, as shown in Exhibit 15.13. Notice how sensitive your savings are to the annual return. Almost $1 million more is accumulated from an annual return of 10 percent than from an annual return of 8 percent. An annual return of 12 percent produces about $1.6 million more in accumulated savings than an annual return of 10 percent. Remember, too, the reinvestment risk discussed earlier. To achieve the results used in these examples, you must be able to obtain that same rate on all earnings.

IN-CLASS NOTES

Estimating Your Future Retirement Savings

- The more you save today, the more money you will have at the time of your retirement.
- The longer your savings are invested, the more they will be worth at retirement.
- Retirement savings are highly sensitive to your annual rate of return.

L.O. 8 MEASURING THE TAX BENEFITS FROM A RETIREMENT ACCOUNT

If you can avoid or defer taxes when investing for your retirement, you will likely be able to save a much larger amount of money. Since registered retirement contributions can be used as a tax deduction, you can reduce the present level of income taxes. In addition, you will not be taxed on your registered investments until they are withdrawn from your retirement account. The potential tax benefits of investing in a retirement account are illustrated in the following example.

EXAMPLE

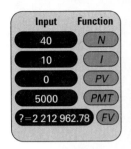

From the previous example, you can see that a $5000 per year investment earning a return of 10 percent per year for 40 years would accumulate to $2 212 950. Using the future value of an annuity (*FVIFA*) table in Appendix A, your savings at retirement would be:

$$\text{Savings at Retirement} = \text{Annual Investment} \times FVIFA \ (i = 10\%, n = 40)$$
$$= \$5000 \times 442.59$$
$$= \$2\ 212\ 950$$

As you withdraw the money from your account after you retire, you will be taxed at your ordinary income tax rate, even though the investment appreciated over time due to capital gains. If you withdraw all of your money in one year, and are taxed at a 30 percent rate, your tax will be:

$$\text{Tax} = \text{Income} \times \text{Tax Rate}$$
$$= \$2\ 212\ 950 \times 0.30$$
$$= \$663\ 885$$

You probably would not withdraw all of your funds in one year, but this lump sum withdrawal simplifies the example. Your income after taxes in this example would be:

$$\text{Income after Taxes} = \text{Taxable Income} - \text{Income Tax}$$
$$= \$2\ 212\ 950 - \$663\ 885$$
$$= \$1\ 549\ 065$$

To compare the return from investing $5000 in the registered retirement account to the return from investing $5000 in a non-registered retirement account, consider first that if your investment is non-registered, you will not be eligible to deduct the $5000 contribution from your taxable income. Assuming that your prevailing marginal income tax rate is 30 percent, you are subject to a tax of $1500 each year that you could have eliminated by depositing the $5000 in a registered account such as an RRSP. After considering taxes, you have $3500 that you can invest each year. Assume that you earn 10 percent on those annual savings invested over the next 40 years. Referring to the future value of annuity (*FVIFA*) table in Appendix A, you will receive:

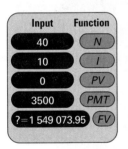

$$\text{Savings at Retirement} = \text{Annual Investment} \times FVIFA \ (i = 10\%, n = 40)$$
$$= \$3500 \times 442.59$$
$$= \$1\ 549\ 065$$

Next, consider that you will have to pay taxes when you cash in this investment. For many investments such as bonds or dividend-paying stocks, you would have been paying taxes every year over this 40-year period. Even if you had minimized taxes by choosing a stock that does not pay dividends, you would still pay a capital gains tax when you cash in the investment. Since you invested $3500 per year, or a total of $140 000 over 40 years, your capital gain is:

$$\text{Capital Gain} = \text{Selling Price of Stock} - \text{Purchase Price of Stock}$$
$$= \$1\ 549\ 065 - \$140\ 000$$
$$= \$1\ 409\ 065$$

Assuming a marginal tax rate of 30 percent, your capital gains tax would be:

$$\text{Capital Gains Tax} = \text{Taxable Portion of Capital Gain} \times \text{Marginal Tax Rate}$$
$$= \$704\ 532.50 \times 0.30$$
$$= \$211\ 359.75$$

Therefore, after 40 years, you have:

$$\text{Value of Investment} = \text{Value of Investment before Taxes} - \text{Capital Gains Tax}$$
$$= \$1\ 549\ 065 - \$211\ 360$$
$$= \$1\ 337\ 705$$

Go to
www.seclonlogic.com/
demo/planning.asp

This website provides
a calculator that will assist
you in planning for your
retirement by displaying
the additional amount you
will need to save based on
the assumptions you enter.

Overall, investing $5000 per year for the next 40 years in your retirement account will be worth over $211 000 more than if you invest $5000 per year on your own. If you withdraw funds gradually from your retirement plan, its benefits will be even greater because you will defer taxes for a longer period of time. If you use a different annual return, you will get different results, but the advantage of the retirement account will remain. If you invest in something other than non-dividend-paying stocks on your own, the advantage of the retirement account will be even greater. Any investments on your own are subject to annual taxes on any ordinary income (dividend or interest payments), while income generated in the retirement account is not taxed until you withdraw the funds.

HOW RETIREMENT PLANNING FITS WITHIN YOUR FINANCIAL PLAN

The following are the key retirement planning decisions that should be included within your financial plan:

- Should you invest in a retirement plan?
- How much should you invest in a retirement plan?
- How should you allocate investments within your retirement plan?

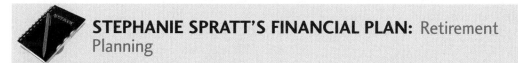

STEPHANIE SPRATT'S FINANCIAL PLAN: Retirement Planning

GOALS FOR RETIREMENT PLANNING

1. Ensure an adequate financial position at the time I retire.

2. Reduce the tax liability on my present income.

ANALYSIS

Type of Retirement Plan	Benefits
Employer's defined-contribution pension plan	*I plan to contribute $2400 of my income (tax-deferred) per year to my employer's defined-contribution pension plan. In addition, my employer provides a matching contribution of $2400.*
RRSP	*I can contribute up to $4000 of income per year (tax-deferred) to an RRSP.*

DECISIONS

Decision on Whether I Should Engage in Retirement Planning

Even if Old Age Security and Canada Pension Plan benefits are available when I retire, they will not be sufficient to provide the amount of financial support I desire. Given the substantial tax benefits of a retirement plan, I should engage in retirement planning. I plan to take full advantage of my employer's defined-contribution pension plan. I will contribute $2400 per year and my employer will match this with $2400. The benefits of an RRSP are substantial. Although I have not contributed to this retirement account in the past, I plan to do so as soon as possible.

Decision on How Much to Contribute to Retirement

I should attempt to contribute the maximum allowed to my employer's defined-contribution pension plan and to an RRSP. These contributions will reduce the amount of money I can dedicate toward savings and investments, but the trade-off favours retirement contributions because of the tax advantages.

Decision on Asset Allocation within the Retirement Account

I plan to invest the money slated for retirement in stock and bond mutual funds. I will invest about 70 or 80 percent of the money in a few diversified stock mutual funds and the remainder in a diversified corporate bond mutual fund.

Discussion Questions

1. How would Stephanie's retirement planning decisions be different if she were a single mother of two children?

2. How would Stephanie's retirement planning decisions be affected if she were 35 years old? If she were 50 years old?

SUMMARY

Old Age Security benefits provide income to qualified individuals to support them during their retirement. In addition, the Canada Pension Plan is a government-sponsored contributory plan that provides a retirement pension to most working Canadians. However, the income provided by these government programs is not sufficient for most individuals to live comfortably. Therefore, individuals engage in retirement planning so that they will have additional sources of income when they retire.

Retirement plans sponsored by employers are normally classified as defined-benefit pension plans or defined-contribution pension plans. Defined-benefit pension plans guarantee a specific amount of income to employees upon retirement, based on factors such as their salary and number of years of service. Defined-contribution pension plans provide guidelines on the maximum amount that can be contributed to a retirement account. With respect to a defined-contribution pension plan, individuals usually have the freedom to make decisions about how much to invest and how to invest for their retirement. In most jurisdictions, an employer will match or exceed the employee contribution to a defined-contribution pension plan. However, the defined-benefit plan does offer security for pensioners in that the final benefit can be calculated and the risk is borne by the employer if the plan does not have enough funds to pay these benefits.

Two key retirement planning decisions are how much to contribute to your retirement plan and how to invest your contributions. When an employer is willing to match your retirement contribution, you should always contribute enough to take full advantage of the match. In addition, you should try to contribute the maximum amount allowed, even if doing so means you will have fewer funds to invest in other ways. Most financial advisers suggest investing most of your contribution in one or more diversified stock mutual funds and putting the remainder in a diversified bond mutual fund.

The specific allocation depends on your willingness to tolerate risk and your overall financial position.

In addition to retirement accounts offered by employers, individuals can establish a registered retirement savings plan (RRSP). Many individuals own a locked-in retirement account (LIRA), which is an individual retirement plan that results from the transfer of pension plan assets from an employer-sponsored pension plan.

At retirement, a number of retirement income conversion options are available. With respect to an RRSP, an individual may cash in or transfer plan assets to a registered retirement income fund (RRIF). The assets from an RRSP can also be used to purchase various types of annuities, including registered term annuities and registered life annuities. Assets from a LIRA may be transferred to a life income fund (LIF) or locked-in retirement income fund (LRIF).

Your future savings from investing in a retirement account can easily be measured based on information regarding the amount you plan to invest each year, the annual return you expect, and the number of years until retirement. The future savings reflect the future value of an annuity.

The tax benefits from investing in a retirement account can be estimated by measuring the amount of retirement savings once they are converted to cash (and the income taxes are paid) versus the amount of savings if you had simply made investments outside a retirement account. The tax benefits arise from deferring tax on income received from your employer until retirement and deferring tax on income earned from your contributions until retirement. Retirement accounts are the preferred investment in any comparison because of the tax advantages.

INTEGRATING THE KEY CONCEPTS

Your retirement planning affects other parts of your financial plan. If you build your retirement account when you are young, any funds you invest in a retirement plan cannot be used to maintain your liquidity (Part 2) or other investments (Part 5). Yet, by contributing to a retirement plan consistently over time, you are not forced to build wealth quickly just before you retire. You will be able to take greater advantage of the power of compounding interest.

If you start saving for retirement at age 50 or later, you may take excessive risk in your efforts to amass substantial wealth for your retirement quickly. For example, you may decide to ignore the need for liquidity (Part 2) so that you can focus on investments that are expected to offer a high rate of return. This strategy could cause you to experience cash shortages in some periods. You may not be able to finance a car or a home (Part 3) because you would need to avoid interest payments and focus on accumulating a lot of money quickly. You may also take excessive risk when making your investment decisions (Part 5), which could backfire. The advantage of retirement planning is that it allows you more time to build wealth for your retirement, so that you can make financing and investment decisions that are based on a long-term perspective.

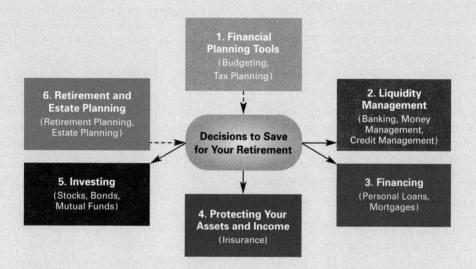

REVIEW QUESTIONS

1. How does Old Age Security (OAS) fit into retirement planning? How is it funded? How does an individual qualify for OAS benefits? When do you receive these benefits?

2. How are OAS benefits calculated? Describe the OAS clawback.

3. Describe the supplemental benefits available under the OAS program. How are OAS benefits taxed?

4. How does the Canada Pension Plan (CPP) fit into retirement planning? How is it funded? When do you receive benefits?

5. What are pensionable earnings? How are pensionable earnings used to determine your CPP contribution? When should you apply for CPP benefits?

6. Describe how a pension assignment works.

7. Discuss some of the concerns about the future of government-sponsored retirement benefits.

8. Describe how employer-sponsored retirement plans work in general.

9. What is a defined-benefit pension plan? What is a flat benefit plan? Describe the various types of unit benefit plans. What is vesting? What does it mean to be fully vested? Describe the tax treatment of a defined-benefit pension plan.

10. What is a defined-contribution pension plan? Why are some employers switching to this type of plan? List the two types of defined-contribution pension plans. List some of the benefits a defined-contribution plan offers to employees.

11. Describe how a pension adjustment works.

12. Describe the process for receiving income from your employer-sponsored retirement plan.

13. Briefly discuss the key retirement planning decisions an individual must make.

14. Describe the features of a registered retirement savings plan (RRSP). What is the purpose of the various RRSP account types? What investments qualify to be held inside an RRSP account? How do you determine the contribution limit for an RRSP? What is a spousal RRSP?

15. Describe the features of the Home Buyers' Plan (HBP) and the Lifelong Learning Plan (LLP).

16. What is a locked-in retirement account (LIRA)? What is its main purpose?

17. Describe the retirement income conversion options for an RRSP account.

18. What is the difference between a registered term annuity and a registered life annuity? What is the main disadvantage of annuities?

19. Describe the retirement income conversion options for a LIRA. Why are the LIRA conversion options different from the RRSP conversion options?

20. What is a reverse mortgage? What are the benefits of a reverse mortgage? What are the disadvantages?

21. Why are retirement accounts more beneficial than other investments that could be used for retirement? Describe an effective strategy for retirement planning.

22. When estimating the future value of a retirement investment, what factors will affect the amount of funds available to you at retirement? Explain.

23. When estimating the future value of a set of annual investments, what factors will affect the amount of funds available to you at retirement?

24. Explain the tax benefits of investing within a retirement account versus investing outside a retirement account.

25. What is the main advantage of retirement planning?

FINANCIAL PLANNING PROBLEMS

1. Barry has just become eligible for his employer-sponsored retirement plan. Barry is 35 and plans to retire at 65. He calculates that he can contribute $3600 per year to the plan. Barry's employer will match this amount. If Barry can earn an 8 percent return on his investment, how much will he have at retirement?

Problem 2 requires a financial calculator.

2. How much would Barry (from Problem 1) have at retirement if he had started contributing to this plan at age 25?

3. How much would Barry (from Problem 1) have if he could earn a 10 percent return on his investment beginning at age 35?

4. Assuming an 8 percent return, how much would Barry (from Problem 1) have if he could invest an additional $1000 per year that his employer would match beginning at age 35?

5. How much will Marie have in her retirement account in 10 years if her contribution is $7000 per year and the annual return on the account is 6 percent? How much of this amount represents interest?

6. Lloyd and his wife, Jean, have no retirement plan at work but they contribute $4000 in total each year to an RRSP. They are in a 30 percent marginal tax bracket. What tax savings will they realize for these contributions annually?

7. In need of extra cash, Troy and Lilly decide to withdraw $8000 from their RRSP. They are in a 30 percent marginal tax bracket. What will be the tax consequences of this withdrawal?

8. Lisa and Mark married at age 22. Each year until their thirtieth birthdays, they put a total of $4000 into their RRSPs. At age 30, they bought a home and started a family. They continued to make contributions to their employer-sponsored retirement plans (they no longer contribute to their respective RRSPs). If they receive an average annual return of 8 percent, how much will they have in their RRSPs by age 60? What was their total investment?

9. Ricky and Sharon married at age 22, started a family, and bought a house. At age 30, they began making an annual contribution of $4000 to an RRSP. They continued making these contributions until age 60. If the average return on their investment was 8 percent, how much was in their RRSP at age 60? What was their total investment?

10. Tilly would like to invest $2500 of before-tax income each year in an RRSP account or in alternative stock investments. She likes the alternative investments because they provide her with more flexibility and a potentially higher return. She would like to retire in 30 years. If she invests money in an RRSP account, she can earn 7 percent annually. If she invests in alternative stock investments, she can earn 9 percent annually. Tilly is in the 30 percent marginal tax bracket.

    a. If Tilly invests all of her money in the RRSP account and withdraws all of her income when she retires, what is her income after taxes?

    b. If Tilly invests all of her money in alternative stock investments, what are her savings at retirement? (Hint: Remember that the income is taxed prior to investment.)

    c. Assuming a marginal income tax rate of 30 percent, what is the after-tax value of the alternative stock investment?

    d. Should Tilly invest her money in the RRSP account or in the alternative stock investments?

ETHICAL DILEMMA

Nancy and Al have been planning their retirement since they married in their early twenties. In their mid-forties and with two children in college, they are finding it harder to save and fear that they will fall short of the savings needed to reach their retirement goals. Nancy's rich Uncle Charlie assures her that she has nothing to worry about: "You are my favourite niece and because you are so good to me, I am leaving my entire estate to you." Nancy and Al begin devoting considerable time and energy to making Uncle Charlie's golden years as enjoyable as possible. Factoring in their anticipated inheritance, Nancy and Al look forward to a comfortable retirement. Ten years later, Uncle Charlie passes away. At the reading of his will, Nancy is surprised to learn that Uncle Charlie made the same comment to her four cousins. As the will is read, all five of them are horrified to find that Uncle Charlie left his entire estate, valued at more than $2 million, to a home for stray cats.

a. Fully discuss your views on the ethics of Uncle Charlie's actions.

b. Looking at Nancy and Al's experience, what lessons about retirement planning can be learned?

FINANCIAL PLANNING ONLINE EXERCISES

1. How you invest your contributions will have a major impact on your annual return and the amount of money you will save toward retirement. Go to www.retirementadvisor.ca/retadv/apps/tools/tools.jsp. Under Investment Tools, click on Portfolio Rates of Return.

a. Select the GRAPHS tab. What is the difference in the annual return among the three asset mixes? Which asset mix shows the highest annual return? Which shows the lowest annual return? Which asset mix is the most diversified? Record the asset mix under each scenario on a piece of paper.

b. Return to the main page. Under Investment Tools, click on Portfolio Accumulations. Change the asset mixes so that they are the same as in part a. Enter $1000 for Amount invested at beginning of period. Now select the GRAPHS tab. Which asset mix results in the highest return? Which asset mix would you choose? Why?

2. Go to http://ca.pfinance.yahoo.com. Under Tools, click on RRSP Contribution Limit. Enter your income earned last year. If you do not have any pension adjustments and/or any unused deduction room, enter 0. What is your RRSP contribution limit?

3. Go to www.mackenziefinancial.com/en. Under Planning Tools, click on Investment Calculators. Then click on RIF/LIF Illustrator. This tool can be used to determine how retirement income will be received from an RRIF, LIF, or LRIF. Under Assumptions, select yes for Deduct Withholding Tax, and yes for New Funds After 1992. Input a Current Plan Value of $100 000, a Plan Type of RRIF, an Annual Rate of Return of 5.00%, a Birth Date of 06/21/1942, and an Issue Date and First Payment Date of 07/14/2007. Payment Type should be Minimum and Payment Frequency should be Monthly.

a. Click on Next. What is the total amount of payments received from the RRIF? Select Graph. How long do RRIF payments last? What is the plan's value at age 80? Age 100?

b. Compare the total payments and graph from the RRIF calculation to those of the LIF and LRIF, respectively.

ON THE STUDENT CD-ROM FOR THIS CHAPTER YOU WILL FIND:

- Building Your Own Financial Plan exercise and worksheets
- The chapter-end Continuing Case about the Sampson family

Read through the Building Your Own Financial Plan exercise and use the worksheets to develop a retirement plan.

After reading the Sampson case study, use the Continuing Case worksheets to help the Sampsons plan for their retirement.

Study Guide

Circle the correct answer and then check the answers in the back of the book to chart your progress.

Multiple Choice

1. Which of the following benefits is not subject to a clawback?
   a. Old Age Security (OAS)
   b. Canada Pension Plan (CPP)
   c. Guaranteed Income Supplement (GIS)
   d. Allowance for the survivor

2. Eleanor is a 63-year-old pensioner who has asked for your advice with respect to what government benefits she may be eligible to apply for. Given no further information, which of the following government benefits is Eleanor not eligible to apply for?
   a. Allowance
   b. Canada Pension Plan (CPP)
   c. Guaranteed Income Supplement (GIS)
   d. Allowance for the survivor

3. Francis is an employee of Hybrid Pipeline. His income for 2007 was $42 000. Determine the amount of CPP contribution he would make for the year. The YMPE and employee contribution rate for 2007 are $43 700 and 4.95%, respectively.
   a. $2079.00
   b. $1989.90
   c. $1905.75
   d. $2163.15

4. Which of the following statements regarding a defined-contribution pension plan is true?
   a. An actuarial valuation is required every three years to ensure that contribution rates are being maintained by the employer and/or employee.
   b. This type of pension plan is non-contributory.
   c. Benefit formula options include a career average earnings option.
   d. This type of pension plan does not guarantee you a specific amount of income when you retire.

5. Serena belongs to a defined-benefit pension plan. For each year of service, she earns an annual pension income of 1.4 percent on her first $35 000 of annual income, and 1.7 percent on any remaining income for the year. In 2007, Serena earned income of $65 000. Calculate the amount of annual pension income she has earned based on her 2007 income.
   a. $1007.50
   b. $1000.00

c. $1105.00
d. $910.00

6. Normand has been a member of a defined-benefit pension plan sponsored by his employer, AVT Technologies, for the past 13 years. Assuming that the defined-benefit pension plan contains no restrictions for employees who leave the company, which of the following is a transfer option that Normand could use if he decides to leave AVT Technologies to work as a self-employed consultant?
   a. He could transfer his pension assets to an individual locked-in retirement account (LIRA).
   b. He could leave his pension assets in AVT's pension account.
   c. He could transfer his pension assets to another employer, assuming that the new employer has an employer-sponsored pension plan that permits this transfer.
   d. Based on the circumstances outlined above, Normand could apply any of these options.

7. When determining the amount of potential savings that will result from contributing to your retirement plan, which of the following assumptions should you take into account?
   a. How much are you able to contribute per year?
   b. What type of return will you earn on your investments?
   c. How many years before you retire?
   d. All of the above.

8. Which of the following is not a qualified investment for RRSP purposes?
   a. Mortgages
   b. Foreign currency
   c. Royalty units
   d. Annuities

9. Which of the following is a retirement income conversion option for a locked-in RRSP?
   a. Registered Retirement Life Income Fund
   b. Registered Term Annuity
   c. Registered Life Annuity
   d. Registered Retirement Savings Plan

10. To estimate the future value of one investment, you will need all of the following information, except:
    a. The gender of the investor.
    b. The amount of the investment.

c. The annual return you expect on the investment.

d. The time when the investment will end.

True/False

1. True or False? A "means test" refers to the concept that if your income exceeds a certain amount, the amount you will receive from any of the OAS program benefits will be reduced.

2. True or False? Olga expects to live to 100 and would like to maximize the amount she will receive from the CPP. Assuming that her retirement income needs are being met by other sources, she should apply for CPP benefits at age 65.

3. True or False? If a married couple contributed to the CPP prior to the start of their relationship, a pension assignment will reduce the CPP income of the low-income pensioner and increase the CPP income of the high-income pensioner by an equivalent amount.

4. True or False? With respect to employer-sponsored retirement plans, any money you withdraw from the retirement account after you retire is taxed according to the source of the income. For example,

income from a stock mutual fund will be taxed as dividend or capital gain income when you withdraw it from your retirement account.

5. True or False? If you are young and far from retirement, you are in a position to take more risk with your investments.

6. True or False? A self-directed RRSP is sufficient for the needs of investors who are opening their first account or have all of their RRSP assets in the mutual funds of a single company.

7. True or False? The main advantage of a registered annuity over an RRIF is that you are no longer exposed to the risk that your investments may decrease in value.

8. True or False? The need to take out a reverse mortgage is reduced if you actively participate in sound financial planning.

9. True or False? The longer your annual savings are invested, the more they may be worth at retirement.

10. True or False? The income generated inside a retirement account is not taxed until you withdraw the funds.

Chapter 16

Estate Planning

D amaris managed to accumulate an estate of more than $2.5 million, including a house worth $500 000 and investment assets of approximately $1 million. Her two children were aware of the value of their mother's estate, but were surprised to learn that her will was no longer valid after her marriage to Paul, her widower. Although it appeared that the children would have inherited the estate assets on a 50–50 basis, this was no longer the case. Since Damaris did not have a valid will at her death, her estate assets will be distributed according to the intestacy provisions of the province in which she lived. As a result, her estate assets are not likely to be distributed in accordance with her wishes. Failure to update her will and take advantage of the estate planning tools available to her may result in a difficult distribution of her estate assets. Without a legally enforceable will, her two children, Paul, and any other potential beneficiaries may each claim a portion of the estate.

Estate planning involves the planning and documentation of how your assets will be distributed either before or after your death. Estate planning is not just a tool for the rich. It is important for all individuals to ensure that their estates are distributed in the manner they desire. This chapter explains several important estate planning concepts as well as methods to reduce estate taxes.

The objectives of this chapter are to:
1. Explain the use of a will
2. Describe the common types of wills
3. Describe the key components of a will
4. Describe estate taxes
5. Explain the use of trusts and contributions
6. Introduce other aspects of estate planning

BACKGROUND ON WILLS

estate
The assets of a deceased person after all debts are paid.

An **estate** represents a deceased person's assets after all debts are paid. At the time of a person's death, the estate is distributed according to that person's wishes, according to his or her will. **Estate planning** is the act of planning how your wealth will be allocated on or before your death. One of the most important tasks in estate planning is the creation of a will, which is a legal document that describes how your estate should be distributed upon your death. It can also identify a preferred guardian for any surviving minor children. The individual who makes a will is known as a testator, if male, or a testatrix, if female.

estate planning
The act of planning how your wealth will be allocated on or before your death.

L.O. 1

will
A legal document that describes how your estate should be distributed upon your death. It can also identify a preferred guardian for any surviving minor children.

Reasons for Having a Will

Having a will is critical to ensure that your estate is distributed in the manner you desire. Once you have a positive net worth to be distributed upon your death, you should consider creating a will. In it you can specify the persons you want to receive your estate—referred to as your **beneficiaries** (or heirs). In addition to allowing you to appoint a guardian for your minor children, a will can be used to specify the age at which the children will receive their inheritance. Any beneficiary that is under the age of 18 is not entitled to receive his or her inheritance directly. In this case, the inheritance is held in trust for the beneficiary. The uses of trusts will be discussed later in this chapter. Finally, a beneficiary can be of any age, and in fact can be unborn at the time the will is made.

beneficiaries (heirs)
The persons specified in a will to receive part of an estate.

intestate
The condition of dying without a will.

If you die **intestate** (without a will), the court will appoint a person (called an administrator) to distribute your estate according to the laws of your province. In that case, one family member may receive more than you intended, while others may receive less. In most provinces, the surviving spouse will receive a **preferential share**. The preferential share refers to the dollar value of estate assets that will be distributed to the surviving spouse before assets are distributed among all potential beneficiaries. Depending on the circumstances of an individual case, the surviving spouse may receive more than the preferential share provided under provincial legislation. Exhibit 16.1 highlights the dollar value of the preferential share in each province. Notice that the amount that may be received varies by province. If there is no surviving spouse, the administrator decides who will assume responsibility for any minor children. Having an administrator also results in additional costs being imposed on the estate.

preferential share
The dollar value of estate assets that will be distributed to the surviving spouse before assets are distributed among all potential beneficiaries.

Creating a Valid Will

To create a valid will in most provinces, you must be at least the age of majority, which is 18 or 19 depending on the province in which you live. Some provinces permit individuals younger than the age of majority to create a legal will in the case of military duty and/or marriage. In all provinces, you must be mentally competent and should not be subject to undue influence (threats) from others. A will is more likely to be challenged by potential heirs if there is some question about your competence or about whether you were forced to designate one or more beneficiaries in the will.

English form will
A will that contains the signature of the testator and of two witnesses who were present when the testator signed the will.

Common Types of Wills

The most common type of will in Canada is the **English form will**, which contains the signature of the testator, as well as the signatures of two witnesses who were present when the testator signed the will. The will may be handwritten or typed. To be valid, a will must be dated and signed. Normally, witnesses to a will do not inherit anything under the will. If this is not the case, witnesses will be denied their status as beneficiaries of the will. Although you are not required to hire a lawyer, you should consider doing so to ensure that your will is created properly. A **notarial will** is a formal type of will that is commonly used in Quebec and is completed in the presence of a notary (lawyer). In most cases, only one witness to this type of will is required. The original copy of the will is left with the notary. A **holograph will** is a will that is written solely in the handwriting of the testator and that does not require the signature of any witnesses.

L.O. 2

notarial will
A formal type of will that is commonly used in Quebec and is completed in the presence of a notary (lawyer).

holograph will
A will that is written solely in the handwriting of the testator and that does not require the signature of any witnesses.

Exhibit 16.1 Provincial Summary of Preferential Share Amounts

	Preferential Share for Spouse	Preferential Share ($)
Alberta	Yes	First $40 000
British Columbia	Yes	First $65 000
Manitoba	Yes	Depends[1]
New Brunswick	No	-
Newfoundland and Labrador	No	-
Nova Scotia	Yes	First $50 000
Ontario	Yes	First $200 000
Prince Edward Island	No	-
Quebec	No	-
Saskatchewan	Yes	First $100 000

[1] If there are a surviving spouse and children, and if all of the children are also children of the surviving spouse, the entire estate goes to the surviving spouse. If there are a surviving spouse and children, and one or more of the children are not also children of the surviving spouse, the surviving spouse receives the first $50 000 plus one-half of any remainder.

Source: CCH Canadian Limited, *Wealth Management and Estate Planning,* Third Edition, pages 19–42, CFP® Education Program, CCH Canadian Limited, 2007. Reprinted with permission of CCH Canadian Limited.

IN-CLASS NOTES

Background on Wills

- Reasons for having a will
  - Ensures that your estate is distributed in the manner you desire and to the beneficiaries you specify
  - Allows you to appoint a guardian for minor children
  - Provides control over the distribution of any inheritance to minor children and other heirs
- Creating a valid will
  - Must usually be at least the age of majority (18 or 19)
  - Must be mentally competent
  - Must not be subject to undue influence
- Common types of wills
  - English form, notarial, holograph

L.O. 3   KEY COMPONENTS OF A WILL

Exhibit 16.2 provides an example of a will that names either one or two alternate executors in case the intended executor is unwilling or unable to do the job of carrying out the will. This sample will leaves almost everything to one beneficiary, but allows for an alternate beneficiary should the original intended beneficiary predecease the person writing

Exhibit 16.2 A Sample Last Will and Testament

LAST WILL AND TESTAMENT

THIS IS THE LAST WILL of me, **James T. Smith,** presently of the City of Brampton, in the Province of Ontario.

1. **I REVOKE** all former wills and codicils and **DECLARE** this to be and contain my Last Will and Testament.

2. **I APPOINT** my Spouse, Karen A. Smith, as sole Executrix and Trustee of this my Will, but if my Spouse should predecease me, or shall refuse or be unable to act or continue to act as Executrix and Trustee or die before the trusts created in this Will shall have terminated, then I APPOINT Edward J. Smith of Brampton, Ontario, to be the Executor and Trustee of this my Will in the place of my Spouse.

3. If my Spouse predeceases me, then **I APPOINT** Edward J. Smith of Brampton, Ontario, and Marie S. Smith of Toronto, Ontario, or the survivor of them, to be the Guardian of the persons of my infant children during their respective minorities.

DISPOSITION OF ESTATE

4. I **GIVE AND APPOINT** to my Trustee all my property wherever located including any property over which I may have a power of appointment, upon the following trusts:

   a. To pay my legally enforceable debts, funeral expenses, and all expenses in connection with the administration of my estate and the trusts created by my Will as soon as convenient after my death.

   b. To deliver, transfer, and pay to Edward J. Smith of Brampton, Ontario, if he shall survive me, for his own use absolutely, the following: my gold watch.

   c. To transfer the residue of my estate to my Spouse, if she survives me for thirty (30) full days, for her own use absolutely.

   d. If my Spouse should predecease me or should survive me but die within a period of thirty (30) days after my death, I DIRECT my Trustee to hold in trust the residue of my estate for my child: Cheryl D. Smith of Brampton, Ontario, if that child is alive at my death, and to keep that share invested and to pay the whole or such part of the net income derived therefrom and any amount or amounts out of the capital that my Trustee may deem advisable to that child or for the maintenance, education, or benefit of that child until she reaches the age of 25 years and thereupon to pay and transfer the remainder of the part of that share to that child.

   e. If my child should predecease me, then the residue set apart for that child shall instead be distributed to Edward J. Smith of Brampton, Ontario, and Marie S. Smith of Toronto, Ontario, equally share and share alike. If one of these named beneficiaries should predecease me, then the equal share set apart for that deceased beneficiary shall be distributed to his or her descendants, equally share and share alike.

ADMINISTRATION OF ESTATE

5. **TO CARRY OUT** the terms of my Will, I give my Trustee the following powers to be used in his or her discretion at any time namely:

   Subject to my express direction to the contrary to use his or her discretion in the realization of my estate, with power to my Trustee to sell, call in, and convert into money any part of my estate not consisting of money at such time or times, in such manner and upon such terms, and either for cash or credit or for part

(continued)

Exhibit 16.2 continued

cash and part credit as my Trustee may in his or her uncontrolled discretion decide upon, or to postpone such conversion of my estate or any part or parts thereof for such length of time as he or she may think best and I HEREBY DECLARE that my Trustee may retain any portion of my estate in the form in which it may be at my death (notwithstanding that it may not be in the form of an investment in which trustees are authorized to invest trust funds, and whether or not there is a liability attached to any such portion of my estate) for such length of time as my Trustee may in his or her discretion deem advisable.

6. Subject to the terms of this my Will, I DIRECT that my Trustee shall not be liable for any loss to my estate or to any beneficiary resulting from the exercise by him or her in good faith of any discretion given him or her in this my Will.

IN WITNESS WHEREOF I, James T. Smith, the within named Testator, have to this my last will contained on this and the preceding pages, set my hand at the City of Brampton, in the Province of Ontario this 13th day of June 2007.

SIGNED, PUBLISHED, AND DECLARED
by James T. Smith,   )
as and for his Last Will and Testament   )
in the presence of us, both present at   ) _____
the same time, who at his request and   ) James T. Smith
in his presence and in the presence of   )
each other have hereunto subscribed   )
our names as witnesses.   )

_____   _____
(Witness' signature)   (Witness' signature)

Name _____   Name _____

Address _____   Address _____

City/Province _____   City/Province _____

Source: Adapted from LawDepot.com, www.lawdepot.com (accessed July 26, 2007). Reprinted with permission of LawDepot.

the will. In addition, a specific bequest is made to one beneficiary. The will also provides instructions in case the alternate beneficiary also predeceases the testator. The key components of a will are described next.

Testator Identification. The initial part of the will in Exhibit 16.2 identifies the person who made the will. In this case, the testator is James T. Smith.

Revocation of Previous Wills. To avoid confusion if more than one will exists, a standard will contains a clause revoking all other wills and declaring this will to be the last will. If two wills are later found to exist, the will with the most recent date will be the valid will.

executor (personal representative)
The person designated in a will to execute your instructions regarding the distribution of your assets.

Appointment of Executor (Personal Representative). In your will, you name an executor (also called a personal representative) to execute your instructions regarding the distribution of your assets. A female executor is referred to as an executrix. An executor may be required to collect any money owed to the estate, pay off any debts owed by the estate, sell specific assets (such as a home) that are part of the estate, and then distribute the proceeds as specified in the will. The executor must notify everyone who has an interest or potential interest in the estate. Most people select a family member, a friend, a business associate, a bank trust company employee, or a lawyer as executor. You should select an executor who will serve your interests in distributing the assets as specified in your will, who is capable of handling the process, and who is sufficiently organized to complete the process in a timely manner. The executor is entitled to be paid by the estate for services provided, but some executors elect not to charge the estate. In many cases, the executor and trustee is the same individual. A trustee is an individual or organization that is responsible for the management of assets held in trust for one or more of the beneficiaries of a will. Recall that any beneficiary under the age of 18 is not entitled to receive his or her inheritance directly. In this case, the inheritance is held in trust by the trustee for the beneficiary. In Exhibit 16.2, the executrix and trustee is the spouse, Karen A. Smith. The alternate executor and trustee is the testator's brother Edward J. Smith. Of course, the executrix/executor can be a beneficiary as well.

trustee
An individual or organization that is responsible for the management of assets held in trust for one or more of the beneficiaries of a will.

Appointment of Guardian for Minor Children. If you are a parent, you should name a guardian who will be assigned the responsibility of caring for your children and of managing any estate left to them. You should ensure that the person you select as guardian is willing to serve in this capacity. Your will may specify an amount of money to be distributed to the guardian to care for the children. Section 3 of Exhibit 16.2 indicates that the guardian will be either the spouse, Karen A. Smith, or the uncle, Edward J. Smith. The guardian does not necessarily have custody of the children. The guardian can choose another for custodial care, but would retain the legal responsibility.

"Does it bother anyone else that we're burying half the Pharaoh's assets with him?"

www.cartoonresource.com

Authorization to Pay Debts. Prior to the distribution of any assets, the debts and expenses of the deceased must be paid. Section 4a of Exhibit 16.2 gives the executor the legal authority to pay the debts and expenses of the deceased.

Authorization to Make Bequests. In the example will, a specific bequest of a gold watch is made to Edward J. Smith. A bequest is a gift that results from the instructions provided in a will. There is no limit to the number of bequests that can be made in a will. A bequest is often made in circumstances where the deceased would like to leave some personal property of sentimental value to a specific individual.

bequest
A gift that results from the instructions provided in a will.

Distribution of Residue. A will details how the estate should be distributed among the beneficiaries. Since you do not know what your estate will be worth, you may specify your desired distribution according to percentages of the estate. For example, you could specify that two people each receive 50 percent of the estate. Alternatively, you could specify that one person receive a specific dollar amount and that the other person receive the remainder of the estate. Residue refers to the amount remaining in an estate after all financial obligations, such as the payment of debts, expenses, taxes, and bequests, have been fulfilled. This clause ensures that all remaining assets of the deceased are accounted for and distributed. As such, it is important to ensure that the individual(s) who will receive the residue of the estate have not predeceased the testator. In Exhibit 16.2, section 4c transfers the residue of the estate to the spouse. If the spouse is predeceased, the residue is held in trust for the child of the testator. If the child is predeceased, the residue is shared equally between the testator's brother and sister. If either the brother or the sister is predeceased, their share of the residue is shared among their descendants.

residue
Refers to the amount remaining in an estate after all financial obligations, such as the payment of debts, expenses, taxes, and bequests, have been fulfilled.

Administration of the Estate. The instructions with respect to the administration of an estate can be very detailed or very simple. In Exhibit 16.2, a single clause is used to provide the trustee with complete authority in dealing with the assets of the estate. Every province provides a set of guidelines for how an estate is to be administered by a trustee. If the testator would like to give the trustee more discretion to deal with estate assets than what is provided for in provincial legislation, it is important to include clear instructions in the will. As a result, a will may contain a number of clauses that deal with the administration of an estate.

Liability. A trustee executor can be held legally liable for any mistakes made in administering a will. As a result, it is common to include a clause in a will, such as the one in section 6 of Exhibit 16.2, that limits the liability of a trustee who acts in good faith.

Signatures. A will must be signed by the testator and by two witnesses in order to be valid. This helps to ensure that someone else does not create a fake will.

Letter of Last Instruction. Some individuals may also wish to prepare a letter of last instruction; a supplement to a will that describes preferences regarding funeral arrangements and indicates where any key financial documents are stored, such as mortgage and insurance contracts.

letter of last instruction
A supplement to a will that can describe preferences regarding funeral arrangements and indicate where any key financial documents are stored.

Focus on Ethics: Undue Influence on Wills
By now, you have learned to be aware of fraudulent or unethical behaviour in all components of financial planning. Fraud and unethical behaviour can even occur during the creation of a will. Consider the following examples:

- Christine, a 60-year-old mother of two, asks her oldest son for estate planning advice. He pressures her to leave much of the estate to him.

- Marguerite has already completed a will, which specifies that most of her estate will go to charity. She becomes terminally ill. Brooke, a frequent visitor at the hospital, pressures Marguerite to include her in the will.

- Jarrod asks his son Jim (who is a lawyer) for advice on creating a will. Jim misrepresents the rules about estates, which causes Jarrod to create a will that leaves a disproportionate amount of the estate to Jim.

- Tamara, a widow, has created a will that leaves her estate to her children and grandchildren. However, she recently met Jim, who has proposed marriage. Jim suggests that she leave her estate to him since he will be her husband.

These types of situations occur more frequently than you might think. If the court determines that there is fraud or some form of undue influence on the creator of the will, it may prevent the person who used fraudulent or unethical behaviour from receiving any benefits. However, someone has to contest the will to have the court pursue an inquiry.

Consider creating a will without consulting potential beneficiaries. Meet with a financial planner or lawyer who specializes in wills and explain how you wish to allocate the estate among your heirs or others. The financial planner can design the will in a manner that achieves your goals. You can include all of your wishes in a will without discussing any of them with persons who are (or are not) named in the will.

Changing Your Will
A will should be updated every two to three years. In addition, specific events should trigger a review of your will. These events include:

- birth or adoption of a child

- marriage

- undertaking of a common-law relationship

- separation from a spouse or common-law partner

- receipt of an inheritance

- death of a child

- relocation to a new province of residence

- changes to provincial legislation

- illness or death of an executor or trustee named in the will

- illness or death of a significant beneficiary

In all provinces except Quebec, the act of marriage will automatically cancel all wills dated prior to the date of marriage. If you do not update your will, your estate will be subject to the intestate succession laws of the province in which you reside. The distribution of your assets will be determined, in part, based on the information provided in Exhibit 16.1 on page 432.

In some cases, a common-law relationship will not trigger the preferential spouse's share under laws of intestacy. If you are in a common-law relationship, you should consider a will to make your intentions clear.

If you wish to make major changes to your will, you will probably need to create a new one. The new will must specify that you are revoking your previous will, so that you do not have multiple wills with conflicting instructions. When you wish to make only minor revisions to your will, you can add a codicil, which is a document that specifies changes in an existing will.

codicil
A document that specifies changes in an existing will.

Executing the Will during Probate

Probate is a legal process that declares a will valid and ensures the orderly distribution of assets. The probate process ensures that when people die, their assets are distributed as they wish, and the guardianship of children is assigned as they wish. To start the probate process, the executor files forms in a local probate court, provides a copy of the will, provides a list of the assets and debts of the deceased person, pays debts, and sells any assets that need to be liquidated. The executor typically opens a bank account for the estate that is used to pay the debts of the deceased and to deposit proceeds from liquidating the assets. If the executor does not have time or is otherwise unable to perform these tasks, a lawyer can be hired to complete them. The courts will also appoint the guardian for minor children. If family members dispute the intended guardian for cause, the court may appoint another.

probate
A legal process that declares a will valid and ensures the orderly distribution of assets.

IN-CLASS NOTES

Key Components of a Will

- Testator identification
- Revocation of previous wills
- Appointment of executor (personal representative)
- Appointment of guardian for minor children
- Authorization to pay debts
- Authorization to make bequests
- Distribution of residue
- Administration of the estate
- Liability
- Signatures
- Letter of last instruction

L.O. 4   ESTATE TAXES

When a taxpayer dies, a final tax return must be filed with the CRA that may require the estate to pay taxes on some of its assets. A deceased taxpayer may have to pay taxes because, for tax purposes, he or she is deemed to have disposed of his or her assets on the date of death. This deemed disposition does not mean that the estate must sell the deceased's assets. Instead, the estate will be responsible to pay the deceased's taxes on income, investment income, and capital gains.

All capital property is deemed to be disposed of when a person dies. This is not an actual sale, but the deemed disposition will trigger capital gains or losses for which the estate will be liable. Such gains or losses can be deferred in some cases. However, the taxpayer must plan ahead to this tax deferral.

Remember that the principal residence of a taxpayer will not trigger capital gains or losses. If the house is owned jointly (with rights of survivorship), the house will pass to the co-owner without tax consequences. RRSPs can be rolled over to a spouse with no tax consequences if they have the spouse listed as the designated beneficiary. RRSPs can also be rolled over to a dependent child with no tax liability. Other assets that are owned jointly with rights of survivorship, such as investments, will simply transfer to the survivor.

The amount of tax payable on estate assets is calculated using the difference between the fair market value of the assets at the date of death and the acquisition cost of the assets.

EXAMPLE

Quang is in the process of writing his will. As a part of this process, he completes an inventory of his assets. Quang is the sole owner of a cottage that he purchased for $150 000 in 1998. It has a current fair market value of $250 000. If Quang bequeaths the cottage to his spouse, Linh, his estate will not have to pay taxes on its increased value. If he bequeaths the cottage to his son, Jackson, a capital gains tax must be paid by Quang's estate on the increased value of the cottage. In the first transfer, a spousal rollover allows Quang's estate to avoid having to pay taxes until Linh has passed away. In the second transfer, a rollover is not permitted.

The amount of tax that Canadians pay upon death is relatively low. First, the increase in value of your principal residence is not subject to tax. Second, RRSPs and other registered retirement accounts can be easily rolled over to a surviving spouse, thereby temporarily delaying taxes payable. Combined, these two asset types usually represent the bulk of most Canadians' net worth. As a result, taxes at death tend to be less of a concern for the average Canadian taxpayer.

Optional Tax Returns

Even though taxes at death may be less of a concern for many Canadians, other estate planning techniques should be considered to reduce the amount of tax payable on estate assets. As mentioned, the executor must file a final tax return on behalf of a deceased taxpayer. This tax return is normally filed within six months of the date of death or on April 30 of the following year, whichever is later. In addition, the executor may be able to reduce the taxes payable by filing separate returns for "rights or things," business income, and income from a testamentary trust. Rights or things is income that was owed to the deceased taxpayer but not paid at the time of death, but that would have been included in income had the taxpayer not died. For example, a bond coupon payment that was earned by the taxpayer while alive that had not been paid by the time of death would qualify as a "right or thing." A deceased taxpayer's share of business income from a partnership or proprietorship that had not been paid by the time of death can be reported on a separate tax return. Finally, if the deceased taxpayer was receiving income from a testamentary trust, the deceased's share of any unallocated income can be reported on a separate tax return. The ability to split income and report it on separate

rights or things
Income that was owed to the deceased taxpayer but not paid at the time of death, but that would have been included in income had the taxpayer not died.

tax returns will reduce the amount of tax payable by the deceased. In addition, some of the non-refundable tax credits available on the final return can be used again on each optional return. The option to use tax credits on each tax form will further reduce the amount of taxes payable by the deceased.

IN-CLASS NOTES

Estate Taxes

- At death → a deceased taxpayer is deemed to have disposed of his or her assets
- Spousal rollover → a mechanism that can be used to delay the payment of tax
- Determination of tax payable based on:
  - Fair market value (FMV) minus acquisition cost
- Optional tax returns
  - Rights or things
  - Business income from a partnership or proprietorship
  - Income from a testamentary trust

L.O. 5 TRUSTS AND CONTRIBUTIONS

Estate planning commonly involves trusts and contributions to charitable organizations. Trusts are an effective estate planning tool that can be used during or after the taxpayer's lifetime to meet a number of different needs. Contributions to charitable organizations, in addition to being effective tax planning tools, can be used to provide for charities that are important to the taxpayer and/or his or her family.

trust
A legal document in which one person, the settlor, transfers assets to a trustee, who manages them for designated beneficiaries.

settlor
The person who creates a trust.

inter vivos trust
A trust in which you assign the management of your assets to a trustee while you are living.

Trusts

A trust is a legal document in which one person, called a settlor, transfers assets to a trustee, who manages the assets for designated beneficiaries. The settlor must select a trustee who is trustworthy and capable of managing the assets being transferred. If a suitable individual cannot be found to act as a trustee, various types of investment firms can be hired to serve as trustees.

Inter Vivos Trusts. An inter vivos trust is a trust in which you assign the management of your assets to a trustee while you are living. You identify a trustee that you want to manage the assets (which includes making decisions on how to invest cash until it is needed or how to spend cash). This type of trust is a useful estate planning tool if you feel that someone will contest your will when you die, as the assets transferred into an inter vivos trust do not form part of your estate when you die. By using a trust, you can maintain some control over how assets are used. In particular, an inter vivos trust may be set up to take care of dependent children or others, to control the use of assets such as a cottage or vacation property, and to maintain control of business interests. Inter vivos trusts are private arrangements, and therefore have no public accountability. If you wish to distribute assets to individuals while maintaining a high level of privacy, inter vivos trusts may be used. Similar to the situation when a taxpayer dies, assets transferred to an inter vivos trust are deemed to be disposed of at fair market value at the time of transfer. Income earned on the assets inside an inter vivos trust is taxed at the highest combined federal and provincial marginal tax rate. To avoid having the trust pay taxes at the highest marginal tax rate, inter vivos trusts normally distribute any income to the trust beneficiaries annually.

revocable inter vivos trust
An inter vivos trust that can be dissolved.

Revocable Inter Vivos Trust. With a **revocable inter vivos trust**, you can dissolve or revoke the trust at any time because you are still the legal owner of the assets. For example, you may revoke an inter vivos trust if you decide you want to manage the assets yourself. Alternatively, you may revoke an inter vivos trust so that you can replace the trustee or beneficiaries. In this case, you would create a new inter vivos trust with a newly identified trustee.

By using a revocable inter vivos trust, you can avoid the probate process. However, the assets are still considered part of your estate, which will reduce some of the tax benefits that would otherwise be available if you set up an irrevocable inter vivos trust.

irrevocable inter vivos trust
An inter vivos trust that cannot be changed, although it may provide income to the settlor.

Irrevocable Inter Vivos Trust. An **irrevocable inter vivos trust** cannot be changed. This type of trust is a separate entity. It can provide income for you, the settlor, but the assets in the trust are no longer legally yours. If the settlor is one of the beneficiaries of the assets, this type of trust will be treated as a revocable inter vivos trust.

testamentary trust
A trust created by a will.

Testamentary Trust. A **testamentary trust** is a trust created by a will. It is popular because it can be used to provide for the needs of dependent children or parents in a manner somewhat similar to the inter vivos trust. Income earned on assets inside a testamentary trust is taxed in a manner similar to that of an individual taxpayer at that same level of income.

Contributions to Charitable Organizations

Contributions to charitable organizations made in the year a taxpayer dies are provided special tax incentives. Normally, charitable contributions up to and including 75 percent of a taxpayer's net income may be claimed against net income. In the year of death, the amount of charitable contributions that may be claimed against net income increases to 100 percent of net income. In addition, any overcontribution to a charitable organization may be used to write off up to 100 percent of the previous year's net income.

EXAMPLE

In 2007, Ruthie donated $200 000 to the local hospital, a registered charity. This same year, Ruthie earned net income of $63 000. If Ruthie died in 2007, how much of the $200 000 donation can her executor claim for charitable donations?

The executor can claim $63 000 (100 percent of her net income) for 2007 on her final tax return and can carry back $137 000 to claim on her 2006 tax return up to a maximum of her net income claim. If Ruthie's net income for 2006 is also $63 000, her executor can claim 100 percent of her net income for 2006 as well.

IN-CLASS NOTES

Trusts and Contributions

- Trust → a legal document in which one person, the settlor, transfers assets to a trustee, who manages them for designated beneficiaries
- Types of trusts
  - Inter vivos trust (revocable or irrevocable)
  - Testamentary trust
- Contributions to charitable organizations
  - Tax benefit is greater in the year of death and in the year preceding death than it is under other circumstances

_____

_____

_____

_____

_____

_____

L.O. 6 OTHER ASPECTS OF ESTATE PLANNING

In addition to wills and trusts, estate planning involves some other key decisions regarding a living will and power of attorney.

Living Will

living will
A simple legal document in which individuals specify their preferences if they become mentally or physically disabled.

A living will, also known as a personal care directive or a health care directive, is a simple legal document in which individuals specify their preferences if they become mentally or physically disabled. A living will speaks for you when you are unable to speak for yourself. For example, many individuals have a living will that expresses their desire not to be placed on life support if they become terminally ill. Without a living will, there may be added conflict and uncertainty as your family members attempt to make a decision regarding your personal well-being.

Go to
www.rbcds.com/
RBC:RsHplo71A8cAGfCqmss/
estate-planning-guide.html

This website provides
a helpful guide to estate planning.

Power of Attorney

limited (non-continuing) power of attorney
A legal document granting a person the power to make specific decisions for you in the event that you are temporarily incapacitated.

A **limited (non-continuing) power of attorney** is a legal document granting a person the power to make specific decisions for you in the event that you are temporarily incapacitated. The decision-making power granted is relative to a specific or defined task. For example, you may name a family member or a close friend to make decisions regarding paying your bills on time while you are out of the country. Once you return, the limited (non-continuing) power of attorney document expires. You should name someone who you believe would act to serve your interests.

general power of attorney
A legal document granting a person the immediate power to make any decisions and/or commitments for you, with specific limitations.

A **general power of attorney** is a legal document granting a person the immediate power to make any decisions and/or commitments for you. Normally, the only restriction placed on the appointed attorney is the inability to make a will or another power of attorney document on your behalf. Otherwise, this document is effective immediately, once it is signed and witnessed.

A general power of attorney document terminates automatically if:

- the grantor dies
- the attorney dies
- the grantor becomes incapacitated due to mental illness

enduring (continuing) power of attorney
A legal document granting a person the immediate power to make any decisions and/or commitments for you, even when you are mentally incapacitated.

The addition of an enduring or continuing clause to a general power of attorney allows the power of attorney to continue even if the grantor becomes incapacitated due to mental illness. This type of document is often referred to as an **enduring (continuing) power of attorney** since it grants a person the immediate power to make any decisions and/or commitments for you, even when you are mentally incapacitated. An enduring power of attorney can also be created such that it is triggered by a specific event, such as the mental incapacity of the grantor, instead of being added as a clause to a general power of attorney document.

durable power of attorney for health care
A legal document granting a person the power to make specific health care decisions for you.

A **durable power of attorney for health care** is a legal document granting a person the power to make specific health care decisions for you. Unlike a living will, a durable power of attorney ensures that the person you identify has the power to make specific decisions regarding your health care in the event that you become incapacitated. While a living will states many of your preferences, a situation may arise that is not covered by it. A durable power of attorney for health care means that the necessary decisions will be made by someone who knows your preferences, rather than by a health care facility. By appointing one or more people to make these decisions, you are reducing the possibility of court involvement with regard to these decisions.

Go to
www.fiscalagents.com/
newsletter/gloss/Glossary/
estategloss.shtml

This website provides
a special glossary of estate planning terms.

Maintaining Estate Planning Documents

Key documents such as your will, living will, and power of attorney should be kept in a safe, accessible place. You should tell the person (or people) you named as executor and granted power of attorney where you keep these documents so that they can be retrieved if and when they are needed. Medical or personal care documents may be copied and provided to your health care professionals. Other copies of such documents may be kept with your lawyer.

A checklist of the important documents you should keep together follows:

- Estate planning information, such as a will, living will, and power of attorney
- Life insurance policies and other insurance policies
- RRSP and other retirement account information
- Home ownership and mortgage information
- Information on ownership of other real estate
- Information on personal property, such as cars or jewellery
- Mortgage information
- Personal loans
- Credit card debt information
- Information on ownership of businesses
- Personal legal documents
- The most recent personal tax filing
- Bank account information
- Investment information

IN-CLASS NOTES

Other Aspects of Estate Planning
- Living will
  - A simple legal document in which individuals specify their preferences if they become mentally or physically disabled
- Limited (non-continuing) power of attorney
- General power of attorney
- Enduring (continuing) power of attorney
- Durable power of attorney for health care

_____

_____

_____

_____

_____

HOW ESTATE PLANNING FITS WITHIN YOUR FINANCIAL PLAN

The following are the key decisions about estate planning that should be included within your financial plan:

- Should you create a will?
- How can you reduce or delay the payment of your estate taxes?
- Should you create a living will or designate an individual to have power of attorney?

STEPHANIE SPRATT'S FINANCIAL PLAN: Estate Planning

GOALS FOR ESTATE PLANNING

1. *Create a will.*

2. *Establish a plan for trusts or charitable contributions if my estate is subject to high taxes.*

3. *Decide whether I need to create a living will or assign power of attorney.*

ANALYSIS

Estate Planning and Related Issues

Issue	Status
Possible heirs to my estate?	*My sister and parents.*
Tax implications for my estate?	*Small estate at this point; there is no need to establish a plan for trusts or charitable contributions.*
Power of attorney necessary?	*Yes; I want someone to make decisions for me if I am unable to.*
Living will necessary?	*Yes; I do not want to be placed on life support.*

DECISIONS

Decision Regarding a Will

I plan to make my parents my heirs if they are alive; otherwise, I will name my sister as my heir. I will designate my sister to be executrix.

Decision Regarding Trusts and Charitable Contributions

My estate is not large enough to require any additional tax planning. Therefore, I do not need to consider establishing trusts or making charitable contributions at this time.

Decision on a Power of Attorney and Durable Power of Attorney

I will assign my mother the power of attorney and the durable power of attorney. I will hire a lawyer who can complete these documents along with my will in one or two hours. I will construct a list of my wishes regarding my estate prior to meeting with the lawyer. This should reduce the expense of making a will.

Discussion Questions

1. How would Stephanie's estate planning decisions be different if she were a single mother of two children?

2. How would Stephanie's estate planning decisions be affected if she were 35 years old? If she were 50 years old?

SUMMARY

A will is intended to ensure that your wishes are carried out after your death. It allows you to distribute your estate, select a guardian for your children, and select an executor to ensure that the will is executed properly. The most common type of will in Canada is the English form will. Other types include a notarial will, which is a will form commonly used in Quebec, and a holograph will, which is a will written solely in the handwriting of the testator.

Key components of a will include clauses that identify the testator, revoke previous wills, appoint an executor and a trustee, appoint a guardian for minor children, authorize the payment of outstanding debts, authorize bequests, direct distribution of the residue of the estate, provide instructions with respect to estate administration, and limit the liability of a trustee who has acted in good faith.

Estate taxes are an issue for individuals who have assets that have increased in value above their acquisition cost. A spousal rollover can effectively delay the amount of tax payable when a taxpayer dies. In addition, your principal residence is exempt from any type of estate tax.

Estate planning involves the use of trusts and charitable contributions. Trusts can be structured so that a large estate can be passed to the beneficiaries without being subjected to estate taxes. A deceased taxpayer's contributions to charity receive favourable tax treatment in the year of death and in the year prior to death, relative to the normal non-refundable tax credit that is provided by charitable contributions.

In the event that you someday may be incapable of making decisions relating to your health and financial situation, you should consider creating a living will and power of attorney. A living will is a legal document that allows you to specify your health treatment preferences, such as life support options. A power of attorney is a legal document that allows you to assign a person the power to make specific decisions

for you if and when you are no longer capable of making these decisions. The availability of a number of different types of power of attorney provides you with some flexibility to choose how this legal document can work for you.

INTEGRATING THE KEY CONCEPTS

Your estate planning decisions are related to other parts of your financial plan. For example, your estate planning decision to make charitable contributions reduces your liquidity. It also reduces the amount of funds available to pay off personal loans or a mortgage (Part 3) or to invest (Part 5). Yet, making charitable contributions may be more appropriate than paying off loans or making more investments because it can help reduce the taxes on your estate. You should also consider the emotional benefits of such contributions.

Your estate planning decisions may also be related to your life insurance decisions because you may not need as much life insurance if you have established a large estate. Conversely, life insurance can provide the necessary cash for tax liabilities upon your death, allowing investments, businesses, and other assets to pass to your beneficiaries undisturbed.

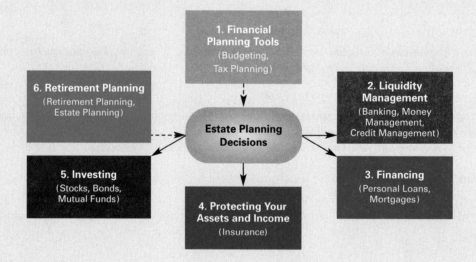

REVIEW QUESTIONS

1. What is an estate? What is estate planning? What is the main goal of estate planning?

2. What is a will? Why is a will important? What happens if a person dies without a will?

3. List the requirements for a valid will.

4. Describe three common types of wills.

5. List and briefly discuss the key components of a will.

6. When would you change your will? How can your will be changed?

7. What is probate? Describe the probate process.

8. With respect to estate taxes, what happens when a taxpayer dies? What is the purpose of a spousal rollover?

9. What information is required to determine a deceased taxpayer's tax payable? Under what circumstances will estate taxes be minimized?

10. Describe the three types of optional tax returns.

11. Beyond having a will, what does estate planning involve?

12. What is a trust? What is the difference between an inter vivos trust and a testamentary trust?

13. What is a revocable inter vivos trust? How can it be used to help your estate? How does it affect estate taxes?

14. What is an irrevocable inter vivos trust?

15. How can contributions to charitable organizations help in estate planning?

16. What is a living will? What are its implications for estate planning?

17. What is a limited (non-continuing) power of attorney?

18. What is the difference between a general power of attorney and an enduring (continuing) power of attorney?

19. What is a durable power of attorney for health care? Why is it needed even if you have a living will?

20. How should estate plan documents be maintained?

ETHICAL DILEMMA

In the nineteenth century, people travelled the country selling tonics that were guaranteed to cure all ailments of mankind. In the twenty-first century, these "snake oil salesmen" have been replaced by individuals making professional presentations on estate planning. At the conclusion of the presentation, they are prepared to sell you, for many hundreds of dollars, a kit that will show you how to do everything they have discussed without the expense of a lawyer or tax professional.

One such group extols the virtues of a device called a charitable remainder trust (CRT). It tells you how you can establish one using the boilerplate template provided in its booklet. The CRT will allow you to make tax-deductible contributions to it during your lifetime, and upon your death will pass to a family foundation managed by your children. This will allow the assets to avoid estate taxes and probate. The presenter presents this as a cost-effective way to pass your assets to your children. All of what is said in the presentation concerning CRTs is true.

However, what the presenter does not explain is that distributions from the family foundation can be made only to recognized charities. In other words, your children will own the estate but will not have access to it. These devices work well for a small percentage of the population, but will not serve the purpose the presenter has alluded to for the majority of people.

a. Discuss how ethical you believe the presenter is being by not telling the full story about CRTs. Keep in mind that what the presenter says is true, just not the whole truth.

b. If these presenters are the modern-day version of snake oil salesmen, whom should you go to for estate planning advice?

FINANCIAL PLANNING ONLINE EXERCISES

1. Go to www.tdcanadatrust.com/planning/tools/index.jsp.

a. Under Estate Planning, click on Executor's Tool. Taking this quiz will enable an executor to determine the amount of assistance he or she will need in administering an estate.

b. Return to the first page. Under Estate Planning, click on Executor Selection Tool. Taking this quiz will help you to determine whom you should select as an executor for your estate.

c. Using the information from these two quizzes, what are some of the important considerations when determining the complexity of an estate and/or the process of selecting an executor?

ON THE STUDENT CD-ROM FOR THIS CHAPTER YOU WILL FIND:

- Building Your Own Financial Plan exercise and worksheets
- The chapter-end running case about the Sampson family
- The sixth part-end Continuing Case about Brad Brooks

Read through the Building Your Own Financial Plan exercise and use the worksheets to help you plan your estate, create a will, and establish a plan for a power of attorney.

After reading the Sampson case study, use the continuing Case worksheets to help the Sampsons determine if they have made sure their children will be properly cared for in the event of their death.

After reading the Brad Brooks case study, use the Continuing Case worksheets to help Brad with his retirement and estate planning.

Study Guide

Circle the correct answer and then check the answers in the back of the book to chart your progress.

Multiple Choice

1. The reasons for having a will may include:
   a. A will helps to ensure that your estate is distributed in the manner you desire.
   b. You can use a will to specify the persons you want to receive your estate, referred to as your beneficiaries (or heirs).
   c. A will can be used to specify the age at which your children will receive their inheritance.
   d. All of the above are reasons for having a will.

2. Which of the following is not a common type of will?
   a. English form will
   b. Notarial will
   c. Holograph will
   d. Valid will

3. Which of the following statements best describes the role of an executor?
   a. An executor may be required to collect any money owed to the estate, personally pay off any debts owed by the estate, sell specific assets (such as a home) that are part of the estate, and then distribute the proceeds as specified in the will.
   b. An executor may be required to collect any money owed to the estate, pay off any debts owed by the estate, sell specific assets (such as a home) that are part of the estate, and then distribute the proceeds as specified in the will.
   c. An executor may be required to collect any money owed to the estate, personally pay off any debts owed by the estate, sell specific assets (such as a home) that are part of the estate, appoint a guardian for minor children, and then distribute the proceeds as specified in the will.
   d. An executor may be required to collect any money owed to the estate, pay off any debts owed by the estate, sell specific assets (such as a home) that are part of the estate, appoint a guardian for minor children, and then distribute the proceeds as specified in the will.

4. Which clause in a will ensures that all remaining assets of the deceased are accounted for and distributed?
   a. Administration of the estate
   b. Letter of last instruction
   c. Distribution of residue
   d. Authorization to distribute remainder

5. Which of the following does not qualify as an optional tax return?
   a. Business income from a partnership, proprietorship, or corporation
   b. Rights or things
   c. Business income from a partnership or proprietorship
   d. Income from a testamentary trust

6. The amount of tax that Canadians pay upon death is relatively low. This statement can be supported because:
   a. The increase in value of your summer cottage is not subject to tax.
   b. RRSPs are only subject to tax when a taxpayer is alive and withdrawing money from them.
   c. Most Canadians would count their principal residence and registered retirement accounts, such as an RRSP, as their largest assets.
   d. The tax payable on RRSPs and other registered retirement accounts can be delayed using a spousal rollover.

7. The characteristics of a testamentary trust include all of the following, except:
   a. It is a type of trust that is created by a will.
   b. The income earned on the assets inside it is taxed in a manner similar to that of an individual taxpayer at that same level of income.
   c. The income earned on the assets inside it is taxed at the highest combined federal and provincial marginal tax rate.
   d. It is a popular type of trust because it can be used to provide for the needs of dependent children or others.

8. Contributions to charitable organizations in the year that a taxpayer dies are provided special tax incentives. Which of the following statements most accurately reflects the tax treatment of charitable contributions in the year of death?
   a. In the year of death, the amount of charitable contributions that may be claimed against net income increases to 100 percent of net income. In addition, any overcontribution to a charitable organization may be used to write off up to 100 percent of the previous year's net income.
   b. In the year of death, the amount of charitable contributions that may be claimed against net income increases to 100 percent of net income.

In addition, any overcontribution to a charitable organization may be used to write off up to 75 percent of the previous year's net income.

c. In the year of death, the amount of charitable contributions that may be claimed against net income remains at 75 percent of net income. However, any overcontribution to a charitable organization may be used to write off up to 100 percent of the previous year's net income.

d. In the year of death, the amount of charitable contributions that may be claimed against net income remains at 75 percent of net income. In addition, any overcontribution to a charitable organization may be used to write off up to 75 percent of the previous year's net income.

9. A(n) _____ is a legal document granting a person the power to make specific decisions for you in the event that you are temporarily incapacitated.
a. general power of attorney
b. limited (non-continuing) power of attorney
c. durable power of attorney for health care
d. enduring (continuing) power of attorney

10. A(n) _____ is a legal document granting a person the immediate power to make any decisions and/or commitments for you, even when you are mentally incapacitated.
a. general power of attorney
b. limited (non-continuing) power of attorney
c. durable power of attorney for health care
d. enduring (continuing) power of attorney

True/False

1. True or False? An estate represents a deceased person's assets, including any debts that are outstanding.

2. True or False? If you die intestate in Canada, your surviving spouse will receive a preferential share of estate assets before assets are distributed among all beneficiaries.

3. True or False? To avoid confusion, a standard will contains a clause revoking all other wills and declaring this latest will to be the last will.

4. True or False? The purpose of the probate process is for the court to declare a will valid, make any necessary changes to ensure the validity of the will, and ensure the orderly distribution of assets.

5. True or False? Under normal circumstances, a deemed disposition means that a deceased taxpayer has to sell his or her assets and pay any tax owing once the assets are sold.

6. True or False? A spousal rollover does not eliminate or reduce the amount of tax payable by the taxpayer; it only delays the payment of tax until the surviving spouse dies.

7. True or False? An inter vivos trust is a trust in which you assign the management of your assets to a trustee while you are living.

8. True or False? An irrevocable inter vivos trust will be treated as a revocable inter vivos trust if the settlor is one of the beneficiaries of the assets of the trust.

9. True or False? A living will, also known as a personal care directive or a health care directive, is a simple legal document in which individuals specify their preferences if they become mentally or physically disabled.

10. True or False? A durable medical power of attorney is similar to a living will in that it ensures that the person you identify has the power to make specific decisions regarding your health care in the event that you become incapacitated.

PART 7

Synthesis of Financial Planning

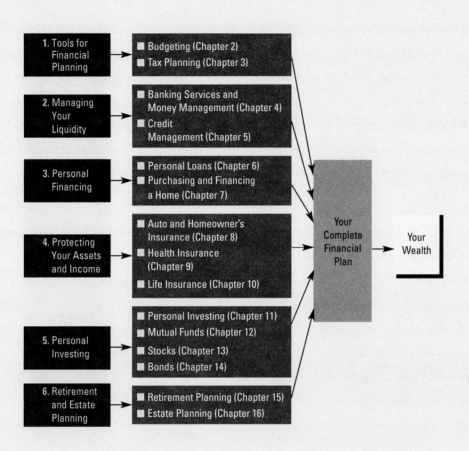

THIS PART SERVES AS A CAPSTONE BY SUMMARIZING THE KEY COMPONENTS of a financial plan. It also illustrates the interrelationships among the segments of a financial plan by highlighting how decisions regarding each component affect the other components.

Chapter 17

Integrating the Components of a Financial Plan

N ow that you have completed your journey through the components of a financial plan, it is time for you to compile all of this information and the many decisions you have made. Regarding your own personal financial situation, you have been asked to complete a number of assignments and online exercises throughout the previous chapters. Your first step is to determine the status of your personal finances. Establish your personal balance sheet, prepare your cash flow statement, establish your financial goals, and address your concerns. From there you can analyze each part of the financial plan—your taxes, insurance, investments, retirement planning, estate planning—and establish a plan of action to help you accomplish your financial goals.

As explained throughout this text, each component of a financial plan affects your ability to build wealth and achieve your goals. You have now learned many of the fundamentals relating to each component of a financial plan. This capstone chapter will help you integrate that knowledge into a cohesive financial plan.

The objectives of this chapter are to:
1. Review the components of a financial plan
2. Illustrate how a financial plan's components are integrated
3. Provide an example of a financial plan

L.O. 1 REVIEW OF COMPONENTS WITHIN A FINANCIAL PLAN

A key to financial planning is recognizing how the components of your financial plan are related. Each part of this text has focused on one of the six main components of your financial plan, which are illustrated once again in Exhibit 17.1. The decisions you make regarding each component of your financial plan affect your cash flows and your wealth. The six components are summarized next, with information on how they are interrelated.

Budgeting

Recall that budgeting allows you to forecast how much money you will have at the end of each month so that you can determine how much you will be able to invest in assets. Most importantly, budgeting allows you to determine whether your expenses will exceed your income so that you can forecast any shortages in that month. Your spending decisions affect your budget, which affects every other component of your financial plan. Careful budgeting can prevent excessive spending and therefore help you achieve financial goals.

Budgeting Trade-Off. The more you spend, the less money you will have available for liquidity purposes, investments, or retirement saving. Thus, your budgeting decisions involve a trade-off between spending today and allocating funds for the future. Your budget should attempt to ensure that you have net cash flows every month for savings or for retirement. The more funds you can allocate for the future, the more you will be able to benefit from compounded interest, and the more you will be able to spend in the future.

Managing Liquidity

You can prepare for anticipated cash shortages in any future month by ensuring that you have enough liquid assets to cover the deficiencies. Some of the more liquid assets include a chequing account, a savings account, a term deposit, and money market funds. The more funds you maintain in these types of assets, the more liquidity you will have to cover cash shortages. Even if you do not have sufficient liquid assets, you can cover a cash deficiency

Exhibit 17.1 Your Financial Transactions

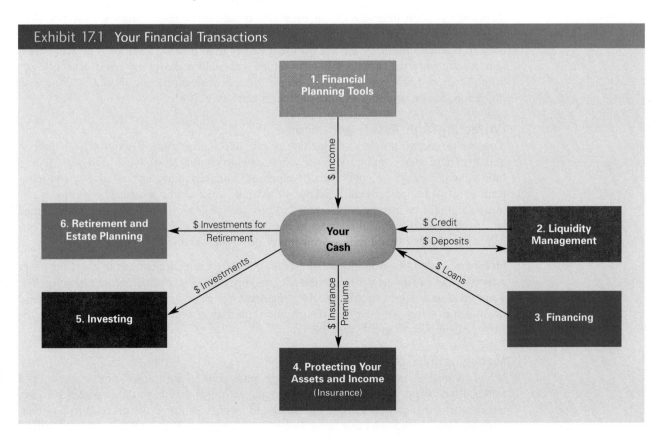

by obtaining short-term financing (such as using a credit card). If you maintain adequate liquidity, you will not need to borrow every time you need money. In this way, you can avoid major financial problems and therefore be more likely to achieve your financial goals.

Liquidity Trade-Off.   Since liquid assets generate relatively low returns, you forgo earning a higher return. A chequing account does not earn very much interest, and the other types of liquid assets have relatively low interest rates. If you choose to earn higher returns by investing all of your money in stocks or bonds, however, you may not have sufficient liquidity. Therefore, you should maintain just enough money in an emergency fund to satisfy your liquidity needs; then you can earn a higher return on your other assets.

Financing
Financing allows you to make purchases now without having the full amount of cash on hand. Thus, financing can increase the amount of your assets. It is especially useful for large purchases such as a car or a home.

Financing Trade-Off.   One of the disadvantages of borrowing funds for a mortgage or home equity line of credit is that financing can cause budgeting problems. When you borrow to pay for a car, to purchase a home, or even to pay off a credit card balance, you affect your future budget, because the monthly loan payment means that you will have less cash available at the end of each month. Although a loan allows you to make purchases now, it restricts your spending or saving in future months while you are paying off the loan. Therefore, an excessive amount of financing can prevent you from achieving your financial goals, even if your consumer needs are met. In addition, excessive financing may prevent you from paying off your loans on time, and therefore could damage your credit rating or cause you to file for bankruptcy.

It is easier to cover monthly loan payments if you select financing with a relatively long maturity. However, the longer the maturity, the longer the loan will be outstanding, and the more interest you will pay.

You may want to consider paying off a loan before its maturity so that you can avoid incurring any more interest expense, especially if the interest rate charged is relatively high. You should not use all of your liquid funds to pay off a loan, however, because you will still need to maintain liquidity. Paying off loans rather than making additional investments is appropriate when the expected after-tax return you could make on the investments is lower than the interest rate you are paying on the loan. Borrowing money should be done with discretion. Saving up for consumer purchases is a wiser choice.

Protecting Your Assets and Income
You can protect your assets and income by purchasing insurance. Recall from Chapters 8 and 9 that property and casualty insurance insures your assets (such as your car and home), health insurance covers health expenses, while disability, critical illness, and long-term care insurance provide financial support if you become disabled, critically ill, or incapacitated. Life insurance (Chapter 10) provides your family members or other named beneficiaries with financial support in the event of your death. Thus, insurance protects against events that could reduce your income or your wealth.

Insurance Trade-Off.   Any money that is used to buy insurance cannot be used for other purposes such as investing in liquid assets, paying off loans, or making investments. Yet, your insurance needs should be given priority before investments. You need to have insurance to cover your car and your home. You may also need life insurance to provide financial support to family members.

Managing Investments
When making investments, recall that your main choices are mutual funds, stocks, and bonds. If you want your investments to provide periodic income, you may consider investing in stocks that pay dividends. The stocks of large, well-known firms tend to pay relatively stable dividends, as these firms are not growing as fast as smaller firms and can afford

to pay out more of their earnings as dividends. Bonds also provide periodic income. If you do not need income and would prefer to see your money grow, you may consider investing in stocks of firms that do not pay dividends. These firms often are growing at a fast pace and therefore offer the potential for a large increase in the stock value over time.

Investment Trade-Off. By investing in the stocks of large, well-known firms, you will receive dividend income. You may be able to sell the stocks easily if you need money, but may risk a loss of capital. Government of Canada bonds or highly rated corporate bonds provide periodic income and can be sold easily if you need money. Again, there may be a loss of capital. However, these investments typically do not generate as high a return as investments in growth-oriented companies.

If you try to earn high returns by investing all of your money in stocks of smaller firms, you forgo liquidity because the prices of these stocks are volatile, and you may want to avoid selling them when prices are relatively low. If you have sufficient liquid assets such as chequing and savings accounts, however, you do not need additional liquidity from your investments.

Another concern about the stocks of smaller firms is that they can be very risky and are more likely to result in large losses than investments in stocks of large, well-known firms. You can invest in small stocks without being exposed to the specific risk of any individual stock by investing in a mutual fund that focuses on small stocks. When market conditions are weak, however, such funds can experience large losses, although not as much as a single stock of a small firm.

Whenever you use money for investments, you forgo the use of that money for some other purpose, such as investing in more liquid assets, paying off existing debt, or buying insurance. You should make investments only after you have sufficient liquidity and sufficient insurance to protect your existing assets. Investments are the key to building your wealth over time. By investing a portion of your income consistently over time, you are more likely to achieve your financial goals. This can be applied to your retirement planning as well.

Retirement Planning

Retirement planning can ensure that you will have sufficient funds at the time you retire. As discussed in Chapter 15, there are a variety of plans available and many tax advantages to retirement savings.

Retirement Account Trade-Off. The more money you contribute to your retirement account now, the more money you will have when you reach retirement age. However, you should make sure you can afford whatever you decide to contribute. You need to have enough money to maintain sufficient liquidity so that you can afford any monthly loan payments before you contribute to your retirement.

When deciding whether to invest your money in current investments or in your retirement account, consider your goals. If you plan to use the investments for tuition or some other purpose in the near future, you should not put this money in your retirement account. Funds invested in a retirement account are not necessarily liquid. Any money withdrawn from an RRSP must be taken into income in the year of withdrawal and will be taxed at your marginal tax rate. The withdrawal is subject to a 10 percent withholding tax, which should be considered as a down payment on the total tax liability. If you need to withdraw money from your RRSP, calculate your total tax payable and save this money for tax owing. Two exceptions are withdrawals with respect to the Home Buyers' Plan and the Lifelong Learning Plan. If your goal is to save for retirement, you should allocate money to a retirement account, such as an RRSP. Contributions to an RRSP are tax deductible and you are not taxed on the growth of your contributions, as long as you leave the money in the account.

Maintaining Your Financial Documents

To monitor your financial plan over time, you should store all finance-related documents in one place, such as in a safe at home or in a safety deposit box. The key documents are identified in Exhibit 17.2.

Go to
www.canadianbusiness.com/my_money/index.jsp

This website provides useful information about financial planning that can help you complete and refine your financial plan.

Exhibit 17.2 Documents Used for Financial Planning

Liquidity

- Guaranteed Investment Certificates
- Bank account balances
- Any other money market securities owned

Financing

- Credit card account numbers
- Credit card balances
- Personal loan (such as car loan) agreements
- Mortgage loan agreement

Insurance

- Insurance policies
- Home inventory of items covered by homeowner's insurance

Investments

- Account balance showing the market value of mutual funds
- Account balance showing the market value of stocks
- Account balance showing the market value of bonds
- Stock certificates
- Bonds

Retirement and Estate Plans

- Retirement plan contracts
- Retirement account balances
- Will
- Trust agreements

IN-CLASS NOTES

Review of Components within a Financial Plan

- Budgeting
- Managing liquidity
- Financing
- Protecting your assets and income
- Managing investments
- Retirement planning

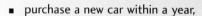

L.O. 2 INTEGRATING THE COMPONENTS

At this point, you have sufficient background to complete all components of your financial plan. As time passes, however, your financial position will change, and your financial goals will change as well. You will need to revise your financial plan periodically in order to meet your financial goals. The following example for Stephanie Spratt illustrates how an individual's financial position can change over time, how a financial plan may need to be revised as a result, and how the components of the financial plan are integrated.

EXAMPLE

Recall from Chapter 1 that Stephanie Spratt established the following goals:

- purchase a new car within a year,
- buy a home within two years,
- make investments that will allow her wealth to grow over time, and
- build a large amount of savings by the time of her retirement in 20 to 40 years.

Stephanie purchased her new car and new home. She also made some small investments. She has clearly made progress toward her goal of building a large amount of savings by the time she retires.

Recall from Chapter 2 that Stephanie originally had a relatively simple personal balance sheet. Her assets amounted to $9000 and she had credit card debt of $2000 as her only liability. Thus, her net worth was $7000 at that time. Since she created the balance sheet shown in Chapter 2, her assets, liabilities, and net worth have changed substantially.

In Exhibit 17.3, Stephanie's current personal balance sheet is compared to her personal balance sheet from Chapter 2. Notice how her personal balance sheet has changed:

1. She purchased a new car for $18 000 that currently has a market value of $15 000.
2. She purchased a home for $165 000 that still has a market value of $165 000.
3. She recently used $2000 of income to invest in two mutual funds, which are now valued at $2100.
4. She recently started investing in her retirement account and has $800 in it.

The main changes in her liabilities are as follows:

1. Her purchase of a home required her to obtain a mortgage loan, which now has a balance of $123 750.
2. Her purchase of a car required her to obtain a car loan (she made a down payment of $1000, has paid $2000 of principal on the loan, and still owes $15 000).
3. She has a $1000 credit card bill that she will pay off soon.

As Exhibit 17.3 shows, Stephanie's total assets are now $190 000. She increased her assets primarily by making financing decisions that also increased her liabilities. Exhibit 17.3 shows that her liabilities are now $139 750. Thus, her net worth is:

Net Worth = Total Assets − Total Liabilities

= $190 000 − $139 750

= $50 250

The increase in her net worth since the beginning of the year is mainly attributable to a bonus from her employer this year, which helped her cover the down payment on her house. Now that she has a car loan and a mortgage, she uses a large portion of her income to cover loan payments and will not be able to save much money.

Exhibit 17.3 Update on Stephanie Spratt's Personal Balance Sheet		
	Initial Personal Balance Sheet (from Chapter 2)	As of Today
Assets		
Liquid Assets		
Cash	$500	$200
Chequing account	3 500	200
Money market fund	0	2 600
Total liquid assets	**$4 000**	**$3 000**
Household Assets		
Home	$0	$165 000
Car	1 000	15 000
Furniture	1 000	1 000
Total household assets	**$2 000**	**$181 000**
Investment Assets		
Stocks	$3 000	$3 100
Mutual funds	0	2 100
Investment in retirement account	0	800
Total investment assets	**$3 000**	**$6 000**
TOTAL ASSETS	**$9 000**	**$190 000**
Liabilities and Net Worth		
Current Liabilities		
Credit card balance	$2 000	$1 000
Total current liabilities	**$2 000**	**$1 000**
Long-Term Liabilities		
Car loan	$0	$15 000
Mortgage	0	123 750
Total long-term liabilities	**$0**	**$138 750**
TOTAL LIABILITIES	**$2 000**	**$139 750**
Net Worth	**$7 000**	**$50 250**

As time passes, Stephanie hopes to invest in more stocks or other investments to increase her net worth. If the value of her home increases over time, her net worth will also grow. However, her car will likely decline in value over time, which will reduce the value of her assets and therefore reduce her net worth.

Budgeting

Stephanie's recent cash flow statement is shown in Exhibit 17.4. The major change in her income from Chapter 2 is that her disposable income is now higher as a result of

Exhibit 17.4 Update on Stephanie Spratt's Monthly Cash Flow Statement

	Initial Cash Flow Statement	Most Recent Cash Flow Statement	Change in the Cash Flow Statement
Income			
Disposable (after-tax) income	$2 500	$3 000	+$500
Interest on deposits	0	0	No change
Dividend payments	0	0	No change
Total income	**$2 500**	**$3 000**	**+$500**
Expenses			
Rent	$600	$0	– $600
Cable TV	50	50	No change
Electricity and water	60	80	+20
Telephone	60	60	No change
Groceries	300	300	No change
Health insurance expenses	130	140	+10
Clothing	100	100	No change
Car insurance and maintenance	200	100	–100
Recreation	600	500	–100
Car loan payment	0	412	+412
Mortgage payment (includes property taxes and insurance)	0	848	+848
Life insurance payment	0	10	+10
Contribution to retirement plan	0	300	+300
Total expenses			
	$2 100	**$2 900**	**+$800**
Net cash flows	**$400**	**$100**	**–$300**

a promotion and salary increase at work. The major changes in her expenses are as follows:

1. She no longer has a rent payment.

2. As a result of buying a new car, she now saves about $100 per month on car maintenance because the car dealer will do all maintenance at no charge for the next two years.

3. Primarily by discontinuing her health club membership and exercising at home, she has reduced her recreation expenses to about $500 per month (a reduction of $100 per month).

4. She now has a car loan payment of $412 each month.

5. She now has a mortgage loan payment, including property tax and homeowner's insurance, of $848 per month.

6. She just started paying for disability insurance ($10 per month) and life insurance ($10 per month).

7. She just started contributing $300 per month to her retirement account.

Budgeting Dilemma.   While Stephanie's monthly income is now $500 higher, her monthly expenses are $800 higher. Thus, her monthly net cash flows have declined from $400 to $100. This means that even though her salary increased, she has less money available after paying her bills and recreation expenses.

Budgeting Decision.   Stephanie reviews her personal cash flow statement to determine how she is spending her money. Some of her cash flows are currently being invested in assets. Even if she does not invest any of her net cash flows now, her net worth will grow over time because she is paying down the debt on her home and on her car each month and is contributing to her retirement account.

Overall, she decides that she is pleased with her cash flow situation. However, she decides to reassess the other components of her financial plan (as discussed below), which could affect her budget.

Long-Term Strategy for Budgeting.   Some of Stephanie's budgeting is based on the bills she incurs as a result of her car and home. Other parts of the budget are determined by the other components of her financial plan:

- The amount of cash (if any) allocated to liquid assets depends on her plan for managing liquidity.

- The amount of cash allocated to pay off existing loans depends on her plan for personal financing.

- The amount of cash allocated to insurance policies depends on her insurance planning.

- The amount of cash allocated to investments depends on her plan for investing.

- The amount of cash allocated to her retirement account depends on her retirement planning.

Managing Liquidity

Every two weeks, Stephanie's paycheque is direct deposited to her chequing account. She writes cheques to pay all of her bills and to cover the other expenses specified in Exhibit 17.4; she also pays her credit card bill in full each month. She normally has about $100 at the end of the month after paying her bills and recreation expenses. Stephanie wants to ensure that she has sufficient liquidity. Her most convenient source of funds is her chequing account; since her paycheque is deposited there, she knows she will have enough funds every month to pay her bills. If she had any other short-term debt, she would use her net cash flows to pay it off. She recently invested $2600 in a term deposit. This account is her second most convenient source of funds; it allows her quick access to cash in the event that unanticipated expenses occur.

Liquidity Dilemma.   Stephanie must decide whether she should change her liquidity position. She considers these options.

Stephanie's Options If She Changes Her Liquidity	Advantage	Disadvantage
Reduce liquidity position by transferring money from her GIC to a mutual fund	May earn a higher rate of return on her assets	Will have a smaller amount of liquid funds to cover unanticipated expenses
Increase liquidity position by transferring money from a mutual fund to her GIC	May earn a lower rate of return on her assets	Will have a larger amount of liquid funds to cover unanticipated expenses

Liquidity Decision. Stephanie determines that she has access to sufficient funds to cover her liquidity needs. If she has any major unanticipated expenses beyond the funds in her GIC, she could sell shares of the stock or the mutual funds that she owns. She decides to leave her liquidity position as is.

Long-Term Strategy for Managing Liquidity. Stephanie's plan for managing liquidity is to continue using her chequing account to cover bills and to use funds from the GIC to cover any unanticipated expenses. She prefers not to invest any more funds in the GIC because the interest rate is low. Thus, she will use any net cash flows she has at the end of the month for some other purpose. If she ever needs to withdraw funds from her GIC, she will likely attempt to replenish that account once she has new net cash flows that can be invested in it.

Financing

Stephanie has a car loan balance of $15 000 and a mortgage loan balance of $123 750. She has no need for any additional loans. She considers paying off her car loan before it is due (about three years from now).

Financing Dilemma. Stephanie wants to pay off the car loan as soon as she has saved a sufficient amount of money. She realizes that to pay off this liability, she will need to reduce some of her assets. She outlines the following options for paying off her car loan early.

Stephanie's Options for Paying Off Her Car Loan Early	Advantage	Disadvantage
Withdraw funds from GIC	Would be able to reduce or eliminate monthly car loan payment	Will no longer have adequate liquidity
Withdraw funds from retirement account	Would be able to reduce or eliminate monthly car loan payment	Will no longer have funds set aside for retirement
Sell stock	Would be able to reduce or eliminate monthly car loan payment	Would forgo the potential to earn higher returns on the stock
Sell mutual funds	Would be able to reduce or eliminate monthly car loan payment	Would forgo the potential to earn higher returns on the mutual fund

Financing Decision. Stephanie needs to maintain liquidity, so she eliminates the first option. She also eliminates the second option because she believes that those funds should be reserved for retirement purposes.

The remaining options deserve more consideration. Stephanie's annual interest rate on the car loan is 7.60 percent. Once she has a large enough investment in stocks and mutual funds that she can pay off the car loan (perhaps a year from now), she will decide how to use that money as follows:

- If she thinks that the investments will earn an annual after-tax return of less than 7.60 percent, she will sell them and use the money to pay off the car loan. In this way, she will essentially earn a return of 7.60 percent with that money because she will be paying off debt for which she was being charged 7.60 percent.

- If she thinks that the investments will earn an annual after-tax return greater than 7.60 percent, she will keep them. She will not pay off the car loan because her investments are providing her with a higher return than the cost of the car loan.

Long-Term Strategy for Financing. Once Stephanie pays off her car loan, she will have an extra $412 per month (the amount of her car loan payment) that can be used to make more investments. She does not plan to buy another car until she can pay for it with cash. Her only other loan is her mortgage, which has a 25-year amortization period. If she stays in the same home over the next 25 years, she will have paid off her mortgage by that time, assuming that interest remains the same. In this case, she will have no debt after 25 years. She may consider buying a more expensive home in the near future and would likely obtain another mortgage amortized over 25 years.

Insurance

Stephanie currently has auto, homeowner's, health, disability, and life insurance policies.

Insurance Dilemma. Stephanie recognizes that she needs insurance to cover her car, home, and health. In addition, she wants to protect her existing income in case she becomes disabled. She also wants to make sure that she can provide some financial support to her two nieces in the future.

Insurance Decision. Stephanie recently decided to purchase disability insurance to protect her income in case she becomes disabled. She also decided to purchase life insurance to fund her nieces' college education if she dies. She is pleased with her current employer-provided health insurance policy.

Long-Term Strategy for Insurance. Stephanie will maintain a high level of insurance to protect against liability resulting from owning her car or home. If she decides to have children in the future, she will purchase additional life insurance to ensure future financial support for her children. She will continue to review her policies to search for premium savings.

Managing Investments

Stephanie currently has an investment in one stock worth $3100 and an investment in two mutual funds worth $2100.

Investing Dilemma. If the one stock that Stephanie owns performs poorly in the future, the value of her investments (and therefore her net worth) could decline substantially. She expects the stock market to do well but is uncomfortable having an investment in a single stock. She considers the following options.

Stephanie's Options If She Changes Her Investments	Advantage	Disadvantage
Sell stock; invest the proceeds in bonds	Lower risk than from her stock	Lower expected return than from her stock
Sell stock; invest the proceeds in her money market fund	Lower risk and improved liquidity	Lower expected return than from her stock
Sell stock; invest the proceeds in a stock mutual fund	Lower risk	Lower expected return than from her stock

Investing Decision. All three possibilities offer lower risk than the stock, but given that Stephanie expects the stock market to perform well, she prefers a stock mutual fund. She is not relying on the investment to provide periodic income at this time and wants an investment that could increase in value over time. She decides to sell her 100 shares of stock at the prevailing market value of $3100 and to invest the proceeds in her stock mutual fund to achieve greater diversification. This transaction reflects a shift of $3100 on her personal balance sheet from stocks to mutual funds. She incurs a transaction fee of $20 for selling the shares.

Long-Term Strategy for Investing. Stephanie considers using most of her $100 in net cash flows each month to purchase additional units of the stock mutual fund in which she recently invested. She does not specify the amount she will invest because she recognizes that in some months she may face unanticipated expenses that will need to be covered. Once her car loan is paid off, she will have an additional $412 in net cash flows per month that she can invest in the stock mutual fund or in other investments.

Protecting and Maintaining Wealth

Stephanie recently started to contribute to a retirement account. This account is beneficial because her contributions will not be taxed until the funds are withdrawn during retirement. In addition, this account should grow in value if she consistently contributes to it each month and selects investments that appreciate in value over time.

Retirement Contribution Dilemma. Recently, Stephanie started contributing $300 per month to her employer's defined-contribution pension plan, which is matched by a contribution from her employer. She could also establish an RRSP. However, she is not likely to use any of the contributed funds until she retires. She considers the following options.

Stephanie's Options Regarding Her Retirement Account	Advantage	Disadvantage
Do not contribute any funds to retirement account	Can use all net cash flows for other purposes	Forgo tax benefits and matching contribution from employer; will have no money set aside for retirement
Continue to contribute $300 per month	Benefit from a matching contribution and achieve some tax benefits	Could use the $300 for other purposes
Contribute $300 per month and establish an RRSP	Increased tax benefits	Could use the funds for other purposes

Retirement Contribution Decision. Stephanie wants to know how much more she will have in 40 years (when she hopes to retire) if she saves an additional $100 per month ($1200 per year). She expects to earn an annual return of 10 percent per year if she invests in an RRSP. She can use the future value annuity table in Appendix A to determine the future value of her extra contribution. The *FVIFA* for a 10 percent interest rate and a period of 40 years is 442.59. In 40 years, her extra contribution of $1200 per year would accumulate to be worth:

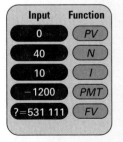

$$\text{Extra Savings at Retirement} = \text{Extra Amount Invested} \times FVIFA_{i,n}$$
$$= \$1200 \times 442.59$$
$$= \$531\ 108$$

She decides to save the additional $100 per month since it will result in $531 108 more at retirement. She also realizes that contributing the extra amount will provide present-day tax benefits. Contributing the extra $100 will reduce her net cash flows, however, so she may have more difficulty meeting her liquidity needs, will be less likely to pay off her existing car loan quickly, and will have less money to spend on recreation. Yet, by accepting these disadvantages in the short term, she can receive major tax benefits and ensure a high level of wealth when she retires. Stephanie's view is that any dollar invested in a retirement account is more valuable than a dollar invested in a non-retirement account because of the tax advantages.

Long-Term Strategy for Retirement Contributions. Stephanie plans to invest the maximum allowed in her retirement account so that she can take full advantage of the tax benefits. The maximum annual limit on her retirement contribution depends on her income. As her income increases over time, she will be able to increase her monthly contribution up to the maximum limit. She would also like to contribute the maximum amount possible to her RRSP, but cannot afford to contribute that amount.

IN-CLASS NOTES

Integrating the Components
- Over time, your financial position and goals will change.
- You will need to revise your financial plan periodically in order to meet your financial goals.

_____

_____

_____

_____

_____

L.O. 3 FINANCIAL PLAN

Stephanie Spratt's financial plan is illustrated below. It incorporates her most recent decisions (discussed in the previous section). Her budget plan determines how she will use her income. Notice that she adjusts her budget plan in response to decisions regarding other components of her financial plan.

A review of Stephanie's financial plan shows that she is building her wealth over time in four ways:

1. She is increasing her equity investment in her car as she makes monthly payments on her car loan.

2. She is increasing her equity investment in her home as she makes monthly payments on her mortgage loan.

3. She is increasing her investment in a mutual fund as she uses her net cash flows each month to buy more units.

4. She is increasing her retirement account assets as she makes monthly contributions.

If Stephanie follows the financial plan she has created, she will pay off her car loan within a year or two. She will also pay off her mortgage loan in 25 years and then will not have any remaining debt. In addition, she will continue to use her net cash flows to make investments in either stock or bond mutual funds. Her retirement account contributions ensure that she will have substantial wealth by the time she retires.

Stephanie's wealth may also increase for other reasons. The value of her home, mutual fund, and any investments she makes within her retirement account may increase over time. Overall, Stephanie's financial plan should provide her with sufficient wealth so that she can afford a very comfortable lifestyle in the future.

STEPHANIE SPRATT'S FINANCIAL PLAN: Budget Plan

My monthly salary of $3000 after taxes is direct deposited to my chequing account. I will use this account to cover all bills and other expenses. My total expenses (including recreation) should be about $2900 per month. This leaves me with monthly net cash flows of $100.

I will use the net cash flows each month to cover any unanticipated expenses that occurred during the month. My second priority is to use the net cash flows to keep about $2600 in my money market fund (MMF) to ensure liquidity. If this account is already at that level, I will use the net cash flows to invest in a registered retirement savings plan (RRSP).

PLAN FOR MANAGING LIQUIDITY

Since my salary is direct deposited to my chequing account, I have a convenient means of covering my expenses. My backup source of liquidity is my MMF, which currently contains $2600; I will maintain the account balance at about that level to ensure liquidity. If I ever need more money than is in this account, I could rely on my net cash flows. In addition, I could sell some shares of my mutual fund, or I could cover some expenses with a credit card since I would have an extra month before the credit card bill arrives. However, I will use other sources before I use the credit card, as interest costs on this form of credit are normally very high.

PLAN FOR FINANCING

I have two finance payments: a monthly car loan payment of $412, and a monthly mortgage payment of $848 (including property taxes and homeowner's insurance). I would like to pay off the car loan early if possible. The interest rate on that loan is 7.60 percent. The principal remaining on the car loan will decrease over time as I pay down the debt with my monthly payments. I may consider selling my units of the mutual fund and using the proceeds to pay off part of the car loan. My decision will depend on whether I believe the mutual fund can provide a higher return than the cost of the car loan. When I pay off the car loan, my expenses will be reduced by $412 per month. Thus, I should have more net cash flows that I can use to make investments or spend in other ways.

INSURANCE PLAN

I have car insurance that covers my car and limits my liability. I have homeowner's insurance that covers the full market value of my home. I have health insurance through my employer. I have disability insurance that will provide financial support if I become disabled. I have life insurance, with my two nieces named as the beneficiaries. If I decide to have children in the future, I will purchase additional life insurance, naming my children as beneficiaries.

INVESTMENT PLAN

I currently have $6000 in investments. This amount should increase over time as I use my net cash flows of about $100 per month to invest in an RRSP or buy more units of my mutual fund. I may sell my units of the mutual fund someday to pay off part of my car loan. Once I pay off the car loan, I will have an additional $412 per month that I can use to make investments. My net cash flows should also increase over time as my salary increases, and most of the net cash flows will be directed toward investments over time.

When I make additional investments, I will consider those that have tax advantages. Since I am not relying on investments to provide me with income at this point, I will only consider investing in mutual funds that do not pay high dividend and capital gain distributions. A stock index mutual fund that focuses on small stocks may be ideal for me because these types of stocks typically do not pay dividends. In addition, an index fund does not trade stocks frequently and therefore does not generate large capital gain distributions. This type of mutual fund provides most of its potential return in the form of an increase in the fund's value over time. I would not pay taxes on this type of capital gain until I sell the mutual fund. I will consider buying such funds in my RRSP for additional tax advantages.

I will focus on mutual funds rather than stocks to achieve diversification. If I invest in any individual stocks in the future, I will only consider stocks that pay no dividends and have more potential to increase in value.

If I consider investing in bonds in the future, I may invest in a Government of Canada bond fund or large-cap corporate bond fund.

RETIREMENT PLAN

I recently began to contribute $300 per month to my retirement account; my employer will provide a matching contribution so that the total contribution will be $7200 per year. If I work over the next 40 years and earn 5 percent a year on this investment, the future value of my contributions will be:

Savings at Retirement = Amount Invested × FVIFA$_{i, n}$

$$= \$7200 \times 120.797$$

$$= \$869\ 738$$

If I have children, I may not work full-time for the entire 40 years, so I may not be able to invest $7200 per year for 40 years. In addition, the return on the retirement fund may be less than 5 percent a year. Therefore, I may be overestimating my future savings. Consequently, I should maximize my contributions now while I am working full-time. Once my cash flow improves, I will consider an RRSP.

SUMMARY

A financial plan consists of a budget (Part 1), a plan for managing liquidity (Part 2), a financing plan (Part 3), an insurance plan (Part 4), an investment plan (Part 5), and a plan for retirement and estate planning (Part 6). The budget determines how you will spend or invest your money. Your plan for managing liquidity will ensure that you can cover any unanticipated expenses. Your financing plan is used to finance large purchases. Financing also involves decisions that affect the interest rate you are charged and the duration of any loans. Your plan for protecting your assets and income involves decisions as to what types of insurance to purchase, how much insurance to buy, how much to invest periodically in your retirement account, and how to distribute your estate to your heirs. Your investment plan determines how much you allocate toward investments and how you allocate money across different types of investments.

The components of a financial plan are integrated in that they depend on each other. The budget plan depends on the other components of the financial plan. The amount of money available for any part of the plan depends on how much money is used for liquidity purposes, to make loan (financing) payments, to make investments, to buy insurance, or to contribute to retirement accounts. The more money you allocate toward any part of the financial plan, the less money you have for the other parts. Thus, a key aspect of financial planning is to decide which components of the financial plan deserve the highest priority, because the decisions made about those components will influence the decisions for the others.

The example featuring Stephanie Spratt's financial plan shows how the plan can be segmented into the six components. The example also illustrates how the components are integrated so that a decision about any one component can only be made after considering the others. As time passes and financial conditions change, you should continuously re-evaluate your financial plan. Re-evaluation should also occur when any major event occurs. These events may include marriage, children, a new job, etc.

INTEGRATING THE KEY CONCEPTS

As this chapter has shown, all parts of the financial plan are related. The financial planning tools (Part 1) allow you to budget, and assess the tax effects of various planning decisions. Your money and credit management (Part 2) allows you to establish liquidity as a cushion in case your expenses exceed your income in a particular month. This cushion should always be maintained before you consider any other financial planning decisions. Your financing decisions (Part 3) determine how much you will borrow and will dictate what you can afford to purchase.

Your insurance decisions (Part 4) determine how much money is needed to protect your assets or income. Therefore, they affect the amount of funds you have available to pay off loans (Part 3) or to make investments (Part 5). Your investment decisions (Part 5) are related to the financing decisions in Part 3, as you should first consider whether the money to be invested could be put to better use by paying off any personal loans. Your investment decisions in Part 5 should take into account whether the money you have to invest should be used for your retirement account (Part 6).

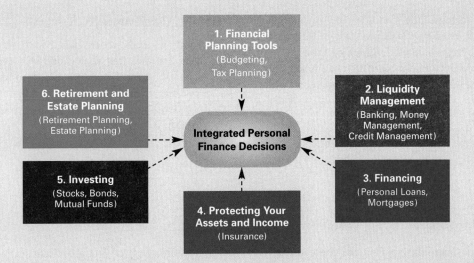

REVIEW QUESTIONS

1. Why is it important to integrate the components of your financial plan?

2. How does budgeting fit into your financial plan? How is your financial plan affected by your spending? What is the budgeting trade-off?

3. Discuss how managing liquidity fits into your financial plan. What is the liquidity trade-off?

4. Describe some advantages and disadvantages of using financing to achieve your financial goals. What is the financing trade-off?

5. How does managing your investments fit into your financial plan? What is the investment trade-off?

6. Discuss some methods for maintaining and protecting your wealth. What is the insurance trade-off? What is the retirement account trade-off?

7. How does time affect your financial plan?

8. What do you think happens to your budget when your financial position changes?

9. You have a $7000 balance on your car loan at 11 percent interest. Your favourite aunt has just left you $10 000 in her will. You can put some of the inheritance in a money market fund at your bank as well as pay off your car loan, or you can invest it in mutual funds. What factors must you consider in making your decision?

10. In the previous question, you decide to pay off the car loan and invest the difference. Now you no longer have a monthly $350 car payment. Suggest some ways you might use these additional funds.

11. You have some extra cash in your budget that you wish to invest. You have narrowed your choices to a single stock, Government of Canada bonds, or stock mutual funds. What characteristics of each investment alternative should you consider in making your decision?

12. How does purchasing car insurance and homeowner's insurance help protect and maintain your wealth?

13. How does purchasing sufficient health insurance help protect and maintain your wealth?

14. How does life insurance protect your wealth? Who needs life insurance?

FINANCIAL PLANNING PROBLEMS

1. Judy has just received $12 500 as an inheritance from her uncle and is considering ways to use the money. Judy's car is one year old, and her monthly payment is $304. She owes 48 more payments. The amount needed to pay off the loan is $12 460. How much will Judy save in interest if she pays off her car loan now?

2. Judy (from Problem 1) is also considering investing the $12 500 in a guaranteed investment certificate (GIC). She is guaranteed a return of 4 percent on a four-year GIC. How much would she earn from the GIC? Which of the two alternatives (Problem 1 versus Problem 2) offers the better return?

3. Judy (from Problem 1) pays off her car loan and now must decide how she wants to invest the extra $3648 per year that she budgeted for car payments. She decides to invest this additional amount in her RRSP. Currently, the plan is averaging a 12 percent annual return. Judy has 15 years until retirement. How much more money will she have at retirement if she invests this additional amount?

4. Judy (from Problem 1) believes that another benefit of investing the extra $3648 per year in her RRSP

is the tax savings. Judy is in a 30 percent marginal tax bracket. How much will investing in this manner save her in taxes annually? Assuming that she remains in a 30 percent marginal tax bracket until she retires, how much will it save her in total over the next 15 years, ignoring the time value of the tax savings?

FINANCIAL PLANNING ONLINE EXERCISE

1. Go to www.creditcounselling.com/assets/files/pdf/10_tips_for_pain-free_savings.pdf. This article provides 10 tips for pain-free investing. Which of these tips can you put into action in the next month in order to begin the process of establishing a plan to improve your financial health?

ON THE STUDENT CD-ROM FOR THIS CHAPTER YOU WILL FIND:

- Building Your Own Financial Plan exercise and work-sheets
- The chapter-end Continuing Case about the Sampson family

    Read through the Building Your Own Financial Plan exercise and use the worksheets to review your financial plan to date.

After reading the Sampson case study, use the Continuing Case worksheets to summarize the Sampsons' plans for budgeting, managing their liquidity, financing large purchases, protecting their wealth, and investing for their children's education.

Study Guide

Circle the correct answer and then check the answers in the back of the book to chart your progress.

Multiple Choice

1. The six main components of the financial plan include:
   a. Budgeting, managing liquidity, financing, protecting your assets and income, personal investing, and retirement and estate planning.
   b. Budgeting, managing liquidity, financing, protecting your assets, personal investing, and retirement and estate planning.
   c. Budgeting, managing liquidity, financing, protecting your assets and income, personal investing, and retirement and will planning.
   d. Budgeting, managing liquidity, financing, protecting your assets, personal investing, and retirement and will planning.

2. Which of the following statements regarding the budgeting trade-off is true?
   a. The more you spend, the more money you will have available for liquidity purposes, investments, or retirement saving.
   b. Your budgeting decisions involve a trade-off between spending today and allocating funds for the past.

   c. Your budget should attempt to ensure that you have net cash flows every month for savings or for retirement.
   d. The more funds you can allocate for the future, the less you will be able to benefit from compounded interest, and the more you will be able to spend in the future.

3. Which of the following would not be considered a liquid asset?
   a. Savings account
   b. Stock mutual fund
   c. Term deposit
   d. Money market fund

4. Which of the following statements with respect to the financing trade-off is incorrect?
   a. An excessive amount of financing can prevent you from achieving your financial goals.
   b. It is easier to cover the monthly loan payment if you select financing with a relatively short maturity.
   c. You may want to consider paying off a loan before its maturity so that you can avoid incurring any more interest expense.

d. Paying off loans rather than making additional investments is appropriate when the expected after-tax return on the investments you could make is lower than the interest rate you are paying on the loan.

5. While playing tennis with a friend, you suffer a debilitating stroke. After three weeks, you are discharged from the hospital. Which of the following types of insurance would have been of the least benefit to you and/or your family?
a. Life insurance
b. Disability insurance
c. Long-term care insurance
d. Critical illness insurance

6. You would like to build a portfolio that will provide periodic income. Which of the following investments may not be appropriate for the portfolio you are trying to create?
a. An investment in stocks that pay dividends
b. The stocks of large, well-known firms
c. An investment in bonds
d. An investment in the stock of a firm that is growing at a fast pace

7. All of the following would be concerns with respect to investing money in the stocks of smaller firms, except:
a. An investment in stocks of smaller firms will require you to forgo some liquidity.
b. An investment in stocks of smaller firms is more likely to result in large losses than investments in stocks of large, well-known firms.
c. By investing in a mutual fund that focuses on small stocks, you can reduce the risk associated with being exposed to the specific risk of any individual small stock.
d. By investing in a mutual fund that focuses on small stocks, you can reduce the risk associated with weakening market conditions.

8. With respect to your investments, which of the following documents should be stored in a safe at home or in a safety deposit box?
a. Stock certificates
b. Will
c. Personal loan (such as car loan) agreements
d. Insurance policies

9. Which of the following is a consequence of reducing your liquidity position by transferring money from a GIC to a growth mutual fund?
a. You will earn a higher return on your assets.

b. You may have a smaller amount of liquid funds to cover unanticipated expenses.
c. You may have a smaller amount of liquid funds to cover anticipated expenses.
d. All of the above.

10. To pay off a car loan, you have decided to reduce the value of one or more of your assets. Which of the following actions is most likely to have the greatest negative impact on your net worth over a period of time?
a. Withdraw funds from a GIC
b. Withdraw funds from a retirement account composed of balanced growth and income investments
c. Sell a bond mutual fund
d. Sell shares of one of the growth stocks in your non-registered portfolio

True/False

1. True or False? Budgeting allows you to determine whether your expenses will exceed your income so that you can forecast any shortages in that month.

2. True or False? The liquidity trade-off refers to the idea that you should maintain as much money as possible in an emergency fund to satisfy your liquidity needs.

3. True or False? Financing can increase the amount of your assets.

4. True or False? Your investment needs should be given priority before insurance.

5. True or False? You should make investments only after you have sufficient liquidity and sufficient insurance to protect your existing assets.

6. True or False? The more money you contribute to your retirement account now, the more money you will have when you reach retirement age.

7. True or False? Without exception, any money withdrawn early from a retirement account is subject to a penalty.

8. True or False? As time passes, your financial goals should remain the same.

9. True or False? To lower your overall portfolio risk and improve your liquidity, you could sell shares from a stock portfolio and invest the proceeds in a money market fund.

10. True or False? You should continuously re-evaluate your financial plan.

Appendix A

Applying Time Value Concepts

This appendix discusses some of the most important concepts regarding finance. Once familiar with these concepts, the student will see the usefulness of these simple formulae.

For the purposes of simplification, we have used a time period (*n*) of one month when calculating the compound interest applicable to credit cards. Credit card companies often compound on a daily basis. For most applications, the small difference in interest payable is not important. However, for large sums of money over long periods of time, the daily calculation of interest can mean a great deal.

THE IMPORTANCE OF THE TIME VALUE OF MONEY

The time value of money is a powerful principle. In fact, it is so powerful that Albert Einstein stated that it was one of the strongest forces on earth. The time value is especially important for estimating how your money may grow over time.

EXAMPLE

To show you the power of the time value of money, consider the situation in which your ancestors may have found themselves in 1694. At that time, let us assume that one of them invested $20 in a savings account at a local bank earning 5 percent interest annually. Also assume that this ancestor never informed his family members of this transaction and that the money remained in the account accumulating interest of 5 percent annually until the year 2007, when the bank locates you and informs you of the account. Over this time period, the $20 would have accumulated to $86 million.

As a more realistic example, consider that an investment today of just $2000 in an account that earns 6 percent a year will be worth about $11 487 in 30 years.

These examples show how money grows over time when you receive a return on your investment. When you spend money, you incur an opportunity cost of what you could have done with that money had you not spent it. In the previous example, if you had spent the $2000 on a vacation rather than saving the money, you would have incurred an opportunity cost of the alternative ways that you could have used the money. That is, you can either have a vacation today or have that money accumulate to be worth $11 487 in 30 years (among other possible choices). Whatever decision you make, you will forgo some alternative uses of those funds.

The time value of money is most commonly applied to two types of cash flows: a single dollar amount (also referred to as a lump sum) and an annuity. An ordinary annuity is a stream of equal payments that are received or paid at equal intervals in time at the end of a period. For example, a monthly deposit of $50 as new savings in a bank account at the end of every month is an annuity. Your telephone bill is not an annuity, as the payments are not the same each month.

ordinary annuity
A stream of equal payments that are received or paid at equal intervals in time at the end of a period.

FUTURE VALUE OF A SINGLE DOLLAR AMOUNT

When you deposit money in a bank savings account, your money grows because the bank pays interest on your deposit. The interest is a payment to you for depositing your money in the account, and is normally expressed as a percentage of the deposit amount and is paid annually.

You may want to know how your money will grow to determine whether you can afford specific purchases in the future. For example, you may want to estimate how your existing bank balance will accumulate in six months when you will need to make a tuition payment. Alternatively, you may want to estimate how that money will accumulate in one year when you hope to make a down payment on a new car. To do this, you can apply the interest rate that you expect to earn on your deposit to the deposit amount.

To determine the future value of an amount of money you deposit today, you need to know:

- The amount of your deposit (or other investment) today

- The interest rate to be earned on your deposit

- The number of years the money will be invested

EXAMPLE

If you created a bank deposit of $1000 that earned 4 percent annually, the deposit will earn an annual interest of:

Interest Rate × Deposit = 4 percent × $1000 = $40

Thus, your deposit will accumulate to be worth $1040 by the end of one year.

compounding
The process of earning interest on interest.

In the next year, the interest rate of 4 percent will be applied not only on your original $1000 deposit, but also on the interest that you earned in the previous year. The process of earning interest on interest is called compounding.

EXAMPLE

Assuming that the interest rate is 4 percent in the second year, it will be applied to your deposit balance of $1040, which results in interest of $41.60 (computed as 4 percent × $1040). Thus, your balance by the end of the second year would be $1081.60.

Notice that the interest of $41.60 paid in the second year is more than the interest paid in the first year, even though the interest rate is the same. This is because the interest rate was applied to a larger deposit balance.

In the third year, a 4 percent interest rate would result in interest of $43.26 (computed as 4 percent of $1081.60). Your deposit balance would be $1124.86 by the end of the third year.

future value interest factor (FVIF)
A factor multiplied by today's savings to determine how the savings will accumulate over time.

In some cases, you may want to know how your deposit will accumulate over a long period of time, such as 20 or 30 years. You can quickly determine the future value for any period of time by using the future value interest factor (FVIF), which is a factor multiplied by today's savings to determine how the savings will accumulate over time. The factor depends on the interest rate and the number of years the money is invested. Your deposit today is multiplied by the FVIF to determine the future value of the deposit.

Using the Future Value Table

Table A-1 shows the *FVIF* for various interest rates (*i*) and time periods (*n*). Each column in the table lists an interest rate and each row lists a possible time period. By reviewing any column, you will notice that as the number of years increases, the *FVIF* becomes higher. This means that the longer the time period in which your money is invested at a set rate of return, the more your money will grow.

By reviewing any row of Table A-1, you will notice that as the interest rate increases, the *FVIF* becomes higher. This means that the higher the rate of return, the more your money will grow over a given time period.

EXAMPLE

Suppose that you want to know how much money you will have in five years if you invest $5000 now and earn an annual return of 9 percent. The present value of money (*PV*) is the amount invested, or $5000. The *FVIF* for an interest rate of 9 percent and a time period of five years is 1.539 (look down the column for 9 percent, and across the row for five years). Thus, the future value (*FV*) of the $5000 in five years will be:

$$FV = PV \times FVIF_{i,n}$$

$$FV = PV \times FVIF_{9\%,5}$$

$$= \$5000 \times 1.539$$

$$= \$7695$$

Using a Financial Calculator

There are a variety of financial calculators available for purchase that greatly simplify time value calculations, as the following example shows.

EXAMPLE

Suppose you have $5687 to invest in the stock market today. You like to invest for the long term and plan to choose your stocks carefully. You will invest your money for 12 years in certain stocks on which you expect a return of 10 percent annually. Although financial calculators can vary slightly in their setup, most would require inputs as shown at left.

Where:

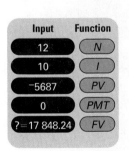

N	= number of periods
I	= interest rate
PV	= present value, which is the initial amount deposited
PMT	= payment, which is not applicable in this example
FV	= future value of the deposit you make today, which is computed by the calculator

The *PV* is a negative number here, reflecting the outflow of cash to make the investment. The calculator computes the future value to be $17 848.24, which indicates that you will have $17 848.24 in your brokerage account in 12 years if you achieve a return of 10 percent annually on your $5687 investment.

Use a financial calculator to determine the future value of $5000 invested at 9 percent for five years. (This is the previous example used for the *FVIF* table.) Your answer should be $7695. Any difference in answers using the *FVIF* table versus using a financial calculator is due to rounding.

Table A-1 Future Value Interest Factors for $1 Compounded at i Percent for n Periods: $FV = PV \times FVIF_{i,n}$

Period	1%	2%	3%	4%	5%	6%	7%	8%	9%	10%	11%	12%	13%	14%	15%	16%	17%	18%	19%	20%
1	1.010	1.020	1.030	1.040	1.050	1.060	1.070	1.080	1.090	1.100	1.110	1.120	1.130	1.140	1.150	1.160	1.170	1.180	1.190	1.200
2	1.020	1.040	1.061	1.082	1.102	1.124	1.145	1.166	1.188	1.210	1.232	1.254	1.277	1.300	1.322	1.346	1.369	1.392	1.416	1.440
3	1.030	1.061	1.093	1.125	1.158	1.191	1.225	1.260	1.295	1.331	1.368	1.405	1.443	1.482	1.521	1.561	1.602	1.643	1.685	1.728
4	1.041	1.082	1.126	1.170	1.216	1.262	1.311	1.360	1.412	1.464	1.518	1.574	1.630	1.689	1.749	1.811	1.874	1.939	2.005	2.074
5	1.051	1.104	1.159	1.217	1.276	1.338	1.403	1.469	1.539	1.611	1.685	1.762	1.842	1.925	2.011	2.100	2.192	2.288	2.386	2.488
6	1.062	1.126	1.194	1.265	1.340	1.419	1.501	1.587	1.677	1.772	1.870	1.974	2.082	2.195	2.313	2.436	2.565	2.700	2.840	2.986
7	1.072	1.149	1.230	1.316	1.407	1.504	1.606	1.714	1.828	1.949	2.076	2.211	2.353	2.502	2.660	2.826	3.001	3.185	3.379	3.583
8	1.083	1.172	1.267	1.369	1.477	1.594	1.718	1.851	1.993	2.144	2.305	2.476	2.658	2.853	3.059	3.278	3.511	3.759	4.021	4.300
9	1.094	1.195	1.305	1.423	1.551	1.689	1.838	1.999	2.172	2.358	2.558	2.773	3.004	3.252	3.518	3.803	4.108	4.435	4.785	5.160
10	1.105	1.219	1.344	1.480	1.629	1.791	1.967	2.159	2.367	2.594	2.839	3.106	3.395	3.707	4.046	4.411	4.807	5.234	5.695	6.192
11	1.116	1.243	1.384	1.539	1.710	1.898	2.105	2.332	2.580	2.853	3.152	3.479	3.836	4.226	4.652	5.117	5.624	6.176	6.777	7.430
12	1.127	1.268	1.426	1.601	1.796	2.012	2.252	2.518	2.813	3.138	3.498	3.896	4.334	4.818	5.350	5.936	6.580	7.288	8.064	8.916
13	1.138	1.294	1.469	1.665	1.886	2.133	2.410	2.720	3.066	3.452	3.883	4.363	4.898	5.492	6.153	6.886	7.699	8.599	9.596	10.699
14	1.149	1.319	1.513	1.732	1.980	2.261	2.579	2.937	3.342	3.797	4.310	4.887	5.535	6.261	7.076	7.987	9.007	10.147	11.420	12.839
15	1.161	1.346	1.558	1.801	2.079	2.397	2.759	3.172	3.642	4.177	4.785	5.474	6.254	7.138	8.137	9.265	10.539	11.974	13.589	15.407
16	1.173	1.373	1.605	1.873	2.183	2.540	2.952	3.426	3.970	4.595	5.311	6.130	7.067	8.137	9.358	10.748	12.330	14.129	16.171	18.488
17	1.184	1.400	1.653	1.948	2.292	2.693	3.159	3.700	4.328	5.054	5.895	6.866	7.986	9.276	10.761	12.468	14.426	16.672	19.244	22.186
18	1.196	1.428	1.702	2.026	2.407	2.854	3.380	3.996	4.717	5.560	6.543	7.690	9.024	10.575	12.375	14.462	16.879	19.673	22.900	26.623
19	1.208	1.457	1.753	2.107	2.527	3.026	3.616	4.316	5.142	6.116	7.263	8.613	10.197	12.055	14.232	16.776	19.748	23.214	27.251	31.948
20	1.220	1.486	1.806	2.191	2.653	3.207	3.870	4.661	5.604	6.727	8.062	9.646	11.523	13.743	16.366	19.461	23.105	27.393	32.429	38.337
21	1.232	1.516	1.860	2.279	2.786	3.399	4.140	5.034	6.109	7.400	8.949	10.804	13.021	15.667	18.821	22.574	27.033	32.323	38.591	46.005
22	1.245	1.546	1.916	2.370	2.925	3.603	4.430	5.436	6.658	8.140	9.933	12.100	14.713	17.861	21.644	26.186	31.629	38.141	45.923	55.205
23	1.257	1.577	1.974	2.465	3.071	3.820	4.740	5.871	7.258	8.954	11.026	13.552	16.626	20.361	24.891	30.376	37.005	45.007	54.648	66.247
24	1.270	1.608	2.033	2.563	3.225	4.049	5.072	6.341	7.911	9.850	12.239	15.178	18.788	23.212	28.625	35.236	43.296	53.108	65.031	79.496
25	1.282	1.641	2.094	2.666	3.386	4.292	5.427	6.848	8.623	10.834	13.585	17.000	21.230	26.461	32.918	40.874	50.656	62.667	77.387	95.395
30	1.348	1.811	2.427	3.243	4.322	5.743	7.612	10.062	13.267	17.449	22.892	29.960	39.115	50.949	66.210	85.849	111.061	143.367	184.672	237.373
35	1.417	2.000	2.814	3.946	5.516	7.686	10.676	14.785	20.413	28.102	38.574	52.799	72.066	98.097	133.172	180.311	243.495	327.988	440.691	590.657
40	1.489	2.208	3.262	4.801	7.040	10.285	14.974	21.724	31.408	45.258	64.999	93.049	132.776	188.876	267.856	378.715	533.846	750.353	1051.642	1469.740
45	1.565	2.438	3.781	5.841	8.985	13.764	21.002	31.920	48.325	72.888	109.527	163.985	244.629	363.662	538.752	795.429	1170.425	1716.619	2509.583	3657.176
50	1.645	2.691	4.384	7.106	11.467	18.419	29.456	46.900	74.354	117.386	184.559	288.996	450.711	700.197	1083.619	1670.669	2566.080	3927.189	5988.730	9100.191

Period	21%	22%	23%	24%	25%	26%	27%	28%	29%	30%	31%	32%	33%	34%	35%	40%	45%	50%
1	1.210	1.220	1.230	1.240	1.250	1.260	1.270	1.280	1.290	1.300	1.310	1.320	1.330	1.340	1.350	1.400	1.450	1.500
2	1.464	1.488	1.513	1.538	1.562	1.588	1.613	1.638	1.664	1.690	1.716	1.742	1.769	1.796	1.822	1.960	2.102	2.250
3	1.772	1.816	1.861	1.907	1.953	2.000	2.048	2.097	2.147	2.197	2.248	2.300	2.353	2.406	2.460	2.744	3.049	3.375
4	2.144	2.215	2.289	2.364	2.441	2.520	2.601	2.684	2.769	2.856	2.945	3.036	3.129	3.224	3.321	3.842	4.421	5.063
5	2.594	2.703	2.815	2.932	3.052	3.176	3.304	3.436	3.572	3.713	3.858	4.007	4.162	4.320	4.484	5.378	6.410	7.594
6	3.138	3.297	3.463	3.635	3.815	4.001	4.196	4.398	4.608	4.827	5.054	5.290	5.535	5.789	6.053	7.530	9.294	11.391
7	3.797	4.023	4.259	4.508	4.768	5.042	5.329	5.629	5.945	6.275	6.621	6.983	7.361	7.758	8.172	10.541	13.476	17.086
8	4.595	4.908	5.239	5.589	5.960	6.353	6.767	7.206	7.669	8.157	8.673	9.217	9.791	10.395	11.032	14.758	19.541	25.629
9	5.560	5.987	6.444	6.931	7.451	8.004	8.595	9.223	9.893	10.604	11.362	12.166	13.022	13.930	14.894	20.661	28.334	38.443
10	6.727	7.305	7.926	8.594	9.313	10.086	10.915	11.806	12.761	13.786	14.884	16.060	17.319	18.666	20.106	28.925	41.085	57.665
11	8.140	8.912	9.749	10.657	11.642	12.708	13.862	15.112	16.462	17.921	19.498	21.199	23.034	25.012	27.144	40.495	59.573	86.498
12	9.850	10.872	11.991	13.215	14.552	16.012	17.605	19.343	21.236	23.298	25.542	27.982	30.635	33.516	36.644	56.694	86.380	129.746
13	11.918	13.264	14.749	16.386	18.190	20.175	22.359	24.759	27.395	30.287	33.460	36.937	40.745	44.912	49.469	79.371	125.251	194.620
14	14.421	16.182	18.141	20.319	22.737	25.420	28.395	31.691	35.339	39.373	43.832	48.756	54.190	60.181	66.784	111.119	181.614	291.929
15	17.449	19.742	22.314	25.195	28.422	32.030	36.062	40.565	45.587	51.185	57.420	64.358	72.073	80.643	90.158	155.567	263.341	437.894
16	21.113	24.085	27.446	31.242	35.527	40.357	45.799	51.923	58.808	66.541	75.220	84.953	95.857	108.061	121.713	217.793	381.844	656.841
17	25.547	29.384	33.758	38.740	44.409	50.850	58.165	66.461	75.862	86.503	98.539	112.138	127.490	144.802	164.312	304.911	553.674	985.261
18	30.912	35.848	41.523	48.038	55.511	64.071	73.869	85.070	97.862	112.454	129.086	148.022	169.561	194.035	221.822	426.875	802.826	1477.892
19	37.404	43.735	51.073	59.567	69.389	80.730	93.813	108.890	126.242	146.190	169.102	195.389	225.517	260.006	299.459	597.625	1164.098	2216.838
20	45.258	53.357	62.820	73.863	86.736	101.720	119.143	139.379	162.852	190.047	221.523	257.913	299.937	348.408	404.270	836.674	1687.942	3325.257
21	54.762	65.095	77.268	91.591	108.420	128.167	151.312	178.405	210.079	247.061	290.196	340.446	398.916	466.867	545.764	1171.343	2447.515	4987.883
22	66.262	79.416	95.040	113.572	135.525	161.490	192.165	228.358	271.002	321.178	380.156	449.388	530.558	625.601	736.781	1639.878	3548.896	7481.824
23	80.178	96.887	116.899	140.829	169.407	203.477	244.050	292.298	349.592	417.531	498.004	593.192	705.642	838.305	994.653	2295.829	5145.898	11222.738
24	97.015	118.203	143.786	174.628	211.758	256.381	309.943	374.141	450.974	542.791	652.385	783.013	938.504	1123.328	1342.781	3214.158	7461.547	16834.109
25	117.388	144.207	176.857	216.539	264.698	323.040	393.628	478.901	581.756	705.627	854.623	1033.577	1248.210	1505.258	1812.754	4499.816	10819.242	25251.164
30	304.471	389.748	497.904	634.810	807.793	1025.904	1300.477	1645.488	2078.208	2619.936	3297.081	4142.008	5194.516	6503.285	8128.426	24201.043	69348.375	191751.000
35	789.716	1053.370	1401.749	1861.020	2465.189	3258.053	4296.547	5653.840	7423.988	9727.598	12719.918	16598.906	21617.363	28096.695	36448.051	130158.687	*	*
40	2048.309	2846.941	3946.340	5455.797	7523.156	10346.879	14195.051	19426.418	26520.723	36117.754	49072.621	66519.313	89962.188	121388.437	163433.875	700022.688	*	*
45	5312.758	7694.418	11110.121	15994.316	22958.844	32859.457	46897.973	66748.500	94739.937	134102.187	*	*	*	*	*	*	*	*
50	13779.844	20795.680	31278.301	46889.207	70064.812	104354.562	154942.687	229345.875	338440.000	497910.125	*	*	*	*	*	*	*	*

*Not shown because of space limitations.

PRESENT VALUE OF A DOLLAR AMOUNT

discounting
The process of obtaining present values.

In many situations, you will want to know how much money you must deposit or invest today to accumulate a specified amount of money at a future point in time. The process of obtaining present values is referred to as **discounting**. Suppose that you want to have $20 000 for a down payment on a house in three years. You want to know how much money you need to invest today to achieve $20 000 in three years. That is, you want to know the present value of $20 000 that will be received in three years, based on some interest rate that you could earn over that period.

To determine the present value of an amount of money received in the future, you need to know:

- The amount of money to be received in the future

- The interest rate to be earned on your deposit

- The number of years the money will be invested

present value interest factor (PVIF)
A factor multiplied by a future value to determine the present value of that amount.

The present value can be calculated by using a **present value interest factor (PVIF)**, which is a factor multiplied by the future value to determine the present value of that amount. It depends on the interest rate and the number of years the money is invested.

Using the Present Value Table

Table A-2 shows the *PVIF* for various interest rates (i) and time periods (n). Each column in the table lists an interest rate, while each row lists a time period.

You will notice that in any column of the table the *PVIF* is lower as the number of years increases. This means that less money is needed to achieve a specific future value when the money is invested for a greater number of years.

Similarly, an inspection of any row in the table will reveal that less money is needed to achieve a specific future value when the money is invested at a higher rate of return.

EXAMPLE

You would like to accumulate $50 000 in five years by making a single investment today. You believe you can achieve a return from your investment of 8 percent annually. What is the dollar amount you need to invest today to achieve your goal?

The *PVIF* in this example is 0.681 (look down the column for 8 percent and across the row for five years). Using the present value table, the present value (*PV*) is:

$$PV = FV \times PVIF_{i,n}$$

$$PV = FV \times PVIF_{8\%,5}$$

$$= \$50\ 000 \times 0.681$$

$$= \$34\ 050$$

Thus, you need to invest $34 050 today to have $50 000 in five years if you expect an annual return of 8 percent.

Using a Financial Calculator

Using a financial calculator, present values can be obtained quickly by inputting all known variables and solving for the one unknown variable.

Table A-2 Present Value Interest Factors for $1 Compounded at i Percent for n Periods: $PV = FV \times FVIF_{i,n}$

Period	1%	2%	3%	4%	5%	6%	7%	8%	9%	10%	11%	12%	13%	14%	15%	16%	17%	18%	19%	20%
1	.990	.980	.971	.962	.952	.943	.935	.926	.917	.909	.901	.893	.885	.877	.870	.862	.855	.847	.840	.833
2	.980	.961	.943	.925	.907	.890	.873	.857	.842	.826	.812	.797	.783	.769	.756	.743	.731	.718	.706	.694
3	.971	.942	.915	.889	.864	.840	.816	.794	.772	.751	.731	.712	.693	.675	.658	.641	.624	.609	.593	.579
4	.961	.924	.888	.855	.823	.792	.763	.735	.708	.683	.659	.636	.613	.592	.572	.552	.534	.516	.499	.482
5	.951	.906	.863	.822	.784	.747	.713	.681	.650	.621	.593	.567	.543	.519	.497	.476	.456	.437	.419	.402
6	.942	.888	.837	.790	.746	.705	.666	.630	.596	.564	.535	.507	.480	.456	.432	.410	.390	.370	.352	.335
7	.933	.871	.813	.760	.711	.665	.623	.583	.547	.513	.482	.452	.425	.400	.376	.354	.333	.314	.296	.279
8	.923	.853	.789	.731	.677	.627	.582	.540	.502	.467	.434	.404	.376	.351	.327	.305	.285	.266	.249	.233
9	.914	.837	.766	.703	.645	.592	.544	.500	.460	.424	.391	.361	.333	.308	.284	.263	.243	.225	.209	.194
10	.905	.820	.744	.676	.614	.558	.508	.463	.422	.386	.352	.322	.295	.270	.247	.227	.208	.191	.176	.162
11	.896	.804	.722	.650	.585	.527	.475	.429	.388	.350	.317	.287	.261	.237	.215	.195	.178	.162	.148	.135
12	.887	.789	.701	.625	.557	.497	.444	.397	.356	.319	.286	.257	.231	.208	.187	.168	.152	.137	.124	.112
13	.879	.773	.681	.601	.530	.469	.415	.368	.326	.290	.258	.229	.204	.182	.163	.145	.130	.116	.104	.093
14	.870	.758	.661	.577	.505	.442	.388	.340	.299	.263	.232	.205	.181	.160	.141	.125	.111	.099	.088	.078
15	.861	.743	.642	.555	.481	.417	.362	.315	.275	.239	.209	.183	.160	.140	.123	.108	.095	.084	.074	.065
16	.853	.728	.623	.534	.458	.394	.339	.292	.252	.218	.188	.163	.141	.123	.107	.093	.081	.071	.062	.054
17	.844	.714	.605	.513	.436	.371	.317	.270	.231	.198	.170	.146	.125	.108	.093	.080	.069	.060	.052	.045
18	.836	.700	.587	.494	.416	.350	.296	.250	.212	.180	.153	.130	.111	.095	.081	.069	.059	.051	.044	.038
19	.828	.686	.570	.475	.396	.331	.277	.232	.194	.164	.138	.116	.098	.083	.070	.060	.051	.043	.037	.031
20	.820	.673	.554	.456	.377	.312	.258	.215	.178	.149	.124	.104	.087	.073	.061	.051	.043	.037	.031	.026
21	.811	.660	.538	.439	.359	.294	.242	.199	.164	.135	.112	.093	.077	.064	.053	.044	.037	.031	.026	.022
22	.803	.647	.522	.422	.342	.278	.226	.184	.150	.123	.101	.083	.068	.056	.046	.038	.032	.026	.022	.018
23	.795	.634	.507	.406	.326	.262	.211	.170	.138	.112	.091	.074	.060	.049	.040	.033	.027	.022	.018	.015
24	.788	.622	.492	.390	.310	.247	.197	.158	.126	.102	.082	.066	.053	.043	.035	.028	.023	.019	.015	.013
25	.780	.610	.478	.375	.295	.233	.184	.146	.116	.092	.074	.059	.047	.038	.030	.024	.020	.016	.013	.010
30	.742	.552	.412	.308	.231	.174	.131	.099	.075	.057	.044	.033	.026	.020	.015	.012	.009	.007	.005	.004
35	.706	.500	.355	.253	.181	.130	.094	.068	.049	.036	.026	.019	.014	.010	.008	.006	.004	.003	.002	.002
40	.672	.453	.307	.208	.142	.097	.067	.046	.032	.022	.015	.011	.008	.005	.004	.003	.002	.001	.001	.001
45	.639	.410	.264	.171	.111	.073	.048	.031	.021	.014	.009	.006	.004	.003	.002	.001	.001	.001	*	*
50	.608	.372	.228	.141	.087	.054	.034	.021	.013	.009	.005	.003	.002	.001	.001	.001	*	*	*	*

*PVIF is zero to three decimal places.

Table A-2 (Continued)

Period	21%	22%	23%	24%	25%	26%	27%	28%	29%	30%	31%	32%	33%	34%	35%	40%	45%	50%
1	.826	.820	.813	.806	.800	.794	.787	.781	.775	.769	.763	.758	.752	.746	.741	.714	.690	.667
2	.683	.672	.661	.650	.640	.630	.620	.610	.601	.592	.583	.574	.565	.557	.549	.510	.476	.444
3	.564	.551	.537	.524	.512	.500	.488	.477	.466	.455	.445	.435	.425	.416	.406	.364	.328	.296
4	.467	.451	.437	.423	.410	.397	.384	.373	.361	.350	.340	.329	.320	.310	.301	.260	.226	.198
5	.386	.370	.355	.341	.328	.315	.303	.291	.280	.269	.259	.250	.240	.231	.223	.186	.156	.132
6	.319	.303	.289	.275	.262	.250	.238	.227	.217	.207	.198	.189	.181	.173	.165	.133	.108	.088
7	.263	.249	.235	.222	.210	.198	.188	.178	.168	.159	.151	.143	.136	.129	.122	.095	.074	.059
8	.218	.204	.191	.179	.168	.157	.148	.139	.130	.123	.115	.108	.102	.096	.091	.068	.051	.039
9	.180	.167	.155	.144	.134	.125	.116	.108	.101	.094	.088	.082	.077	.072	.067	.048	.035	.026
10	.149	.137	.126	.116	.107	.099	.092	.085	.078	.073	.067	.062	.058	.054	.050	.035	.024	.017
11	.123	.112	.103	.094	.086	.079	.072	.066	.061	.056	.051	.047	.043	.040	.037	.025	.017	.012
12	.102	.092	.083	.076	.069	.062	.057	.052	.047	.043	.039	.036	.033	.030	.027	.018	.012	.008
13	.084	.075	.068	.061	.055	.050	.045	.040	.037	.033	.030	.027	.025	.022	.020	.013	.008	.005
14	.069	.062	.055	.049	.044	.039	.035	.032	.028	.025	.023	.021	.018	.017	.015	.009	.006	.003
15	.057	.051	.045	.040	.035	.031	.028	.025	.022	.020	.017	.016	.014	.012	.011	.006	.004	.002
16	.047	.042	.036	.032	.028	.025	.022	.019	.017	.015	.013	.012	.010	.009	.008	.005	.003	.002
17	.039	.034	.030	.026	.023	.020	.017	.015	.013	.012	.010	.009	.008	.007	.006	.003	.002	.001
18	.032	.028	.024	.021	.018	.016	.014	.012	.010	.009	.008	.007	.006	.005	.005	.002	.001	.001
19	.027	.023	.020	.017	.014	.012	.011	.009	.008	.007	.006	.005	.004	.004	.003	.002	.001	*
20	.022	.019	.016	.014	.012	.010	.008	.007	.006	.005	.005	.004	.003	.003	.002	.001	.001	*
21	.018	.015	.013	.011	.009	.008	.007	.006	.005	.004	.003	.003	.003	.002	.002	.001	*	*
22	.015	.013	.011	.009	.007	.006	.005	.004	.004	.003	.003	.002	.002	.002	.001	.001	*	*
23	.012	.010	.009	.007	.006	.005	.004	.003	.003	.002	.002	.002	.001	.001	.001	*	*	*
24	.010	.008	.007	.006	.005	.004	.003	.003	.002	.002	.002	.001	.001	.001	.001	*	*	*
25	.009	.007	.006	.005	.004	.003	.003	.002	.002	.001	.001	.001	.001	.001	.001	*	*	*
30	.003	.003	.002	.002	.001	.001	.001	.001	*	*	*	*	*	*	*	*	*	*
35	.001	.001	.001	.001	*	*	*	*	*	*	*	*	*	*	*	*	*	*
40	*	*	*	*	*	*	*	*	*	*	*	*	*	*	*	*	*	*
45	*	*	*	*	*	*	*	*	*	*	*	*	*	*	*	*	*	*
50	*	*	*	*	*	*	*	*	*	*	*	*	*	*	*	*	*	*

*PVIF is zero to three decimal places.

EXAMPLE

Loretta Callahan would like to accumulate $500 000 by the time she retires in 20 years. If she can earn an 8.61 percent return annually, how much must she invest today to have $500 000 in 20 years? Since the unknown variable is the present value (*PV*), the calculator input will be as shown at left.

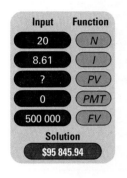

Where:

N	= 20 years
I	= 8.61 percent
PV	= present value, or the amount that would have to be deposited today
PMT	= payment, which is not applicable in this example
FV	= $500 000

Thus, Loretta would have to invest $95 845.94 today to accumulate $500 000 in 20 years if she really earns 8.61 percent annually.

Use a financial calculator to determine the present value of a single sum by calculating the present value of $50 000 in five years if the money is invested at an interest rate of 8 percent. This is the example used earlier to illustrate the present value tables. Your answer should be $34 050. Your answer may vary slightly due to rounding.

FUTURE VALUE OF AN ANNUITY

Earlier in the chapter, you saw how your money can grow from a single deposit. An alternative way to accumulate funds over time is through an ordinary annuity, which represents a stream of equal payments (or investments) that occur at the end of each period. For example, if you make a $30 deposit at the end of each month for 100 months, this is an ordinary annuity. As another example, you may invest $1000 at the end of each year for 10 years. There is a simple and quick method to determine the future value of an annuity. If the payment changes over time, the payment stream does not reflect an annuity. You can still determine the future value of a payment stream that does not reflect an annuity, but the computation process is more complicated.

An alternative to an ordinary annuity is an annuity due, which is a series of equal cash flow payments that occur at the beginning of each period. Thus, an annuity due differs from an ordinary annuity in that the payments occur at the beginning instead of the end of the period.

The best way to illustrate the future value of an ordinary annuity is through the use of timelines, which show payments received or paid over time.

ordinary annuity
A series of equal cash flow payments that occur at the end of each period.

annuity due
A series of equal cash flow payments that occur at the beginning of each period.

timelines
Diagrams that show payments received or paid over time.

EXAMPLE

You plan to invest $100 at the end of every year for the next three years. You expect to earn an annual interest rate of 10 percent on the funds you invest. Using a timeline, the cash flows from this annuity can be represented as follows:

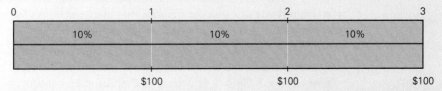

You would like to know how much money will be in your investment account at the end of the third year. This amount is the future value of the annuity. The first step in calculating the future value of the annuity is to treat each payment as a single sum and determine the future value of each payment individually. Next, add up the individual future values to obtain the future value of the annuity.

Since the first payment will be invested from the end of year 1 to the end of year 3, it will be invested for two years. Since the second payment will be invested from the end of year 2 to the end of year 3, it will be invested for one year. The third payment is made at the end of year 3, the point in time at which we want to determine the future value of the annuity. Hence, the third-year payment will not accumulate any interest. Using the future value in Table A-1 to obtain the *FVIF* for two years and 10 percent ($FVIF_{10\%,2} = 1.21$) and the *FVIF* for one year and 10 percent ($FVIF_{10\%,1} = 1.10$), the future value of your annuity can be determined as follows:

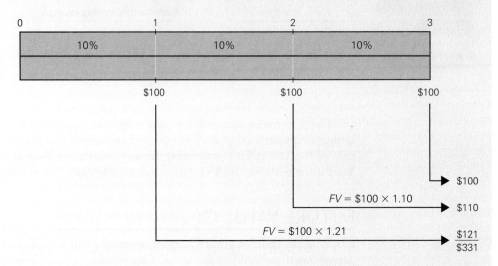

Adding up the individual future values shows that the future value of this annuity is $331 (that is, you will have $331 in your account at the end of the third year). Notice that $300 of the $331 represents the three $100 payments. Thus, the remaining $31 of the $331 is the combined interest you earned on the three payments.

Using the Future Value Annuity Table

future value interest factor for an annuity (FVIFA)
A factor multiplied by the periodic savings level (annuity) to determine how the savings will accumulate over time.

Computing the future value of an annuity by looking up each individual single-sum *FVIF* is rather tedious. Consequently, Table A-3 lists the factors for various interest rates and periods (years). These factors are referred to as future value interest factors for an annuity ($FVIFA_{i,n}$), where i is the periodic interest rate and n is the number of payments in the annuity. The annuity payment (*PMT*) can be multiplied by the *FVIFA* to determine the future value of the annuity ($FVA = PMT \times FVIFA$). Each column in the table lists an interest rate, while each row lists the period of concern.

EXAMPLE

Suppose that you have won the lottery and will receive $150 000 at the end of every year for the next 20 years. As soon as you receive the payments, you will invest them at your bank at an interest rate of 7 percent annually. How much will be in your account at the end of 20 years (assuming that you do not make any withdrawals)?

To find the answer, you must determine the future value of the annuity. (The stream of cash flows is in the form of an annuity since the payments are equal in value and equally spaced in time.) Using Table A-3 to determine the factor, look in the $i = 7\%$ column and the $n = 20$ periods row. Table A-3 shows that this factor is 40.995.

(continued)

Table A-3 Future Value Interest Factors for $1 Annuity Compounded at i Percent for n Periods: $FVA = PMT \times FVIFA_{i,n}$

Period	1%	2%	3%	4%	5%	6%	7%	8%	9%	10%	11%	12%	13%	14%	15%	16%	17%	18%	19%	20%
1	1.000	1.000	1.000	1.000	1.000	1.000	1.000	1.000	1.000	1.000	1.000	1.000	1.000	1.000	1.000	1.000	1.000	1.000	1.000	1.000
2	2.010	2.020	2.030	2.040	2.050	2.060	2.070	2.080	2.090	2.100	2.110	2.120	2.130	2.140	2.150	2.160	2.170	2.180	2.190	2.200
3	3.030	3.060	3.091	3.122	3.152	3.184	3.215	3.246	3.278	3.310	3.342	3.374	3.407	3.440	3.472	3.506	3.539	3.572	3.606	3.640
4	4.060	4.122	4.184	4.246	4.310	4.375	4.440	4.506	4.573	4.641	4.710	4.779	4.850	4.921	4.993	5.066	5.141	5.215	5.291	5.368
5	5.101	5.204	5.309	5.416	5.526	5.637	5.751	5.867	5.985	6.105	6.228	6.353	6.480	6.610	6.742	6.877	7.014	7.154	7.297	7.442
6	6.152	6.308	6.468	6.633	6.802	6.975	7.153	7.336	7.523	7.716	7.913	8.115	8.323	8.535	8.754	8.977	9.207	9.442	9.683	9.930
7	7.214	7.434	7.662	7.898	8.142	8.394	8.654	8.923	9.200	9.487	9.783	10.089	10.405	10.730	11.067	11.414	11.772	12.141	12.523	12.916
8	8.286	8.583	8.892	9.214	9.549	9.897	10.260	10.637	11.028	11.436	11.859	12.300	12.757	13.233	13.727	14.240	14.773	15.327	15.902	16.499
9	9.368	9.755	10.159	10.583	11.027	11.491	11.978	12.488	13.021	13.579	14.164	14.776	15.416	16.085	16.786	17.518	18.285	19.086	19.923	20.799
10	10.462	10.950	11.464	12.006	12.578	13.181	13.816	14.487	15.193	15.937	16.722	17.549	18.420	19.337	20.304	21.321	22.393	23.521	24.709	25.959
11	11.567	12.169	12.808	13.486	14.207	14.972	15.784	16.645	17.560	18.531	19.561	20.655	21.814	23.044	24.349	25.733	27.200	28.755	30.403	32.150
12	12.682	13.412	14.192	15.026	15.917	16.870	17.888	18.977	20.141	21.384	22.713	24.133	25.650	27.271	29.001	30.850	32.824	34.931	37.180	39.580
13	13.809	14.680	15.618	16.627	17.713	18.882	20.141	21.495	22.953	24.523	26.211	28.029	29.984	32.088	34.352	36.786	39.404	42.218	45.244	48.496
14	14.947	15.974	17.086	18.292	19.598	21.015	22.550	24.215	26.019	27.975	30.095	32.392	34.882	37.581	40.504	43.672	47.102	50.818	54.841	59.196
15	16.097	17.293	18.599	20.023	21.578	23.276	25.129	27.152	29.361	31.772	34.405	37.280	40.417	43.842	47.580	51.659	56.109	60.965	66.260	72.035
16	17.258	18.639	20.157	21.824	23.657	25.672	27.888	30.324	33.003	35.949	39.190	42.753	46.671	50.980	55.717	60.925	66.648	72.938	79.850	87.442
17	18.430	20.012	21.761	23.697	25.840	28.213	30.840	33.750	36.973	40.544	44.500	48.883	53.738	59.117	65.075	71.673	78.978	87.067	96.021	105.930
18	19.614	21.412	23.414	25.645	28.132	30.905	33.999	37.450	41.301	45.599	50.396	55.749	61.724	68.393	75.836	84.140	93.404	103.739	115.265	128.116
19	20.811	22.840	25.117	27.671	30.539	33.760	37.379	41.446	46.018	51.158	56.939	63.439	70.748	78.968	88.211	98.603	110.283	123.412	138.165	154.739
20	22.019	24.297	26.870	29.778	33.066	36.785	40.995	45.762	51.159	57.274	64.202	72.052	80.946	91.024	102.443	115.379	130.031	146.626	165.417	186.687
21	23.239	25.783	28.676	31.969	35.719	39.992	44.865	50.422	56.764	64.002	72.264	81.698	92.468	104.767	118.809	134.840	153.136	174.019	197.846	225.024
22	24.471	27.299	30.536	34.248	38.505	43.392	49.005	55.456	62.872	71.402	81.213	92.502	105.489	120.434	137.630	157.414	180.169	206.342	236.436	271.028
23	25.716	28.845	32.452	36.618	41.430	46.995	53.435	60.893	69.531	79.542	91.147	104.602	120.203	138.295	159.274	183.600	211.798	244.483	282.359	326.234
24	26.973	30.421	34.426	39.082	44.501	50.815	58.176	66.764	76.789	88.496	102.173	118.154	136.829	158.656	184.166	213.976	248.803	289.490	337.007	392.480
25	28.243	32.030	36.459	41.645	47.726	54.864	63.248	73.105	84.699	98.346	114.412	133.333	155.616	181.867	212.790	249.212	292.099	342.598	402.038	471.976
30	34.784	40.567	47.575	56.084	66.438	79.057	94.459	113.282	136.305	164.491	199.018	241.330	293.192	356.778	434.738	530.306	647.423	790.932	966.698	1181.865
35	41.659	49.994	60.461	73.651	90.318	111.432	138.234	172.314	215.705	271.018	341.583	431.658	546.663	693.552	881.152	1120.699	1426.448	1816.607	2314.173	2948.294
40	48.885	60.401	75.400	95.024	120.797	154.758	199.630	259.052	337.872	442.580	581.812	767.080	1013.667	1341.979	1779.048	2360.724	3134.412	4163.094	5529.711	7343.715
45	56.479	71.891	92.718	121.027	159.695	212.737	285.741	386.497	525.840	718.881	986.613	1358.208	1874.086	2590.464	3585.031	4965.191	6879.008	9531.258	13203.105	18280.914
50	64.461	84.577	112.794	152.664	209.341	290.325	406.516	573.756	815.051	1163.865	1668.723	2399.975	3459.344	4994.301	7217.488	10435.449	15088.805	21812.273	31514.492	45496.094

Table A-3 (Continued)

Period	21%	22%	23%	24%	25%	26%	27%	28%	29%	30%	31%	32%	33%	34%	35%	40%	45%	50%
1	1.000	1.000	1.000	1.000	1.000	1.000	1.000	1.000	1.000	1.000	1.000	1.000	1.000	1.000	1.000	1.000	1.000	1.000
2	2.210	2.220	2.230	2.240	2.250	2.260	2.270	2.280	2.290	2.300	2.310	2.320	2.330	2.340	2.350	2.400	2.450	2.500
3	3.674	3.708	3.743	3.778	3.813	3.848	3.883	3.918	3.954	3.990	4.026	4.062	4.099	4.136	4.172	4.360	4.552	4.750
4	5.446	5.524	5.604	5.684	5.766	5.848	5.931	6.016	6.101	6.187	6.274	6.362	6.452	6.542	6.633	7.104	7.601	8.125
5	7.589	7.740	7.893	8.048	8.207	8.368	8.533	8.700	8.870	9.043	9.219	9.398	9.581	9.766	9.954	10.946	12.022	13.188
6	10.183	10.442	10.708	10.980	11.259	11.544	11.837	12.136	12.442	12.756	13.077	13.406	13.742	14.086	14.438	16.324	18.431	20.781
7	13.321	13.740	14.171	14.615	15.073	15.546	16.032	16.534	17.051	17.583	18.131	18.696	19.277	19.876	20.492	23.853	27.725	32.172
8	17.119	17.762	18.430	19.123	19.842	20.588	21.361	22.163	22.995	23.858	24.752	25.678	26.638	27.633	28.664	34.395	41.202	49.258
9	21.714	22.670	23.669	24.712	25.802	26.940	28.129	29.369	30.664	32.015	33.425	34.895	36.429	38.028	39.696	49.152	60.743	74.887
10	27.274	28.657	30.113	31.643	33.253	34.945	36.723	38.592	40.556	42.619	44.786	47.062	49.451	51.958	54.590	69.813	89.077	113.330
11	34.001	35.962	38.039	40.238	42.566	45.030	47.639	50.398	53.318	56.405	59.670	63.121	66.769	70.624	74.696	98.739	130.161	170.995
12	42.141	44.873	47.787	50.895	54.208	57.738	61.501	65.510	69.780	74.326	79.167	84.320	89.803	95.636	101.840	139.234	189.734	257.493
13	51.991	55.745	59.778	64.109	68.760	73.750	79.106	84.853	91.016	97.624	104.709	112.302	120.438	129.152	138.484	195.928	276.114	387.239
14	63.909	69.009	74.528	80.496	86.949	93.925	101.465	109.611	118.411	127.912	138.169	149.239	161.183	174.063	187.953	275.299	401.365	581.858
15	78.330	85.191	92.669	100.815	109.687	119.346	129.860	141.302	153.750	167.285	182.001	197.996	215.373	234.245	254.737	386.418	582.980	873.788
16	95.779	104.933	114.983	126.010	138.109	151.375	165.922	181.867	199.337	218.470	239.421	262.354	287.446	314.888	344.895	541.985	846.321	1311.681
17	116.892	129.019	142.428	157.252	173.636	191.733	211.721	233.790	258.145	285.011	314.642	347.307	383.303	422.949	466.608	759.778	1228.165	1968.522
18	142.439	158.403	176.187	195.993	218.045	242.583	269.885	300.250	334.006	371.514	413.180	459.445	510.792	567.751	630.920	1064.689	1781.838	2955.783
19	173.351	194.251	217.710	244.031	273.556	306.654	343.754	385.321	431.868	483.968	542.266	607.467	680.354	761.786	852.741	1491.563	2584.665	4431.672
20	210.755	237.986	268.783	303.598	342.945	387.384	437.568	494.210	558.110	630.157	711.368	802.856	905.870	1021.792	1152.200	2089.188	3748.763	6648.508
21	256.013	291.343	331.603	377.461	429.681	489.104	556.710	633.589	720.962	820.204	932.891	1060.769	1205.807	1370.201	1556.470	2925.862	5436.703	9973.762
22	310.775	356.438	408.871	469.052	538.101	617.270	708.022	811.993	931.040	1067.265	1223.087	1401.215	1604.724	1837.068	2102.234	4097.203	7884.215	14961.645
23	377.038	435.854	503.911	582.624	673.626	778.760	900.187	1040.351	1202.042	1388.443	1603.243	1850.603	2135.282	2462.669	2839.014	5737.078	11433.109	22443.469
24	457.215	532.741	620.810	723.453	843.032	982.237	1144.237	1332.649	1551.634	1805.975	2101.247	2443.795	2840.924	3300.974	3833.667	8032.906	16579.008	33666.207
25	554.230	650.944	764.596	898.082	1054.791	1238.617	1454.180	1706.790	2002.608	2348.765	2753.631	3226.808	3779.428	4424.301	5176.445	11247.062	24040.555	50500.316
30	1445.111	1767.044	2160.459	2640.881	3227.172	3941.953	4812.891	5873.172	7162.785	8729.805	10632.543	12940.672	15737.945	19124.434	23221.258	60500.207	154105.313	383500.000
35	3755.814	4783.520	6090.227	7750.094	9856.746	12527.160	15909.480	20188.742	25596.512	32422.090	41028.887	51868.563	65504.199	82634.625	104134.500	325394.688	*	*
40	9749.141	12936.141	17153.691	22728.367	30088.621	39791.957	52570.707	69376.562	91447.375	120389.375	*	*	*	*	*	*	*	*
45	25294.223	34970.230	48300.660	66638.937	91831.312	126378.937	173692.875	238384.312	326686.375	447005.062	*	*	*	*	*	*	*	*

*Not shown because of space limitations.

480

The next step is to determine the future value of your lottery annuity:

$$FVA = PMT \times FVIFA_{i,n}$$
$$= PMT \times FVIFA_{7\%,20}$$
$$= \$150\ 000 \times 40.995$$
$$= \$6\ 149\ 250$$

Thus, after 20 years, you will have $6 149 250 if you invest all of your lottery payments in an account earning an interest rate of 7 percent.

As an exercise, use the future value annuity table to determine the future value of five $172 payments, received at the end of every year, and earning an interest rate of 14 percent. Your answer should be $1137.

Using a Financial Calculator to Determine the Future Value of an Annuity

Using a financial calculator to determine the future value of an annuity is similar to using the calculator to determine the future value of a single dollar amount. As before, the known variables must be input in order to solve for the unknown variable.

The following example illustrates the use of a financial calculator to determine the future value of an annuity.

EXAMPLE

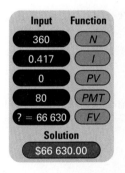

Input	Function
360	N
0.417	I
0	PV
80	PMT
? = 66 630	FV
Solution	
$66 630.00	

You have instructed your employer to deduct $80 from your paycheque every month and automatically invest the money at an annual interest rate of 5 percent. You intend to use this money for your retirement in 30 years. How much will be in the account at that time?

This problem differs from the others we have seen so far, in that the payments are received on a monthly (not annual) basis. You would like to obtain the future value of the annuity and consequently need the number of periods, the periodic interest rate, the present value, and the payment. Because there are 12 months in a year, there are 30 × 12 = 360 periods. Furthermore, since the annual interest rate is 5 percent, the monthly interest rate is 5 ÷ 12 = 0.417 percent. Also, note that to determine the future value of an annuity, most financial calculators require an input of 0 for the present value. The payment in this problem is 80.

The input for the financial calculator would be as shown at the left.

Thus, you will have $66 630 when you retire in 30 years as a result of your monthly investment.

PRESENT VALUE OF AN ANNUITY

Just as the future value of an annuity can be obtained by compounding the individual cash flows of the annuity and then totalling them, the present value of an annuity can be obtained by discounting the individual cash flows of the annuity and totalling them.

Referring to our earlier example of an ordinary annuity with three $100 payments and an interest rate of 10 percent, we can graphically illustrate the process as follows:

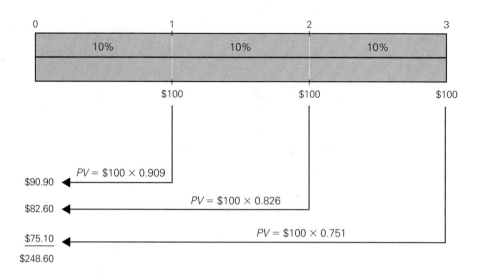

Adding up the individual present values leads to the conclusion that the present value of this annuity is $248.60. Therefore, three $100 payments received at the end of each of the next three years are worth $248.60 to you today if you can invest your money at an interest rate of 10 percent.

present value interest
factor for an annuity
(PVIFA)
A factor multiplied by a
periodic savings level
(annuity) to determine the
present value of the annuity.

Using the Present Value Annuity Table

Table A-4 shows the present value interest factors for an annuity ($PVIFA_{i,n}$) for various interest rates (i) and time periods (n) in the annuity. Each column in the table lists an interest rate, while each row lists a time period.

EXAMPLE

You have just won the lottery. As a result of your luck, you will receive $82 000 at the end of every year for the next 25 years. A financial firm offers you a lump sum of $700 000 in return for these payments. If you can invest your money at an annual interest rate of 9 percent, should you accept the offer?

This problem requires you to determine the present value of the lottery annuity. If the present value of the annuity is higher than the amount offered by the financial firm, you should reject the offer. Using Table A-4 to determine the factor, look in the $i = 9\%$ column and the $n = 25$ periods row. Table A-4 shows that this factor is 9.823.

The next step is to determine the present value of the annuity:

$$PVA = PMT \times PVIFA_{i,n}$$

$$= PMT \times PVIFA_{9\%,25}$$

$$= \$82\ 000 \times 9.823$$

$$= \$805\ 486$$

Thus, the 25 payments of $82 000 each are worth $805 486 to you today if you can invest your money at an interest rate of 9 percent. Consequently, you should reject the financial firm's offer to purchase your future lottery payments for $700 000.

As an exercise, use the present value annuity table to determine the present value of eight $54 payments, received at the end of every year and earning an interest rate of 14 percent. Your answer should be $250.50, which means that the eight payments have a present value of $250.50.

Table A-4 Present Value Interest Factors for $1 Annuity Discounted at i Percent for n Periods: $PVA = PMT \times PVIFA_{i,n}$

Period	1%	2%	3%	4%	5%	6%	7%	8%	9%	10%	11%	12%	13%	14%	15%	16%	17%	18%	19%	20%
1	.990	.980	.971	.962	.952	.943	.935	.926	.917	.909	.901	.893	.885	.877	.870	.862	.855	.847	.840	.833
2	1.970	1.942	1.913	1.886	1.859	1.833	1.808	1.783	1.759	1.736	1.713	1.690	1.668	1.647	1.626	1.605	1.585	1.566	1.547	1.528
3	2.941	2.884	2.829	2.775	2.723	2.673	2.624	2.577	2.531	2.487	2.444	2.402	2.361	2.322	2.283	2.246	2.210	2.174	2.140	2.106
4	3.902	3.808	3.717	3.630	3.546	3.465	3.387	3.312	3.240	3.170	3.102	3.037	2.974	2.914	2.855	2.798	2.743	2.690	2.639	2.589
5	4.853	4.713	4.580	4.452	4.329	4.212	4.100	3.993	3.890	3.791	3.696	3.605	3.517	3.433	3.352	3.274	3.199	3.127	3.058	2.991
6	5.795	5.601	5.417	5.242	5.076	4.917	4.767	4.623	4.486	4.355	4.231	4.111	3.998	3.889	3.784	3.685	3.589	3.498	3.410	3.326
7	6.728	6.472	6.230	6.002	5.786	5.582	5.389	5.206	5.033	4.868	4.712	4.564	4.423	4.288	4.160	4.039	3.922	3.812	3.706	3.605
8	7.652	7.326	7.020	6.733	6.463	6.210	5.971	5.747	5.535	5.335	5.146	4.968	4.799	4.639	4.487	4.344	4.207	4.078	3.954	3.837
9	8.566	8.162	7.786	7.435	7.108	6.802	6.515	6.247	5.995	5.759	5.537	5.328	5.132	4.946	4.772	4.607	4.451	4.303	4.163	4.031
10	9.471	8.983	8.530	8.111	7.722	7.360	7.024	6.710	6.418	6.145	5.889	5.650	5.426	5.216	5.019	4.833	4.659	4.494	4.339	4.192
11	10.368	9.787	9.253	8.760	8.306	7.887	7.499	7.139	6.805	6.495	6.207	5.938	5.687	5.453	5.234	5.029	4.836	4.656	4.486	4.327
12	11.255	10.575	9.954	9.385	8.863	8.384	7.943	7.536	7.161	6.814	6.492	6.194	5.918	5.660	5.421	5.197	4.988	4.793	4.611	4.439
13	12.134	11.348	10.635	9.986	9.394	8.853	8.358	7.904	7.487	7.013	6.750	6.424	6.122	5.842	5.583	5.342	5.118	4.910	4.715	4.533
14	13.004	12.106	11.296	10.563	9.899	9.295	8.745	8.244	7.786	7.367	6.982	6.628	6.302	6.002	5.724	5.468	5.229	5.008	4.802	4.611
15	13.865	12.849	11.938	11.118	10.380	9.712	9.108	8.560	8.061	7.606	7.191	6.811	6.462	6.142	5.847	5.575	5.324	5.092	4.876	4.675
16	14.718	13.578	12.561	11.652	10.838	10.106	9.447	8.851	8.313	7.824	7.379	6.974	6.604	6.265	5.954	5.668	5.405	5.162	4.938	4.730
17	15.562	14.292	13.166	12.166	11.274	10.477	9.763	9.122	8.544	8.022	7.549	7.120	6.729	6.373	6.047	5.749	5.475	5.222	4.990	4.775
18	16.398	14.992	13.754	12.659	11.690	10.828	10.059	9.372	8.756	8.201	7.702	7.250	6.840	6.467	6.128	5.818	5.534	5.273	5.033	4.812
19	17.226	15.679	14.324	13.134	12.085	11.158	10.336	9.604	8.950	8.365	7.839	7.366	6.938	6.550	6.198	5.877	5.584	5.316	5.070	4.843
20	18.046	16.352	14.878	13.590	12.462	11.470	10.594	9.818	9.129	8.514	7.963	7.469	7.025	6.623	6.259	5.929	5.628	5.353	5.101	4.870
21	18.857	17.011	15.415	14.029	12.821	11.764	10.836	10.017	9.292	8.649	8.075	7.562	7.102	6.687	6.312	5.973	5.665	5.384	5.127	4.891
22	19.661	17.658	15.937	14.451	13.163	12.042	11.061	10.201	9.442	8.772	8.176	7.645	7.170	6.743	6.359	6.011	5.696	5.410	5.149	4.909
23	20.456	18.292	16.444	14.857	13.489	12.303	11.272	10.371	9.580	8.883	8.266	7.718	7.230	6.792	6.399	6.044	5.723	5.432	5.167	4.925
24	21.244	18.914	16.936	15.247	13.799	12.550	11.469	10.529	9.707	8.985	8.348	7.784	7.283	6.835	6.434	6.073	5.746	5.451	5.182	4.937
25	22.023	19.524	17.413	15.622	14.094	12.783	11.654	10.675	9.823	9.077	8.422	7.843	7.330	6.873	6.464	6.097	5.766	5.467	5.195	4.948
30	25.808	22.396	19.601	17.292	15.373	13.765	12.409	11.258	10.274	9.427	8.694	8.055	7.496	7.003	6.566	6.177	5.829	5.517	5.235	4.979
35	29.409	24.999	21.487	18.665	16.374	14.498	12.948	11.655	10.567	9.644	8.855	8.176	7.586	7.070	6.617	6.215	5.858	5.539	5.251	4.992
40	32.835	27.356	23.115	19.793	17.159	15.046	13.332	11.925	10.757	9.779	8.951	8.244	7.634	7.105	6.642	6.233	5.871	5.548	5.258	4.997
45	36.095	29.490	24.519	20.720	17.774	15.456	13.606	12.108	10.881	9.863	9.008	8.283	7.661	7.123	6.654	6.242	5.877	5.552	5.261	4.999
50	39.196	31.424	25.730	21.482	18.256	15.762	13.801	12.233	10.962	9.915	9.042	8.304	7.675	7.133	6.661	6.246	5.880	5.554	5.262	4.999

Table A-4 (Continued)

Period	21%	22%	23%	24%	25%	26%	27%	28%	29%	30%	31%	32%	33%	34%	35%	40%	45%	50%
1	.826	.820	.813	.806	.800	.794	.787	.781	.775	.769	.763	.758	.752	.746	.741	.714	.690	.667
2	1.509	1.492	1.474	1.457	1.440	1.424	1.407	1.392	1.376	1.361	1.346	1.331	1.317	1.303	1.289	1.224	1.165	1.111
3	2.074	2.042	2.011	1.981	1.952	1.923	1.896	1.868	1.842	1.816	1.791	1.766	1.742	1.719	1.696	1.589	1.493	1.407
4	2.540	2.494	2.448	2.404	2.362	2.320	2.280	2.241	2.203	2.166	2.130	2.096	2.062	2.029	1.997	1.849	1.720	1.605
5	2.926	2.864	2.803	2.745	2.689	2.635	2.583	2.532	2.483	2.436	2.390	2.345	2.302	2.260	2.220	2.035	1.876	1.737
6	3.245	3.167	3.092	3.020	2.951	2.885	2.821	2.759	2.700	2.643	2.588	2.534	2.483	2.433	2.385	2.168	1.983	1.824
7	3.508	3.416	3.327	3.242	3.161	3.083	3.009	2.937	2.868	2.802	2.739	2.677	2.619	2.562	2.508	2.263	2.057	1.883
8	3.726	3.619	3.518	3.421	3.329	3.241	3.156	3.076	2.999	2.925	2.854	2.786	2.721	2.658	2.598	2.331	2.109	1.922
9	3.905	3.786	3.673	3.566	3.463	3.366	3.273	3.184	3.100	3.019	2.942	2.868	2.798	2.730	2.665	2.379	2.144	1.948
10	4.054	3.923	3.799	3.682	3.570	3.465	3.364	3.269	3.178	3.092	3.009	2.930	2.855	2.784	2.715	2.414	2.168	1.965
11	4.177	4.035	3.902	3.776	3.656	3.544	3.437	3.335	3.239	3.147	3.060	2.978	2.899	2.824	2.752	2.438	2.185	1.977
12	4.278	4.127	3.985	3.851	3.725	3.606	3.493	3.387	3.286	3.190	3.100	3.013	2.931	2.853	2.779	2.456	2.196	1.985
13	4.362	4.203	4.053	3.912	3.780	3.656	3.538	3.427	3.322	3.223	3.129	3.040	2.956	2.876	2.799	2.469	2.204	1.990
14	4.432	4.265	4.108	3.962	3.824	3.695	3.573	3.459	3.351	3.249	3.152	3.061	2.974	2.892	2.814	2.478	2.210	1.993
15	4.489	4.315	4.153	4.001	3.859	3.726	3.601	3.483	3.373	3.268	3.170	3.076	2.988	2.905	2.825	2.484	2.214	1.995
16	4.536	4.357	4.189	4.033	3.887	3.751	3.623	3.503	3.390	3.283	3.183	3.088	2.999	2.914	2.834	2.489	2.216	1.997
17	4.576	4.391	4.219	4.059	3.910	3.771	3.640	3.518	3.403	3.295	3.193	3.097	3.007	2.921	2.840	2.492	2.218	1.998
18	4.608	4.419	4.243	4.080	3.928	3.786	3.654	3.529	3.413	3.304	3.201	3.104	3.012	2.926	2.844	2.494	2.219	1.999
19	4.635	4.442	4.263	4.097	3.942	3.799	3.664	3.539	3.421	3.311	3.207	3.109	3.017	2.930	2.848	2.496	2.220	1.999
20	4.657	4.460	4.279	4.110	3.954	3.808	3.673	3.546	3.427	3.316	3.211	3.113	3.020	2.933	2.850	2.497	2.221	1.999
21	4.675	4.476	4.292	4.121	3.963	3.816	3.679	3.551	3.432	3.320	3.215	3.116	3.023	2.935	2.852	2.498	2.221	2.000
22	4.690	4.488	4.302	4.130	3.970	3.822	3.684	3.556	3.436	3.323	3.217	3.118	3.025	2.936	2.853	2.498	2.222	2.000
23	4.703	4.499	4.311	4.137	3.976	3.827	3.689	3.559	3.438	3.325	3.219	3.120	3.026	2.938	2.854	2.499	2.222	2.000
24	4.713	4.507	4.318	4.143	3.981	3.831	3.692	3.562	3.441	3.327	3.221	3.121	3.027	2.939	2.855	2.499	2.222	2.000
25	4.721	4.514	4.323	4.147	3.985	3.834	3.694	3.564	3.442	3.329	3.222	3.122	3.028	2.939	2.856	2.499	2.222	2.000
30	4.746	4.534	4.339	4.160	3.995	3.842	3.701	3.569	3.447	3.332	3.225	3.124	3.030	2.941	2.857	2.500	2.222	2.000
35	4.756	4.541	4.345	4.164	3.998	3.845	3.703	3.571	3.448	3.333	3.226	3.125	3.030	2.941	2.857	2.500	2.222	2.000
40	4.760	4.544	4.347	4.166	3.999	3.846	3.703	3.571	3.448	3.333	3.226	3.125	3.030	2.941	2.857	2.500	2.222	2.000
45	4.761	4.545	4.347	4.166	4.000	3.846	3.704	3.571	3.448	3.333	3.226	3.125	3.030	2.941	2.857	2.500	2.222	2.000
50	4.762	4.545	4.348	4.167	4.000	3.846	3.704	3.571	3.448	3.333	3.226	3.125	3.030	2.941	2.857	2.500	2.222	2.000

Using a Financial Calculator to Determine the Present Value of an Annuity

Determining the present value of an annuity with a financial calculator is similar to using the calculator to determine the present value of a single-sum payment. Again, the values of known variables are inserted to solve for the unknown variable.

EXAMPLE

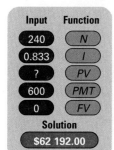

Input	Function
240	N
0.833	I
?	PV
600	PMT
0	FV
Solution	
$62 192.00	

A recent retiree, Dave Buzz receives his $600 pension monthly. He will receive this pension for 20 years. If Dave can invest his funds at an interest rate of 10 percent, he should be just as satisfied receiving this pension as receiving a lump sum payment today of what amount?

This problem requires us to determine the present value of the pension annuity. Because there are 20 × 12 = 240 months in 20 years, $n = 240$. The monthly (periodic) interest rate is 10 ÷ 12 = 0.833 percent. Thus, $i = 0.833$. Using these inputs with a financial calculator, we obtain the inputs shown to the left.

The present value is $62 192. If Dave is offered a lump sum of $62 192 today, he should accept it if he can invest his funds at a minimum of 10 percent annually.

Appendix B

Your Career

DETERMINING YOUR CAREER PATH

What career path is optimal for you? Review the factors described here that you should consider when determining your career path. Then, access the sources of information that are identified below to help make your selection.

Factors That May Affect Your Career Path

Perhaps the obvious first step in determining your career path is to consider your interests, and then identify the careers that fit those interests. Most people identify several possible career interests, which makes the decision difficult. However, you may be able to screen your list based on the following factors.

Educational and Skill Requirements. Some jobs may seem interesting but require more education and training than you are prepared to acquire. For example, the training required to be a doctor may be too extensive and time consuming. In addition, the entrance requirements are very high. Review the education and skills needed for each career that appeals to you. From your list of possible career paths, focus on those in which you already have or would be willing to achieve the necessary background, education, and skills.

Job Availability. There are some career paths that people think they would like to follow and could do so successfully, but the paths have a limited supply of open positions relative to applicants. For example, many people want to be actors or actresses, or waiters at very expensive restaurants. Consider the number of job positions available compared to the number of applicants pursuing those jobs.

Compensation. Most people consider compensation to be an important criterion when considering job positions. Some career tracks may be enjoyable but do not provide sufficient compensation. Information on compensation for various types of jobs is available on many websites. For example, at www.workopolis.com you can insert the type of job position you are curious about and obtain salary ranges for that position in a particular location in Canada.

Sources of Information That Can Help You Select Your Career Path

Consider the following sources of information as you attempt to establish your list of career options from which to select your optimal career path.

Books on Careers. There are many books that identify careers and describe the necessary skills for each one. Some books provide a broad overview, while others are more detailed. A broad overview is usually ideal when you are first identifying the various types of careers that exist. Then, once you narrow down the list, you can find a book that focuses on your chosen field, such as medicine, engineering, social work, and so on.

Courses.   Your college or university courses are a vital source of information about related careers. Courses in finance can help you understand the nature of the work in the financial services industry, accounting classes provide insight into the nature of the work that accountants do, and courses in entrepreneurship may help you understand the job skills required of a self-employed individual. Even courses that are broader in scope (for example, courses in management) may be applicable to many different types of jobs, including those of financial advisers, accountants, and entrepreneurs. If you enjoyed your basic management course, you may like a job in which you are involved in managing people, production processes, or services.

Job Experience.   Management trainee positions allow some exposure to a particular type of job and allow you to learn what tasks people in a field do as part of their daily work. Such experience is especially useful because many jobs are likely to differ from your perception.

Contacts.   For any specific job description in which you are interested, identify people whom you know in that field. Set up an informational interview so that you can ask detailed questions about the job.

The Internet.   A great deal of information on careers is available on the Internet. To explore the types of careers that are available, and the skills needed for each, go to www.monster.ca. Here you can learn about jobs in numerous fields, including finance, law, management, construction, health, agriculture, and broadcasting. Be careful, however, to note the size of the pool of applicants for any type of job you are interested in. It is much easier to land the job you want (assuming that you have the requisite skills) when the number of openings is large compared to the number of qualified people interested in that position. Your expectations with respect to your first job should be reasonable given your knowledge and experience.

At some point, you have to narrow your choices so that you can focus more time on the careers that intrigue you the most. The Internet is very valuable in offering insight even after you narrow your choices.

Personality Tests.   You can get feedback on the type of career that fits you based on a personality test. Some of these tests are expensive, and there are mixed opinions about whether they can more accurately pinpoint a job that fits your personality than if you simply use the criteria described above. Some tests are offered for free online, such as the personality test at www.typefocus.com. Be aware that free tests normally do not offer as detailed an analysis as tests that you pay for.

GETTING THE SKILLS YOU NEED

Once you decide on the type of position you want, your next step is to determine the training and education you will need to qualify for it.

Training
To gather general information, go to websites such as the Service Canada Training and Careers site (www.jobsetc.ca). There you can learn about the training needed for a specific job description and how to obtain it.

Be careful when reviewing information about various training courses that are available. Much information found on websites specifically devoted to training is provided by companies that want to sell you training. For this reason, carefully evaluate whether the training offered will get you the job that you want. As an extreme example, some companies provide training for modelling or acting. People are well aware of celebrities who became very rich by modelling or acting. However, taking a few courses is unlikely to lead to major success in those fields. Try to determine whether the market truly rewards people who pay for training by a particular company before you pay for it.

The training by some companies may be certified, which could distinguish it from others. However, a certificate does not always mean that the training is valuable or will lead to employment. In some cases, there may simply be fewer jobs than the number of people who are properly trained. In other cases, the training might not qualify you for a specific job position.

Education

A degree in a career-oriented major, such as accounting or business, will prepare you for a job in that specific field. A liberal arts degree, on the other hand, will allow you to choose from a broad range of careers in areas such as marketing, journalism, teaching, and publishing.

The reputations of post-secondary institutions vary substantially, and some schools may be much more credible than others in preparing you for a specific job position. Some jobs require that your degree be acquired from an accredited university, while other jobs require you to have the applied training that is available from technical institutes. It may be important to learn about the accreditation standards of any post-secondary institution that you wish to attend. Because there are different accreditation agencies, it is important to determine the type of accreditation that would be important for the specific type of job you plan to pursue.

Learn as much as you can about the college or department of the university in which you are considering taking courses. What percentage of recent graduates passed a standardized exam that must be taken after graduation (for fields like financial services and accounting)? Are recent graduates being hired in the field that you wish to enter when you graduate? You may be able to get answers to these questions from the department where you would be taking courses.

Expanding Your Education

A master's degree or a doctorate provides you with additional knowledge and skills that may allow you to qualify for better jobs. However, there are costs associated with pursuing such degrees, and you must weigh them against the potential benefits.

Costs. The cost of a graduate degree is substantial, and should be estimated carefully before you make your decision to pursue one. Because the cost varies substantially among programs, you may find a program that is less expensive than others and yet satisfies your needs. Consider tuition and fees, room and board, and the opportunity cost of pursuing the degree. If you enrol in a full-time program, your opportunity cost is the salary you could have earned if you had worked during that time. You may also find it necessary to give up some social activities.

Benefits. Individuals often pursue a master's degree or doctorate to increase their marketability. There are many job positions that require a degree beyond a bachelor of arts or a bachelor of science. If your goal is to increase your marketability, determine whether an additional degree truly results in better job opportunities. In addition, determine what type of degree would make the biggest difference. For example, engineers commonly obtain a master's in business administration (MBA) rather than a master's in engineering because the MBA is intended to give them stronger management skills.

If you decide to pursue a master's degree or doctorate, determine whether the university you select would make a big difference in your marketability. Some programs have a national or international reputation, while others are known only within a local area.

CHANGING YOUR CAREER

Many people do not realize what career would make them happy until they have pursued the wrong one. In some cases, they can use their existing experience in a new career, while in other cases they must be retrained. The obvious barrier to switching careers is the amount of time already invested in a particular career. In addition, if training is necessary, the costs of changing careers may be high. Nevertheless, people should seriously consider switching if they truly believe a different career would be more satisfying, but first they should obtain detailed information about the new job description.

Be realistic in assessing any career switch; look closely at your expectations. Would you really be more satisfied? How much training is involved? Would you have to stop working while you are retrained? How long will it take you to get a job once you are retrained? Is the compensation higher or lower in the new career versus your existing career? Are there more chances for advancement? Is there more job security?

Self-Employment

At some point in your life, you may decide that you want to leave your current job to become self-employed. There are millions of people who started their own businesses and are much more satisfied than when they were employed by a firm or government agency. Self-employment, however, is not for everyone; some people are excellent workers but are not effective at creating business ideas or running a business.

To start your own business, you need a business plan that will be successful. Normally, this requires the creation of a product or service that is more desirable to customers than other products or services already offered in the marketplace. Your advantage may be creating a product that you can offer at a lower price than similar products in the marketplace. Alternatively, your advantage may be higher quality. Keep in mind that competitors may be quick to adjust once you start your business and it may be more difficult than you anticipated to gain market share. A business is accountable to its customers, and if it does not satisfy customers, it will not survive.

CRITERIA USED TO ASSESS APPLICANTS

When you pursue a job, you will likely be competing against many other applicants. By recognizing what the employer is seeking, you may be able to distinguish yourself from the other applicants. Understanding the criteria that employers use to assess applicants will help you determine whether you possess the right qualifications for the job.

Your Application

An application may request general information about your education background, such as the schools you attended and your major and/or minor in college. It may also request information about your previous work experience. Applications are used to determine whether applicants have the knowledge and the experience to perform well in the job position.

Your Resumé

Your resumé should provide your educational background and work experience. Companies receive numerous resumés for job positions, so it helps to describe succinctly the skills that may help you stand out from other applicants. If you obtain the skills and training that you need to pursue the job you desire, creating a resumé is relatively easy. Most career websites offer tips on how you can improve your resumé (for example, http://resume.monster.ca/6920_EN-CA_p1.asp). You can also post your resumé on many job websites such as www.monster.ca and www.careerbuilder.ca.

Job Interviews

The interview process helps an employer obtain additional information such as how you interact with people and respond to specific situations. Various personality traits can be assessed, such as:

- your punctuality
- your ability to work with others

- your ability to communicate
- your ability to grasp concepts
- your listening skills
- your ability to recognize your limitations
- your ability to take orders
- your ability to give orders
- your potential as a leader

There are numerous books and websites that offer advice about various aspects of job interviews, such as grooming, body language, etiquette, and even answering tough questions about deficiencies in your resumé. Another source of up-to-date information on interviewing is the career centre at your college or university, which often offers seminars on effective interview techniques.

You may be asked to provide references during the interview process. You should be prepared to provide a list of business and personal references with addresses and contact numbers upon request. You should ask your references for permission before using them and be sure to thank them if they are contacted.

CONCLUSION

You have control over your career path. If you follow guidelines such as those described in this appendix, you can increase your chances of achieving the job and career path you want. However, keep in mind that your career aspirations and opportunities change over time. Therefore, your career planning does not end with your first job but continues throughout your career path, and even plays a role in your decision to retire someday.

Glossary

accident benefits coverage Insures against the cost of medical care for you and other passengers in your car.

add-on interest method A method of determining the monthly payment on a loan; it involves calculating the interest that must be paid on the loan amount, adding together interest and loan principal, and dividing by the number of payments.

all perils coverage Protects the home and any other structures on the property against all events except those that are specifically excluded by the policy.

allowable capital loss The portion of a capital loss that you can deduct from taxable capital gains.

amortization The expected number of years it will take a borrower to pay off the entire mortgage loan balance.

amortize To repay the principal of a loan (the original amount borrowed) through a series of equal payments. A loan repaid in this manner is said to be amortized.

annual percentage rate (APR) Measures the finance expenses (including interest and all other expenses) on a loan annually.

annuity due A series of equal cash flow payments that occur at the beginning of each period.

asset allocation The process of allocating money across financial assets (such as mutual funds, stocks, and bonds) with the objective of achieving a desired return while maintaining risk at a tolerable level.

asset turnover ratio A measure of efficiency; computed as sales divided by average total assets.

assets What you own.

auto insurance policy Specifies the coverage provided by an insurance company for a particular individual and vehicle.

automated banking machine (ABM) A machine individuals can use to deposit and withdraw funds at any time of day.

average collection period A measure of efficiency; computed as accounts receivable divided by average daily sales.

average tax rate The amount of tax you pay as a percentage of your total taxable income.

back-end load mutual funds Mutual funds that charge a fee if units are redeemed within a set period of time.

balance sheet A financial statement that indicates a firm's sources of funds and how it has invested those funds as of a particular point in time.

banker's acceptances (BAs) Short-term debt securities issued by large firms that are guaranteed by a bank.

beneficiaries (heirs) The persons specified in a will to receive part of an estate.

beneficiary The named individual who receives life insurance payments upon the death of the insured.

bequest A gift that results from the instructions provided in a will.

board lot Shares bought or sold in multiples of typically 100 shares. The size of the board lot depends on the price of the security.

bodily injury liability coverage Protects you against liability associated with injuries you cause to others.

bond mutual funds Funds that sell units to individuals and use this money to invest in bonds.

bonds Certificates issued by borrowers to raise funds.

bonds Long-term debt securities issued by government agencies or corporations that are collateralized by assets.

budget A cash flow statement that is based on forecasted cash flows (income and expenses) for a future time period.

budget method (or needs method) A method that determines how much life insurance is needed based on the household's future expected expenses and current financial situation.

budget planning (budgeting) The process of forecasting future income, expenses, and savings goals.

buy stop order An order to buy a stock when the price rises to a specified level.

call (prepayment) risk The risk that a callable bond will be called.

call feature A feature on a bond that allows the issuer to repurchase the bond from the investor before maturity.

Canada Health Act Establishes the criteria and conditions related to insured health care services that provinces and territories must meet in order to receive money from the federal government for health care.

Canada Health and Social Transfer (CHST) The largest federal transfer of money to the provinces and territories, providing them with cash payments and tax transfers in support of health care, post-secondary education, social assistance, and social services, including early childhood development.

Canada Savings Bonds (CSBs) Short-term to medium-term, high-quality debt securities issued by the Government of Canada.

capital gain Money earned when you sell an asset at a higher price than you paid for it.

capital loss Occurs when you sell an asset for a lower price than you paid for it.

captive (or exclusive) insurance agent Works for one particular insurance company.

cash value The portion of the premium in excess of insurance-related and company expenses that is invested by the insurance company on behalf of the policy owner.

cash value policy Pays you the value of the damaged property after considering its depreciation.

certified cheque A cheque that can be cashed immediately by the payee without the payee having to wait for the bank to process and clear it.

chartered banks Financial institutions that accept deposits and use the funds to provide business and personal loans. These banks are federally incorporated.

cheque register A booklet in your chequebook where you record the details of each transaction you make, including deposits, cheque writing, withdrawals, and bill payments.

clawback Used to reduce (i.e., clawback) a particular government benefit provided to taxpayers who have an income that exceeds a certain threshold amount.

closed mortgage Restricts your ability to pay off the mortgage balance during the mortgage term unless you are willing to pay a financial penalty.

closed-end funds Funds that sell units to investors but will not redeem these units; instead, the fund's units are traded on a stock exchange.

codicil A document that specifies changes in an existing will.

collateral Assets of a borrower that back a loan in the event that the borrower defaults. Collateral is a form of security for the lender.

collision insurance Insures against costs of damage to your car resulting from an accident in which the driver of your car is at fault.

commercial paper A short-term debt security issued by large firms that is guaranteed by the issuing firm.

common stock A certificate issued by a firm to raise funds that represents partial ownership in the firm.

comprehensive coverage Insures you against damage to your car that results from something other than a collision, such as floods, theft, fire, hail, explosions, riots, vandalism, and various other perils.

compounding The process of earning interest on interest.

consumer price index (CPI) A measure of inflation that represents the increase in the prices of consumer products such as groceries, household products, housing, and gasoline over time.

consumer proposal An offer made by a debtor to his or her creditors to modify his or her payments.

conventional mortgage A mortgage where the down payment is at least 25 percent of the home's appraised value.

conversion option Allows you to convert your term insurance policy into a whole life policy that will be in effect for the rest of your life.

convertible bond A bond that can be converted into a stated number of shares of the issuer's stock at a specified price.

corporate bonds Long-term debt securities issued by large firms.

correlation A mathematical measure that describes how two securities' prices move in relation to one another.

cost of insurance The insurance-related expenses incurred by a life insurance company to provide the actual death benefit, sometimes referred to as the pure cost of dying.

credit Funds provided by a creditor to a borrower that the borrower will repay with interest or fees in the future.

credit management Decisions regarding how much credit to obtain to support your spending and which sources of credit to use.

credit reports Reports provided by credit bureaus that document a person's credit payment history.

credit unions/caisses populaires Provincially incorporated co-operative financial institutions that are owned and controlled by their members.

creditor An individual or company to whom you owe money.

creditor insurance Term life insurance where the beneficiary of the policy is a creditor.

current liabilities Personal debts that will be paid in the near future (within a year).

current ratio The ratio of a firm's short-term assets to its short-term liabilities.

day traders Investors who buy stocks and then sell them on the same day.

death benefit The total amount paid tax-free to the beneficiary upon the death of the policy owner.

debentures Long-term debt securities issued by corporations that are secured only by the corporation's promise to pay.

debit card A card that is not only used for identification for your bank, but also allows you to make purchases that are charged against an existing chequing account.

debt ratio A measure of financial leverage that calculates the proportion of total assets financed with debt.

declining redemption schedule A fee schedule where the back-end load charge reduces with each year an investor holds the fund.

decreasing term insurance A type of creditor insurance, such as mortgage life insurance, where the life insurance face amount decreases each time a regular payment is made on debt that is amortized over a period of time.

deductible A set dollar amount that you are responsible for paying before any coverage is provided by your insurer.

deduction An expense that can be deducted from total income to determine taxable income.

default Occurs when a company borrows money through the issuance of debt securities and does not pay either the interest or the principal.

default risk Risk that the borrower of funds will not repay the creditors.

defined-benefit pension plan An employer-sponsored retirement plan that guarantees you a specific amount of income when you retire, based on your salary and years of employment.

defined-contribution pension plan An employer-sponsored retirement plan where the contribution rate, not the benefit amount, is based on a specific formula.

demutualization Refers to the transformation of a firm from a member-owned organization to a publicly owned, for-profit organization.

depository institutions Financial institutions that accept deposits from and provide loans to individuals and businesses.

disability income insurance A monthly insurance benefit paid to you in the event that you are unable to work as a result of an injury or an illness.

discount A bond that is trading at a price below its par value; the amount by which a closed-end fund's unit price in the secondary market is below the fund's NAVPU.

discount brokerage firm A brokerage firm that executes transactions but does not offer investment advice.

discounting The process of obtaining present values.

dividend income Income received from corporations in the form of dividends paid on stock or on mutual funds that hold stock. Dividend income represents the profit due to part owners of the company.

dumpster diving Occurs when an identity thief goes through your trash for discarded items that reveal personal information that can be used for fraudulent purposes.

durable power of attorney for health care A legal document granting a person the power to make specific health care decisions for you.

economic growth The growth in a country's economy over a particular period.

efficient stock market A market in which stock prices fully reflect information that is available to investors.

emergency fund A portion of savings that you have allocated to short-term needs such as unexpected expenses in order to maintain adequate liquidity.

Employment Insurance (EI) Government benefits that are payable for periods of time when you are away from work due to specific situations.

enduring (continuing) power of attorney A legal document granting a person the immediate power to make any decisions and/or commitments for you, even when you are mentally incapacitated.

English form will A will that contains the signature of the testator and of two witnesses who were present when the testator signed the will.

equity The market value of your home less any outstanding mortgage balance and/or debts held by others that are secured against your property.

equity mutual funds Funds that sell units to individuals and use this money to invest in stocks.

equity of a home The market value of a home minus the debt owed on the home.

estate The assets of a deceased person after all debts are paid.

estate planning Determining how your wealth will be distributed before and/or after your death. A financial statement that measures a person's income and expenses.

estate planning The act of planning how your wealth will be allocated on or before your death.

exchange rate risk The risk that the value of a bond may drop if the currency denominating the bond weakens against the Canadian dollar.

exchange traded fund (ETF) A portfolio of securities whose value moves in tandem with a particular stock index. Unlike a mutual fund, these funds trade on an exchange or stock market.

excise taxes Special taxes levied on certain consumer products such as cigarettes, alcohol, and gasoline.

exclusion A term appearing in insurance contracts or policies that describes items or circumstances that are specifically excluded from insurance coverage.

executor (personal representative) The person designated in a will to execute your instructions regarding the distribution of your assets.

extendible bond A short-term bond that allows the investor to extend the maturity date of the bond.

face amount The amount stated on the face of the policy that will be paid on the death of the insured.

Facility Association Ensures that drivers unable to obtain insurance with an individual company are able to obtain the coverage they need to operate their vehicles legally.

Federal Crown corporation bonds Debt securities issued by corporations established by the federal government.

finance and lease companies Non-depository institutions that specialize in providing personal loans or leases to individuals.

finance charge The interest and fees you must pay as a result of using credit.

financial conglomerates Financial institutions that offer a diverse set of financial services to individuals or firms.

financial leverage A firm's reliance on debt to support its operations.

Financial Planners Standards Council (FPSC) A not-for-profit organization that was created to benefit the public through the development, enforcement, and promotion of the highest competency and ethical standards in financial planning.

fiscal policy How the government imposes taxes on individuals and corporations and how it spends tax revenues.

fixed-rate mortgage A mortgage in which a fixed interest rate is specified for the term of the mortgage.

front-end load mutual funds Mutual funds that charge a fee at the time of purchase, which is paid to stockbrokers or other financial service advisers who execute transactions for investors.

full-service brokerage firm A brokerage firm that offers investment advice and executes transactions.

fundamental analysis The valuation of stocks based on an examination of fundamental characteristics such as revenue, earnings, and/or the sensitivity of the firm's performance to economic conditions.

future value interest factor for an annuity (FVIFA) A factor multiplied by the periodic savings level (annuity) to determine how the savings will accumulate over time.

general power of attorney A legal document granting a person the immediate power to make any decisions and/or commitments for you, with specific limitations.

global bond funds Mutual funds that focus on bonds issued by non-Canadian firms or governments.

Government of Canada bonds Debt securities issued by the Canadian government.

grace period The period the insurance company extends to the policy owner before the policy will lapse due to nonpayment.

gross debt service ratio (GDSR) Your mortgage-related debt payments—including mortgage loan repayments, heating costs, property taxes, and any condo fees—divided by your total monthly gross household income.

gross domestic product (GDP) The total market value of all products and services produced in a country.

group term insurance Term insurance provided to a designated group of people with a common bond that generally has lower-than-typical premiums.

growth stocks Shares of firms with substantial growth opportunities.

guaranteed investment certificate (GIC) An instrument issued by a depository institution that specifies a minimum investment, an interest rate, and a maturity date.

health insurance A group of insurance benefits provided to a living individual as a result of sickness or injury.

hedge funds Limited partnerships that manage portfolios of funds for wealthy individuals and financial institutions.

high ratio mortgage A mortgage where the down payment is less than 25 percent of the home's appraised value.

high-yield bonds Bonds issued by less stable corporations that are subject to a higher degree of default risk.

holograph will A will that is written solely in the handwriting of the testator and that does not require the signature of any witnesses.

Home Buyers' Plan (HBP) A tax-free RRSP withdrawal option that is available to Canadians who would like to buy their first home.

home equity loan A loan in which the equity in a home serves as collateral.

home inspection A report on the condition of the home.

home inventory Contains detailed information about your personal property that can be used when filing a claim.

homeowner's insurance Provides insurance in the event of property damage, theft, or personal and third party liability relating to home ownership.

household assets Items normally owned by a household, such as a car and furniture.

identity theft Occurs when an individual uses personal, identifying information unique to you, such as your Social Insurance Number, without your permission for their personal gain.

income method Determines how much life insurance is needed based on the policyholder's annual income.

income statement A financial statement that measures a firm's revenues, expenses, and earnings over a particular period of time.

income stocks Stocks that provide investors with periodic income in the form of large dividends.

income trust A flow-through investment vehicle that generates income and capital gains for investors.

indemnification The concept of putting an insured individual back into the same position he or she was in prior to the event that resulted in insurance benefits being paid.

independent insurance agent Represents many different insurance companies.

index funds Mutual funds that attempt to mirror the movements of an existing equity index.

individual investors Individuals who invest funds in securities.

inefficient stock market A market in which stock prices do not reflect all public information that is available to investors.

inflation The increase in the general level of prices of products and services over a specified period.

initial public offering (IPO) The first offering of a firm's shares to the public.

insider information Non-public information known by employees and other professionals that is not known by outsiders. It is illegal to use insider information.

insolvent A person who owes at least $1000 and is unable to pay his or her debts as they come due.

instalment credit Credit provided for specific purchases, with interest charged on the amount borrowed. It is repaid on a regular basis, generally with blended payments.

instalment payments settlement The payment of life insurance benefits owed to a beneficiary as a stream of equal payments over a specified number of years.

institutional investors Professionals responsible for managing large pools of money, such as pension funds, on behalf of their clients.

insurance agent Represents one or more insurance companies and recommends insurance policies that fit customers' needs.

insurance companies Non-depository institutions that sell insurance to protect individuals or firms from risks that can incur financial loss.

insurance planning Determining the types and amount of insurance needed to protect your assets.

insurance policy Contract between an insurance company and the policy owner.

insured health care services Medically necessary hospital, physician, and surgical-dental services provided to insured persons.

insured person An eligible resident of a province. Does not include someone who may be covered by other federal or provincial legislation.

inter vivos trust A trust in which you assign the management of your assets to a trustee while you are living.

interest adjustment Occurs when there is a difference between the date you take possession of your home and the date from which your lender calculates your first mortgage payment.

interest income Interest earned from investments in various types of savings accounts at financial institutions; from investments in debt securities such as term deposits, GICs, and CSBs; and from loans to other individuals, companies, and governments.

interest payments settlement A method of paying life insurance benefits in which the insurance company retains the amount owed to the beneficiary for a specified number of years and pays interest to the beneficiary.

interest rate risk The risk that a bond's price will decline in response to an increase in interest rates; the risk that occurs because of changes in the interest rate. This risk affects funds that invest in debt securities and other income-oriented securities.

interest rate strategy Selecting bonds based on interest rate expectations.

intestate The condition of dying without a will.

inventory turnover A measure of efficiency; computed as the cost of goods sold divided by average daily inventory.

investment dealers Non-depository institutions that facilitate the purchase or sale of various investments by firms or individuals by providing investment banking and brokerage services.

investment objective In a prospectus, a brief statement about the general goal of the mutual fund.

investment risk Uncertainty surrounding not only the potential return on an investment but also its future potential value.

investment strategy In a prospectus, a summary of the types of securities that are purchased by the mutual fund to achieve its objective.

irrevocable inter vivos trust An inter vivos trust that cannot be changed, although it may provide income to the settlor.

letter of last instruction A supplement to a will that can describe preferences regarding funeral arrangements and indicate where any key financial documents are stored.

liabilities What you owe; your debt.

life annuity A financial contract that provides regular payments for one's lifetime.

life insurance Insurance that provides a payment to a specified beneficiary when the insured dies.

life insured The individual who is covered in the life insurance policy.

Lifelong Learning Plan (LLP) A tax-free RRSP withdrawal that is available to full-time students who temporarily would like to use an RRSP to finance their education.

limit order An order to buy or sell a stock only if the price is within limits that you specify.

limited (non-continuing) power of attorney A legal document granting a person the power to make specific decisions for you in the event that you are temporarily incapacitated.

limited payment policy Allows you to pay premiums over a specified period but remain insured for life.

liquid assets Financial assets that can be easily converted into cash without a loss in value.

liquidity Access to ready cash, including savings and credit, to cover short-term or unexpected expenses; the ease with which the investor can convert the investment into cash without a loss of capital.

living benefits (accelerated death benefits) Benefits that allow the policyholder to receive a portion of death benefits prior to death.

living will A simple legal document in which individuals specify their preferences if they become mentally or physically disabled.

loan contract A contract that specifies the terms of a loan as agreed to by the borrower and the lender.

locked-in retirement account (LIRA) A private pension plan that is created when an individual transfers vested money from an employer-sponsored pension plan.

long-term care insurance Covers expenses associated with long-term health conditions that cause individuals to need help with everyday tasks.

long-term liabilities Debt that will be paid over a period longer than one year.

lump sum settlement A single payment of all benefits owed to a beneficiary upon the death of the policyholder.

management expense ratio (MER) The annual expenses incurred by a fund on a percentage basis, calculated as annual expenses of the fund divided by the net asset value of the fund; the result of this calculation is then divided by the number of units outstanding.

margin call A request from a brokerage firm for the investor to increase the cash in the account in order to return the margin to the minimum level.

marginal tax rate The percentage of tax you pay on your next dollar of taxable income.

market analysis An estimate of the price of a home based on the prices of similar homes in the area.

market makers Securities dealers who are required to trade actively in the market so that liquidity is maintained when natural market forces cannot provide sufficient liquidity.

market order An order to buy or sell a stock at its prevailing market price.

market risk The susceptibility of a mutual fund's performance to general market conditions.

marketability The ease with which an investor can convert an investment into cash.

maturity matching strategy Investing in bonds that will generate payments to match future expenses.

maturity or term With respect to a loan, the life or duration of the loan.

medicare An interlocking system of ten provincial and three territorial health insurance plans provided by the governments, including the federal government.

monetary policy Techniques used by the Bank of Canada (central bank) to affect the economy of the country.

money management A series of decisions made over a short-term period regarding income and expenses; decisions regarding how much money to retain in liquid form and how to allocate the funds among short-term investment instruments.

money market funds (MMFs) Accounts that pool money from individuals and invest in securities that have short-term maturities, such as one year or less.

money market mutual funds Funds that sell units to individuals and use this money to invest in cash and investments that can be converted to cash quickly (very liquid investments).

money orders and drafts Products that direct your bank to pay a specified amount to the person named on them.

mortality rate The number of deaths in a population or in a subgroup of the population.

mortgage backed securities Represent a pool of CMHC-insured residential mortgages that are issued by banks and other financial institutions.

mortgage companies Non-depository institutions that specialize in providing mortgage loans to individuals.

mortgage refinancing Paying off an existing mortgage with a new mortgage that has a lower interest rate.

mortgage term The period of time over which the mortgage interest rate and other terms of the mortgage contract will not change.

Multiple Listing Service (MLS) An information database of homes available for sale through realtors who are members of the service.

municipal bonds Long-term debt securities issued by local government agencies.

mutual fund companies Non-depository institutions that sell units to individuals and use the proceeds to invest in securities to create mutual funds.

mutual funds Investment companies that sell units to individuals and invest the proceeds in an overall portfolio of investment instruments such as bonds or stocks.

named perils coverage Protects the home and any other structures on the property against only those events named in the policy.

net asset value (NAV) The market value of the securities that a mutual fund has purchased minus any liabilities and fees owed.

net asset value per unit (NAVPU) Calculated by dividing the NAV by the number of units in the fund.

net cash flows Disposable (after-tax) income minus expenses.

net profit margin A measure of profitability that measures net profit as a percentage of sales.

net worth The value of what you own minus the value of what you owe.

no-load mutual funds Funds that sell directly to investors and do not charge a fee.

non-depository institutions Financial institutions that do not offer federally insured deposit accounts but provide various other financial services.

non-forfeiture options The options available to a policy owner who would like to discontinue or cancel a policy that has cash value.

non-participating policy A life insurance policy that is not eligible to receive policy dividends.

non-refundable tax credits The portion of the credit that is not needed to reduce your tax liability will not be paid to you and cannot be carried forward to reduce your tax liability in the future.

normal retirement age The age by which employees are entitled to receive 100 percent of the pension income they are eligible for.

notarial will A formal type of will that is commonly used in Quebec and is completed in the presence of a notary (lawyer).

odd lot Less than a board lot of that particular stock.

on margin Purchasing a stock with a small amount of personal funds and a portion of the funds borrowed from a brokerage firm.

on-stop order An order to execute a transaction when the stock price reaches a specified level; a special form of limit order.

open mortgage Allows you to pay off the mortgage balance at any time during the mortgage term.

open-end mutual funds Funds that sell units directly to investors and will redeem those units whenever investors wish to "cash" in.

operating profit margin A firm's operating profit divided by sales.

opportunity cost What you give up as a result of a decision.

ordinary annuity A stream of equal payments that are received or paid at equal intervals in time at the end of a period.

overdraft protection An arrangement that protects a customer who writes a cheque for an amount that exceeds their chequing account balance; it is a short-term loan from the depository institution where the chequing account is maintained.

over-the-counter (OTC) market An electronic communications network that allows investors to buy or sell securities.

paid-up insurance A permanent life insurance policy that results from exercising a non-forfeiture option on a policy that has accumulated cash value.

par value For a bond, its face value, or the amount returned to the investor at the maturity date when the bond is due.

participating policy A life insurance policy that is eligible to receive policy dividends.

passive strategy Investing in a diversified portfolio of bonds that are held for a long period of time.

payday loan A short-term loan provided in advance of receiving a paycheque.

pension adjustment Calculates the remaining annual contribution room available to an individual after taking into account any employer-sponsored pension plan contributions.

pension assignment Occurs when a married or common-law couple decides to share their CPP retirement pensions in order to reduce their income taxes.

pensionable earnings The amount of income you earn between the year's basic exemption (YBE) and the year's maximum pensionable earnings (YMPE).

per capita debt The amount of debt each individual in Canada would have if total debt (consumer debt plus mortgages) was spread equally across the population.

peril A hazard or risk you face.

permanent insurance Life insurance that continues to provide insurance for as long as premiums are paid.

personal balance sheet A summary of your assets (what you own), your liabilities (what you owe), and your net worth (assets minus liabilities).

personal cash flow statement A financial statement that measures a person's income and expenses.

personal finance (personal financial planning) The process of planning your spending, financing, and investing activities, while taking into account uncontrollable events such as death or disability, in order to optimize your financial situation over time.

personal financial plan A plan that specifies your financial goals, describes the spending, financing, and investing activities that are intended to achieve those goals over time, and the risk management strategies that are required to protect against uncontrollable events such as death or disability.

personal income taxes Taxes imposed on income earned.

personal property floater An extension of the homeowner's insurance policy that allows you to itemize your valuables.

pharming Similar to phishing, but targeted at larger audiences, it directs users to bogus websites to collect their personal information.

phishing Occurs when pretexting happens online.

policy dividend A refund of premiums that occurs when the long-term assumptions the insurance company made with respect to the cost of insurance, company expenses, and investment returns have changed.

policy owner The individual who owns all rights and obligations to the policy.

portfolio A set of multiple investments in different assets.

pre-approval certificate Provides you with a guideline on how large a mortgage you can afford based on your financial situation.

preferential share The dollar value of estate assets that will be distributed to the surviving spouse before assets are distributed among all potential beneficiaries.

preferred stock A certificate issued by a firm to raise funds that entitles shareholders to first priority to receive dividends.

premium A bond that is trading at a price above its par value; the amount by which a closed-end fund's unit price in the secondary market is above the fund's NAVPU; the cost of obtaining insurance.

present value interest factor for an annuity (PVIFA) A factor multiplied by a periodic savings level (annuity) to determine the present value of the annuity.

prestige cards Credit cards, such as gold cards or platinum cards, issued by a financial institution to individuals who have an exceptional credit standing.

pretexting Occurs when individuals access personal information under false pretenses.

price–earnings (P/E) method A method of valuing stocks in which a firm's earnings per share are multiplied by the mean industry price–earnings (P/E) ratio.

price–sales (P/S) method A method of valuing stocks in which the revenue per share of a specific firm is multiplied by the mean industry ratio of share price to revenue.

primary market A market in which newly issued securities are traded.

prime rate The interest rate a bank charges its best customers.

probate A legal process that declares a will valid and ensures the orderly distribution of assets.

property damage liability coverage Protects against losses that result when the policy owner damages another person's property with his or her car.

provincial bonds Debt securities issued by the various provincial governments.

put feature A feature on a bond that allows the investor to redeem the bond at its face value before it matures.

range of returns Returns of a specific investment over a given period.

real estate investment trusts (REITs) Income trusts that pool investments from individuals and use the proceeds to invest in real estate.

real estate Rental property and land.

real return bonds Long-term debt securities issued by the Government of Canada that protect you from inflation risk.

refundable tax credit The portion of the credit that is not needed to reduce your tax liability (because it is already zero) may be paid to you.

registered annuities Annuities that are created using assets from a registered plan, such as an RRSP.

registered retirement savings plan (RRSP) A type of private pension that enables you to save for your retirement on a tax-deferred basis.

reinstatement The process of completing a reinstatement application to restore a policy that is in lapse status.

renewability option Allows you to renew your policy for another term once the existing term expires.

rental property Housing or commercial property that is rented out to others.

replacement cost policy Pays you the actual cost of replacing the damaged property.

residue Refers to the amount remaining in an estate after all financial obligations, such as the payment of debts, expenses, taxes, and bequests, have been fulfilled.

retail (or proprietary) credit card A credit card that is honoured only by a specific retail establishment.

retirement planning Determining how much money you should set aside each year for retirement and how you should invest those funds.

return on assets A measure of profitability; computed as net profit divided by total assets.

return on equity A measure of profitability; computed as net profit divided by the owners' investment in the firm (shareholders' equity).

reverse mortgage A secured loan that allows older Canadians to generate income using the equity in their homes without having to sell this asset.

revocable inter vivos trust An inter vivos trust that can be dissolved.

revolving open-end credit Credit provided up to a specified maximum amount based on income, debt level, and credit history; interest is charged each month on the outstanding balance.

riders Options that allow you to customize a life insurance policy to your specific needs.

rights or things Income that was owed to the deceased taxpayer but not paid at the time of death, but that would have been included in income had the taxpayer not died.

risk Exposure to events (or perils) that can cause a financial loss.

risk management Decisions about whether and how to protect against risk.

risk premium An additional return beyond the risk-free rate you could earn from an investment; the extra yield required by investors to compensate for default risk.

risk tolerance A person's ability to accept risk, usually defined as a potential loss of return and/or loss of capital.

safety deposit box A box at a financial institution in which a customer can store documents, jewellery, and other valuables. It is secure because it is stored in the bank's vault.

second mortgage A secured mortgage loan that is subordinate (or secondary) to another loan.

secondary market A market in which existing securities such as debt securities are traded.

sector funds Mutual funds that focus on stocks in a specific industry or sector, such as technology stocks.

secured loan A loan that is backed or secured by collateral.

sell stop order An order to sell a stock when the price falls to a specified level.

settlement options The ways in which a beneficiary can receive life insurance benefits in the event that the policyholder dies.

settlor The person who creates a trust.

shoulder surfing Occurs in public places where you can be readily seen or heard by someone standing close by.

simple interest Interest on a loan computed as a percentage of the existing loan amount (or principal). Compounding is not taken into account.

simplified prospectus A document that provides financial information about a mutual fund, including expenses and past performance.

skimming Occurs when identity thieves steal your credit or debit card number by copying the information contained in the magnetic strip on the card.

spousal RRSP A type of RRSP where one spouse contributes to the plan and the other spouse is the beneficiary, or annuitant.

standard deviation The degree of volatility in the stock's returns over time.

stock exchanges Facilities that allow investors to purchase or sell existing stocks.

stocks Certificates representing partial ownership of a firm.

stop payment A financial institution's notice that it will not honour a cheque if someone tries to cash it; usually occurs in response to a request by the writer of the cheque.

strip bonds Long-term debt securities issued by the Government of Canada that do not offer coupon payments.

student loan A loan provided to finance a portion of a student's expenses while pursuing post-secondary education.

T4 slip A document provided to you by your employer that displays your salary and all deductions associated with your employment with that specific employer for the previous year. Your employer is required to provide you with a T4 slip by February 28.

T4A slip A document provided to you when you receive income other than salary income.

tax avoidance A term used to describe the process of legally applying tax law to reduce or eliminate taxes payable in ways that the CRA considers potentially abusive of the spirit of the Income Tax Act.

tax credits Specific amounts used directly to reduce tax liability.

tax evasion Occurs when taxpayers attempt to deceive the CRA by knowingly reporting less tax payable than what the law obligates them to pay.

tax planning Involves activities and transactions that reduce or eliminate tax.

taxable capital gain The portion of a capital gain that is subject to income tax. The portion included in income is called the inclusion amount and currently stands at 50 percent.

T-Bills Short-term debt securities issued by the Canadian government and sold at a discount.

technical analysis The valuation of stocks based on historical price patterns using various charting techniques.

tenant's insurance An insurance policy that protects your possessions within a house, condominium, or apartment that you are renting.

term annuity A financial contract that provides regular payments until a specified year.

term insurance Life insurance that is provided over a specified time period and does not build a cash value.

term to 100 insurance A form of permanent life insurance designed for the sole purpose of providing a benefit at death.

testamentary trust A trust created by a will.

third party liability A legal term that describes the person(s) who have experienced loss because of the insured.

ticker symbol The abbreviated term used to identify a stock for trading purposes.

times interest earned ratio A measure of financial leverage that indicates the ratio of the firm's earnings before interest and taxes to its total interest payments.

timelines Diagrams that show payments received or paid over time.

total debt service ratio (TDSR) Your mortgage-related debt payments plus all other consumer debt payments divided by your total monthly gross household income.

total income All reportable income from any source, including salary, wages, commissions, business income, government benefits, pension income, interest income, dividend income, and capital gains received during the tax year. Income received from sources outside Canada is also subject to Canadian income tax.

traveller's cheque A cheque written on behalf of an individual that will be charged against a large, well-known financial institution or credit card sponsor's account.

trust A legal document in which one person, the settlor, transfers assets to a trustee, who manages them for designated beneficiaries.

trust and loan companies Financial institutions that, in addition to providing services similar to a bank, can provide financial planning services, such as administering estates and acting as trustee in the administration of trust accounts.

trustee An individual or organization that is responsible for the management of assets held in trust for one or more of the beneficiaries of a will.

trustee in bankruptcy A person licensed to administer consumer proposals and bankruptcies and manage assets held in trust.

umbrella personal liability policy A supplement to auto and homeowner's insurance that provides additional personal liability coverage.

underinsured motorist coverage Insures against the additional cost of bodily injury when an accident is caused by a driver who has insufficient coverage.

underwriters Employees of an insurance company who determine the risk of specific insurance policies and decide what policies to offer and what premiums to charge.

underwriting The process of evaluating an insurance application based on the applicant's age, sex, smoking status, driving record, and other health and lifestyle considerations and then issuing insurance policies based on the responses.

uninsured motorist coverage Insures against the cost of bodily injury when an accident is caused by another driver who is not insured.

universal life insurance A form of permanent life insurance for which you do not pay a fixed premium and in which you can invest the cash value portion in a variety of investments.

unsecured loan A loan that is not backed by collateral.

value stocks Stocks of firms that are currently undervalued by the market for reasons other than the performance of the businesses themselves.

variable-rate mortgage (VRM) A mortgage where the interest charged on the loan changes in response to movements in a specific market-determined interest rate. The rate used is usually referred to as prime. Lenders will add a percentage to prime for the total mortgage rate.

vendor take-back mortgage A mortgage where the lender is the seller of the property.

venture capital Refers to investors' funds destined for risky, generally new businesses with tremendous growth potential.

vested Having a claim to the money in an employer-sponsored retirement account that has been reserved for you upon your retirement, even if you leave the company.

waiting period The period from the time you become disabled until you begin to receive disability income benefits.

whole life insurance A form of permanent life insurance that builds cash value based on a fixed premium that is payable for the life of the insured.

will A legal document that describes how your estate should be distributed upon your death. It can also identify a preferred guardian for any surviving minor children.

yield to maturity The annualized return on a bond if it is held until maturity.

Index

Note: Keywords and the pages on which they are defined are in bold.

Answers to Study Guide Questions

Chapter 1

Multiple Choice

1. c 2. d 3. b 4. c 5. d 6. b 7. a 8. c 9. a 10. d

True/False

1. T 2. T 3. F 4. T 5. F 6. F 7. F 8. T 9. T 10. F

Chapter 2

Multiple Choice

1. b 2. c 3. a 4. d 5. d 6. g 7. d 8. c 9. d 10. a

True/False

1. F 2. T 3. F 4. F 5. F 6. F 7. T 8. F 9. T 10. T

Chapter 3

Multiple Choice

1. c 2. c 3. b 4. d 5. d 6. b 7. d 8. b 9. d 10. d

True/False

1. F 2. F 3. T 4. T 5. T 6. F 7. T 8. F 9. F 10. F

Chapter 4

Multiple Choice

1. c 2. d 3. b 4. a 5. b 6. b 7. d 8. d 9. c 10. a

True/False

1. F 2. T 3. F 4. F 5. T 6. F 7. T 8. F 9. F 10. T

Chapter 5

Multiple Choice

1. b 2. b 3. a 4. d 5. b 6. a 7. a 8. d 9. c 10. e

True/False

1. F 2. F 3. T 4. T 5. T 6. T 7. T 8. F 9. F 10. T

Chapter 6

Multiple Choice

1. b 2. c 3. a 4. b 5. a 6. c 7. c 8. d 9. b 10. c

True/False

1. F 2. T 3. T 4. F 5. F 6. T 7. F 8. T 9. T 10. F

Chapter 7

Multiple Choice

1. b 2. a 3. a 4. d 5. a 6. c 7. d 8. c 9. a 10. b

True/False

1. T 2. F 3. F 4. T 5. T 6. F 7. F 8. F 9. F 10. T

Chapter 8

Multiple Choice

1. c 2. d 3. b 4. a 5. d 6. b 7. b 8. a 9. c 10. d

True/False

1. T 2. F 3. T 4. F 5. T 6. F 7. F 8. T 9. F 10. T

Chapter 9

Multiple Choice

1. a 2. d 3. b 4. c 5. b 6. d 7. c 8. a 9. b 10. d

True/False

1. F 2. F 3. T 4. F 5. F 6. T 7. T 8. T 9. T 10. F

Chapter 10

Multiple Choice

1. d 2. a 3. b 4. b 5. c 6. a 7. a 8. d 9. b 10. c

True/False

1. F 2. T 3. F 4. F 5. T 6. T 7. T 8. F 9. T 10. T

Chapter 11

Multiple Choice

1. c   2. b   3. a   4. a   5. d   6. d   7. c   8. b   9. c   10. a

True/False

1. F   2. T   3. T   4. F   5. T   6. F   7. F   8. T   9. F   10. T

Chapter 12

Multiple Choice

1. d   2. d   3. a   4. c   5. c   6. b   7. d   8. a   9. b   10. d

True/False

1. T   2. T   3. F   4. T   5. F   6. F   7. T   8. T   9. F   10. T

Chapter 13

Multiple Choice

1. a   2. c   3. d   4. c   5. b   6. a   7. b   8. d   9. b   10. a

True/False

1. F   2. F   3. F   4. T   5. F   6. F   7. T   8. F   9. T   10. F

Chapter 14

Multiple Choice

1. c   2. d   3. a   4. d   5. b   6. b   7. c   8. a   9. a   10. d

True/False

1. F   2. T   3. F   4. T   5. F   6. T   7. T   8. F   9. T   10. F

Chapter 15

Multiple Choice

1. b   2. c   3. c   4. d   5. b   6. a   7. d   8. b   9. c   10. a

True/False

1. T   2. F   3. F   4. F   5. T   6. F   7. T   8. T   9. T   10. T

Chapter 16

Multiple Choice

1. d   2. d   3. b   4. c   5. a   6. d   7. c   8. a   9. b   10. d

True/False

1. F   2. F   3. T   4. F   5. F   6. T   7. T   8. T   9. T   10. F

Chapter 17

Multiple Choice

1. a   2. c   3. b   4. b   5. a   6. d   7. c   8. a   9. b   10. d

True/False

1. T   2. F   3. T   4. F   5. T   6. T   7. F   8. F   9. T   10. T

Credits

pp. 126–127, information on the response to identity theft, adapted from Fact Sheet: Identity Theft: What it is and what you can do about it, Privacy Commissioner of Canada, 2004. Reproduced with the permission of the Minister of Public Works and Government Services Canada, 2008; pp. 172–174, information on closing costs, adapted from *Gimme' Shelter* Brochure, ATB Financial. Reprinted with permission of ATB Financial; pp.175–176, information on mortgage options, adapted from *Gimme' Shelter* Brochure, ATB Financial. Reprinted with permission of ATB Financial; p. 208, information on If You Are In an Auto Accident, adapted from www.ibc.ca/en/Car_Insurance/What_to_do_Accident.asp. Reprinted with permission of Insurance Bureau of Canada; pp. 374–375, information on types of bonds, adapted from www.tdcanadatrust.com/invest/fixedinc/index.jsp. Reprinted with permission of TD Canada Trust. Note that some content has been edited for this publication; pp. 432–437, information on the key components of a will, adapted from www.lawdepot.com. Reprinted with permission of LawDepot; pp. 436–437, information on changing your will, adapted from *Wealth Management & Estate Planning*, Third Edition, pp. 19–36, CFP® Education Program, CCH Canadian Limited, 2007. Reprinted with permission of CCH Canadian Limited.

"AS IS" LICENSE AGREEMENT AND LIMITED WARRANTY

READ THIS LICENSE CAREFULLY BEFORE OPENING THIS PACKAGE. BY OPENING THIS PACKAGE, YOU ARE AGREEING TO THE TERMS AND CONDITIONS OF THIS LICENSE. IF YOU DO NOT AGREE, DO NOT OPEN THE PACKAGE. PROMPTLY RETURN THE UNOPENED PACKAGE AND ALL ACCOMPANYING ITEMS TO THE PLACE YOU OBTAINED THEM. THESE TERMS APPLY TO ALL LICENSED SOFTWARE ON THE DISK EXCEPT THAT THE TERMS FOR USE OF ANY SHAREWARE OR FREEWARE ON THE DISKETTES ARE AS SET FORTH IN THE ELECTRONIC LICENSE LOCATED ON THE DISK:

1. GRANT OF LICENSE and OWNERSHIP: The enclosed computer programs and any data ("Software") are licensed, not sold, to you by Pearson Canada Inc. ("We" or the "Company") in consideration of your adoption of the accompanying Company textbooks and/or other materials, and your agreement to these terms. You own only the disk(s) but we and/or our licensors own the Software itself. This license allows instructors and students enrolled in the course using the Company textbook that accompanies this Software (the "Course") to use and display the enclosed copy of the Software for academic use only, so long as you comply with the terms of this Agreement. You may make one copy for back up only. We reserve any rights not granted to you.

2. USE RESTRICTIONS: You may not sell or license copies of the Software or the Documentation to others. You may not transfer, distribute or make available the Software or the Documentation, except to instructors and students in your school who are users of the adopted Company textbook that accompanies this Software in connection with the course for which the textbook was adopted. You may not reverse engineer, disassemble, decompile, modify, adapt, translate or create derivative works based on the Software or the Documentation. You may be held legally responsible for any copying or copyright infringement that is caused by your failure to abide by the terms of these restrictions.

3. TERMINATION: This license is effective until terminated. This license will terminate automatically without notice from the Company if you fail to comply with any provisions or limitations of this license. Upon termination, you shall destroy the Documentation and all copies of the Software. All provisions of this Agreement as to limitation and disclaimer of warranties, limitation of liability, remedies or damages, and our ownership rights shall survive termination.

4. DISCLAIMER OF WARRANTY: THE COMPANY AND ITS LICENSORS MAKE NO WARRANTIES ABOUT THE SOFTWARE, WHICH IS PROVIDED "AS-IS." IF THE DISK IS DEFECTIVE IN MATERIALS OR WORKMANSHIP, YOUR ONLY REMEDY IS TO RETURN IT TO THE COMPANY WITHIN 30 DAYS FOR REPLACEMENT UNLESS THE COMPANY DETERMINES IN GOOD FAITH THAT THE DISK HAS BEEN MISUSED OR IMPROPERLY INSTALLED, REPAIRED, ALTERED OR DAMAGED. THE COMPANY DISCLAIMS ALL WARRANTIES, EXPRESS OR IMPLIED, INCLUDING WITHOUT LIMITATION, THE IMPLIED WARRANTIES OF MERCHANTABILITY AND FITNESS FOR A PARTICULAR PURPOSE. THE COMPANY DOES NOT WARRANT, GUARANTEE OR MAKE ANY REPRESENTATION REGARDING THE ACCURACY, RELIABILITY, CURRENTNESS, USE, OR RESULTS OF USE, OF THE SOFTWARE.

5. LIMITATION OF REMEDIES AND DAMAGES: IN NO EVENT, SHALL THE COMPANY OR ITS EMPLOYEES, AGENTS, LICENSORS OR CONTRACTORS BE LIABLE FOR ANY INCIDENTAL, INDIRECT, SPECIAL OR CONSEQUENTIAL DAMAGES ARISING OUT OF OR IN CONNECTION WITH THIS LICENSE OR THE SOFTWARE, INCLUDING, WITHOUT LIMITATION, LOSS OF USE, LOSS OF DATA, LOSS OF INCOME OR PROFIT, OR OTHER LOSSES SUSTAINED AS A RESULT OF INJURY TO ANY PERSON, OR LOSS OF OR DAMAGE TO PROPERTY, OR CLAIMS OF THIRD PARTIES, EVEN IF THE COMPANY OR AN AUTHORIZED REPRESENTATIVE OF THE COMPANY HAS BEEN ADVISED OF THE POSSIBILITY OF SUCH DAMAGES. SOME JURISDICTIONS DO NOT ALLOW THE LIMITATION OF DAMAGES IN CERTAIN CIRCUMSTANCES, SO THE ABOVE LIMITATIONS MAY NOT ALWAYS APPLY.

6. GENERAL: THIS AGREEMENT SHALL BE CONSTRUED AND INTERPRETED ACCORDING TO THE LAWS OF THE PROVINCE OF ONTARIO. This Agreement is the complete and exclusive statement of the agreement between you and the Company and supersedes all proposals, prior agreements, oral or written, and any other communications between you and the company or any of its representatives relating to the subject matter.

Should you have any questions concerning this agreement or if you wish to contact the Company for any reason, please contact in writing: Permissions, Pearson Education Canada, a division of Pearson Canada Inc., 26 Prince Andrew Place, Toronto, Ontario M3C 2T8.